T0301456

# ECONOMIC RELATIONS BETWEEN EGYPT AND THE GULF OIL STATES, 1967–2000

*To My Mother*

Ruth

# Economic Relations between Egypt and the Gulf Oil States, 1967–2000

*Petro-Wealth and Patterns of Influence*

Gil Feiler

sussex
ACADEMIC
PRESS

*BRIGHTON • PORTLAND*

2 4 6 8 10 9 7 5 3 1

*First published in 2003 in Great Britain by*
SUSSEX ACADEMIC PRESS
PO Box 2950
Brighton BN2 5SP

*and in the United States of America by*
SUSSEX ACADEMIC PRESS
920 NE 58th Ave          Suite 300
Portland, Oregon  97213-3786

*British Library Cataloguing in Publication Data*
A CIP catalogue record for this book is available from the British Library.

*Library of Congress Cataloging-in-Publication Data*
Feiler, Gil.
Economic relations between Egypt and the Gulf oil states, 1967–2000 :
petro wealth and patterns of influence / Gil Feiler.
p. cm.
Includes bibliographical references and index.
ISBN 1–903900–40–9 (acid-free)
1. Egypt—Economic conditions—1952–  2. Egypt—Foreign economic relations.  3. Egypt—Foreign relations—United Arab Emirates.  4. United Arab Emirates—Foreign relations—Egypt.
I. Title.
HC830.F445  2003
337.620536'09'045—dc21
2003003865

Typeset and designed by G&G Editorial, Brighton
Printed by MPG Books Ltd, Bodmin, Cornwall
This book is printed on acid-free paper.

# Contents

---

# *Preface*

_____

The upheaval in oil prices in the early 1970s gave prominence to an arresting and interesting phenomenon in inter-Arab relations – a serious and prolonged imbalance between the economies of Arab countries and increasing inequality in terms of social advantages as a result of the economic imbalance. As the oil-producing countries grew rich and their citizens enjoyed one of the highest standards of living in the world, Egypt was enmeshed in an economic morass, barely managing to finance the import of foodstuffs for its population.

There is controversy in the professional literature regarding the definition of the term "aid." Some define aid as grants that do not have to be repaid, others include loans[1] and/or investments in aid. In the research presented in this book, aid includes (civil and military) *grants* and medium-term and long-term *loans* from Arab governments and inter-Arab aid institutions.

An attempt is made to accurately examine the real magnitude of foreign aid and investments from the 1970s onward, and to describe its structure, its quality in terms of effectiveness, and the conditions of delivery. The research endeavors to understand the considerations, the demands, and the policy of each side toward the economic relations between giver and receiver. Central to the study is the phenomenon of Egyptian workers in the Gulf States, and the (direct) influences and the (indirect) implications of these ties on national policy. Expatriate workers are scrutinized in the light of two focal questions: what impact did the relationship between the expatriate workers have on relations between the countries, on an economic/social/political level? And how did they reflect on the striving for the Arab ideal of unification, cooperation, and mutual accountability? Furthermore, what were the implications of Sadat's decision to take a new and independent road – a road to peace with the State of Israel? Did Egypt's considerably diminished hegemony – after the June 1967 defeat – strengthen or weaken economic cooperation with the oil states?[2] The central questions to be addressed are:

- What was the underlying logic in the web of economic relations between the countries?
- Did economic relations reinforce political relations?
- Was the Egyptian worker, returning home from the Gulf to Egypt, imbued with an intensified Arab orientation or was his Egyptian orientation strengthened?

- How much did Arab aid to Egypt influence Sadat's steps toward peace?
- How should the range of economic relations between Egypt and the Arab Oil Countries (AOC) in the 1970s be viewed: Was Arab aid generous, as they claimed, or was it trifling, as claimed by Egypt, which stressed that the Arabs had become wealthy by Egyptian blood?
- Was the web of economic relations on the popular level influenced by economic relations on the official level? Did the governments involved have a deliberate policy in this context?
- Why did the oil-producing countries grant Egypt large amounts of aid? How was this aid doled out and was the timing critical in any way?
- Did Egypt renounce the independent formation of its foreign policy in exchange for aid?

Traditional literature portrays the poor as weak, and the poor countries of the world as dependent on rich countries, which provide them with military, as well as technological and economic, assistance.[3] In the case of Egypt and the rich oil-producing countries matters were different: a country strong from a military standpoint and rich from a demographic, human resources and cultural viewpoint, Egypt required economic aid from countries (the oil-producing states) that were financially wealthy but poor in other spheres. Globally, very few cases exist along similar lines. Those that do are generally found to be South–South, as opposed to North–South, relations. India, for example, in spite of its poverty, is richer than its neighbors: the relationship between India, and, for example, Pakistan, is similar to the global relations between North and South. In contrast, the oil countries, notwithstanding their vast revenues from oil, were dependent on the huge population, and the demographic, technological and intellectual potential of poor Egypt, and this created a relationship of mutual dependency.[4]

The ties between four Arab conservative and rich oil states – Saudi Arabia (SA), Kuwait, the United Arab Emirates (UAE) and Qatar – and Egypt are examined. Libyan and Iraqi aid (although these two nations were oil states, they were not conservative) to Egypt will also be discussed.

June 1967 was a turning-point in the history of the Arab states and the beginning of a period in which pragmatic relations between Egypt and its rich neighbors replaced the previous "prestige" relationship that existed prior to 1967. Egypt now recognized the legitimacy of its neighbors as separate nations in the Arab world and the latter, as wealthy, oil-producing countries, granted Egypt economic assistance. From 1967 onward, Egypt began to receive institutionalized Arab aid,[5] which replaced Soviet aid (which in turn replaced American aid) as the principal source of economic assistance to the country.

An additional reason for the choice of the June 1967 date is the lack of important distinctions in the economic relations between Egypt and the AOC, such as migration of laborers, assistance and investments, prior to 1967; if they existed at all, their scope was minor. Although 1967 is the point of reference for this study, each chapter is treated to a historical (and methodological) introduction.

Economic relations between Egypt and the AOC took several forms, principally economic and military aid, investments, worker migration, tourism and commerce.

The present research focuses on aid and investment, because of their centrality and their considerable influence on many criteria in the Egyptian economy and in those of the oil countries considered. The flow of commerce and tourism, whose importance to the Egyptian economy was secondary, is taken into account when analyzing the sum total of Egypt's relations with the AOC and the influence of the economic boycott imposed on Egypt following the peace treaty with Israel.

## Structure of the book

*Chapter 1* presents a picture of the magnitude of civil and military aid granted by the Arab conservative oil countries to Egypt in the years 1967–78. A major task will be to resolve some of the many differences of opinion with respect to the amount of aid given, as detailed by the professional literature. A full comparison of primary and secondary sources relating to the aid issue, and other sources, is presented.

*Chapter 2* begins by explaining the Egyptian government's policy regarding foreign investments. It then goes on to deal with Arab investments in Egypt on three levels: (1) the governmental level; (2) the inter-Arab level; and (3) the private level. Governmental and civil investments of the AOC in Egypt, both as individual states as well as a joint initiative of several Arab countries, are investigated. The Arab Military Industrialization Authority (AMIO), which was established (and then liquidated) in Egypt, is an important example of a multilateral Arab investment. The reaction of AOC citizens to investment statute 43 will be examined (the *Infitah* law, 1974), and the sectors in which they invested their money will be scrutinized and comparisons made with those of Western investors in Egypt. Assistance from Arab aid funds for specific investment purposes in Egypt will also be investigated.

*Chapter 3* focuses on one of the most important phenomena in the 1970s and 1980s – the migration of Egyptian laborers to the Arab oil economies and their remittances to the home country. The extent and distinctive qualities of Egyptian migration before and after the oil boom, and the motivation for migration and the migration policy of the Egyptian and Arab oil countries, will be analyzed. Remittances of the Egyptian migrants, both via official and unofficial channels, will be compared to economic criteria in the Egyptian economy.

*Chapter 4* deals with the aid policy of the Arab oil-producing countries to Egypt. Motives for aid to Egypt, and the way its magnitude and timing were determined, are examined in the light of whether the AOC succeeded in influencing Egyptian policy-making by dint of their assistance.

*Chapter 5* examines Egypt's position on petro-dollar aid, on both the ideological and practical levels. The main theme is how Egypt formed its policy in light of its wish to receive aid at the beginning of the period, and its dissatisfaction with the unwillingness of the AOC to grant aid toward the end. Egyptian disappointment is generally thought to have led to Egypt's pursuit of the path to peace. The subsequent boycott imposed on Egypt by the Arab countries, and the causes for its failure, are also discussed.

*Chapter 6* brings the study up to date by surveying Arab aid and investment inflows into Egypt up to the year 2000. This chapter covers changes in the number of Egyptian workers employed in the Gulf Cooperation Council (GCC) countries and the volume of their remittances. It also provides the latest figures on exchanges of trade and tourism between Egypt and the Arab world.

*Chapter 7* concludes the study, providing a macro-examination of aid to Egypt since the evolution of the AOC, and reviewing the reasons for its decline. Could Egypt have been better served in terms of aid by the AOC? Was it right to seek peace with Israel? And, finally, has its new relationship with the US been more beneficial, in the short and long term? The current economic slump Egypt finds itself in is placed against the historical background of the study.

The role of foreign capital in the economic development of Third World countries has been the subject of extensive empiric and theoretical studies, many of which reached contradictory conclusions.[6] Much has been written on foreign aid to Egypt and aid's influence on its economy. Most studies on Egypt focus solely on the economic aspect of aid. But substantial aid to any country impacts on the nation as a whole, and has political and social ramifications that cannot be ignored. Further, the economic analysis of many studies was based on insufficient data, especially with regard to the scope and type of Arab aid; such analyses therefore remain incomplete.

Abou Settit, in his "Foreign Capital and Economic Performance: The Case of Egypt," stated that his aim was "to examine in depth the influence of foreign capital on the Egyptian economy in the years 1967–83."[7] His research centered on total foreign capital flow into Egypt, not necessarily on Arab capital. Abou Settit assembled data on foreign aid and investments from the annual publication of the International Monetary Fund (IMF) Balance of Payments Statistics, and from the OECD, but these sources do not provide full details on Western aid, hardly anything on Arab investments, only partial details on civil Arab aid, and nothing at all on military assistance. According to Abou Settit's findings, Egypt did not receive any aid whatsoever from the OPEC countries in the years 1971–2 and 1978;[8] in fact, Egypt received more than $1 billion in those years **(see chapter 1)**. Abou Settit wrote that Egypt received loans from all parties to the amount of $12 million in 1979 and that he has no data for 1975–6.[9] In fact Egypt received much larger loans in 1979 and in 1975–6 – years on which he has no information at all; all told, Arab loans to Egypt totaled more than $1 billion. Abou Settit also wrote that Arab investments in Egypt declined after the peace agreement with Israel; in fact they increased **(see chapter 2)**.[10]

Economic relations between countries, principally foreign aid and investment, impact on foreign policy. Economic ties involve political relations – it is not possible to understand the workings of one without the other.[11] Although scholars have documented ties between Egypt and the Gulf oil states,[12] their research emphasis on the sum total of economic relations has been limited.[13]

In order to mobilize aid from the conservative oil countries and from the West, Nasser (toward the end of his rule) and Sadat enacted legal and institutional changes in the Egyptian economy and political structure. The fact that the AOC did not hasten to Egypt's assistance to the extent desired by that country inspired foreign policy-making and marked a decisive turn toward a political process *vis-à-vis* Israel. The subject of economic ties between Egypt and the AOC was put on the Arab agenda by Egypt; it brought about an in-depth discussion among politicians of all parties, as well among intellectuals and the Egyptian public. Various aspects of economic relations were discussed: the AOC's duty to compensate Egypt for the sacrifices made for the sake of joint Arab interests; the implications of these ties on the Egyptian economy and Egypt's capacity to maintain independent foreign policy-making; and issues of national identity following heavy economic dependence on the rich Arab states.

Notwithstanding that aid was pivotal in the relations between Egypt and the Arab oil countries, to date there has been no comprehensive study of its magnitude. Much research on Egypt has ignored the impact that aid had on the political economy of Egypt. In his article "The New Arab Political Order: Implications for the 1980s," Dessouki mentions Wien's research project, "A comprehensive review of Saudi economic assistance to Egypt,"[14] but this latter work was neither comprehensive nor accurate. Wien based his data on UNCTAD and OECD information up to 1976. He did not compare different sources, and without such comparison it is impossible to obtain a correct picture of aid data. In his conclusions, Wien asserted that it would not be possible to give an exact evaluation of the level of Saudi military and civil aid to Egypt since 1973.[15] The chapters that follow herewith nevertheless provide this information.

In Dawisha's *Egypt in the Arab World: The Elements of Foreign Policy*, which examines Egypt's relations with the Arab world (principally the revolutionary countries) in the years 1952–70 (in the last chapter he also examines the Sadat period), there is barely any mention of the topics dealt with in the present study.[16] It is the same situation in Ragsdale's doctoral thesis, "Egypt and the Persian Gulf: A Study of Small States in Coalition," which examines Egypt's relations with the Gulf States. Ragsdale does not deal with important topics such as the AOC's investments in Egypt and the migration of Egyptian workers to the Gulf States. Although she does occasionally mention the economic importance of Egypt's relations with the Gulf States, statistical data is not provided, except for a single table with data on aid the AOC had granted Egypt in the years 1974–5, albeit that her research deals with a period of more than a decade.[17] Similarly al-Fiki does not mention Arab aid in his doctoral thesis, "Economic Foreign Aid and the Egyptian Economy," except for a few lines about Arab aid in the years 1967–73 and reference to the establishment of the Gulf Fund for the Development of Egypt (GFDE) in 1976. Al-Fiki does not attribute any great importance to Arab assistance granted to Egypt in the period of 1966–73, asserting that assistance from the Eastern bloc continued to be the main source of aid to the Egyptian economy,[18] while in fact Arab aid was of decisive importance in those years and it surpassed all others (**see chapter 1**). More comprehensive works of research on Arab aid to Egypt are the studies of Ayubi, who based his work on World Bank data on civil aid, and Barkai, who analyzes military aid.[19] Neither of the latter two studies mentioned Arab (governmental and private) investment in Egypt. As we shall see in **chapter 2**, many books dealing with Arab investment do not even mention investments in Egypt.

Several research works have been written on OPEC aid to the Third World and on inter-Arab aid, but these were mostly surveys of data – principally aid from funds and not bilateral aid, which actually constituted the major part of Arab aid to

Egypt; military aid was not included in these studies. In any case, it has not been possible to derive any significant data on aid to Egypt.[20] OECD and UNCTAD published part of the OPEC aid data, but without mentioning military aid. Their data is not complete and it is difficult to determine from their publications the distribution and the donors of aid for the whole period.[21] In this regard it should be noted that to date, no comprehensive or partial studies have been published that provide figures on aid or investments in Egypt in the 1990s. Moreover, several international agencies stopped covering Arab aid figures in their reports.

Verification of the authenticity of sources and their statistical data as it relates to Third World countries is well known, and the Arab states are no exception to this rule. In spite of the great improvement (in quality and quantity) attained in the sources/statistical field in the Arab world, there is still a lack of information, and supporting data is often inconsistent. Certain countries publish much larger volumes of data than others. There are many reasons for this, and some of them will be discussed in the framework of the methodological introduction to the chapters that follow.

The present research relies on primary sources not hitherto utilized. Findings in other research works are here analyzed in a different way. The Arab oil countries and Egypt have yet to reveal official documents, and it is doubtful whether they will do so in the near future or indeed if ever. Although many official documents published by these countries remain unavailable to the public, many official documents pertaining to international bodies – such as the OECD, UNCTAD, the IMF, the World Bank – nevertheless exist. Personal interviews with senior personalities of the OECD (Paris) substantiated various claims made in the reports, the data of which was supplied by Arab countries. Correspondence between the makers of Egyptian and Saudi economic policy and other bodies is also used in the present study, as are some Egyptian official reports. Other sources include: the memoirs of Arab statesmen who played an active role in political events; and personal interviews with policy-makers (including two Egyptian prime ministers, Sadat's spokesman, and a minister in his government). The documents and interviews helped to uncover new facts; they also confirmed various details essential to clarifiying the whole picture. Material relating to the discussions of American congressional committees, particularly the committee for Foreign Affairs, contributed significantly to a deeper understanding. Other valuable material was derived from reports of the American Embassy in Cairo and from the headquarters of the American Aid Agency in that city. Finally, assistance from Arab aid funds to Egypt is utilized in the form of the funds' reports.

Several research scholars have cast doubts on the usefulness of autobiographies for research purposes. The most common claims are that the author of an autobiography usually paints an image with emphasis on the positive sides of character and contribution to policy-making. For example, Sadat wrote his autobiography[22] at the time of his regime, and his book was aimed, inter alia, at presenting a figure loved by his Egyptian constituency; the aim was to increase public support for his policies, especially after the food riots in 1977. Often, the autobiography serves as a platform for retired leaders to justify their actions when they were in office. Nevertheless, autobiographies can be useful sources to the historian. Memoirs constitute a good starting point, albeit that further information and different view-points for the verification of facts is essential.

Arab press reports were also very useful in the present research, particularly the Lebanese press up to the mid-1970s. Articles exposed motives and issues that were not yet promulgated through official channels, and many times reporters' percep-tions and analysis were subsequently proved accurate.

The original study was written as a doctorate dissertation at Tel Aviv University in 1989. The text has been updated continually over a period of twelve years. Since 1989, the author has taught at various academic institutions in Israel and co-founded Info-Prod Research (Middle East) Ltd. (IPR), a business consultancy serving Fortune 500 companies. IPR operates its own news agency, which supplies business information to Reuters, Lexis-Nexis, Dow Jones, Gale, Genios, Financial Times, Proquest, EBSCO and more. The author's publications include *Rethinking Business Strategy in the Middle East and North Africa* (Economist Group), *The Middle East in the New Millennium* (Kluwer) and *From Boycott to Economic Cooperation: The Political Economy of the Arab Boycott of Israel* (Frank Cass).

# Acknowledgments

———

I owe a special debt of gratitude to my mentors, Professor Shimon Shamir and Professor Gad Gilbar, for their guidance and encouragement.

Many individuals and institutions responded favorably to my requests for information. They allowed me to open a window to their knowledge, thereby helping me to carry out this research. Some individuals asked to remain incognito and I have expressed my gratitude to them in other ways. I sincerely thank all of them.

I also wish to thank Alfred Atherton, the United States Ambassador to Egypt in the years 1979–83; Jürgen Bartsh, who was in charge of the Arab Aid Department on behalf of the OECD; the late Eliyahu Ben-Elisar, Israel's first Ambassador to Egypt; Dr. Tahsin Bashir, Sadat's spokesman; Arnon Gafny, Governor of the Bank of Israel at the time of the peace treaty; A. Jacobini, the economic attaché at the US embassy in Cairo; Dr. Ali Hillal Dessouki, professor of political science at Cairo University; Dr. 'Abd al-'Aziz Hijazi, Egypt's Minister of Finance in the late 1960s and early 1970s, and Egypt's Prime Minister until April 1975; Dr. Mustafa Khalil, Egypt's Prime Minister at the time of the peace agreement; Hasan Mansur, the Egyptian Minister of Information in the late 1970s; 'Abd al-Sattar Tawila, assistant editor of *Ruz al-Yusuf*; 'Abduh Mubashir, military correspondent of *al-Ahram*; Anis Mansur, editor of *October* until 1985; Sa'id 'Ashmawi, judge of the Supreme Court in Egypt; Professor 'Abd al-'Azim Ramadan, Egyptian historian; and Professor Mahmud Sha'lan, head of the Faculty of Psychiatry at al-Azhar University.

During several of my visits to Egypt, with the help of grants from the Israeli Academic Center in Cairo, I received considerable help from the heads of the center and their wives. Mrs. Rachel and Professor Gabriel Warburg and later Mrs. Ruth and Professor Asher Ovadia helped making my visits in Egypt fruitful and pleasant. The contribution of the Department for Information at the American Aid Agency in Cairo was substantial. I am especially grateful in this context to the head of the Department, Mrs. Lou-Anne MacNeil. Professor Itamar Rabinovitch of Tel Aviv University helped me in setting up fruitful contacts with the American Aid Agency, and in the granting of Moshe Dayan research scholarships. A special word of thanks to Mr. and Mrs. Hostfeld of Venezuela, who made a generous contribution to this research. Moreover, I wish to thank the Ben-Gurion Research Promotion Fund of the Histadrut, and the Kaplan Chair for Israel and Egypt for the research scholarships they granted me.

I wish to thank the staff at the Haifa University library, of the Dayan Center (Tel Aviv University), and at the Truman Institute (Hebrew University) for the assistance accorded to me.

I owe a special debt to Ms. Noa Schonmann for her dedicated work in bringing this book to light.

The understanding of the subject matter displayed in this research should be regarded as my personal outlook. I accept total responsibility for any error in facts, considerations or understanding.

# List of Tables and Figures

**Tables**

## Figure

# Abbreviations

---

| | |
|---|---|
| ACDA | The Arms Control and Disarmament Agency |
| ADFAED | The Abu Dhabi Fund for Arab Economic Development |
| AFDB | Arab Development Bank |
| AFESD | Arab Fund for Economic and Social Development |
| AIB | Arab International Bank |
| AMF | Arab Monetary Fund |
| AMIO | Arab Military Industrialization Organization |
| AOC | Arab Oil Countries |
| ARE | Arab Republic of Egypt |
| *ARR* | *Arab Report and Record* |
| *ASQ* | *Arab Studies Quarterly* |
| ASU | Arab Socialist Union |
| BADEA | The Arab Bank for Economic Development in Africa |
| *CSM* | *Christian Science Monitor* |
| ECB | Egyptian Central Bank |
| EgP | Egyptian Pound |
| EIA | Egyptian Investment Authority |
| EIU | Economist Intelligence Unit |
| ESCWA | UN Economic and Social Commission for Western Asia |
| *FT* | *Financial Times* |
| FY | Financial Year |
| GAFIZ | General Authority for Investment and Free Zones |
| GFDE | Gulf Fund for Development of Egypt |
| IBRD | International Bank for Reconstruction and Development |
| IFED | Iraqi Fund for External Development |
| *IHT* | *International Hearald Tribune* |
| IISS | The International Institute for Strategic Studies |
| *IJMES* | *International Journal of Middle East Studies* |
| ILO | International Labour Organization |
| IFS | International Financial Statistics |
| IMF | International Monetary Fund |
| ISDB | Islamic Development Bank |
| IMF | International Monetary Fund |

| | |
|---|---|
| GCC | Gulf Cooperation Council |
| KD | Kuwaiti Dinar |
| KFAED | Kuwaiti Fund for Arab Economic Development |
| *KCA* | *Keesings' Contemporary Archive* |
| LAFB | Libyan Arab Foreign Bank |
| *MECS* | *Middle East Contemporary Survey* |
| *MEED* | *Middle East Economic Digest* |
| *MEES* | *Middle East Economic Survey* |
| *MEJ* | *Middle East Journal* |
| MENA | Middle East News Agency (Egyptian News Agency) |
| NIEO | New International Economic Order |
| *NYT* | *New York Times* |
| ODA | Official Development Assistance |
| OECD | Organization of Economic Cooperation and Development |
| OPEC | Organization of Petroleum Exporting Countries |
| SFD | Saudi Development Fund |
| SIPRI | Stockholm International Peace Research Institute |
| SWB | Summary of World Broadcasts |
| WB | The World Bank |
| *WSJ* | *Wall Street Journal* |
| UN | United Nations |
| UNCTAD | United Nations Committee for Trade and Development |
| USAID | United Sates Agency for International Development |

# Economic Relations between Egypt and the Gulf Oil States, 1967–2000

*Petro-Wealth and Patterns of Influence*

# 1

# Aid to Egypt, 1967–1978

Contrary to aid given by Western countries, the extent of aid allotted by the oil-producing countries to Egypt is difficult to establish. Data on aid and the way it has been doled out constitutes an important link for understanding the range of ties between Egypt and its neighbors. Arab aid to Egypt is particularly confusing after the October 1973 War. Aid from the Gulf oil states to Egypt in the period 1967 to 1978 has been documented in a number of forms, some of which provide conflicting data. Two ministers of the Sadat government dealt with aid over this period, but their data is inconsistent. Former Prime Minister Kamal Hasan 'Ali wrote that "the Arabs gave [Egypt] $5 billion from 1973 up to November 1977, out of which $2 billion as a deposit at seven percent interest. Besides this, they also [provided] arms valued at $3.5 billion." However, the Egyptian Minister of Economy, Salah Hamid, declared before the Egyptian Parliament that "Egypt received $3,287 million from the Arab states, in loans and grants [including military assistance and without deposits]."[1] The oil countries, though, reported much higher amounts of aid. *ARAMCO World Magazine* claimed that Egypt received $17 billion from the end of 1973 until 1978, and the UPI agency quoted Saudi officials in Jedda in May 1979, stating that Egypt had received $13 billion in cash from Saudi Arabia, Kuwait, Qatar and the UAE in the "past six years." According to this report, the amount did not include arms purchases for the Egyptian army – which were entirely financed by the four oil countries – nor the repayment of Egypt's debts.[2] *al-Ahram* editor-in-chief Ibrahim Nafi' claimed that his information was the most reliable of all the data available, and that "Arab aid [to Egypt] in all its forms [including military assistance] in the years 1967–79 did not exceed . . . $12 billion."[3]

Many reasons contributed to the conflicting information: military aid data was classified for strategic reasons, mainly to make it harder for the enemy to trace arms purchases. Sadat once commented: "There are many things between us and the Saudis which are still not for publication." According to Muhammed Hassanein Heikal, former *al-Ahram* editor-in-chief, the conflicting data emanated from Sadat's demand to transfer part of the aid money to a separate fund under his control, and not to the Central Bank. Sadat insisted that this money was not to be viewed as part of the regular income of the Egyptian treasury; these funds were supposed to be kept for an emergency. Heikal pointed to aid granted to Egypt in accordance with the resolutions of the Arab summit conference in Khartoum.

According to him, some of the donor countries agreed to transfer the aid money to a special fund. Only the Kuwait government refused to go along with this demand, transferring its aid funds to the Egyptian Central Bank. Added to this, military aid of a sensitive nature never appeared in regular reports.[4]

Although Heikal's comments sit within the framework of his criticism of the Sadat regime, his data provides clear evidence that in Egypt there was an "emergency fund" to which, inter alia, grants from Arab governments were channeled. This fund was activated at the end of the 1960s after the rout in the June 1967 War. The resources of this fund were applied to security and rehabilitation purposes and were not included in the national budget.[5] Egypt, like many other countries, did not publish data on its military imports and the financing thereof, nor was this data included in the official balance of payments. Occasionally the governments of Egypt and the donor countries reached secret agreements on economic and military aid funds. Egypt received most aid at talks in the periods between the Arab summit conferences. Furthermore, at some of these meetings cheques were given directly to the Egyptian president, and not by regular transfer from one central bank to the other. Once, Saudi King Faysal – shortly before his demise – presented Sadat with a cheque for $125 million at a meeting in Egypt. In spite of Egypt's shaky economic situation, the cheque was deposited only after several weeks.[6] It is quite probable that after this cheque and others were endorsed, they were transferred directly to arms suppliers in Europe and the USSR. In several cases, the oil countries even transferred funds directly to the Europeans and the Russians, before and after the October 1973 War. These purchases were effected only after finalizing matters with the Egyptian president and his associates, which made identifying the extent of aid more difficult. The Egyptian leadership did not always reveal the magnitude of aid, because they wanted to avoid embitterment among the Egyptian poor over their substandard living conditions.

Another problem with obtaining comprehensive data on aid can be attributed to the inconsistency of reports on small amounts. All together, these amounts add up to significant sums. Similarly, the aid data is obscure, as the researcher does not always know if commitments for aid by the AOC to Egypt were upheld – wholly or partly.

As aid data published in literature, in official publications in Egypt, in the AOC and in publications of various international bodies is completely contradictory, it is necessary to examine, step by step, most of the information mentioning anything about the AOC's aid to Egypt, and to question the way the various research works arrived at their results and the origin of their sources. Commitments for aid and the actual doling out of monies were traced. In order to reach a realistic evaluation, diverse sources were accessed and assessed: (a) official Egyptian reports; (b) personal interviews with Egyptian personalities who fulfilled various functions in the political and economic leadership, such as prime ministers or ministers of finance; (c) reports and hearings which had been presented for perusal to committees of the American Congress – principally to the committee for Foreign Affairs; (d) reports of international financial bodies, e.g. OECD, UNCTAD, the IMF, the World Bank; (e) declarations by Egyptian and AOC personalities regarding aid; (f) the Arab and Western press; (g) the memoirs of

Egyptian dignitaries who had taken an active part in obtaining aid from the AOC; and (h) secondary research works.

Because of extensive reliance on official sources detailed above, it is necessary to answer a possible criticism as to research reliance on reports of news agencies and the Arab and Western press. The importance of the news agencies' coverage, particularly in light of the nature of Arab aid, is that the AOC provided two kinds of assistance: open and covert. Information on open aid was passed on to international bodies, whereas the second kind was politically sensitive. Covert aid sometimes exceeded official aid and no information on the former was supplied to international bodies, but occasionally it received publicity via various news agencies. Naturally, any such data should be viewed with extreme caution, and efforts need to be made to verify or to disprove the data in various ways. Such research efforts are essential to the follow-up and the analysis of the motives for aid, and the manner in which the donor countries related to Egypt's requests (its timing, the dates when Egypt's requests were rejected, and so on).

A first step was to analyze the data of Arab aid to Egypt, not including official reports, and to make an evaluation, and then to compare this information to other reports and studies, while at the same time examining and comparing the components of each report. This method enabled an accept/reject decision to be made, and to qualify the reasons behind the decision. A fundamental element of the evaluation was to find information – from both sides, the donor and the recipient – on promised aid actually being delivered. Approval given at meetings of the Kuwaiti National Council for providing aid to Egypt, for example, is accurate information only when it is supplanted by Egypt's confirmation that aid had indeed arrived. It is not always possible to obtain data from both sides, but in most cases confirmation from one side only proved reliable. Commitments to aid without any confirmation of the receipt thereof are sometime mentioned in the text, but are not taken into account.

The final data presented here is most certainly not one hundred percent accurate. According to a former principal economic policy-maker, it is extremely doubtful that the Egyptian government itself possesses totally accurate data. Only after examining dozens of both official and unofficial reports, can one attempt to present, as much as possible, realistic and well-founded data.

## Prior to the June 1967 War

Many scholars dealing with the economy of the Middle East in general – and in the relations between Egypt and the Arab oil-producing countries in particular – ignored or diminished the value of Arab aid to Egypt before June 1967. In an article in the *International Journal of Middle East Studies* (*IJMES*) on the role of foreign capital in the development of the Egyptian economy in the years 1960–72, Nazem Abdalla discussed loans and grants that Egypt received in this period. According to Abdalla, Egypt had the benefit of loans from three groups: Soviet, American and "other countries." The author did not include the AOC as a separate group, and by "other countries" he meant first and foremost aid provided to Egypt by Eastern

European countries and China. Arab aid, he wrote, should be disregarded as far as it concerned the period before 1967, because of its minor scope.[7] Kanovski stated that between 1961 and 1975, the Kuwaiti Fund paid out about $14 million annually – to all Arab countries combined, and that loans from the Kuwaiti treasury in that period amounted to less than the above sum.[8]

**Table 1.1** Kuwaiti loans to Egypt, December 1963–April 1965 (in millions of KD)

| Date of Agreement | Amount | Repayment date (years) | Interest (%) |
|---|---|---|---|
| 2.12.63[1] | 3.00 | 12 | 0 |
| 5.4.64[2] | 0.75 | 18 | 4 |
| 12.4.64[2] | 25.00 | 15 | 4 |
| 29.3.65 | 5.00 | 18 | 4 |
| Total | 33.75 | | |

*Sources*: Kuwait Ministry of Finance and Energy, as quoted by: Hassan Ali al-Ibrahim, *Kuwait and the Gulf* (London: Croom Helm, 1984), p. 99; *Middle East Economic Digest*, Statistical and Documentary Service (London, March 1966).

[1] Loan approved in late November 1963 was destined for the relocation of the Abu-Simbel Temple. See: *al-Ahram*, November 24, 1963. This report also mentioned that the loan had been granted for a period of 12 years, interest-free.

[2] On March 15, April 8 and 15 *al-Ahram* wrote about aid that Egypt received from the Kuwaiti Fund in the amount of KD 35 million, but there was a mistake in its report – a mistake in terminology, not in the figures. As can be seen in the above table, the Kuwaiti government signed in one week in April 1964, two loan agreements with Egypt, totaling KD 25.75 million, and the Kuwaiti Development Fund signed on another agreement for KD 9.8 million, totaling KD 35.55 million, as reported by both *al-Ahram* and the *New York Times* News Agency. See: *NYT News Service*, June 23, 1965, derived from the "Misr-Kuwait" file in the *al-Ahram* archives. The above sources reported that the whole amount was granted by the KFAED, whereas the Kuwaiti government had in fact provided the lion's share of the loan.

A study of official sources will point to conflicting data in the above-mentioned studies, and will show that Egypt benefited from extensive Arab aid already from the early 1960s: from the Kuwaiti Development Fund – which, in April 1964, provided a loan of KD 9.8 million ($27.5 million) for the widening and deepening of the Suez Canal[9] – as well as from direct governmental aid, which by far exceeded the assistance provided by the Kuwaiti Fund. According to reports from the Kuwaiti Ministry of Finance (table 1.1), the Kuwaiti government granted Egypt loans in the amount of KD 33.75 million ($94.5 million) in less than a year-and-a-half (December 1963–April 1965)[10], in addition to the loan of $27.5 million from the Kuwaiti Fund. These loans, considered as substantial in the contemporary Arab world, were granted at long-term repayment conditions.

From official Kuwaiti data, it appeared therefore that up to April 1965 Kuwait provided Egypt loans for a total of KD 43.55 million, divided up as follows: KD 33.75 million from national reserves (table 1.1) and another KD 9.8 million from the Kuwaiti Development Fund. This amount was equal to $121.9 million. In addition to the data provided by the Kuwaiti government, it appears that Egypt received two other big loans up to 1966: the first for $98 million in February 1965, which Kuwait allocated to Nasser to help extricate him from his financial difficulties;[11] and the second one for KD 15 million ($42 million) in late January 1966, during the visit to Kuwait of the Egyptian Vice-Premier, 'Abd al-Mun'im al-Qaysuni. This loan was granted for a period of ten years.[12]

**Table 1.2**   Kuwaiti aid to Egypt, December 1963–January 1966 (in millions of US dollars)

| Date of loan | Amount |
|---|---|
| Four loans from monetary reserves, December 1963–April 1965 | 94.5 |
| Loan from the Kuwaiti Fund for Arab Economic Development, April 1964 | 27.5 |
| Loan in February 1965 | 98.0 |
| Loan in January 1966 | 42.0 |
| Total | 262.0 |

*Sources*: See data detailed in table 1.1.

According to table 1.2, Egypt received loans totaling $234.5 million from the Kuwaiti government and another $27.4 million from the KFAED, totaling $261.9 million, up to the beginning of 1966. *MEED*, which mentioned the loan of January 1966 (see above), added that before this loan Egypt received other, partly unreported loans, totaling £80 million ($224 million).[13] If we add to this amount the loan of KD 15 million ($42 million), then according to the *MEED* data Kuwait loaned Egypt a total of $266 million, as compared to my figure of $262 million.[14] On top of this figure, Egypt also received a grant of $1 million for the financing of medical research equipment for the Cairo University.[15]

Kuwaiti aid in this period exceeded aid from the Soviet bloc, which amounted to about $135 million in the years 1964–6 **(see chapter 5)**, and American aid, which from 1956 was minimal. It should be remembered that at this time Kuwait did not benefit from the revenues it received after the Teheran Agreement of February 1971, nor from the first oil boom. Kuwait's income in 1965/6 totaled $610 million,[16] and in July 1965 its total investments abroad, according to the Kuwaiti Minister of Finance, amounted to $1.52 billion.[17] Furthermore, Kuwaiti aid constituted a significant contribution to the Egyptian economy: Egypt's commercial deficit in the years 1964–5 stood at an average of $310 million annually[18] and Kuwaiti aid in those years, at an annual average of $110 million, covered more than 35 percent of the deficit.

The question remains as to whether the above-mentioned data is reliable (loans totaling $234.5 million from the Kuwaiti government and $27.4 million from the KDF, up to early 1966); there is no argument about the total of $121.9 million granted to Egypt up to April 1965, because this was reported by the Kuwaiti government and the KDF. However, there is no official confirmation for the additional $140 million, as reported by the *New York Times* News Agency and by *MEED*. Notwithstanding that these sources confirmed the reliability of their information,

it is difficult to rely only on data presented by them. An IMF document[19] contradicted Abdallah, who stated that loans provided to Egypt by Arab governments
before 1967 were of no consequence. Data for the IMF document were provided by
Egypt's Ministry of Economy, and accordingly, on June 30, 1967, Egypt's accumulated debt to Kuwait totaled about $252 million.[20] (At the same time, its debt to
the US amounted to about $185 million, and to Iraq about $9 million.)[21]

Up to early 1966 the Kuwaiti government granted Egypt loans totaling $234.5
million (not including the KDF), and IMF documentation mentions an amount of
$252 million, including the period up to the end of June 1967. The discrepancy of
$17.5 million stems from the fact that the IMF report included a longer period,
during which (in June 1967) Egypt received additional loans, to be detailed in due
course.

## From June 1967 until Sadat's rise to power

After the June War, Egypt received aid from nearly all the oil-producing countries.
Immediately after the war, the Kuwaiti Peoples Council approved a grant of
KD 25 million for "the Arab war effort," out of which KD 10 million ($28 million)
were allocated to Egypt;[22] on June 18, the Libyan government decided to grant £20
million to the confrontation states, out of which £10 million went to Egypt ($24
million);[23] and Algeria provided 30 million Algerian Dinars (ca. $6 million).[24]
Altogether, Egypt received in June $58 million as Arab governmental aid, as well
as popular donations (cash, gold and medical assistance). The committee for
popular contributions (established in Kuwait after the war) transferred KD 3
million to Egypt (ca. $8.5 million).[25] Likewise, Kuwait sent medicine and food as a
gift to "the victims of Israeli aggression."[26] The jewellery and food Egypt received
had no great fiscal value, but carried great symbolic, propaganda value. Similarly,
Bahrain's small contribution of $1 million to the confrontation states – divided up
between Egypt, Syria, Iraq and Jordan – had symbolic significance, when Sheikh
Muhammad Bin Mubarak, the director-general of the Bahraini Ministry of
Information, personally flew to these four countries to present his country's contribution.[27]

In June Egypt received $60 million from the Arab oil countries. This data is based
on several official statements by the governments of Kuwait, Libya, Algeria and
Egypt. Additional support for the above appears in a report by the IMF, which
stated that in June 1967 Egypt received assistance from governments and private
parties totaling $69 million. The document stresses that aid was furnished mainly
by Arab governments, as grants.[28] In an interview given by the Egyptian Minister
of Planning, 'Abd al-Mun'im al-Qaysuni, to the London *Times* in early July 1967,
he declared that since the armistice Egypt had received aid amounting to $100
million, provided mainly by Arab countries.[29]

On August 4, the resolutions of the Arab Summit conference in Khartoum were
published.[30] In addition to a summary of seven items, a separate decision stipulated
that Saudi Arabia, Kuwait and Libya would provide an annual grant, in quarterly
payments, of £135 million ($365 million) to Egypt and Jordan, from mid-October

1967 until "the elimination of the results of Israeli aggression." The three donor countries' share was determined as follows: Kuwait, £55 million; Saudi Arabia, £50 million; and Libya, £30 million.[31] The conference did not decide how the aid would be divided up between Egypt and Jordan. Mahmud Riyad, the Egyptian Foreign Minister at the time, described in his memoirs how aid was divided up between the two countries; in a separate meeting, with the participation of the donor and the recipient countries, Jordan's minister of finance requested £40 million ($108 million). Riyad informed Nasser of the talks and he proposed increasing Jordan's share of aid from £15 million to £20–25 million. According to Riyad, Nasser rejected this proposal, claiming that King Hussein was honest with Egypt and he would be able to get £40 million.[32] Accordingly, Egypt's share of the "Khartoum Aid" amounted to £95 million ($257 million) annually. Heikal, Sadat and Mahmud Riyad stated that Nasser was, at this early stage, surprised at the relatively large amount of the Khartoum aid, as he had anticipated a much lower total.[33]

The Khartoum conference was a landmark in the history of aid relations between the AOC and Egypt. It is true that Egypt did benefit from loans and grants before the Khartoum resolutions, but there were innovations: (a) At the Khartoum conference only grants were discussed; (b) Saudi Arabia joined the group of Arab states assisting Egypt; (c) a permanent basis was created for institutionalized financial aid from the Arab oil countries to Egypt "until the elimination of the results of Israeli aggression." The conference created an explicit commitment on the part of the oil countries to render assistance to the confrontation states, without written conditions.

On October 10 the Kuwaiti People's Council approved the Khartoum aid law, according to which aid would be provided to Egypt until the opening of the Suez Canal, and to Jordan until the return of the West Bank.[34] The Saudi cabinet had approved the allotment of aid on October 5. An examination of the budget and balance of payments of Egypt, Kuwait and Saudi Arabia reveals that these countries, as well as Libya, kept up their quarterly payments, both in the amounts and the schedule (attempts to obtain Libya's data were unsuccessful, but from the Egyptian budget it appears that Libya honored its commitment). The Arab media made a big and festive occasion of each quarterly payment. Aid cheques started arriving in mid-October. The Saudi cheque for £8.3 million ($22 million) arrived on October 16, and one day later a cheque for £3.255 million (ca. $9 million) from Kuwait and one for £5.278 million (ca. $14 million) from Libya was forthcoming.[35]

The AOC paid out the entire amount committed by them, and on time. They even increased Khartoum aid in December 1967, after the pound sterling was devaluated by 14.3 percent, about three months after the aid resolutions were passed. Faysal informed Hasan 'Abbas Zaki – the Egyptian Minister of Economy who was visiting in Saudi Arabia – that the Saudis would increase aid proportionately to the rate of devaluation. Libya acted likewise.[36] The Kuwaiti authorities were looking into a proposal to impose taxes on various products, to enable them to keep their aid commitments;[37] this was because Kuwait lost ca. £27 million as a result of the devaluation, as a substantial part of its monetary reserves were held in sterling deposits.[38]

It was usual for the actual amount of aid received to be less than the commitment, but that is not the case here. Egypt received an annual grant of $251 million as per the Khartoum resolutions and adjustments for devaluation. Saudi Arabia granted $98 million, Kuwait, $94 million, and Libya, $59 million.[39] In the 1967/8 fiscal year Egypt received, in accordance with the above resolutions, $190 million and in 1968/9 $251 million.[40] Besides financial aid, during 1967 Egypt received oil shipments from Algeria and Kuwait valued at $10 million.[41] The Khartoum aid continued also after the opening of the Suez Canal to shipping, until the second Baghdad conference, when an economic boycott was imposed on Egypt (March 1979).[42] Libya, as we will see later, ceased providing assistance following the interim agreements with Israel.

Up to the Rabat Summit conference (which convened on December 21, 1969), Egypt continued to receive the Khartoum grant,[43] as well as other small amounts, like the grant of $75,000 from the Emirate of Dubai.[44] A study of Abu Dhabi's Five Year Plan for 1968–72 indicates that it budgeted $63.5 million as aid to other Arab countries[45], but the share of this given to Egypt is not clear. In any case, these figures are insignificant; from data presented by the Egyptian government to the IMF it appears that in the 1968/9 fiscal year Egypt received, in addition to $251 million (the Khartoum grant), one-time aid from Arab countries totaling $30 million.[46] This amount reflects in part the loan of EgP 10 million ($23 million) that the Libyan king, Sanusi, sent to Nasser, after the USSR demanded payment in cash for arms deliveries. Nasser sent an envoy to Libya with a request for a loan of EgP 20 million. Sanusi sent EgP 10 million, with a promise that the remainder would be transferred three months later, after Libya received payment for oil exports.[47]

Riyad mentioned that Nasser's pride made it difficult for him to request aid from the conservative oil states after the June war.[48] However, not long before the Rabat Summit in late 1969, Egypt declared that it would demand an increase in aid to the confrontation states from £135 million to £400 million. According to the Egyptian proposal, it would receive £200 million, or in other words double the Khartoum grant; Jordan, £100 million; Syria, £50 million; and Lebanon, £50 million. According to this proposal, Saudi Arabia would provide £100 million; Kuwait, £100 million; Iraq, £50 million; and Algeria, £50 million sterling.[49]

At the summit, Nasser insisted on a guarantee for manpower and military equipment from the Arab states, and for the financing of the struggle with Israel.[50] The Egyptian General Fawzi proposed that the AOC raise a sum of EgP 500 million. His proposal was rejected in its entirety. Gaddafi announced he would give an immediate grant of £40 million, and another £300 million for the war. On the other hand, the Saudi King and the Emir of Kuwait declared they were willing to continue the Khartoum aid payments, but they said nothing about an increase. Iraq claimed that it was also a confrontation state and therefore it would not participate in the financing of the war.[51] Algeria and Saudi Arabia proclaimed that priority should be given to the Palestinians over increasing aid to Egypt.[52]

On the third day of discussions, Nasser attacked Faysal and al-Sabah for their refusal to increase aid,[53] warning the participants that he would take an independent stand if they stood by their refusal;[54] he left the meeting in a rage. After some persuasion, Nasser returned to the meeting, but overall, in contrast to the Khartoum Summit, Egypt's expectations were unfulfilled. The assistance that

Egypt obtained at the Rabat Summit was significantly less – but just how much less is open to debate.

*Al-Nahar* wrote that Libya agreed to increase its share of aid to the confrontation states by £60 million and Kuwait by £30 million.[55] This report tends to exaggerate facts, and is not corroborated by other reports presented herewith: *al-Jarida*, supported by a Kuwaiti report, mentioned Kuwait only and noted that it agreed to increase its aid to the front-line states by £10 million.[56] *MEED* stated that Libya was ready to increase its aid to Egypt and Jordan by £20 million.[57] Saudi Arabia was not mentioned in these reports. In late December 1969, *al-Ahram* wrote that the three big oil countries had agreed to finance "a new arms agreement" at a cost of £35 million (ca. $85 million), divided up as follows: Libya, £20 million; Saudi Arabia, £10 million; and Kuwait, £5 million sterling.[58] A few days later, the Kuwaiti *al-Siyasa* reported that Egypt would receive £10 million, and it stressed that this sum would be given as a one-time grant, and not as an annual commitment.[59]

A different history of the amount of oil received was given by Sadat nine years after the closing session of the summit. He said that Nasser asked for EgP 20 million only ($46 million) to pay for an arms deal with the USSR. Gaddafi offered his services and he blamed Faysal and al-Sabah. Faysal replied that Libya had a population of only 1.5 million people as against 8 million of Saudi Arabia. Sadat stated that after lengthy discussions Gaddafi offered to pay EgP 10 million, and the Kuwaiti Emir pledged a further EgP 5 million. Sadat added that Gaddafi never sent the money promised to Nasser, so that in the end Egypt only received EgP 5 million out of the 20 million it had asked for.[60]

**Table 1.3**  Kuwaiti aid according to the Khartoum and Rabat agreements (in millions of KD)

| Fiscal year[1] | 1968/9 | 1969/70 | 1970/1 | 1971/2[2] |
|---|---|---|---|---|
| Khartoum remittances | 47.1 | 47.1 | 45.7 | 47.5 |
| Rabat remittances | 8.6 | 2.5 | — | — |
| Gulf States/South Arabian peninsula Aid | 1.6 | 1.9 | 1.7 | 2.3 |
| Other | 5.5 | 0.4 | 3.7 | 0.7 |
| Total | 54.2 | 58.0 | 53.7 | 50.5[3] |

*Source*: Kuwaiti Ministry of Finance and Energy, as quoted in a document of the IMF, Kuwait p. 30.

[1] Terminates on March 31.
[2] An evaluation by the Kuwaiti Ministry of Finance and Energy, as manifested by its budget.
[3] The decline in Kuwaiti aid in 1970/1 reflects the freezing of remittances to Jordan.

The confusion over Kuwaiti assistance was cleared up: on February 25, 1970, the Kuwaiti National Assembly approved additional aid to Egypt totaling KD 10 million ($28 million), and an announcement to that effect was published in the media.[61] A study of the Kuwaiti budget and IMF documentation reveals that Kuwait paid a total of KD 11.1 million for the Rabat aid package and spread out its payments over two budget years.[62] According to Kuwaiti documents, in Rabat

Kuwait had committed itself to paying a total of KD 15 million – 10 million to Egypt and 5 million to the PLO[63]. According to most reports, Libya guaranteed to increase its support by £20 million (ca. $48 million). This amount received official Libyan approval: after Nasser had made a stop-over in Libya on his way back to Cairo from the Rabat Summit, it was officially announced on December 27, that Libya had increased its annual grant to Egypt by £20 million. In addition, a Libyan tank battalion would be sent to the Suez Canal front.[64] In early 1970 Libya did indeed transfer its quarterly payment to Egypt (as it had guaranteed in Khartoum), which was larger than usual and which included some of the guarantees it had taken upon itself in Rabat. Earlier it had transferred an additional grant of $2 million to Egypt.[65]

Besides the "Khartoum aid"[66] and the "Rabat aid," the AOC did not provide Egypt with any other direct assistance, except for small sums such as $2.5 million which it received jointly from Libya and Kuwait in late March.[67] Nevertheless, Egypt benefited from indirect aid: in June 1970, the financial committee of the Kuwaiti National Assembly agreed to postpone indefinitely repayment of loans to Egypt totaling $162 million, to enable it to deal with its economic difficulties.[68]

## Sadat's rise to power (September 1970) to the October 1973 War

When Sadat took over the reins of power in September 1970, relations and cooperation with the leaders of the conservative oil states were strengthened. Indeed, initially there were still some points of controversy between Egypt and the AOC **(see chapters 4 and 5)**, which precluded the supply of massive aid to Egypt; however, the nature of relations changed with the expulsion of the Soviet advisors in July 1972, and from that time on until just before the October War Egypt received substantial financial and military assistance.

Toward the end of Nasser's regime, Egypt received only minor military aid from Libya after Gaddafi came to power. However, the talks over extensive military aid that commenced during Nasser's time bore fruit during Sadat's regime. Egyptian military experts posed as Libyan officials at talks between Libya and France over the sale of French arms to Libya. Fathi al-Dib, an Egyptian intelligence officer, initiated negotiations with the French Ministry of Defense. Al-Dib pressured the Libyan government into purchasing the Mirage fighter plane, which the Egyptians had unsuccessfully tried to obtain from France after the June defeat under Nasser. The Mirage was faster than anything in the Egyptian air force, and had a range exceeding 375 miles – the range of the MIG 21 supplied by the Soviets.[69] France was not disposed to the offer from Egypt, because it did not want to violate the arms embargo which had just been activated. Furthermore, France had no confidence in Egypt's ability to finance the deal.[70] On Gaddafi's rise to power on September 1, 1969, Nasser sent Fathi al-Dib to him, in addition to a motorized battalion, as support for the new regime. Negotiations between France and Libya commenced in early November 1969,[71] and the Mirages finally arrived in Egypt at the beginning of 1972.

Libya purchased arms for Egypt in the West and in the communist bloc countries. After Sadat's visit to Moscow in February 1972 he paid a visit to Libya. Notwithstanding the differences of opinion that came up between Sadat and Gaddafi, one of the results of this visit was Jalud's mission to Moscow at the head of an arms-purchasing delegation, representing Libya and Egypt. In Moscow, Jalud looked into the possibility of payment in cash and in foreign currency, in exchange for expediting the supply of arms.[72] Heikal did not mention the results of the talks with the delegation, and if, and at what price, the Libyans had ordered arms for Egypt, but on another occasion he said that Libya contributed no less than $1 billion to the preparations for the battle.[73] On February 24, 1972, the Israeli Chief-of-Staff, General David Elazar, declared that the Mirage planes France sold to Libya were transferred to the Egyptian air force and that Egyptian pilots, posing as Libyans, were sent to France for training. He said that Libya had also transferred other types of weapons to Egypt.[74] This information was verified by Egypt: in early August Sadat reported to a Defense Staff meeting that Libya had put a squadron of Mirages at Egypt's disposal, as well as twenty-four 155 mm guns, twelve 120 mm guns and 100 armored cars.[75] In addition to Libyan military aid, Egypt received a grant of $7 million for arms purchases from Iraq[76] and $1 million from Bahrain.[77]

Similarly, Saudi Arabia joined in supplying Egypt with military aid. In May 1972 Fahd, the Saudi Crown Prince, announced after a visit to Cairo that Saudi Arabia was putting all its military, material and political potential at Egypt's disposal.[78] After Soviet experts had left Egypt, Sadat sent military missions to the Gulf oil states to discuss arms transactions, to be financed by them. These missions were successful and the AOC started supporting the Egyptian armed forces, although they denied this at first. The Kuwaiti Minister of Interior and Defense denied reports claiming the Kuwaiti air force had loaned planes to Egypt. He added, however, that Kuwait was always ready to expand its military cooperation with Egypt in any way.[79] In late August 1972, a delegation of the Egyptian air force visited Kuwait and Saudi Arabia to inspect their Lightning fighters.[80] At the same time, a Kuwaiti report stated that "two civilians from another Arab country" were discussing arms orders at a cost of $200 million with arms manufacturers in several European countries. The report did not mention Egypt, but it noted that the European arms manufacturers inquired, on exchanging documents, if the arms were destined for Kuwait or for another country financed by Kuwait.[81]

During November and December 1972 contacts on aid between Egypt and the oil countries intensified, and besides the military delegations, high-level officials such as Ashraf Marwan, a close associate of Sadat, and 'Aziz Sidqi, the Prime Minister, were sent to the AOC.[82] In addition to military aid and the financing of the arms transaction with Britain at a cost of £100 million ($250 million) in October[83], Egypt also requested civilian aid, following the deterioration of its economy: its external debt was growing, its foreign currency reserves were dwindling and its imports were increasing (chapter 5). Egypt's requests were successful, and it received significant civil and military aid. Kuwait committed itself to aid totaling £65 million ($163 million), and Qatar and Abu Dhabi each guaranteed aid for £20 million ($50 million), a total of $263 million, destined for arms purchases from the UK. Over and above this amount, Abu Dhabi granted a long-term loan of $38 million for the financing of development projects in Egypt. At the time,

Egyptian pilots were training on Lightning planes in Kuwait and in Saudi Arabia and on MIGs in Libya.[84] Kuwait granted Egypt a loan of $38 million for the purchase of four civilian Boeing planes.[85] In the last months of 1972 Egypt received aid totaling $340 million.

In mid-December 1972, Egypt gained another achievement at a meeting of the Arab Chiefs-of-Staff in Cairo: Arab states not defined as confrontation states pledged to send arms shipments to Egypt. Saudi Arabia and Kuwait each pledged to send two squadrons of Lightnings, and Libya promised to consign three squadrons of Mirages. Besides military aid, Egypt was promised substantial financial assistance, to enable it to enter arms deals with Moscow and with other arms suppliers.[86]

The Arab states did not fulfill all their commitments at the conference of Chiefs-of-Staff regarding consignments of military equipment – mainly planes[87] – but they kept their financial obligations. Moreover Faysal agreed to assist Egypt with purchases of Soviet weaponry. Egypt had experienced difficulties with buying arms from Western states and was forced to turn again to the USSR, especially since its weapon systems were adapted to the Soviet system. Saudi Arabia allowed Egypt to negotiate a large arms deal with the USSR, to be financed in hard currency by the oil countries. So after the meeting, Faysal, who had organized the aid package, arranged $300–$500 million for Egypt's arms purchases, and $400–$500 million in economic support. In February 1973, General Hafiz Isma'il, Sadat's National Security advisor, arranged an arms deal with the USSR, which was finalized in March of that year. This was the largest shipment of arms ever agreed between the two countries.[88] In late March 1973 Sadat stated that bilateral contacts with the USSR had led to positive, practical results, but that it wasn't the right time to reveal them. "It would be preferable to keep silent so as not to reveal anything to our enemies, as we are concerned about the war, which is more important than anything else."[89] And so from the second day of the October War, enormous shipments of arms were airlifted to Egypt from the USSR, including about 100 fighter planes, 600 tanks and equipment for 30 batteries of SAM missiles,[90] most of which was paid for by petro-dollars.

In addition to these considerable funds, in February and March 1973 Egypt received aid totaling $10 million from Abu Dhabi and $7 million from Iraq. The Iraqi *al-Jumhuriyya* made this grant, stating that "the grant to Egypt points to the Iraqi victory in the nationalization of the IPC pipeline, a step benefiting the entire Arab cause."[91] Besides financing arms deals for Egypt, the AOC purchased Western arms for Sadat. In late March 1973 the Kuwaiti Foreign Minister admitted that Kuwait had purchased two squadrons of Lightnings for Egypt, according to the resolution taken at the summit meeting of Arab foreign and defense ministers.[92] At the beginning of April Libya transferred 18 Mirage planes to Egypt,[93] and a few months later Saudi Arabia purchased 30 Sea King helicopters from the British Westland Aircraft Co., which were destined for Egypt.[94] The American Secretary of State, Henry Kissinger, declared that he received reports from various agencies in early 1973, according to which Arab arms were moving in the region, which included Libyan and Saudi aircraft to Egypt.[95]

The oil-producing countries rendered aid to Egypt in additional ways, such as further postponement of debts and interest payments to Kuwait of $115 million, up to the end of 1975.[96] On August 23, 1973 Sadat visited Riyadh in order to coordinate positions with King Faysal regarding the war **(see chapter 4)**. Besides the promise to mobilize the oil weapon for the struggle against Israel, Saudi Arabia, Kuwait, Qatar and Abu Dhabi promised $500 million for further arms purchases from European countries and the USSR.[97] Later the AOC paid $700 million directly to the USSR for an arms transaction.[98] During and after the October War, Egypt received from the USSR MIG SU-7 aircraft, T-62 tanks and other armored vehicles.[99]

**Table 1.4**   Aid from the oil-producing countries to Egypt 1967–October 1973 (in millions of US dollars)

| Details of aid | Amount |
| --- | --- |
| Khartoum and Rabat aid | 1,590 |
| Additional economic aid | 220 |
| Military aid | 1,250 |
| Total | 3,000 |

*Source*: Data as presented in tables 1.1–1.3.

Egypt received massive aid even before the first shot was fired in the October War. Up to 1967, Egypt received aid totaling $260 million, of which a major proportion was from Kuwait in the form of loans, and a smaller amount from Iraq. The "Khartoum" and "Rabat" aid packages, bestowed as grants, amounted to $1,590 million in the years 1967–73. Other economic aid in this period stood at $220 million, while military aid came to ca. $1,250 million (mainly in 1973). In other words, up to the beginning of the October War Egypt received, according to the aforementioned data, more than $3 billion,[100] which is an enormous sum. Even if we break up this amount over a period of six years, Egypt still received an average of $500 million annually, a significant amount of money (especially as this refers to the period up to 1973, when inflation was still low). Additionally, Egypt benefited from indirect aid, such as the postponement of debts.

In past and contemporary studies, most researchers disregarded this major aid factor. It was acceptable to think that in this period, aid was minor and included only the Khartoum and Rabat aid packages, as indicated by a study of the oil countries' budgets. However, as already remarked, not all aid funds to Egypt were reflected in its budget. Irregular military and economic aid was usually drawn from the huge defense budgets of the oil states or from their monetary reserves.

## October 1973 to December 1975

### Civil Aid

The day after the October War broke out, Sadat ordered Sayyid Mar'i to head a delegation to the Arab oil countries in order "to coordinate their strategy." On

October 10 – after deciding on the participants and the strategy of the delegation – Mar'i, Ashraf Marwan, Mustafa Khalil and General Sa'ad al-Qadi flew to the Gulf States. Sadat wanted to coordinate the way the oil weapon would be exploited and obtain additional aid, but, as Mar'i wrote in his memoirs, he did not give the delegation any specific requests, and he left the decision to the Arab leaders.[101] The delegation's first stop was in Saudi Arabia. Mar'i remarked that Saudi Arabia's decision regarding aid to Egypt was most important, because of its influence on the oil Emirates. If the Saudis allocated substantial aid, he wrote, the other oil states would do likewise. Right from the start of its talks with Faysal (October 10), the Egyptian delegation made it clear that it had every intention of obtaining aid, when Marwan made a request for "a small amount" of arms and immediately received a positive reply.[102]

At another meeting with Faysal – after discussing the oil boycott and agreeing to cut oil production by 5 percent – the King said: "You have made all Arabs proud – is there anything you need?" Mar'i stressed that Sadat had instructed the delegation not to request anything: He only mentioned that Gaddafi had sent oil to Egypt. Faysal's reaction was to declare that Saudi Arabia would immediately grant $200 million to Egypt. After the meeting, Faysal's advisor, Rashid Far'un, accompanied the Egyptian delegation and he asked Mar'i if he was satisfied with the magnitude of aid. Mar'i replied: "I am not satisfied, do you know how much costs one hour of fighting taking place at this moment in Sinai? 10 million dollars . . . In any case, we are extremely grateful to Saudi Arabia for its generosity, but you should realize that the other oil states will not contribute more than Saudi Arabia . . . even less."[103] Far'un asked how much exactly Egypt needed, and according to him Mar'i avoided giving him a clear answer, as "Sadat had instructed them not to ask for assistance." Following this conversation, Faysal sent an envoy to the Egyptian delegation before their departure, who informed them that Faysal had decided to double the amount to $400 million.[104]

The delegation also visited Kuwait, Qatar, Bahrain and Abu Dhabi. The Emir of Kuwait declared that he would immediately grant Egypt $200 million; the Emir of Qatar decided at first to give $50 million, but before the delegation left Qatar, he doubled the amount to $100 million; and Zayd, the Emir of Abu Dhabi, borrowed $100 million from British banks to give to Egypt.[105] Later, Zayd stated that this money was paid to the USSR for arms for Egypt.[106] Algeria gave its support, when Boumedien paid $200 million to the USSR for tanks shipped to Egypt and Syria.[107] The delegation's other destinations were Bahrain, Dubai and Oman, but Mar'i did not mention if these countries also provided aid.

In total, the Egyptian delegation received commitments for aid totaling $800 million. Sadat declared on many occasions that in the first week of the war Egypt received $500 million.[108] Precise calculations show that aid received by Egypt in that period stood at $920 million, as per the following details: Saudi Arabia, $300 million; Kuwait, $250 million; Libya, $170 million; and Qatar and Abu Dhabi, $100 million each.[109] Egypt did not receive the whole amount in cash. Some of it was transferred directly to the arms suppliers for military equipment for Egypt. Aside from this aid, the Kuwaiti government also decided to continue to defer the repayment of debts.[110]

According to Riyad, an agreement was reached at the Arab summit conference, held on November 26, 1973, to purchase arms for Egypt and it was determined that continued consolidation would be effected through bilateral agreements, to prevent publication of the resolutions.[111] In January 1974, Sadat travelled to the Gulf States to try and obtain financial aid to cover the commercial deficit anticipated in 1974, financing for the reconstruction of the Canal zone and direct Arab investments in Egypt.[112] Three months after his visit, Egypt received $100 million from Saudi Arabia, designated for the reconstruction of the Canal cities,[113] and Arab aid funds contributed to various development projects **(see chapter 2)**.

Libya donated its aid to Egypt on the condition that Egypt would continue the fighting. Although in January 1974 'Abd al-Salam Jalud, the Prime Minister, pledged to assist Egypt with $700 million (in grants, loans and investments),[114] except for a loan of $18.5 million in February 1974,[115] he did not fufil his obligation. In late March 1974, following Libya's failure to transfer the Khartoum aid which it was supposed to have provided at this time,[116] it discontinued oil shipments to Egypt. Jalud announced that the end of the war had made oil shipments super-fluous, but he denied Libya had suspended payments of the Khartoum grant.[117] Only after Sadat sent a sharply-worded letter to Gaddafi and to the members of the Libyan Revolutionary Council in early May 1974 – stating that Libya had shipped 800,000 tons of oil during the war (out of its total commitment for 4 million tons), and that it had violated its commitment on the Khartoum grant[118] – did Libya admit that it had indeed discontinued aid. The reason given was because Egypt had not honored the resolutions of the Khartoum Summit, which determined that there would be no negotiations with, or recognition of, Israel.[119]

In late 1974 Saudi King Faysal came to Cairo for talks. His visit gave rise to antic-ipations of significant aid: the media talked about a grant of $1 billion and a loan of $500 million. But they made a mountain out of a molehill: the joint statement at the end of his visit said that Saudi Arabia would provide "an immediate financial grant of $300 million,"[120] which Egypt received immediately after his visit.[121] However, this amount did not constitute a suitable response to its economic straits. Egypt tried to obtain massive financial aid which would alleviate its trade deficit, but the AOC preferred to assist Egypt in other ways, such as arms purchases or application of resources to joint investments in Egypt, which in themselves were very important, but insufficient to extricate the Egyptian economy from its chronic difficulties.

In November 1974, Hijazi, the Egyptian Prime Minister, visited Saudi Arabia, the UAE, Bahrain and Qatar, with the purpose of raising substantial aid. On his visit he received commitments totaling $1,195 million.[122] A large proportion of this sum was allocated to joint projects and investment companies, a further amount was granted as credit possibilities for the financing of these projects and only a small percentage of the total sum was promised as a loan: the Saudi Fund, $161 million; the Abu Dhabi fund, $33 million; and the Qatar government, $10 million.[123] Hijazi continued on to Kuwait, and the spectacle repeated itself: it was agreed that, for a number of years, Kuwait would finance projects for housing, industry, maritime traffic, tourism and other projects, at a cost of $1.3 billion. In fact, only a part of this amount was agreed on for that year,[124] and the total amount mentioned in the joint statement at the end of the visit was destined to serve the propaganda purposes of the parties involved. At first, pledges received by Egypt during the November 1974 visit were impressive: it is not every day that a country receives commitments for $2,495 million, but examination of the components of this aid show why Egypt was not entirely satisfied: most of this aid added up to "try to get too much, you finish up with nothing." Much of the aid was promised for specific projects, and as such, it was to be allocated according to the rate of progress on these projects. Considering Egypt's ponderous bureaucracy, it was difficult to anticipate how and when Egypt could utilize this assistance in its entirety.

Without minimizing the importance of the assistance promised to Hijazi, it should be noted that this was not immediate aid that Egypt could have used for its most pressing needs. The Egyptian leadership sought a comprehensive solution for the economy in the form of an Arab Marshall Plan. Sadat and others in the government spoke a great deal about the need for this solution to carry benefits equivalent to the original Marshall Plan. One of its originators was Sayyid Mar'i, who proposed that subscribers to this fund would make donations on the basis of their national income or on the basis of their exports. Mar'i proposed that the capital for this fund be set at $3 billion in the first stage, and that it would gradually grow to $20 billion within a decade.[125] This plan never took off. The Egyptian government, as we shall see in chapter 5, was not comfortable with being forced to beg every time they approached the AOC, who on their part did not make any effort to find a comprehensive solution for the Egyptian economy, being satisfied with a strategy of trickles of aid.

The state of the Egyptian economy deteriorated steadily in 1975: the Egyptian people were called to tighten their belts in light of a shortage of basic foodstuffs and the crisis in public services **(chapter 5)**. While the joint communiqués after visits – such as Hijazi's to the Gulf – spoke about massive aid to Egypt, in actual fact it received minor portions of civil aid. There were those among the Egyptian people who, after the impressive announcements on support, thought that the time had come to demand welfare instead of a belt-tightening. Their leaders were aware of this. Sadat remarked: "They have forgotten that these billions are not liquid funds but sources of financing, whose fruits can be picked only after a considerable period of time, and that this investment plan is still being prepared by the Minister of Planning, to be ratified by the People's Council"; and Hijazi accused the establishment press of planting false hopes among the masses by way of "huge headlines about openness, about . . . the millions we are receiving from abroad." He said people "thought that the heavens would rain gold."[126]

In mid-January 1975 Egypt received the first part of aid agreed on at the Arab Summit conference at Rabat (October 26–29, 1974). The aid resolutions at this conference caused many disputes. At the meetings it was decided to allocate $2.35 billion to the confrontation states, distributed as follows: Egypt and Syria, $1 billion each; Jordan, $250 million; and the PLO, $100 million.[127] However, the final resolution indicated a sum of $1,369 million only, which was supposed to have been provided by Saudi Arabia and Kuwait, $400 million each; the UAE, $300 million; Qatar, 150 million; Iraq, 100 million; Oman, 15 million; and Bahrain, $4 million.[128] It appears that they decided to allocate the larger sum, but the amount that the above-mentioned countries proposed was lower. Algeria, Tunisia, Morocco and Libya did not pledge specific sums and their representatives declared that first they would raise the matter before the political authorities in their respective countries. So it turned out that the final aid total would be only 58 percent of the original sum.[129] Heikal indicated that Egypt and Syria together were supposed to receive $1 billion according to the distribution to be determined by a subcommittee. The normal custom, according to Heikal, was to distribute the sum proportionately to the populace of the two countries, but as there was no Egyptian representative in the subcommittee, Syria succeeded in obtaining half the amount.[130]

The final decision on assistance did not indicate the share of each recipient, but in April the amount of Kuwaiti aid to Egypt was announced, when the Kuwaiti National Assembly approved an advance expenditure of $415 million from the state reserves for support of the confrontation states – as decided in Rabat. Egypt's share of the pie came to $170.2 million[131] and it received $42.5 million from Iraq.[132] One year later official approval was granted to the exact amount of aid. The Egyptian Minister of the Treasury stated that Egypt had received $582 million, as a one-time grant, as per the Rabat resolution. This figure matches the aforementioned report, according to which the final amount of aid was set at 58 percent of the original Rabat resolution.[133]

From data obtained by the OECD from the Saudi Treasury it appears that, at the Rabat conference, the Saudis pledged to provide assistance totaling $391 million to Egypt, Jordan and Syria.[134] Egypt's share in this amount is not immediately apparent, but it is possible to calculate Egypt's portion by adding up all sums allocated by the other countries, and then to deduct this amount from the total sum Egypt received in 1975 for the Rabat aid. It transpires that the Saudi part of this support amounted to $213.5 million, minus a donation of $27 million by Libya to Egypt,[135] leaving Saudi Arabia's share at $186 million. The Egyptian Central Bank's statement indicated that Saudi Arabia granted $170 million;[136] the minor discrepancy apparently stemmed from differences in exchange rates, or from small sums of aid bestowed on Egypt by other countries, such as Qatar. From this statement, it appears that every oil state acted as it saw fit in regard to this aid. There were countries which provided aid on one occasion only, and others, such as Kuwait, which continued to allocate aid to Egypt on an irregular basis.[137]

In early January 1975, workers' riots broke out in Cairo in protest against the high cost of living, the shortage of food and inferior services. These riots were not as widespread as the riots of January 1977. But they were a clear sign of the dissatisfaction of the population. The security forces acted rapidly and arrested hundreds of demonstrators. Prime Minister Hijazi, appointed in 1974, was fired in April,[138] and Mamduh Salem, the Minister of Interior, replaced him. Several days after the riots, Faysal visited Cairo and he promised a grant of $100 million for the purchase of vital products, especially food, and 2 million tons of oil.[139]

Once again the Egyptian government was disappointed by the size of the Saudi grant. Saudi Arabia and the other oil-producing states allocated additional aid to Egypt, but in small amounts and for specific purposes: Saudi Arabia granted $100 million – half in cash and half in construction materials – for the financing of construction projects[140], the UAE, $60 million for the financing of the purchase of seven Boeing planes[141], and Kuwait, Abu Dhabi and Qatar gave support for the costs involved in the reopening of the Suez Canal.

Egypt's large repayments of foreign debts – totaling $1,184 million in the period of May to August 1975[142] – and the continuing deterioration of the economic situation in Egypt caused Saudi Arabia to evince greater generosity, in a calculated way. In July 1975 Khaled visited Egypt as the head of a delegation, consisting of, among others, the Saudi Ministers of Defense and Foreign Affairs. This was Khaled's first visit to Cairo since his rise to power after the murder of Faysal, and as a gesture to the king, Egyptian Mirages – purchased by Saudi Arabia and Libya – put on an air show.[143] During this visit, Khaled pledged to grant Egypt a loan of $600 million, and to participate in the financing of a housing project in Hilwan. An agreement was reached for the repayment of this loan over a period of thirty years, at a low rate of interest.[144] Several weeks after the visit, Fahd, the Saudi Crown Prince, appealed to the Arab states to assist Egypt, and Fahmi, the Egyptian Foreign Minister, stated that Egypt considered this "a declaration of principles."[145]

In the summer of 1975 the AOC reached an agreement in principle to render aid to Egypt for an amount of $1 billion.[146] In late September 1975 – in spite of the political problematics encountered by the oil countries following the signing of the Sinai II agreement **(chapter 4)** – the Egyptian Finance Minister proclaimed that Egypt had obtained long-term loans totaling $1.2 billion from three Arab countries. As mentioned before, Saudi Arabia pledged $600 million in July, Kuwait loaned $500 million (after it was supposed to have given a larger sum) and Qatar gave another $100 million. Loans were allocated for a period of twenty years, including a "grace period" of five years, at low interest rates.[147] At the end of October 1975, Kuwait and Egypt signed an agreement for an additional loan of $34 million.[148]

In early October 1975, the Kuwaiti al-Qabas reported Saudi agreement to grant Egypt an interest-free loan of $1 billion. The report stated that this agreement was reached after the signing of the Sinai treaty, and added that the Saudis insisted that this aid be kept secret.[149] This information is unreliable, because of the lack of confirmation from an official source, or from an unofficial source. But there are two plausible explanations for this report: first, that Saudi Arabia had increased its aid from $600 million (Khaled's commitment of July 1975) to $1 billion; and secondly, that this was a new pledge for aid, granted in addition to Khaled's commitment. It could very well be that this was a commitment for a later stage. Moreover, World Bank data shows that Egypt did not receive the loan. The bank noted that in 1975 Egypt received loans totaling $1,420 million from the AOC[150], which is in accord with the declarations of the Egyptian Treasury ($1.2 billion), in addition to the assistance Egypt received at the beginning of the year.

## Military aid

There was less resistance to military aid provided by the AOC to Egypt than to financial aid. The AOC financed Egypt's preparations for the October 1973 War, provided cash for arms purchases and bought arms before and during the war. They agreed to supply 120 planes that Egypt had failed to acquire from the Russians. They exploited the termination of the French embargo on arms shipments to the confrontation states in the Middle East, and they purchased military equipment for

Egypt. But, as noted above, even before the cancellation of the embargo, at the end of 1973, they ordered military items for Egypt. Appearing before students on August 26, 1974, Sadat referred to arms shipments financed by the AOC, declaring that new fighter planes, "purchased for us by several friendly Arab governments," were on their way to Egypt, as replacements for the 120 planes that were shot down in the October war.[151]

In November 1974, Mirages that had been purchased by Saudi Arabia landed in Egypt. Between thirty and thirty-six planes had been ordered, as part of the framework of an arms transaction totaling $700–$1,000 million, destined for Egypt. Further military equipment – part of which had already been received – included British Lightnings and Sikorsky helicopters, American tanks and Belgian military products.[152] Similarly, Kuwait and Abu Dhabi ordered at least thirty Mirages for Egypt. In January 1975 Sadat flew to Paris to purchase arms and presented the French with a long shopping list. During this visit, the members of the Egyptian mission signed contracts for arms purchases and opened discussions on future arms transactions.[153] In June 1975, during the Egyptian Foreign Minister Fahmi's visit, the UK and Egypt signed an agreement on an arms deal at a cost of £450 million (ca. $1 billion). In this deal, Britain dropped its former demand for a credit note covering the entire amount, principally because most of the financing would come from Saudi Arabia and Kuwait.[154]

In May 1975, Sadat referred to the military aid supplied by the AOC:

Immediately after the cease-fire and until January 1975, the USSR discontinued [arms] shipments. Therefore, in mid-1974 we signed several contracts with various arms dealers in other countries. Some of these items have already reached Cairo. I wish to thank our brothers in Saudi Arabia, Kuwait, Abu Dhabi and Qatar for their part in these transactions. Formerly I mentioned Saudi assistance with the purchase of Mirages and helicopters, but we did not reveal what our brothers in Kuwait had sent, or what others had done for us, because normally Kuwait acts without much fanfare or public declarations.[155]

On his trip to Kuwait in May 1975, Sadat, in an interview to a local television station, again mentioned that Kuwait had bought "certain weaponry" for Egypt, but refused to elaborate. At first, France denied the reports on the purchase of Mirages for Egypt by the AOC, until it was finally forced to admit to the fact: "We would not be surprised if these planes remained in Egypt for an extended period of time."[156] The subject of the Mirages again embarrassed the French government on another occasion: in one of the verbal clashes between Sadat and Gaddafi during the summer of 1975, the former accused Libya of delivering to Egypt Mirages without spare parts, which in the end were paid for by Saudi Arabia (who later on requested Egypt to return the planes to it). This came out after *MENA* published the contents of another letter sent by Sadat to the Libyan Revolutionary Council on July 31, 1975.

In early November 1975, Sadat paid a visit to England. Referring to his visit, he said he was absolutely satisfied.[157] Sadat had good reason to be. Britain, Egypt and Saudi Arabia had arrived at a series of agreements, inter alia, on the sale of 200 Jaguar planes, a joint English–French product, to Egypt,[158] financed by the AMIO

(Arab Military Industrialization Authority) **(see chapter 2)**. Tables 1.5–1.6 present a summary of arms deals closed by Egypt with Britain and France in 1975. The tables are based on data as presented above and on publications by bodies dealing in the subject, such as: SIPRI, IISS and JANE.

**Table 1.5** British arms sales to Egypt, 1975

| Item | Number | Comments |
|---|---|---|
| Sea King helicopters | 6 | Ordered January 1975. Financed by SA. |
| Westland helicopters | 24 | Ordered on October, 23 by SA. |
| Westland helicopters | 4 | Ordered in December 1975. |
| Hawk training planes | 100 | Ordered in October 1975. |
| Jaguar planes | 200 | Ordered in November. Financing by the AMIO. One part was supposed to have been delivered to Egypt, and one part to be assembled in Egyptian plants. |
| Lynx helicopters | 250 | Ditto. |
| Swinger missiles | 10,000 | Finalized on Sadat's trip to London (November). |
| HS 748 | 18 | Saudi financing. |
| SRN 6 | 3 | Hovercraft. Ordered end of 1976. |
| VOSPER/BR | 9 | High-speed patrol boats. |

*Sources*: IISS, Military Balance; SIPRI; *AWST*; *Jane's* Yearbooks and the sources presented in this chapter.

**Table 1.6** French arms sales to Egypt, 1975

| Item | Number | Comments |
|---|---|---|
| Mirage | 30–36 | Transferred to Egypt via SA |
| Gazelle heli. | 42 | Ordered in mid-1975. Received in January 1977. |
| Super Frelon heli. | — | — |
| Exocet missiles | — | — |
| Mirage F-1C | 22 | Ordered in Jan. 1975, delivered in 1977. Price/unit $5.6 million. |
| Mirage F-1E | 22 | Ordered in Jan. 1975. Delivery: 1979. |

*Sources*: See table 1.5.

Note: All the above items were part of a package deal totaling ca. $1 billion, most of which was to have been financed by SA.

## Interim Summary

An interim summary of civil and military aid Egypt received from October 1973 up to December 1975, shows that it received over $6 billion, of which $2 billion was made up of military aid. Table 1.7 presents the details.

**Table 1.7**  Civil and military aid: October 1973–December 1975 (in millions of US dollars)

| Conditions for aid | Amount |
|---|---|
| The Mar'i–Khalil mission (October 1973) (grant) | 350[1] |
| Libyan grant in first week of the war | 170 |
| Libyan loan, February 1974 | 18 |
| Faysal grant for reconstruction of Canal cities, April 1974 | 100 |
| Faysal grant, August 1974 | 300 |
| Qatar loan, November 1974 | 10 |
| Faysal grant for essential products, February 1975 | 100 |
| Saudi construction grant 1975 (50% in building materials) | 100 |
| Loan after Khaled visit, July 1975 | 600 |
| Kuwaiti loan for opening of the Canal, 1975 | 33 |
| Kuwaiti loan, September 1975 | 500[2] |
| Kuwaiti loan, October 1975 | 34 |
| UAE grant for purchase of 75 Boeing planes | 60[3] |
| Qatar grant, September 1975 | 100 |
| Khartoum grants, 1974–5 | 450[4] |
| Rabat grant, 1975 | 582 |
| Saudi and Iraqi oil grants | 150[5] |
| Arms purchases for Egypt by SA, Kuwait, UAE | 2,000[6] |
| Aid funds: bilateral and multilateral | 350[7] |
| Total civil and military aid: composed of: | 6,007 |
| Military grant | 2,000 |
| Grants | 2,372 |
| Loans | 1,635 |
| Grand total | 6,007 |

*Sources*: Data as presented in this study.

[1] The mission obtained a commitment for $800 million, but a part of this amount was paid for arms, and therefore appears under item "arms purchases" in this table. This data also corroborates Hijazi's statements in a personal interview, as well as Sadat's statements.

[2] In a personal interview, Hijazi stated that in April 1975 Kuwait granted $100 million, after Egypt had demanded $500 million. He said he remembered this aid package very well, as it was granted just before the end of his term as Prime Minister. It seems that in the end Kuwait relented and supplemented the amount up to $500 million.

[3] Hijazi advised that the planes were purchased by the UAE itself.

[4] In 1974 Libya did not fulfill all its Khartoum obligations, so that the total amount of aid that Egypt received by the spring of 1974 was lower than in previous years. It should be noted that Libya granted Egypt $27 million for the Rabat aid package in 1975. On the cessation of the Libyan remittances, see also the statements of the Egyptian Treasury Minister to the budgets committee of the Egyptian People's Council, on February 1, 1976, as quoted by: *ARR*, 1976, p. 71.

[5] A cautious estimate. $82 million from Iraq, SA provided 750,000 tons, but every now and then it substantially increased shipment tonnage. See, as example, Sadat's remarks, *al-Ahram*, June 13, 1976.

[6] According to a cautious estimate. Various reports mentioned larger amounts: *MEED* (July

25, 1975, p. 13) reported that SA alone granted $2.5 billion in military assistance, but this report also included aid received by Egypt before the war, which is included in data presented up to the war (see above). It could be that the AOC had not paid the European suppliers in full, having only signed contracts with them, and that full payment was to be made only after receipt of the goods. Besides data presented in this work regarding arms purchases for Egypt in the West, the AOC made substantial payments to the USSR in exchange for arms for Egypt, during and after the war. The SIPRI report (1974, p. 152) pointed out that the AOC paid ca. $2 billion for military equipment destined for Egypt and Syria. SIPRI did not differentiate between the two countries. The report including Syria is up-to-date only until 1974, but as we saw, in 1975 Egypt received further military assistance. Egyptian Treasury data showed that an item of the Egyptian Emergency Fund budget, financed by Arab grants and which covered a considerable slice of the military budget, indicated that in 1973 Egypt received $1 billion, in 1974 $1.25 billion and in 1975 $1 billion. See: *Financial Times*, June 28, 1976. As we will see presently, official Egyptian data pointed to $3.6 billion provided as military aid in the period between 1973 to 1978.

[7] For exact details of the amounts, according to distribution of funds and projects, see chapter 2.

[a] A more detailed analysis of data will be furnished, while comparing them to primary and secondary sources, at the conclusion of the presentation of aid details for the whole period under discussion.

## Drop in aid, 1976 to 1977

### Civil aid

In the period 1976–7 there was a significant drop in the magnitude of Arab aid to Egypt, in the civil as well as in the military sector. There was an especially sharp decline in 1976. In 1977 the extent of aid increased again, but this was caused by the food riots in January 1977, not by the AOC's decision to provide massive support to the Egyptian economy (see chapter 4). In February 1976, Sadat made a tour of the Gulf States. The Egyptian economy's difficulties and its arrears in payment of its debts compelled him to spell out the realities of the difficult economic situation to the leaders of the AOC, and the social and political implications stemming therefrom, and to try and obtain substantial assistance (see chapters 4 and 5). Sadat was again disappointed by the AOC on this trip: the Kuwaiti Emir proclaimed that it was the national duty of every Arab country to assist Egypt, but toward the end of his visit, Kuwait agreed to provide a mere $200 million. Even this relatively small sum was paid in instalments, the last one in August 1976.[159] The UAE agreed to a loan of $150 million in instalments, the last one in October 1976; Qatar, $70 million;[160] and Saudi Arabia, $300 million. It was decided during this tour to establish a special aid fund for the Egyptian economy.[161]

Over the course of this visit, the oil-producing countries displayed a patronizing attitude toward Egypt. For the first time, they conditioned their aid on Egypt putting its monetary affairs under external supervision, in exchange for aid amounting to $720 million (Saudi, Kuwaiti, UAE and Qatari aid).[162] Sadat had no option but to agree to their conditions, as this aid – notwithstanding its relatively minor scope and that it would be paid in installments – comprised a temporary solution for the Egyptian economy. In a speech at an Egyptian air force base, Sadat said that this aid "prevented an economic catastrophe."[163]

After Sadat's visit, discussions were initiated on the establishment of the special fund. Sadat demanded that the fund's capital be fixed at $10–$12 billion for a period of five years. On April 1, 1976, the session of Arab Finance Ministers in Riyadh, in which the proposed fund was discussed, was adjourned. Reports on this meeting in the Egyptian media were optimistic: *Akhbar al-Yawm* wrote that it had been decided to allocate $10 billion to the fund.[164] It is fair to suppose that this optimistic report was only used as an instrument, to pressure the AOC to react positively to Sadat's demands. In the end, the Finance Ministers of Saudi Arabia, Kuwait, the UAE and Qatar signed a protocol for the establishment of "The Gulf Fund for the Development of Egypt" (*Hay'at al-Khalij lil-Tanmiya fi Misr*) with a capital of $2 billion. They decided that the funds would be channeled to development investments in Egypt for a period of five years. The countries contributed to the fund's capital as follows: Saudi Arabia, 40%; Kuwait, 35%; the UAE, 15%; and Qatar, 10%.[165]

Sadat was not pleased with the size of the fund, nor with the dictates of the AOC, especially when Egypt was suffering from a severe payments crisis – the result of bank credits Egypt had taken out in the period 1973–6. These credits had been allotted at tough repayment terms: the average term for repayment was six months at commercial interest rates. Egypt took out this kind of credits before 1973, but for small sums. The turning-point came in 1973 following the war and the global rise in prices of raw materials. Egypt took out large loans – as it needed to import large quantities of food to feed its rapidly-growing population – and the trend continued in 1974. One year later, Egypt reduced its commercial loans, because of aid it was receiving, primarily from the AOC, and its rising debt settled. However, in 1976 the situation repeated itself, when Egypt once again increased the level of bank credits. These kinds of credits forced Egypt into a vortex of debts, whose end was difficult to foresee. The economy needed a high level of liquidity in order to handle the burden of short-term debts: in 1975 Egypt needed to repay $2,184 million in bank debts (principal and interest).

In order to demonstrate the importance of this sum, one should realize that it comprised around 78 percent of Egypt's total export revenues (products and services). It should be remembered that Egypt earned more than half of its export revenues through bilateral agreements with various countries – in other words, they did not bring in foreign currency.[166] In 1975 Egypt got lucky, when it won generous medium- and long-term credits from the oil countries, but in 1976 those generous credits did not repeat themselves, and Egypt could not meet its commitments. According to World Bank data, Egypt's debts to commercial banks in late 1976 amounted to $1.4 billion[167] (not including its medium- and long-term debts – ca. $5.8 billion – or its military debt).

In the interim period, between talks on the establishment of the Gulf Fund and the commencement of its aid activities, the AOC were in no hurry to provide any significant economic assistance. Saudi Arabia allocated $50 million to the rehabilitation of the Suez Canal area, and Kuwait agreed to again postpone repayment of loans until the end of 1978.[168] Sadat did not share a common language with the contributors to the fund, even after its establishment. He tried to determine the goals of the fund's capital, but the AOC leaders saw things differently. In October 1976, the directors of the fund rejected Egypt's request for a loan of $1.2 billion to support its balance of payments, on the pretext that fund capital was designated for development projects. The fund directors only agreed – another novelty on their part – to guarantee a loan of $250 million which Egypt was supposed to receive from the Chase Manhattan Bank, instead of according Egypt any direct aid. The AOC even conditioned their guarantee on a counter-guarantee from the Egyptian Central Bank.[169]

In light of the Gulf Fund's directors' refusal to help Egypt financially, the Egyptian Finance Minister held urgent talks with his Saudi counterpart, the chairman of the Fund, to convince him to provide additional aid on top of the guarantee given by them. Just before the end of 1976, the managers of the Fund agreed to the Finance Minister's plea to grant Egypt a loan of $250 million, destined to reduce the deficit in the current account. The loan was given for a period of ten years, including a three-year grace period, at an annual interest of 5 percent. Egypt tried to reduce the rate of interest, but it was turned down.[170]

In late 1976 Egypt's civil and military debts increased greatly, and it was in arrears with its short-term debts by $400 million.[171] Aid received from the Gulf Fund and directly from the AOC was minor – relative to its needs – and it was doled out on hard terms. At a conference of Foreign Ministers from the AOC, Egypt and Syria, held in Riyadh on January 9–10, 1977, Fahmi requested an increase of aid. The AOC refused and Fahmi stormed out of the meeting.[172] On January 18, 1977, a few days after the conference, the Egyptian pressure cooker exploded with the beginning of the "food riots" (**see chapter 5**). That same day, Sadat secretly flew to Saudi Arabia and demanded urgent assistance.[173] As the AOC feared that the situation in Egypt would have negative ramifications for them, they were relatively generous. Two weeks after the food riots, Finance Ministers of the Gulf Fund met with their Egyptian counterpart and agreed to loan Egypt $1 billion for the 1977 budget year.[174] In April 1977, the managers of the Fund decided to put $1.474 billion at the disposal of the ECB, in instalments, instead of the original sum ($1 billion).[175] Saudi Arabia and Kuwait also postponed the withdrawal of their deposits from the ECB (ca. $2 billion), as well as repayment of Egypt's debts.[176]

## Military aid

During Sadat's visit to the Gulf in February 1976, Saudi Arabia decided to allocate additional sums to Egypt for arms purchases from the US, on top of civil aid. There is no way of accurately assessing the magnitude of military aid promised to Egypt, for two reasons: first, reports give versions of between $250 and $700 million, and second, it was determined that this aid would depend on the willingness of the Americans to cancel the embargo on weapons sales to Egypt.[177] Several months after his tour, Sadat shed some light on military aid he obtained during his visit to the Gulf. In a speech at the Maritime Academy in Abu Qir, he said that Saudi Arabia paid the US for Egyptian arms purchases, but the former postponed its decision at this stage. Sadat added: "I wish to express my heartfelt gratitude to Saudi Arabia for their aid to our armed forces, which was not published for security reasons. This was for the purpose of keeping my promise to you . . . that I would not burden you with further duties, before you received state-of-the-art weapons."[178] Later in 1976, the US supplied Egypt with six C-130 cargo planes, financed by the Saudis **(chapter 5)**. Furthermore, during 1976/early 1977, Saudi Arabia financed Egypt's order for thirty-eight Mirage planes.[179]

In the summer of 1977 Sadat revealed, that "the previous year" Saudi Arabia had pledged to finance all expenses involved in the development of the Egyptian armed forces for a period of five years, "without asking Egypt for one penny."[180] In December 1977, it was reported that Saudi Arabia financed the purchase of four-teen Hercules planes at a cost of $250 million from Lockheed.[181] Besides direct Saudi financing, in the years 1976–7, Egypt closed several arms transactions with Western European countries, and the financing body was supposed to have been the AMIO. These deals included both direct arms supply to the Egyptian army as well as transfer of technology to the AMIO, to enable the latter to assemble, and at a later stage to manufacture, the weapons **(chapter 2)**. Intelligence data from the American State Department show that at least $835 million was furnished by the AMIO for Egyptian weapons purchases: $70 million to West Germany, $765 million to the UK.[182]

According to a State Department report, Egypt signed tentative or formal agree-ments with West European countries in the years 1976–8 (the report did not differentiate between the years), for over $2.9 billion in weapons purchases, including military equipment, ammunition, spare parts, logistic aid, training, joint manufacture and assembly of weapons. They also purchased arms from communist countries for over $120 million, mostly from China.[183] In accordance with ACDA data, Egypt bought arms from all sources in the period of 1974–8 at a cost of $1.2 billion.[184] This seems to contradict the classified data of the State Department report; it could be that ACDA referred to arms Egypt actually received, while the State Department report referred to tentative and formal agreements. It is more likely that ACDA did not relate to agreements on assembly of Western weapons in Egypt. Another possibility is that the ACDA deliberately published incorrect data.

## Sadat's trip to Jordan, 1978

### Civil Aid

Sadat's trip to Jerusalem, in November 1977, prompted various reactions from the oil-producing countries. Before Sadat's trip, the AOC were in no hurry to provide massive economic aid to Egypt, and even less after this event. Nevertheless, aid was never completely discontinued, but, as indicated, there was already a major decline in scope by 1976. As we will see in chapters 4 and 5, Egypt continued to receive mili-tary and civil aid from the conservative oil states, even after the Camp David agreement, and subsequently after the economic boycott imposed on it.

The GFDE's managers' agreement to loan Egypt $1.48 billion in the summer of 1977 made it clear that the major part of the Fund's capital ($1.75 billion out of $2 billion) was actually meted out to Egypt as a guarantee, or it was promised as loan. Egypt therefore tried to persuade the AOC to allot additional resources to the Gulf Fund. In April 1977 Kuwait announced that it would be willing to do so,[185] but as the talks dragged on, it became clear that the AOC were not willing to increase fund capital. The Fund managers were furious that capital had been used by Egypt prematurely (in a year-and-a-half instead of five years), for repayment of short-term debts and imports, instead of applying these funds to development projects. The Saudi and Kuwaiti finance ministers stressed that they were not ready to increase the Fund's capital in order to subsidize consumer products.[186] In the end, members of the Fund and Egypt reached an agreement in the summer of 1978. After a meeting with 'Abd al-Rahman al-'Atiqi, the Kuwaiti Finance Minister, who was acting chairman of the Fund at the time, and an Egyptian delegation, headed by its economic ministers, it was agreed that Egypt could utilize interest it was supposed to repay to the Fund for its previous loans.[187]

In the course of 1978, Egypt received the balance of Fund capital, about $500 million, as guaranteed by the AOC in 1977, and in August 1978 they agreed to loan Egypt another $250 million up to the end of the year, in the following manner: $100 million in deferred interest payments and $150 million as a guarantee from the Fund to the international monetary markets in exchange for their loans to Egypt.[188] Besides the balance of the Gulf Fund – which was funneled to Egypt in 1978 – it also received a part of the Khartoum and Rabat aid package. Saudi Arabia provided its share of the Khartoum obligation with a $150 million grant, while Kuwait paid for the Rabat commitment, and transferred $175 million.[189] So that total civil aid received by Egypt from the AOC in 1978 came to $825 million. Out of this more than $300 million was bilateral aid, and the rest was the balance of the Gulf Fund.[190] This data does not include a loan of $17.7 million – as support for the balance of payments – that Egypt received from the Arab Monetary Fund in August.[191] This amount is insignificant, but it was the first loan that the Fund had made since its founding, and it is worth noting that Egypt received it in spite of its intensive direct talks with Israel.

## Military aid

Military cooperation between Egypt and the AOC continued in 1978. Egypt signed agreements with several European manufacturers for transfer of military know-how to the AMIO, for the assembly of military equipment in Egypt, with one of the outstanding agreements being a letter of intent for the purchase of 160 Alpha fighter planes at a cost of $800 million – of which a major part were to be assembled in Egypt.[192] In February 1978, Egypt received most of the Mirage F-1s, out of the forty-four planes ordered for it, financed by the Egyptian AMIO.[193]

In early 1978, General Fish, of the Foreign Affairs Committee of the American Congress, was questioned about information that had reached members of the committee, according to which Egyptian pilots, stationed in Saudi Arabia, were training on Saudi F-5 planes, in order to transfer them afterwards to the Egyptian air force. The General evaded a direct answer, stating that the laws of Congress oblige a country to notify the US in advance of any transfer of arms to a third country, and according to him Saudi Arabia had not done so. The members of the committee made matters difficult for the General: Gillman repeated his question on the matter of the training of Egyptian pilots in Saudi Arabia, and after further pressure, Fish replied he would look into the matter and send a report to the committee.[194] The report that was sent later also avoided clear answers: "we have no knowledge of any arrangements between Egypt and Saudi Arabia regarding transfer of any kind of weapon or military equipment." The report also indicated, that six Egyptian pilots received training on F-5 planes in 1975, but they finished their course after two months and since then no Egyptian pilot had received any training.[195]

In August 1978, several months after the discussion in the Congressional committee, it transpired that the information received by the committee was correct. Saudi Arabia had pledged to finance for Egypt the purchase of fifty F-5 planes from the US at a cost of $525 million. The Saudis agreed to this transaction, even after the first Baghdad conference in late 1978.[196] Even after the signing of the peace treaty and the adoption of the anti-Egyptian diplomatic and economic boycott in the fall of 1979, the American administration saw signs that Saudi Arabia would finance the deal: in a discussion in the Congressional Foreign Affairs Committee (late April 1979), Senator Glenn asked the Secretary of Defense, Harold Brown, about the deal, and the latter replied that there were positive indications that it would be honored.[197] Only in early July 1979 did American officials declare that Saudi Arabia would not pay for the planes[198]. The Carter administration then delayed the shipment of F-5s, but Egypt did not come out a loser: the US granted Egypt a credit of $594 million, for the purchase of thirty-five F-4E planes, which were more advanced than the F-5s.

## Aid in 1976–1978: An interim summary

In this period (thirty-six months) Egypt received $5.2 billion compared to more than $6 billion in the period October 1973–December 1975, which was shorter (twenty-seven months). The exceptional aid during this period was granted following the food riots in January 1977, and it is doubtful if Egypt would have received it otherwise.

Table 1.8   AOC aid to Egypt, 1976–1978 (in millions of US dollars)

| Circumstances of aid | Amount |
| --- | --- |
| Grants following Sadat's trip, Feb. 1976 | 720[1] |
| Saudi grant for reconstruction of Canal area, 1976 | 50 |
| Khartoum and Rabat grants (1976–8) | 930[2] |
| Gulf Fund loans (1976–8) | 2,000[3] |
| Military aid | 1,000 |
| Loans from bi- and multilateral aid funds | 500[4] |
| Total | 5,200 |
| breakdown: | |
| Military grant | 1,000 |
| Grants | 1,700 |
| Loans | 2,500 |
| Total | 5,200 |

*Sources*: Data presented in this chapter.

*Notes to table 1.8*
[1] The amount was paid in full in the course of that year.
[2] As we saw, Rabat aid alone should have exceeded $500 million annually, but the AOC reduced it, after they initially claimed that this assistance was destined for one year only. Similarly, Khartoum aid should have exceeded $250 million annually, but Libya stopped paying its share, so that Egypt received somewhat less than $200 million annually. Therefore total Khartoum aid in this period should have reached $600 million; but in 1978 Egypt received only $150 million, so that above aid amounted to $550 million. From an ECB report it appears that Egypt received $964 million in the period of 1975–8, as Rabat aid. See: Nafi', *Nahnu wal-'Alam*, pp. 122–4. In 1975 Egypt received $582 million, so that during this period it received the difference – $382 million. In accordance with this data, Egypt received $930 million for Khartoum and Rabat aid in this period. This is a much lower sum than AOC commitments for these clauses. From aid that should have amounted to $750 million annually, Egypt received in this period an annual average of $310 million. For example, in 1977 it received $375 million. See: WB, *ARE, Recent Economic Development and External Capital Requirements* (May 19, 1978), p. 5.
[3] Including a guarantee of $250 million provided as a loan to Egypt, $1,075 million as a cash loan to Egypt for the payment of its debts, and a loan of $650 million for imports and payment of short-term debts.
[4] Including 1979. See details on aid funds in chapter 2.

After Sadat's trip to Jerusalem, aid to Egypt declined sharply, but this view could be misleading. Already in 1976 there was a sharp decline in the magnitude of Arab aid (table 1.9), and in fact, besides aid from the Gulf Fund, provided under special circumstances, Egypt did not receive any significant assistance in 1977.

**Table 1.9**  Arab government and civil aid[1] to Egypt, October 1973–1978, and its share of total GNP (in millions of US dollars and percentages)

| Year | Grants | Loans | Total | GNP | % of GNP |
|------|--------|-------|-------|-----|----------|
| 1973 | 520[2] | —     | 520   | 8,820[3] | 5.9 |
| 1974 | 600    | 28    | 628   | 10,210   | 6.2 |
| 1975 | 1,342  | 1,167 | 2,509 | 9,540    | 26.3 |
| 1976 | 1,073  | 250   | 1,323 | 10,680   | 12.4 |
| 1977 | 302    | 1,250 | 1,552 | 12,950   | 12.0 |
| 1978 | 325    | 500   | 825   | 15,520   | 5.3 |

*Sources to table 1.9*: Arranged in accordance with data quoted in this chapter and tables 1.8–1.9. GNP data as per: World Bank, *WB Atlas*, various issues.

[1] This does not include military and aid fund assistance, except for the GFDE.
[2] October–December.
[3] Data refers to the entire year.

## 1967–1978: A summary

Many of the studies and reports listed in this chapter do not deal at all with aid that Egypt received after this period, not least because of their assumption that Egypt received no direct, official aid whatsoever after the 1979 Baghdad boycott. Actually, Egypt did receive aid after this time, but in much smaller amounts than it had received up to 1978, albeit irregularly. In chapter 4, which examines, inter alia, the policy of the Arab oil-producing countries toward Egypt after the peace treaty, and in chapter 5, which examines the influences of the economic boycott on Egypt, aid to Egypt after the peace agreement will be discussed, as well as the continuing employment of Egyptian workers in the AOC and their remittances to the Egyptian economy.

According to the data presented in this chapter, the extent of military aid in the period of June 1967–December 1978 amounted to $4.25 billion. Most of this was doled out in 1973, during and after the preparations for the October War. This data is more conservative than other sources, as we will see below. The main reason for this conservative choice is the difficulty in tracing the amounts of arms purchases the AOC made for Egypt: even when extensive details of these purchases were published, the amounts were not always indicated, and it is not clear whether all arms ordered actually reached Egypt.

Some of the research works listed below, refer to the period of January 1973–December 1978; others refer to more constricted timeframes, such as: October 1973–December 1978, 1974–8 and so on. The following are data reached in several variations:

1   Total aid Egypt received in the period June 1967–December 1978: $14.2 billion.
2   Total aid in the period of January 1973–December 1978: $12.2 billion, of which $4.072 million in grants, $4.135 million in loans, and $4,000 million in military aid (the balance of $250 million represents the difference in military aid, supplied before 1973).
3   Total aid in the period October 1973–December 1978: $11.2 billion.

These amounts do not include the deposits the AOC (principally Saudi Arabia and Kuwait) kept in the Egyptian Central Bank, which totaled $2 billion. Several reports included these deposits in their aid calculations, claiming they had been deposited in Egypt for an extended period, and at rates of interest which were lower than the customary rates on international monetary markets. If one wishes to include them in aid calculations, the sum of $2 billion must be added to the total amount.

Table 1.10 shows the oil countries' aid to Egypt from mid-1967 to the end of 1978.

**Table 1.10**   Oil-countries' aid to Egypt, June 1967–December 1978 (in billions of US dollars)

| | |
|---|---|
| June 1967–October 1973 | 3.06 |
| October 1973–December 1975 | 6.00 |
| January 1976–December 1978 | 5.20 |
| Total (not incl. deposits) | 14.26 |
| Total (incl. deposits) | 16.26 |

**Table 1.10** (*continued*)

| | |
|---|---|
| Breakdown: | |
| Military aid | 4.25 |
| Grants | 5.875 |
| Loans | 4.135 |
| Deposits | 2.00 |
| Total incl. deposits | 16.26 |

*Sources*: Data presented in this chapter.

## A comparative analysis

In this section various official reports are analyzed, both those that dealt with actual aid and those that analyzed other economic data (with no direct indication of aid), which enabled the indirect location of data on loans. An example for this data is the breakdown of Egypt's foreign debts – analysis that highlights the basic contradictions in the published literature, and allows a more rounded evalution of aid contribution.

### Official data/reports

**Data from the Egyptian National Bank and the World Bank**  An important method for locating Arab aid to Egypt is an examination and an analysis of its foreign debts.[199] This method does not give us a full picture, because it only enables us to pinpoint loan data. To complete the picture we need details of grants and military aid. From an Egyptian National Bank report for the fiscal year 1982/3 it appears that, up to June 30, 1982, Egypt's medium- and long-term civil debts amounted to $20.8 billion. Out of this amount, Egypt actually received $14.9 billion.[200] Aid in the delivery stage is Western aid – largely American – which Egypt had difficulty in absorbing. It succeeded in absorbing the major part of Arab aid, as most of it was bestowed in cash, to support its balance of payments, as compared to Western civil aid, which was provided according to progress achieved on various projects **(see chapters 2 and 5)**.

According to the report, 57 percent of total debts ($11.9 billion – out of which $8.8 billion were actually transferred) were bilateral debts. In the years 1975–9, most of these debts were owed to Arab states and, after the signing of the Camp David agreement, to the United States. The US was the principal bilateral creditor – 40 percent; Kuwait came second – 13 percent; and Saudi Arabia came third – 11 percent. Other debts were owed to bi- and multilateral institutions (20%), international monetary markets (7%) and economic relief (16%).[201] As per this data, Saudi Arabia and Kuwait loaned Egypt 24 percent out of $8.8 billion, which is slightly more than $2.1 billion. The report did not indicate loans granted by the UAE, Qatar, Libya and Iraq. This data was supplemented by a World Bank report from 1979 – whose data on debts to Saudi Arabia and Kuwait match those of the Egyptian Central Bank – according to which Egypt owed Iraq $31 million; Libya, $138 million; Qatar, $88 million; and the UAE, $295 million.[202] A combination of the two reports shows that Egypt received loans totaling $2.7 billion from the Arab oil states.

A study of an OECD document shows that Egypt's debts to the OPEC states in 1983 amounted to $3.141 billion.[203] This figure exceeds the total reached in this study – $2.7 billion – but it should be remembered that Iran also gave loans to Egypt totaling $320 million.[204] Therefore total debts to the AOC amounted to $2.8 billion, according to OECD data, compared to the figure of $2.7 billion, which the combination of the ENBO and World Bank reports gives us. The latter data are more specific than the OECD data. To this data, multilateral aid (including the Gulf Fund), bilateral grants and military aid should be added. Multilateral aid (loans) amounted to $2.8 billion – out of which $2 billion was provided by the Gulf Fund[205] – multilateral grants in the years 1973–8 came to slightly more than $4.1 billion.[206]

**Table 1.11**    AOC grants to Egypt, 1967–1976 (in millions of US dollars)

|  | Amount |
|---|---|
| 1967–72 (annual average) 261 x 6 = | 1,566 |
| 1973 | 648 |
| 1974 | 1,035 |
| 1975 | 1,077 |
| 1976 | 711 |
| 1977 (first quarter) | 63 |
| Total for 1967–March 1977 | 5,100 |
| Total for 1973–March 1977 | 3,534 |

*Source*: Egyptian Central Bank, *al-Taqrir al-Sanawi* (1967–76), quarterly bank statements for 1967–77.

The sum total up to now indicates that Egypt received loans and grants totaling $9.6 billion in the years 1973–8, as against my figure of $8.2 billion. For a final computation, only military aid data is still required. None of the reports mentioned so far included any details on military assistance. If we add military aid data to the final figure as calculated in this study ($4 billion – see below for different evaluations on military aid), we will find that Arab aid to Egypt in the years 1973–8 came to $13.6 billion, compared to $12.2 billion, according to my calculations. The discrepancy in the data – ca. 11 percent – is not so conclusive as to change the general picture decisively. This is a result of excluding unconfirmed aid to Egypt.

ECB quarterly documentation reveals the following information: in the years 1967–72 Egypt received an average of $261 million annually (a total of $1,566 million for the whole period), and in the period from 1973 until the first quarter of 1977, a total of $3,496 million (table 1.11). This data confirms the findings in my research for the period of June 1967–October 1973; up to 1972 Egypt received, according to information from the Egyptian bank, grants totaling $1.6 billion, and in 1973, $648 million. Total grants (excluding military aid) came to $2.2 billion. This research reached a figure of just over $3 billion, including military aid received by Egypt just before the October 1973 War. The figures agree, without military aid.

**Table 1.12**    Arab aid to Egypt (in millions of US dollars)

| Year | 1973 | 1974 | 1975 | 1976 | 1977 | 1978 |
|---|---|---|---|---|---|---|
| Grants | 700 | 1,243 | 1,002 | 700 | 350 | 148 |
| Loans and deposits | 175 | 360 | 1,750 | 285 | 1,243 | 573 |
| Loans for projects | 30 | — | 22 | 87 | 158 | 164 |
| Total | 905 | 1,603 | 2,774 | 1,072 | 1,751 | 885 |

*Source*: K. Ikram, *Egypt – Economic Management,* p. 351.

The World Bank published data which included grants, general loans, deposits and loans for specific projects provided by the AOC to Egypt in the years 1973–8. The bank did not differentiate between loan and deposit details, neither did it include assistance by the bi- and multilateral funds, except for the Gulf Fund for the Development of Egypt (GFDE).[207] Table 1.12 shows that total aid in this period amounted to $8.99 billion (excluding military aid). If we add on aid from the various funds ($850 million), military aid ($4 billion), and we deduct the deposits of the AOC on the ECB ($2 billion), we arrive at a total of $11.84 billion, that Egypt received between 1973 and 1978. These figures almost match data presented here, $12.2 billion – a difference of less than 3 percent. These figures are comparable with World Bank data only by the parameters indicated by the World Bank: therefore, by deducting military aid ($4 billion) and fund aid ($0.85 billion) from the total of $12.2 billion, and adding to this sum the deposits ($2 billion), we arrive at a figure of $9.35 billion, compared to the World Bank figure of $8.99 billion. The discrepancies are not significant, even when compared to the components of the aid package. Thus,

1    Total grants received by Egypt, according to the World Bank, amount to $4,143 million. This study arrives at a figure of $4,072 million – a difference of $71 million. In comparison with the data in table 1.12, in which the amount of grants is similar, but the annual breakdown is different.

2    For a breakdown of grants by countries for the years 1973–8, see the World Bank report, with the same caption as the source of this table (The World Bank, May 8 1978), volume 4, p. 48.

3    Loans for projects were funds channeled directly from the oil governments' budgets – and not via aid funds – to projects such as the development of the Suez Canal area, the construction of new cities, e.g. the city of Sheikh Zayd (named for the ruler of Abu Dhabi). Aid funds also provided assistance for these purposes.

4    Total loans and deposits in table 1.12 amount to $4,847 million (excluding aid from various funds, except for the Gulf Fund). If we deduct from this amount the deposits held by the AOC on the ECB ($2 billion), we arrive at an amount of $2,847 million. This study calculates loans totaled at $4,135 million, but this amount also included aid from the various funds ($850 million). If we deduct this sum, we get $3,285 million.

In late 1979, the Egyptian Minister of Planning, 'Abd al-Raziq 'Abd al-Majid, declared that in the years 1973–8 Egypt received grants and loans (excluding military aid) totaling $7.5 billion from the Arab countries.[208] This study shows loans and grants in this period amounted to $8,107 million. If we deduct aid from this amount ($850 million), we arrive at a figure of $7,257 million, which very nearly approximates the minister's data.

**OECD and UNCTAD data**    OECD data are neither detailed nor clear: they indicate that from 1974 to 1978 Egypt received $5,307.7 million as "bilateral concessional aid" from the OPEC states.[209] OECD did not differentiate between grants and loans, and it did not mention which countries rendered aid to Egypt. The figures give no indication of aid provided to Egypt by non-Arab OPEC members. Nigeria and Venezuela did not provide any assistance to Egypt, which leaves only Iran – from whom Egypt did not receive any substantial aid. In the mid-1970s there was talk of joint projects by the two countries, but little was said about aid. Iranian foreign aid focused mainly on the subcontinent of India,[210] and Egypt received $320 million.[211] This figure should be deducted from OECD data. Therefore total aid received by Egypt from the AOC in this period was ca. $4.9 billion. To this amount we must add aid from the Gulf Fund ($2 billion), and the assistance from the Arab aid funds and institutions ($850 million), totaling $7.7 billion in civil aid, compared to $7.3 billion in the corresponding period.

UNCTAD data indicate that in the years 1973–8 Egypt received civil aid amounting to $5,980 million from OPEC member countries[212]. After deduction of Iranian aid ($320 million) and addition of aid from the Gulf Fund and other funds ($2.85 billion), we arrive at a figure of $8.48 billion, compared to $8.2 billion in my research, in the corresponding period.

**Official American data**    The US closely monitored aid received by Egypt, because it had also rendered assistance to that country. In discussions in Congressional committees who approved aid and its extent to Egypt, committee members inquired into the magnitude of aid furnished by other countries. Data provided by AID to the subcommittee for foreign affairs of the American House of Representatives, revealed that Saudi Arabia, Kuwait, the UAE and Qatar had granted Egypt $7.2 billion in civil aid during the years 1974–7, out of a total aid package of more than $12 billion from all sources. This report indicated the components of aid, but not the amounts of each item separately. This sum included grants, loans, bank deposits and loan guarantees.[213] The report of the AID covered a period of only four years, without the data for the regional aid funds or military aid. For a comparison between the agency estimate and the present research, we will add aid figures for the years 1973 and 1978 data of funds aid (except for the Gulf Fund) and military aid.

To the basic figure ($7.2 billion) was added civil aid that Egypt received in 1973 ($900 million); aid received by Egypt in 1978 (the balance from the Gulf Fund, and a part of the Khartoum and Rabat commitments – $825 million); aid from regional funds ($850 million); and military aid ($4 billion). Egypt received a total of $13.78 billion from 1973–8. The last stage in the calculation is the deduction of deposits ($2 billion) and the final figure comes to $11.78 billion, compared to the $12.2 billion in this study's findings.

### Secondary sources

Waterbury quoted a news item published in the Saudi *al-Riyad* (May 1979), which indicated that Saudi assistance to Egypt in 1973 amounted to $7 billion. In his opinion, this sum is exaggerated, even if military aid and unpublished grants are taken into account. To reinforce his contention, Waterbury quoted a report from the IMF, according to which AOC credits to Egypt up to September 1977 totaled $4.4 billion (Saudi Arabia and Kuwait were the principal creditors; Egypt owed them jointly $2.4 billion).[214] Waterbury did not take into account several significant factors, which change the picture: first, the report he based his research on does not indicate a method for a comprehensive evaluation of Arab aid to Egypt – in this case Saudi aid – as it did not include the grants, which were bigger than the credits, and military aid. From data supplied by the IMF, the World Bank and data presented in this research, it appears that the Saudi grants to Egypt amounted to at least $2 billion; second, Waterbury rejected an estimate published in 1979, in favor of data published in September 1977. The Arab boycott was imposed eighteen months after this date, and Saudi Arabia, as we saw, assisted Egypt in this period; third, Waterbury quoted only Egypt's bilateral debts from the IMF report, and not the multilateral debts, in which the Saudis had a major part. Waterbury also neglected to mention the Saudi role in Gulf Fund aid to Egypt ($800 million). In any case, he did not give an alternative all-inclusive evaluation for Saudi assistance, or for the other oil countries' aid to Egypt.

Gouda 'Abdel Khalek quoted in his article reports from Egypt's Ministry of Economy and Economic Cooperation, and the Egyptian Central Bank. He examined the extent of aid in the period 1952 to June 1977. Khalek did not give a breakdown of aid according to years, only each country's global share over the whole period. Up to the beginning of the 1960s, Egypt did not receive aid from these countries. According to the findings of the reports Khalek investigated, Egypt received EgP 1,322.3 million from the AOC, including aid funds, which amount to $3,379 million, adjusted to the 1977 rate of exchange. Khalek added that this figure does not include military aid Egypt received as a grant – EgP 1,928.9 million ($4,929 million).[215] According to this data, Egypt received civil and military aid totaling $8,308 million. An examination of the data presented by Khalek shows that the Gulf Fund granted EgP 259 million ($662 million) in this period.[216]

The amount of Gulf Fund aid included in these figures has been reduced, as Khalek quoted data endorsed up to June 1977, but the Gulf Fund granted the balance of aid ($1.35 billion) only after this date. If we add to the total amount the remainder of Gulf Fund aid and the aid Egypt received from July 1977 until the end of 1978 ($2 billion), we reach a total of $10.3 billion, in civil and military assistance received by Egypt from the AOC since 1967. This figure is lower than other official Egyptian estimates. Khalek did not indicate on which specific reports he based his findings, but other reports from the ECB demonstrated that up to March 1977 Egypt received $1.5 billion in grants only, and this data compares favorably with World Bank figures for the years 1973–7. Khalek's data indicated about half of this figure. One possibility is that Khalek only took into account aid given to Egypt according to the resolutions of the Arab summits, and in that case the amount would be realistic.

Sayigh wrote that, in the period of October 1973–December 1974, Egypt received $3,026 million from the oil-producing countries, as per the following breakdown (in millions of US dollars): Iraq, 875; Kuwait, 615; Saudi Arabia, 1,045; the UAE, 139.5; Qatar, 161.5; Libya, 10. The author added that aid to Egypt, including aid from bilateral and multilateral funds, totaled $3,269 billion. Moreover, he mentioned that there were reports that Egypt and Syria jointly received $3–$4 billion in military aid, and on top of that all confrontation states combined received $1,369 million, with no clear breakdown between them. (In the sum of $1,369 million, Sayigh apparently referred to "Rabat aid," in which Egypt's share came to $582 million.)[217]

These inflated figures create several problems:

1   The author included pledges for aid, but not actual payment.
2   Iraq never granted Egypt aid in the amount of $875 million. This sum does not represent aid, but an agreement on investments between Egypt and Iraq **(see chapter 2)**, of which not even a small part had been realized up to the end of 1974.
3   Up to the end of 1974, Egypt did not receive one cent of the $1,369 million promised to the confrontation states. It received its share of Rabat aid only in mid-January 1975.
4   The author considerably underestimated Libyan aid to Egypt.

No attempt was made to separate military aid to Egypt from that given to Syria.

McLaurin and Price devoted an article on OPEC aid to the confrontation states. According to their research, during the years 1974–7 these countries granted $11.8 billion to Egypt in civil and military aid.

These figures and their details are astonishing: a table with specifications of this aid shows that total aid to Egypt came to $12.83 billion,[218] and not $11.8 billion as indicated before. The table illustrates that in the years 1974–5, Iran assisted Egypt with a total of $1,785 million. It should be stressed that Iran's aid to Egypt did not amount to even 20 percent of this amount; the authors indicated that in 1975 Egypt received $1 billion from Saudi Arabia and Kuwait as payment for the 1974 Rabat aid package. This sum was only an initial proposal, before it was reduced to $580 million. Furthermore, besides Saudi Arabia and Kuwait, Libya, Iraq and the UAE also participated in this aid. McLaurin and Price mentioned that total military aid to Egypt came to $6 billion, most of which was bestowed in 1974–5. They based their findings, among other sources, on the Kuwaiti *al-Watan*, which mentioned this figure. An inquiry in *al-Watan* (March 18, 1975) reveals that Saudi Arabia independently provided this military aid ($6 billion) in the period October 1973–March 1975. During this time Egypt did not benefit from anywhere near this amount of military aid, even if civil aid is included. Egypt never received $6 billion in military aid from Saudi Arabia during the whole period up to 1978.

Other surprising data presented in McLaurin and Price's table are those on Libyan and Iraqi aid to Egypt in 1975. In that year Libya granted $2,078 million and Iraq $1,693 million to Egypt. In actual fact, because of a cooling of relations between Egypt and Libya in this period, the latter hardly provided any assistance at all to Egypt, except for proportionally smaller donations. Moreover, even if we add up all "the good years" in the ties between these two countries, we still find that aid granted by Libya to Egypt does not even approach this figure. The same can be said of Egypt's relations with Iraq. The amount of aid Iraq granted to Egypt in 1975 came to less than 10 percent of the sum mentioned in McLaurin and Price's research, and total aid figures for the above countries over the years were less than 30 percent of the above-mentioned $1,693 million. To compound the errors in their research McLaurin and Price's data contends that Saudi Arabia never provided any aid to Egypt, except for the Rabat aid package.[219]

In his book *Nahnu wal-'Alam* ("We and the World"), Ibrahim Nafi' emphasized that he had the "most up-to-date and accurate" data of aid to Egypt. He stated that the time had come "that we open the file, so that all parties will know what rights and obligations they have."[220] The following are details of aid as presented by Ibrahim Nafi': Khartoum aid, £1,079 million sterling; Saudi Arabia, £479 million; Kuwait, £445 million; Libya, £155 million. In addition, from 1973 to 1979 the AOC furnished the following aid: Saudi Arabia, $1,655 million ($170 million in Rabat aid, $940 million in additional aid and $545 million as its share of the Gulf Fund loans), and $837 million in deposits on the ECB; Kuwait, $1,472 million ($517 million; Rabat, $478 million; additional aid, $477 million, Gulf Fund), and $926 million, deposits; Libya, $137 million ($27 million, Rabat; $110 million additional aid), and $106 million, deposits; the UAE, $733 million ($102 million, Rabat; $458 million additional aid; $203 million, Gulf Fund), and $230 million in loans to various authorities in Egypt; Qatar, $171 million ($106 million, Rabat; $65 million, additional aid), and $75 million, loans to Egyptian authorities; Iraq, $48 million ($42 million, Rabat; $6 million, additional aid).

Total aid, according to Nafi', amounted to £1,079 and $6,101 million (in accordance with his data the figure should be $1,859 million). According to Nafi', to this figure the sum of $3.6 billion in military aid should be added, so that the sum total of all kinds of Arab aid during the years 1967–79 "did definitely not exceed $12 billion."[221]

Nafi' based his findings on data in reports from the ECB and the Egyptian Ministry of Defense, but nevertheless his figures referring to aid from 1967 to 1979 are low, and it seems that Nafi' relied on partial data only. The Gulf Fund aid to Egypt, Nafi's data apparently shows, bestowed a total of $1,225 million, but it granted $2 billion only, as confirmed and declared by Egyptian officials, Arab organizations that financed the fund and international financial bodies. If we add to this Nafi's mistaken calculations (as we saw, he omitted about $350 million), and the difference between his data on deposits and the actual figure ($150 million), we arrive at a total of $1.3 billion omitted by him.

Besides these data, Nafi' omitted other details: in accordance with ECB data, from 1967 to March 1977 Egypt received grants totaling $1.5 billion, and from an Egyptian National Bank report, reviewing its bilateral debts (excluding the funds), it appeared that Egypt's debts to the AOC amounted to $2.7 billion. According to these reports, the sum total of bilateral grants and loans that Egypt received added up to $7.8 billion. Nafi', of course, omits the figures for deposits ($1,869 million as he claimed), the Gulf Fund ($1,225 million), military aid ($3.6 billion) and the small loans provided by the UAE and Qatar to various bodies in Egypt ($305 million), to arrive at a total of $5 billion, compared to $7.8 billion. If, added to Nafi's estimate, the sums he did not compile ($4.1 billion), a total is arrived at $16.1 billion, including deposits. This study calculates a total of $16.2 billion (including deposits) in the years 1967–78.

Many other details of aid were published in the Arab and Western media and in research works, but they were neither consistent nor complete. They often presented too generalized data, or they presented data without breaking down for periods of time. They also refrained from furnishing details of their source, making it difficult to verify the material. Jabber, for example, stated that in the years 1973–8, according to a conservative estimate, Arab aid to Egypt totaled $15 billion. In support of this sum, he declared that he would give a breakdown of the figures in his article. However, later on Jabber wrote that in the years 1973–6 Egypt received $1.5 billion and that from 1976 on, aid declined steadily, so that billions of dollars disappeared without any details in his research;[222] in mid-1979 EIU quoted Kuwaiti sources, according to which Arab countries granted Egypt civil aid worth $8.5 billion in the years 1974–8[223]; the Saudi *al-Fajr* declared in May 1979, that Saudi Arabia assisted Egypt from 1973 onward with a total of $7 billion;[224] in April 1979 *al-Watan al-'Arabi* wrote that Egypt received Arab aid totaling $4 billion, as per the resolutions of the summit conferences;[225] Ghantus only mentioned the credits Egypt received from the AOC in 1975–6 – $1,872.8 million in 1975 and $1,028.2 million in 1976;[226] Ragsdale quoted data from the American State Department for 1974 and 1975, which stated that, in 1974, Egypt received $1,013 million from the Gulf countries and $2,524 million in 1975;[227] and Mattes declared that from 1969 to 1975 Egypt received $184 million from Libya, out of which $138 million was issued as a grant for military purposes.[228]

Adel Hussein attempted to deal with Arab aid in a more comprehensive framework, with solid resources regarding aid from Arab funds to Egypt. His data for governmental aid, however, which constitutes the major part, is less well-grounded. Hussein did not include Saudi aid – which was the largest source of governmental aid to Egypt – on the pretext that "its government does not usually publish data." According to his data, from the October War until November 30, 1977, Egypt received loans from Kuwait totaling $115 million, from Abu Dhabi, $230 million, and from Qatar, $88 million. Furthermore, in October 1973 Kuwait rendered aid amounting to $700 million for the purchase of Soviet arms; in June 1974 it granted $175 million, and $150 million for the war effort and development projects, without mentioning a specific date; the UAE granted $103 million for development projects, financed the purchase of Boeing planes in June 1974, and granted $33 million for works on the Canal in late 1974; in June 1974, Qatar granted $50 million for development, $60 million for various projects up to 1976, and a loan for an amount of $3.5 million for Egyptian industry.[229]

Hasanein Heikal had said that there has never been a clear picture of aid from Arab or European sources, or from the commercial banks. He quoted two estimates on Arab aid to Egypt: the first one was for $22 billion in the years 1971–80, by the Kuwaiti Minister of Finance, 'Abd al-Latif al-Hamid; and the second one was for $14 billion in the years 1971–7, "a reliable figure," by 'Abd al-Mun'im al-Qaysuni, the previous Minister of Finance. Heikal added that the Qaysuni data referred to the period up to 1977, compared to the Kuwaiti Finance Minister's data, which was valid up to 1980. But after Sadat's visit to Kuwait, Egypt received minimal aid. [230]

After the imposition of the economic boycott on Egypt at the second Baghdad conference in 1979, Sadat launched an unprecedented tirade against the governments of the oil-producing countries, and he commented bitterly about the minimal aid they had extended to Egypt **(see chapter 5)**. As a result of his complaint, the AOC leaders leaked information to the media on the magnitude of their aid to Egypt. In May 1979 *al-Riyad* wrote, quoting "other sources," that during the past six years Egypt had received $13 billion in cash from Saudi Arabia, Kuwait, Qatar and the UAE. *Al-Riyad* added that this sum included grants, bank credits and long-term loans provided by the governments in question and by regional funds and institutions. The paper quoted that this sum did not include arms purchases for the Egyptian army, which were financed entirely by the four Arab oil states, nor did it include repayment of Egyptian debts and additional capital provided to support the Egyptian economy. Moreover, the article gave the following breakdown of aid according to states: Saudi Arabia, $7 billion; Kuwait, $2 billion; Qatar, $1.9 billion; the UAE, $2.15 billion.[231]

The Kuwaiti *al-Qabas* quoted "an official source" in April 1979 and mentioned a higher figure than *al-Riyad*. The paper claimed that "during the past five years," Egypt received loans and investments totaling $17 billion from the AOC, of which Kuwait had granted $5.5 billion. The Kuwaiti official was quoted as declaring: "We have in our possession documentation, proving the amount of aid we granted. But we will not publish classified material." The source attacked the Egyptian economy and compared it "to a bottomless pit managed by unbending economists . . . the only thing they are interested in is our aid in cash, without their being able to repay us."[232]

During the Baghdad conference in 1978, the figure of $17 billion was mentioned several times.[233] This is a realistic figure if we include all civil and military aid (as well as deposits) that Egypt received from the AOC starting in 1967 until the imposition of the economic boycott. However, this figure is too high when referring to the period from the October War and after, not even including military aid. *Al-Qabas* claimed aid also included investments, but this does not change the picture significantly: as we will see in chapter 2, the extent of Arab investments in Egypt did not exceed $2 billion.

Arab military aid to Egypt was wrapped in great secrecy. The Egyptian leaders – Sadat, Kamal Hasan 'Ali and Egyptian Minister of Defense 'Abdul Ghani Gamasi – mentioned the importance of Arab military aid and that it comprised the main source for Egypt's arms purchases.[234] The AOC leaders allocated to military aid to Egypt, especially after the peace agreement, [235] but neither side provided accurate details. Only partial data was published by SIPRI and in the memoirs of Egyptian dignitaries.

Details on military aid are conflicting, and make determining of the total Arab aid to Egypt difficult. There are reports on arms items ordered by Egypt (e.g. SIPRI,

ACDA, JCSS, IISS), but the purchase figures are not always listed. Hence much unreliable data was published. *The Economist* wrote that Saudi Arabia put £1 billion ($2.2 billion) sterling annually at Egypt's disposal for the purchase of military equipment;[236] an even higher sum was given by the Kuwaiti *al-Qabas* in March 1975. It wrote that, from October 1973, Saudi Arabia financed arms transactions for Egypt at a cost of $6 billion.[237] Ayubi, quoting Tuma, stated that up to the end of 1977 Egypt obtained pledges for military aid from Saudi Arabia alone totaling $5.14 billion, on top of aid from Libya, Kuwait and other Gulf States.[238]

Barkai proposed a method for evaluating Arab military aid to Egypt. He based his method on the Israeli Ministry of Defense model to calculate the main supply of arms on a certain date. Barkai applied the principle to Egypt. Military equipment (tanks, artillery, armored troop carriers, missile boats, torpedo boats, planes and helicopters) was compiled and sorted, and assuming that 75 percent of Egyptian military equipment had been bought from 1974 onwards, an estimate for military aid was made at $3.5 billion in the years 1974–7.[239] Barkai had reservations about this model: in his opinion, the figures underestimated the total aid, as they excluded all naval equipment, imported ammunition, surface-to-air missiles and trucks bought by Egypt. This did not prevent Barkai from contending that the assumption that 75 percent of military supplies had been purchased in a short period of four years was exaggerated. He declared that the figure of $750 million a year, as an average annual computation for arms imports to Egypt, was reasonable, and he added that Arab military aid amounted to about $1 billion annually during this time, at the very most – assuming that these countries financed all defense imports to Egypt. In his opinion this is also the maximum data for 1978.[240]

Gouda Abd al-Khalek, quoting from Ministry of Economy and Central Bank reports, declared that Arab states furnished Egypt with military grants totaling EgP 1,928.9 million ($4.93 billion, at the 1977 rate of exchange) from 1967 until June 30, 1977.[241] This figure matches Kamal Hasan 'Ali's figure, who said that the Arabs allocated $3.5 billion in the years 1973–8.[242] If we add this sum to military supplies provided by the AOC to Egypt before the October War (ca. $1.25 billion), we arrive at approximately $4.75 billion, the above-mentioned sum. Tahsin Bashir expounded his evaluation of military aid, "after closely following each separate transaction," at $4.5 billion.[243] Nafi', as detailed above, came up with a total of $3.6 billion, as representing military aid to Egypt in the years 1967–79.

It is very difficult to find an accurate figure: even so, Abd al-Khalek's official Egyptian data ($4.9 billion) and Kamal Hasan 'Ali's data lead to a comparable figure, and Barkai's method of calculation and Tahsin Bashir's data likewise support this figure. However, as we saw, there are other reports, such as Nafi's ($3.6 billion).

## Summary

Arab aid to Egypt (civil and military) in the years 1973–8 totaled between $12.2 and $13 billion. If we add to this sum the deposits, we arrive at a figure of between $14.2 and $15 billion. Total aid (civil and military) Egypt received from the AOC during the years 1967–78, amounted to $14.2–15 billion, without deposits, or $16.2–$17 billion including deposits.

As the data has demonstrated so far, the extent of aid Egypt received from the AOC in 1976 declined drastically, down to half of that supplied in 1975. Even in 1975, however, with the sharp increase of Arab aid, the percentage of loans was high. The sharp decline of Arab aid in 1976 forced the Egyptian government to reduce its imports. It began to fall behind in debt repayment and started borrowing capital at commercial conditions, and in so doing, caused further deterioration of the Egyptian economy, as we will see in chapter 5. By 1977, the magnitude of Arab aid to Egypt had again increased, but this was during the food riots in January of that year. In any case, even after the increase of aid in 1977, it was nowhere near as much as donated in 1975, when Arab aid figures equaled ca. 26 percent of the Egyptian GNP. In 1977 that figure had fallen to 12 percent, and in 1978 only 5 percent of the nation's GNP was Arab aid.

The AOC grants after the June 1967 War were the only significant financial source for Egypt, and this aid prevented it from going completely bankrupt. Arab aid enabled Egypt to go to war in October 1973, and after the war to maintain a higher level of investment. In 1975 investments grew to $2,867 million, compared to $1,373 million in 1973 (in 1975 prices).[244] Also its balance of payments deficit in 1974–6 was largely covered by AOC aid – which was substantial until 1976, relative to other aid sources – and Iranian and American aid. [245] Arab aid enabled Egypt to import large quantities of food and raw materials, even when global prices were skyrocketing, and although the Egyptian government had not significantly increased its export revenues, aid prevented a reduction in the GDP following the import of capital products and the increase of industrial products, particularly because of the low level of Egypt's savings accounts. According to World Bank data, (civil) Arab grants alone covered 111, 78, 40 and 41 percent of the current account deficit in the years 1973–6, respectively.[246] Before the 1979 Baghdad reso-lutions, Arab aid was the dominating factor, enabling the Egyptian government to apply resources to civil investments and at the same time to continue with plans for the modernization of the army.[247] From mid-1977 the Egyptian economy continued its recovery from the liquidity crisis as a result of this aid, and the remittances from Egyptian workers in the oil-producing countries.

However, it should be emphasized that, relative to the needs of the Egyptian economy and the expectations of the Egyptian leadership because of its sacrifices, the level of aid was insignificant. Assistance from the Gulf Fund in the years 1977–8 helped, for example, to solve the problem of the arrears in repayment of short-term debts and the import of vital products, but it was not a springboard for the economic rehabilitation of Egypt. As we will see in chapters 4 and 5, both the change of the trends in Arab aid to Egypt after 1975, as well as the disappointment of the Egyptian leaders with the magnitude of Arab aid and the way it was doled out, had political implications.

# 2

## Arab Investment in Egypt

_____

The rise to power of the officer regime in 1952 did not constitute a turning-point in the Egyptian economy. Until 1956 the regime continued to carry out the same economic policy that had prospered before the revolution. Indeed one minister declared that the Egyptian economy would prosper only under conditions of private enterprise.[1] In 1953 the government passed the Foreign Investment Law (no. 156) in order to expand investment and industrial activities, which were perceived by Egyptian policy-makers as the main levers for economic development and a means of expanding employment, output and income. The Law allowed a foreign investor to take out profits, up to a maximum of 10 percent of the company's registered capital. One year later Law 475 was enacted, revising the previous Law, enabling a foreign investor to take out all profits. Despite this Law, the level of foreign investment was minimal, totaling only EgP 1.9 million ($5.5 million) up to 1957, and EgP 8 million ($23 million) up to 1960.[2]

On top of minor foreign investments, the extent of local savings was very low. After the US retracted its commitment to assist in the construction of the Aswan High Dam (July 1956), it became necessary to mobilize different resources for the financing of extensive industrialization plans, and to attain rapid economic growth. In the years 1957–60, the revolutionary regime embarked on a new economic plan, which O'Brien called "guided capitalism"; in July 1960, private enterprise entered into its final stage, and a socialist economic system was established – "Arab socialism."[3] The role of the private sector was substantially reduced from the period under the monarchy.

Nasser nationalized foreign property (1956, 1957, 1960), and carried out an agrarian reform – in the framework of which 717,000 fedans were confiscated from the Egyptian elite and redistributed.[4] In July 1961, he nationalized the property of most of the non-agrarian companies in the private sector (foreign and local) that employed more than fifty workers, or whose assets exceeded EgP 10 million in value (about $28 million). Other companies were compelled to sell at least 50 percent of their shares to the public sector. The compensation offered by the Egyptian government to foreign investors was low by any standards: the rate was determined by the registered value of the company (not by its market value), and compensation was given in debentures quoted in Egyptian pounds, payable in fifteen years. These bonds failed to inspire the recipients' confidence, to the point where even public sector banks refused to accept them as collateral on loans. In 1963 and 1964 most shares that were still privately owned were transferred to the government.[5]

Many researchers (except for Abd al-Khalek, Ajami, Dessouki and Waterbury)[6] have argued that whereas Sadat was the primary initiator in attracting foreign investments, Nasser's economic policy acted as a deterrent to that goal. This is not entirely true – the roots of *infitah* would not be sewn for some years yet. Nasser was well aware of the importance of foreign investment, and, up to 1956 and during the length of his term in office, he strove to attract investment. Waterbury remarks that Nasser acknowledged the failure of his policy even before the June 1967 War, and adds moreover that the war resulted in diminished activity in the public sector, while the private sector found new opportunities for growth. Waterbury perceives the seeds of the *infitah* already in this period,[7] and states elsewhere that the *infitah* was not planned to destroy the Nasserist experiment but to adapt it.[8] Baker wrote that Sadat's policy was no more than Nasserism with a liberal façade.[9] Maybe Baker and Waterbury exaggerated in their statements, as we will see further on, but Waterbury's basic thesis is well-founded. In late October 1966, the Egyptian Minister of Industry announced the annulment of some of the export bans, as well as listing exemptions from import taxes for raw materials and spare parts for the promotion of exports. In November 1966, *MEED* declared that the Egyptian media viewed this step as a continuation of the trend to enlarge the private sector.[10] In 1967, statute 97 was passed, enabling citizens to possess foreign currency, without having to declare its source,[11] preventing deposits on foreign banks and attracting foreign currency to Egyptian banks. However, these steps did not produce any substantial effect on the Egyptian economy, which suffered from a paucity of foreign investments until the end of Nasser's rule.

In Weinbaum's opinion, Sadat's announcement that he intended to reform the Egyptian economy (October 1974), was almost as dramatic as the "crossing" in 1973 and his trip to Jerusalem in 1977.[12] Weinbaum does not give sufficient weight to the steps preceding 1974. Even if one disregards the contributions to the economy and its restructuring under Nasser, the "October 1974" announcement was still not a one-time and knee-jerk reaction; signs of the beginning of liberalization existed before Sadat's time, and his step was more a gradual realization of his economic policy since his rise to power – that is, to increase the role of the private sector and attract foreign investment.

After his rise to power, Sadat instructed Prime Minister Mahmoud Fawzi to set up a committee to look into ways of terminating the state of nationalization in place in Egypt. The new Egyptian constitution of September 11, 1971 determined that private and common public property would enjoy the state's protection, guaranteeing private investments and banning the nationalization of property without fair compensation.[13] On May 31, 1971 the People's Council approved a law that stripped the government of its authority to confiscate private property[14] and on September 13, 1971 the Coucil enacted the law for foreign investment and free-trade zones (statute 65).[15] The statute also granted Arabs priority over foreign investors: they could purchase real estate in Egypt (forbidden for non-Arab nationals by law); and the process for approval of Arab investments was made easier than for other nationals. Arab investments were to be approved by the Egyptian Investment

Authority, while non-Arab national investments would have to be approved first by a committee of ministers, and then by the President.

Despite Sadat's steps to ensure the political, military and economic future of Egypt, investment – in addition to being less attractive to non-Arab investors – failed to reach desirable levels. Sadat even hurt the process, when he declared that 1971 and 1972 would be "the years of decision," declarations that contributed to the creation of an atmosphere of anxiety and crisis, which made it unsuitable for investment.

Following the October 1973 War, Sadat pressed for a new economic policy based upon the earlier Foreign Investment Act (1971). In "The October Paper" (1974), Sadat formulated a comprehensive framework for changes in his economic and political policy **(see chapter 5)**, and he strove to bring together (mainly Western) industrial and agricultural technology, the capital reserves of the Arab oil countries, and Egyptian manpower and physical resources. He said: "the Arabs have the capital, and the industrialized countries have the technology." Sadat went on to say that Egypt must rein in these two facets in order to create a super-nation, a "Sixth World Power."[16] The *infitah* strategy was anchored in statute 43, which was approved by the Egyptian People's Council in June 1974.

Sadat and Hijazi saw the *infitah* as a necessity for several reasons: internationally, Egypt had endeavoured to reach an agreement on the settlement of its debts to the USSR so as to obtain further aid from it, but the USSR showed itself to be inflexible to Egypt's request (Hijazi noted that this was a major reason for the concept of the *infitah*[17]); on a regional level, Egyptian policy-makers considered trying to attract AOC capital, in view of rising oil prices and their growing wealth.

Sadat defended his *infitah* policy and refuted his critics, who claimed that he was neglecting socialism in favor of capitalism.[18] Sadat declared that Egypt would attract foreign capital, as long as it was the master of its economy. He explained that the purpose of the *infitah* was to reduce the suffering of the Egyptian people from a period of twenty years to five years by a flow of Arab and foreign capital.[19] Sadat explained that the only solution to the problem of the Egyptian economy was the *infitah*: "We have come to realize that we cannot close the door behind us and claim we are building up the economy . . . as all our reserves have been used up during the previous seven years . . . therefore we are maintaining the *infitah*." [20] Sadat cited other countries who had opted for an open-door policy and, not without reason, he mentioned the USSR – the leader of socialism – and Iraq:

> It was only natural that new economic problems, e.g. rehabilitation, would crop up after the war. The *infitah* has been devised specifically to solve these problems. The whole world is adopting an open-door policy. The USSR has opened its door to the West, signing loan agreements worth billions of dollars. Iraq, an Arab oil producer, has been granted loans from France and Japan. Why shouldn't we take a similar policy without compromising our independence? We stand by our declarations, that we welcome, first of all, Arab capital . . . at the same time, we have no objection to receiving foreign aid . . . This is what the *infitah* policy implies.[21]

Much has been written on the causes, the steps and the legal ramifications of the *infitah* policy in Egypt,[22] and there is no need to repeat the details in this framework.

The Law granted foreign, non-Arab, investors rights equal to those given to Arab investors, except for the right to buy real estate in Egypt, and to participate in housing projects – even with an Egyptian national as partner. The Law laid out in detail the sectors in which the Egyptian government wanted to attract investors, the ways of investment, the procedures for transferring funds to and from Egypt, tax and customs statutes for *infitah* projects (including rebates and tax-free items) and procedures for mobilizing workers. Item 7 of the Law stated that in no case would it be possible to nationalize or confiscate foreign capital, except by a court decision. The Law emphasized that investments according to statute 43 would be considered as private investments, even if the partner or partners owning the largest part of the investment represented the public sector in Egypt. In some sectors, minimal Egyptian participation in joint ventures was requisite: in construction and contracting 50 percent, and in banking 51 percent, if the bank wished to do business in local currency.

The Egyptian government was not satisfied with statute 43, and in 1975 it announced that Western companies listed under the Arab boycott[23] would be able to invest in Egypt, on condition that they invest at least twice as much as they had invested in Israel. Major Western firms initiated negotiations with the Egyptian government such as Leyland, Ford, Coca Cola, Colgate, Motorola, Revlon and others.[24] Besides Sadat's efforts to attract foreign investments, Egypt had some "natural" advantages, which made it attractive to foreign capital: (a) its geographical location as a junction of trade routes between Europe, India and the Far East enabled investors to export their products to many parts of the world in a minimal period of time; (b) almost unlimited skilled and unskilled, relatively inexpensive, manpower; and (c) a relatively advanced infrastructure of roads, railroads, river transport and power supplies.[25]

Despite the hopes and efforts that the Egyptian policy-makers put in statute 43, levels of investment remained stagnant. According to Investment Authority data, up to the end of June 1977 there were 161 operational plans worth EgP 242.4 million, mainly in the banking sector and in investment companies. Industrial initiatives whereby the Egyptian government hoped to combine Arab capital with Western technology, were few and far between,[26] for several reasons: besides its advantages, the Egyptian economy also presented some unfavorable conditions to the foreign investor, principally the bureaucracy rife in the country. Though the Egyptian political elite passed many resolutions with the purpose of easing matters for foreign investors, many of these resolutions did not translate into practical assistance to investors. This phenomenon had several causes, but the root problem was believed to be psychological. The head of the Arab Investment Co., Abd al-Rahman al-Sai, stated: "It seems that all countries with a deficit feel humiliated because of their need to seek foreign investments. On the personal level, officials are tempted . . . to try to make an impression that they [as representatives of their country] . . . do not need foreign investments, and that they do not find it necessary to go out of their way to make this possible [and in so doing, to facilitate matters for investors]."[27] The head of the Kuwaiti corporation for real estate investments and a major investor in Egypt, Ahmad al-Duweij, declared in an interview to the Kuwaiti *al-Hadaf*: "[Investors in Egypt] come up against an inner wall of hostility. Even investors make mistakes, they are not angels, but many of them have the feeling that they are suspect until proven innocent. They tend to ask themselves if Egypt really needs them."[28] On another occasion al-Duweij said that it was not necessarily advantageous to do business with their Arab brothers, because they sometimes tended to be apprehensive of each other's interests. To be an Arab investor (in an Arab country) usually complicated matters. Dwueij reported that he was unconvinced by the need to invest in Eypt.[29]

The Arab League, in an attempt to increase capital flow between the Arab countries, drafted regulations and made agreements to remove obstacles obstructing capital transfers between their nations, such as transfer of profits, restrictions on foreign currency and taxation. Agreements were reached on investments and capital transfers (1971); on obviating double taxation and on tax exemption (1975); on settling disputes between the investing and the recipient countries (1976); and on Arab capital investment in Arab countries (1981).[30] However, even after the above treaties, difficulties with capital flow between the poor and the rich countries in the region continued. Joint agreements depended on a change in legislation on the national level, which was not always forthcoming. The lack of a body which could grant investors guarantees against non-commercial risks likewise kept the level of investments low. In January 1975 an inter-Arab corporation guaranteeing investments was established, but its low capital level meant that it could not grant investors reasonable security. The corporation started with initial capital of KD 10 million ($36 million), which was increased to $87 million in May 1976. Its main goal was to guarantee "reasonable" compensation for "non-commercial risks" for potential Arab investors, both on the national and private level. The risks covered included nationalization, revolution, new laws and military operations .[31]

Since the beginning of the 1970s, joint ventures between the Arab countries had been undertaken, principally through the Arab League and OAPEC. The authorized capital of these joint initiatives from the early 1970s until 1982 totaled $18 billion (this figure includes partnerships between the rich oil-producing countries),[32] compared to the hundreds of billions of dollars the AOC invested in the West (table 2.2). The extent of investments in Egypt was very low.

As well as a cumbersome Egyptian bureaucracy, the lack of private investments also emanated from a concern with the political instability in the Arab region (even when referring to Egypt under Sadat's rule) and a fear of nationalization. Abd al-Wahab Galdari, an investor from the UAE and one of the owners of the Delta Bank in Egypt, clearly expressed this feeling in the late seventies: "What if something happens to Sadat? . . . His successor could very well confiscate all foreign property. He would most likely start with Arab property, as the easiest target."[33]

In order to overcome the multitude of practical and psychological difficulties it faced, the Egyptian government discussed legal issues with foreign companies and investors, and in 1977 changed several clauses in statute 43 – in accordance with the criticism of investors and accumulated experience – and passed statute 32,[34] which was in fact an adaptation of statute 43. Statute 32 clarified and removed obstacles encountered by foreign investors, and symbolized the beginning of a new and more dynamic phase in the *infitah* policy. The basic change in statute 32 was that Egyptian investors could now enjoy all benefits and exemptions given to foreign investors.

This brought about a substantial increase of Egyptian investment in their own economy, and turned nationals into a major influence in the statute for foreign investment. The Egyptian government, as we will see later on, did not rest on its laurels, and passed additional regulations to facilitate foreign investment, under Sadat's regime as well as that of Mubarak.

With all the Egyptian government's concessions and efforts to attract foreign investment, the AOC leaders did not allocate any significant funds to investment in Egypt. This was not only because of Egyptian bureaucracy or a fear of re-nation-alization. The opening sentence in Law's research amply illustrates the reason for the AOC's investing a major portion of their "reserves" in the West, and not with their neighbors. One should never forget, he wrote, that Arab investors are no different from investors in any other part of the world,[35] in that they seek maximum profits from their investments. AOC policy-makers and their subjects did not view their overseas investment as aid or charity. On the contrary, they expected high profits which would support them "in the post-oil era." Feelings of Arab solidarity were marginal, and as the chairman of the Kuwaiti Investment Co. stated: "Despite our government's ties with the [Arab states], we are not a charity organization. Our business is to invest and make money."[36]

**Table 2.1**   Investment revenues for Saudi Arabia, Kuwait and the UAE (in millions of US dollars)

|  | 1974 | 1975 | 1976 | 1977 | 1978 |
|---|---|---|---|---|---|
| Saudi Arabia | 900 | 1,962 (2,200)[1] | 3,227 | 4,447 | 6,000 |
| Kuwait | 800 | 1,361 (1,300) | 1,821 | 2,111 | 2,700 |
| UAE | 300 | 268 (700) | 470 | 731 | 1,000 |

*Sources*: 1974 and 1975 data in brackets: United States Central Intelligence Agency (CIA), Research Department, *OPEC Countries: Current Account Trends, 1975–76* (ER 76–10370, June 1976), p. 18. 1975–8 data: *Arab Oil and Economic Review* (vol. 2, no. 6, June 1979), p. 22.

[1] Figures in brackets are CIA data. Disparities for SA and Kuwait from the two sources are insignificant, excluding the figures for the UAE. The CIA document also included revenues earned by Libya and Qatar from their investments: Libya – in 1974 – $200 million and, in 1975, $300 million; Qatar – in 1974 – $100 million and, in 1975, $200 million.

It is true that, in the second half of the 1970s, the oil-producing countries enjoyed good profits from their investments. But it was in the early 1980s – with the decline in revenues from oil exports and the current account deficits – that the proceeds from foreign investment began to fulfill a major role in the Arab oil countries' economies. Kuwait's investment revenues came to 54 percent (around $5 billion) of its oil and gas revenues in the 1982/3 fiscal year, and $4 billion in 1985;[37] in 1983, between $15 and $20 billion flowed into Saudi Arabia's coffers – the fruits of its investments.[38] Table 2.1 presents details of revenues for Saudi Arabia, Kuwait and the UAE from their investments in the years 1974–8.

## Governmental and public investment

There was a very low level of public investment made by the AOC in Egypt. The governments comprising the AOC initiated bilateral investments of no more than $400 million, through joint ventures with the Egyptian government from 1973–83, compared to their enormous surplus funds and the hundreds of billions of dollars invested in the West (see tables 2.2–2.3). To this figure AOC deposits on the Egyptian Central Bank, totaling $2 billion, should be added **(see chapter 5)**.

**Table 2.2** Total accumulated surplus funds in the AOC current account for the period of 1974–1982 (in billions of US dollars)

| State | Total | Percentage |
|---|---|---|
| Saudi Arabia | 166.8 | 52.6 |
| Kuwait | 79.7 | 25.1 |
| UAE | 39.7 | 12.5 |
| Qatar | 12.9 | 4.0 |
| Libya | 17.9 | 5.6 |
| Total | 317.0 | 100.0[1] |

*Sources*: The calculations for SA (1974–82), Kuwait (1975–82), and Libya (1974–82) are based on IMF data: IMF, *International Financial Statistics (IFS) Yearbook 1983*, pp. 327, 335, 443; *IFS*, December 1986, pp. 308, 325, 439. Figures for Kuwait 1974, UAE and Qatar (for the entire period) are based on OPEC data: OPEC secretariat, *Annual Statistical Bulletin* (Vienna: OPEC, 1985), p. 10.

[1] Total amounts to 99.8 and not 100 percent through rounding off.

Many studies have been devoted to AOC investments.[39] These studies focused on their investments on the international money markets, particularly in the US and in Europe. The attention given to their investments in Third World countries was minimal, to say the least. No (published) research work has specifically examined their governmental or civil investments in any Third World country. Mattione, who dealt in his research with OPEC investments, overlooks AOC investment in Arab countries.[40] Law, who wrote a whole volume specifically about Saudi Arabia, Kuwaiti and UAE investments in Arab countries, does not present any clear data on investments of their citizens in the Arab world in general, nor in Egypt specifically. Out of hundreds of investments made by citizens of the Gulf States in Egypt, Law indicates about fifteen. His data on governmental investments in Egypt is far more comprehensive.[41]

This scant attention is in direct proportion to the very small amount of investment, and stems from the fact that the AOC and their peoples allocated only a tiny fraction of their capital to the Third World, when compared to their investments in Europe, North America and other developed countries. Two-thirds of the Kuwaiti government's financial surpluses – amounting to around $65 billion in 1980 – were invested in the US and in Western Europe, little more than one-fourth in its own economy, and only 4.8 percent ($3.1 billion) in all Arab countries combined.[42]

**Table 2.3** Evaluations of the geographic breakdown of OPEC surplus funds (deposits, securities and assets)[9] (in billions of US dollars)

| Breakdown | US Treasury 1974–82[1] | Bank of England 1974–9[3] | OPEC 1974–80[2] |
|---|---|---|---|
| USA[4] | 85.5 | 55.4 | 65.4 |
| Developed[5] | 232.3 | 56.9 | 212.5 |
| Developing | 75.7[6] | 123.7 | 46.4 |
| Total | 393.5 | 236.0 | 324.3 |

*Sources*: US Treasury – Mattione, p. 12. The Bank of England: "The Surpluses of the Oil Exporters," *Bank of England Quarterly Bulletin* (June 1980), p. 159. OAPEC evaluation: OAPEC, *Secretary General's Eighth Annual Report* (Kuwait: OAPEC, 1982), p. 66

[1] The US Treasury evaluation refers to a longer period. If we exclude figures for the years 1981–2, we reach a total of $336.4 billion.

[2] In both cases figures refer to OPEC investments, even though evaluation was made by OAPEC.

[3] The Bank of England summated OPEC surpluses according to three categories: US, the UK and other countries and organizations. Therefore, in this case only England should be included in the "developed" group in the table. The large difference between Bank of England figures and other data stems from the different periods in question. It should be remembered that in 1980 SA's oil revenues alone amounted to $84.5 billion, and in 1981, $102 billion (after that there was a substantial decline of revenues). See: Saudi Arabia Monetary Agency (SAMA), Research and Statistics Department, *Statistical Summary 1407* (1987), table 2, p. 70. Another study of the English bank (published in March 1985) indicated that in the period of 1974–83, the OPEC countries invested $380 billion, divided up as follows: UK – 63.1 billion; US – 85.9 billion; West Germany – $21.6 billion; other industrialized states: 117.3 billion; developing countries – 58.3 billion; IMF and the World Bank – 20.8 billion; various credits – 13 billion. See: "Deployment of oil exporters' surpluses," *Bank of England Quarterly Bulletin* (vol. 25, no. 1, March 1985), p. 71.

[4] Includes bonds, securities, shares, deposits, direct investments.

[5] The industrialized nations (including developed countries without a free-market economy), and investments in international financing institutions.

[6] Evaluation no. 1 includes grants in this figure.

[7] Evaluation no. 2 breaks up this figure as follows: short-term investments – $155.6 billion (48%), long-term investments $168.6 billion (52%).

[a] See for a more detailed breakdown above-mentioned sources. For data of previous years, see e.g.: *Bank of England Quarterly Bulletin*, various issues: *MEES*, April 23, 1979; *Newsweek*, February 10, 1975.

[b] According to a study conducted by 'Abd al-Wahab al-Thamar, in 1981 the financial assets alone of Saudi Arabia, Kuwait, the UAE and Qatar totaled $256 billion, as per the following breakdown: SA – $145 billion; Kuwait – $72 billion; UAE – $22 billion; and Qatar – $8 billion. See: 'Abd al-Wahab al-Thamar, 'Nadwat al-Tanmiya li-Aqtar al-Jazira al-'Arabiyya al-Muntija lil-Naft' (Kuwait, 1985), p. 98, as quoted by Jasim Khalid al-Sa'dun, "Mustaqbal al-Naft wal-Maliya al-'Amma fi Aqtar Majlis al-Ta'awun al-Khaliji," *al-Mustaqbal al-'Arabi* (al-Sana 10, al-'Adad 99, May 1987), p. 9.

The AOC preferred not to publicize the magnitude of their overseas investment, and data on this subject was published in the framework of the overall extent of OPEC investments without a breakdown of states (table 2.3). As this study deals only with Arab oil-producing countries, it is necessary to separate AOC investment figures from the total sum of OPEC investments. The difficulty in doing this is not surprising, considering the sensitivity of the AOC leadership over the extent of their investments. There is also the problem of separating state funds from royal funds, as laid out before an American Congressional committee regarding monies belonging to the Saudi government and funds "belonging" to the Saudi Royal family. This sensitivity brought about, inter alia, secret arrangements between the American Treasury and the oil countries – as, for example, the agreement reached in early 1974 between William Simon, the US Secretary of the Treasury, and the Saudi and Kuwaiti governments, and the agreement between the US Treasury and the Saudi Monetary Agency (SAMA) signed in 1975, stipulating that separate investment data for each Arab country would not be made public, and would remain a broad regional framework, e.g. "other Asian countries" or "other African states." In the 1970s and the 1980s the various Congressional committees tried to obtain up-to-date information on each separate oil country's investments in the United States, but the CIA and the US Treasury prevented any possibility of disclosure, and Reagan vetoed publication of the data in 1982. At first, the US Treasury denied the existence of these agreements, but later it confirmed that Arab investors had made it clear that any investment in the US must remain absolutely confidential. So, while the US Treasury publishes the portfolio of every foreign country with investments within its own borders, this is not the case when it concerns the oil countries. Data for the latter is published in the comprehensive framework of the "OPEC countries." [43]

### Kuwaiti investment in Egypt

According to IMF data, Kuwait's foreign assets in 1979 amounted to $39.9 billion, compared to $11 billion in 1974.[44] In 1981 Kuwait's foreign property values totaled $51 billion[45] on top of that. Other assets include: Central Bank overseas assets of $4,310 million; commercial banks overseas assets of $7,975 million; and the overseas properties of "other financial institutions" – $3,543 million (all data from late 1981).[46] Kuwait's overseas properties amounted to $66.6 billion in 1981, a figure which matches the announcement of the chairman of the Kuwaiti National Assembly's Finance Committee in mid-1983, who indicated a figure of $66.7 billion for total Kuwaiti reserves by the end of 1981;[47] in 1985 its investments abroad came to $80 billion;[48] and in 1986, according to the Kuwaiti National Bank, $86 billion.[49] Table 2.4 shows the extent of Kuwait's foreign assets .

Kuwait is the only Arab oil-producing country which set aside a part of its annual revenues for "The Reserve Fund for Future Generations," established in 1976. Kuwaiti policy-makers believed that Kuwait would have to supplement its budget in the post-oil era with its income from overseas investment. The Kuwaiti government funneled $3 billion to the fund on its establishment, and decreed that 10 percent of oil revenues be added to the fund annually. It was determined that no monies were to be withdrawn from the fund for a period of twenty-five years.[50] Kuwait made the largest investments in Arab countries, more than its richer neighbors. Most of its investments were made by the Finance Ministry, managed by two government-controlled companies: The Kuwaiti Company for Foreign Trade,

Contracting and Investments (KCFCI) established in 1965, and The Kuwaiti Corporation for Real Estate Investments, established in 1975.[51]

**Table 2.4**  Kuwait's foreign assets, 1974–1986 (in billions of US dollars)

| Year | Total[1] |
|------|----------|
| 1974 | 11.0 |
| 1975 | 15.1 |
| 1976 | 18.3 |
| 1977 | 24.1 |
| 1978 | 27.2 |
| 1979 | 39.9 |
| 1981 | 66.7 |
| 1982 | 71.6 |
| 1985 | 80.0 |
| 1986 | 86.0 |

*Sources*: 1974–9 data: IMF, *Kuwait – Recent Economic Developments* (SM/80/146, June 20, 1980), table 24, p. 55. 1981–2 data: *MEES*, June 6, 1983, p. B5. 1985 data: *The Middle East*, July 1986, p. 22. 1986 data: *MEES*, September 21, 1987.

[1] Data include Finance Ministry reserves, "The Reserve Fund for Future Generations," Central Bank, commercial banks' and other Kuwaiti government institutions' assets. See last note in table 2.3.

On January 29, 1974, an agreement was signed for industrial cooperation between Egypt and Kuwait. The Kuwaiti government agreed to participate in the financing of joint development projects with Egypt for a total of $700 million. The projects would enhance the economy by building a fertilizer factory, exploitation of fish in Lake Nasser, and a sugar and a paper factory.[52] Six months later, Egypt unexpectedly rejected the Kuwaiti investments proposals, reasoning that unfavorable conditions had been offered, and that it had received superior investment offers from American and European companies. Kuwait did not conceal its disappointment with Egypt's decision.[53]

In December 1974, during Hijazi's visit to the Gulf, an amicable settlement was reached between the two nations. On terminating his visit to Kuwait (December 3), a joint announcement was issued, with Egypt and Kuwait agreeing on joint investments in Egypt amounting to $1.3 billion, for housing projects, industrialization, shipping, tourism and other plans.[54] This amount included the $700 million agreed upon in February 1974. But as we will see below, the practical results of the projects were minimal, and most of these investments never got beyond the proposal stage.

The Kuwaiti and Egyptian governments jointly established a number of companies but many of them ran into difficulties and operating speeds were slow: e.g. in May 1974, the two governments decided to establish a joint shipping company with a capital of $30 million. Egypt found it difficult to finance its share of the partnership, and it requested a loan on easy terms from Kuwait to finance its part. Kuwait refused, but it agreed to grant a loan at global market conditions. In May 1975, the company was finally established, with the two governments contributing 50 percent each.[55]

In July 1974, the KCFCI together with the Egyptian government established The Kuwaiti–Egyptian Investment Co., on a 50–50 partnership basis, with authorized capital of $25 million. It was agreed that the corporation would be based in Cairo. The Egyptian share-holders were the General Investment Authority, 26%; the Misr Insurance Co., 12% and the al-Sharq Insurance Co., 12%. This company set up, inter alia, a shoe and leather-wear factory (The Kuwaiti–Egyptian Shoe Co.), which commenced operations in 1980. In July, the bi-national corporation decided to found a joint building material firm with a capital of $5.8 million. The jointly-owned corporation also owned a marble and granite company and a hotel in Cairo.[56]

Further joint, low-capital projects included The Arab Ceramic Co., established with a capital of $4.4 million. The partners were: The Kuwaiti Corporation for Real Estate Investments (KCREI), 13%; the Saudi private sector, 12%; the Egyptian private sector, 20%; the Egyptian Ceramic Co., 30%; the International Financing Corporation, founded by the World Bank, 10%.[57] A joint Egyptian–Kuwaiti fishery company was also established in 1976, for the exploitation of fish in Lake Nasser, with a capital of $10 million.[58]

The Kuwaiti government concentrated its investments on Egyptian real estate. On March 3, 1975, the Egyptian Minister for Rehabilitation and Housing, Othman Ahmad Othman, announced the establishment of the Egyptian–Kuwaiti Real Estate Development Co. (Cairo). This was finalized during Hijazi's visit in Kuwait in December 1974. The company was slated to carry out projects for up to $500 million in Egypt. The Kuwaiti Treasury's share in the project was 61.2 percent of total paid-up capital of $12.4 million (authorized capital came to $100 million). The Egyptian partner was the Madinat Nasser Housing and Rehabilitation Co., owned by Cairo municipal institutions. Egypt contributed to its share of the partnership by supplying the land, with the purpose of constructing a commercial centre in Nasser City. In September 1982, after a long delay, the company started building the centre in Madinat Nasser.[59] The Egyptian–Kuwaiti Co. also held ownership of 200 square kilometers of real estate on the banks of the Nile (south of Cairo) designated for the building of a suburb, and 200 sq/km at Mount Muqtam (Cairo), designated for the construction of thousands of housing units for intermediate level income families.[60]

In 1975 the Alexandria–Kuwait Real Estate Investment Co. was established, with a capital of $14 million. The Kuwaiti government holds ownership of half the shares, and its partner – the Alexandria Municipal Area Authority – owns the other half. The aim of the company was to develop about 12 sq. km of land, contributed by the Alexandria district as its share in the project, for the construction of a hotel and a commercial center. By the end of 1982 work had still not started. The main obstacle was the dispute between the parties involved over land values.[61]

Besides the partnership with the two Egyptian companies, the Kuwaiti government independently established several projects in Egypt, such as a hostel in Cairo, serving 600 female Kuwaiti students studying at Egyptian universities, and the construction of housing projects in the Zamaleq and Aguza quarters (Cairo). Furthermore the Kuwaiti government owns land in prestigious areas – Garden City and Al-Giza; a 5 percent share in the Kuwaiti–Egyptian Investment Bank in Cairo; and it built and managed, through a Kuwaiti corporation, the two four-star Sabir hotels in Cairo.[62] Initially the Kuwaiti companies in Egypt did not prosper. As a result their joint projects with the Egyptian government (as well as their independent plans) were seriously delayed. Although a decision had been taken to start work on Madinat Nasser in 1974, works did not commence before September 1982. Most of Kuwait's investment plans in the real estate sector encountered difficulties, causing their cancellation and/or extended delays. In February 1976, the Kuwaiti Investment Co. decided to freeze all its activities in Egypt, following a plan by the Egyptian National Council to restrict foreigners' rights to purchase real estate.[63]

On top of the bureaucratic difficulties in Egypt, Kuwaiti plans came up against opposition in Egyptian government circles. One of the leading opponents to these projects was the Minister for Rehabilitation, Othman, who opposed "the sale of Egypt," as he wrote in his memoirs. Othman noted that at one of the government meetings (probably 1974), a Kuwaiti company's request to purchase land in Cairo for $40 million, for the construction of low-priced housing, was brought up for discussion. Hijazi, the vice-premier, supported approval of the transaction, proclaiming that the buyers were "fellow Arabs," and that the transaction was part and parcel of the *infitah* policy. Othman opposed the deal, comparing the land (*ardh*) to Egyptian honor (*'ardh*). He added that it was not the purpose of the *infitah* to sell Egypt and that "Palestine was lost in a similar way." No final decision on the subject was taken at the meeting.[64]

In his memoirs, Othman wrote about a similar episode in connection to this incident. Hijazi called him a few days later, and invited him to a meeting in his office with the Kuwaiti Finance Minister. When Othman arrived for the meeting, the Kuwaiti minister addressed Othman as follows: "We are having problems with you," he said, complaining that in Ismailiya the Madinat al-Sheikh al-Zayd (named after the UAE president) was under construction, as well as the Madinat al-Malik Faysal in Suez, towns and the quarters built as a gesture to these countries, for their assistance in the rehabilitation of the Canal. They were upset that Kuwait had not been granted a similar honor. After Othman had explained that the Madinat al-Sabah in honor of Kuwait was being constructed in Port Said, but work had been delayed because of land problems in the area, the Kuwaiti minister said that a Kuwaiti company wanted to build a hotel on the banks of the Nile. Othman replied he wished to ponder the matter. A heated discussion arose, with Hijazi siding with the Kuwaiti minister. According to Othman, Sadat at first approved the land purchase plan by the Kuwaiti company, but cancelled it after further discussions.[65]

After the imposition of the economic boycott on Egypt at the Baghdad Summit in March 1979, Kuwait continued to invest in Egypt, distinguishing between "politics and business," in the words of 'Awad al-Khalidi, the representative of the KCREI in Cairo.[66] In 1981 the Egypt–Gulf Bank was established by the Cairo Bank, the Egyptian Insurance Co. and the KCREI. The bank was a business success, and in 1984 showed a profit of $3.8 million, and one year later, $5.9 million. In May 1986, the bank's management decided to increase its capital to $50 million.[67]

Mubarak's policy of promoting Arab investments and Kuwait's desire to support the Egyptian economy **(see chapter 4)**, brought with it a renewed momentum of Kuwaiti investments in Egypt. In early 1982 Kuwait and Egypt founded a joint investment company – The Sabah al-Awwal Investment Co. – with a capital of $40 million. Kuwait's share in the partnership came to 75 percent and Egypt's part, 25 percent. It was determined that at first, the company would concentrate on development of tourism and housing projects in Egypt, and at a later point, a commercial bank would be established with a capital of $100 million.[68] In July 1982 the Kuwaiti Oil Corporation invested in oil exploration in the Gulf of Suez. Besides the Kuwaiti Corporation, APICORP – Arab Petroleum Investment Corp. – in which several other Arab countries were partners and other European companies also participated in this project.[69] The largest official Kuwaiti investment in 1982 was by the KCREI – the Kuwaiti Corporation for Real Estate Investments. This company presented the Egyptian government with investment plans totaling $150 million, intended for the tourism sector. Kuwait had decided to allocate this sum five years before, but it was not before November 1982 – after many bureaucratic difficulties – that the Egyptian Ministry of Tourism and Aviation approved the first two plans (on the Red Sea shores) proposed by the Kuwaiti Corporation.[70] In March 1984 the Kuwaiti government decided to invest $120 million in a TV factory in Ismailiya, in partnership with Japanese investors.[71]

Ironically, Kuwaiti government investments in Egypt had increased after the imposition of the economic boycott. Although there were less projects, capital investment after the boycott increased. As time passed, Kuwait openly invested in Egypt. This level of investment is relatively insignificant, because Kuwait's investments did not exceed $200 million (excluding its deposits on the Egyptian Central Bank) in the decade after the October War – a very low figure compared to its investments in the West.

## Saudi Arabian investment in Egypt

Kuwaiti bilateral investments, even if they were relatively insignificant, still exceeded those of Saudi Arabia and the UAE. The latter were not eager to invest in other Arab countries, and they sufficed with transferring cash for assistance and to aid funds investing in Arab countries.

According to IMF data, in February 1984 the Saudi Monetary Agency was managing foreign assets totaling Saudi Riyals 464.48 ($132.5 billion) for the Saudi government; in late 1983 the commercial banks were managing foreign assets totaling $17.9 billion.[72] Total foreign investments exceeded $150 billion (this figure does not include direct investments by Saudi citizens in the West). In mid-1983, Saudi overseas investment amounted to between $110 and $180 billion.[73] In 1986, after a decline in oil revenues, Saudi reserves totaled $80 billion, according to a survey by the Kuwaiti National Bank.[74]

After the rise in oil prices in 1973, Saudi policy-makers assumed that their country would be compelled to utilize all its reserves to finance its development,[75] and they did not allot any part of their revenues to "a retirement fund," as Kuwait had done. Saudi Arabia wanted to maintain the liquidity of its resources by short-term investments, while increasing security; as the Governor of the Saudi Central Bank declared: "We wish to be able to withdraw our money when we need it."[76] So most of its capital was invested in financial assets, and a small part in real estate.

The only restriction on monetary reserves, part of the first Five-Year Plan, was that the kingdom was required to leave reserves to cover its needs for a period of at least eighteen months.[77]

Total Saudi investments in Egypt were very small, amounting to two companies jointly owned with the Egyptian government, which they had decided to set up on April 1, 1975, in an agreement between government representatives. These companies were established after Hijazi's visit to the Gulf in December 1974. The Saudi–Egyptian Reconstruction Co. was a joint venture between the Saudis, who, through the Treasury, owned 50 percent of shares in the company, and the Egyptian government which – through the Ministry of Reconstruction – owned the other half. The capital of the joint company was $50 million. It was agreed that the Saudis would participate with American dollars and Egypt with Egyptian pounds. Moreover it was agreed that Saudi Arabia would grant the company $200 million credit for investment and housing plans in Egypt. The goal of the company was real estate development, mainly in the Suez Canal area. The second jointly owned company, The Saudi–Egyptian Company for Investment and Finance, was established with paid-up capital of $23 million (authorized capital of $100 million). Sixty percent of the paid-up capital was provided by the Saudi side and 40 percent by the Egyptians. The company's aim was to invest in various projects in Egypt. The company's first project was the construction of the Semiramis Hotel in Cairo at a cost exceeding $40 million.[78] The company drew up plans for a large tourism project near the pyramids, but it never got off the drawing-board. Aside from these two major companies in 1975 two other joint Saudi–Egyptian ventures were established in Alexandria, with a capital of $1.3 million each. One specialized in beach development in Egypt, the other in shipping.[79]

After the boycott on Egypt, the Saudi partners on the board of directors of the Saudi–Egyptian Reconstruction Co. refrained from participating in meetings, but they continued to keep in touch with matters behind the scenes. The Saudi government had no intention of liquidating the company; it even refused a proposal by a Saudi investor, Salah Kamal, to purchase its share in the company.[80]

## UAE and Qatar investment in Egypt

The UAE made long-term investments in the West with a major proportion of its surplus funds, which in 1986 amounted to $22 billion,[81] though it did not establish a "Future Generation Fund." Its investment in Egypt consisted of an investment company, owned jointly with Egypt, and with a capital of $100 million.[82] The UAE was also associated with a number of Egyptian banks and insurance companies, using its links to establish the Joint Arab Investment Corporation in June 1979, with a paid-up capital of $13 million (authorized capital, $50 million). The aim of the corporation was to promote tourism and commercial banking in Egypt. The UAE government's share was 50 percent and the remaining 50 percent share was split between: the Cairo Bank, the Egyptian National Bank, the National Egyptian Insurance Co., the al-Sharq Insurance Co., the Alexandria Bank, the Misr Bank and the Egyptian Insurance Co. The UAE government paid its part in dollars, and the Egyptian partners in local currency.[83] The founding of the corporation occurred after the imposition of the boycott on Egypt.

The investments in Egypt of the Qatar government, whose reserves in 1986 amounted to $12 billion,[84] consisted of the establishment of a jointly-owned company with the local government in 1975 – The Egyptian–Qatari Investment Co. (in Egypt) – with authorized capital of $25 million .[85]

## Joint investments of Arab governments in Egypt

During Nasser's reign the first joint investments of the oil-producing countries were made, and came in the main in banking. In 1964 the Arab African Bank was founded and it was followed soon after in 1971 when the International Arab Bank was established in Cairo. The banks received various benefits and exemptions at a time when the *infitah* policy was not yet in force. The Arab African Bank was initially set up as a joint shares company by the ECB and the Kuwaiti Treasury. The governments of Iraq, Algeria, Jordan and Qatar immediately joined the partnership. In 1977 the bank's capital was increased from $40 million to $100 million. In 1978 the bank changed its name to the International Arab African Bank, to demonstrate its international orientation.[86]

After the Camp David agreement, the bank's partners arranged a way to overcome the obstacle the peace treaty had placed against a continuing partnership. A solution was found: by establishing a subsidiary in Bahrain, The Bahraini Arab African Bank, it was determined that the infant company would manage the bank's international transactions. The owners of its capital were the African Arab Bank (Cairo), 60.7%; the Kuwaiti Treasury, 9%; the ECB, 9%; the Rafidayn Bank (Iraq), 2%; the Qatari and Jordanian Treasuries, 2% each; the Algerian Central Bank, 1.3%; the Saudi al-Jazira Bank, 4%; and the Arab Finance Co. (Luxemburg), 10%.[87] In April 1978, the chairman of the bank declared that it would loan Egypt $80 million for the carrying out of development plans.[88]

The second inter-Arab bank, The International Arab Bank, was established in early September 1971 as The International Egyptian Bank for Foreign Trade and Development. By 1974 Libya, Oman, the UAE and Qatar had joined the partnership. Its capital in 1976 stood at $100 million. Egypt, Libya and the UAE each held 28.7 percent of its share capital. The bank provided banking services in foreign currency, participated in the financing of industries and various projects and transferred Arab workers' remittances in the Arab countries. It participated in the establishment of the Arab–European Bank, and it was the principal shareholder (60 percent) in the International Arab Finance Co. Both these institutions are located in Luxemburg. The bank also owns 15 percent of shares in the Suez Canal Bank.[89]

The largest joint initiative between the AOC and Egypt was the setting up of the Authority for Arab Military Industrialization (AMIO) in 1975, with a capital of $1.04 billion,[90] which will be examined separately later on. Another large joint project was the laying of an oil pipeline (320 km) between Suez and Alexandria, for piping oil from the Red Sea to the Mediterranean.[91] Sadat claimed that he, along with Faysal and the Iranian Shah, dreamed of piping Iranian oil to the Mediterranean and Europe, after Israel had laid a pipeline between Eilat and the Mediterranean.[92] The oil pipeline was the first time that a number of Arab states jointly invested in an Egyptian venture other than the banking sector, and cooperated in using Western technology.

The plan of the Suez–Alexandria pipeline and its financing underwent many alterations: the idea was first mooted in 1968. In March 1971 the cost was evaluated at $200 million, and the governments of France, the UK, Belgium and Spain, as well as Dutch and Japanese companies, agreed to finance the project, through credit grants to Egypt.[93] Due to such a wealth of overseas investment, the share of the Arab oil countries in the venture would have been marginal. Saudi Arabia agreed to loan $20 million and the Arab African Bank $4 million.[94]

Up to mid-1973, economic policy-makers in Egypt spent a long time looking for a suitable company to execute the plan: at first, a proposal came up for a conglomerate of eight European countries, but in late July 1973 the talks, which had been going on for two years, broke down.[95] Thereafter, the perspective on financing and executing of the plan changed: in the summer of 1973, Saudi Arabia and Kuwait agreed to finance all foreign currency expenditures; and in December of that same year, Bechtel Inc. of Los Angeles was chosen to carry out the work, at a cost of $398 million. The involvement of Bechtel would have been the first large American economic involvement in Egypt since Dulles decided to cancel aid for the financing of the Aswan High Dam project,[96] but for a dispute between the Egyptian government and Bechtel over the Egyptian governments's refusal to increase the cost price of the project following the devaluation of the dollar. As a result, in April 1974 the work was contracted to an Italian company, with Bechtel fulfilling an inspection role.[97]

To finance the plan, Egypt, Saudi Arabia, Kuwait, Qatar and Abu Dhabi established a joint company – the Arab Petroleum Pipelines Co. – with a capital of $400 million.[98] Egypt contributed $200 million; Saudi Arabia, Kuwait and Abu Dhabi $60 million each; and Qatar $20 million.[99] The project was completed by the end of 1976: in January 1977, crude oil first started flowing through the pipeline, and in mid-June 1977 Sadat officially inaugurated the project.[100] From this date on, the pipeline became an important factor in oil transport and commerce, and it was an economic success: in 1977 – the first year of operations – revenues amounted to around $19 million; in 1980 more than 1.5 million barrels a day flowed through the pipeline to world markets, and shareholders earned a considerable dividend of 20 percent.[101]

In August 1982 the oil countries set up another joint investment company in Egypt, this time called The Arab Gulf Investment Co. Later, many citizens of the AOC joined the partnership by buying shares. The founders of the company – the governments of Kuwait, Saudi Arabia, the UAE, Oman and Qatar – decided to concentrate on the construction of low-cost housing and on projects in tourism, industry and agriculture in Egypt. The company was headed by the Kuwaiti businessman Al Dueij, and had a paid-up capital set at $120 million (though the actual sum remitted to Egypt by mid-1984 totaled only $30 million).[102] Egypt also participated in inter-Arab bodies, as it remained a member of the Arab League until 1979. Nearly all Arab countries participated in these bodies, which had been founded by the Arab League. Their scope of activities – such as the Arab Federation of Shipping, the Arab Mineral Company, the Arab Company for Mining – was very limited, especially in Egypt.[103]

## The Arab military industrialization authority

The Arab Military Industrialization Authority was an outstanding example of the combination of AOC capital with Egyptian manpower and industrial experience (and Western technology). The authority was of one of the few pan-Arab endeavors in extensive joint manufacturing projects, and as a result there were high expectations both from Egypt and the AOC accompanying the project. The subsequent bitter failure of the joint authority constituted another link in the long chain of pan-Arab industrial failures.

The concept of establishing a joint Arab military industry in an all-Arab framework was submitted at a meeting of the Arab Defense Council, which convened in Kuwait on November 13, 1972.[104] Egyptian policy-makers had previously discussed the subject at a meeting of the Egyptian High Command in August 1972, where Sadat declared that Egypt's dependence on external arms suppliers must cease, and that Egypt must manufacture planes, helicopters, small vessels and missiles. Sadat announced that France and the UK were willing to cooperate with the Egyptian military industry on this matter.[105] At the November 1972 meeting of the Arab Defense Council, Shazli, the Egyptian commander-in-chief, proposed a joint Arab military industry, with each country allocating 2 percent of its GNP to the project for a period of five years.[106] At the 1974 Rabat Summit it was decided to promote the project,[107] and on April 29, 1975, Egypt, Saudi Arabia, the UAE and Qatar established the Military Industrialization Authority, with a capital of $1.04 billion.[108]

The partners in the project wanted to establish a sophisticated, independent industry that would serve the military needs of the Arab countries.[109] Their purpose was to gain independence from the West in terms of the supply and maintenance of arms, at lower prices than that of imported arms, and a diversification of arms sources. The ultimate goal was to reduce Arab dependence on any particular world power. Up to 1978, the US refused to supply sophisticated weaponry to Egypt; Sadat's experience with Soviet arms supplies had also been fraught with difficulties. After the approval of the American Congress to supply Egypt with F-5 planes in 1978 (with Saudi financing), the Egyptian Minister of War stated: "With the arrival of these planes, we will succeed in our policy of diversifying our arms sources, as then we will possess American, Soviet and French planes. No other country will be able to control us, as was the case before and after 1952. We will persevere in this policy."[110]

Among the further (unstated) aims of the founders of the authority was to catch up with the Israeli military industries, to equalize as much as possible the Egyptian–Arab–Israeli power balance of routine arms production and to get another chance to cool relations between Egypt and the USSR – the authority signed contracts with Western countries only. The oil countries wanted to have military strength in order to boost their diplomatic power and autonomy; before the authority was established, Arab diplomacy and political bargaining was based solely around financial wealth. It is also possible that the oil countries expected the AMIO to bring with it improvement of the civil industry infrastructure in their countries. Egypt already possessed a military industry in the 1950s. Establishing a "joint industry" with the AOC was an important instrument for obtaining financing of the authority's operations, and also for utilizing AOC ties with European countries to sign agreements for arms supply and know-how.

The AMIO was based on the *infitah* model, maintaining the triangle of a combination of Arab capital, Western technology and Egyptian manpower. Saudi Arabia, the UAE and Qatar allocated $260 million each to authority capital, and Egypt's share in the partnership was given in land, existing military industrial structures and its experience in the arms industry. At the time, Egypt had about twenty factories manufacturing arms, of which four, with a workforce of 15,000 workers, were chosen to serve the authority: Saqr, Helwan (two factories) and Qader.[111]

Prior to the establishment of the AMIO, Egypt was the only Arab country with a serious military industry. Development of its industry had started under the monarchy. Following the 1948 war and complaints about defective arms contributing to defeat, Egyptian army officers opened negotiations with European countries, dealing with, inter alia, assistance in the setting up of an Egyptian military industry. In 1949, the Egyptian government outlined ambitious plans for the development of an aircraft and munitions industry, and in 1950 two factories were set up: an aeronautic plant in Helwan and the Qader plant. After the officers' revolution, the military industry received an extra boost, not least thanks to Hassan Rajib – the chief scientist of the Egyptian army – who was appointed as deputy minister for military industry affairs. In 1953 the Saqr factory was built and in 1960 a second factory was set up in Helwan. From the late 1940s, Egypt received assistance from West German,[112] Swedish, Spanish and Indian experts. The factories manufactured, by contract, sixty-five planes based on a Spanish model, 200 Jumhuriyya training planes (partly for export), spare parts for Soviet planes, surface-to-surface and surface-to-air missiles, armored personnel carriers and explosives.[113] The departure of the German scientists in 1964, financial problems and lack of Soviet support hurt Egyptian military industry. And by the end of the 1960s, several factories had been closed down, and the remaining factories manufactured only light arms and conducted repairs and maintenance of imported arms.[114]

The AMIO established in 1975 was not subject to the regulations of the general and fiscal administration (including administration laws, customs, salaries and local taxes), and its workers were not permitted to form a professional union.[115] The joint authority was managed by a High Committee comprised of the four defense ministers of the member states. Also involved was a board of directors with twelve representatives, three from each country, which acted on the High Committee's directives.[116] Sadat appointed Ashraf Marwan – Nasser's son-in-law and one of his close advisors – as chairman of the authority. This appointment received the blessings of the AOC leadership, with whom Marwan had close ties from his many visits to the Gulf. On October 9, 1978, Cairo Radio announced that Sadat had fired Marwan.[117] Sadat had taken his decision without consulting the other partners. Riyadh insisted that Marwan be kept on, and the day after his dismissal, Adnan Khashoggi, Saudi Businessman, arrived in Cairo and tried, without success, to annul this unfortunate event.[118]

Arab sources saw Sadat's action as an attempt to engineer the collapse of the authority.[119] According to *Foreign Report*, in October 1978, during a visit to France,

French officials conveyed to Mubarak that they had heard that Sadat had spoken to senior Egyptian military personnel about postponing the establishment of the AMIO. The source also mentioned that the Saudi leadership knew about America's military commitment to Egypt at Camp David, and, unhappy about the deal between the US and Egypt, threatened to stop financing Egyptian arms purchases until further notice. As for Marwan, the reason for his dismissal was an "exaggerated loyalty" to Saudi Arabia, looking out for its interests at Egypt's expense.[120] The Cairo *al-Akhbar* argued that Marwan's dismissal stemmed from his enormous salary and the generous perks he received.[121]

After Marwan's dismissal, a conflict developed between Saudi and Egyptian policy-makers over the choice of his successor. The Saudi elite refused to accept another Egyptian, and instead they proposed the Saudi economist al-Tariki, later bringing up the name of Faysal al-Qasimi of the UAE. Egypt initially rejected both suggestions and they offered the job to the Egyptian Hasan 'Abd al-Fattah Ibrahim. In the end, they chose al-Qasimi,[122] but he would not keep his position for very long; shortly after his appointment there was the peace treaty and the dismantling of the authority.

Initial operations in the authority's first year concentrated on the mobilizing and the training of a cadre of personnel. Students and professionals were sent abroad – mainly to the US, England and France – to receive training in technology, administrative and financial organization. In 1978 about 2,500 employees participated in various courses in the West.[123] Before the authority was dismantled, it signed six large contracts for joint production of arms, the majority with West European companies, whose participation in joint projects was usually 30 percent. The board of directors of each joint project was headed by an Arab representative and the operational manager was the representative of the foreign company. Many agreements were only signed after a period of lengthy discussions (a result of technical and political delays). In the case of the assembly of the Alpha-Jet planes politics held back production, as these planes were a joint French–German product, and the German government did not wish to get involved in exporting them. The French, however, urged all parties to finalize the transaction.

In March 1978 an agreement worth $595 million was signed with the British Westland company for setting up in Egypt an assembly line for Lynx attack helicopters. The agreement determined that initially they would produce fifty helicopters, with production increasing to 230 helicopters, subject to the success of the contracts. It was determined that the first twenty helicopters would be produced in the UK and thirty would be assembled in the Helwan plants with a supply of British parts. Some of these helicopters were supposed to have been purchased by the Saudi air force.[124] For this purpose a joint company was set up by the Arab authority and Westland: The Arab–British Helicopter Co., with a capital of $30 million. The British share amounted to 30 percent and included a cash input and providing a managerial and technical cadre.[125]

Further contracts with British companies were signed with Rolls-Royce and British Aerospace Dynamics Group. The agreement with Rolls-Royce stipulated that 750 engines for Lynx helicopters would be produced staggered across time: initially, 150 engines would be produced in the UK and the balance in the Helwan plants. Again, a joint company was established: the Arab–British Co. Rolls-Royce pledged to train Egyptian workers in England and to provide technical and managerial personnel for supervising the initial production stages.[126] The contract with British Aerospace (December 1977) agreed upon the assembly, and later on the production, of "Swingfire" anti-tank guided missiles.[127]

**Table 2.5** Principal characteristics of the joint companies

| Company | Establ. date | Foreign co. | Products | Final qty |
|---|---|---|---|---|
| 1. Arab–British Helic. Co.[1] | 1978 | Westland | Lynx | 230 |
| 2. Arab–British Engine Co. | 1978 | Rolls-Royce | Engines | 750 |
| 3. Arab. Electr. Industries Co. | 1978 | Thomson | Aerospace systems | — |
| 4. Arab–British Co. | 1978 | British Aerospace | Swingfire missiles | — |
| 5. Arab–French Aircraft Co. | 1978 | Dassault-Breguet | Alpha-jet | 160 |
| 6. Arab–French Engine Co. | 1978 | Snecma | Larzac engines | — |
| 7. Arab–American Vehicle Co. | 1978 | American Motors | Jeeps | 10–12,000 |

*Source*: Data presented in the chapter.

[1] By the mid to late 1980s, the Arab-British company assembled French Gazelle helicopters, and the British-Arab Engine Co. manufactured engines for these helicopters, instead of engines for the British Lynx. See: *Defence and Foreign Affairs Handbook* (1986), p. 213.

In September 1978, the AMIO signed an agreement in principle with the French Dassault-Breguet Co., for the manufacture of Alpha-Jet planes in its plants.[128] To begin with, Egypt wanted to produce 200 Mirage F-1s, but in the end it agreed to produce 160 Alpha-Jets, the manufacturing process of which was far simpler than that of the Mirage. It was decided that fourteen planes would be manufactured in France, with 146 planes assembled in Egypt. Furthermore, the agreement included initial details on the possibility of manufacturing the Mirage 2000 in Egypt.[129] In November 1978, the authority reached an agreement in principle with another French company, SNECMA, for the manufacture of LARZAC engines for the Alpha-Jet planes in the AMIO factories. There was also a long-term plan for the authority to manufacture jet-engines for the Mirage 2000.[130]

In the 1970s the United States did not play a significant role in the Arab countries' military production. The only agreement the AMIO signed with an American company was the contract with American Motors for the assembly of 10,000–12,000 jeeps and other mechanized equipment for military use in late 1977. It was agreed that, initially, the American company would supply most of the parts for assembly, and in the second stage the authority would produce a major proportion of the components. The plant was not officially opened until January 1979. Once more, a joint company was set up – the Arab-American Vehicles Co. – with 51 percent of the capital held by the AMIO[131] (for a full list of the pan- and inter-Arab companies established, see table 2.5).

The AMIO factories were set up and operated in Egypt, except for a few plants in Saudi Arabia. One of these was established when, in February 1978, the heads of the AMIO decided to establish a plant for military electronic components in al-

Kharej, Saudi Arabia. In July 1978, a contract was signed with the French Thomson-CSF company for the construction of the plant.[132] A joint company, Arabian Electronics Industries, was set up, in which the AMIO owned 70 percent and the French company 30 percent.[133]

The fact that the Arab oil countries were partners in the AMIO gave rise to great commercial interest on the part of arms manufacturers in the West – mainly in the UK, France and the US. The European countries were the first to sign contracts with the authority, but American arms producers soon penetrated this market, leading to fierce competition between French and American companies. French commercial policy concentrated on those Arab countries with whom it had a large commercial deficit because of oil imports,[134] and attempts by American companies to compete in this field worried France's policy-makers. Their anxiety was compounded because of the central role taken by the US in the peace talks between Egypt and Israel. A spokesman for the French Dassault arms factory accused American industrialists of putting pressure on Sadat to prioritize US companies,[135] and *Le Monde* claimed that part of the American game in the Middle East was to wrest control of the arms market by driving out the French.[136]

After the peace agreement and the withdrawal of the conservative Arab countries from the AMIO, the US became Egypt's principal partner in its military industries. In June 1979 the American Agency for Aid pledged to help Egypt renovate its plants, and in August and October Egypt and America reached an agreement for cooperation in the military field. Inter alia, it was agreed that the US would assist Egypt with the repair and renovation of its stock of Soviet arms, as well as with production of artillery, electronic equipment, naval vessels and armored vehicles, with the construction of a plant for optical equipment and with expanding and renovating factories for missile production.[137]

After Sadat's visit to Jerusalem and the Camp David agreement, the AOC leaders continued to endorse the activities of the AMIO.[138] It was only after the 1979 Baghdad conference that the AOC withdrew from the authority. On May 13, 1979, Sultan, the Saudi Minister of Defense, announced that the authority would be dismantled on July 1, 1979. In June 1979, al-Qasimi, chairman of the AMIO, proposed that the partners convene to finalize dismantling procedures. The dismantlement process saw anti-Egyptian political views expressed by both Sultan and Qasimi.[139] Qasimi gave contradictory signals: shortly after his first announcement, he said that the AMIO must continue to operate, notwithstanding the peace agreement, in Egypt, because "it was an ideal base for the authority. It has manpower, factories, professional expertise and above all, it is less expensive than any other country."[140] Qasimi also noted that the dismantling of the authority was a serious blow to the whole Arab world, throwing to the winds all hopes of achieving self-reliance in arms supply.[141]

The Egyptian elite condemned the AOC decision. Sadat accused them of trying to impose an arms boycott on Egypt, similar to the one imposed by the USSR, and he warned the Arab leaders that Egypt might be forced to violate agreements with foreign companies.[142] The AMIO partners convened on June 17, 1979 in Paris to finalize dismantling procedures, but they did not succeed in reaching a solution satisfactory to all sides. Before the Paris meeting, Sadat and Kamal Hasan 'Ali declared that Egypt would freeze AMIO assets and it would establish an independent industry.[143] After Sadat's declaration, Egypt briefly considered bringing the dispute with the other partners to arbitration by World Bank institutions,[144] but in August 1979 Hassan Ali announced that Egypt had indeed frozen AMIO assets.[145] Expressing a determination to continue military production without Arab financing, Egypt changed the name of the authority from Arab Industrial Authority to Egyptian Industrial Organization. Sadat headed a new High Committee he had set up with Mubarak, Mustafa Khalil – the incumbent Prime Minister – and the ministers of defense and finance as members. Ahmad Zandu, the former Governor of the Egyptian Central Bank, was appointed chairman of the steering committee, assisted by General Ahmed Badawi.[146]

The establishment of the AMIO had symbolized the strengthening of ties between Egypt and the conservative oil states. The goals that authority policy-makers set for themselves – such as reducing dependence on foreign countries – were ambitious, but their achievements were limited. Although the authority was given control of joint companies, this control was illusory. Western companies had exclusive control over the technologies crucial to the daily operations of the military industry. Without their technology, not a single project would have been carried out.

The actual output of the AMIO was also limited: up to the end of 1978, it was involved mainly in building and renovating existing factories in Egypt.[147] In January 1979 a plant for the manufacture of jeeps was opened, in partnership with American Motors,[148] and in early September 1979 (after the liquidation), the first Swingfire missile, assembled on a jeep, was presented, both manufactured by AMIO plants in Egypt.[149] These were the sole achievements of the authority before Egypt's partners withdrew from the project. As far as Egypt was concerned, however, the venture was relatively successful in the field of military industry. In the autumn of 1982, for example, the Egyptian air force received its first Alpha-Jet made in Egypt.[150]

Could the failure of the AMIO be attributed only to the peace agreement between Egypt and Israel? What is beyond doubt is that it was the peace agreement which caused the conservative oil states to withdraw from the AMIO. But, as the Marwan dismissal has demonstrated, prior to the Egypt–Israeli deal the authority was deeply troubled, and its achievements were very modest. The authority encountered technical problems (such as the crash of the prototype of the Alpha-Jet), manpower shortages and financial crises emanating from commitments not honored by AMIO founders. Political obstacles also contributed to the situation, especially conflicts of interest between Egypt and the other partners.[151]

One of the aims of the AMIO was, as stated previously, to reduce dependence on arms supply from the world powers: by the time of the liquidation of the authority, the partner countries not only failed to reduce their dependence, but actually became more reliant on foreign arms.[152] The withdrawal of the AOC from the AMIO forced the cancellation of agreements with French companies. Contracts with British companies were also in doubt, but Egypt managed to receive financing for fifty Lynx helicopters from its former AOC partners. The plan to assemble Lynx helicopters in Egypt was removed from the agenda, but the jointly-owned factory for the assembly of Swingfire missiles continued to operate, and in the 1980s it produced some 500 missiles annually. In the 1980s Egypt renewed its joint initiative with the French company for the assembly of Alpha-Jets, and in November 1982, the first planes became operational in the Egyptian air force. In the mid-1980s the Egyptian plants turned out more than a plane a month.[153]

Egypt suffered substantial financial losses as a result of the liquidation of the partnership, but the AOC's losses were greater. Egypt acquired a well-developed military industry supported mainly by the US. It manufactured ammunitions, artillery pieces, anti-tank missiles, vehicles, rocket-launchers, bombs, vessels for the Navy, armored vehicles, Alpha-Jet and Tocano planes, Gazelle helicopters, and even negotiated the possibility of building F-20 planes and other equipment.[154] In comparison, the oil countries found it difficult to establish a military industry without Egyptian experience and know-how. The AOC tried to set up a military industry without Egypt,[155] but they failed utterly.[156] Saudi Arabia did establish its own arms industry, but it lacked Egyptian military expertise.[157] Establishing a military industry in the AOC became a matter of top priority after the outbreak of the Iran–Iraq War. At a meeting of the ministers of defense of the Gulf Defense Council (GCC) which convened in Riyadh in January 1982, a decision in principle was taken to promote the subject, but nothing practical came of it.[158] In the following years many declarations were made on this subject,[159] but they never progressed beyond the stage of vital discussions: two years after the Riyadh resolution, Sultan stated that the GCC "would study" the possibilities for establishing a military industry;[160] at a conference of GCC countries in Kuwait in late November 1984, the matter was again discussed without any real decisions being taken,[161] and at the Doha Summit in 1985, one of the resolutions dealt with the setting up of a joint military industry, though nothing came of it.[162]

The significant delays and problems encountered by the GCC in establishing an independent military industry strengthen the conclusion that the oil countries lost more than Egypt by the liquidation of the AMIO, an act which was for the AOC "self-defeating" (as remarked by a senior Egyptian official, who added, "too much has been invested to be thrown away, it will be like a Greek tragedy if nothing comes of all our efforts.").[163] Ibrahim Nafi' noted with a little degree of bitterness in *al-Ahram* in May 1982 about Iraq's difficult situation in its war with Iran: "If Egypt had received aid in the last few years instead of being punished and boycotted, like in the AMIO matter, it would now have been able to render large-scale assistance [to Iraq]."[164] The irony was not lost on the AOC that Egypt supplied military equipment to Iraq, but also sold its locally-produced military hardware to other Arab countries, among them ex-members of the AMIO.[165]

## Activity of the Arab investment funds

Development plans in Egypt were financed in one of two ways: either by one Arab fund, or through joint financing by several Arab funds. A number of development projects were also jointly financed by the World Bank and a number of Arab funds, who, together with the World Bank, supplied the foreign currency needed for the execution of these plans, with the Egyptian government financing costs in local currency. Operations involving Arab funds in cooperation with the World Bank in Egypt were affected, in most cases, by the Egyptian government requesting the World Bank for assistance in the financing of a certain project. After the Bank's experts had conducted a feasibility survey for the proposed project, the Bank would discuss with Arab funds the measure of their willingness to support the project, and then it would determine its own contribution. In many cases, expenditures greatly exceeded forecasts – mainly as a result of delays in the start of work and/or a shortage of local capital.

The Arab funds also sent delegations to check on the proposed projects, but they encountered difficulties in evaluating the plans, because of their lack of a professional and skilled staff, so they cooperated with the World Bank. The Arab funds, with the exception of the Kuwaiti Fund, which was established in 1961 and whose personnel had therefore gained experience, were established after the October 1973 War, and they were immediately forced to deal with many requests for aid from the Arab states. The competition for aid between the states meant that a disproportionate number of Egyptians were employed by the various funds in senior positions. As indicated by Bartsh (in charge of the OPEC aid department at the OECD), it can be assumed that the employment of Egyptians in senior positions in government offices and administration in the oil countries, coupled with their employment by the Arab funds on the other hand, played a certain role in influencing the decision-making process regarding resources transferred by the funds to Egypt.[166]

All Arab funds combined allocated some $850 million to development projects in Egypt in the decade following the October War. Most of this was given before the peace treaty with Israel. After the Baghdad boycott, Egypt's membership in the multilateral funds was suspended. Some of the funds discontinued all activities in Egypt, while others continued to finance projects which were already being carried out. In 1984 a number of funds renewed their activities in Egypt.

### National aid funds

The oldest Arab fund was the Kuwaiti Fund for Arab Economic Development. This was an independent public institution, and the chairman of the board of directors was the Kuwaiti prime minister. The fund's loan conditions varied according to the economic circumstances of the recipient country and the type of project. The range of conditions were: interest rates – including 0.5 percent for management fees – varied between 0.5 and 5.5 percent; grace periods ran from 2 to 11 years, and the repayment period was from 9.5 to 50 years; the grant component in loans varied between 17 and 86 percent.[167] According to the fund's twenty-third annual report, until late June 1985 Egypt received from the fund ten loans, totaling KD 59.712 million ($200 million). Out of this sum, seven loans totaling KD 40.917 million (about $140 million) were channelled to the transport and communications sector; two loans amounting to KD 8.795 million (about $30 million) to the industrial sector; and one loan of KD 10 million (about $34 million) was applied to the electric network.[168] Among the Arab countries, only Tunisia and Jordan received larger amounts than Egypt (table 2.6).

**Table 2.6** Kuwaiti Funds' commitment to Arab countries until the end of June 1985 (in millions of KD and US dollars)[1]

| Country | No. of loans | Amount (KD) | US $ |
| --- | --- | --- | --- |
| Algeria | 2 | 9.998 | 34 |
| Bahrain | 7 | 30.959 | 105 |
| Djibouti | 5 | 12.500 | 43 |
| Egypt | 10 | 59.712 | 203 |
| Iraq | 2 | 6.386 | 22 |
| Jordan | 17 | 92.319 | 314 |
| Lebanon | 2 | 2.564 | 8 |
| Mauritania | 8 | 41.620 | 142 |
| Morocco | 10 | 55.545 | 189 |
| Oman | 7 | 36.273 | 123 |
| Somalia | 4 | 30.044 | 102 |
| Sudan | 13 | 57.078 | 194 |
| Syria | 7 | 39.563 | 135 |
| Tunisia | 23 | 102.043 | 347 |
| North Yemen | 15 | 38.545 | 131 |
| South Yemen | 10 | 33.008 | 112 |
| Total | 142 | 648.058 | 2204 |

*Source*: KFAED, *Twenty-Third Annual Report 1984/5*, table D.

[1] Original figures were quoted in KD. The amounts in dollars were rounded off in hundreds, and were calculated according to IMF, *IFS* data.

With the largest loans allocated to the transport and communications sectors in Egypt, the Suez Canal received the most funding: in July 1964, the Kuwaiti Fund granted Egypt a loan of $27 million for development of the Canal[169], for a period of 16 years, including a three-term grace period, at an interest rate of 4 percent annually.[170] In March 1974, the fund put an additional loan of $33 million at the disposal of the Canal authorities for reconstruction and purification. This loan was provided for a period of 17 years, including two years' grace, at 4.5 percent interest annually.[171] In the first quarter of 1978 the Kuwaiti Fund then guaranteed an additional loan of KD 6 million ($22 million) for the widening of the Canal, for a period of 22 years, including four years' grace, at an annual interest rate of 4 percent.[172]

Kuwait also provided other loans, in the shape of funds to aid Egypt's development, including assistance for a ship-building project, with an amount of $10 million; two loans for the development of gas fields in Abu-Kir, totaling $27 million, furnished in July 1973 and July 1975; a power station in Abu Kir ($34 million) in October 1975; a fertilizer project in Talkha ($22 million) in 1976; and the oil pipeline of Ras Shakir ($24 million) in February 1977. Annual interest rates for these loans came to 4 percent, and they were provided for periods of between 15 to 20 years, including a grace period of between 3 to 5 years.[173] After the Baghdad boycott, the fund stopped granting new loans to Egypt, a situation that continued until late 1984.[174]

**Table 2.7** Geographical analysis of Kuwaiti Fund's commitments up to June 30, 1985 (in millions of KD and US dollars)

| Countries | Total (KD) | Total (US $) | % |
|---|---|---|---|
| Arab | 648.058 | 2,203 | 49.6 |
| Africa | 248.033 | 843 | 19.0 |
| Asia | 393.386 | 1,338 | 30.2 |
| Others | 15.950 | 54 | 1.2 |
| Total | 1305.427[1] | 4,438 | 100.0 |

*Source*: See table 2.6, table C.

[1] The fund actually granted KD 868.958 million ($2,954 million). See: *Ibid.*, p. 67.

Saudi Arabia established the Saudi Fund for Development in September 1974. Their late establishment of a fund was triggered by the October War and the increase in oil prices. The fund, which commenced operations in February 1975, was managed by a board of directors headed by the Saudi Minister of Finance, the other members being appointed for a period of three years by the Saudi council of ministers, on the recommendation of the finance minister. Because the fund was a late arrival in the Arab world, its directors showed a preference for participation in financing projects only jointly with other bodies, and preferably the World Bank.[175] The fund's loan conditions varied according to the type of plan and the recipient country. Repayment terms varied between 15 to 30 years; grace periods from 3 to 12 years; interest rates – called "service fees" by the fund – amounted to between 2–4 percent; the grant component came to between 30 and 67 percent.

**Table 2.8** Obligations and aims of Saudi Fund's loans to Egypt until the end of the 1984/85 fiscal year (in millions of Saudi Riyals and US dollars)

| Plan | SDR | US $ |
|---|---|---|
| Reconstruction of the Suez Canal | 175.00 | 50 |
| Railway – second stage | 193.253 | 55 |
| Cotton gin | 89.60 | 27 |
| Development of telephone network[1] | 80.50 | 23 |
| Widening of the Suez Canal | 117.33 | 34 |
| Freeway[2] | 50.00 | 14 |
| Total | 705.68 | 203 |

*Source*: SDF, *Annual Report*, 1404/05 A.H., (vol. XI), appendix III, p. 33.

[1] Telephone connection between Cairo, Ismailiya, Port Said and Suez.
[2] Helwan-Misr al-Jadidah
[a] The fund's annual report for 1982/3, in appendix I indicated that the commitment for this plan stood at SR 226 million. Accordingly, total commitments amounted to SDR 738.43 million. See also: *MEES*, August 8, 1975, p. 7.

In November 1974, about a month after the establishment of the fund was announced, Hijazi paid a visit to Saudi Arabia. At the end of his visit a joint statement was issued, stating that the Saudi Fund would provide Egypt with aid, an amount of $161 million for works on the Suez Canal, setting up a cotton gin and developing a railroad network and telephone system.[176] The fund kept its agreement to the letter and financed its share in all the plans. The Saudi government also rendered assistance for the telephone network project. In the years 1975–7 this included renovating equipment, replacing damaged cables and expanding the number of local and overseas lines. The execution of these projects required $318 million, including $107.9 million in foreign currency. The Saudi government offered a loan of $13.4 million for this purpose,[177] on top of financing by the Saudi Fund totaling $23 million (table 2.8).

**Table 2.9**  Abu Dhabi fund loans to Egypt (millions of Dirham and millions of US dollars)

| Plan | Date of agreement | Dirham | US $ |
|------|-------------------|--------|------|
| Amar Khiyam hotel | 9.11.1974 | 16.6 | 4 |
| Talkha fertilizer plant | 24.9.1974 | 58.4[1] | 15 |
| Abu Qir power station | 28.10.1975 | 130.0 | 33 |
| Suez Canal development | 8.12.1977 | 60.0 | 15 |
| Total | | 265.0 | 67 |

*Source*: Abu Dhabi Fund for Economic Development, *Annual Report*, 1983 and 1984, p. 65; *MEES*, June 27, 1975, p. 6.

[1] 40 million Dirham were granted in 1974, 18.4 million Dirham in 1976.

The development plan for the railway network in Egypt was divided into two parts: the first, a comprehensive survey of the transportation sector in Egypt; and, second, continuing the reconstruction, renovation and expansion of railway lines. The Egyptian government financed the cost in local currency, with the World Bank, West- and East-European countries[178] and the Saudi Fund (which allocated $55 million to the project) financing the required foreign currency of $150 million (out of a total cost of $296 million) (table 2.8). The fund also assisted with the reconstruction and the widening of the Suez Canal, the development of a cotton gin, and with the paving of the Helwan–Misr al-Jadida highway. The plan for the reconstruction of the cotton gin, financed jointly by the Saudi Fund and the World Bank, ran into difficulties when Egypt failed to raise local capital. The Saudi Fund and the World Bank provided part of their loans in foreign currency, but when it was Egypt's turn to complete the financing with Egyptian pounds, it could not keep to the timetable.[179]

The loan was granted for a period of 20 years, including a grace period of 5 years, at 3 percent annual interest.

The Abu Dhabi Fund for Arab Economic Development, which was established in July 1971, commenced activities in March 1973 and signed its first loan agreement in 1974. The fund was managed by a board of directors with seven members, headed by the UAE prime minister. Its loan conditions varied according to country and project, but its conditions were tougher than those of the other funds, and some of its loans were granted at commercial rates. The fund granted Egypt four loans, which were channelled to construction of a luxury hotel, a fertilizer plant and a power station, and to the development of the Suez Canal (table 2.9).

## Inter-Arab aid funds

**Table 2.10**   Arab Fund's activities in Egypt (millions of KD and US dollars)

| Year | Plan | Commitment | | Actual | | Terms | |
|------|------|-----------|-----|-----|-----|----------|-----------|
| | | $ | KD | KD | $ | Int. rate | Repayment |
| 1974 | Fertilizer Talkha 2 | 6.5 | 22 | 6.5 | 22 | 6 | 25$^2$ (5) |
| 1975 | Tura cement plant | 6.7 | 23 | 5.0 | 17 | 6 | 25 (5) |
| 1975 | Cairo–Fustat water | 9.7 | 33 | 7.9 | 27 | 6 | 25 (5) |
| 1975 | Helwan sewage system | 8.3 | 28 | 0.7 | 2 | 6 | 20 (6) |
| 1976 | Talkha fertilizer factory | 2.7 | 9 | 1.6 | 5 | 4 | 17 (3) |
| 1976 | Abu Qir power station | 12.0 | 41 | 8.9 | 30 | 4 | 20 (5) |
| 1976 | Al-Dawar textile plant[1] | 10.0 | 34 | 1.3 | 4 | 4 | 20 (5) |
| 1977 | Suez Canal development | 12.0 | 42 | 3.2 | 11 | 4 | 20 (5) |

*Source*: AFESD, annual report 1980 (Kuwait), pp. 70, 72, 74, 76, 82. Figures converted into dollars according to IMF data and rounded off in hundreds.

[1] Expansion of the textile conglomerate in the village.
[a] Figures in brackets refer to postponement period included in repayment term.
[b] The fund also financed a study for the development of water and sewage systems in Cairo – KD 300,000 ($1 million) and scholarships – KD 20,000 ($72,000).

The Arab Fund for Social and Economic Development, founded in 1968, is the oldest multilateral fund, although it did not grant its first loan until April 1973. Sixteen Arab states, including Egypt, were contributing members to the fund. The oil countries donated the major portion of its capital, totaling $2.6 billion. Kuwait, Saudi Arabia and Libya contributed 58 percent of its capital; Egypt should have contributed 5.5 percent, but in the event it allocated only half that amount. In 1979 Egypt's membership of this fund and of other Arab aid funds was suspended, following the Baghdad boycott. The fund was managed by a board with a representative of each country, elected for a term of five years. Most aid for development projects received by Egypt from the inter-Arab funds was provided by the Arab Social and Economy Development Fund. In the years 1974–80 Egypt received commitments for eight loans, totaling KD 67.9 million ($224 million), comprising 19.8 percent of all commitments granted by the Arab Development Fund. Until the end of December 1980 Egypt actually received KD 35.1 million ($126 million) – 52 percent of commitments (table 2.10).

The textile project in the village of al-Dawar warrants special attention because of the controversy that surrounded it. The purpose of the project was to expand production of the textile companies in the villages of al-Dawar and al-Bayda, with the overall aim of improving Egypt's export potential in the textile market. The ASED Fund was slated to give a loan of $34.5 million, comprising 23 percent of the financing costs of the plan, and the World Bank supplementing the figure with an additional $52 million. The World Bank's terms for the loan were as follows: repayment period of 15 years, including four years' grace, at an annual rate of interest of 8.85 percent.[180]

**Table 2.11**   Analysis of funds'[1] aid to Egypt up to June 1982, according to sectors (in millions of US dollars)

| Economic sector | Amount |
|---|---|
| Transportation, communication, storage | 373.72 |
| Energy (electricity, oil, gas) | 135.59 |
| Water and sewage | 62.07 |
| Agriculture and animal husbandry | 25.38 |
| Industry and mining | 147.02 |
| Others[2] | 18.99 |
| Total | 762.77 |

*Source*: AFESD, coordination of Arab national and regional development institutions, "Development financing operations of Arab regional and national institutions to developing countries up to 30/6/1982" (Safat: Kuwait, 1983), p. 13.(hereinafter: "Comprehensive funds report").

[1] Institutions included are the national funds of Kuwait, Abu-Dhabi and S.A., the Arab Development Fund, the OPEC Development Fund, the Islamic Bank, the Iraqi Fund for Foreign Development and the Arab Bank for Economic Development in Africa. Not included are the Arab Monetary Fund, the Libyan-Arab Bank, and inter-Arab banks, such as the International Arab Bank. Hence the discrepancy of about $90 million between the totals of table 2.11 and table 2.12.
[2] Support of the balance of payments, financing of foreign trade, tourism, education and training.

In December 1976, the loan and its conditions were finalized by Egyptian representatives and ASED Fund managers. It was determined that for a loan of $34.5 million Egypt would pay annual interest of 4 percent. The fund managers stipulated a number of conditions for managing the loan. When the agreement was brought before the Egyptian National Council for ratification, several delegates strongly criticized the high rate of interest and the fund's conditions and demanded the agreement be cancelled. In the end the loan was ratified,[181] but the members of the Council and the government were not happy with the terms dictated to them by the oil countries. The interest rate demanded by the ASED Fund was actually quite reasonable in the global market, but what irked Egypt was the fact that the Americans, who were not "brothers," offered much lower interest rates for development projects in Egypt. In September 1978, the American Aid Agency had signed a loan agreement with the Egyptian government for $96 million, destined for reconstruction plans of the water and sewage systems in the Suez Canal cities. The repayment term was for 40 years, with 10 years' postponement. Annual interest was set at 2 percent for the 10 years' grace period and at 3 percent thereafter.[182]

The ASED Fund worked in close cooperation with the World Bank in allotting resources to projects in Egypt and supervising the rate of progress. Besides the textile project, the two institutions also consulted each other over the plan for enlarg-

**Table 2.12**   Analysis of funds' aid to Egypt up to June 1982 (in millions of US dollars)

| Institution | Amount |
| --- | --- |
| Islamic Bank | 18.00 |
| Abu Dhabi Fund | 67.48 |
| OPEC Fund | 23.20 |
| Saudi Fund | 212.25 |
| Arab Fund | 233.70 |
| Kuwaiti Fund | 214.13 |
| Arab Monetary Fund | 17.50 |
| Libyan–Arab Bank | 25.81 |
| African Bank | 46.00 |
| Total | 858.07 |

*Sources*:  Comprehensive Funds Report (see table 2.11); *MEES* (vol. 21, no. 4, 1978), p. 13 and (no. 27), p. 10: UNCTAD, *Financial Solidarity* (1984); AMF, the First Annual Report; Ayubi, in Kerr, p. 372 (data converted into dollars).

ing the cement factory in Tura. Financing the project by the World Bank was conditional on the procurement of the ASED Fund's loan to explore the project. At a cost of $93 million, including $55 million in foreign currency, the plan was designed to expand production of cement by 660,000 tons annually, using modern technologies, and so increasing Egypt's production capacity from 1.35 million tons to 2.05 million tons of cement per year, as well as for the renewal of machinery.[183] The Egyptian government had good reason for wanting to increase cement production. In the period 1960–73 cement output was adequate for the supply of local demand and even for export. However, with the reconstruction boom in Egypt after the October 1973 War and the increase in local consumption, Egypt was forced to import cement, paid for in foreign currency.[184] Commencement of works on both the cement factory in Tura and the textile factories was delayed for more than a year-and-a-half, and costs increased by $21 million. This was caused, inter alia, by increased labor costs.[185]

The OPEC Fund for International Development was established in 1976 by OPEC members, with Iran, Saudi Arabia, Venezuela, Kuwait and Nigeria contributing the lion's share of its capital, though Iran's donation declined drastically in 1980. The OPEC Fund granted loans to Third World countries for support of their balance of payments, not necessarily just for specific development projects. Moreover the fund provided grants to the poorer element among the developing countries.[186] In 1977, the fund granted Egypt three loans at especially easy terms: in January the fund and the Egyptian government reached an agreement for a loan of $14.45 million as support for the balance of payments, for a period of 25 years, including five years' postponement, interest-free; in October the fund agreed to loan $14.45 million for the fertilizer project in Talkha; and in mid-December 1977 Egypt received an interest-free loan of $8.75 million for 20 years. This loan was granted as a line of credit to the Industrial Development Bank, set up in Egypt in 1975 to assist in the financing of small industries.[187]

Aside from ASEC and OPEC funds, Egypt also received aid from the Libyan Arab Bank (for the Talkha fertilizer plan); the Arab Monetary Fund (a loan for support of the balance of payments); the African International Bank (covering 50 percent of the costs of four generators for the Canal cities); and the Islamic Bank for Development.[188] Egypt also received loans from banks owned jointly by inter-Arab and European parties, such as the UBAF (Union of French and Arab Banks).[189]

### Effectiveness of aid fund utilization by the Egyptian economy

Two projects received large amounts of the loans which the funds donated to Egypt: the development of the Suez Canal and the fertilizer plant in Talkha. The first loans Egypt received were designated for the purification and the reopening of the Suez Canal, which had closed down after the June 1967 War and had been damaged in the October 1973 War. The Egyptian government's revenues from Canal transit fees were a vital source of foreign currency income for the economy. The opening of the Canal to commerce was also essential to the oil countries, as a means of receiving and shipping their oil, and other products, to Western markets. The extensive participation of all Arab funds in assisting Egypt with the purification, opening and widening of the Canal is therefore understandable. Suez Canal Authority data demonstrates that Saudi Arabia and Kuwait were among the main exporters of petroleum, and also generated income by importing goods via the Canal before and after the Camp David agreement.[190]

Widening of the Canal was essential to safeguard foreign income from international vessels of large tonnage that could not, at the time, pass through the Suez Canal. This meant such vessels sailed via the Cape of Good Hope, taking away valuable Egyptian profits. The widening of the Canal would augment Egypt's foreign currency revenues by increasing traffic and hence the quantities of merchandise passing through.[191] After the completion of the first stage of works to widen the Canal in December 1980, Egypt's income grew substantially – by 50 percent in one year (table 2.14). This increase in revenues was not due to moderate price increases on passage through the canal, but because of the vast increase in traffic.

**Table 2.13**   Population growth in Canal cities, 1966, 1975 (in thousands)

| City | 1966 | 1975 |
| --- | --- | --- |
| Port Sa'id | 283 | 300 |
| Isma'iliya City | 144 | 180 |
| Isma'iliya (other parts) | 200 | 220 |
| Suez | 264 | 150 |

*Source*: ARE, UNDP, *Suez Canal Region Plan 1976* (n.d.), p. 61.

The reopening of the Canal to traffic on June 5, 1975 had great significance for the economy and the Egyptian national psyche. Its opening symbolized the beginning of a reconstruction process in the Egyptian economy and a new era in its political history. Besides the resumption of foreign currency revenues, the opening of the Canal accelerated the reconstruction process in the whole region. Port Tawfiq, Port Fu'ad and Qantara, with about one million inhabitants and which had been almost completely destroyed after the 1967 war, were rebuilt in conjunction with reconstruction works on the Canal. By 1975, the number of inhabitants in the

Canal cities, excluding Suez City, exceeded the number before the June 1967 War (table 2.13). Economic development attracted foreign investments and investors viewed the opening of the Canal as a sign of stability.

**Table 2.14**   Suez Canal Authority transit fee revenues (in millions of Saudi Riyals and US dollars in current prices)

| Year | Total | |
|------|-------|------|
|      | SDR   | US $ |
| 1975 | 70  | 58  |
| 1976 | 269 | 233 |
| 1977 | 366 | 314 |
| 1978 | 410 | 327 |
| 1979 | 456 | 353 |
| 1980 | 510 | 392 |
| 1981 | 753 | 639 |
| 1982 | 851 | 771 |
| 1983 | 907 | 848 |

*Source*: IMF, *Balance of Payments Statistics* (vol. 34, part 1, 1983), p. 161 (vol. 38, 1987), p. 198.

[a] Figures given in dollars (rounded off in hundreds) converted according to IMF data in its publication: IMF, *IFS*, November 1984, p. 18, June 1987, p. 514.

The Talkha project, in which many inter-Arab institutions participated, was less successful. The fertilizer factory was set up in Talkha (135 km north of Cairo), close to the oil fields in Abu-Mehdi, which supplied products for producing fertilizers. A World Bank report in May 1974 estimated the cost of the project at $132.4 million, of which $93.4 million was in foreign currency. After talks held by World Bank institutions with the aid funds and Arab governments, an agreement was reached on shared financing of the project: the Abu Dhabi Fund, 7.6% of the total cost; the Arab Development Fund, 16.6%; the Kuwaiti Development Fund, 17.9%; the International Libyan Bank, 7.6%; the Qatar government, 2.6%; the Egyptian government financed 32.6%; and World Bank institutions, 15.1%. It was determined that the Arab lenders would provide $69.3 million in total, to be used for financing costs of equipment and material and for interest payments during construction.[192] The project was to have been finished in the autumn of 1978, but delays in work and in purchasing of equipment resulted in the project being completed more than two-and-a-half years later than planned.[193]

Egypt exploited Arab fund aid with relative success. This was in marked contrast to its unsuccessful exploitation of assistance for specific projects from foreign countries or financial bodies. While Egypt had no problem acquiring aid to provide for support of the balance of payments, or support in accordance with statute 480 (which grants American aid in the form of food and products), it encountered great difficulties in securing aid for specific purposes. The most common bottleneck was in raising local capital to complement foreign capital provided for various projects. On several occasions, foreign capital would arrive on schedule, but a chronic shortage of local capital would delay the project and instigate a rise in costs, because of the time factor and inflation. Further bottlenecks were the Egyptian administration;[194] problems with infrastructure which would harm the realization of agricultural and industrial plans, such as a defective transportation system in the periphery; and the need to increase electric power supply and water salinity. The report of the American Comptroller General (September 1977), which dealt with Egypt's capacity to absorb aid for specific purposes, illustrated Egypt's difficulties. In accordance with its findings, in the period of February 1975–March 1977, American aid for certain projects amounted to $905 million, of which Egypt exploited only $186 million,[195] or less than 21 percent.

An examination of the exploitation of loans granted to Egypt by the World Bank gives a similar picture: from the October War – after which Egypt enjoyed closer ties with the World Bank – until May 1979, the World Bank participated in the financing of thirty-three projects in Egypt, with loans totaling $1.2 billion. Of this amount of aid, Egypt succeeded in using only 34.4 percent, and World Bank experts specified that extensive delays were caused mainly by a shortage of building materials – delaying the construction of factories – and delays in the ratification of agreements by the Egyptian National Council.[196]

Compared to these bleak figures, Arab aid funds' money was absorbed with considerable success. Ayubi asserts that of the funds Egypt was provided, it succeeded in exploiting 74 percent for industrial, economic and social purposes. Ayubi adds that, if aid intended for the textile plants in al-Dawar and al-Bidha villages from the Arab Fund is deducted, the exploitation rate would have been even higher, reaching almost one hundred percent. In his opinion, the reason for this apparently lies in the freedom enjoyed by the recipients of Arab aid in choosing suppliers, machinery and technology involved in the project, which accorded them flexibility in the exploitation of resources.[197] Ayubi claims that he based his facts on data from the Egyptian Ministry of Economy. However, the aid funds' own reports appear to show that the level of exploitation of loans estimated by Ayubi is exaggerated. There were other plans besides the textile conglomerate in al-Dawar which the Egyptians failed to complete because of their inability to maximize aid resources. For example, up to the end of 1980 Egypt managed to exploit only 8 percent of aid intended for the sewage system in Helwan (the agreement was signed in 1975), and only 27 percent of aid granted for the development of the Suez Canal (signed, 1977).

In all, according to Arab Fund data, Egypt succeeded in exploiting only 52 percent of aid designated for it by the fund, compared to 78.8 percent indicated by Ayubi (table 2.15). Salacuse presents figures that suggest both the above estimates are pure hyperbole. Based on unofficial figures from the Ministry of Economy, he claimed that up to late October 1977, Egypt had succeeded in exploiting only $275 million out of commitments for $695 million[198], or only about 40 percent. In any case, the discrepancy between aid funds' data and Ayubi's figures doesn't challange the trend indicated by Ayubi: relative to loans from other sources, Egypt succeeded in exploiting Arab fund aid with greater efficiency.

**Table 2.15**  Exploitation of Arab Fund monies up to September 30, 1978

| Institution | Total loan (EgP millions) | Expl. amount | % Expl. |
|---|---|---|---|
| Arab Fund | 230.6 | 181.8 | 78.8 |
| Kuwaiti Fund | 217.7 | 206.4 | 94.8 |
| Saudi Fund | 213.6 | 192.0 | 89.8 |
| Abu Dhabi Fund | 99.0 | 98.2 | 99.1 |
| African Bank[1] | 24.0 | 18.0 | 75.0 |
| OPEC Fund | 23.2 | 15.6 | 67.2 |
| Arab Monetary Fund | 17.7 | 17.7 | 100.0 |
| Islamic Bank[2] | 12.0 | 12.0 | 100.0[3] |
| Libyan Arab Bank | 10.1 | 10.1 | 100.0 |

*Source*: Egypt's Ministry of Economy and Economic Cooperation, as quoted by Ayubi, in Kerr and Yasin, table 2.12, p. 372.

[1]  African Bank for Development.
[2]  Islamic Bank for Development.
[3]  A check of this figure shows that the entire amount was provided but not before September 1978. Commitment was given in 1977 and Egypt received the money in instalments, the last one in late 1981. See: UNCTAD, *Financial Solidarity*, 1984, annex table 23, p. 80. The Islamic Bank granted Egypt an additional loan of $6 million in early 1978, on commercial terms, destined for a sugar refinery in a factory in al-Sheikh village. See: *Ibid.*, p. 82; *MEES*, Januray 30, 1978, pp. 12–13 (vol. 21 no. 4, 1978), p. 15.

## Arab investment in conformance with Egyptian law

### Sources and clarifications

During the later part of the seventies, investments in Egypt were classified into two categories: local and foreign. This kind of classification gave no indication of the Arabs' share, because they were categorized in the framework of "foreign investments," which did not distinguish between nationalities. From the late seventies on, however, the Egyptian Investments Authority began to publish figures for three categories: local, foreign and Arab investments, though no breakdown of Arab investors by countries was indicated. Political considerations held back the release of such information, and after the Camp David agreement many Arab investors, some of whom were related to the royal families in the oil countries, preferred their investments in Egypt to remain confidential. Another efficient source shedding light on investments is the US Aid Agency (USAID) in Cairo. The information they provide on foreign companies has a high level of credibility, but there is a shortage of data on Arab investments.

Other sources on this kind of investment in Egypt exist in the form of reference books on investments published by foreign banks, the US embassy in Cairo and by commercial firms.[199] The books can sometimes fail to disclose important information such as Arab capital flow to Egypt by indirect means – e.g. via European companies – without being registered as an Arab investment. Furthermore, in their reports on the establishment of joint companies – e.g. Arab-American – the specific share of each group of investors is not identified.[200] This chapter is based on Egyptian Investment Authority data, as published in its annual report. The paucity of details is supplemented with additional information from the authority, published in domestic reports and in data provided by the EIA to Egypt's Central Statistics Authority.

## Investment laws and free-trade zones: Definitions

**Investment authority**   Item 26 of statute 43 determined that an authority for the promotion of foreign investments in Egypt was necessary to increase national income in Egypt. For this purpose The General Authority for Arab and Foreign Investments and Free-trade Zones was established. The authority was directly responsible for the promotion and approval of investments. It operated in the framework of the Ministry of Economy and International Cooperation until the mid-eighties, when it was transferred to the Ministry of Planning.[201]

**Free-trade zones**   Laws distinguished between domestic investments and those in free-trade zones. One of the objectives of free-trade zones was to "revive" the Canal zone, which was damaged in the 1967 and 1973 wars. There are a number of differences between domestic investments and investments in free-trade zones, but the essential difference is the domestic ban on foreign entrepeneurs investing on their own (without an Egyptian partner) in the country; an Egyptian partner with at least a 25 percent share in the project is mandatory. Construction plans and investments in the banking sector require an Egyptian partner or partners, with a share of at least 51 and 50 percent of the business, respectively.

In contrast, in the free-trade zones there are no such restrictions, and a foreign investor can make any kind of investment without Egyptian partners; domestic projects must have the status of a company without branches. In the free-trade zones there are no limitations on the setting up of branches and subsidiaries; as opposed to domestic plans, plans in these zones are exempt from customs duties, as long as they import from and export to foreign markets. Customs duties do apply to transactions between domestic companies and companies in the free-trade zone; transactions in the latter must be carried out entirely in foreign currency, except payments for local products, contrary to domestic companies, which usually work with local currency; management of projects in the free-trade zone is decentralized – each zone has its own board of directors and staff – as opposed to centralized management in domestic companies, with all management procedures executed in the Cairo offices of the investment authority. Some projects are not accepted in the free-trade zones, such as tourism and housing construction, whereas they are acceptable as domestic projects.[202]

**Table 2.16**   Outstanding private investors

| Name | Nationality | Field of economic activity in Egypt |
| --- | --- | --- |
| Mas'ad al-Salah | Kuwaiti | Real estate and main owner of shares in several industries |
| Shabukshi family | Saudi | Co-owners of Egypt Co. for Investment and |

**Table 2.16**   *(continued)*

|  |  | Development, Faysal Bank, Egypt-Abu Dhabi Real Estate Dev. Co., Arabiyeh Airlines |
|---|---|---|
| Mahmad Said Farsi | Saudi | Arabiyeh Airlines |
| Salah Kamal | Saudi | Tourism, Gulf Investments Co., National Video Co., Faysal Bank |
| Abd al-Rahman Sharbatli | Saudi | Egypt-Saudi Contracting Co., glass and beverage industries, Egypt Gulf Bank |
| Abd al-Wahab Galdari | UAE | Co-owner of Delta Bank, Cairo tourism companies. |
| Ali al-Duweij | Kuwait | Owner of extensive property in Egypt |
| Kamal Adham | Saudi | Owns 4 percent of Delta Bank in Egypt |
| Khaled Ibn Turki | Saudi | Investments in banking in Egypt |

*Sources*: Law, vol. 2, pp. 135–88; *La Documentation Africaine* (Paris), *Fichier des Banques Arabes*, "Delta," May 1985 and "Societ, Arabe," September 1985. Following data does not include investments in the oil sector, as it does not belong in the category of Investment Law 43.

The free-trade zones have been divided into two groups: special and general free-trade zones.[203] Special free-trade zones include domestic plans, approved by the investment authority, but under free-trade zone regulations.

Free-trade zones were established following the passing of the 1971 Investment Law, primarily serving the needs of private investment plans. The second group, general zones, includes zones established within special borders, determined by the investment authority as per statute 43. These zones usually serve export industries, and are located in a specific part of certain cities – like in the case of Cairo, Alexandria and Suez – or in any part of town – as in Port Said.

Sometimes the investment authority would approve investment plans with a certain amount of capital, and one year later publish data showing approval of plans with lower accumulated capital, and this despite additional new plans. The reason for this is that the authority sometimes cancelled plans approved for various reasons, such as: the investor's decision to withdraw from the financing of the plan, or a cancellation initiated by the Egyptian investment authority itself – as allowed by clause 27 in statute 43 – when the rate of progress towards the approved plan becoming operational is unsatisfactory. That was the case when, in late 1977 the authority cancelled permits for 121 projects. In accordance with the report published by the authority, the reason for this was the lack of effective practical steps taken by the investors toward completing their plans.[204] Other discrepancies between yearbooks arose from special free-trade zone plans sometimes changing to domestic or regular free-trade zone status, and vice versa.[205]

**Private Arab investment**   Private Arab investors came to Egypt on their own initiative, or by prior referral via branches of the EIA in Kuwait, Saudi Arabia and Abu Dhabi.[206] Rich subjects of the Gulf States exploited the free-trade zones in Egypt for setting up customs-exempt companies, and a major portion of their investments were in the hotel industry. Outstanding personalities among the investors were the Saudi Kamal Adham (King Faysal's brother-in-law), the Shabukshi family, Prince Khaled Ibn Turki, Adnan Khashoggi and Prince Muhammad al-Faysal, one of King Faysal's sons. Prince Muhammad al-Faysal engaged primarily in Islamic banking, and his role in the establishment of the Islamic Faysal Bank was significant. Table 2.16 lists some of the most eminent private investors in Egypt

*Extent, analysis and goal of investments*

**1972–1977**  The EIA started receiving investment offers as of 1972. Up to late 1973 the authority approved plans with a capital of EgP 76 million, but not a single one of these plans came to fruition. With the passing of statute 43, the authority received more proposals for investment, but not to the extent anticipated by the Egyptian leaders. Until late 1977, the authority commissioned investment projects with a capital of EgP 1,422 million. This figure was the total amount of capital for approved projects, but it is not to be understood from this that these projects were operational, or that they were in an advanced stage of planning before starting production. Up to June 30, 1977, 161 plans with a capital of EgP 242.4 million were operational.[207] In certain sectors, the percentage of projects completed up to that time was close to zero. For example, up to the end of 1977, twenty-four building plans were approved, of which only one was realized.[208]

**Table 2.17**  Analysis of capital investments of approved domestic plans, by nationality of investors, up to December 31, 1977 (in EgP millions)

| Nationality | Local | For. Curr. | Total | % |
|---|---|---|---|---|
| Egyptians | 437 | 280 | 717 | 50.5 |
| Arabs | 6 | 336 | 342 | 24.0 |
| EEC | — | 145 | 145 | 10.0 |
| USA | — | 87 | 87 | 6.0 |
| Others | 4 | 127 | 131 | 9.5 |
| Total | 447 | 975 | 1422 | 100.0 |

*Sources*: GAFIZ, *Report until 31/12/1977*, p. 44; Federation of Egyptian Industries (Cairo), *Yearbook 1977*.

The Arab investors' share constituted the largest foreign contribution, totaling 24 percent of all approved capital. Most investment capital – 50.5% – was applied by Egyptian citizens; EEC countries allocated 10%; US, 6%; and other countries, 9.5% (table 2.17). Table 2.18 shows that the largest numbers of plans were approved in 1977. That year Egypt improved its investment regulations, and equalized benefits for Egyptian investors to those bestowed on foreign investors. Egyptian investors lost no time and started investing in their country as per statute 43. At this point Egyptian investments now comprised the dominant part of all investments under this law. Arab investors applied their capital to three primary sectors (see table 2.19): investment corporations, tourism companies and housing projects.

**Table 2.18**    Plans and capital approved up to the end of 1977

| Year | Number of plans | Index ('72–3=100) | Capital (EgP millions) | Index |
|---|---|---|---|---|
| 72–73 | 29 | 100 | 76 | 100 |
| 1974 | 68 | 235 | 178 | 234 |
| 1975 | 104 | 359 | 202 | 266 |
| 1976 | 80 | 275 | 222 | 292 |
| 1977 | 191 | 659 | 744 | 979 |
| Total | 472 | — | 1,422 | — |

*Source*: GAFIZ, Statistics and Information Department, *Report on Arab and Foreign Investment until 31/12/1977.*

**Table 2.19**    Participation of Arab investors in domestic projects (in EgP millions)

| Sector | No. of projects | Participation of Arab capital |
|---|---|---|
| Investment companies | 28 | 113 |
| Banking institutions | 11 | 14 |
| Tourism projects | 50 | 71 |
| Housing projects | 20 | 45 |
| Transportation projects | 4 | 3 |
| Health projects | 6 | 9 |
| Agricultural enterprises | 12 | 14 |
| Construction plans | 4 | 2 |
| Educational projects | 1 | 3 |
| Textile projects | 23 | 9 |
| Food enterprises | 12 | 2 |
| Chemicals | 61 | 26 |
| Engineering projects | 19 | 15 |
| Construction material | 12 | 5 |
| Metal | 11 | 9 |
| Pharmacies | 2 | 2 |
| Total | 276 | 342 |

*Source*: GAFIZ, *Report until 31/12/1977*, p. 48.

**1978–1979**    Up to the end of 1979, 766 domestic projects were approved. Of these 280 were in or about to begin production, and 273 plans were in various stages of construction. Capital originating from Egyptian nationals or companies constituted more than 57 percent (EgP 1,316.2 million) of total authorized capital involved in investment plans; capital originating in Arab countries amounted to less than 16 percent (EgP 356.4 million); capital originating in the US, EgP 167.4 million; European Common Market countries, EgP 104 million; and other countries, EgP 283.7 million.[209] According to these figures, more than 70 percent of approved projects were operational or in the first stages of production. But behind these figures, a less encouraging trend, from the point of view of the Egyptian economy, was taking place. Out of total capital involved in all approved plans (EgP

2,27.7 million – see table 2.20), only EgP 614.5 million (27%) belonged to projects that had commenced operations, and EgP 874.1 million (38%) to projects still in the preliminary stages of production.[210] The term "preliminary stages of production" is vague, covering a wide range of project statuses: it was often the case that such a project was still a long way from starting production. Therefore, the only meaningful figures are those referring to companies that had initiated production.

**Table 2.20**  Participation of countries in regular free-trade zone plans approved by end of 1978, compared to plans approved by end of 1979 (in millions of EgP)

| Country | 1978 | | 1979 | | change | |
|---------|------|------|------|------|--------|------|
| | EgP | % | EgP | % | EgP | % |
| Egypt | 103 | 45.3 | 84.260 | 44.2 | −18.740 | −18.2 |
| Arab | 72 | 31.6 | 43.980 | 23.0 | −28.020 | −23.6 |
| USA | 7 | 2.9 | 15.663 | 18.2 | 8.663 | 123.8 |
| EEC | 36 | 15.7 | 31.268 | 16.4 | −4.732 | −31.1 |
| Others | 10 | 4.5 | 15.707 | 8.2 | 5.707 | 57.1 |
| Total | 228 | 100.0 | 190.878 | 100.0 | −37.122 | −12.9 |

*Source*: Al-Hay'a al-'Amma lil-Istithmar wal-Manatiq al-Hurra, *al-Taqrir al-Sanawi, 1979* (Cairo: 1980), p. 147.

**Table 2.21**  Participation of countries in plans in the special trade zones, approved up to end of 1978 and comparative to 1979 (in millions of EgP)

| Country | 1978 | | 1979 | | change | |
|---------|------|------|------|------|--------|------|
| | EgP | % | EgP | % | EgP | % |
| Egypt | 88 | 45.4 | 87.963 | 42.4 | -0.037 | −0.04 |
| Arab | 11 | 5.7 | 11.151 | 5.4 | 0.151 | 1.40 |
| USA | 81 | 41.8 | 79.198 | 38.1 | −1.802 | −2.20 |
| EEC | 9 | 4.6 | 7.140 | 3.4 | −1.860 | −20.70 |
| Others | 5 | 2.6 | 22.562 | 10.8 | 17.562 | 351.20 |
| Total | 194 | 100.0 | 208.014 | 100.0 | 14.014 | 7.20 |

*Source*: Al-Hay'a al-'Amma lil-Istithmar, *al-Taqrir al-Sanawi, 1979*, p. 156.

In the special free-trade zones, the EIA approved plans for EgP 208 million up to the end of 1979. The Arab states' share in these plans came to EgP 11.1 million, constituting 5.4% of total capital; the Americans' share, 38%; EEC countries, 3.4%; and other countries, 7.2%. Capital originating in Egypt made up the lions' share, or 42.3%.[211] The absolute and the relative share of investment by the Arab countries in the regular free-trade zones also declined. In 1978, Arab capital in these projects amounted to EgP 72 million or 31.6%, but by 1979 this amount had dropped to EgP 43.9 million or 23 percent (table 2.21). The Arab capital decline stemmed in the main from cancellation of plans and free-trade zones changing status to that of domestic investment plans.

**1980/1981**   In the early 1980s the Arab states' share in overall investment in Egypt once more increased significantly, both in absolute and relative terms, in the amount of capital as well as compared to other investors. It should be stressed that this was despite the Arab boycott imposed on Egypt after the peace treaty. During the period of "close ties" between Egypt and the oil countries, the level of Arab investment was low, whereas after the "boycott" it remained low relative to the possibilities open to citizens of oil-producing countries, but now we perceive a significant growth in their investments in Egypt (the reasons for this are explained in **chapters 4 and 5**).

**Table 2.22**   Analysis of all approved projects and their capital up to December 31, 1981: Domestic plans and free-trade zones (in millions of EgP)

| Location | No. of plans | Capital | plans | Percentage Capital |
|---|---|---|---|---|
| Domestic plans | 1,266 | 4,043.3 | 77.9 | 87.1 |
| Special free trade | 63 | 357.9 | 3.9 | 7.7 |
| Regular free trade | 297 | 238.7 | 18.2 | 5.2 |
| Total free trade | 360 | 596.6 | 22.1 | 12.9 |
| Total | 1,626 | 4,639.9 | 100.0 | 100.0 |

*Source*: ARE, CAPMAS, *Status of the Open-door Economy* (Cairo: February 1982), p. 24.

Up to the end of 1980, the Arab countries' share came to EgP 225 million or 11 percent of EgP 1,974 million – the total amount of capital approved for domestic plans. Seventy percent of this amount was applied to agriculture and construction plans – mostly for office space – and EgP 89 million was allocated to industrial projects.[212] In the special free-trade zones, approved investment capital amounted to EgP 210 million. In this period the Arab states' share went up by about 21 percent totaling EgP 14 million compared to EgP 11 million in 1979. Despite this increase, Arab capital represented a small part of total investments in this sector (6%) when compared to Egyptian capital (EgP 115 million) 55%. The rest of special free-trade zone investment was divided: US (EgP 37 million) 18%; EEC countries (EgP 11 million) 5%; and other countries (EgP 33 million) 16%.[213] In the regular free-trade zones plans worth EgP 211 million were approved up to the end of 1980. The Arab share of investments amounted to EgP 40 million or 19%, and they ranked below Egyptian capital totaling EgP 95 million (45%) and above EEC capital – EgP 32 million (15%), and the United States – EgP 18 million (15%). The other countries' part came to EgP 26 million (12%).[214]

**Table 2.23**   Analysis in percentages of capital for domestic projects that commenced production, according to fields of activity and investors' nationality, up to the end of 1981 (in thousands of EgP)

| Activity | EgP | % | Nationality Egypt | Arab | Europe | US | Other | % |
|---|---|---|---|---|---|---|---|---|
| Investment | 337,869 | 10 | 64.5 | 27.0 | 3.1 | 0.3 | 5.1 | 30.9 |
| Banks | 281,100 | 100 | 75.0 | 3.9 | 8.6 | 4.6 | 7.9 | 25.7 |

**Table 2.23** (continued)

| | | | | | | | | |
|---|---|---|---|---|---|---|---|---|
| Tourism | 54,482 | 100 | 62.2 | 20.8 | 13.6 | 0.1 | 3.3 | 5.0 |
| Housing | 14,868 | 100 | 68.7 | 31.1 | — | — | — | 1.4 |
| Transportation[1] | 32.594 | 100 | 53.2 | 18.0 | 18.1 | — | 10.7 | 3.0 |
| Agriculture[2] | 77,428 | 100 | 78.1 | 10.3 | 6.0 | — | 5.6 | 7.1 |
| Contracting | 42,806 | 100 | 66.4 | 10.5 | 18.6 | 0.3 | 4.2 | 3.9 |
| Tech. Cons. | 3,785 | 100 | 63.4 | 2.8 | 17.0 | 7.8 | 9.0 | 0.7 |
| Services | 14,385 | 100 | 80.8 | 1.6 | 10.5 | 5.3 | 1.8 | 1.3 |
| Spinning[3] | 28,357 | 100 | 53.6 | 25.0 | 3.6 | 13.3 | 4.5 | 2.6 |
| Food | 43,736 | 100 | 74.4 | 11.1 | 13.3 | — | 1.2 | 4.0 |
| Chemicals | 56,383 | 100 | 65.2 | 22.9 | 5.5 | 6.2 | 0.2 | 5.2 |
| Wood | 9,147 | 100 | 60.4 | 27.1 | 11.9 | 0.6 | — | 0.8 |
| Engineering | 20,339 | 100 | 50.2 | 19.6 | 30.0 | 0.2 | — | 1.9 |
| Construction | 22,759 | 100 | 63.3 | 30.5 | 6.2 | — | — | 2.1 |
| Metal | 27,240 | 100 | 49.0 | 38.4 | 9.9 | 0.8 | 1.9 | 2.5 |
| Mining | 1,250 | 100 | 83.0 | 13.9 | 3.1 | — | — | 0.1 |
| Oil | 14,334 | 100 | 14.6 | — | 85.4 | — | — | 1.3 |
| Health | 2,494 | 100 | 88.8 | 11.2 | — | — | — | 0.2 |
| Total | 1,092,399 | 100 | 66.7 | 17.0 | 8.9 | 2.4 | 5.0 | 100 |

Source: CAPMAS, 1982, p. 40.

[1] Also includes communications industry.
[2] Agriculture and animals.
[3] Spinning and weaving.

The Egyptian Central Bureau of Statistics, documenting Arab investments in domestic plans (tables 2.22–2.25) in Egypt up to the end of 1981, reveals the following:

1　The Egyptian part of approved *infitah* plans was the largest, and amounted to 66.7%. Arab investments came to 17%; European subjects represented 8.9% of the total; US citizens, 2.4%; and people from other countries, 5%.

2　Most Egyptian capital was directed into economic activity in the investment, banking, agriculture, chemicals and tourism sectors. The Arabs funnelled their capital to tourism, banking, chemicals and mining. The Europeans chose first and foremost banking, investment and oil sectors, whereas the Americans invested mostly in banking, spinning and weaving, medical industries and chemicals.

3　Up to late 1981, the Arab share of investment in domestic plans amounted to only EgP 186 million out of a total of EgP 1,092.4 million.

4　Of all the Arab nations, the Saudis invested the largest amount, 29.1%; Kuwaitis, 23.6%; and UAE citizens, 18.7%.

5　Investments by Saudis, UAE subjects, Kuwaitis, Palestinians, Libyans and Yemenites centered on activities in investment, banking and tourism; Jordanians concentrated mainly on metal and chemical industries; the Syrians on spinning and weaving and tourism; the Sudanese on transportation, agriculture and livestock; and the Lebanese and the Iraqis on chemical industries.

6　Arab investors did not show an interest in industries such as oil and medicine.

**Table 2.24** Capital distribution in domestic projects, which began production, by nationality of investor (in thousands of EgP)

| Activity | Capital | UAE | Jordan | Kuwait | Syria | SA | Sudan | Lebanon | Iraq | Palestine | Libya | Yemen | Others |
|---|---|---|---|---|---|---|---|---|---|---|---|---|---|
| Investment | 91,117 | 33,741 | 13 | 20,067 | 565 | 26,340 | — | 1,797 | — | 2,268 | 2,800 | 391 | 3,135 |
| Banks | 10,954 | 700 | 1,200 | 4,338 | — | 1,384 | — | — | 49 | — | — | — | 3,283 |
| Tourism | 11,357 | — | — | 5,251 | 580 | 3,622 | — | 1,459 | — | 23 | — | 9 | 413 |
| Housing | 4,650 | — | — | 4,025 | 180 | 150 | 45 | — | — | — | — | — | 250 |
| Transportation[1] | 5,852 | — | — | — | — | 4,200 | 1,652 | — | — | — | — | — | — |
| Agriculture[2] | 8,013 | — | — | 321 | — | 6,188 | — | 18 | 18 | — | — | 170 | 1,298 |
| Contracting | 4,481 | — | 30 | 720 | — | 1,392 | 21 | — | 350 | 75 | 93 | — | — |
| Technical consulting | 207 | — | — | — | — | — | 35 | 70 | — | — | — | — | — |
| Services | 224 | — | — | 102 | — | 109 | — | 115 | — | — | — | — | — |
| Spinning[3] | 7,079 | 379 | 627 | 2,135 | 1,744 | — | 213 | 1,576 | 394 | — | 390 | — | — |
| Food | 4,871 | — | — | 280 | 111 | 974 | 878 | 1,229 | — | — | — | — | 1,020 |
| Chemicals | 12,916 | — | 4,100 | — | 339 | 2,012 | 107 | 4,734 | 1,106 | 68 | — | — | 450 |
| Wood | 2,474 | — | 7 | — | — | 2,249 | 89 | 125 | — | 4 | — | — | — |
| Engineering | 3,975 | — | — | 1,456 | 132 | 1,724 | — | 213 | — | — | 450 | — | — |
| Construction | 6,941 | — | 188 | 4,300 | 309 | — | — | 1,500 | — | 212 | 320 | — | 112 |
| Metal | 10,463 | — | 6,600 | 678 | 397 | 1,734 | — | 1,040 | — | 14 | — | — | — |
| Medicines | — | — | — | — | — | — | — | — | — | — | — | — | — |
| Mining | 173 | — | — | 173 | — | — | — | — | — | — | — | — | — |
| Oil | — | — | — | — | — | — | — | — | — | — | — | — | — |
| Health | 280 | — | — | — | — | 280 | — | — | — | — | — | — | — |
| Total | 186,027 | 34,820 | 12,765 | 43,846 | 4,357 | 54,158 | 3,040 | 13,876 | 1,917 | 2,664 | 4,053 | 570 | 9,961 |
| In % | 100 | 18.7 | 6.9 | 23.6 | 2.3 | 29.1 | 1.6 | 7.5 | 1.0 | 1.4 | 2.2 | 0.3 | 5.4 |

*Source:* CAPMAS, 1982, p. 41

See notes to table 2.23.

**Table 2.25** Distribution of places of employment and annual salary of domestic projects, which began operation by the end of 1981, according to employees' nationality (in thousands of EgP)

| Activity | No. of programs | No. of employees | % Egypt | % Foreign | % Total | Annual salary Egypt | Annual salary Foreign | Annual salary Total | Average salary Foreign | Average salary Egypt | Average salary Total |
|---|---|---|---|---|---|---|---|---|---|---|---|
| Investment | 52 | — | — | — | — | — | — | — | — | — | — |
| Banks | 44 | 911 | 92.0 | 8.0 | — | 1,275 | 348 | 1,623 | 4,767 | 1,521 | 1,782 |
| Tourism | 27 | 1,128 | 98.6 | 1.4 | 100 | 853 | 68 | 921 | 4,250 | 767 | 816 |
| Housing | 13 | — | — | — | 100 | — | — | — | — | — | — |
| Transportation[1] | 9 | 1,306 | 94.3 | 5.7 | 100 | 2,144 | 1,457 | 3,601 | 19,427 | 1,742 | 2,757 |
| Agriculture[2] | 17 | 4,022 | 99.9 | 0.1 | 100 | 2,844 | 75 | 2,919 | 15,000 | 708 | 726 |
| Contracting | 48 | 27,709 | 98.6 | 1.4 | 100 | 16,283 | 4,852 | 21,135 | 12,130 | 596 | 763 |
| Technical consulting | 17 | 716 | 90.5 | 9.5 | 100 | 1,069 | 138 | 1,202 | 2,029 | 1,650 | 1,686 |
| Services | 18 | 4,905 | 98.8 | 1.2 | 100 | 5,896 | 1,539 | 7,435 | 26,534 | 1,216 | 1,516 |
| Spinning[3] | 31 | 4,641 | 98.5 | 1.5 | 100 | 3,210 | 307 | 3,517 | 4,324 | 702 | 758 |
| Food | 30 | 3,853 | 99.5 | 0.5 | 100 | 3,102 | 157 | 3,259 | 7,476 | 809 | 846 |
| Chemicals | 53 | 5,065 | 98.9 | 1.1 | 100 | 4,741 | 215 | 4,956 | 3,839 | 946 | 978 |
| Wood | 8 | 1,440 | 98.8 | 1.2 | 100 | 1,100 | 83 | 1,183 | 4,611 | 477 | 822 |
| Engineering | 21 | 2,014 | 99.0 | 1.0 | 100 | 2,926 | 397 | 213 | 18,905 | 1,468 | 1,650 |
| Construction | 14 | 2,319 | 99.7 | 0.3 | 100 | 2,143 | 94 | 3,323 | 13,429 | 927 | 965 |
| Metal | 21 | 2,897 | 98.7 | 1.3 | 100 | 2,544 | 346 | 2,890 | 8,872 | 890 | 998 |
| Medicines | 2 | 115 | 100.0 | — | 100 | 101 | — | 101 | — | 878 | 878 |
| Mining | 1 | 50 | 100.0 | — | 100 | 10 | — | 10 | — | 200 | 200 |
| Oil | 5 | 349 | 94.0 | 6.0 | 100 | 1,934 | 109 | 2,043 | 5,190 | 5,896 | 5,854 |
| Health and hospitals | 5 | 137 | 98.5 | 1.5 | 100 | 69 | 10 | 79 | 5,000 | 511 | 577 |
| Total | 436 | 63,577 | 98.5 | 1.5 | 100 | 52,244 | 10,195 | 62,439 | 10,720 | 834 | 982 |

*Source:* CAPMAS, 1982, p. 48.

See notes to table 2.23.

Free-trade zone data shows two interesting diversions from the above results, listed below:

1   Egyptians invested the largest amount of capital compared to other investors, and their share came to 38%; the Arabs invested 13.5%; the Europeans, 9.7%; the Americans, 12.5%; other investors, 0.6%.
2   Up to late 1981, the Arabs applied about 50 percent of their investments to the food, beverage and tobacco sectors, with business in meat products, vegetable processing, cereals and tea mixing predominating. Second in line was chemical products.[215]

**Table 2.26**   An analysis of the number of jobs and salary in free-trade zone projects starting production up to the end of 1981, according to nationality of employees

| | |
|---|---|
| Number of projects in free-trade zones (special and regular) | 215 |
| Number of positions | 12,995 |
|     positions held by locals | 12,323 |
|     positions held by foreigners | 672 |
| relative percentage of locals | 94.8 |
| relative percentage of foreigners | 5.2 |
| Inclusive annual salary (in thousands of EgP) | |
| Locals | 15,006 |
| Foreigners | 3,540 |
| Total | 18,546 |
| Average annual salary (in thousands of EgP) | |
| Locals | 1,218 |
| Foreigners | 5,268 |
| All employees | 1,42 |

*Source*: CAMPAS, 1982, p. 66.

One of the aims of the *infitah* policy was to provide more employment opportunities for the large Egyptian labor force, and to improve working conditions and salary levels. Table 2.26 presents an estimate of the percentage of locals and foreigners in the workplace, in both special and regular free-trade zones, along with annual salaries. From the table, the following can be deduced: nearly all jobs (94.8%) created as a result of investment projects in the framework of statute 43 were filled by Egyptians, who received the bulk of the money paid out in salaries. However, the foreign workers' salaries were higher than that of their Egyptian colleagues. The reason for this was that foreign workers were employed in the most needed skilled jobs. In any case, salaries paid to Egyptian nationals working in projects in the framework of statute 43 were higher than salaries paid to those employed by firms not connected to this law. This was due to the government enacting laws concerning the share of Egyptian employees and their salaries in investment projects. In the first half of 1981 the government approved a regulation stating that companies operating in free-trade zones were bound to employ at least 75 percent Egyptians in their staff, and their overall salary aggregate must be set at no less than 65 percent of all employee salaries. The regulation further stipulated that the company was required to provide its Egyptian employees with professional training.[216]

**1982/1983**  The EIA registered a notable achievement in 1982/3, compared with previous years: 51 percent of approved plans commenced operations, as compared to 32 percent that were operational up to the end of June 1982 (table 2.27).[217] Until late June 1983, Arab capital approved for domestic plans amounted to EgP 1,247 million, comprising 23 percent of overall investments in this sector. The free-trade zones registered greater substantial growth, with Arab capital totaling EgP 679 million approved up to June 1983, comprising 58 percent of all investments in this sector. This even exceeded approved Egyptian investments, totaling EgP 282 million or 24 percent (table 2.28). The term 1983 was a year for investment growth, and as noted by Wagih Shindy, Egyptian Minister of Investment, most of the increase could be credited to Arab investments.[218]

**Table 2.27**  Performance of plans: domestic and free-trade zone up to end of June 1982 (in thousands of EgP)

| Status of plan | Number | % | Capital | Investment costs |
|---|---|---|---|---|
| Started operations | 834 | 51 | 2222 | 3,310 |
| Preliminary stages | 420 | 25 | 1573 | 3,691 |
| Not carried out | 252 | 15 | 1236 | 2,683 |
| Approved | 147 | 9 | 1489 | 1,797 |
| Total | 1,653[1] | 100 | 6520[1] | 11,481 |

*Source:* Wizarat al-Istithmar wal-Ta'awun al-Dawli, al-Hay'a al-'Ammah lil-Istithmar wal-Manatiq al-Hurra, *al-Taqrir al-Sanawi, 1982/1983* (Cairo: April 1984), p. 36.

[1] In the quarterly journal of the EIA – October 1983 – slightly different data was given. Number of plans – 1654, total capital – EgP 5.9 billion. But official figures of April 1984 are more up-to-date. See: Gafiz, *Investment Review* (vol. 4, no. 3, October 1983), p. 8.

Up to the end of June 1983 most Arab investments (72 percent) were directed to financing projects – primarily in the banking and investment sectors; 10 percent were directed to industrial projects; and 2 percent of all Arab capital was destined for agricultural plans. This is in stark contrast to other foreign investors, who applied most of their investments to the industrial sector. Table 2.29 highlights the distribution, by sector, of Arab investments in Egypt, compared to other foreign investors.

According to investment authority calculations, investment plans approved up to this time were to have supplied 224,000 jobs at a combined annual salary of EgP 349 million, after the approved plans had commenced operations. In actual fact, up to late June 1983, 74,000 people were employed in investment projects in the country. Their total salary amounted to EgP 149 million EgP, and the workers' average annual salary came to EgP 2011.[219]

**Table 2.28** Analysis of investment sources, domestic plans and free-trade zones up to late June 1983 (in millions of EgP)

| Country | Domestic plans EgP | % | Free-trade zones EgP | % |
|---|---|---|---|---|
| Egypt | 3,361 | 63 | 282 | 24 |
| Arab | 1,247 | 23 | 679 | 58 |
| USA | 207 | 4 | 45 | 4 |
| EEC | 274 | 5 | 48 | 4 |
| Others | 249 | 5 | 118 | 10 |
| Total | 5,348 | 100 | 1,172 | 100 |

*Source*: Al-hay'a al-'Ammah lil-Istithmar wal-Manatiq al-Hurra, *al-Taqrir al-Sanawi, 1982/83* (Cairo), pp. 36, 69, 84.

**Table 2.29** Arab investment trends compared to other foreign investment trends

| Sector | Arabs relative % | Foreigners % |
|---|---|---|
| Financing | 72 | 21 |
| Services | 1 | |
| Industry | 10 | 41 |
| Development and construction | 6 | 4 |
| Agriculture | 2 | 3 |
| Total | 100 | 100 |

*Source*: Al-Hay'a al-'Amma lil-Istithmar wal-Manatiq al-Hurra, *Al-Taqrir al-Sanawi, 1982/83*, pp. 73–4.

**1983/1984** The previous year's trend of a steady increase in the number of projects starting production continued. Fifty-nine percent of all approved domestic and free-trade projects were functional, as table 2.30 indicates. However, there is also a slow rise in the cancellation of some plans. This brought with it a cutback in investment capital. Until the end of June 1984, the EIA approved 1,608 plans, with a capital of EgP 5,973.3 million, of which 1,298 were domestic plans with a capital of EgP 5,335.8 million, and 327 plans in the free-trade zones with a capital of EgP 637.5 million (see table 2.31).[220]

The sharp rise in Arab investment in 1982/3 was only temporary, and represented more an increase in potential activity than in real investments. Testimony to this is the fact that the absolute and relative share of Arab investments in 1983/4 registered a steep decline compared to the previous year. Compared to capital for domestic and free-trade zone investments approved up to late June 1983 (amounting to EgP 1,936 million), total Arab investments approved up to the end of June 1984 came to only EgP 997 million. The reason for this drop was the cancelling of approved projects. A drop in the overall number of approved investments also saw the Americans, Europeans and other countries experience a decline in relative and absolute investment capital. The sole source of capital that increased its investments was Egypt.

**Table 2.30**  Execution of domestic and free-trade zone projects (in millions of EgP)

| Status of project | Number | % | Total capital | Invest. costs |
|---|---|---|---|---|
| Started production | 948 | 59 | 2,754.4 | 4,374.2 |
| In prelimin. stages | 326 | 20 | 1,164.0 | 2,773.6 |
| Not yet operational and recently approved plans | 334 | 21 | 2,054.9 | 4,445.9 |
| Total | 1,608 | 100 | 5,973.3 | 11,603.7 |

*Sources*: Al-Hay'a al-'Amma lil-Istithmar wal-Manatiq al-Hurra, *Al-Taqrir al-Sanawi, 1983/1984* (Cairo: September 1984), p. 31; EIA (vol. 5, no. 4, January 1985), p. 8.

**Table 2.31**  Sources of capital for approved investments until late June 1984 (in millions of EgP)

| Country | Domestic plans | | Free-trade | |
|---|---|---|---|---|
| | EgP | % | EgP | % |
| Egypt | 3,781.8 | 71 | 242.9 | 38 |
| Arab | 800.9 | 15 | 196.1[1] | 31 |
| USA | 235.9 | 4 | 45.3 | 7 |
| EEC | 305.0 | 6 | 38.6 | 6 |
| Others | 212.2 | 4 | 114.6 | 18 |
| Total | 5,335.8 | 100 | 637.5 | 100 |

*Source*: Al-Hay'a al-'Amma lil-Istithmar wal-Manatiq al-Hurra, *Al-Taqrir al-Sanawi, 1983/1984*, pp. 31, 55, 83.

[1] EgP 67.5 million in regular zones and EgP 128.6 million in special zones. *Ibid.*, p. 121.

Arab investment capital in domestic plans was applied mainly to finance and service sectors. This year saw the doubling in the share of Arab investments in industrial plans, as compared to the corresponding period in the year before (table 2.32). Up to the end of 1983, 84,000 Egyptian workers were employed in domestic projects, their total annual salary amounting to EgP 198.6 million. The annual average salary per worker stood at EgP 2,358.[221] Another 18,000 workers were employed in the free-trade zones. Their total annual salary amounted to EgP 41.7 million.[222]

**Table 2.32**  Arab investment distribution (in millions of EgP)

| Sector | Amount | % |
|---|---|---|
| Financing[1] | 344.3 | 43.0 |
| Services[2] | 178.9 | 22.3 |
| Industry | 160.7 | 20.1 |
| Construction | 75.3 | 9.4 |
| Agriculture | 41.7 | 5.2 |
| Total | 800.9 | 100.0 |

*Source*: Al-Hay'a al-'Amma lil-Istithmar wal-Manatiq al-Hurra, *Al-Taqrir al-Sanawi, 1983/1984*, pp. 56, 61.

[1] Most of the capital was destined for joint financing companies and banks.
[2] Most of the capital was destined for tourism projects. *Ibid.*, p. 60.

**1984/1985**   Up to the end of June 1985, the EIA and the free-trade zones approved the establishment of 1,649 businesses with a total capital of EgP 7.2 billion, and with estimated investment costs of $13.3 billion. As of June 1985, 1,034 projects were operational with paid-up capital of EgP 3.9 billion (62.7%), as compared to 948 projects with a capital of $2.8 billion in late 1984.[223] The Egyptian contribution to investment was considerable, amounting to EgP 4.368 billion, or 60.7% of all capital; the Arabs' share came to EgP 1,829.7 million, 25.4%; the Americans, 402.9 million EgP, 6.5%; European countries, 408.4 million, 5.7%; and the share of other countries came to 307.5 million EgP, 4.3%. In this year, Arab investors also tripled their share, especially in the free-trade zones. Hence, their investment constituted more than 65% of total capital designated for these zones (table 2.33). The EIA estimated that approved projects would provide 243,000 jobs. The real number was much lower: a little over 110,000 workers were employed in 615 domestic companies, and their overall annual salary amounted to more than EgP 311 million.[224]

### The correlation between Egyptian investment in Egypt and their work in the oil-producing countries

A close connection exists between Egyptian investments, and the remittances from Egyptians working in the oil countries. (This connection is explored later in chapter 3.) This capital, some of which was funneled to investment projects in Egypt, was remitted by the Egyptian workers both during the period they were employed in the Gulf States, and upon their return to Egypt. The investment trend of Egyptian nationals in their economy reached significant proportions after changes were effected in statute 43 in 1977, changes that enabled Egyptian investors to benefit from the same advantages enjoyed by foreign investors. From 1977, there was a substantial increase in investments by Egyptians. Table 2.33 reveals some startling facts: Egyptian capital constituted the central factor in total investments in the framework of statute 43, exceeding the investments by citizens from the oil countries, or any other country, in both domestic and free-trade projects. Hereby a situation was created where Egyptian policy-makers highlighted foreign investment – mainly Arab – as being vital to boost the Egyptian economy, but in fact the most valuable sources of investments were made by Egyptian nationals.

The EIA did not release details of Egyptian investors operating in the oil countries, but it appears that a considerable part of Egyptian investments stemmed from savings from the period of their employment in the Gulf. Millions of Egyptians worked at different times in the AOC and remitted tens of billions of dollars to Egypt. The domestic investment of the foreign savings of Egyptian emigrants was therefore a valuable contribution to the Egyptian economy.[225]

**Table 2.33**   Sources of capital approved for investments up to end of June 1985 (in millions of EgP)

| Country | Domestic plans | | Free-trade zones | |
|---|---|---|---|---|
| | EgP | % | EgP | % |
| Egypt | 4052.4 | 70.0 | 315.6 | 22.1 |
| Arab | 914.8 | 15.8 | 914.9 | 64.0 |

**Table 2.33** *(continued)*

| | | | | |
|---|---|---|---|---|
| USA | 350.7 | 4.3 | 52.2 | 3.6 |
| EEC | 370.1 | 6.4 | 38.3 | 2.7 |
| Others | 199.4 | 4.5 | 108.1 | 7.6 |
| Total | 5787.4 | 100.0 | 1429.1 | 100.0 |

*Sources*: Al-Hay'a al-'Amma lil-Istithmar wal-Manatiq al-Hurra, *Al-Taqrir al-Sanawi, 1984/1985*, pp. 21, 36; *Investment Authority Quarterly Journal* (vol. 7, no. 1, April 1986), p. 8.

Accumulated information, published by the EIA, *MEED* and the *FT*, indicates a similar trend. Since 1983, Egypt has arranged a yearly meeting of Egyptian emigrants, under the auspices of the president. A large part of the discussions revolved around the migrants' investments in Egypt. A result of these talks was the Egyptian Emigrants Co. for Investments and Development, established in August 1983, with an authorized capital of EgP 100 million ($121 million), and paid-up capital totaling EgP 10 million ($12.1 million). This company, as similar businesses had done before, channelled the migrants' funds to investments in Egypt and set up several firms dealing with housing, commerce and food processing.[226] The EIA regularly apprised Egyptian embassies in the Gulf States for information on investment plans for distribution among Egyptian workers. Egyptian emigrants investment in their native land had taken place before the emigrant meetings were held. Egyptian doctors working in Kuwait participated in the construction of the Abu-Sina Medical Centre in Egypt; Egyptians working in the UAE contributed 50 percent of the capital of the Bank for Commerce and Investments; The Nile Bank was founded in 1978 by Egyptians working in Saudi Arabia (75% of capital) and local Egyptians (25%); Egyptians working in the UAE held 50 percent of Delta Bank shares; the Alexandria–Kuwait Bank was also founded with the assistance of Egyptians working in the Gulf States.[227]

It should not be forgotten that the public sector in Egypt also invested in plans under the framework of statute 43, but EIA figures reveal that the Egyptian private sector's share of total Egyptian investments in statute 43 plans amounted to around 62 percent, compared with 38 percent by the public sector, at the end of 1984.[228] A notable fact is that a major proportion of approved, private Egyptian investments (33.5%) were intended for industrial plans.[229]

## *Obstacles to attracting investments*

The ability of a country to attract foreign capital depends on its policy and the climate it creates for foreign and domestic investments. Egypt's reputation in this field was not an encouraging starting-point for statute 43. Investors were mindful of the nationalization program undertaken during Nasser's reign. Egypt's geographical location worked against, as well as for, the economy: besides the advantages, there were problems, because Egypt was located in a region fraught with political instability.

Another difficulty encountered by foreign investors was the relatively low level of development, especially in remote areas far from centrally located cities. Nasser had devoted enormous resources to the military sector and, in so doing, had neglected the development of peripheral areas. Most attention was focused on improving urban development, mainly Cairo, with an eye to better control of the population in the cities, where most government institutions were situated.[230] The contrast in levels and extent of development between the periphery and the centrally located cities widened the gap in income levels, so that purchasing power was in the hands of a relatively small number of groups in the upper middle-class. This meant that there was no real incentive for private investment in the periphery, because of the population's limited purchasing power, as well as the inadequate physical infrastructure.

The Egyptian psyche proved as additional obstacle to the promotion of foreign investments: the combination of anti-colonialist feelings, pride in their cultural heritage and the change in the thrust of Egypt's foreign policy, led to concern among the Egyptian people about foreign involvement in their economy. These anxieties were manifested in the government's attitude toward foreign investment. As Othman wrote in his memoirs, difficulties arose even when it concerned investments by "brothers" from Kuwait, with Othman himself against the selling of Egypt to foreigners.[231]

The Egyptian bureaucracy constituted one of the central problems in attracting foreign capital to Egypt. Foreign investors had to contend with a rigid and inefficient bureaucracy, and many chose not to get involved and invested elsewhere. Egypt did succeed in resolving the problem of its diminished credibility following the period of nationalization: its policy-makers constantly proclaimed that Egypt welcomed foreign investments, and that it would guarantee them and pass relevant legislation. The two interim agreements in Sinai and the peace treaty with Israel greatly enhanced the investment climate. But the government had greater difficulties solving the bureaucratic obstacle. The changes in legislation relating to foreign investments would fail to attract new investors if the bureaucracy did not act in the spirit of the law. A foreign banker warned in September 1975: "When you talk to a minister or a senior official, there is absolutely no doubt of their sincerity and their desire to cooperate. But when you reach the lower ranks, you really become frustrated."[232]

When a foreign investor contacted the EIA with an offer to invest in a specific project, the authority would study the offer, and then accept or reject it. After being approved by the EIA, the proposal was distributed to any government office concerned in any way with the subject. This drawn-out process of confirmation and notification generated a scenario in which an offer that should have been approved within three months at the latest, was sometimes delayed for a long period of time. According to EIA data, up to the end of 1978, 75 percent of proposed plans were approved. It took one month to study 10 percent of the proposals, between one to two months for 55 percent, 4–5 months for 30 percent, and it took 6 months or more to study 4 percent of the plans.[233] Even after a positive reply is given to any proposed deal, the bureaucratic tangle continues, and the investor is obliged to take out work and visiting permits, various stamped licenses, exemptions from customs and taxes, and so forth (see table 2.34).

**Table 2.34** Bureaucratic procedure for approval of plans in the framework of statute 43

| Department | Function |
| --- | --- |
| Work permits – Ministry of Labor | Director General |
| Commercial registration | Director General |
| Legal registr. (notary) | Director General |
| Passp. and migration – Min. of Interior | Director General |
| General industrial authority | Manager |
| Taxation – Treasury | Director General |

Additional necessary permits are needed from the following government ministries (according to specific type of project): ministry of health, tourism, transportation, reconstruction, agriculture and the Central Bank of Egypt.

In 1974, the year statute 43 was ratified, *al-Ahram al-Iqtisadi* criticized the "amateurish approach" of the Egyptian economy to the execution of the law:

> One of our major problems is our approach to all matters, usually characterized by temporary enthusiasm, by noisy and sudden energy, without any scientifically planned or calculated supervision . . . we will not be able to attract Arab and foreign capital to Egypt, just by waving the flag of development and by passing a law protecting foreign capital, without removing obstacles in the way.[234]

A decade after statute 43 was passed, the bureaucratic situation had not changed significantly, and Madhat Hasanein wrote: "Would it be possible to get rid of the large numbers of functionaries handling investments in Egypt . . . the problems facing the investor in Egypt have passed the stage of administrative and formal arrangements. Now there are serious and basic problems."[235]

The Egyptian bureaucracy suffered from several serious problems: many employees did not turn up for work, left early, read newspapers and ate during working hours; often there was a general feeling of disorganization. According to Ayubi, "it is not unusual . . . to find a document of a plan, a budget and a file of laws, used as a cushion on a rocking-chair. Other documents are found under tables, behind doors, on balconies and sometimes even in the bathroom!"[236] Though Ayubi's description is probably exaggerated, the bureaucracy was cumbersome and made reasonable progress on projects difficult.

Other delays were caused by disputes concerning investments between the EIA and other local authorities. As revealed by a report from the American consulting company Arthur Little in 1981 – drawn up at the request of the EIA – statute 43 did not give any extra clout to the EIA which would give it preference over other agencies involved in investments.[237] The authority's inability to take decisions were detrimental to both foreign investors and the Egyptian economy.

The Egyptian leadership tried to simplify the process of approval for investments by consolidating the various bureaucratic procedures within the EIA, instead of having to obtain different permits from poorly linked offices and departments. A regulation of May 1983, which specified that a plan was to be approved within a maximum period of four months, also helped to quicken the process.[238] Attempts at reorganization continued apace: in July 1984, Mubarak set up a High Committee for investments headed by Prime Minister Kamal Hasan 'Ali. The committee issued new regulations, which ruled, inter alia, that the maximum time period for approval of a project should not exceed six months. It also determined that the EIA would be responsible for obtaining permits from all departments and institutions involved in the investment, easing matters for the investor. In order to enhance the status of the EIA, Mubarak decided to transfer authority to the Ministry of Economy and Foreign Trade from the Ministry of Investment and International Cooperation.[239] An amendment to this dictated that the time for approval of plans was shortened to one month, and if this was not met, the investor's project would be automatically accepted. The prime minister took reponsibility for following up slow procedures. Furthermore, the Egyptian government issued a list of benefits to which foreign investors were entitled.[240]

In spite of all efforts and relative progress, investors were still faced with many difficulties. In October 1986, discussions between Saudi investors in Cairo, at the Marriot Hotel, revealed old problems facing the businessmen: complaints that the execution of their projects was seriously delayed because of disputes and a lack of cohesion among the various bodies; the large number of exchange rates; and the low rate of the dollar for promotion of investments, which was lower than the rate on the free market. Al-Ghrib, vice-chairman of the EIA, brokered familiar promises: "In the near future, all restrictions on Arab investments will be lifted . . . investment policy must facilitate customs regulations and taxation on manufacturing equipment . . . Egypt is striving to implement reforms and we are working on a uniform rate of exchange . . . we have difficulties in enforcing the law, but we are working on it." He gave a typical example to the gathering of a list of proposed investment projects: "Lately the EIA drew up a list of investment projects which can be implemented immediately . . . but . . . the list will not be ready for another month."[241]

## Summary

Investments in Egypt were not uppermost on the list of priorities of the AOC governments and their citizens. The costs of security and development in their countries, investment in the West and foreign aid took preference over their investments in Egypt. The governments of the AOC funneled their capital to the West, so Egypt benefited only from an insignificant part of AOC funds (an amount of around $300 million in the decade following October 1973 ). To this sum, we can add another $2 billion held by the oil country governments in the Egyptian Central Bank, although some people viewed these deposits as aid and not as investments. Furthermore, inter-Arab investment projects in Egypt were not substantial, except for the Suez–Alexandria oil pipeline, and a number of jointly-owned banks. The AMIO, which presented ambitious plans and with a capital of about $1 billion, ended up as a total failure and most of its capital was never exploited. Overall, inter-Arab investments in Egypt did not exceed $1.75 billion, of which the Arab aid funds allocated $850 million to development plans in Egypt. A further $500 million was invested by AOC governments and citizens in Egypt according to statute 43, up to 1985. Total

Arab investment in Egypt – including public, inter-Arab and private sectors and deposits and aid fund investment – amounted at the very most to $4.5 billion, compared to the hundreds of billions of dollars invested in the West (table 2.35).

**Table 2.35**   Total Arab investments in Egypt up to 1985 (in millions of US dollars)

| | |
|---|---|
| Public sector investments (bilateral) | 300 |
| Deposits on the Central Bank | 2,000 |
| Inter-Arab investments | 900 |
| Aid funds | 850 |
| Investments based on statute 43 | 500 |
| Total | 4,550 |

*Source*: Data presented in this chapter.

After the implementation of the *infitah* policy in Egypt, the oil countries evinced what turned out to be short-lived enthusiasm. On Hijazi's visit to the Gulf in late 1974, he received commitments for joint investments for over $2 billion; in February 1974, Libya promised to invest $800 million in development projects in Egypt;[242] and from August 1974 up to the signing of a pact in June 1975, Iraq held protracted talks on a series of agreements for investing $700 million in partnership with Egypt. They decided to establish joint Egyptian–Iraqi industries for the manufacture of cars, tractors and trucks, and Iraq also pledged to grant $45 million for building the "Iraq quarter" in Port Said.[243] Out of all these sums (about $3.5 billion) a very small part was applied to investments in the Egyptian economy, though in this Egypt was hardly blameless, owing to various administrative difficulties that came up: Al-Khaled, Director General of the Kuwaiti Corporation in Egypt, claimed that in November 1982, out of $580 million that the Kuwaiti government had budgeted for development plans in Egypt during 1977, by late 1982, only $50 million had actually been invested because of bureaucratic difficulties.[244]

The Egyptian government was optimistic about AOC investments in Egypt. However, just as its expectations for aid were not met, investment income also fell short. But whereas they had provided aid to Egypt after developments threatening its stability (such as the riots in 1977) this was not the case when it came to investments. Their prime consideration now was economic. There were also security considerations and concern for their future; the Arab oil-producing countries were seeking an optimum combination of growth, profits and security. The difference between the AOC's separate nations in the application of their investments was in the strategy implemented by each country for the realization of these aims: Kuwait gave priority to long-term, low-risk investments, with reasonable profits, with concern for future generations; Saudi Arabia considered the liquidity of its investments as all-important. Oil countries with a fragile economy[245] invested a major proportion of their surplus monies on Western markets. It should be noted that Kuwait, as well as Saudi Arabia, made minor investments in Egypt, but also made the biggest investments. The reason for this was that Kuwait was the first oil producer that had accumulated surplus capital and it had the most experience in investments. In time, Kuwait developed a sophisticated financial system, which sometimes took on investments with a high-risk factor. It had made investments in poor countries such as Mauritania and North Yemen, while other oil countries were not willing to invest in these nations, except for very small sums.[246]

Besides the fact that the AOC did not make any major investments in Egypt, they also refused to drop Western companies from the Arab boycott list. As a result, a number of foreign companies cancelled their intention to invest in Egypt.[247] The economic boycott imposed on Egypt in 1979 caused some anxiety to Western companies which were not listed under the boycott. Many of these businesses had invested in Egypt in order to export their products later to markets in the Arab countries (see table 2.36). In an attempt to allay their fears, Sadat assembled their envoys in May 1979, and he promised them that their businesses would not be harmed, notwithstanding the anticipated boycott.[248]

**Table 2.36**  Revenues from free-trade zones 1975 to mid-1980 (in thousands of EgP)

| Income | 1975 | 1976 | 1977 | 1978 | 1979 | mid-1980 |
|---|---|---|---|---|---|---|
| Taxes | — | 47.4 | 638.8 | 2,048.6 | 2,681.1 | 1,939.1 |
| Rental fees | 85.3 | 405.4 | 317.7 | 945.4 | 1,061.5 | 1,025.6 |
| Total | 85.3 | 452.8 | 956.5 | 2,994.0 | 3,762.6 | 2,964.7 |

*Source*: Farouk Shakweer, Mona Ghaleb Mourad, *Cost/Benefit Assessment of Free Zones: A case study on Egypt* (Cairo: May 1981), p. 104.

As with the poverty of government aid and investments, the Egyptian economy did not benefit greatly from private investment and AOC citizens preferred investing in the West; overall, Arab commitments for investments since the beginning of the *infitah* policy until mid-1985 did not exceed EgP 1.9 billion (most of this funding came after Sadat's peace initiative). Although this figure constituted the capital of approved projects, in reality less than 50 percent of these projects were operational. Furthermore, Arab investments were made mainly in the services sector and not in manufacturing. According to Egyptian Five Year Plan data for the years 1982/3–1986/7, 72.2 percent of Arab investment capital was applied to services and 27.8 percent to the production sectors. Arab investors were not very different in this matter from other foreign investors, who appropriated 62.2 percent and 37.8 percent, respectively. Moreover the Five-Year Plan indicated that most new projects approved according to statute 43 were built in Cairo and Alexandria, increasing the already overloaded burden on the infrastructure in these areas.[249]

In accordance with calculations by government economists, the scope of foreign investment in the Egyptian economy was much lower than that of the government. Up to the mid-seventies, for example, Egypt invested EgP 176.8 million in the infrastructure of the free-trade zones, compared to foreign operational investments of EgP 14.4 million. The period of time it took a typical project to yield a return on its investment (infrastructure costs, less real estate rental fees and 1–3 percent fee on transactions charged by the EIA) was between five and six years.[250]

**Table 2.37** Comparison between the national investment plans and the plans authorized by the Egyptian Investment Authority, 1975, 1979 (in percentages)

| Field of activity | 1975 | | 1979 | |
|---|---|---|---|---|
| | 1[1] | 2 | 1 | 2 |
| Banks and financ. instit. | 1.3 | 22.8 | 1.7 | 26.3 |
| Tourism and services | 9.1 | 27.7 | 8.3 | 27.3 |
| Housing and construction | 14.8 | 16.0 | 19.8 | 10.7 |
| Transport and communicat. | 30.4 | 1.4 | 24.7 | 1.5 |
| Agriculture | 15.0 | 2.0 | 18.0 | 4.2 |
| Industries | 30.4 | 30.1 | 27.5 | 33.0 |
| Total | 100.0 | 100.0 | 100.0 | 100.0 |

*Source*: Government accountant report as quoted by Shakweer, p. 28.

[1] Column 1 indicates the relative part of each sector as planned in the Egyptian Five-Year Plan. Column 2 indicates the relative part of each sector as approved by the EIA.

Considerable criticism of the foreign banks was voiced in Egypt. These banks were established to promote foreign investments, but instead they were engaged in financing of commercial activity, boosting imports and competing with Egyptian commercial banks. Asma Rashid, in his article headlined "Are foreign investments building Egypt," noted that foreign banks transferred profits earned from their activities in Egypt to overseas subsidiaries.[251] In a 1979 report the government indicated that levels and distribution of foreign investment did not conform to the national investment plan, the net result being that domestic savings, skilled manpower and other national resources were not properly exploited. Table 2.37 compares the relative part of each sector in the national investment plan (column 2), to that approved by the EIA in 1975 and 1979 (column 1).

The rate of foreign investment compared to domestic investments was 5 percent in 1974, 13 percent in 1979 and 11 percent in 1984/5, as shown in table 2.38. The foreign oil companies, who supplied most direct foreign investments in Egypt, concentrated on oil exploration (which was not included in the framework of statute 43). The American share in oil investment was far greater than the Arabs' share, which was marginal. With regard to investments within the framework of statute 43, the Arabs' share was larger, totaling about 25 percent of all commitments for this kind of investment, compared to less than 6 percent by the US and about 4 percent by EEC countries. A dominant part of investments in this framework was taken by Egyptian investors – about 60 percent. A substantial part of Egyptian investments ensued from the migration of millions of Egyptians to the oil countries, who invested their capital in their homeland.

Most Arab investments were made in the tourism and housing sectors. Tourism projects were important because they were one of the prime sources of foreign currency for the Egyptian economy. Likewise, foreign investments in the manufacture of consumer products had potential benefits, as policy-makers strove to reduce the balance of payments deficit with the help of foreign investment, by having local industry produce goods formerly imported by Egypt. Even the setting up of a soft-drink company like 7-UP brought with it savings in foreign currency: an imported can of 7-Up cost 35 piastre in foreign currency, compared to a local price of 6 piastre.[252]

**Table 2.38**  Investment costs (in millions of current EgP)

|                                                        | 1974 | 1977  | 1979  | 1984/85[1] |
|--------------------------------------------------------|------|-------|-------|------------|
| Investments costs (local and foreign) of which:        | 680  | 1,838 | 3,705 | 8,718      |
| foreign investment                                     | 34   | 204   | 497   | 1,037      |
| Oil companies                                          | 32   | 155   | 371   | 876        |
| Statute 43 costs                                       | 2    | 49    | 126   | 161        |

*Source*: World Bank, ARE, *Current Economic Situation and Economic Reform Program* (Report no. 6195–EGT, October 22, 1986), p. 90.

[1] Estimate.

Investments by AOC nationals, both in relative and absolute terms, exceeded investments in Egypt by their native governments (excluding deposits), even though government resources were considerably larger. Nationals not only did not stop investing in Egypt after the peace treaty with Israel, they even increased their investments. Organized groups of investors headed by senior dignitaries from the Gulf traveled to Egypt, and met with their counterparts of the Egyptian leadership, including President Mubarak.[253] In fact, as the Secretary-General of the Chamber of Commerce commented in Jedda in October 1986, "Saudi investments were never discontinued."[254] The AOC governments did not stop investing in Egypt after the boycott, and they did nothing to prevent their people from continuing to do so, or from expanding their investments. In late May 1979, a senior Kuwaiti official said that Kuwaiti citizens would make their own decisions about their money invested in Egypt, "as the government has no control over these matters."[255] A spokesman for the Kuwaiti development fund stated at the time that private investors in his country considered Egypt and Kuwait as the best places for investing their money.[256]

AOC citizens invested in Egypt because of cultural and geographical incentives: things like the proximity of the country and familiarity with the language and culture were important to investors. Mustafa Khalil notes other reasons for their investing in Egypt: many Arab investors were married to Egyptian women, like the Saudi businessman Shabukshi; many had received their education in Egypt, or from Egyptian teachers working in the Gulf; the Arabs diversified their investments (especially after the start of tension between the US and Iran, with the resulting confiscation of Iranian property in the US); the Arab investors felt secure that nothing would happen to their investments, and that Egypt had always made every effort to create a positive atmosphere.[257] Gamal al-Nasser, the Egyptian minister of the economy, cited the influence of marital relations, as well as the lack of supervision on foreign currency in the Gulf States, making it easier for their citizens to spend their money as they saw fit.[258] Three other points attracted Arab investors to Egypt: the Lebanon War, the Iran–Iraq War and the collapse of the Suq al-Manakh in Kuwait,[259] which made Egypt a more attractive place for investment at the expense of nations like Lebanon, whose own economies were badly hit by these crises. It is very probable that private investors from countries with poor diplomatic relations with Egypt were attracted to the idea of investing in Egypt after the signing of the peace treaty, which created the comfort of knowing that there was little chance of war breaking out between these two countries, thus giving added security to their investments.

# 3

# Labor Migration to the Arab Oil Countries

Of particular interest from a historic socio-economic and regional point of view is the worker migration from the poor Arab countries to the rich countries in the 1970s and 1980s. This subject crudely reflected the disproportionate wealth division between the oil-producing countries in the Gulf and the poor countries in the region. Worker migration from Egypt to the AOC constituted one of the most important aspects in the economic relations between the two sets of countries. The phenomenon of temporary migration is dramatic because of its magnitude, the resulting capital flow and its socio-economic and political influences on the Egyptian economy and society. Millions of Egyptians seized the chance to emigrate to the oil countries, and they remitted over $15 billion (via official channels) to the Egyptian economy from 1973 to 1983. Egyptian migration to the AOC in the early 1980s included, directly and indirectly, at least one-third of Egypt's total population of around 48 million people. In 1983, approximately three million Egyptians worked in the Arab oil countries. Assuming that every emigrant had three dependants (some, obviously had many more than that), it is evident that about nine million Egyptians were directly dependent for their livelihood on the migration process. There was also constant exchange of workers: those that had terminated their work in the Gulf returned to Egypt and others left to try their luck.

In the past, people had been of the opinion that Egyptians – especially the Egyptian *fellahin* – were not inclined to leave their land to emigrate to another country, even if they had the possibility to do so.[1] Indeed, until the 1960s, the number of Egyptian migrants was insignificant: according to El-Badri, in the 1940s their number came to about 25,000;[2] in the mid-1960s there were about 100,000 Egyptians living abroad, most of whom had emigrated for good,[3] compared to 91,000 foreign residents in Egypt in 1966;[4] in 1973, before the "oil boom," about 160,000 Egyptians – of whom 35,000 were on government assignment in the Arab countries[5] – were working abroad, and about 219,000 Egyptians temporarily migrated for working purposes.[6]

The accelerated levels of emigration to the Arab countries were precipitated by the economic consequences of the October 1973 War, and the subsequent improvement of relations between Egypt and the AOC nations. If, in the fifties and sixties, most of the emigrants were intellectuals, post-"oil boom," Egyptians from all strata of society migrated to the AOC: intellectuals, skilled and unskilled workers, refuting the traditional claim that Egyptians were not inclined to transmigrate. Once the AOC started providing well-paid employment possibilities, the Egyptians overcame their dislike of settling outside Egypt, and massive emigration became common-place. At least a part of the Egyptian communities who emigrated to the AOC would end up settling there permanently.[7]

## Egyptian migration movement after the oil price rise

The exact extent of Egyptian migration – the total number of migrants for a specific year, the annual number of migrants, as well as their age, sex and economic activity – is simply not known. Owing to the spontaneous nature of migration, government records do not detail an accurate picture of the migration process. Many more migrants were involved than the number agreed between the Egyptian and AOC governments (a number which comprises about 5 percent of the total). Existing records regarding migration in the framework of official agreements do not comprise any kind of criterion for evaluating the total number of migrants.[8]

**Table 3.1**   Total number of pilgrims to Saudi Arabia and the Egyptian quota

| Year | Total | Egyptian quota |
|------|-------|----------------|
| 1979 | 862,520 | 48,297 |
| 1980 | 812,892 | 66,106 |
| 1981 | 879,368 | 83,907 |
| 1982 | 853,555 | 98,408 |
| 1983 | 1,003,911 | 121,171 |
| 1984 | 919,671 | 133,071 |

*Source*: Saudi Arabian Monetary Agency (SAMA), Research and Statistics Department, *Statistical Summary 1402*, p. 98, *1403*, p. 115, *1407*, p. 100.

Illegal emigration was the most prominent factor in making estimates on the number of emigrants. Many migrants arrived in the Gulf States masquerading as tourists or visiting family, but with a firm intention to illegally remain in the AOC, or they would arrive originally on a Hajj and then decide to remain and to find work.[9] The Hajj movement is of particular interest, because there was a significant increase in the number of Egyptians fulfilling this religious commandment, an increase considerably higher than the rise in the number of pilgrims from all countries: in 1979, 48,000 Egyptians made the pilgrimage; in 1982, 98,000; whereas in 1984, their number rose to 133,000 (table 3.1). This represented an increase of 177 percent in five years. In comparison, the total number of pilgrims from all countries in 1979 stood at 863,000 and in 1984 they totaled 920,000, an increase of less than 7 percent for the same period.[10] A substantial number of the Egyptian pilgrims remained to work illegally in Saudi Arabia. Saudi Arabia occasionally pardoned illegal immigrants and enabled them to register and remain in the kingdom, or to leave the country without punishing them.

A further difficulty in the evaluation of the number of emigrants lies in the fact that Egyptians were not required to present a visa on arrival in the various Arab countries, such as Jordan or Iraq, where the authorities only required an identity card.[11]

The World Bank and the International Labor Organization attempted to assess the total number of migrants in the Near East. The findings of both organizations, marred by incomplete data, also saw the AOC deliberately distort figures, in an attempt to conceal, for political purposes, the real number of immigrants relative to their own indigenous populations (primarily because, in several cases, the number of foreigners exceeded the locals). In 1975, *MEED* cited official Saudi data indicating 400,000 foreigners in the Kingdom for that year, while a Saudi expert estimated that more than one million foreigners were living in the country.[12] As far as Saudi Arabia was concerned, even the size of its own population was open to debate.[13] The problem of determining the actual number of Egyptian workers in the AOC is made even more difficult because of conflicting data presented by the various authorities in Egypt.

**Table 3.2**  Egyptian workers abroad and their percentage relative to the Egyptian labor force 1975–1982/1983 (in thousands)

| Year | Egyptians abroad | Labor force | % of Egyptians abroad |
|------|------|------|------|
| 1975 | 520 | 9,606 | 5.4 |
| 1976 | 750 | 9,946 | 7.8 |
| 1978 | 1,400 | 10,216 | 13.7 |
| 1980 | 1,600 | 11,057 | 14.4 |
| 1981 | 2,300 | 11,600 | 19.8 |
| 1982/83 | 2,900 | 12,110 | 23 |

*Source*: Gil Feiler, "The number of Egyptian workers in the Arab oil countries, 1974–1983: A critical discussion" (Dayan Center, Occasional Papers: October 1986), p. 20.

Estimates from the various sources – World Bank, ILO, Egypt and the AOC countries – are conflicting, and sometimes the disparity between estimates is huge. For 1978, the ILO gives two estimates for the number of Egyptians working in the AOC. The first one estimates there to be 404,000 Egyptian workers in the AOC, and the second report claimed the figure was closer to 600,000; a research project on migration conducted at the Massachusetts Institute of Technology (MIT) gave a figure of one million Egyptian workers in the AOC for 1978; and *al-Ahram* (1978), quoting data from the Egyptian ministries for foreign affairs and migration, went as far as to claim the number was 1.4 million.[14] In 1982, the gap between estimates grew. *Al-Siyasa al-Duwaliyya* cited three totally conflicting official Egyptian evaluations: the Central Bureau of Statistics estimated that in late 1982 1.6 million Egyptians were working abroad; the Foreign Ministry assessed their number at 2.9 million; and the National Councils (*al-Majalis al-Qawmiyya al-Mutakhassisa*) estimated 2.6 million.[15] That same year, *al-Ahram* quoted the Egyptian ministry of labor, which contended that 3 million Egyptians were working abroad.[16] Table 3.2 presents the summary of conflicting data, and a survey and analysis of relevant sources.[17] The table highlights an impressive increase in the number of Egyptians working in the Arab oil states – from 520,000 to about 3 million – in less than a decade.

Until the oil boom, these Egyptians who did emigrate went chiefly to Libya and Sudan. Between the October War and the Iran–Iraq War, Egyptians moved mainly to Saudi Arabia, Kuwait, the UAE, Libya and Jordan (in Jordan, they replaced the locals who had gone to work in the Gulf States). During the Iran–Iraq War, Egyptian emigration to Iraq soared. The war brought more than 1 million Egyptian migrants to Iraq, quite a staggering number given the political tension existing between the two countries at the time. Iraqi policy-makers preferred to mobilize an Egyptian workforce for several reasons: Egypt supplied arms to Iraq's military **(see chapters 4 and 5)**; the Egyptians were not thought to be a potential source of political disturbance, compared to Palestinian workers, for instance; Syrians could not be considered because the Syrian regime supported Iran. The fact that the Iraqi government imposed limits on the number of foreign Asian workers[18] also worked in favor of mobilizing Egyptian manpower.

The Egyptian Foreign Ministry estimated that 500,000 Egyptians were employed in Libya, and the same number in Saudi Arabia, in 1978; 150,000 each in Kuwait and the UAE; 50,000 in Iraq; and 15,000 in Qatar.[19] In 1982/3, according to data from the Egyptian Foreign and Migration Ministries, 1.25 million Egyptians were employed in Iraq; in Saudi Arabia, 800,000; in Libya, 300,000; in Kuwait, 200,000; in the UAE, 150,000; in Jordan, 125,000; in Algeria, 35,000; in Qatar, 25,000; in Sudan, 20,000; in Syria, 15,000; in North Yemen, 12,000; in Oman and Morocco, 11,500 each; in Bahrain, 6,000; and 12,000 in Somalia, Lebanon, Mauritania and Tunisia.[20]

## Causes of migration

Emigration contributed to a more balanced sharing of human capital resources, and to a lesser degree, to the sharing of financial resources, via the remittance of tens of billions of dollars paid by the rich oil states to the labor force from the poor Arab countries. The causes for the migration of Egyptian workers to the wealthy AOC can be analyzed according to the classic model of supply and demand. The rise in oil prices in late 1973 heightened the numerous disparities between the rich, under-populated states and the poor, overpopulated countries. In 1976, per capita GNP in Kuwait came to $15,480; in Saudi Arabia, $15,480; in Libya, $6,310 and in Egypt, only $280. The Saudi GDP in 1982 amounted $153.6 billion; in the UAE, S29.9 billion; in Kuwait, $20 billion; and in Egypt, $26.4 billion (table 3.3). The gap between Egypt and the AOC was so big that Egypt's GDP was lower than that of the UAE, a country whose total population was a fiftieth the size of Egypt's.

As a result of the petro-dollar revenues, which exceeded one trillion dollars in the decade after the October 1973 War, the AOC invested $323 billion in extensive development projects.[21] The AOC wanted to diversify their economies, which were, at that point, based primarily on the oil sector. Their policy-makers set up development projects, which included petro-chemical plants, power stations, the construction of airports and harbors, road construction and many other projects. In the years 1973–80, Saudi Arabia alone devoted $180 billion to these works. Even very small countries, such as Qatar and the UAE, spent considerable sums: $10 billion and $9 billion, respectively.[22]

**Table 3.3**  Egypt and the oil countries: GNP per capita (1976) and GDP (1982)

| State | GNP per capita (US) $ | GDP (US $ millions) |
| --- | --- | --- |
| Saudi Arabia | 16,000 | 153,590 |
| Kuwait | 15,480 | 20,060 |
| UAE | — | 29,870 |
| Libya | 6,310 | 28,360 |
| Oman | — | 7,110 |
| Egypt | 280 | 26,400 |

*Source*: World Bank, *World Development Report*, various issues (Oxford University Press).

**Table 3.4**  Age group below 15 years in 1975

| Country | Percentage |
| --- | --- |
| Kuwait | 47.28 |
| Iraq | 48.89[1] |
| Saudi Arabia | 44.72 |
| Libya | 44.39 |
| Egypt | 40.66 |

*Source*: Taken from author's data, ILO, *Yearbook of Labor Statistics 1978*, pp. 19, 21, 37–8.

[1] Data refers to 1977.

The conservative oil countries' problem was that their enormous financial wealth was in stark contrast to their meagre resources in the areas of manpower, social development, economic diversity and military capacity.[23] Local manpower did not fit the requirements to achieve socio-economic development in the AOC, either in quality or in quantity; therefore, these countries were compelled to mobilize large numbers of foreign workers in all spheres of industry. In many instances, the number of foreigners exceeded the total number of citizens in the oil states, sometimes filling as much as 80 percent of all available jobs (e.g. the UAE). The combination of oil revenues and the massive migratory movement enabled the AOC to carry out ambitious development projects, in spite of the qualitative and quantitative limitations of their populations.

Apart from Saudi Arabia, the local population of the conservative oil states was less than 500,000 inhabitants in 1975, compared to 37 million citizens in Egypt. UN population estimates for 1975 (showing a population of one million in Kuwait; 766,000 in Oman; 171,000 in Qatar; 505,000 in the UAE; and 256,000 people in Bahrain)[24] were exaggerated, as the figures also include foreigners. The actual number of local civilians was much lower. A report from the IMF indicates that foreigners in the UAE constituted almost 75 percent of its total population[25], and a

Kuwaiti population census in 1975 revealed that local citizens comprised only 45 percent of all inhabitants.[26]

The shortage of workers across industries in the conservative oil states was not due merely to their small population, but – and in certain cases, primarily – because of the distinctive demographic, social and cultural qualities of the local inhabitants:

1    About 50 percent of the population were children below the age of 15, compared to one-quarter of the industrialized nations (see table 3.4). As a result, a large portion of the populace was not very active in the labor market. In Saudi Arabia, 5.9 percent of this age group was employed in 1975, and in Kuwait the figure was 0.2 percent.[27]

2    The percentage of women employed in the modern work sector was very low, and most of them were engaged in traditional household functions, as Islamic society is rooted in tradition. This also explains the low rate of participation among women in the educational system. In Saudi Arabia, only 113,000 women were employed in 1975, out of a total of 4.43 million women – less than 3 percent. Kuwait, in the same year, saw only 25,000 women, out of a total of 492,000 women in a form of employment.[28] Research illustrates that there is a strong link between a woman's level of education and its future employment prospects: the rate of employment amongst Kuwaiti female university graduates in 1975 was 83%, compared to 48% among high-school graduates, 5.6% among those who finished elementary school, and only 1.1% for illiterate women.[29]

3    Additional factors that contributed to the low level of local participation in the AOC labor market included the nomadic peoples, who were not generally involved in modern places of employment; and the rapid development of educational institutions in the AOC, which was responsible for attracting many young people who would have otherwise joined the pool of job-seekers.

The traditions and demographics of the local population, the percentage of women in the labor force, the development of the educational system and the nomadic population, conspired to bring about a very low rate of local participation in the AOC labor pool. In 1975, the rate of local employment stood at about 20 percent in the conservative countries and 26 percent in Iraq and Algeria, compared to about 50 percent in the Western industrialized nations (see table 3.5). In Egypt, the rate of participation was slightly higher – 30 percent, according to a 1976 population census.[30]

With the AOC's local human resources stretched to the limit, and ever-reliant on emigrant employment, the AOC plans to focus on development projects meant that even more pressure would be placed on local and foreign recruitment. After the oil boom, the AOC expanded their educational system, but training highly skilled professionals requires at least a decade, and in the mid-1970s there was already a very limited number of skilled local citizens. In the early 1980s – after a decade of enormous expansion of the educational system – the AOC were still faced with a shortage of skilled personnel in the fields of science and technology. In 1980, the number of students studying scientific and technological professions increased, and represented a relatively high percentage of total higher education, but the actual number of students was quite low. In Bahrain, for instance, 44 percent of students specialized in science and technology in 1980, but in absolute terms this amounted to only 840 students. In comparison, in Egypt only 35 percent were studying in these fields, but the absolute figure was more than 185,000.[31]

**Table 3.5**   Countries importing workers: local manpower (in thousands), and rate of participation in the workforce (in percentages) in 1975

| State | National manpower | Rate of participation |
|---|---|---|
| Bahrain | 50 | 21.4 |
| Kuwait | 87 | 19.4 |
| Libya | 454 | 20.2 |
| Oman | 89 | 19.0 |
| Qatar | 12 | 18.4 |
| Saudi Arabia | 1,300 | 23.0 |
| UAE | 45 | 22.5 |
| Algeria | 3,037 | 26.1 |
| Iraq | 3,008 | 26.0 |

*Source*: World Bank, *Manpower and International Labor Migration in the Middle East and North Africa* (Document of the World Bank, final report of research project: June 30, 1981), p. 59.

The educational system in the AOC of the 1970s failed to meet the needs of the ambitious development plans conceived by their policy-makers. Even by the early 1980s, in spite of the expansion of the educational system, technological education was still in its infancy stage, with many people intimidated by the new technologies and sciences. The majority of the population still preferred to work in the service and administrative sectors. Most of the jobs in production were therefore carried out by foreigners.[32] Unskilled labor was shaped by the local citizenry, who preferred not to engage in manual, low pay work, for reasons of prestige. Even people with a poor education still preferred to work as drivers, eschewing a career in construction.[33] The Kuwaiti labor pool was indicative of this: in the mid-1970s, 80 percent of Kuwaitis were working in white-collar jobs, the majority employed in Kuwaiti governmental institutions.[34]

The structural changes in the regional economy, which brought demand for laborers in the AOC, allied with the political and demographic strength that Egypt possessed, in spite of its economic troubles, enabled it to react positively to the demand for workers. Two factors played to Egypt's advantage: about 40 percent illiteracy among the general populace, and, comparative to the AOC, a well-developed educational system, made it possible for Egypt to export both skilled and unskilled manpower. Egypt, however, had to deal with problems on its labor market as well. The Egyptian government encouraged young people to take advantage of the higher education system. What they did not do was take into consideration the extremely limited demand of the local market for university graduates, caused mainly by sociopolitical considerations and faulty planning. The result was that very few young Egyptians with a university education were absorbed into the local market, and many of those that did find a job were employed in overqualified positions and/or earned a low salary. Conversely, employers experienced great difficulty in finding workers of the level they required. This created a situation of overt and covert unemployment: the Egyptian administration was expanded, with the purpose of providing employment for university graduates, while at the same time there was a shortage of professional and skilled labor force.[35]

Like the oil countries, there was a high number of underage (under 15) youngsters in Egypt, though less than in the AOC. Because of Egypt's large population, however, this does not carry the same significance as in the AOC. Similarly, the percentage of women in the workforce was low compared to Western standards; but, in 1975, the number of Egyptian women in employment was five times higher than the number of working women in Libya, Kuwait and Saudi Arabia combined. The number of women employed in Egypt in 1975 (795,000), exceeded the total number of men and women employed in Bahrain, Kuwait, Libya, Oman, Qatar and the UAE (737,000).[36]

The economic incentives that the Egyptian workers in the AOC received had a major influence on the migration process. The fact that the AOC needed foreign workers, and that Egypt could supply their demand, did not, by itself, cause mass emigration. Conditions in Egypt, and in the AOC, made migration possible, but it was the wages paid to foreign workers that convinced many to transmigrate. In 1975, an Egyptian teacher, living in Egypt, earned (permanent job and private lessons) an annual salary of EgP 250 ($625). In comparison, the average salary of an Egyptian teacher in the AOC came to $8,250.[37] There was a major gulf in salaries between Egypt and the rich oil countries: in the teaching and construction sectors, the gap was six- to ninefold, with Egypt on the bottom rung.[38] In the mid-1970s, a professor in Egypt could earn EgP 150 per month, which, over a period of thirty years, came to EgP 48,600. By contrast, on a four-year assignment in Kuwait he could earn EgP 84,000, double the amount he could earn during a thirty-year career in Egypt.[39] Egypt's migration policy was also a factor in facilitating the migration of millions of Egyptians to the rich oil states. In the 1970s and 1980s the Egyptian government promoted this movement, and turned it into an integral part of its open–door policy.

## Migration policy

### The policy of the Egyptian government

The Egyptian government made sweeping changes to its policies and laws regarding migration in the period between the 1950s and the 1980s. Dessouki highlighted each of the three main development phases of Egyptian migration policy: first, a ban on migration from the fifties until 1967; unrestricted migration in the late 1960s; and promotion of migration with Sadat's rise to power.[40] The Egyptian government had in fact, already decided in the fifties to promote migration, but its policies were delayed until the 1970s and 1980s.[41]

Since the mid-1960s the Egyptian government had made increasing efforts to attract foreign currency. Naturally, remittances by migrant workers comprised one of its goals. Up to 1965, every unmarried migrant was required to convert 25 percent of his income through the Egyptian banking system at the official rate of exchange; a married migrant was required to convert 10 percent on the same conditions; and a migrant with a free profession was required to convert 50 percent. In 1965 migrants were given the option to convert their money at a rate of exchange about 35 percent higher than the official rate.[42] In the late 1960s the government continued easing conditions for potential emigrants, by agreeing to grant six months unpaid vacation to every citizen wishing to leave Egypt to look for work: if the citizen did not succeed in finding employment abroad, they were free to return to their place of employment in Egypt.[43] In resolution 364 of 1968, the Egyptian government decided to drop the ban on the flow of capital belonging to Egyptians working abroad.[44] This policy created problems for the Egyptian government: a majority of Egyptians who exploited the opportunity to emigrate held positions or were in professions that were highly specialized, and many who had been sent to work abroad by the Egyptian government refused to return.[45] This was the reason behind the decision of July 1969 to prohibit the migration of technicians employed in various sectors of Egyptian industry.[46]

Notwithstanding the relative easing of restrictions for Egyptian emigrants, from the fifties until the mid-1960s migration was regulated by special decrees. Egyptian laws made it possible to compel members of essential professions, such as engineers, doctors and technicians, to serve for a number of years after the termination of their studies in governmental offices. Leaving for employment abroad could be arranged only after receiving an exit visa issued by the Ministry of the Interior, which was a complicated procedure.[47] It was not before the 1970s that the Egyptian government passed new legislation, encouraging both temporary and permanent emigration.[48] This legislation befitted the change in the economic and political policy in Egypt as from the late 1960s. In the constitution of 1971, the citizen's right to emigrate was recognized: "a citizen has the right to emigrate permanently or temporarily."[49] In 1974, emigration was made even easier: the exit visa was annulled in favor of a traveller's visa, issued by the Egyptian employer; passport issue procedures were facilitated; and Egyptian embassies abroad were permitted to renew passports for Egyptians employed there, without having to apply to the Interior Ministry.[50] Further steps were the removal of travel restrictions in passports, as was the case in the 1960s; the possibility for an Egyptian to hold dual nationality;[51] tax exemption for emigrants' income; and keeping open the emigrant's job for two years after his resignation.

In the 1970s and 1980s Egypt's policy-makers announced that migration to Arab countries would not be halted. This was in spite of the shortage of professionals in several sectors claimed by the Minister of Labor, Sa'ad Muhammad Ahmad, in February 1982.[52] Referring to the shortage of certain categories of professionals in Egypt, he said that Egyptians working abroad should be perceived as a branch of export, and investments in expansion of educational facilities and professional training should be made accordingly, to preclude a shortage of manpower. The minister repeatedly stressed that leaving for employment abroad was anchored in the individual's basic rights and this was not to be denied to him.[53] At a meeting of Egyptian nationals residing abroad, held in Egypt in the summer of 1983, Mubarak's speech amply illustrated the policy of promotion of Egyptian migration: "The days when a citizen living abroad was regarded with suspicion, as if he had not fulfilled his national duties, are over . . . we must all guarantee, in deeds and not in words, that an Egyptian working abroad is a good citizen, who has not renounced his identity."[54]

The Egyptian leaders continued to promote migration, despite criticism that it brought about a "brain drain," accelerated inflation and undercut the work ethic.[55] The government assumed that, in the long run, emigration engendered positive results for the Egyptian economy, and Sa'ad Muhammad Ahmad, the Egyptian Minister of Labor, expressed this extremely well in May 1983: "Even if only 100,000 Egyptians were working abroad, this would constitute a national contribution to Egypt and its economy."[56] This policy of promoting emigration was also expressed by Egypt's elementary educational system: according to Kemal Gabala, study books documented Egyptian migration as a natural process, and schoolchildren were taught that "people migrate just like the birds."[57] Egypt's liberal migration policy was shaped by socio-economic and political considerations. The government was trying to ease the problem of overcrowding and unemployment by migration. As Mubarak said: "I am not opposed to emigration, as we are a nation of 45 million [people]."[58] The opportunity to raise large amounts of foreign currency ($4 billion in 1984), and to reduce the deficit in the balance of payments, meant that the policy was beneficial to all parties. The government considered migration "a safety valve," enabling millions of Egyptians of all classes – frustrated academics who could not find suitable employment, skilled and unskilled workers – to go abroad and to improve their standard of living; through this policy the government was able to avoid tension and remove potential dangers from the Egyptian political scene.

Emigration also had the desired effect of enhancing cooperation between Egypt and Third World countries. and with the oil countries in particular.[59] The presence of Egyptian workers, many in senior positions in the AOC, led to a strengthening of ties between Egypt and the host countries, especially after the Camp David agreement. Migration and the interdependence of Egypt and the AOC definitely served as a political and economic tonic that soothed relations between them. There were other reasons for the promotion of migration, although not mentioned in the various sources. One was Egypt's desire to curtail expenditure on food imports. For example, in 1977 the Egyptian economy spent $2 billion on food imports.[60] The presence of millions of Egyptians abroad eased the steadily increasing demand for food and the spending of much-needed foreign currency on expensive imports. Moreover, liberal migration policy suited the image of openness which Egypt was trying to create in the international community. The policy-makers also hoped that an increase in the number of women seeking employment (left in Egypt after their husbands' departures abroad) would result in a diminished birthrate.

## Migration policy of the oil countries

The migration policy of the oil countries also changed, but unlike Egypt's, it followed a path towards stricter rules in migration. Until the end of the seventies the AOC policy was fairly liberal. Obtaining work permits was easy, because the development plans of these countries necessitated large numbers of foreign laborers, though their citizenship laws were very strict, making it difficult to get permanent stay permits. In the late seventies, in order to cope with the growing flow of immigrants, the AOC authorities decided to prohibit the migrant worker from bringing his family with him, except for certain essential skilled workers.[61]

In the late 1970s, the AOC authorities stepped up their control of migrant laborers – particularly those who entered their countries illegally. The oil countries feared the migrants (who constituted a majority in some nations) would undermine the stability and balance of power in the region. The Saudi Minister of the Interior stated that his ministry viewed the non-Muslim element of the migrant workers as a potential threat to national stability.[62] Saudi Arabia started deporting illegal immigrants, many of whom were pilgrims, and they put obstacles in the way of contractors who regularly received collective work permits for foreign workers.[63] At the same time, the Saudi Five-Year Plan for 1980–5 called for increased professional training and education for Saudi citizens, so that they would gradually replace foreign workers.[64] The AOC established "workers camps" in industrial zones, remote from residential areas, such as Jebel and Yanbu' in Saudi Arabia, set up to deal with the influx of foreigners. These "workers camps" isolated the migrant workers from the local population, reduced the host countries' expenses for social services for the foreigners, and discouraged the migrant from bringing his family with him.[65]

The oil countries made Egyptian workers an exception in the workplace to the treatment of other foreigners in the 1970s as well as in the 1980s, after deciding to curtail the foreign labor force in the wake of a decrease in oil revenues. Egyptian workers were rarely sacked, and were laid off in small numbers when compared to other foreigners. In line with the policy of the 1980–5 Saudi Five-Year Plan, the Saudi Ministry of Labor decided to reduce the number of foreign workers, primarily in construction, but Egyptians were hit less hard than others.[66] Similarly, the decision in other oil countries to replace Asian laborers with Arab manpower, as in Kuwait in 1980,[67] worked in the Egyptians' favor. As a consequence, the Egyptians became the first eligible candidates for the resulting job openings. Despite the priority given to the Egyptians over other workers, however, many of them suffered discrimination in working conditions, compared to local subjects.

The favorable treatment shown to Egyptians partly resulted from the fact that Egypt fulfilled a traditional role as go-between for Western technology and the technical needs of the Arabs, as well as possessing cultural similarity.[68] Egyptian workers were also preferred for other reasons: first, Egypt could provide manpower in a variety of professions, and second, they were considered to be politically neutral, in contrast with the Palestinians, who were viewed as political agitators. Kuwait, the UAE and Qatar used any means at their disposal to prevent the growth of the Palestinian community in their countries. Kuwait even ordered special computer software for screening Palestinian passport data to check if place and date of birth had been altered, to identify Palestinians entering Kuwait with false Arab passports.[69] The AOC viewed the migration of Egyptian workers to their countries as an important factor in the strengthening of relations with the Egyptian regime, and in so doing, making it dependent on them. Their governments saw the migrant workers' remittances as another way of strengthening the Egyptian economy, especially after the formal breaking off of diplomatic and economic relations between the countries. The AOC needed Egyptian assistance, following the tension created in the region during the Iran–Iraq War. After the economic boycott imposed on Egypt at the second Baghdad conference (March 1979), the number of Egyptians working in the oil countries increased, and monetary remittances attained new records after the boycott.

The primary reason for the increase in the number of Egyptian migrant workers after the Baghdad boycott was the Iran–Iraq War, which saw Iraq bring in more than one million Egyptian workers to replace Iraqi citizens who had been mobilized. Relations between Egypt and Iraq were not great, but even though Iraq had played a major role in securing the boycott against Egypt, Iraq still had a policy of hiring Egyptian workers. In the initial phase of the war Egypt did not openly admit to a special work relationship with Iraq, but the facts spoke for themselves. In June 1983, the first vice-president of Iraq, Tah Yasin Ramadan, announced that Iraq had a policy of absorbing Egyptian workers rather than other foreigners.[70] Aside from manpower, Iraq also needed Egypt for the supply of arms manufactures, or to act as mediator in arms purchases. Egyptian military experts gave tactical assistance to Iraq in the war, and some Egyptians even joined the Iraqi army on their own initiative (with their government's unofficial approval). According to the Iraqi vice-president, their numbers reached between 12,000 and 15,000 "fighters" in 1983, comprising about 50 percent of all Arab volunteers. These volunteers – from among the Egyptian workforce in Iraq – served for up to half a year in the Iraqi army, later returning to their civilian jobs. Ramadan added that up to June 1983 there were about twenty Egyptian casualties.[71]

## The extent of remittances

### Official remittances
The change in the migration trend, from permanent migration in the mid-1960s to temporary migration for working purposes in the late 1960s, and the subsequent increase in the number of Egyptians working in the AOC, brought in its wake vast capital remittances to the Egyptian economy. A remittance worked thus: part of the salary of a native Egyptian working abroad, usually in the AOC, was transferred from the host country to Egypt. Just before the large emigration waves of 1973, official remittances by Egyptians working abroad amounted to just $123 million. Within one year this amount increased by 150 percent, totaling $310 million in 1974, and by 1984 it had reached $4 billion, constituting the main source of foreign currency for the Egyptian economy.[72]

Remittances have a multifaceted influence on the economy of the recipient state: they ease the shortage of foreign currency and improve the balance of payments; they directly and indirectly raise the standard of living of millions of people; and they are a potential source for the improved distribution of income, particularly for unskilled migrant workers. But remittances also have negative connotations. Levels of remittance income vary wildly, as they are dependent on migrant income: migrants and their families spend a large part of their income on consumer goods, increasing demand and the rate of inflation, and raising the wage level and the high rate of imports created by increased demand for imported goods amplifies the dependence on imports, exhausting foreign currency reserves and exacerbating the balance of payments situation.[73]

**Table 3.6**   Remittances in the years 1967–1973 (in millions of US dollars)

| Year | Amount |
|------|--------|
| 1967 | 12 |
| 1968 | 3 |
| 1969 | 8 |
| 1970 | 33 |
| 1971 | 38 |
| 1972 | 110 |
| 1973 | 123 |

*Source*: IMF, *IFS, 1983 Yearbook*, pp. 204–5.

A study of remittance payments in tables 3.6–3.7 evinces a consistent, yearly increase punctuated by the occasional year when political events influenced income levels. In the mid-1960s, remittances from abroad did not play a leading role in the Egyptian economy. In 1965 they came to $10 million; in 1966 they declined to $6 million and in 1967 they totaled $12 million, which amounted to 2 percent of Egypt's commercial exports.[74] In 1968 and 1969 the sum of remittances went down to $3 million and $8 million, respectively.[75] The reason for these declines did not stem from a decrease in the number of Egyptians working abroad, but from a reluctance to funnel capital to Egypt following the June 1967 rout. The "intellectuals' crisis" that followed the war caused many emigrants to opt for permanent residence abroad; once they had done so, personal ties to Egypt – including remittances – were brought to a halt. In 1970–1 remittances actually increased to $33 and $38 million respectively, but their contribution to the Egyptian economy was still not significant. In the years 1972–3 the extent of remittances increased threefold compared to 1971 (table 3.6); these were the first years that the payments made a tangible contribution to the Egyptian economy.

The most substantial increase of remittances came in the wake of Egypt's upsurge in economic fortunes, following the October 1973 War and the sharp rise in oil prices. In the first year after the war, a marked change occurred in the level of remittances by Egyptians working abroad (the majority in the Arab oil states): in 1974 remittances amounted to $310 million, and thereafter remittances increased substantially from year to year; in 1977, they totaled $988 million; in 1979 they exceeded the $2 billion barrier, amounting to $2.3 billion; in 1981–2 there was another decline. There were two main reasons for this: the murder of Sadat in 1981, and changes made to the foreign currency sector by the Egyptian government, in an attempt to attract the migrants' money. The political instability caused by Sadat's murder meant that many Egyptians working abroad were apprehensive of transferring large amounts of money to Egypt. Most non-domestic workers sent only enough for their families to subsist on.[76] In 1983 things picked up again, and the level of remittances passed the $3 billion barrier; in 1984 they came to almost $4 billion (table 3.7).

**Table 3.7** Remittances in the years 1974–1984 (in millions of US dollars, at 1984 and 1987 prices)

| Year | 1987 prices | 1984 prices |
|------|-------------|-------------|
| 1974 | 310 | 602 |
| 1975 | 445 | 790 |
| 1976 | 842 | 1,421 |
| 1977 | 988 | 1,576 |
| 1978 | 1,824 | 2,709 |
| 1979 | 2,269 | 3,102 |
| 1980 | 2,791 | 3,494 |
| 1981 | 2,230 | 2,547 |
| 1982 | 2,481 | 2,672 |
| 1983 | 3,688 | 3,826 |
| 1984 | 3,981 | 3,981 |

*Source*: current prices – IMF, *IFS*, 1983 and 1987 *Yearbooks*. 1984 prices were calculated by the author in accordance with: *Economic report of the President* (Washington, D.C.: GPO, 1985), table B-3, p. 236.

[a] Besides workers' remittances, data also includes total private remittances. However, nearly all private remittances were made by workers, yearly increasing their percentage of the total. In 1975 they comprised about 80 percent of the total; in 1982 – 98 percent; and in 1984 – they exceeded 99.5 percent of total private remittances. These figures are based on the following data: IMF, *Balance of Payments Statistics Yearbook* (vol. 34, part 1, 1983), pp. 160–4; World Bank, *World Tables from the Data Files of the World Bank* (1984, vol. 1: Economic data, Baltimore, 1984), p. 283; World Bank, *World Development Report 1984*, pp. 244–5, 1986, p. 206.

From the mid-1970s on, except for a few years during the 1980s when revenues from oil exports rose dramatically, remittances constituted Egypt's principal source of foreign currency. In 1978, remittances exceeded the combined income from tourism, passage fees from the Suez Canal and oil export revenues.[77] These remittances increased the government's options for financing the import of essential goods. Despite a sharp increase in commercial imports in the 1970s and '80s, there was no substantial increase in the current account deficit (table 3.8). The deficit even showed a decline in some years, largely attributed to the remittances.

The rate of worker remittances in the 1980s was more than thirty times higher than in the late 1960s and the early 1970s. The Egyptian "laborers' export industry" had a greater impact in the 1970s and '80s in comparison to other microeconomic gauges of the Egyptian economy, such as the GNP and the GDP, and compared to the levels of export and import. In 1970 remittances were equal to 4 percent of Egypt's commercial exports; in 1975 this went up to 29 percent; and in 1978, they amounted to 94 percent of exports. In 1983 they were on a level with total commercial exports. Similarly, the ratio of remittances compared to Egypt's commercial

**Table 3.9** Ratio of remittances compared to commercial export/import, as well as export/import of goods and services (in millions of US dollars and percentages)

| | 1970 | 1975 | 1976 | 1977 | 1978 | 1979 | 1980 | 1981 | 1982 | 1983 |
|---|---|---|---|---|---|---|---|---|---|---|
| Commercial exports | 817 | 1,567 | 1,609 | 1,974 | 1,939 | 2,424 | 3,854 | 3,999 | 4,018 | 3,693[1] |
| Remittances/comm.exp. | 4 | 29.0 | 52.3 | 50.1 | 94.1 | 93.6 | 72.4 | 55.8 | 61.7 | 99.9 |
| Commercial imports | 1,084 | 3,941 | 3,842 | 4,038 | 4,743 | 6,002 | 6,814 | 7,918 | 7,333 | 7,515[1] |
| Remittances/ Commercial imports | 3.0 | 11.5 | 21.9 | 24.5 | 38.5 | 37.8 | 41.0 | 28.2 | 33.8 | 49.1 |
| Export of goods and services | 960 | 1,295 | 2,758 | 3,576 | 3,573 | 4,210 | 4,246 | 6,534 | — | —[1] |
| Remittances/ export of goods and services | 3.0 | 20.7 | 30.5 | 27.6 | 51.0 | 53.9 | 65.7 | 34.1 | — | — |
| Import of goods and services | 1,381 | 4,937 | 4,842 | 5,486 | 6,290 | 7,774 | 9,156 | 10,404 | — | —[1] |
| Remittances/ Import of goods and services | 2.1 | 9.2 | 17.4 | 18.0 | 29.0 | 29.2 | 30.5 | 21.4 | — | — |

*Sources:* IMF, *IFS* (various issues); World Bank, *World Tables* (vol. 1, 1984), p. 283; Table nos. 7–8.

[1] Commercial export and import data (FOB) were taken from source no. 1; Data of export and import of goods and services were taken from source no. 2; Remittance data were taken from source no. 3. Calculations in percentages were made by the author. Import and export of goods and services data in source no. 2 are given until 1981 only. In source no. 1 these figures are also to be found for the years 1982–3, but the data include "goods, services and additional income," while source no. 2 includes "goods and services" data only. The differences are insignificant, but for the sake of uniformity, I did not include this data in the table. It should be noted, that the remittances also represent payment for export of laborer services, but the World Bank and the IMF do not include this item under "Export of goods and services."

imports increased impressively: from 3 percent in 1970 to 11 percent in 1975 and to 49 percent in 1983. The same goes for the ratio of remittances compared to export and import of goods and services (table 3.9).

**Table 3.8**   Current account (in millions of US dollars)

| Year | Amount |
|------|--------|
| 1977 | −1200 |
| 1978 | −1220 |
| 1979 | −1542 |
| 1980 | −438 |
| 1981 | −2136 |
| 1982 | −1852 |
| 1983 | −411 |

*Sources*: IMF, *IFS* (November 1984), p. 184 (December 1986), p. 175.

*Note*: See table 3.9 for import and export data.

   The proportions of Egyptian remittances are significant not only in the perspective of the Egyptian or Middle Eastern economies, but also by global standards: in 1977, remittances by Egyptian migrants constituted 3.8 percent of all global transfers, and 21 percent of the total in the Middle East; in 1983 there was a marked increase, with the Egyptian remittances totaling 8.6 percent of global and 78 percent of all Middle Eastern transfers (table 3.10).
   Remittances also influenced the level of investments, the rate of inflation, level of wages and all of the macro- and microeconomic gauges of Egypt. The construction boom in the 1970s was caused, both directly and indirectly, by migration.[78] The rise in the consumption level in Egypt was a result of the process of migration for employment purposes: growing numbers of Egyptians who worked abroad, earning high wages, became consumers on their return to their homeland, preferring to spend rather than save or invest.[79] The Egyptian National Bank found that not only were large bulks of remittance payments being spent on consumer goods, but that the investment sector was failing to attract the migrants or, more specifically, their money. Investors preferred to buy real estate and land, instead of saving their earnings in productive channels. This caused land prices to skyrocket.[80] Egyptians earned a comparatively high salary in the oil countries, far more than anything they earned back home, and this in turn encouraged patterns of consumption. People who were previously unable to afford certain electric appliances before their migration, used their new-found wealth to improve their standard of living and their social standing. Those who owned electric appliances or a car before their emigration increased their consumption, buying an extra TV set, another car and so on.[81] The number of imported cars increased from 1,400 in 1966/7 to 40,000 in 1975/6, soaring to 74,000 cars in 1982; in the years 1971–9, the number of TV sets purchased went up from 71,000 to 480,000; the number of refrigerators went up, in the same period, from 36,000 to about 215,000.[82] Although migrants and their families were not the only ones buying these appliances, they did represent a large portion of the

consumers. Further reasons for consumption increase included the reduction in prices of some products like TVs and refrigerators, as well as the population growth in Egypt, both local and foreign.

**Table 3.10** Private remittances in global terms, in the Middle East and in Egypt, and the ratio of Egyptian remittances compared to the above (in millions of SDR and in percentages)

| Region | 1977 | 1980 | 1981 | 1982 | 1983 |
|---|---|---|---|---|---|
| Globally | 22,059 | 34,677 | 37,278 | 38,832 | 36,663 |
| ME | 4,032 | 5,475 | 5,520 | 5,790 | 4,059 |
| Egypt | 846 | 2,145 | 1,891 | 1,917 | 3,166[1] |
| Egypt/glob.% | 3.8 | 6.2 | 5.1 | 4.9 | 8.6 |
| Egypt/ME% | 21.0 | 39.2 | 34.3 | 33.1 | 78.0 |

*Sources*: IMF, *Balance of Payments Statistics Yearbook* (vol. 35, part 2, 1984), pp. 68–9; IMF, *IFS, 1984 Yearbook*.

[1] This figure was taken from the second source and appears in dollars. Conversion to SDR according to IMF data.

**Table 3.11** An indication of the flow of remittances by Egyptian workers 1980–1983/84 (in millions of US dollars and in percentages of the total)

| Year | 1980 | 1980/1 | 1981/2 | 1982/3 | 1983/4 |
|---|---|---|---|---|---|
| Imports | 1,802 | 1,724 | 1,396 | 2,046 | 2,150 |
| % | 43 | 43 | 41 | 49 | 44 |
| Cash | 1,110 | 1,130 | 686 | 1,120 | 1,750 |
| % | 26 | 28 | 20 | 27 | 36 |
| Foreign Currency Accounts | 1,289 | 1,142 | 1,300 | 978 | 1,000 |
| % | 31 | 29 | 39 | 24 | 20 |
| Total | 4,201 | 3,997 | 3,382 | 4,144 | 4,900 |

*Source*: IMF, *Arab Republic of Egypt – Recent Economic Development* (June 15, 1984), p. 59.

[a] It must be stressed that above figures are only an indication. Figures in this table are higher than figures published by the IMF (see table 3.8). The reason for discrepancies is that the IMF include data omitted from the earlier table, and they apparently also include transfers by unofficial channels, as evaluated by the IMF.

The migrants' cash flow brought with it direct and indirect imports: direct imports were generated by the workers bringing in goods for themselves and their families, and indirect imports were caused by currency traders buying their foreign currency, which in turn financed imports to Egypt. According to a survey conducted by the IMF, the component of imports financed by the migrants' transfers amounted to 43 percent in 1980, went up to 49 percent in 1982/3, and dropped to 44 percent in 1983/4; remittances in cash came to 20% in 1980 and increased to 36%

in 1983/4; the inflow into foreign currency accounts, totaling 31 percent in 1980, dropped to 20% in 1983/4. The rate of cash transfers compared to total transfers went up, but exports, exceeding 40%, were very high (table 3.11). The Egyptian Central Bank also examined the breakdown of transfers; it found that in 1979 and 1981 cash transfers amounted to 43%, and goods transfers about 57% (table 3.12).

**Table 3.12**   The share of cash and goods transfers in 1979 and 1981 (in millions of EgP)

|  | 1979 | 1981 |
| --- | --- | --- |
| Total remittances | 1,549.5 | 1,887.2 |
| Cash transfers | 666.2 | 817.2 |
| Goods transfers | 888.3 | 1,070.0 |

*Source*: Central Bank of Egypt, *Economic Review* (vol.21, no. 1, 1981), p. 43.

## Remittances via unofficial channels

So far we have touched on official remittances, but the extent of transfers to Egypt by unofficial channels was also a significant factor in the Egyptian economy. The Egyptian migrants found endless ways to circumvent the official system, channeling their money back to Egypt by various means, converting their money through dealers in foreign currency, transferring funds to their families via friends going home on vacation, even depositing their money in foreign banks. The total remittance transfer value to the Egyptian economy was perhaps double the official figure given. In the seventies and eighties, Egyptian migrants and their families could convert their money on the free market (until the new steps taken in May 1987)[83] for higher rates of exchange, up to 50 percent (sometimes even more) above the official rate. The system of "free" banking was an established entity against which the Egyptian authorities did not take strong measures. Money-changers could often be found near the entrances of many banks in Cairo, offering prospective bank clients more attractive exchange rates.[84]

It is difficult – if not impossible – to evaluate the amount of transfers that found their way to the free market in Egypt. Researchers and statesmen gave various data, but there are no completely reliable figures: the IMF estimated that the amounts channeled in this way ranged from between 20 to 100 percent of the amounts remitted by official channels.[85] In the early 1980s the Egyptian minister of migration declared that approximately 50 percent of transfers were effected via unofficial channels,[86] whereas *Mideast Markets*, quoting the Egyptian minister of the economy, noted that amounts transferred through the black market in the mid-1970s came to between $300 to $400 million annually, compared to the 1980s, when more than $3 billion annually were transferred to the black market.[87] Other less reliable figures exist, but which nonetheless agree on a common figure of between $2.5 billion to $3 billion.[88] Besides these remittances, capital from other sources, such as tourism, was likewise channeled to the free market. The major component of capital, however, was issued from Egyptians working abroad.[89]

## Summary

Egypt's income levels were not evenly distributed in the 1970s and 1980s. AOC aid was minimal, petro-dollar wealth was also low. But worker migration proved a salvation to the Egyptian economy. In the period of 1974–84, remittances to Egypt, via official channels only, amounted to almost $22 billion. This figure was larger than the combined amounts of civil and military foreign aid that Egypt received from the AOC in this period, more than both government and private Arab invest-ments in Egypt, as well as exceeding its revenues from Arab tourism and exports to the oil countries.

The AOC gave priority to attracting Egyptian workers: besides the rapproche-ment between Sadat's regime and that of the AOC, after Sadat's rise to power, Egyptian workers were viewed as being disciplined, free from the pollution of revo-lutionary ideas; the AOC, not wanting to harm Egypt following the economic boycott imposed on it in 1979, found a suitable channel to transfer large amounts of hard currency to Egypt, and at the same time to abide by the policy of the confrontation states and to impose an economic boycott on that country. The Iran–Iraq War forced Iraq to bring in large numbers of Egyptian workers, even after the boycott. Post-boycott remittance payments in the period of 1980–4 were twice as high as transfers from 1974–9: $15 billion compared to less than $7 billion. Egyptian policy-makers were aware of the importance of the remittances to the Egyptian economy and so they promoted migration. Beginning in the late 1960s, migration became an integral part of Egypt's economic policy. The Egyptian government encouraged its citizens to migrate, ignoring the many warnings that only a negative outcome would result through an increase in consumption, foreign imports and the "brain drain."

# 4

# *Aid Policy of the Arab Oil Countries toward Egypt: Containment and the Construction of Arab Unity*

The conservative oil countries' aid policy to Egypt was directed toward moderating Nasser's regime (after abetting attempts to overthrow him), supporting Sadat's pro-Western regime, voicing concerns about Egypt's military potential, and fending off Soviet influence and economic considerations. The amount of aid granted, and the reasons for the aid being given, differed from year to year. Supporting Egypt's pro-Western political and economic orientation was aimed at eliminating revolutionary power groups and preventing the seizure of power by a radical leader. The purpose of maintaining a strong Egyptian military and cooperating with its army was the elimination of subversive elements in the region, and to guard against an Israeli attack on Arab countries. The AOC and Egypt also presented a front of Arab unity. The economic aims of aid to Egypt were designed to bring economic prosperity to the oil countries, with the help of Egyptian workers employed by them, by maintaining an independent oil policy, without Egyptian interference and by profitable joint investments of both parties.

## The initial period of aid: 1962–June 1967

Up to the beginning of the 1960s, Egypt received no Arab aid, except for an annual grant of $4 million, and a one-time grant of $1 million from Saudi Arabia, after Egyptian funds in British banks were frozen following the nationalization of the Suez Canal.[1] The reason that the oil countries were not able to offer Egypt any substantial aid was because their income from oil revenues, though it actually doubled in the fifties, was eroded by foreign oil companies and production costs (see table 4.1). This meant Saudi Arabia, and other AOC nations, had small reserves. Kuwait was the only country with relatively large reserves – $1.5 billion in 1965[2] – and in 1952 it granted aid to Yemen and the Emirates (which were later to become the UAE).[3] Saudi Arabia's oil revenues in 1950 amounted to less than $57 million, and in 1961 approximately $378 million. The blockading of the Suez Canal in 1956 reduced their oil revenues, and only in the early 1960s did reserves reach their level of 1955. During the 1940s and '50s it was, ironically, Egypt who assisted the oil countries, giving aid in the form of medicine, education and technology. Libya also received financial aid – in addition to the salaries paid by the Egyptian government to the teachers it had loaned to Libya.[4] Saudi Arabia received military aid in the form of an Egyptian military cadre and eight Vampire planes in 1957, as part of the framework of their mutual military alliance.[5]

**Table 4.1**  Saudi Arabia's oil revenues (in millions of US dollars)

| Year | Amount | Year | Amount |
|------|--------|------|--------|
| 1939 | 3.2    | 1957 | 296.3  |
| 1946 | 10.4   | 1958 | 297.6  |
| 1950 | 56.7   | 1959 | 313.1  |
| 1951 | 110.0  | 1960 | 333.7  |
| 1952 | 212.2  | 1961 | 377.6  |
| 1953 | 169.8  | 1962 | 409.7  |
| 1954 | 236.3  | 1963 | 607.7  |
| 1955 | 340.8  | 1964 | 523.2  |
| 1956 | 290.2  | —    | —      |

*Sources*: Kingdom of Saudi Arabia, Ministry of Planning, *Third Development Plan, 1400–1405 (1980–1985)* (Riyadh), p. 11; OPEC, *Annual Statistical Review*, 1978 (Vienna), p.161; Kingdom of Saudi Arabia, Saudi Arabia Monetary Agency, *Annual Statistical Report*, various issues; IMF, *Saudi Arabia – An Economic and Financial Survey* (SM/75/157: June 24, 1975), p. 10.

[a]  These revenues reflect the Saudi government's share given to her by ARAMCO, Getty Oil, Arabian Oil and other oil companies (incl. Tanco Saudia, Tapline and Petromin).

At the beginning of the 1960s, only Kuwait provided Egypt with aid. As long as Egypt was involved in the Yemen War, there was no chance of it receiving Saudi aid: from November 1962 until June 1967, the Egyptian air force attacked Saudi military and civilian targets incessantly.[6] The border town of Najran – one of many attacked by Egypt during the war – was bombed at least forty-five times. Bombardments similar to this struck at the oil flowing from the Gulf oil fields to the Middle East through the Trans-Arabian pipeline, causing material damage and casualties.[7] Egypt also "organized" subversive activities throughout Saudi Arabia, such as the sabotaging of the Saudi Ministry of Defense and the American military headquarters in Riyadh in early 1967.[8] The Egyptian government also harnessed the power of the media in their propaganda war against the Saudi government.[9] Saudi Arabia tried to strike back at Nasser, but was hampered by an ill-equipped military; instead, it sent materials and financing to the Muslim Brotherhood in Egypt, a group involved in plotting to overthrow Nasser.[10]

Hostile relations between Saudi Arabia and Egypt did not prevent Kuwait from granting aid to Egypt from December 1963. Kuwait had gained independence just two years earlier and had already been threatened by Iraq. It was therefore interested in retaining good relations with the Egyptian and Iraqi regimes, in order to "buy" its independence, obtain international recognition, and to gain the favor of revolutionary, and potentially dangerous, leaders. Kuwait's only way of realizing these ambitions was to pay protection money and distribute practical aid to neighboring countries.[11] Data from the Kuwaiti Ministry of Finance indicated that the greater the perceived threat, the more aid Kuwait granted to the "threatening" country. The revolutionary regimes of Egypt, Iraq and Algeria received the largest amounts of aid, while the other Arab countries received much smaller amounts (see table 4.2).

In spite of Iraqi President General Abd al-Karim Qasim's aggressive reaction, all the other Arab countries agreed to recognize Kuwait as an independent state, and Kuwait was accepted as a member of the Arab League. But the price for this pan-Arab benevolence was a share of Kuwait's oil revenues. It was widely understood that this was Kuwait's first payment on account of sponsorship fees. This was complemented by other and more open forms of bribery, such as interest-free loans for unspecified needs, straight from the Kuwaiti Treasury.[12]

**Table 4.2**   Kuwaiti loans to Arab countries up to early 1966 (in millions of KD)

|          | Amount |
|----------|--------|
| Egypt    | 33.75  |
| Iraq     | 30.00  |
| Algeria  | 20.00  |
| Lebanon  | 10.00  |
| Morocco  | 10.00  |
| Jordan   | 6.00   |
| Sudan    | 5.00   |
| Tunisia  | 4.00   |
| Dubai    | 0.80   |
| Total    | 119.55 |

*Source*: *MEED*, Statistical and Documentary Service, March 1966.

[a]  These figures do not include the loans of the Kuwaiti Development Fund (KFAED).

Egyptian influence on various strata of Kuwaiti government and society contributed to the relatively high level of aid to Egypt. From the 1950s, Egypt sent teachers and doctors to Kuwait, whose contribution to the educational and the medical system in the sheikhdom was decisive. For example, 95 percent of the 3,575 teachers employed in Kuwait in the 1963/4 school year were foreigners.[13] In 1961 approximately 17,000 Egyptians were living in Kuwait,[14] and many of them held key positions in the Kuwaiti administration. This foothold in Kuwait politics worked in Egypt's favor in two ways: first, Kuwaiti aid was granted to Egypt as a result of cooperation between the two countries, and second, Nasser was able to apply pressure on Kuwaiti leaders through the Egyptian and Palestinian workers in Kuwait, who saw him as their natural leader, and through the extensive foreign population in that country (see table 4.3). In the Kuwaiti National Assembly, elected in 1961, there were ten Nasserist–Ba'athist delegates[15] out of fifty. To gauge how great Nasser's influence was, it is worth pointing out that Kuwaiti regulations did not give voting rights to foreigners, even if they had been resident in the sheikhdom for over ten years. Nasser therefore carried a certain amount of influence over larger segments of the domestic population. Already in 1959, Nasser had made it clear to Kuwait (and to the other oil countries) that if they would not willingly share their oil wealth with Egypt, there would come a day that Egypt would force them to do so.[16]

**Table 4.3**  The population of Kuwait 1957–1970 according to population census[1]

| Year | Total | Kuwaitis | Foreigners |
|------|-------|----------|------------|
| 1957 | 206,473 | 113,622 | 92,851 |
| 1961 | 321,621 | 161,909 | 159,712 |
| 1965 | 467,339 | 220,059 | 247,280 |
| 1970 | 733,662 | 391,266 | 347,397 |

*Source*: Population censi of 1957, 1961, as made up by *al-Ra'y al-'Amm*, May 3, 1970: M.W. Khouja and P.G. Sadler, *The Economy of Kuwait: Development and Role in International Finance* (London: Macmillan, 1979), p. 38; censi of 1965, 1970 as made up by: IMF, *Kuwait – Recent Economic Development* (SM/75/113, May 19, 1975), p. 7.

[1] The first census was held in February 1957, the second in May 1961, the third in April 1965 and the fourth in April, 1970. Kuwait is one of the few Arab countries to hold a regular population census (every five years) and to publish its results.

Besides its direct aid to Arab countries, Kuwait gave assistance to the Joint Arab Command, more than any other Arab country,[17] and to the Palestine Liberation Army.[18] Kuwait also supported Egypt's political stands in several cases, even when they were in conflict with Saudi Arabia's position. For instance, Egypt demanded the imposition of an economic boycott on West Germany, following its recognition of the State of Israel in March 1965. Saudi Arabia and Libya opposed this step, while Kuwait supported the proposal.[19] The Egyptian regime appreciated Kuwait's assistance, and omitted it from most of its verbal attacks on Arab countries – whether they were conservative or revolutionary.[20]

The Egyptian government received, up to April 1965, loans totaling $192.5 million (not including loans from the Kuwaiti Development Fund). On the other hand, during the period of April 1965–June 1967, Kuwait's aid to Egypt decreased sharply, totaling only $60 million. What was the reason for Kuwait's drastically reduced aid to Egypt as from April 1965 until the termination of their financial honeymoon? There were two principal causes: (a) The tightening of supervision by Kuwait's People's Council (whose Nasserist element had been heavily eroded in the 1965 elections) over Kuwait's monetary reserves, and the requirement that all future loans be channelled through the Kuwaiti Fund;[21] and (b) the question of compensation for Kuwaiti citizens whose possessions had been confiscated in Egypt in 1961, and which came up for discussion at the beginning of 1966.

In February 1966, the Kuwaiti leadership rejected a request by the Egyptian delegation, headed by al-Qaysuni, Assistant Prime Minister for Economic Affairs, for a separate loan of KD15 million, stating that a loan not originating from the Kuwaiti Fund was in contravention of the People's Council's constitution.[22] It is conceivable that the Saudis also influenced Kuwaiti reduction of aid to Egypt. After the Emir al-Sabah's visit to Saudi Arabia on February 9, 1966,[23] aid to Egypt virtually ceased, in spite of Egypt's economic difficulties.[24] The aid package was renewed only in June 1967.

In February 1967, nobody imagined that a few months later Egypt would also receive aid from the Saudis. After the Egyptian air force had bombarded the Saudi capital, igniting a total breakdown in relations between the two regimes, the Saudi authorities issued a governmental decree in early February 1967 which ordered the closure of Egyptian bank branches in Saudi Arabia (the Misr Bank and the Cairo Bank). This step was justified by Saudi leaders as a response to the nationalization of Saudi citizens' property in Egypt in 1961 and 1965, to the Egyptian banks' exceeding their function as bankers and their harming the security of the state.[25] In reaction to this, one week after the Saudi ruling, the Egyptian government nationalized the property of 210 Saudi nationals worth EgP 15–20 million as well as the property of some Saudi companies. The property of King Faysal and his family, worth EgP 3 million, was confiscated, as well as that of the Saudi Minister of Defense, Prince Sultan 'Abd al-'Aziz and the Saudi ambassadors in Cairo, Rabat, Tokyo and Washington. The Egyptian government even suggested that Saud, the deposed Saudi king living in Cairo, move into Faysal's confiscated palace.[26]

The bombings, the subversive activities and the nationalizations served as a grave reminder to Faysal of his futile efforts in the long political struggle with the President of Egypt. Faysal realized that these attacks were perpetrated in spite of American guarantees, and in spite of his extensive military purchases from the UK and US; he therefore tried to cool the difficult relations between the regimes. On March 27, 1967, Faysal declared: "The death of an Egyptian or a Yemenite is as tragic to us as the death of a Saudi. We feel nothing but love for our Egyptian brothers. Our only wish is for them to leave Yemen, and to leave the responsibility for their own destiny to the Yemenite people."[27] One week before the Six Day War in June 1967, Faysal declared that he would support Nasser in any campaign against Israel, and on the outbreak of war Faysal sent Nasser a message, in which he wrote among other things: "We will help you with whatever you need in this important campaign in the history of the Arab nation."[28]

## The period of institutionalized aid:
## Aid from Khartoum to Rabat

The June 1967 defeat, followed by the economic crisis in Egypt, forced Nasser to request aid from the oil countries. Before the summit conference in Khartoum, which was convened on August 29, 1967, Mahmud Riyad met with members of the Saudi delegation – Prince Sultan and the Saudi Minister of State for Foreign Affairs, 'Umar al-Saqqaf – and explained to them that Egypt needed £120 million (ca. $324 million) to cover the drop in revenues following the closing of the Suez Canal and the loss of its oil fields. Riyad proposed that the Saudis name the amount of aid they would be prepared to extend, so that the other oil countries would donate a similar amount. At a second meeting between the parties, the Saudi foreign minister informed Riyad that Faysal refused to specify any amount before the opening of discussions, and that he would extend aid to Egypt on the basis of a fixed percentage of Saudi Arabia's oil revenues.[29] The unofficial meeting held by Nasser and Faysal on August 30 at the residence of the President of Sudan, host of the summit conference, served to ease somewhat the tense relations between the two. Nasser and Faysal agreed to honor the resolutions of the Jedda Treaty of 1965; to remove Egyptian forces from Yemen (Nasser had already started pulling out his forces before the conference); and to abolish the economic sanctions the two countries had taken against each other. Immediately after this meeting, Egypt released Saudi property confiscated in February 1967, while Saudi Arabia abrogated the boycott of Egyptian banks operating in their country.[30] At the meeting, Nasser agreed also to discontinue his support of King Saud's attempts to return to Saudi Arabia.[31]

After eliminating some of the obstacles at the meeting between Faysal and Nasser, the path for aid to Egypt lay open. At the summit it was decided that Egypt and Jordan would receive an annual grant of $365 million in quarterly payments. The instalment condition was inserted: (a) because the Saudis did not trust Egypt to keep its promises, especially regarding the pullout from Yemen, so the instalment clause acted as a kind of guarantee; and (b) to encourage a slow but steady turn-around in economic fortune in the aid countries. Two critical questions regarding the aid commitments to Egypt are discussed below.

### Compensation for Egypt's war losses at the Khartoum Summit: A fair deal?

If the intention was to compensate the Egyptian economy for the loss of revenues because of the closing of the Suez Canal and loss of the oil fields, this aid would have compensated Egypt. Heikal maintained that aid received by Egypt was 10 percent higher than its estimation of losses suffered as a result of the war.[32] The World Bank agreed with this estimate.[33] But if one considers the aid package amount in comparison to the true total damages and costs sustained by Egypt as a result of the war, then the aid figure does not even begin to compensate Nasser. Besides losses from the closing of the Suez Canal, loss of the oil fields, the decline in income from tourism, and damages to industry and infrastructure in the Suez Canal area, the Egyptian government drastically increased their outlay on defense. In order to meet the cost of these developments, the government was compelled to reduce its investments, to cut down on the civilian budget and to raise direct and indirect taxes, which entailed raising the prices of a number of controlled products. Although these steps reduced the budget deficit, this severe policy triggered a period of economic stagnation and negative growth in the budgetary years of 1966/7 and 1967/8.[34] The data shown in table 4.4 illustrates the economic hardships suffered by Egypt after the war. Defense costs in a period of six years increased by 2.5 percent, while civilian expenses increased nominally in the same period by less than 3 percent.

In light of the above figures, the question is: for what purpose did the oil countries send their aid? Was it to compensate Egypt for loss of revenues due to the closing of the Suez Canal, the loss of the oil fields and reduced tourism? Or was it for absolute compensation, including its direct and indirect military expenses?

Before the summit conference, Riyad requested £120 million to compensate the Egyptian economy for loss of revenues, and the oil countries agreed to allocate £95 million, and further compensated the Egyptians after the devaluation of the pound sterling. It should not be forgotten that Riyad presented the sum (£120 million) at his first meeting with representatives of the oil countries, and it is highly probable that the amount he presented as an opening position was higher in the first place, to enable him to receive a realistic amount after negotiations. Riyad reported to Nasser after the war that Egypt had suffered losses worth EgP 120 million, equal to £95 million.[35]

**Table 4.4**  Defense expenditure in Egypt (normal budget): 1965/66–1970/71 (in millions of EgP)

| Year | Defense costs | Change in % | Total expense not applied to defense | Annual change in % |
|------|------|------|------|------|
| 1965/6 | 175 | −1 | 810 | 23 |
| 1966/7 | 167 | −5 | 768 | −5 |
| 1967/8 | 224 | 34 | 659 | −14 |
| 1968/9 | 268 | 20 | 695 | 5 |
| 1969/70 | 386 | 44 | 801 | 15 |
| 1970/1 | 423 | 10 | 832 | 4 |

*Source*: IBRD, *Current Economic Position and Prospects of the Arab Republic of Egypt* (December 30, 1972).

## Underlying motives for the aid package

Why did the oil countries come to Egypt's help after the June rout? There is a strong possibility that the oil countries assisted Egypt because of its military and political concessions. Egypt's monetary dependence forced Nasser to abandon the application of his ideology, to retreat from Yemen and to recognize the monarchist regimes, in return for support. Sela remarked:

> Egypt's defeat and the closing of the Suez Canal forced Nasser to abandon his unifi-
> cation slogans and to look for a basis for cooperation with the conservative regimes
> under the leadership of Saudi Arabia . . . At the Khartoum summit conference a new
> type of cooperation based on "give and take" was created: the oil countries agreed to
> provide increased financial aid, for which in return the confrontation states agreed to
> recognize the conservative regimes and to honor the sovereignty of their leaders.[36]

Dawisha wrote that, in the wake of the 1967 war, Egyptian economic welfare was dependent on the financial support of the oil countries. This dependence began with the Arab summit in Khartoum.[37] Waterbury stated that at the Khartoum summit Nasser had to submit to Faysal's financial power,[38] whereas 'Ajami claimed that the oil countries did not want to hear any more about pan-Arabism in return for aid.[39] Choucri asserted that the oil countries consented to provide aid, and in return they demanded that Egypt reassess its role as the dominant political force in the region.[40]

Was Egypt's dependence on the oil countries so great that they merely accepted whatever terms the AOC dictated? Were the oil countries not also dependent on Egypt? Was the give and take aid a quid pro quo for concessions from Nasser's side only? It is correct to say that Nasser suffered a heavy economic blow in addition to the military débâcle, and the desperate need to attract capital to revive an ailing economy certainly influenced his decision, but it would be incorrect to think that the oil countries assisted Egypt only because Nasser eased off on his revolutionary vitriol. Their aid was not only the result of Nasser's recognizing their conservative regimes, or his pullout from Yemen, but, just as Nasser wanted to receive aid, the oil countries desperately sought to provide it, because of economic–political–strategic considerations. Lacking Egypt's military clout or cultural appeal, the AOC had little choice but to give aid in order to distribute power (and wealth) more equally throughout the region.

After the June 1967 War, the oil countries felt threatened not only by revolutionary Arab ideology, but also by Israel – even if this was only a theoretical threat. Israel, in the period immediately after the war, represented a major power and opposed the AOC. If Egypt, the largest and strongest of the Arab countries, could not hold the breach, then Saudi Arabia or Kuwait could definitely not stand up against Israel. The postwar situation, which saw Israeli borders redefined, only heightened their Arab anxieties. Safran noted that the oil countries supported Egypt after the war, seeing response as an investment in geopolitical stability. Nasser was quick to exploit the Israeli threat felt by the weak oil countries. Even after their defeat, the Egyptian army was far superior to the oil countries' military potential and, if necessary, could offer valuable support.[41] Such a perspective on matters – the Israeli threat scenario – begs the question as to why Arab nations didn't invest more heavily in Egypt, given that their own domestic security was at stake.

Vatikiotis added another variant to Safran's interpretation. In his opinion, this aid should be seen as protection money to the troublemakers.[42] If the Yemen problem had not been solved, a defeated Nasser would have been close to the Saudi oil fields, and in Egypt's deteriorating economic situation, the Saudis feared that Nasser would have had no other choice but to threaten their oil fields. The summit conference, of course, had come only a few months after the bombing of Saudi territory by the Egyptians. Another point of view is given by Kerr, who argued that the oil states supported Egypt, while at the same time urging it to resume its strong stand against Israel. They hoped to focus Nasser on his conflict with Israel, forestalling his desire to renew old habits and take on the Arabs.[43] The Saudis also feared that defeat would leave Nasser with no option but to strengthen his ties with and his dependence on the Soviet Union, which would strengthen their influence in the region.[44] There were good reasons for the decision to support Egypt and Jordan at the Khartoum summit. Support meant that the oil countries won greater influence in inter-Arab politics, and wider recognition of their dedication to the common Arab cause. The Khartoum aid also provided their regimes with political legitimacy – what Hudson called "the central problem of governments in the Arab world"[45] – after their regimes had been challenged by Arab revolutionary states.

Besides the oil countries' fear of an Egyptian attack on the oil fields, they were apprehensive of Egypt dictating oil policy to them, as it had endeavored to do in the past; for example, when Nasser tried to dictate an economic boycott on West

Germany after they recognized the State of Israel. Egypt's proposed boycott was opposed by the AOC.[46] On realizing the innate wealth and power in oil, the oil countries wanted to create an independent oil policy. They were fully aware that without oil exports their regimes could collapse, as nearly all of their income stemmed from this product. The oil countries declared that it was their wish to exploit the oil weapon in a "positive" way, i.e. with aid from their oil income to the confrontation states; exploiting the oil weapon through a boycott would very likely harm their economies.[47]

At the conference of the Arab ministers of finance and energy which convened in Baghdad, August 15–20, 1967, the oil countries exploited their support of the confrontation states by opposing a proposal tabled by Iraq and Algeria to impose a total boycott on oil exports. Saudi Arabia, Kuwait and Libya, fearing the loss of their revenues, declared that oil exports should be continued in order to support the confrontation states until such a time as they would regain their lost territories. Finally, it was decided to transfer the decisions in this matter to the summit conference,[48] and at the Khartoum summit the conservative oil countries consolidated their stance with the support of Nasser.[49] Agreement on this issue was probably reached between Nasser and Faysal before the start of discussions at the summit. The agreement meant the oil countries could continue to export oil and protect their income, and Nasser secured financial aid. The conservative oil countries drew up a draft of pan-Arabism, which called for continuing oil exports, "in order to support the confrontation states," and also serving their own interests.

The deal that secured Egypt aid and the oil countries their export industry was a compromise on mutual interests, producing a kind of pragmatism, adopted by Egypt and the oil countries. Nasser, his views moderated by defeat (and not necessarily by aid), was interested in obtaining financing to rehabilitate the deteriorating Egyptian economy, and he saw that moderation could work in Egypt's favor. Faysal wanted to obtain concessions from the Egyptian side, mainly on the subject of Yemen, to guarantee his dominance in the Gulf area, and to strengthen the Egyptian army against an Israeli threat, to which he was also susceptible. Nasser's defeat enabled him to obtain these goals, and at the same time to be portrayed as showing concern for the common Arab cause. Though Nasser was, politically, in a weak position, he used his weakness as his strength, as the Israeli threat to both Egypt and the oil countries brought the two sides closer.

In 1967, economic ties between Egypt and the oil countries were strengthened. In addition to financial aid, Egypt received oil shipments from Algeria and Kuwait[50], and Egyptian economic missions visited Saudi Arabia frequently.[51] Furthermore, a decision was taken to employ Egyptian workers in Saudi Arabia and to establish a joint Egyptian–Saudi bank, based in Saudi Arabia.[52] Saudi Arabia was not indifferent to the steps taken by Egypt after the June defeat, which included the adoption of a new attitude toward the US and the budding of concern for the private sector. Their spokesman declared: "Egypt is not standing on its own, the Saudi government, which never hesitated to assist its big sister in the various stages of its conflict with the enemy . . . feels today, as always, that it is supporting Egypt."[53]

Unlike the Khartoum summit, Egypt attended the Rabat summit, which convened on December 21, 1969, determined to raise additional substantial aid from the AOC. Before the summit assembly, Nasser sent several economic missions to Saudi Arabia,[54] in an attempt to reach agreement on an increase of the Khartoum aid. The oil countries objected to this, and they expressed their position on the subject well before contacts were made for the convening of the summit. Up until the summit, Egypt and the oil countries waged a "war of nerves": Saudi Arabia threatened to reduce its aid to Egypt and Jordan after the sabotaging of the Tapline pipeline. 'Umar Saqqaf, the Saudi Minister of State for Foreign Affairs, announced in early December 1969 that aid was influenced by oil revenues, and that the oil flow after the act of sabotage was irregular. The minister threatened that "we will be forced to reduce aid" in case of any further acts of sabotage.[55]

Immediately after the Khartoum summit, Kuwait indicated that it did not intend to increase aid to the confrontation states. In contrast to Libya and Saudi Arabia, Kuwait did not compensate Egypt for the devaluation of the Egyptian pound in November 1967, after the conclusion of the summit. In June 1968, al-'Atiqi, the Kuwaiti Minister of Finance, declared that although Kuwaiti oil revenues were considerable, its capacity for aid was limited, because most capital was being spent on developing the economy.[56] In January 1969, during a discussion held by the Kuwaiti People's Council, critical questions were raised: how long would Kuwait have to support the confrontation states? As long as Israel occupied Arab territories? And why was the Kuwaiti economy suffering as a result of this aid?[57] Several members proposed that if Kuwait really wanted to combat Israel, then they should transfer some or all of the aid that Egypt and Jordan had received, to Palestinian organizations; and anyway, the Egyptian economy was no longer in a recession.[58] One month after the Council's meeting, the Kuwaiti press criticized the aid provided to Egypt and Jordan. *Al-Ra'y al-'Amm* denounced the Arab summit conferences, and declared that they were not in Kuwait's interest: "The time and money wasted could be used more efficiently."[59] In May 1968, pro-monarchist Libya joined the debate by claiming that aid to Egypt and Jordan hurt its economy. The Libyan Prime Minister, Bakush, declared that Libya "would reconsider continuation of aid." In June 1968, Bakush stated that the Libyan government was "not in a position to consider increased aid," as the government "itself was in need of resources" and its aid to Arab countries amounted to 20 percent of its budget.[60]

At Nasser's request, Faysal made a stopover in Cairo, on his way to Rabat, and met Nasser for the first time since their Khartoum meeting about two years ago.[61] The two men had many issues to discuss which they did not agree upon. Faysal claimed that Egypt had a hand in the attempted revolt in the Saudi air force, and mentioned Sami Sharif, head of Nasser's office, as one of the main instigators in the attempt. Nasser denied the allegation and mounted an offensive on financial matters, stating that Egypt was in need of additional aid. Faysal retorted that Saudi Arabia was going through a period of financial difficulties and it had to choose between a loan from the IMF or cessation of aid. These difficulties, Faysal added, were caused by the Tapline sabotage carried out by friends of Nasser, George Habash and others, who were operating in collaboration with the Zionists.[62] Nasser and Faysal therefore arrived at the Rabat summit without having reached prior agreement on the question of aid, and at the summit the conservative oil countries opposed increasing their aid sums to Egypt. The atmosphere at this summit was much tenser and more highly charged than at the Khartoum conference. Why did this change come about? And why were the oil countries being so parsimonious?

**Table 4.5**   Saudi Arabia's oil revenues, 1965–1969 (in millions of US dollars)

| Year | Revenues |
| --- | --- |
| 1965 | 664.1 |
| 1966 | 789.9 |
| 1967 | 903.6 |
| 1968 | 926.4 |
| 1969 | 949.2 |

*Source*: IMF, *Saudi Arabia, Report no. SM/75/157*, p. 10.

The AOC governments were not willing to grant Egypt aid in addition to the regular figures already agreed upon at the Khartoum summit, plus additional small amounts over and above the Khartoum agreement. For example, Saudi Arabia's oil revenues for 1967 came to $904 million, and for 1969, to $949 million.[63] Egypt alone received regular aid of $100 million from the Saudis, i.e. more than 10 percent of that country's oil revenues. Egypt would have no doubt been satisfied if it had been granted a similar percentage of Saudi Arabia's oil revenues during the 1970s. We should not forget that it was not only Egypt enjoying Saudi aid, but also Jordan, the PLO and the Saudi brigade stationed in Jordan. The official amount that Saudi Arabia granted in aid to Arab countries, amounted at that time to SAR 662 million ($150 million),[64] i.e. more than 15 percent of its oil revenues, which actually comprised the lion's share of its total income. On top of that, Saudi Arabia's balance of payments showed a deficit in the years 1968 and 1969.[65] Kuwait also allocated large amounts to aid relative to its income from oil. From the end of the 1960s up to the fiscal year 1970/1, its oil revenues totaled less than $900 million annually, while it allocated $135 million in aid to Arab countries,[66] which amounted to 15 percent of its oil revenues. A study of the Kuwaiti budget showed that the Kuwaiti government's actual development costs amounted to only KD 37 million ($104 million) in the 1968/9 fiscal year;[67] that is, less than its aid to Arab countries.

Although lack of money was a major reason for the AOC's decision, other factors did come into play. Although they allocated the Khartoum aid without prior written conditions, they wanted to supervise the way their aid money was spent. In May 1968, about eight months after the Khartoum aid decision was taken, a Libyan daily editorial asserted that Libya had every right to express its opinion about the way aid was utilized by Egypt and Jordan, as this aid had been allocated directly from their budget, and not from surplus monetary reserves.[68] An identical demand was officially made in September 1968, at the conference of Arab foreign ministers, where the AOC delegates demanded that Egypt give an account on how the Khartoum aid was being spent.[69] Saudi Arabia and Kuwait demanded that their aid money to Jordan be transferred to British banks, through which Jordan would purchase arms, to prevent the spending of aid funds on internal needs,[70] and it is quite likely that this demand was made of Egypt as well. At the summit Faysal said that he was ready to provide aid, but he demanded that he be kept informed of the manner in which these funds were spent and for what purpose.[71]

In the 1968/9 and 1969/70 fiscal years Egypt actually channeled substantial amounts of aid funds to internal needs, in an attempt to initiate economic growth, after the harsh economic policy it had adopted in 1966/7 and 1967/8, which caused economic stagnation. An IMF report on Egypt stated that in an attempt to revive its economy, the government increased its investment funding up to a certain level. This increase was financed by extensive aid from Arab countries and higher local revenues. As a result, the budget deficit has been kept within reasonable bounds.[72] Besides the dissatisfaction of the oil countries with the manner in which Egypt used the aid funds, a paradoxical situation had been created. Whereas the Saudis, as we saw, suffered from a balance of payments deficit in 1968 and 1969, Egypt showed a small surplus in its 1968/9 balance of payments, in addition to a relative upward trend in its economy. In a letter sent by Hasan Zaki, the Egyptian Minister of Economic Affairs and Foreign Trade, to Schweitzer, the executive director of the IMF, Zaki pointed out the increased economic activity in Egypt, was the direct result of Arab aid funds.[73]

Saudi Arabia and Kuwait were not comfortable with the slight improvement shown in the Egyptian economy, not least because it was Nasser who stood at the head of the Egyptian elite. The basic differences between Nasser and Faysal remained the same. The agreement they reached at the Khartoum summit in 1967 did not signify the end of conflict between the two leaders; rather, it represented the mere murmur of an amicable resolution. Faysal was still suspicious of Nasser's subversion and of his part in the attempted revolt in the Saudi air force and in the sabotaging of the Tapline pipeline. The oil countries feared that Nasser's increasing power would result in a triumphant march toward an anti-Western, pro-nationalization dictatorship, especially after the military coups in Sudan in May 1969 and in Libya in September 1969. Nasser was quick to recognize Gaddafi's regime, and Heikal dedicated several articles to the Libyan coup, which he described as "one of the most significant events in the Arab world in recent years."[74] Gaddafi repaid him in kind and declared in early October that his government would increase its aid to Egypt.[75] Saudi Arabia and its neighbors in the Gulf were not happy with this constellation, while at the same time they noted the steadily growing Soviet presence in Egypt, which included operational advice.[76] Less than two weeks before the assembly of the Arab summit conference in Rabat, an Egyptian delegation arrived in Moscow, and the two parties agreed on steps for comprehensive collaboration in the political, military and ideological spheres. Nasser's dependence on the Soviets was never greater than at that time.[77]

These factors combined to deter the oil nations from increasing aid to Egypt, with the economic situation of the AOC being the central factor. Even if they had ignored all the other issues, until 1971 (the year of the Teheran Pact and increased oil revenues), the AOC were not really capable of offering much more aid than they had done in Khartoum whilst simultaneously carrying out development plans in their own countries. Further, they did not feel like committing themselves to additional established aid and they preferred to provide this – if at all – in ways and at a time of their own choosing. Aid on an ad hoc basis served their interests in a better way.

## Aid from Sadat's rise to power until the peace initiative:
## September 1970–November 1977

On September 28, 1970, Nasser passed away. A new chapter was opened in the history of political relations in general, and especially in economic relations, between the AOC and Egypt, and the "Cairo–Riyadh" axis was created.[78] The Saudis felt more at ease after Nasser's death. In spite of their improved relations with Nasser, the Saudis could not erase the events of the past, for Nasser had adopted a foreign policy which was not consistent with Saudi Arabia's interests. Sadat's rise to power introduced a different dimension to relations between the two states. Faysal was interested in establishing close contact with Sadat, with whom he had been acquainted for some time, and he hoped to establish an Arab conservative consensus based on Egyptian muscle and Saudi money. Faysal believed that this consensus, allied with the special relationship with Washington, would create the best Saudi guarantee for stability.[79] The aspiration for security was especially strong in light of the expected British withdrawal from the Gulf.

### Involvement in the expulsion of the Soviet advisors

After Sadat had been sworn in, Faysal sent him his brother-in-law Kamal Adham, Chief of Saudi Intelligence and his close advisor, to explore the possibility of an understanding between them. The primary subject of the talks was the Saudi regime's fear of the growing Soviet presence and influence in Egypt. Sadat noted that the Soviets had supplied him with arms, and added that his priority was Egyptian security, and whether it was the Soviets or Satan offering their services was not his concern. Nevertheless, Sadat remarked that after the first stage of the Israeli withdrawal had been completed, he would be willing to expel the Soviets.[80] He permitted Adham to convey this message to the US administration.[81]

According to Cordesman, Faysal and Adham tried to persuade Sadat to disrupt Egyptian–Soviet relations as early as December 1969.[82] The *Washington Post* wrote that the CIA fostered relations with Adham, who was described as the CIA's Saudi contact man and as having close relations with the Saudi royal family and with Sadat. Adham was known to have arranged a fixed private income for Sadat already at the time of his vice-presidency.[83] Such actions question whether the Saudis befriended Sadat before his rise to power, with the ulterior objective being the removal of the Soviet presence from Egypt. Events in the region after Sadat's rise to power certainly lead to the possibility that the Saudis had a hand in the removal of the Soviets from Egypt, and this was in exchange for immediate aid and commitments for future support.

Egypt was no longer dangerous from Faysal's point of view in the early 1970s, because it was poor and weak, and, in the aftermath of Nasser, had lost its ambitions to interfere in the Arabian Peninsula.[84] However, the situation was in fact one still coated in suspense and suspicion, mainly due to Egypt's relations with the USSR, and to Faysal's fear that Egypt still entertained political ambitions in the region. Despite the close nature of the personal relationship between Faysal and Sadat, 1971 was marked by Saudi wariness toward Egypt. The Saudis had two reasons to be suspicious: one was the Federation Agreement between Egypt, Syria and Libya signed on April 10, 1971 – a move that threatened to return radical Arab nationalism to the Arab world; the other was Egypt's relationship with the Soviet Union, which included the presence of Soviet advisors in Egypt and a mutual information agreement between the two countries on May 27, 1971. Another problem that clouded relations between Egypt and Saudi Arabia was the future of the Gulf sheikdoms following the British withdrawal from the Gulf. Faysal wanted to ensure his freedom of action without interference from Cairo, but Egypt had not only signed agreements with Libya and Syria and a friendship pact with the USSR, it was also in close contact with the sheikdoms' rulers. In view of these developments, Faysal made a week-long visit to Cairo at the end of May 1971. Sadat attempted to reassure him that the friendship pact was no more then a "piece of paper" and that Egypt's goal in signing this Soviet deal was solely to receive military aid. In addition, Sadat clarified that he had no political or other ambitions in the Gulf region.[85] Faysal was thus put at ease by this visit, which, for many observers, symbolized the real rapprochement between the two regimes. The understanding reached between the two leaders carried with it a promise for increased Saudi financial aid,[86] beyond the extent agreed in Khartoum.

During this period, Faysal responded positively to Sadat's request to put Lightning fighters at his disposal. On October 10, 1971, just one day before Sadat's visit to the USSR, Faysal sent him a cable in which he informed him that Saudi Arabia would supply Egypt with the requested bombers.[87] The timing of the cable had been planned in advance. Heikal gives a different version of events. He claims that Sadat did in fact fly not once, but twice, and it was after the second trip, on February 2, 1972 that he returned and told Heikal: "Who would have thought that the turning-point [in relations with the USSR] would be King Faysal?" According to Heikal, the Saudis informed them of the supply of the bombers a few days before the second visit, when Faysal said: "I hope that this will persuade a few other [states] to increase their aid [to Egypt]."[88] It could very well be that Saudi Arabia repeated this promise before both Sadat's trips to Moscow. In any case, Faysal's timing for approving the supply of the bombers was obvious. According to Heikal, Sadat demonstrated the depth of his gratitude by ordering General Muhammad Sadiq to cable the Saudi Minister of Defense, Prince Sultan, advising him that the Egyptian armed forces would be at Faysal's disposal in case of an emergency, during Sadat's stay in Moscow. This message, it was reported, left a deep impression on senior Saudi officials.[89]

In the spring of 1972, Washington officials made it clear to Faysal that if he would help them to erode the heavy Soviet presence in Egypt by gentle persuasion of Sadat, the US would apply more pressure on Israel to relinquish the occupied territories.[90] The Saudis were interested in getting the Russians out of Egypt, first, because of their anti-Soviet views in general, and secondly, to encourage Egypt to adopt a more pro-American (and pro-Western) attitude. However, in the spring of 1972, the decision to get the Soviets out of Egypt became even more critical when Iraq and the USSR signed a treaty of friendship in April 1972. The Iraqi media celebrated the boost in relations between the two countries and added that the treaty had Egypt's blessing.[91] Saudi diplomacy went into overdrive. In June, after the Saudi Crown Prince's visit to Egypt, the Saudi Minister of Defense, Prince Sultan, met with President Nixon and with Rogers in the US, made a stopover in Egypt before returning to Saudi Arabia for talks with Sadat; after a brief stop in Saudi Arabia he again flew to Cairo in early July 1972[92] and stayed in Egypt until just before the announcement of the Soviets' ouster from the country. Adham also remained in Cairo, next to Prince Sultan. There is no evidence to prove whether Saudi officials colluded with Sadat in expelling the Soviets, or if Faysal was informed in advance of the imminent retreat of the Russians.[93] In any case, the Soviets criticized Saudi Arabia and the other conservative countries and accused them of causing the dispute between Egypt and the USSR.[94]

It is difficult to judge precisely what role the Saudis played in the expulsion of the Soviets. Relations between Egypt and Saudi Arabia were shrouded in secrecy, with the president and his aides maintaining the nature of political contact, especially Ashraf Marwan (Nasser's son-in-law), and Sadiq, Minister of Defense. Shadhli noted that during his term of office (1971–3), Sadat's envoys paid about thirty visits to Saudi Arabia, but he never knew the purpose of these visits. Shadhli claimed he was told only that Sadiq would be in charge of receiving the arms promised by the Saudis, and that before the October War Marwan advised him that all contacts between Egypt and Saudi Arabia would be handled directly between President Sadat and King Faysal, and not by the two ministers of defense.[95] After the Soviet withdrawal was announced, Kissinger claimed that he had had no advance knowledge of this move: "I don't understand President Sadat. If he had come to me and told me about it before this [expulsion] happened, I would have felt an obligation to give him something in exchange. But now I got it for free." Saudi sources at the time reported that Faysal urged the Americans to make a substantive offer to Egypt. Faysal made it clear to the Americans that his personal prestige would be hurt if they did not give some kind of reward, now that the main obstacle to American–Egyptian–Saudi negotiations was gone.[96]

It was not only Egypt's relationship with the Saudis that caused the expulsion of the Soviets. There were several factors behind this retreat: the many crises in the Egyptian–Soviet relationship, after Sadat did not receive the military hardware he had requested; the tension between Soviet and Egyptian officers; failure to honor commitments by the USSR; Russian interference in Egypt's internal affairs; Egypt's desire to strengthen relations with the US, etc.[97] But considerable importance should be attached to the ties between Egypt and Saudi Arabia, between Sadat and Faysal, with the brokers' roles fulfilled by Saudi Arabia, and the anti-Soviet dogmatic stance taken by Faysal – whose support had been crucial to the success of the Egyptian military option (because of financial aid and the use of the oil weapon) – in terms of influencing Sadat's decision-making process. There was good reason for Sultan's and Adham's presence in Cairo just before the expulsion was announced and even at the time of the communiqué. Sadat declared that "Faysal's intention was to make me tell the Russians 'get out,' and that is what happened."[98]

After the Soviet expulsion, a Saudi delegation flew to Cairo to assess the infrastructure damages caused by the withdrawal, with the main aim being to look at possible ways of softening the blow to Egypt's military power. It was decided that Saudi Arabia would grant additional financial aid to help Egypt sever itself from Soviet political and military influence.[99] From hereon in, the AOC gave Egypt considerable support, strengthening the argument that Riyadh played a substantial part in ejecting the Russians from Egypt,[100] in the same way that it tried to keep Soviet influence out of other countries in the region. Tahsin Bashir, Sadat's spokesman, would only declare that Sadat had wanted to expel the Russians and that he consulted many important people on this subject, and that the Saudis had but a minor part in his decision. At the same time, Sadat had no objection to glorifying the Saudi role in this matter, to exploit this to Egypt's interest and to obtain more aid. Statements implying that the Saudis played an important part in the expulsion and that this influenced Sadat in his decision only increased the Saudi authorities' provision of aid to Egypt.[101]

Rustum, without referring specifically to the ousting of the Russians, claims that, as Faysal did not wish to assist regimes which "mixed communism with Islam," Egypt adopted an anti-communist political stance for the purpose of obtaining aid.[102] This conclusion is only partly correct because two other factors came into consideration: first, Saudi Arabia did provide aid to countries who "mixed Islam with communism" in the Arab as well as in the non-Arab world; and secondly, Egypt was also uncomfortable with the Soviet presence on its soil – ousting the USSR was not, therefore, contrary to its interests. Korany's theoretical research on Egypt's foreign relations in terms of aid from January 1967 until September 1970 shows that Egypt's stand *vis-à-vis* the USSR was influenced by Saudi Arabia's own stance on communism. Korany comes to the conclusion that there is not sufficient evidence to confirm the existence of mutually exclusive interrelationship between aid recipients (such as Egypt) and foreign relations on a global level. There was, however, a tangible Middle Eastern, regional level economic dependence, which expressed itself in Egypt's rapprochement and its improved relations with the conservative states.[103] According to Korany's theory, already in 1970 there were signs pointing to the potential influence of the Saudi stand *vis-à-vis* the USSR on Egyptian international relations, though at that time it remained only a possibility. Decisive changes occurred in the region following Korany's study: the rise to power in Egypt of a man with a markedly different personality to Nasser, and a significant change in the AOC's economic status after the Teheran Pact of February 1971.[104] Hence, the possibility of Saudi Arabia influencing Egypt's relations with the USSR, which had been unlikely during Nasser's regime, became very likely under Sadat, whose economic and political strategy took the oil countries' wealth into consideration.

After the expulsion of the Soviet experts, Egypt continued to adopt a policy compatible to the interests of the conservative oil countries. On the outbreak of civil war in Yemen (September 1972), Sadat ordered to send military supplies to North Yemen, including five MIG-17 fighters, four T-28 bombers and twenty-two tanks of the T-34 class. This was the price Egypt paid to utilize Saudi wealth and power.[105]

## Aid before the October War (1973)
In mid-December 1972, the Arab chiefs of staff convened in Cairo. At this meeting, Saudi Arabia, Kuwait and Libya pledged to provide Egypt with military and financial assistance, to be used in part for purchasing arms from Moscow and from other sources. The decisions made at this meeting established a precedent: at all former

meetings of the Joint Arab Defense Council enthusiastic speeches were made in favor of mutual aid, but these speeches were not followed by any practical achievement. The primary obstacle had always been that the representatives at these meetings had not been authorized to take independent decisions and they were subject to approval from the highest echelons on their return to their country. At the December meeting, operational decisions were made: on January 27, 1973, the Arab Defense Council convened for a special sitting in Cairo and confirmed the decisions made at the meeting of the chiefs of staff.[106] Moreover, the expulsion of the Russians from Egypt contributed to the strategic alliance which had started to develop between Egypt and the AOC.

Shadhli, who acted as the Arab League's Assistant Secretary-General for defense matters as of June 1971, described in his memoirs the relative dynamics between the Arab confrontation states and the other Arab nations and the change that occurred in the AOC's attitude to aid to Egypt after the expulsion of the Soviet advisors, and after their reconciliation with Sadat. On assuming his position Shadhli's first act was to establish an Arab Defense Fund, which advocated that the wealthier the Arab state, the more money it would contribute to the Fund. States with an annual income of less than $200 per capita would donate 10 percent of their GNP to the Fund, and states with an annual income of between $1,000–$2,000 per capita would contribute 25 percent to the fund. The accumulated sum, according to Shadhli, was to be divided up between the countries, so that at least 50 percent would go to the confrontation states.[107] Shadhli himself called his plan a utopian dream and an official approach to the Arab League had already rejected the idea, so it was unsurprising that as an official proposal it was rejected outright.[108] Shadhli remained an ambitious thinker and was not deterred from his plans, sometimes coming up against Egyptian opposition.[109]

In January 1973 the chief of staffs' decisions from the end of 1972 were approved, and from that time on until the October War, Egypt received extensive financial and military aid from the AOC. Saudi Arabia even agreed to allow Egypt to use aid money for purchasing arms from the USSR,[110] since there was a lack of an alternative supplier – Egypt had no diplomatic relations with the US and Western countries refused to sell substantial military supplies to Egypt. Added to that, Egyptian weapons systems were already adapted to the Soviet system. In late April 1973, Ahmad Isma'il, the Egyptian Minister of Defense, paid a visit to Saudi Arabia and Kuwait to discuss Saudi aid to Egypt in the event of war. Saudi Arabia had already pledged to maintain the present level of oil production in the event of a continued stalemate in the Middle East. Saudi Arabia promised to stop oil exports in the event of war. Ahmed Isma'il used his visit to inspect the Egyptian pilots who had been undergoing training on the Saudi air forces' Lightning aircraft.[111] Intensive contacts at the highest level between Egypt and the AOC governments continued until the outbreak of the October War. In July 1973, Marwan paid three visits to Saudi Arabia, and in early August the Saudi Foreign Minister visited Egypt. Adham also visited Cairo several times. After these preparatory visits, Sadat paid a visit to Saudi Arabia on August 23, 1973.[112] Faysal promised him additional military and civil aid after the outbreak of hostilities in return for a pledge to block any proposed unification with Libya.[113] During this visit Sadat asked Faysal to use the oil weapon;

Faysal's reply was that it was too early: "Give us time. We do not want to exploit our oil as a weapon for a war lasting only two or three days. We want to see a conflict lasting long enough for us to mobilize world public opinion."[114] Salim Luzi, the editor of *al-Hawadith*, wrote in late August 1973, that Faysal and Sadat reached an agreement, according to which "the Arabs would create a formula which would turn the oil into a source of arms instead of a weapon in itself". Faysal told Sadat:

> There have been attempts to thwart the Arabs by creating an illusion that cutting off the oil [flow] is the only way that this [oil] weapon can be manipulated. Nobody asked where we would obtain the funds that we would need in the event we reduced oil supplies, not only to finance the needs of our country but [also] to provide aid to our brothers on the front line.[115]

Another report supported Luzi's version that money and not oil would be used as a weapon. Heikal claimed that Faysal agreed to finance about half of Egypt's arms purchases and promised to assist Egypt in repaying its debts to the USSR.[116] Heikal's and Luzi's versions both agree that Faysal agreed to exploit oil for the war. Where they differ is that Heikal reported that Faysal agreed to use the boycott, whereas Luzi wrote that Faysal preferred to donate aid from oil revenues. James Akins, the new US ambassador to Saudi Arabia, stated at the end of September 1973:

> In the past . . . Faysal said . . . that the Arabs would not exploit oil as a weapon and would not cut supplies. He is still saying this, but he also says "we will not increase output in order to fulfill your [USA's] demands as long as your policy is sympathetic to Israeli expansion at the Arab's expense." I always took Faysal's declarations . . . very seriously. Until such a time as he sees political change from the American side, I am afraid that he will impose sanctions on output.[117]

In the first stage of planning the October War, Sadat did not succeed in obtaining a Saudi commitment to exploit the oil weapon. Saudi Arabia agreed to provide financial and military aid, but not to involve oil in global diplomacy. The change in the Saudi attitude probably came about after its failure to gain preferred access status to the American energy market, in exchange for a Saudi guarantee of oil supply to the US.[118] Until late July 1973, Faysal was still ostensibly against using oil as a diplomatic weapon,[119] but doubts had already crept into his mind, as seen when Faysal agreed, in principle, in late April 1973 to exploit the political uses of oil. The other oil countries had also implied that they would exploit the oil weapon if necessary.[120] After Sadat's visit to Riyadh, the Kuwaiti head of state arrived in Cairo, and the two leaders reached agreement for the exploitation of all Arab resources, including oil, "in the face of the Zionist–imperialist challenge".[121] The contacts of the Mar'i delegation, which visited Saudi Arabia and the Gulf States from October 10, 1973, had the important purpose of finally imposing the oil boycott on October 17, 1973.[122]

The aid dispensed by the AOC to Egypt until the October War was less, from a global perspective, than aid after the October War. In comparison to the GNP and other parameters, however, the aid was substantially greater than in the period immediately after the war; Arab assistance was then of great importance because of the cessation of Western aid to Egypt. Without the massive level of aid (civil and military) provided by the AOC to Egypt and their commitment to increase it after the outbreak of war, Sadat would have found it difficult to start the campaign of the October War.

## Aid from the October War until 1975

The first positive blows struck in the October War inspired the AOC with a new spirit of patriotism and self-belief, heralding a new era of full cooperation with Egypt. Sadat felt that the AOC did not believe he would actually go to war, and his declarations since 1971 about "the year of decision" merely added to their incredulity. Saudi Arabia and Kuwait extended massive economic and military aid to Egypt just before the war, and their willingness to help increased after the war, but in strictly calculated amounts. According to Crecelius, the Saudi treasury was willing to provide Egypt with any amount it asked for. He added that after the war, Faysal increased his grant to Egypt to such an extent that it enabled Sadat to promise "arms and butter" to the Egyptian people.[123] Crecelius's analysis was not entirely accurate, however. The oil countries had provided relatively small amounts of civil aid to Egypt and their investments in Egypt were minor in scope, although their oil revenues had increased ten-fold after the October War and they were holding hundreds of billions of dollars in the West.

The euphoria that the leaders of the oil countries were originally caught up in soon waned, with the AOC's willingness to donate massive aid amounts diminished after the end of the war. Even in their initial enthusiasm, the oil countries' donations were not so big as to single-handedly rehabilitate the Egyptian economy or make any significant steps in that direction. A few days after the beginning of the war, Faysal expressed to the Mar'i delegation his willingness to assist Egypt;[124] he offered just $400 million, in spite of Mar'i's explanation that the cost of one hour of warfare was $10 million.[125] After the war, the conservative oil countries did not extend any significant economic aid to Egypt and they did not make any meaningful investments in this country, contrary to the expectations of the policy-makers and the Egyptian people. Faysal's visit to Cairo in late July 1974 was symptomatic of excessive Egyptian expectations being dashed. The Egyptian media came out with huge headlines just before his visit, claiming that Faysal would grant them $1 billion and a loan of half that sum. But great expectations produced only big disappointments. Faysal declared he would grant Egypt $300 million only. An exception to this was military aid, which was given to Egypt with greater open-handedness, to cover its war losses.

In spite of the Egyptian government's unrelenting efforts to rehabilitate the economy, the AOC chose to grant it limited amounts of economic assistance and to concentrate on military aid. They had no desire to extricate Egypt from its chronic economic difficulties, which worked in their favor by ensuring its continued reliance on the AOC's financial benevolence. Most of the financing for military aid was transferred directly to arms suppliers by Saudi Arabia and Kuwait precisely because these nations wanted to circumvent Egypt appropriating aid for non-military purposes. The AOC hastened to buy military equipment to cover the Egyptian army's losses in the war (table 4.6), because they wanted to safeguard the military balance between Egypt and Israel (which received massive armament shipments from the US). Egypt could not buy Western arms on its own, so the oil countries took steps to help it by financing the transactions and by serving as a go-between for transferring the equipment to Egypt. The military and civil aid granted by the AOC to Egypt did enable Sadat to allocate valuable resources to other under-funded sectors in the Egyptian economy besides the military, but most important, this enabled him to maneuver more freely on the international stage. Besides strengthening the Egyptian armed forces, the AOC's main intention was to reduce Egypt's reliance on Soviet arms. The AOC strove to strengthen Egypt's Western orientation, while continuing to reject Soviet influence in the region. The Saudi Crown Prince stated in November 1975 that Egypt's turning to new sources of arms, e.g. the US, was in the framework of the arms diversification strategy and appropriate to Saudi strategy.[126]

**Table 4.6**  Egypt's losses of military equipment in the October War 1973

| Type of equipment | Total |
|---|---|
| Aircraft | 223 |
| Helicopters | 42 |
| Tanks | 1000 |
| Armoured vehicles | 450 |
| Artillery | 300 |
| SAM missile batteries | 44 |
| Missile boats | 6 |
| Torpedo boats | 4 |

*Sources*: Israeli Intelligence Data, as quoted by: S. Gazit, "Arab Forces two years after the Yom Kippur War," in *Military Aspects of the Israeli–Arab Conflict* (proceedings of an international symposium, October 12–17, 1975, Tel Aviv: University Publishing Projects, 1975), pp. 188–90.

The resolutions at the Rabat summit conference (October 26, 1974) and their subsequent implementation indicated once again the AOC's attitude toward supporting Egypt. The amount of aid Egypt received following the summit ($582 million), was only half of the $1 billion agreed upon at the summit. These sums were destined for the military and not for the economic sector, as emphasized in the summit resolutions. Although the amounts were not particularly large, compared to the AOC's total revenues, some of the donor countries indicated that the Rabat aid package was a one-time affair, whereas Egypt and the other confrontation states claimed that this aid was granted on a permanent basis.

In an attempt to mobilize generous aid for Egypt's economy, Hijazi, the Egyptian Prime Minister, visited the Gulf States in November 1974, but he found that the AOC's resolve on the matter of aid was firm. During this visit he received commitments for aid and investments to the tune of $2.5 billion. But this sum was essentially fictitious: agreement was reached on the establishment of joint Egyptian–Saudi investment companies, and on the Saudi and the Abu Dhabi Funds providing aid to Egypt for specific ventures and with Kuwait, and Hijazi agreed on the setting up of a series of projects in the industrial and food branches of the economy – but the oil countries did not provide hard cash for the immediate needs of the Egyptian economy. Aid was to have been granted pro rata to progress on the project, and the Egyptian and the AOC governments could not have foreseen when, if at all, these funds would be absorbed by the Egyptian economy.

As Shazli wrote in his memoirs, the AOC were not interested in far-reaching plans for the build-up of military forces before the October War, and likewise, they did not want to commit themselves to a comprehensive solution for the Egyptian economy, as a kind of "Arab Marshall Plan." Egypt did begin to establish such a fund soon after the war, with Sa'id Mar'i, one of the plan's initiators, tabling a proposal in 1975, according to which the AOC would donate to a specially-established fund a certain percentage of their national income or their exports,[127] but his proposal did not gain practical support from the AOC leaders.

In the summer of 1975, Egypt and Israel initiated contacts, negotiated by Kissinger, toward a second separation agreement in Sinai. The United States and several European countries implied that they would render Egypt extensive aid in the event that the Kissinger talks were successful, and the AOC expressed their agreement in principle to assist Egypt with an amount of $1 billion.[128] The US kept its promise immediately after the official signing of the interim agreement in Geneva, on September 4, 1975,[129] and on the same day, at a White House press conference, a grant of $650 million in economic aid to Egypt for the 1975/6 fiscal year was announced. The conservative AOC did not lag in aid grants, and in late September 1975 the Egyptian Minister of Finance announced that Egypt had obtained long-term loans for a total of $1.2 billion from three Arab countries.

The aid accorded to Egypt after the second Sinai agreement was problematic from the AOC's point of view. Though they supported any settlement that would bring stability to the region, especially if obtained under the auspices of the US and not that of the USSR, the open dispute between Syria and Egypt threatened: (a) the possibility of reaching a solution to the Arab–Israeli dispute; and (b) the precarious regional stability, which the AOC feared could be undermined.[130] The signing of the interim agreement aggravated Egyptian–Syrian relations and threatened Arab understanding and solidarity, which had been achieved after a long struggle by Saudi ruler Khaled, who paid his first visit to Cairo as King on July 16, 1975. During his visit, King Khaled expressed his support for the agreement,[131] and promised Egypt a loan of $600 million **(see chapter 1)**, but in the end he was forced to dissociate himself from the second Sinai deal. Kuwait even joined an anti-Egyptian coalition headed by Syria[132] (but Saudi Arabia and Kuwait together continued supporting Egypt, both openly and covertly). The Kuwaiti *al-Qabas* wrote that the Saudis guaranteed aid to Egypt after the interim agreement, but demanded that this be kept secret.[133] This was not the first time that Kuwait openly expressed its opposition to Egyptian policy, while continuing to give aid to Sadat. When Egypt decided to support the cease-fire agreement after the October War of 1973 (October 21),[134] Kuwait notified Egypt that it would continue aid in spite of its opposition to resolution 242 of the UN Security Council.[135] Unlike Kuwait, Libya's aid was based on condition of Egypt remaining at war with Israel; following the second Sinai agreement, Libya suspended virtually all aid. There were also voices of discontent in

Kuwait calling for a cessation of aid to Egypt. 'Abd al-'Aziz Mas'ud, a member of the Council for Foreign Affairs in the National Assembly, announced on September 17, 1975, his intention to propose a motion for a law suspending aid to Egypt after the Israeli deal; and on November 4, 1975, he tabled a motion at the Council, arguing that "Egypt was no longer a confrontation state."[136] But Kuwaiti opinion was deeply divided over this issue. Another member of the council, Khalid al-Mas'udi, countered with a proposal for a $1 billion interest-free loan to Egypt, for reimbursement of debts and arms purchases.[137] In the end, neither resolution was passed.

## AOC changes in aid policy: 1976

In 1976 basic changes occurred in the amount, the conditions and the channels of aid extended by the AOC, all of which were unfavorable to Egypt. Up to the end of 1975, the AOC had provided most of their aid to Egypt bilaterally, but as from the second half of 1976 they funneled most of their aid through the Gulf Fund for the Development of Egypt (GFDE), and every Egyptian request for aid was examined by the managers of the Fund. The AOC also laid down an explicit condition that assistance would be extended only if Egypt adopted the reforms proposed to it by the IMF.

The first repercussions of the AOC's new aid policy were felt in early 1976. Sadat flew to the Gulf during February 1976 to give an in-depth review of the economic situation in Egypt to the AOC leaders. Sadat's visit proved to be disastrous on all fronts. No substantial aid package was obtained, adding to the woes experienced by other Egyptian dignitaries in Saudi Arabia, and by Faysal's tour of Egypt. But the most damaging result of discussions was the fact that the AOC granted aid to Egypt on condition of it adopting the reforms proposed to it by the IMF. This constituted nothing less than interference in Egypt's internal affairs, although the donor states had no intention of providing the substantial aid needed by Sadat to reach some kind of salvation from the current economic crisis. Tahsin Bashir, Sadat's spokesman and companion on the tour, stated that the AOC, having received the IMF reports on the state of the Egyptian economy and its misman-agement, pointed out the inadequacies to Sadat, and demanded that any future loans to Egypt be managed by external financial bodies such as Morgan Stanley.[138]

Sadat was forced to swallow the bitter pill the AOC had handed out, because the severe situation of the Egyptian economy gave him no political leeway. He had to place Egypt's monetary affairs under external supervision, against a guarantee of aid to the tune of $700 million, to be paid in instalments over the entire year. Although this aid was not a massive sum, Sadat declared in a speech at an Egyptian air force base that it had prevented an economic catastrophe.[139] Sadat declined to react to the conditions dictated to him by the AOC, in the hope that, after his visit to the Gulf, an Arab fund with substantial capital would be set up in 1976, which would be used to rehabilitate the Egyptian economy, and would help Egypt finance its Five-Year Plan for the years 1976–80.[140] From the time of Sadat's visit to the Gulf in February 1976 up to the establishment of al-Hay'a al-Khalijiyya lil-Tanmiya fi Misr (The Gulf Fund for the Development of Egypt – GFDE) on July 18, 1976, this matter was never off the agenda in Egypt. They had great expectations: Sadat demanded between $10–$12 billion for a period of five years, and the *Akhbar al-Yawm* wrote that the AOC would probably allocate $10 billion.[141] But they allocated only $2 billion to the Fund, for a period of five years, and they stipulated that the funds should be channeled to specific projects in Egypt, and not as support for the balance of payments.

The setting up of the Gulf Fund constituted a milestone in AOC–Egypt economic relations. Sadat and Egypt had been humiliated by the AOC, thinking that they would receive "a fund of billions"; there was bitter disappointment at the AOC's refusal to give massive support. The financiers of the Fund hardened their position even after its establishment, and serious disagreement emerged between Sadat and the Fund's managers. Egypt wanted a fund with a simple and flexible structure, which would enable it to utilize credits as it saw fit, but the financiers saw matters differently. In October 1976, the Fund rejected Egypt's request for a loan of $1.2 billion to alleviate the balance of payments difficulties. The Fund's managers again stated that they had no intention of providing capital to support the balance of payments, but only for development projects. A further request for aid from Egypt was granted by the AOC, but not directly: instead, they agreed to guarantee a loan of $250 million that Egypt was hoping to borrow from the American Chase Manhattan Bank.[142] Moreover, the AOC conditioned their guarantee on a counter-guarantee of the Egyptian Central Bank [143], and at one stage they even demanded that they supervise Egypt's revenues from the Suez Canal as a guarantee of debt reimbursement.[144] Only after pressure was brought to bear and after urgent negotiations between the Egyptian and the Saudi ministers of finance – the latter was chairman of the Fund – did the Fund's managers agree, in late 1977, to grant Egypt a loan of $250 million to reduce the deficit in the current balance of payments, at an annual rate of interest of 5 percent. The Fund managers also rejected Egypt's request to reduce the rate of interest.

The AOC's aid to Egypt was limited, granted on hard terms and did not enable Egypt to solve the problems of its difficult economic situation at the end of 1976. Therefore, at the conference of foreign ministers of the AOC, Syria and Egypt (Riyadh, January 9), Isma'il Fahmi demanded that the AOC increase their aid. Sela writes that at this conference, the AOC agreed to renew their monetary aid to the front line states in accordance with the criteria of the 1974 Rabat Summit, and "so they terminated the argument that existed in 1976 between the front-line states and the PLO on one side and the AOC on the other side, over the question whether this aid was for one year only or multi-annual . . . However, the argument on the extent of aid was not settled."[145] The atmosphere at this conference was still simmering with hostility. The AOC flatly rejected Fahmi's request to increase aid to Egypt, and Fahmi voted with his feet.[146] In the end, discussions were renewed five days later, with Fahmi participating, but Egypt did not find a remedy to its problems. Sela notes that the final resolution merely reconfirmed the resolutions of the 1974 Rabat Summit; this meant a cut in aid funds by about 58 percent. Egypt was allotted $570 million in military aid.[147]

What brought about the change in policy of the AOC? Until 1976 the AOC granted Egypt limited aid, on condition of its moderation, without any supervision of its economic policy. AOC spokesmen said in 1975, for example, that they were ready to increase their aid if Egypt would first arrange its own affairs, and stabilize its regime.[148] But after Sadat's visit to the AOC in February 1976 and the setting up of the Gulf Fund, the AOC conditioned their aid on the adoption of the IMF resolutions and on monetary reforms in Egypt. In an interview given by the Saudi Foreign Minister, Mahmud Aba al-Kha'il, he was asked why Saudi Arabia had linked its aid to Egypt to the IMF directives. Al-Kha'il answered that there was no direct connection between Saudi aid and the IMF's directives, but "Egypt and the IMF had decided on a specific plan. It's only natural that Egypt should adhere to the fulfillment of its commitments."[149] From the Saudi minister's words one might think that Saudi Arabia was keeping Egypt's promise to a third party. Why, therefore, did the AOC act as they did? The conditions for carrying out reforms could very well create problems of instability in Egypt. Saudi Arabia probably joined forces with Western financiers, considering a dictate of financial conditions to Egypt as a policy that would ensure long-term stability in that country. According to this explanation, although Saudi Arabia and the Western countries feared that conditional reforms could very well cause instability in Egypt, they feared even more the serious economic, social and political consequences resulting from a lack of reforms. Wheeler stated at a hearing of the Committee for Foreign Affairs in Congress in March 1979, when asked about the pressure being brought to bear on Egypt to carry out reforms: "We feel that it is essential that these [reforms] be carried out, [when considering] long-term stability."[150]

According to Jabber, the AOC reduced their aid to Egypt after 1975, because, in their opinion, Egypt was not properly managing the resources put at its disposal.[151] Mustapha Khalil declared that the reason for this was that the AOC knew Sadat intended to sign a peace treaty with Israel.[152] The AOC was annoyed that Egypt should reconcile with Israel, but quite possibly it was more irate over Sadat's independent policy toward Israel, dating back to the second Sinai agreement (September 1975), which was considered an affront to nations of Arab unity. The AOC feared that an overly independent policy by Sadat could lead to a renewal of Egypt's attempts to achieve hegemony in the Arab world, which they wanted to avoid at all costs.

In Anis Mansour's opinion, American officials advised the Saudis to reduce their aid to Egypt, as the US was keen also to keep Egypt from growing stronger and hoped to apply political pressure on the Egyptian leadership by reducing aid via the Saudis,[153] but there is no additional evidence for this, and the proposition is also illogical, considering the increased American aid to Egypt since 1974. After all, it was not only Egypt that suffered from reduced aid in 1976, and as the Saudi Minister of Planning put it in August 1976: "Saudi aid reached its peak and then started diminishing."[154] In any case, the question still remains: why didn't the AOC provide increased aid to Egypt in 1976 as well as in the period after the October War? And why did they give it on an ad hoc basis, and not systematically? This line of inquiry leads on to several other key issues: was the AOC leadership really interested in the recovery of Egypt's economy? And what was the red line the AOC leaders had drawn themselves, if any, in helping Egypt?

Waterbury claims that the AOC wanted Egypt as their tamed client, and feared an Egypt enjoying economic prosperity. As far as they were concerned, a prosperous

Egypt, with its large population, its industrial base and its vast army could pose a deadly threat to the conservative regimes, as it had done in the sixties. Conversely, they were not interested in the collapse of Sadat's government, a situation which could, from their point of view, radicalize Egyptian society and politics, and lead to regional instability.[155] In order to maintain such a delicate balance, the AOC did not want to commit themselves to permanent aid to Egypt in the form of an "Arab Marshall Plan." They wanted Egypt to request aid intermittently, and in exchange it would be forced to take AOC requests into consideration. The AOC, as they conveyed to several public figures in Egypt, granted aid to Egypt to keep it alive, but "just barely."

It should be remembered that the AOC did not grant aid only to Egypt. In order to protect their global interests, they provided assistance also to the other confrontation states – Syria, Jordan and the PLO. Increased aid to Egypt could bring in its wake demands for greater funding from the other states, especially from Syria. Saudi Arabia had already experienced this once before, when the PLO claimed that Saudi Arabia was withholding necessary support. Salah Khalaf (Abu Iyad), Arafat's deputy, attacked Saudi Arabia in August 1974 for not granting them aid worthy of a guerilla movement, while it was "piping millions" to Egypt.[156] Saudi Arabia avoided strengthening the PLO too much, because it opposed strengthening any revolutionary body whatsoever, while at the same time it feared a strong Palestinian reaction to limited aid to the PLO as compared to Egypt's allocation.

The decrease in aid to Egypt stemmed likewise from the fact that the AOC found it necessary to spread out their aid in order to gain influence in other regions. Up to the mid-1970s the AOC dedicated the greater part of their aid to the Arab states, with Egypt receiving the lion's share. However, after this period Arab aid was divided up between a larger number of states, including Asian, African and South American countries. Aside from this, 1977 saw Saudi Arabia suffer from a budget deficit, resulting in a decline in its financial reserves. The AOC almost certainly subscribed to the belief that Egypt would not be satisfied with the assistance it received, even if it was given additional billions of dollars, as this amount would not save its economy.[157] Possibly they also feared that Egypt would become accustomed to receiving aid from them any time it asked for it, which over a period of time could lead to the AOC losing control over their resources.

As we have seen, the AOC struggled with potential and practical dangers until 1977. The size of the threat became more tangible in 1980, with the outbreak of the Iraq–Iran war, which meant that they could not increase aid to Egypt. The Arab–Israeli conflict illustrates this point. Geographically, the oil countries are located in another sub-region of the Middle East. In spite of them being relatively remote (and hence the Israeli threat is minimal), the AOC felt threatened, and they supported Egypt and other confrontation states. But the AOC did not go through the painful experience of the Iran–Iraq War, when Kuwait was bombed by the Iranian air force, and there was agitation by the Shi'ite minority in their territories, nor did they suffer from acts of sabotage or a threat to their oil exports. Therefore, they quickly and "generously" volunteered to help the Iraqi treasury and they "loaned" them huge sums to fend off any potential threat. Up to 1983, Iraq received aid, as calculated by the Americam Embassy in Baghdad, for a total amount of

$20–$30 billion, mainly from Saudi Arabia and Kuwait,[158] and up to end 1985, according to Kamal Hasan 'Ali, about $50 billion.[159] These enormous sums were allotted in spite of lower oil prices and their considerably lower revenues. The proximity of the war, in addition to a real potential threat, determined the scope of their aid.[160] Egypt never attained the level of aid received by Iraq – after the outbreak of war with Iran – not even during the October War.

Several persons close to Sadat, among them Tahsin Bashir,[161] placed part of the "blame" for the low volume of aid with Sadat. Anis Mansur writes that Sadat, as a *fellahin*, was very sensitive to the subject of aid because of a strong sense of dignity bred in Egyptian peasants. Sadat did not make an ultimatum for aid, like the Syrians and the PLO, nor did he properly exploit the opportunity that came his way after the 1973 October War to obtain "appropriate" aid. Another claim brought up by Sadat's close circle[162] was that the Saudis presented Sadat with "protocol favors," and this fact reduced his bargaining power when discussing the subject of aid with them. Tahsin Bashir said:

> The Sheikhs do not pay the tribe, they pay to the chief of the tribe. When Sadat received money, he reduced the effectiveness of his aid request. Syria demanded and received more aid, relative to its population, and so did the PLO, who did not use pleasantries and obtained aid. Remember the OPEC conference, where the PLO forced the ministers to their knees.

Another prominent factor behind the AOC's decision not to grant "too much" aid to Egypt was, ironically, the interests they had in common with Egypt – the communist threat perceived by both nations and Egypt's desire to develop the Egyptian economy and to maintain regional stability. Logically speaking, common interests should have been used as leverage for increasing, not reducing, aid to Egypt, but such was not the case in this matter. The AOC saw that Egypt would act to neutralize any communist influence and strive for regional stability, only in order to realize its own specific interests, such as an economic revival that would empower Egyptian attempts to regain cultural and political hegemony. The conservative oil countries noted a change in Egypt's political–economic orientation since Sadat came to power, seen in statements made by Sadat that stressed that regional stability must be maintained in order to realize Egypt's economic goals.

The makers of Egyptian defense policy shaped their plans around a central theme, one shared by Saudi Arabia; that is, the Egyptian fear of Soviet expansionism in the region – both direct and indirect.[163] Sadat, since coming to power, feared that the Kremlin had been involved in the planning of several attempts to overthrow him,[164] and he was convinced that the Soviets and Egyptian communists were responsible for acts of sabotage, assaults and riots, including the food riots in January 1977.[165] Sadat declared that "Russia is after Numeiry in Sudan, and after me,"[166] and he told Senator Pell that the main purpose of Soviet activity in Africa was to topple his government.[167] Because both the Saudis and Egypt feared the communists,[168] Saudi Arabia took the opportunity to kill three birds with one stone: Egypt carried out a foreign policy which fell in with the requirements of Saudi foreign policy, Egypt remained dependent on the Saudi treasury, and Saudi Arabia pumped smaller amounts of aid to Sadat. Saudi Arabia was more concerned with

Egypt's military might than with its economic development, so, although it was not conducive to effectively eliminating Soviet influence in the region, the Saudis did not grant Egypt unlimited, or even reasonable, resources.

It is possible that Egypt had exaggerated the communist threat in a manipulative way, to attract more aid from the conservative countries as well as from the US, but the "Red Menace" was real enough in the view of Sadat and Egypt's policymakers. The Saudi and Egyptian regimes' "Russophobia" contributed considerably to the strengthening of ties between the regimes. It would, however, be incorrect to say that Sadat was always acting only on behalf of the Saudis. In certain cases, Sadat operated strictly on his own interests. Thus, for example, he provided aid to various African countries in order to keep them away from Soviet influence and from the danger of a revolution. In other instances, he certainly acted in close cooperation with Saudi Arabia, e.g. in supporting the Omani Sultan against the Dhofar rebels. Sadat also joined a Saudi attempt to moderate the South Yemen leadership by channeling Saudi aid to South Yemen through Egypt. In fact, part of this aid ($10 million annually) paid in leasing fees for an Egyptian military base on the island of Prim, was transferred to Egyptian authority in 1974.[169]

Even after Saudi–Egyptian relations came to a point of crisis, following Sadat's peace initiative, the two countries continued to cooperate in fighting off revolutionary movements in the region. Such actions were certainly welcomed by the Saudis; nonetheless it was not Saudi aid that primarily motivated Sadat to act, but rather his own interest in the matter. Thus, for example, while Saudi Arabia favored Egypt's military intervention in Sudan and the removal of communist influence there, it was also clearly in Egypt's interest to do so. Stability in Sudan was important to Egypt, no less than to Saudi Arabia, considering that Sudan had long been regarded by Egypt as its backyard in terms of strategic and economic opportunities.[170] In light of the above, it is clear that Saudi Arabia was not required to pay much to secure Egypt's cooperation.

### Increased aid after the 1977 food riots

In spite of the continuing aid "trickle" policy, there were times that Egypt received increased assistance, usually after a political or economic crisis that had hit Egypt and threatened the oil states' stability. The food riots on January 18–19, 1977 resulted in the oil states showing greater generosity, but even so under strict supervision. The riots, in which seventy-nine people died, occurred after a failed attempt by the Egyptian government to cut subsidies and to raise the prices of basic products by up to 60 percent. The government was forced to make this move after both the US and Saudi Arabia explained that these steps were a sine qua non for their continuing aid as well as that of the IMF's.[171] On the very same day the riots started, Sadat paid a secret flying visit to Saudi Arabia to demand urgent assistance.[172] Sadat explained that the demands for reforms made by the IMF with the support of the oil states could not be achieved in the current social crisis. With the support of Egyptian intellectuals, Sadat argued, further postponement of aid by the AOC would threaten regional stability.[173]

The media in the AOC were divided in their opinion on the riots in Egypt: *al-Ra'y al-'Amm* called for the assembly of an Arab Summit, in which continued aid to Egypt would be outlined;[174] and *al-Wahda* pressed for the AOC to assist Egypt because "its security was closely connected with the security and the stability of the whole Arab region." Nonetheless, *al-Wahda* recommended that aid not be granted for the purpose of improving the state of the Egyptian economy, only to alleviate the military burden caused by the conflict with Israel.[175] Some Kuwaiti newspapers speculated that Sadat staged the riots in order to receive aid without preconditions.[176] On January 25, 1977, *al-Ra'y* rejected the claim that the Egyptian Communist Party was strong, and declared that the Egyptian media were promoting the myth of the communist menace after the riots in order to move the AOC to provide increased aid to Egypt.[177]

The AOC leaders followed developments in Egypt with concern, and they sent their ministers of finance to a meeting with the Egyptian minister of finance in Riyadh about two weeks after the riots. This time they decided to agree to Egypt's request for a loan of $1 billion for the 1977 fiscal year,[178] and they also agreed that this assistance be granted for the financing of the expected budgetary deficit, and not for specific development projects. In late March – one month after the meeting in Riyadh – the Egyptian government was surprised when the financial backers of the GFDE agreed to increase their aid to Egypt over and above the sum agreed on at Riyadh. This message was given to the Egyptian Minister of Economy and Planning, Abdel Moneim Kaissouni, during his visit to the Gulf States. Kaissouni was surprised by this step, so much so that he interrupted his visit to the Gulf States in order to report to President Sadat, and he returned to the Gulf after three days of consultations in Egypt.[179]

In April 1977, the managers of the Fund announced officially that the sum to be put at Egypt's disposal would be $1.474 billion, which would be transferred to the Egyptian Central Bank in several instalments.[180] Moreover, to facilitate matters for Egypt the oil countries agreed to postpone the withdrawal of their deposits with the Egyptian Central Bank ($2 billion), so Egypt could continue to use these deposits, and they postponed the repayment of Egypt's debts on its previous loans, including another $2 billion.[181] But the AOC leaders refused Egypt's request to increase the capital of the GFDE, in spite of Kaissouni's pleas for a moderate increase during his visit to the Gulf, proposing to increase the Gulf Fund capital by $4 billion, compared to an original request for $10–$12 billion.[182]

Concerning military aid to Egypt, the oil countries continued to donate as generously as ever: on July 16, 1977, Sadat revealed that the previous year Saudi Arabia had taken on itself the burden of covering all expenses involved in the development of Egypt's armed forces for a period of five years, "without Egypt having to pay one penny."[183] Saudi Arabia had already urged the US to supply Egypt with arms at its (Saudi Arabia's) expense[184] as well as purchasing weaponry in Europe for Egypt, but 1976 represented an all-encompassing, long-term commitment. Part of this commitment was the financing of the purchase of fourteen Hercules aircraft from the American Lockheed company in 1977, at a cost of $250 million.[185] It is important to note that the Saudi decision was made after a further deterioration in relations between Egypt and the USSR, and the abrogation of the friendship treaty with the Saudis in March 1976, a step which was later accompanied by the cancellation of preferential treatment for the Soviet navy in Egypt's ports.[186]

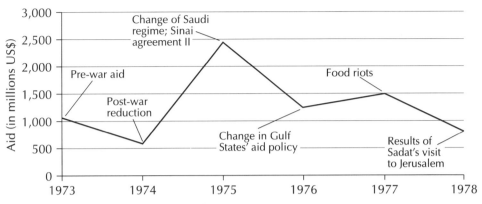

**Figure 4.1**   Oil countries' civilian aid to Egypt, 1973–1978

## The oil countries' economic relations with Egypt: 1977–1984

### A period of doubt: November 1977–March 1979

The Saudi leadership was among the first Arab governments to show signs of accepting Israel's legitimacy, on condition that it retreat from the Arab conquered territories and recognize the rights of the Palestinian people.[187] But the Saudi leadership was not happy with the idea that Sadat, who met with King Khaled in Saudi Arabia in early November, did not inform them of his peace initiative. Moreover, the Saudis were afraid that Sadat's agreement with the Israelis would be interpreted as having Saudi, and generally Arab, backing. Fahd remarked later that he took offense from the fact that Sadat had not informed him in advance of his initiative[188], and he noted that "[Sadat] came here and I stayed with him until three o'clock in the morning and he did not mention anything, except that he was determined [to go] to the Geneva conference."[189]

From the time of Sadat's visit in Jerusalem up to the Camp David agreement, the Saudi government had no idea how things would turn out in the end, and therefore they did not take a firm stand over the delicate matter of Israeli negotiations.[190] As the American Secretary of State Vance remarked, Saudi Arabia and Jordan were torn between private hopes for peace and concerns over Sadat's initiative, which they feared would fail, and dampen their burning desire to restore Arab solidarity.[191] Saudi Arabia emphasized that any solution to the Arab–Israeli conflict should be reached in an all-Arab framework, while maintaining the Arab consensus and avoiding disunity.[192] Fahd was also apprehensive that a separate peace treaty with Israel would hurt "vulnerable" regimes in the area, would cause a renunciation by Egypt of military aid to the Arab world and would bring with it increasing Soviet penetration of the Arab world.[193]

The Saudi leadership stressed that they would continue to support the Egyptian military after the Camp David agreement, and denied the rumors that they intended to abrogate their commitment to finance the needs of the Egyptian army for a period of five years.[194] In December 1977 Fahd declared that "as Egypt's and President Sadat's brothers, we will never cut off our relations with Egypt."[195] The Saudi leadership kept to its word, and in early 1978 Egypt signed an agreement with Italy for a total of $225 million for the purchase of two or three Lupo class frigates, the lion's share of which was supposed to be paid for by the Saudis;[196] at the end of February 1978, Saudi Arabia further agreed to finance for Egypt the purchase of fifty American F-5E fighters, at a cost of over $500 million; and in 1978 the oil countries transferred the balance of funds from the GFDE to Egypt, as well as part of the aid commitments from the Khartoum and Rabat Summit conferences.[197]

The Camp David agreement caused a shock to the Arab nations. In spite of the peace talks, they hoped that Egypt would "return to the fold," especially because of the impasse that the negotiations between Israel and Egypt had reached in the summer of 1978.[198] This belief was expressed by the Saudi leaders in the presence of Alfred Atherton – the American special envoy to the Middle East.[199] Following the Camp David agreement, Iraq called for the convening of an Arab Summit, to decide on sanctions against Egypt.[200] Saudi Arabia did everything in its power to prevent "irreversible" actions against Egypt, in spite of its dissatisfaction with Sadat's moves.[201] In spite of the Camp David agreement, economic ties between the AOC and Egypt continued. On September 30, the Saudi Minister of Finance, Mahmud Aba al-Kha'il, declared that Saudi Arabia did not intend to reduce its aid to Egypt, and added: "Saudi Arabia is very pleased with the rate of progress of the development projects in Egypt, many of which will receive Saudi financial aid."[202] In mid-October 1978 Fahd declared in a message to Sadat, that he would move to prevent Egypt's isolation in the Arab world,[203] and *al-Riyad* wrote that Saudi Arabia would object to imposing severe sanctions against Egypt.[204] The Saudi Foreign Minister, Sa'ud al-Faysal, on a visit to Kuwait and the Emirates to coordinate positions with them for the Baghdad Summit, declared that "I cannot imagine Egypt being isolated . . . the aim of the summit is not to punish Egypt, but to close ranks because of the peace treaty."[205] In a different context, the minister argued that Egypt's isolation would harm the Arab world.[206]

Before the convening of the first Baghdad conference (November 2, 1978), Carter received good news from Khaled and Fahd, pointing to a possibility of Saudi support for the Camp David talks.[207] But in spite of its declarations before the conference and its messages to Carter, Saudi Arabia joined the hardline states at the conference in condemning the Camp David agreement. The Summit resolutions determined that, in the event that Egypt signed a peace treaty with Israel, the Arab states would cease their aid and break off diplomatic relations with Egypt and cancel its membership of the Arab League; Arab financial institutions would be suspended and an oil boycott would be imposed on it.[208] Moreover, it was decided at the Summit to establish a fund of $3.5 billion for aid to the confrontation states and the PLO, from which Syria would receive $1.85 million.[209] This was an attempt to signal to Sadat that refuting the Camp David agreement would be economically profitable. The previous attempt was on November 4 – one day before the termination of the Summit – when a delegation on their behalf, headed by Salim al-Hus, the Lebanese Prime Minister, arrived in Cairo and offered Sadat "everything" to enable him to continue the struggle against Israel, in exchange for the abrogation of the Camp David agreement. Sadat refused even to meet the delegation, which returned to Baghdad the very same day.[210]

According to Carter, Saudi Arabia claimed that more extreme anti-Egyptian resolutions would have been passed at the Summit, if it were not for its moderating influence, and that Sadat was encouraged, in spite of reports from the Summit, after he conferred "directly" with the Saudis.[211] Saudi Arabia continued supporting Egypt after the first Baghdad conference, in spite of the hard words between Sadat and the AOC leaders. Senator Pell, who met Sadat on November 25, 1978, declared that Egypt enjoyed the support of moderate Arab governments, mainly Saudi Arabia, in important fields, such as financial aid needed for the welfare of the Egyptian economy.[212] In late December 1978, *Cairo Radio* announced that the Saudi ambassador in Cairo delivered a missive from Khaled, which stated that "Saudi Arabia feels bound to honor its commitment in the framework of Arab aid to Egypt . . . [and] to supply it with military and material assistance."[213] The testimony given at the subcommittee of the American Foreign Relations Committee in February 1979, confirms that the Saudis gave continued support:

> *Hamilton* (chairman of the subcommittee for European and Middle-Eastern affairs): Were there, for instance, grants from OPEC countries [to Egypt] since Camp David?
>
> *Wyler* (senior clerk at the Agency for American Aid): Yes.
>
> *Hamilton*: Since the Baghdad conference [November 1978]?
>
> *Wyler*: Yes, to the best of my knowledge.
>
> *Hamilton*: Have they been delayed because of this?
>
> *Wyler*: It seems that the Khartoum and Rabat payments have been affected.[214]

In mid-March 1979 Sadat agreed to accept the peace treaty after meeting in Cairo with a high-level American delegation, including President Carter, his National Security advisor Brzezinski, Vance and Brown. After their return to Washington, the president instructed Brzezinski to fly to Saudi Arabia, Jordan and Cairo, to inform their governments about the agreement and to convey their reactions to Sadat. In talks with Brzezinski in Saudi Arabia (March 17–18) the Saudis pledged not to impose sanctions on Egypt. The Saudis stated that they would limit themselves to a formal, negative reaction and protest against a separate peace treaty with Israel.[215] The Saudis tried to keep their promise to Brzezinski: Fahd and Sa'ud said that after signing the peace treaty on March 26, 1979, Saudi Arabia would "limit its sanctions" against Egypt,[216] and at a summit conference of Arab foreign and finance ministers which convened in Baghdad on March 27, 1979, the Saudis endeavored to limit the actions taken against Egypt by other Arab nations.[217] But they retreated from this position, and ended up joining in the political and economic boycott against Egypt, enshrined in several resolutions. The political resolutions included suspension of diplomatic relations, moving the headquarters of the Arab League to Tunisia, Egypt's removal from inter-Arab institutions and organizations, and an attempt to exclude it from the Organization of Non-aligned States.[218] Economic sanctions were agreed upon, with all assistance to Egypt suspended, the imposition of an oil boycott and the cessation of commercial traffic.[219]

Saudi Arabia was forced to harden its official position toward Egypt, and to adopt the stand of the Arab hardline states for the following reasons:

1     The hardline states applied pressure backed up by genuine threats. Arafat accused Sa'ud al-Faysal of being "a traitor to his father's heritage";[220] Abdul Halim Khaddam, the Syrian Foreign Minister, threatened to strengthen Syrian relations with the USSR and to support Palestinian terrorism against Arab governments supporting Sadat; Iraq threatened before and during the conference, that any country not fulfilling the boycott resolutions would be considered a traitor and a collaborator with Sadat; and Saddam Hussein threatened that the hardline states would incite the population of "deviating" states and help them to topple their regimes in any way possible.[221] Saudi Arabia did not want to become a victim of the hardline states while the following developments were on the agenda: the Somali–Ethiopian conflict, the revolution in Iran, the strengthening of the Soviet position in South Yemen, internal subversion in the Gulf States and agreement between Iraq and Syria.

2     Saudi Arabia felt that its wealth was not an effective political lever against Egypt, and that its power to influence Sadat was extremely limited, if any.

3     Saudi Arabia felt that its "special relationship" with the US was being steadily undermined, and its government sensed an opportunity to strengthen its policy of Arab solidarity. Quandt claims that the Saudis felt Egypt had become the preferred partner of the US in the Arab world at its own expense. Egypt and Saudi Arabia competed with each other, and Saudi Arabia was bitter that Egypt received American arms as aid, while it purchased arms at exorbitant prices.[222] The Saudi leaders were also doubtful of the US's ability and willingness to defend their Kingdom: testifying before the Senate Foreign Relations Committee, Secretary of Defense Brown declared that the US had not pledged to defend Saudi Arabia.[223] One month later Brown retracted that statement,[224] but the damage had been done: the Saudis remembered how the Americans did not come to the assistance of the Shah of Iran. One of Fahd's close circle even blamed the US in January 1979 for the expansion of Soviet influence in the region.[225]

4     Israeli Prime Minister Menachem Begin's speech in the Knesset on March 20, 1979, did not make matters any easier for Saudi policy-makers. The day after the Israeli government had ratified the peace treaty, Begin declared that Israel would never give up Jerusalem, that it would not permit the establishment of a Palestinian state in the West Bank and in the Gaza Strip and that it would not retreat from the occupied territories.[226] Saudi Arabia and the other Gulf States, who had large Palestinian populations, could not agree with these statements because of their potential consequences.[227]

5     The religious aspect played an important role in Saudi Arabia's official policy toward Egypt and the peace treaty. Saudi Arabia could not afford to ignore the Jerusalem problem, after having preached unstintingly – in its role as the traditional defender of the holy places – the religious right of the Arabs to sovereign rule in East Jerusalem. Ignoring the problem of Jerusalem would have harmed its legitimacy as the guardian of the holy places of Islam, from which the Saudi elite derived great political strength. Faysal had said in 1970: "Resolution 242 . . . may be good enough for others. But what are we Saudis in the eyes of Muslims and in the eyes of God, without the liberation of Palestine and the

restoration of the Arab character of Jerusalem?"[228] Even before Sadat's deal with the Israelis, Saudi Arabia was already insisting on East Jerusalem's Arab character and roots.[229]

Anis Mansur best described the situation in which the AOC found themselves at the foreign ministers conference in Baghdad: "In the same way as their hands trembled, so did their voices and resolutions." The AOC feared that agreeing to any resolutions would isolate them from Egypt, but this fear, was compounded by other problems the oil countries faced: the Saudis feared the Palestinians, the Palestinians feared Syria, the Gulf States feared Iraq and Iran, Morocco feared Libya and Algeria, and they all feared the US.[230] A senior Saudi official compared the Saudi position toward Egypt as one who was compelled to cut off a limb to stay alive .[231]

The amphibological nature of relations between the Saudis and Egypt was a further result of the dispute within the royal family as to the approach to be adopted toward Egypt and the US.[232] The dispute stemmed from two different points of view: "the American approach" and the "Arab approach." Fahd was in favor of keeping an open line to Egypt and to the US, even if this would lead to conflicts with the hardline states. On the other hand, Khaled and 'Abdallah feared that a moderate stand, opposing the Arab bloc, would harm the Kingdom's security and they championed the "Arab approach."[233]

## Continuing economic relations vis-à-vis diplomatic isolation: April 1979–1984

According to Safran, Sela and Law, Saudi Arabia cut off its aid to Egypt after the second Baghdad Summit. Safran wrote that Saudi Arabia ceased almost all kinds of cooperation with Egypt.[234] Qatar's Minister of Information told the American ambassador in early May 1979, as recorded in the American Secretary of State's report, that Qatar had ceased all aid to Egypt.[235] But although diplomatic relations between Egypt and the oil states had been suspended, and the AOC's repeated statements that they were committed to resolutions for an economic boycott of Egypt, the AOC and Egypt continued to maintain informal relations, both in the political and economic spheres. The maintenance of bilateral relations between states lacking diplomatic relations is a well-known phenomenon in international diplomacy.[236] Sharply reduced official aid does not disguise the fact that nearly all kinds of cooperation between Egypt and the AOC continued, such as the employment of Egyptian workers in the AOC, their citizens' investments in Egypt, leaving their deposits on the Egyptian Central Bank and in commercial activity and tourism (see chapter 5). Moreover, Saudi Arabia and the other Gulf States "temporarily" waived reimbursement of loans and the interest on them.[237] Deferring reimbursement of loans – even temporarily – to the tune of $5 billion[238] constituted a great help.

Saudi Arabia suspended diplomatic relations with Egypt on April 23, 1979,[239] but carefully omitted any mention of a suspension in economic relations between the two countries. By suspending diplomatic relations Saudi Arabia hoped to appease the hardline states, whilst trying not to harm the Egyptian or its own economy (Saudi Arabia did not, for example, dismiss the hundreds of thousands of Egyptian workers employed within its boundaries). Several factors reinforced this approach: their promise to Brzezinski; their declarations before the convening of the Baghdad Summit; their moderate attitude toward Egypt at the time of the Summit; the resolve of senior Saudi officials to prevent a situation in which Egypt would suffer irreversible damage as a result of the boycott; the Saudi announcements that Egyptian citizens would enjoy free entry to the Kingdom and that the contracts of Egyptians working in Saudi Arabia would be renewed;[240] and the Saudis' practical attitude after the suspension of relations. The conservative Arab states' policy of non-suspension of economic relations was deliberate from the very beginning. It can be argued that the extent of economic relations between Egypt and the AOC was greater and more significant after the boycott than before. Sadat himself declared in the last year of his life that Saudi Arabia took a moderate stand to the Camp David agreement, although Khaled condemned his visit to Jerusalem, publicly and privately.[241] Before he died, he urged the Americans to help his Saudi friends.[242] He supported the sale of the AWACS to Saudi Arabia, and he said that before his visit to Sudan, he wanted to know what was going on in Libya, Sudan and Chad; "the Saudis loaned me an [AWACS] plane with the help of the Americans."[243]

After the second Baghdad conference it seemed that the Saudis would continue supporting the Egyptian economy and army and honor their commitment to finance the purchase of F-5 fighters for Egypt. In accordance with a report of the American State Department, about one month after the Summit, Saudi Arabia declared its intention of honoring its standing commitment;[244] and at the end of April 1979, replying to Senator Glenn, Harold Brown declared that all signs pointed to the deal having been honored. Moreover, a senior Saudi official said in the months after the conference that Saudi Arabia had not cancelled its guarantee to cover Egyptian arms purchases in the US, France and England.[245] In June 1979, Saudi Arabia agreed to finance for Egypt the purchase of jeeps and military trucks from the US for the sum of $100 million.[246] The administration, together with Rockefeller, President of the Chase Manhattan Bank, exerted all their influence to persuade Saudi Arabia to finance this transaction.[247]

According to *al-Kifah al-'Arabi*, the Saudis – mainly Kamal Adham's assistants (among them Egyptians) – held continuous talks with Egyptian dignitaries after the Summit. The Egyptians Hasan Mansur and Usama al-Baz played an important part at these meetings. The crowning achievement of the discussions was the Sadat–Fahd meeting in May 1979 at a Saudi military base, which was organized by Kissinger, after he warned the Saudis that "the USSR will take the oil fields." Sadat flew to Saudi Arabia in an American plane and he was accompanied by Eilts, the American ambassador. At this meeting Fahd promised Sadat that he would reimburse him for despatching Egyptian armed forces to Chad to help the Chad Minister of Defense, Hussein Habré, and that he would finance the Egyptian forces that had been sent to Zaire and Morocco (to suppress the Polisario).[248] In late June 1979, a highly-placed Saudi delegation led by King Khaled's brother, Prince 'Abdallah, arrived secretly in Egypt, accompanied by the Foreign Minister. The delegates assured the Egyptians that Saudi Arabia did not intend to discontinue aid. The Saudi authorities' public statements were, they assured the Egyptians, just a front, and part of a sort of "double talk" policy (official vs. covert relations demanded use of such a system).[249]

In mid-1979, Saudi Arabia breached for the first time the commitment made to Egypt in the summer of 1977, to cover all expenses for the Egyptian armed forces for a period of five years. In July 1979 Saudi Arabia withdrew its commitment to finance the F-5 fighter deal for Egypt. A report from the Intelligence and Research Division of the American State Department (July 2, 1979) stated that Egypt also would probably lose considerable financing for other military purchases. According to this report, the discontinuation of aid was forecasted to adversely affect roughly 50 percent of the $5.3 billion arms purchase transactions concluded by Egypt since 1976, "including the F-5 planes."[250]

Nonetheless, Saudi Arabia continued to show concern, in its own way, for the Egyptian army's strength. It seems that Saudi Arbia deliberately put out a smoke-screen regarding its intention to pay for Egypt's planes and up to the official announcement of the commitment's withdrawal, there were widespread rumors on the matter. The Saudis breached their commitment to Egypt with the anticipation that the US would soon after announce its intention to supply Egypt with F-4E planes – which were more advanced fighters. Hereby Saudi Arabia indirectly achieved its goal of sustaining the strength of the armed forces, whilst simultaneously appeasing the hardline states.

Saudi Arabia conducted its foreign policy more covertly than overtly, and as asserted by Herman Eilts, who was well-versed in the mysteries of Saudi diplomacy, it excelled in "behind the scenes" diplomacy. Therefore, Saudi Arabia's official statements concerning relations with Egypt should be taken with a grain of salt. And in Eilts's words: "Their leaders' cautious language sometimes confuses persons not familiar with their real intentions."[251] Kissinger stated that the double-edged thrust of Saudi policy was forced on it by events and not by preference.[252] After Ayatollah Khomeini's rise to power in Iran, Khaled declared: "The new regime in Iran has removed all obstacles . . . to cooperation between Saudi Arabia and the Iranian Islamic Republic. We are united by Islam . . . we are pleased with Iran's policy . . . of preserving Islam."[253] Khaled's statement was typical of the nature of Saudi politics and foreign relations: official comments covering an underbelly of deceit and false intentions.

Saudi Arabia could not afford, in the delicate political situation prevailing in the area after the fall of the Shah, to finance the plane transaction for Egypt, all the more so because this deal received wide publicity well before it was officially announced. But the financing of undisclosed transactions to Egypt by Saudi Arabia continued. Saudi Arabia cut off various kinds of assistance to Egypt, mainly the kind that required cooperation with other Arab states, such as Arab aid funds and the Arab arms industry, but it did not harm other sources of capital for the Egyptian economy, such as the Egyptian workers in the kingdom, who pumped enormous amounts of foreign currency into the Egyptian state coffers. Saudi Arabia even requested that Egypt loan it – after the suspension of diplomatic relations – another 3,568 teachers for the 1980 school year.[254] A few months later it decided to increase the number of flights between Riyadh and Cairo from nine to twelve weekly flights.[255] These facts corroborate an American State Department report of May

1979, which asserted that the moderate nations adopted the boycott resolutions for purely show purposes, and they endeavored to reduce the damage that Egypt might possibly suffer in the long run.[256]

A secret letter from the Saudi Minister of Finance, Mahmud Aba al-Kha'il, to the administrative director of the IMF dated December 15, 1979 (the letter was a sharp complaint about Egypt's freezing of Saudi deposits on the Egyptian Central Bank), confirmed that Saudi Arabia had not restricted capital flow to Egypt. The letter read:

> The Kingdom did not take any military or economic action whatsoever, or even threaten to take any kind of action which could have implications on Egypt's security. No Egyptian assets have been frozen and the capital flow between the two countries has not been disrupted in any way. The Saudi government did not even request the Egyptian Central Bank to pay out its deposits before payment was due.[257]

Saudi Arabia's continued contacts with Egypt resulted in its winning Sadat's enduring support. In May 1980, Ibrahim Sa'ada wrote in the *al-Akhbar* daily (a paper well known for relaying official Egyptian policy), about the "real essence of the secret contacts between Egypt and Saudi Arabia," such as high-level contacts between Badawi and Sultan, the Egyptian and Saudi Ministers of Defense, and between Mubarak, the Egyptian Vice-President and members of the Saudi royal family. Meetings were held in Oman, Egypt and Switzerland, with "Oman playing an important role in bringing the parties together." The article mentioned that Fahd's declarations verified the rumours about the meetings.[258] The transactions between the countries were effected under a heavy veil of secrecy, and only a few of the deals leaked out, such as the C-130 cargo plane that Saudi Arabia presented to Egypt in 1981 and a loan of $180 million to the Egyptian military industry, to help in the manufacture of armored troop carriers.[259] Furthermore, the AOC found indirect channels to provide Egypt with civil aid, such as involving Arab banks in a loan for the sum of $400 million in the spring of 1982. Of this amount, $200 million transferred from the London branch of the Chase Manhattan Bank to the Egyptian Central Bank and the other $200 million transferred by Saudi Arabia through the Cairo–Saudi Bank in Jedda.[260] Nor did Egypt reimburse its loans to the AOC. In 1981 Egypt was supposed to have commenced reimbursing its debts to the GFDE but did not begin to repay the debt for some time.[261] Saudi policy-makers denied that they assisted Egypt,[262] nor did Sadat mention the aid he continued to receive from the AOC. Sadat maintained the covert nature of Saudi–Egyptian relations for two reasons: first, Saudi Arabia insisted that its aid be kept a secret, and second, Sadat felt that if he did reveal this matter, he might very well endanger his plans for increasing Western aid.[263] From data received by the OECD from the AOC, it is evident that Egypt, indirectly and covertly, continued to receive aid, although how much is not clear. The AOC gave the organization information about the principal recipients of their aid in 1983. At the top of the list of aid recipients were Arab countries such as Syria ($922 million) and Jordan ($307 million). After detailing aid to other countries, under the title "[aid to] other Arab countries," a sum of $440 million is listed, and the largest amount of aid is recorded under another heading, without any subdivisions – $1,369 million.[264]

The Baghdad conference certified that, despite the boycott, relations between the AOC and the Egyptian people should not be impaired. That is, Egyptian workers, at home or (especially) abroad in the other Arab States, would not be laid off or harmed in any way. This resolution was intended to soften the expected negative impact of the boycott on the Egyptian economy. The Kuwaiti Minister of Foreign Affairs and Information gave a speech to the National Assembly in February 1984, stating: "The political–economic boycott, imposed on Egypt by the Baghdad reso- lutions, is still valid, and Kuwait is committed to it, without disregarding the interests of our brothers, the Egyptian people."[265] The oil country governments did everything in their power to prevent a situation arising which would see Egypt severely suffer from the boycott. Besides taking care of the Egyptian workers in their countries, they also permitted their citizens to invest in Egypt. Sa'ud al-Faysal said explicitly that Saudi Arabia would not interfere in private investments in Egypt,[266] and the governments did not liquidate their companies which were jointly owned with Egypt. It is interesting to note that even some Arab governments of the hard- line states continued to maintain economic relations with Egypt: Algeria and Iraq increased their capital in a joint Arab banking project – the Arab African International Bank – in which Egypt was a partner; and Khomeini – who accused Egypt of sheltering the deposed Iranian Shah – agreed in July 1979 to double the capital of the Egyptian–Iranian Bank from $20 million to $40 million.[267]

The confrontation states were aware of the double-faced relations between Egypt and the AOC, and of the continuing flow of capital to Egypt through the Egyptian workers, and they termed such politics an "exploitation of loopholes by Egypt." They presented memoranda to the General Secretariat of the Arab League at the summit conference of the confrontation states, held in Tripoli in April 1980. Iraq and Syria's memoranda stated that Arab investments in Egypt should be prohib- ited – even if they were private – because Egypt, which had frozen Arab League accounts and deposits of the Arab countries after the boycott, would not hesitate to also freeze Arab citizens' property. The Syrian memorandum emphasized that "Egypt should be boycotted . . . in such a way that the boycott terms on Israel would also apply to it, without distinguishing between the state and its administration, its institutions or its citizens." The Syrian memorandum went on to argue that people should not be allowed to travel between the Arab League countries and Egypt, and that the remittances of Egyptian workers to Egyptian banks or to Egyptian govern- ment accounts, both directly and indirectly, should be forbidden.[268]

The oil countries rejected the Syrian–Iraq memoranda: besides their unwilling- ness to hurt the Egyptian economy, the AOC governments recognized that Egyptian workers were indispensable to their economies. Even if they could have discharged the Egyptians' services and expelled such enormous human masses, they would have been forced to import other professional workers, such as the Syrians and the Palestinians, who were considered to be politically active. Hassan Mansour, the Minister of Information in Sadat's government, raised another reason for the AOC's unwillingness to harm the Egyptian workers: the leaders of these countries wanted to gain the Egyptian workers' political support and turn them against Egypt.[269] It is perhaps more likely that the policy-makers of the AOC feared that a serious lack of resources in the Egyptian economy would leave the government with no other choice but to cast "covetous" eyes in their direction, leading to possible war against Arab neighbors, and/or that the serious state of the economy would be exploited to overthrow the present regime in Egypt, a situation which could be disastrous from their point of view. Therefore, the AOC did not touch the flow of capital to Egypt.

All this points to the central question concerning the AOC's position: if aid to Egypt given before the peace treaty was in part to guarantee stability in Egypt, why did they make the choice to reduce their aid to Egypt after the peace agreement? A situation of tremendous economic pressure in Egypt could cause the political radicalization of the whole area. There are several answers to this issue: first, after the Khomeini revolution there was a cooling of relations between Saudi Arabia and the US, which influenced the state of Egyptian–Saudi relations. If, before the final banishment of the Shah, Saudi Arabia tried to moderate the resolutions taken against Egypt because of its security interests, after Khomeini's rise to power, Saudi Arabia was disappointed by the US and the Western countries, which, in its opinion, demonstrated how powerless they were during the events in Iran. Therefore, Saudi Arabia was forced to join the hardline states, lest it remain isolated and exposed to their threats, the more so as certain members of the Saudi royal family supported a cooling of relations with Egypt.

The main reason for the reduction of their official aid, however, was that the AOC knew that Egypt would not remain out in the cold. They were aware of the contacts developing between Washington and Cairo, mainly the American guarantee to support Egypt's economy and its army and to cover its economic losses sustained as a result of the peace treaty. They were convinced that the US was collaborating with the Egyptians. The Americans prevented a collapse in the Egyptian economy (which would endanger national security) by pouring in greater financial aid as well as by military supplies, and assisting the Egyptian military industry – after the AOC withdrew their commitment to finance planes for Egypt and after withdrawing from the Military Industrialization Authority.

It is not surprising, however, that even after the suspension of relations Saudi Arabia remained concerned with Egypt's military strength. The Saudis were well aware that Egypt's peace agreement with Israel had not changed the reality of their own dependence on Egypt. They did not need the Egyptian media to remind them of their weak spot. "In a personal letter" to the Saudi Crown Prince which the editor of *Ruz al-Yusuf* published in January 1980, he wrote:

> If I may give some advice, I would like to say to Fahd: Beware of arrogance, don't judge by externals! Learn the moral lesson of what happened to the Shah: you must know that the Shah had the same kind of wealth as you have, and also that the Shah had many times the amount of arms that you have purchased with your petro-dollars. All this did not help him when his time came! [270]

Saudi Arabia was interested in a continued policy of cooperation and strategic consultation with Egypt after the peace agreement, in order to maintain regional stability and to keep the Soviets out. Somalia continued to receive shipments of Egyptian arms, as of 1977, and Egypt even threatened to intervene or to send armed forces in the event that Ethiopia invaded Somalia. The same went for Zaire, to whom Egypt shipped arms, pilots, military advisors and instructors, after the Angolan invasion of Shaba Province;[271] Chad, Morocco and Sudan, which received Egyptian military aid;[272] and the Afghan rebels, who received joint Egyptian–Saudi–American aid. Egypt assisted in the transfer of American funds to the Afghan rebels after the Soviet invasion, in training some of them in boot camps, as well as supplying Egyptian arms – mainly Soviet or spare parts manufactured in Egypt.[273]

Even if the AOC wished, in all sincerity, to also suspend its relations with Egypt on the informal level, events such as the Soviet invasion of Afghanistan and especially the Iran–Iraq War ruled out this possibility. Egypt's strategic contribution to the conservative Gulf States, after the peace agreement, was not theoretical, but real. The Iranian–Shi'ite threat was tangible, and the Gulf States could have done very little, if anything at all, to defend themselves against an Iranian assault on their oil fields. Sadat emphasized that peace with Israel did not nullify Egypt's commitment to defend other Arab states. After the Soviet invasion of Afghanistan, Sadat and his spokesmen declared that Egypt, and only Egypt, could and would defend the Gulf region against any danger.[274]

With the outbreak of the Iran–Iraq War (September 22, 1980), Egypt proved its strategic value. The AOC needed clarification from the Egyptian policy-makers concerning Egypt's position on the war. When the war broke out, Egypt declared itself neutral, but Sadat – although he never stopped his scathing personal attacks against the AOC leaders until the day he died[275] – stated, tentatively at first, then overtly, that Egypt would assist the oil countries in the event they were exposed to external threats.[276] In November 1980, Ahmed Badawi, the Egyptian Minister of Defense, declared that Egypt would help the Gulf States in strengthening their defenses,[277] and during that month an Egyptian military delegation arrived in Riyadh to discuss military coordination between Riyadh and Cairo, in view of the war in the Gulf.[278] In February 1981 the Kuwaiti *al-Siyasa* quoted Mubarak on its front-page, stating: "The Gulf is full of communists and we already warned them . . . we will immediately defend any Arab nation exposed to threats and danger."[279] Various reports hinted at further secret contacts between the higher echelons of Egyptian and Saudi politics[280] during the Sadat period, but there is no further evidence to substantiate these reports.

Egypt also offered Iraq substantial military aid. In January 1981, Sadat was still denying reports on arms supplies to Iraq.[281] But on April 1, 1981 Cairo Radio confirmed that weapons had been sold, stating that in contrast "to those who tried to harm Egypt," it would not turn its back on the Arab people. In response, the *Iraqi News Agency* admitted, on the same day, that Iraq had purchased military equipment from Egypt through a third party.[282] The first arms shipments to Iraq were flown by air shuttle from Cairo and Amman, and from there it was transferred to Iraq. But with an increasing need for arms, Iraq dropped the secrecy of the shipments, and Iraqi cargo planes landed in Cairo to load military equipment.[283] Israel's attack on the Iraqi nuclear reactor in the second half of 1981 further encouraged the Saudi trend to a reconciliation with Egypt. Saudi Arabia felt threatened, especially after Israeli aircraft penetrated its airspace on their way to Baghdad, and the Saudi AWACS had not been able to spot these planes. In July 1983 Egypt agreed to put sophisticated early-warning planes at Saudi Arabia's disposal, in case of a threat to the Kingdom.[284]

President Sadat was assassinated on October 6, 1981. His successor, Muhammad Hosni Mubarak, paved the way for better relations with the AOC. Saudi newspapers called for the Arab countries to help Mubarak "turn over a new page," and to help Egypt to return to the Arab fold. Moreover, the Saudi media praised Mubarak, who "ordered the Egyptian media to stop the war of words against the Arab countries."[285] The Saudis saw in Mubarak's rise to power a convenient opportunity for a further rapprochement between their countries. In an article on the front-page of *al-Madina*, which regularly expressed government policy, the Arab states were called to avoid putting pressure on Egypt to repudiate the Camp David agreement, and to give Mubarak – "with his clean Arab past" – a year "to arrange matters in Egypt." The paper claimed that Mubarak could not renunciate the agreement "for several understandable reasons," mainly the imminent Israeli pullout from Sinai.[286]

After Mubarak came to power, Abu Ghazala declared that his country was willing to assist the oil countries,[287] and that Egypt considered the Gulf as providing added depth to the country's strategic defenses from the east.[288] Mubarak stated in April 1982, that "the security of the Gulf is part of Egyptian strategic security and it will not tolerate a threat to the stability of the region."[289] Abu Ghazala and Kamal Hasan 'Ali added, hinting broadly, that Egypt had no problem in defending the Gulf except for the financial issue,[290] and that "the Egyptian military should be reinforced for the sake of regional security."[291]

Egypt supplied Iraq with ammunition, military equipment, cannon, tanks, planes, missiles, technical staff, training in its military institutions and military advisors. The value of arms shipped by Egypt was evaluated by foreign diplomats at more than $1.5 billion up to mid-1982. Egypt also supplied arms to Oman and through it to the other Gulf States. In 1983 Kuwait negotiated directly for the purchase of 20 Alpha Jet planes manufactured in Egypt.[292] Egypt also acted as arms broker for Iraq, and agreed to the transfer through its territory of European armaments destined for Iraq.[293] The AOC paid Egypt, both directly and indirectly, for the supply of most arms to Iraq.

The Gulf States wanted a specific Egyptian guarantee that its forces would fight in the war: Yusuf al-'Alawi, the Omani Foreign Minister, flew to Egypt in late April 1982, after a meeting of the GCC, followed by Qabus, the Sultan of Oman, in the first half of May 1982. Egypt turned down their request,[294] but it was willing to allow the participation of its citizens in the war. However, their policy-makers took care to make it quite clear that Egyptian citizens working in Iraq would choose to participate in the war of their own free will, without any official Egyptian guidance or consent whatsoever.[295] Moreover, Kuwait and the other Gulf States secretly employed Egyptian military advisors on personal contracts.[296]

## Summary

Aid granted to Egypt varied in sums, and in the reasons it was given, which differed from country to country. Libyan aid to Egypt in the years 1967–73 (principally military aid) was relatively large and was granted to help Nasser with his internal and external problems. Gaddafi tried to fulfill a central role in the Arab world by influencing Egypt. Alan McGregor has quoted Gaddafi as stating in January 1973: "Egypt is a country without a leader and I am a leader without a country."[297] The conservative oil countries mainly wanted to moderate Egypt's political attitudes; to guarantee that they would be defended by the Egyptian military, if necessary; to gain active Egyptian assistance in rejecting the communist influence; to be able to employ Egyptian manpower; and to keep their pan-Arab image. The AOC were dependent on Egypt as much as, perhaps more than, Egypt depended on their aid.

The small states – mainly the UAE and Qatar – provided aid to Egypt in gratitude to their "big sister," Saudi Arabia, whose policies they often followed. In spite of the good relations existing between Saudi Arabia and its neighbors, the leaders of the UAE and Qatar had not forgotten their sister's attempts to subdue the Gulf region in the 1920s and the many territorial disputes between them and Saudi Arabia even as late as the mid-1970s (Oman, Abu-Dhabi). The smaller states believed that, if they provided aid to Egypt, it would come to their help when necessary. Some of them also wanted Egypt to continue to fulfill the leading role in the Arab world, as opposed to Saudi Arabia, which feared Egyptian hegemony and did everything possible to reduce Egyptian influence in the inter-Arab arena.[298]

The aid meted out by the AOC to Egypt was calculated and was originally intended to serve their own interests, not to support the Egyptian economy. As indicated by Tuma, the rich countries were not bothered by the gap in the standard of living between "the Arab brothers," and they had no intention of changing the status quo and of narrowing the gap in favor of the poor countries in the region. In order to maintain the distance between the rich and poor Arab nations, the rich countries' aid to the poor countries was minimal, or it was granted for specific projects.[299] Egypt illustrated both these intentions: aid was indeed relatively minimal, coming in "trickles"; and from 1976 on, the AOC concentrated their aid through the GFDE and demanded that Egypt apply the greater part of this aid to specific development plans. In their speeches the AOC leaders agreed on their duty to support their "Egyptian sister," but they disagreed on the extent of their aid, its direction, its targets and its use. Sometimes, during crises in the Egyptian economy, the AOC increased their aid, fearing that these crises could overflow into their territory.

After imposing an economic and political boycott on Egypt, events in the Middle East, especially the Gulf War and the Iranian threat it exposed, gave the AOC leaders a good illustration of why they continue to cooperate with Egypt, even if contacts were held under a veil of secrecy. As mentioned by Quandt, whatever ups and downs there may be in the relations between Saudi Arabia and Egypt, "Saudi Arabia cannot ignore Egypt."[300] Since the suspension of diplomatic relations between Egypt and the AOC, there existed a separation between political and economic considerations in their relations, and as time passed, their political relations grew stronger – albeit informally. In fact, these bilateral relations existed behind the scenes on an almost continuous basis.[301] Kerr compared the transformation in the relations between Egypt and Saudi Arabia after the peace treaty to that of a divorced couple still in "friendly" contact.[302] The other oil countries also maintained their relations with Egypt, and they openly declared the Arab world's need for Egypt. The Kuwaiti *al-Ra'y al-'Amm* wrote in April 1984: "One of the fatal mistakes was the idea that getting rid of Egypt would solve Arab problems. But... Egypt is vital to the Arab world and being excluded from the Arab League does not harm it, but it does harm the Arab world."[303] Sheikh Isa Ibn Salman al-Khalifa, Prince of Bahrain, added:

> People talk about suspension and renewal of relations with Egypt. Who can break off relations with Egypt? . . . The question of diplomatic relations is nothing more than just a formality. What matters are the real relations between Egypt and the Arab countries. These relations can never be severed, no matter what happens. Who can suspend relations with Egypt, the backbone of the Arab people? Look at conditions in the Arab world without Egypt. The return of Egypt to the Arab world – which is a must – will again strengthen the Arab people.[304]

In spite of these declarations, the AOC leaders took care to emphasize the importance of an Arab consensus, as mentioned, for example, by Sa'ud al-Faysal, the Saudi Foreign Minister: "We want Egypt to return to the Arab fold, but it is essential that its return should not cause a new rupture in the Arab nation. This is also the position taken by the [other] Gulf States."[305]

The economic relations between the AOC and Egypt did not cease after the peace agreement, and even increased in some areas. Official Arab assistance to Egypt did not stop completely, although it was diminished somewhat. The AOC transferred aid to Egypt covertly, and after 1984 this aid became steadily more overt. Aid was provided by inter-Arab bodies and by political aid institutions, such as: the African Development Bank, the Kuwaiti Development Fund, the Arab Gulf Project for aid to UN organizations and further direct aid from Saudi Arabia and Kuwait. In the Arab media, published mainly in Europe, news items started appearing from early 1981 on topics such as: "Arab monies are finding their way back [to Egypt]"; "Egypt's economy is renewing its connections with the Arab world"; "Increase in Egyptian exports to Arab countries in 1980"; and many similar items. Private investments continued to flow into the Egyptian economy. As for commerce – not only it did not stop, it even expanded in certain cases, as did Arab tourism to Egypt. The oil countries continued employing Egyptians and even increased their number, which caused a significant augmentation of Egypt's foreign currency revenues.

Covert cooperation between the Saudis and Egypt existed, and in fact it hardly ever stopped at all after Sadat came to power. In July 1986 *al-Kifah al-'Arabi* wrote that an agreement for inter-state military cooperation had been reached, one of its clauses referring to the dispatch of Egyptian forces to Saudi Arabia in case of need.[306] Mubarak referred to the nature of the covert relations between Egypt and the AOC, declaring in January 1987: "I am not interested in revealing all our cards on the subject of our support of the Gulf States."[307] In the first four months of 1987 – just before the assembly of the Islamic Congress which convened in Kuwait and afterwards – Egyptian officials declared that Kuwait and Saudi Arabia "would purchase" Egypt's military debts to the West, so that Egypt could defray its debts at easier terms. Moreover the AOC offered Egypt large amounts of aid in return for its commitment to stand by them in times of need.[308] And so, after the 1987 riots in

Mecca, Egyptian anti-terrorist forces arrived in Saudi Arabia, which openly expressed its gratitude to Egypt for its helpful position in this critical period.[309]

Strategic–political considerations were first and foremost the AOC's guidelines for providing aid. But did their wealth and aid give them any political influence on the decision-making process of the confrontation countries in the region that received the aid? The answer is no. Egypt signed a separate peace treaty with Israel, and this in spite of the AOC's threats to suspend aid. There were some isolated cases of the AOC succeeding in neutralizing the radicalism of revolutionary Arab states, but their wealth never managed to give them any decisive influence on the decisions made in any Arab country. It is true that in several cases, in order to attract petro-dollars to its economy, Egypt adopted a policy similar to that of the AOC, but this was first and foremost to promote its own interests, like getting rid of the centers of communist influence in the region. On these occasions, as mentioned by Tahsin Bashir, Egypt's leaders did not object to presenting the facts in such a way that Saudi Arabia's role in pushing out the Soviets seemed larger than it was in reality.

When referring to the limitations of the Arab oil countries' influence, by dint of their aid, on Egypt's position, we must first of all take into account the size of the recipient states and their demographic and military power; and second, Egypt's relations with the US. Egypt's economic dependence on the AOC was not one-sided: the AOC were themselves dependent on Egypt for manpower and its military forces. Starting from the mid-seventies, especially since the peace treaty with Israel, Egypt had secured an alternative source of aid, in the form of American assistance, and it was no longer dependent solely on its Arab "patrons." (As a matter of fact, any country in this region could receive (at that time) aid from one of the two Great Powers, a fact which limited the influence of Arab aid on the outlining of the recipient countries' policy.)

One argument dictates that Egypt did not allow its decision-making process to be "mortgaged" because of the – in its opinion – limited aid it received from the AOC. But even if aid had been much more substantial, the picture would not have been very different. It is possible to measure this through other states that received aid from the AOC: "radical" Syria and "conservative" Jordan both received significant amounts of aid after the 1973 war. And at the second Baghdad conference (March 1979), it was decided to increase aid to these countries substantially. This assistance did not go hand in hand with political reconciliation between the regimes. Moreover, Syria supported Iran in the Iran–Iraq War, and at the same time it continued to receive aid from the conservative oil states, in spite of its totally contradictory position to that of Saudi Arabia and of the Gulf security council members, who considered the Islamic regime in Iran a direct threat to their stability. Syria, which received considerable aid, and relative to its population more than Egypt, maintained its alliance with the USSR, although this was clearly opposed to Saudi Arabia's interests. Also South Yemen, a recipient of Saudi aid, continued its connections with the USSR. Other countries, much weaker than Syria, acted contrary to the AOC's position, in spite of the aid they received from them. For instance, Mauritania made a separate peace treaty with the Polisario guerrillas in Marocco, although Kuwait threatened to reduce aid[310] and Saudi Arabia did not succeed, through its aid, in persuading Algeria to stop supporting the Polisario front in the Western Sahara.[311]

These facts illustrate that aid supplied by the Gulf States had a very limited capability in terms of influencing the positions of the recipient states. Aid was provided as a sort of defense mechanism, a guarantee against invasion or attack. As a Saudi source exclaimed: "How can you demand conditions for aid that you are granting to a country, when your aim is to prevent its taking subversive action against you?"[312] This does not mean that aid was not accompanied by petitions and requests, but, in terms of influence over the recipient state's political make-up, the oil countries' aid was extremely limited. The principal explanation for this situation is very simple. A country whose sole power lies in its financial wealth cannot enforce its demands by that standard alone. The country needs additional elements of power, such as an efficient and strong army, technological sophistication and a large and developed population. Even the Soviet Union, as Rubinstein indicated, had only limited influence on Egypt's key decisions.[313] Furthermore, the AOC's strictly limited influence stems from the fact that they themselves were dependent on Egypt, for security as well as for Egyptian manpower, and also because of their external and internal vulnerability.[314]

# 5

# *Egypt and the Arab Petro-Dollar Influence*

A nation's interests are shaped by political, economic, ideological and strategic considerations. *Vis-à-vis* the Arab world, Egypt was guided by multiple, often contradictory considerations: it sought to lead Arab nationalism, whilst struggling at the same time with its own considerable domestic difficulties. This chapter examines whether Egypt formed its national and international policy with one eye on attracting some of the petro-dollars of the conservative oil countries, and if so, to what degree; what steps Egyptian policy-makers took to get the AOC to share their wealth with it; how they acted after the AOC agreed to share their revenues with Egypt; and how they acted when it became clear to them that their hopes for what they perceived as a fair distribution of wealth were dashed.

Egyptian foreign policy was not conducted solely in accordance with economic considerations. However, economic considerations, and the will to secure a substantial part of the AOC's wealth, played a central, if not decisive, role in recent events in Egypt's history and that of the whole region, especially during the regimes of Sadat and Mubarak.[1] In "The October Paper" Sadat argued that Arab unity "had passed from an obligatory framework to practical, viable steps . . . mainly in the field of economic cooperation";[2] in a speech in July 1976 he said that "the economy is the kingpin of our policy";[3] and in June 1977 he compared the struggle to rehabilitate the Egyptian economy to the October War of 1973: "the struggle to build the Egyptian economy is absolutely comparable to the October War, as without building an economy, we will not be independent, we will continue to be subject to those who pay us for the purchase of food, and we will not be able to enjoy either our economy or our freedom."[4] Moreover, Kamal Hasan 'Ali emphasized the importance of economic considerations, mentioning that Egypt's foreign relations "are determined in accordance with its economic interests . . . and separating policy from the economy or from culture negates their meaning."[5]

## The ideological field: Egypt's demand for a new regional distribution of oil revenues

### *The period before June 1967*
The ideological dispute over the distribution of the oil revenues between the rich

and the poor Arab states dates back to far before the 1973 escalation of oil prices. It broke out not only between Egypt and the AOC, but also among other states and bodies in the Arab world. The philosophy of the pan-Arabs – the most ardent among them coming mostly from non-producing states (Gaddafi being an exception in this sense) – considered oil as jointly owned wealth, belonging to the entire Arab nation, and therefore its purpose was to serve the needs of the *Ummah*. In the economic field this meant that the oil profits should be divided up among the Arab nation, under the slogan *"Zayt al-'Arab lil-'Arab."* Emile Bustani said that the future welfare of the Arabs depended largely on the logical division of oil wealth, and in the 1950s he proposed establishing a fund, to which the AOC would contribute 5 percent of their revenues, for the welfare of the entire Arab nation.[6] The poor Arab states, which did not produce oil and through whose territory the oil flowed, demanded compensation for this from the AOC. They declared that Arab oil could never reach its destination without their cooperation; as far as they were concerned, the oil transportation industry was an integral part of the oil industry, and their cooperation enabled the oil producers to carry out development projects.[7] Therefore, they had every right to benefit from oil revenues.

Egypt's stand in the 1950s and 1960s on aid stemming from oil revenues was, in the opinion of Hirst, ambiguous. Though it tried to create an impression that it was not interested in profiting from the AOC's oil revenues, it savagely attacked the rulers of the AOC for their corruption. Hirst is not quite correct: Nasser, as in the framework of his discussion in the "Arab Circle" in *The Philosophy of the Revolution*, attributed great importance to oil, which belonged to the whole Arab nation.[8] Egypt also threatened to obtain by force what it saw as being owed: at the first Arab Oil Congress, which convened in Cairo in April 1959 – initiated by Egypt – the Egyptian delegation turned to the Kuwaiti delegation and declared: "We are not asking for favors, but our national rights, and if the AOC refuse to share with us God's gift to them, then the time will come when we will take our share by force."[9]

Up to the early 1960s, although Egypt was not a rich country, it did provide financial aid to the Arab countries (e.g. Jordan) and technical assistance through delegations of teachers and medical teams. Egypt financed the lion's share of the Arab League's budget, from the start of the League's activities until the early 1960s,[10] and in the 1970s, Egypt turned its past generosity into a propaganda weapon. As an example, Sadat stated: "Before they found oil, Kuwait used to receive teachers, books, notebooks and erasers [from Egypt]. [After the oil price rise] they want to starve the Egyptian people . . . [notwithstanding that the price of] oil has quadrupled at [the expense] of our sons' blood in Sinai."[11]

## June 1967–October 1973

Just after the June 1967 War, an Egyptian spokesman implied that it was the AOC's duty to come to Egypt's assistance. Heikal argued that "we have no choice but to apply the oil revenues to development in a comprehensive and integral Arab framework."[12] At first Nasser did not warm to the idea of having to ask for aid from the conservative oil states, but he was forced to change his attitude in the wake of the deteriorating economic situation in Egypt, the war of attrition and the rise to power in Libya of Gaddafi. At the Rabat Summit in late 1969, Nasser insisted that the

AOC increase their aid to the confrontation states, and in May 1970 he expressed his disappointment with the Arabs, stating that losses in the 1967 war cost the Egyptian economy £180 million, while it received only £95 million, so that it had to cover its own losses.[13]

When Sadat rose to power, he talked a lot about oil wealth, and he implied that it was the AOC's duty to assist Egypt. The media and the Egyptian intellectuals discussed heavily this subject. The intellectuals and the Egyptian leadership raised two central arguments for the sharing of wealth: first, in the name of "justice" in the Arab world; and second, as a sacrifice to bear the burden of the struggle against Israel. Their main arguments emphasized Egypt's human and material sacrifice for the sake of the entire "Arab nation," its cardinal contribution to the build-up of Arab wealth following the 1973 war and the duty of the AOC to compensate and to assist Egypt.

In June 1971, while comparing Egypt and Israel, Sadat said that Israel received all its requirements from the US, "from bread to Phantom planes," while "there is nobody who gives us cheques every year or at fixed periods . . . Arab aid we received lately was for £109 million [only] as compensation for loss of revenues from the Suez Canal."[14] In September 1971 Sadat expressed the hope that "more oil capital would flow to us for the financing of tourism [projects] and the construction of magnificent buildings, to enable us, as a state, to dedicate our resources to housing projects for the masses."[15] Sadat spoke with moderation, but Egyptian writers and politicians were not so moderate. The elite of Egyptian writers and intellectuals, such as Tawfiq al-Hakim, Louis Awad, Hassin Fuzi, Lutfi al-Khuli and Ahmad Baha Al-Din declared that "Egypt must fight for its honor and its interests and not be dependent on Arab chivalry"; "Egypt paid a high price and this was not appreciated by the Arabs"; and that "the Arabs want Egyptians to die, so they can live."[16]

In 1972 Egyptian writers and politicians brought up, with renewed vigor, the problem of sharing the burden of the wars with Israel, generated by Arab interests and for Arab benefit, and they claimed that the AOC should compensate Egypt for its sacrifices. Anis Mansur wrote: "We did everything we could. Thousands of our sons have fallen in the defense of Egypt and the Arabs. What did the other [Arabs] do?"[17] Shazli, the Egyptian Chief of Staff, attacked the Arab countries who were not on the front line, for not providing adequate financial support. According to him, Egypt spent 50 percent of total defense expenditure of the Arab states, notwithstanding that Egypt's part of the GNP among the Arab nation came to only 26 percent.[18]

## November 1973–November 1977

The October 1973 War inspired the Egyptian policy-makers and intellectuals, who found a new spirit and enthusiasm in the wake of the conflict. Tawfiq al-Hakim said in November 1973, that Egypt "had erased its shame";[19] Naguib Mahfouz said, that the day of October 6 "testified to Arab unity, such as had not been seen in Arab history since Muhammad's mission";[20] and al-Tali'a outlined great plans for the development of the Egyptian economy in its April 1974 edition, which would be carried out, it wrote, by applying a substantial part of the AOC's wealth to aid and investments in Egypt. However, disappointment over the low amount of aid provided to the Egyptian economy was soon rife. In an article in November 1974, Yussuf Idris presented the economic distress of the Egyptian citizen. He accused the AOC of not doing its best to alleviate this distress, remarking ironically: "We will continue dreaming until money falls out of the heavens or from the oil countries."[21] In early 1975 *al-Tali'a* changed its tone, and in the February and March issues that year, the optimism of 1974 was replaced with open disappointment over the aid given by the AOC, who (it was claimed) preferred to turn their backs on the Egyptian people, and to invest their money in the countries of the West. Fuad Mursi said: "It is a mistake to see the AOC's investments in a different light from that of private investors. These countries are interested only in profits without taking into account the purpose or the quality of the investment."[22]

The war and its results strengthened Egypt's claims to regional wealth. Intellectuals and politicians claimed that the quadrupling of oil prices came about because of their victory in the war, and that the oil countries had become rich on Egypt's back. Another consequence of the war was that, with the rise in prices of oil and raw materials worldwide, another burden had been added to Egypt's balance of payments.[23] Egyptian spokesmen spoke of the sharing of oil wealth as a God-given right, and occasionally reminded the world of Egypt's many casualties who fell on the battlefield in the name of the Arab cause. Makram Ahmad mentioned the high price the Egyptian people paid in exchange for Egypt's status and its function as the leader of Arab nationalism:

> The fact that we alone bear the heavy burden of Arab nationalism is to blame for our [economic and social] problems, and not the Egyptian people and we ask the Arabs: why do they delay the development of Arab power? And where are they investing those millions and billions [of dollars]? And until when will the Egyptian people alone bear this burden, while others are satisfied with giving aid and with [minimal] participation?[24]

Egypt felt that its participation in a war for the Arab cause resulted in massive Egyptian losses while the Gulf States profited handsomely from such distress. Egypt felt that the rich Arabs wanted it, as 'Ajami indicated, to starve alone, to die alone, to fight alone, and to go bankrupt alone.[25] In December 1974, Wahid Rif'at made a presentation of the crises and the economic problems of the Egyptian people, and he quoted Prime Minister 'Abd al-'Aziz Hijazi: "We have almost become the poorest people in the region, while our fellow Arabs in the neighboring countries are becoming steadily richer, with a burgeoning construction and development activity and signs of material prosperity."[26] The Egyptian press expressed its own anger at its Arab neighbors, writing that: "Our patience is wearing thin" and "we should not allow them to continue to ignore the great historical sacrifice [of the Egyptians]."[27] The Egyptian ideological struggle to mobilize aid had two main goals that, through extensive media publicity, became widely known: first, gaining part of the oil wealth to alleviate economic hardship, and second, as indicated by Wien, to turn the existing fury and frustration of the Egyptian masses, suffering under difficult economic conditions, toward the rich Arab states, who had not provided aid to Egypt in spite of their great wealth.[28]

Sadat chose not to commit himself to either an anti-Arab extremist position, or to side too much with the Arabs. In a speech he made in October 1974 before the People's Council, he said: "The war continues with all arms and the concurrent necessary expenses . . . in spite of our Arab brothers' help . . . and we are deeply grateful to them . . . we must all realize that we carry this heavy burden, not only of sweat and toil, but we also spend one third of our national income . . . for the benefit of the whole Arab nation."[29] At another occasion he stated: "There are some people who think that it [the aid] is not much, but I believe that this is a good beginning, auguring well for the future."[30] Sadat further mentioned the minimal Arab investments in Egypt and stated that the AOC "must establish something similar to the Marshall Plan [for Egypt]."[31]

The "semi-official" Egyptian press proposed that the Arab League convene a special meeting to assess Egypt's sacrifices for the Arab cause since the June 1967 war, in order to ascertain "equitable" financial responsibility of the AOC governments.[32] This was after Egypt had claimed many times, that Arab aid had amounted to only about 10 percent of all economic damages incurred by Egypt as a result of the wars with Israel.[33] 'Abd al-Fattah Qindil brought up for discussion the matter of oil revenues, stating that "Kuwait contributed 6 percent of its oil revenues to the aid funds . . . Saudi Arabia contributed 2.7 percent . . . and Libya 2.2 percent." Hence, Qindil indicated, "the confrontation states alone sustained heavy sacrifices, borne by their citizens, their most important possession. Since the beginning of the conflict, Egypt has suffered more than 50,000 casualties, many of them highly educated people."[34] On the subject of losses, Egyptian spokesmen remarked bitterly, that "the Arabs are determined to fight to the last Egyptian."[35] The controversy over Egyptian losses was contrasted with the AOC's wealth – "petro-dollar" opposite "petro-blood" – a theory advanced by Lutfi al-Khuli, which was hotly discussed in the mid-1970s:

> Petro-blood and petro-dollars – two faces of a new currency ruling the Arab world today . . . at a time when the AOC have attained enormous wealth, the Arab states fighting the Zionist, imperialist enemy have fallen into an abyss of poverty and misery . . . [the AOC] converted every drop of blood spilt in Sinai, on the Golan Heights and in Palestine into increased oil prices . . . up to 400 percent in less than a year . . . the Egyptian people economized on its essential needs and its daily bread by the sweat of its brow . . . the fourth war [October] left many parties rolling in wealth and others continued to live in dire poverty. The first ones picked the fruit, while the others reaped the whirlwind.[36]

The Egyptian authors sought to invoke other arguments, fanning the flames of ideological conflict. They claimed that Iran, a non-Arab country, had been more generous with them than their Arab brothers. During a visit to Egypt in early 1975, Saudi Arabia's Faysal had granted $100 million to Egypt. Several weeks before, the Iranian Shah had guaranteed Egypt a credit of $1 billion.[37] The claim that non-Arab Iran granted more aid than the Arab sister states, carried more weight than pan-Arab ideology, which had actually been weakened during Sadat's reign. In the "October Paper" Sadat emphasized the rehabilitation process of Egyptian nationalism, the concept of "the Egyptian personality," and Egyptian historical continuity,[38] but when Egyptian leaders referred to Arab aid, they chose, rather conveniently to emphasize Arab unity.

In the first quarter of 1976, the ideological campaign stopped almost completely. In January Sadat announced that in 1976 Egypt would need aid that would amount to at least $4 billion,[39] and he hoped to receive substantial aid from the oil countries. In March 1976 he made the following statement before the People's Council, while on a tour of the AOC:

> On your behalf and on behalf of the entire people I want to thank the six Arab countries, who not only agreed to participate for many years in a fund of billions to save the Egyptian economy, but also assisted us during our visit to them, although I had not asked them to do so, as I had gone there to negotiate long-term loans for the execution of joint projects, but on top of that they granted us immediate aid.[40]

"The billions fund" Sadat had been alluding to was the Gulf Fund for the Development of Egypt (GFDE). Sadat was optimistic about the future of this Fund. He believed that its establishment would help the Egyptian economy recover from its serious predicament, and he hoped that once and for all a remedy would be found for its economic malaise. At a military base in Suez, Sadat said: "On my last visit to the Arab countries, we agreed on a solution to the economic difficulties that we have been burdened with since 1962 . . . so [we can] revive our economy";[41] to the editors of the London *Times* and the French *L'Expansion* Sadat stated that Arab aid would finally extricate Egypt from its economic straits.[42] The Fund was set up in July 1976, but Sadat was bitterly disappointed, as the Fund's capital for a period of five years was $2 billion only, compared to the $12 billion he had demanded. Instead of receiving serious aid which would extricate him – so he hoped – once and for all from his economic difficulties, he received "trickles" of aid. After this event, Sadat took the unprecedented step of publicly expressing bitterness. In a speech made to mark the twenty-fourth anniversary of the revolution, while expressing his appreciation for Arab aid, he immediately added: "I definitely want to say to our brothers, that the fund has taken on a totally different character from what we envisaged."[43] The AOC reacted angrily to his words, and Sadat moderated his criticism. In an interview to the Kuwaiti *al-Siyasa* he said: "Egypt needs the sum mentioned [$12 billion] . . . this sum is not exaggerated. If they could help us, we would be grateful; if they do not want to do so, it's their choice . . . I am not interested in making an issue of the matter."[44]

The Egyptian media relented for a short time from criticizing the Fund, as they waited to see its real contribution, when they saw the final amount, they started to attack the AOC again. Egyptian author 'Abd al-Rahman al-Sharqawi lambasted the oil countries for widening the gap between the rich and the poor Arab nations, notwithstanding that Egypt safeguarded their political, military and economic stability, and that it had sacrificed "the blood of its holy ones" and its citizens' standard of living for the Arab cause. Al-Sharqawi also attacked the AOC for making investments in the West and not in Egypt, which offered the Arabs "greater profits and . . . the honor of participating in Arab development." Al-Sharqawi ended on an almost threatening note: "Oil is not an inexhaustible source, so do not put your unreserved hopes on it, as there is an end to everything ."[45] In this atmosphere of accusations, Egypt also protested against the AOC's conditions for aid. *Al-Ahram al-Iqtisadi* called these conditions "disgraceful,"[46] and Ibrahim Nafi' – the economic editor of *al-Ahram* at the time – wrote: "It is inconceivable that a rich Arab country . . . would impose such conditions on a poor Arab country."[47]

The food riots in Egypt on January 18–19, 1977 caused immediate criticism against the AOC. On January 20, 1977, Tawfiq al-Hakim warned that any conflagration in Egypt would cause those "sitting on wells of gold to sit on wells of fire." In order to prevent a revolt in their oil fields, Hakim added: "The Arabs must finance 80 percent of the Egyptian military budget."[48] The Egyptian press published reports of Egypt's casualties in its wars with Israel, and the minimal Arab contribution,[49] and there were many publications condemning Arab nationalism. Naguib Mahfouz asked: "Why should our nationalism create hunger and suffering only? . . . I implore with all my strength that we abandon the Arabs if they have decided to abandon us."[50] The *Ruz al-Yusuf* concurred, writing:

> Who would believe that after more than twenty-five years in which Egypt was the leader of the Arab Nationalist movement . . . the people of Egypt are again wondering if they are Arabs or only Egyptians. If they are Arabs, why are the other Arabs threatening them, and if our people are only Egyptian, why do they accept responsibility, as if they were Arabs? And if they [our people] accept Arab responsibility, why don't the rest of the Arabs acknowledge the Arab character of the struggle? And if the other Arabs do not acknowledge the Arab character of the campaign, why don't the Egyptians just acknowledge their Egyptian character – and accept a unilateral solution?[51]

*Al-Ahram al-Iqtisadi* drew comparisons between South Africa and Egypt, blaming the "economic apartheid" in Egypt, with "new groups" enjoying enormous riches, while at the same time most of the people lacked a basic standard of living. Among the new groups it mentioned the Arab tourists, "visiting Egypt with great purchasing power, dividing and ruining Egyptian society from within."[52] Egyptian officials reminded the leaders of the Arab countries that their past prosperity was due, at least in part, to Egyptian aid.[53] Nafi' argued that, up to 1967, Egypt extensively assisted Arab states, in finance, education, enriching the socio-cultural anatomy of Arab life, while in Egypt's hour of need "the AOC have forgotten the aid they received from it and they only speak about the financial aid they granted Egypt."[54]

## November 1977–1979

After the Arab states' criticism of Sadat's peace initiative, an ideological debate emerged in the press, engineered by Tawfiq al-Hakim, in which the author called for Egyptian "neutrality" in the events unfolding in the Middle East. His theory was based on the notion that the Arab sister states urged Egypt to partake in the wars, but they did not share their riches with it: "the way to peace and quiet," he said, "is by neutrality." Al-Hakim emphasized that Egypt had paid its Arab dues, but it had not received its Arab rights, so "that Egypt had squandered its life and its money, it had become impoverished and had become the servant in the houses of the wealthy Arab countries."[55] Al-Hakim also said that "some of the states are thinking about peace conferences, and others – about oil conferences."[56]

Besides al-Hakim, other writers were similarly in favor of ditching the concept of Arab unity; Naguib Mahfouz expressed a similar sentiment after the food riots, and Louis 'Awad also supported Hakim's approach. In April 1978, 'Awad said that Egypt had every right to take care of its own affairs, even if this would necessitate "turning its back on the Arab world, to facilitate matters for itself . . . I agree with Tawfiq al-Hakim when he says that the statement that the Arabs are one people with a common interest – has no basis in reality." 'Awad called for unification of the Egyptian identity "to solve the problems. Doesn't Egypt – after the blood it has spilt, the money it has spent and the victims it has sacrificed – have the right to reexamine its strategy?"[57] It should be noted, that there were also people opposed to al-Hakim's approach, and a short statement by Yussuf Idris illustrated this sharply: "Pardon me, my father, teacher and friend – Tawfiq al-Hakim – no!"[58]

On May 1, 1979, Sadat attacked the Saudi regime, for the first time since the days of Nasser,[59] but his attacks had really started much earlier, going back to the first Baghdad conference (November 1978). Then, Sadat had said: "The Egyptian people are not at all like the 'nouveaux riches' and their logic, according to which money is everything . . . the Egyptian people . . . had a culture many thousands of years before the other Arabs awakened from their slumber."[60] Sadat accused the AOC of "investing in the West," adding: "They deposit [the petro-dollars] in Jewish banks – it is no secret that the Jews control the world's economy . . . – and I have to borrow their Arab money at 12 or 15 percent and pay the interest to Jews."[61] Sadat further criticized the AOC leaders for squandering their people's money on matters that would not help the Arab people's welfare, and that they were depositing petro-dollars in secret accounts. These funds, it was argued, were to be used after the people in the AOC finally realized, that their governments were totally corrupt, in order to buy them (the populace) out.[62]

## 1979–1984

After the peace treaty with the Israelis and its ratification, the Egyptian ideological attack switched its focus from the AOC's duty to compensate them, instead concentrating ferocious criticism against the oil countries' governments. After the second Baghdad conference (March 1979), during which the resolutions for the economic and diplomatic boycott of Egypt were confirmed, Sadat launched an unprecedented sharp attack on the AOC rulers, starting with the King of Saudi Arabia. In his speech on May 1, 1979 (after the severing of diplomatic relations between Egypt and Saudi Arabia), he accused the Saudis of bribing the Arab countries to break off their relations with Egypt:

"The Arabs who broke off relations with us told me that they did so after being bribed by Saudi Arabia. Who benefited from this? The Alawi's in Syria? The Takriti family in Iraq, who threatened to attack and to occupy Kuwait? . . . Suppose Iraq attacks Kuwait tomorrow, what would be Saudi Arabia's position? What will the new leaders of the Arab world [Saudi Arabia] do? . . . Everyone must know his worth . . . Saudi Arabia had a place in the sun in Faysal's time, but these people are losing their place."[63] Sadat's attack was so fierce and confrontational that the Saudis, who usually did not react to these attacks, retorted with criticism of their own, stating that Sadat was "a liar" and that his vitriolic abuse was apparently caused by "mental problems."[64] Until the day he died, Sadat and his team did not stop throwing harsh criticism at the AOC leadership. The Americans did actually succeed – through their mediations between Fahd and Sadat[65] – in moderating the arguments and temporarily stopping them, but they were powerless, to prevent Sadat's continued attacks against the AOC leaders with great venom and sarcasm in the Arab press as well as in the Western press. He declared that the attack on the Great Mosque in Mecca (November 1979), was a sign of the lack of stability of the Saudi leadership "in absolute contrast to the stability during Faysal's regime," and he added that "there was something inherently wrong with the regime, a small number of families controlling countries so rich in oil, that one is unavoidably reminded of the example of the Iranian collapse." The Saudi regime, according to Sadat, had lost its legitimacy as the leader of Islam.[66] Sayyid Mar'i, a close friend of Sadat's, noted that Egypt had succeeded in regaining territories that had been occupied for thirteen years, while Saudi Arabia was threatening Egypt with an economic boycott, without investing any effort in regaining Arab Jerusalem.[67]

Egyptian officials criticized the AOC for not only donating minimal aid, but also causing delays in providing it, resulting in an increased price tag for projects after inflation (the AOC did not compensate it for this delay).[68] Sadat accused the "midgets" [the AOC rulers] of attempting "to starve the Egyptian people by stopping aid" and "of strangling Egypt in times of shortages."[69] In a speech given at Alexandria in May 1981, Sadat gave thanks to Allah, that had saved him from the indignity of receiving aid from the "midgets." In response, the Saudis attacked him, through *al-Riyad*, noting that the midgets Sadat referred to would be happy to alleviate the Egyptian people's plight with job openings.[70] Kamal Hasan 'Ali said that the oil states thought that their aid to Egypt would be reason enough for continuing the Arab–Israeli conflict, and furthermore, that with the end of this conflict, there would be no justification for continuing aid.[71] The Arabs, therefore, had some difficulty in comprehending the fact that Egypt had succeeded in ending its sacrifices through peace after more than thirty years, a difficulty that was criticized by Egyptian officials.[72] Ali indicated that the Arabs provided Iraq with $50 billion in aid, while some of them were stating that Egypt was a bottomless pit.[73]

Mubarak, unlike his predecessor, chose not to launch scathing attacks against the AOC regimes, and he generally avoided openly discussing ideological matters regarding Arab aid to Egypt, and, for his respect and restraint, the AOC praised him. The official media in Egypt followed Mubarak's policy. Virtually the only direct mention on the topic of Arab aid was made, though, in a speech broadcast to the Egyptian people celebrating the day of the revolution in 1985, Mubarak attacked the Arabs for not providing financial aid to Egypt, and for causing instability in Egypt. He added: "If our Arab brothers have decided, for known or unknown reasons, not to participate [in carrying the burden], Egypt who always gave a helping hand, will never reach out to request help."[74]

## The response of the Arab oil states to Egyptian claims

The AOC were not overly concerned with the Egyptians' various claims – of duty, of sacrifice, of Arab unity – and generally refrained from associating themselves with such ideals (Iraq was more involved than the conservative oil states). Their answers to the claims brought against them focused mainly on economic and religious issues. They emphasized the fact that it was their countries' duty to assist Egypt, which was fighting in the name of the whole Arab nation,[75] while stressing their internal problems. The reactions of the conservative and the revolutionary oil states were similar; although the latter stressed that the economic resources belonged to the whole Arab nation, their bottom line remained that aid was very limited because of internal difficulties. In August 1975, Saddam Hussein stated that the Egyptian people, whose task it was to liberate Sinai, needed economic aid, and this in spite of differences of opinion with Sadat concerning his policy:

> We cannot ignore basic facts. Egypt plays an important role among the Arab nation, from a political standpoint and because of its large population . . . We believe that the whole Arab nation has a right to enjoy our resources and that when we bring up the slogans of liberation, battle and reinforcing the fronts and when we call for the Egyptians to stand fast, it is unacceptable to let our people in Egypt suffer economic hardship. Because when one part of our people is hungry and you yourself overeat ad nauseam, how can you ask them to fight and liberate Sinai . . . if you demand this from the Egyptian people, they must have food in their bellies.[76]

In another interview with Ahmed Khamroush in April 1976, Saddam Hussein repeated the slogan that the Arab nation had joint ownership of all its resources, a sly criticism that the conservative oil states were not acting by this axiom. As for Iraqi aid, Hussein said "although the Iraqi economic situation has improved, nonetheless a substantial part of the Iraqi people still goes barefoot and suffers from anemia, and we are dependent on our oil revenues, which tend to fluctuate strongly. However, we consider aid to Egypt as our duty, in accordance with our capabilities."[77]

The main defense used by the AOC was that they were not as rich as everybody claimed; oil is not in endless supply, and even with all their oil reserves, the day will come when these reserves will dry up, and therefore present income from oil must be used for future needs, to guarantee the future of the oil countries in the post-oil period. Officials from the oil producing countries declared that even if they were rich in oil, that was not the case in other sectors such as human and industrial resources. This attitude was best described by Mahmud 'Imadi and by Sheikh Ahmad Zaki Yamani. 'Imadi, the general manager and chairman of the board of the Arab Fund for Economic and Social Development, stated that the AOC were not rich, and that they had only just started amassing their capital. They would continue to amass capital from oil for a limited period only, and therefore they were bound to apply this capital to the obtaining of a balanced, economic structure;[78] Sheikh Yamani, the Saudi Minister of Oil, said:

> I declare that we are still a poor country. Not only are we lacking industry, agriculture and manpower . . . we send our students to foreign universities, but it takes years to obtain a degree or a technical diploma. In the meantime we have to import engineers, technicians, expert manpower, and because of our lack of hotels, we do not know where to lodge them. To build hotels we need building contractors, but these contractors themselves have to live somewhere. This is an exhausting, vicious circle. We need,

among other things, cement. We don't have ports because we don't have the cement to build them . . . we don't have water. We don't have any rivers or lakes. We are totally dependent on rain water. In the last one hundred years, rainfall has decreased, with a steadily lowering frequency, and in the last twenty-five years it has hardly rained at all.[79]

Fahd stressed that one of the main priorities was to give aid to Egypt. In April 1977 he rejected Egypt's claims that it was not getting the aid it deserved, stating: "The AOC have supported you in the past and they will not spare any effort to do so in the future, their only limitations being their capabilities and their commitments to the development of their citizens. They feel that this support is a natural and sacred duty dictated by a common Arab destiny, and by the hopes and aspirations of the Arab world."[80] AOC countries claimed that they had provided extensive aid to their brethren who "had been less fortunate," in spite of domestic financial limitations.[81]

Nevertheless, they were not willing to reveal the exact amount of their aid to Egypt; the one time they did publish figures was in May 1979, after Sadat's sharp attack on the Saudis, and the publication was a deliberate play. The AOC declared that they acted this way for reasons of modesty and because the receiving party had suffered casualties in war, and you could not pay for blood with money. Furthermore the AOC governments stated that corruption, bureaucratic problems, the low absorption ability of the Egyptian economy and the future dangers of nationalization meant that the size of their aid and their investments in Egypt were never very high. They also said that Egypt had not been able to absorb large amounts of aid provided by Western sources.[82]

From Ibrahim Nafi's book *We and the World*, according to the AOC, additional aid was accorded to Egypt by way of payments to Egyptian workers in their countries, who transferred their salaries in hard currency to Egypt. They declared that these payments amounted to between $50 and 60 billion in the decade between 1975–85. Nafi' disputes this claim:

> Those of our Arab brothers who enjoy exercises in accountancy are mistaken. In the last ten years the Egyptian workers have transferred to Egypt yearly amounts of $2 billion only . . . These people's mistake . . . is that they are confusing the Egyptian workers' production yields in building Arab economies from an economic and social point of view with their salaries.

Nafi' adds that the Egyptians had spent a lot of money on purchases in the Arab countries, which the AOC had classified as "economic aid to Egypt." Moreover, Nafi' states:

> We could say that the AOC are providing economic aid to the USA, France, India, Pakistan, the UK, Japan and to every country whose citizens are working in these countries . . . Furthermore, those who think this way forget that the Arab countries chose highly skilled Arab professionals and artisans, that the influx of Egyptian workers to their country brought about a 100 percent salary increase in the years 1960–73, and later an increase of 500 percent from 1973 to 1983, and this in addition to the considerable negative influences on the Egyptian economy.[83]

Nafi' also argues that Egypt allowed, in spite of its economic difficulties, 600,000 pilgrims to fulfill the religious commandment of the Hajj, and they gave them $1.2 billion a year. According to him, every pilgrim spent an average of $2,000, hereby contributing to the Saudi economy.[84]

Sa'ad al-Din Ibrahim declares that the AOC used religion to defend their aid policy, quoting verses from the Koran, such as: "Allah gives to whom he wants to and renounces in the same way." The poor countries responded with another Koranic verse: "Both those who ask and those who are destitute have an explicit right to your riches."[85] However, the religious dispute played only a secondary role in the ideological debate on Arab aid. Egypt, as we saw, did not play the Islamic card when making its own case. Sa'ad al-Din Ibrahim claims that in the debate between the rich Arab countries and the poor, neither actually appealed against the validity of the basic argument. Both regarded the subject of sharing Arab wealth as a legitimate issue for discussion and none considered state sovereignty as a justification for withholding oil riches, although in Ibrahim's opinion, this was the most convincing argument.[86]

## Pragmatic considerations and realpolitik

### Positive changes during Nasser's regime
From 1961 onward, the public sector controlled most of Egypt's economic branches. The government fixed prices and supervised output and investment in most sectors.[87] During the decade of 1955–64, the Egyptian economy showed an annual GDP growth rate of 6 percent. But after this initial period, the growth rate decreased considerably, and the Egyptian economy started to show a deficit in the current account. Some of these deficits were covered by medium- and long-term loans. The debt burden became so severe that Egypt defaulted on some of its debts. By the end of 1965, Nasser had begun to admit openly the serious economic difficulties in which the Egyptian economy found itself.[88] In early 1966 the US postponed discussions with Egypt regarding its request to receive American foodstuffs in the amount of $150 million, while the IMF refused to grant it a loan of $70 million.[89] Because of its difficult economic situation, Egypt adopted a thrift policy in the two years after 1966.[90]

Egypt's dependence on external resources contradicted its state socialist slogans. The need to bring about a quick change to its international economic status forced the leadership to look for foreign investment. Nasser attached great importance to foreign policy, through which he could mobilize foreign capital needed for the development of his country. In late 1964 he stated: "We have no other alternative but to become an industrial force in the shortest possible time . . . the economic resources needed for this can only come from foreign aid."[91] Copland – who was employed by the CIA and by the American state department, to examine Nasser's policy – noted that Nasser was formulating a policy of "positive neutrality" not as a goal in itself, but as a way of winning international favor, and with it the prospect of obtaining aid, after he understood that the Egyptian economy needed extensive foreign aid for its very existence. Copland reported that the aid Egypt received from communist and Western countries, and from international financing bodies, since the officers' revolution up to the early 1960s, amounted to EgP 1,794 million (not including military and technical aid, industrial equipment and foodstuffs), and he also observed that if Nasser had not adopted a policy of "positive neutrality," he would have received, at the most, $50 million annually from the US and Great Britain, and not a penny from the Russians. The foreign policy chosen by Nasser, Copland added, produced a financial yield of ten times more than the above amount.[92]

Other studies support Copland's approach. Rivlin remarks that Egyptian foreign policy in the 1960s was formed according to its economic needs, and especially noted its close ties with the USSR – who shipped its economic and military aid;[93] Hamid Ansari writes that the policy of neutrality in the years 1958–64 reduced the gap between state resources and its requirements for economic growth;[94] and Heikal characterized Egyptian foreign policy in Nasser's time "as the moving force of the Egyptian economy."[95] Nasser himself explained to the People's Council in late 1964, that his global foreign policy was meant to obtain foreign aid from "America, Russia, Japan, Germany, Czechoslovakia, Yugoslavia, Romania, as published in the press," to realize Egypt's goals.[96]

The regime of the Free Officers needed economic resources to realize its ideological concepts. Nasser adopted the Arab national identity, as illustrated by Zilberman, not only as a joint Arab ideological and strategic policy, but also in order to obtain aid through the resources of the Arab countries.[97] His active intervention in the Arab peninsula was a deviation from his ideology. Because of its dire economic situation, Egypt was interested in attaining, through force, a part of the oil revenues of the Arab peninsula states, and Yemen's geographical location ("at Saudi Arabia's back door") suited his purposes.[98]

Nasser, aware that he would not be able to realize Egypt's development projects without outside help, sometimes adopted a policy of appeasement (even before his crushing defeat in June 1967) toward conservative Kuwait, notwithstanding his revolutionary policy. Nasser omitted Kuwait from his verbal attacks against the conservative Gulf States, because Kuwait was the only Arab country in the early 1960s that granted him substantial aid. In June 1964, Nasser even apologized to the Kuwaiti Emir, Sheikh 'Abdallah Salam al-Sabah, after a verbal attack by Khrushchev on the leaders of the Arab peninsula during his visit in Cairo, when the Soviet leader had said that the small Emirates were bases of imperialism, and that they were accepting bribes from the Western oil companies.[99]

From the mid-1960s till the defeat in the June 1967 War, Nasser failed to make any significant economic changes to prevent further decline in Egypt's economy. Nasser did make some minor tweaks to the economic and political scenes: he turned Port Said into a custom free-trade zone and in so doing, made it easier for foreign investors to do business; on the political level, he showed relative moderation and he agreed to invite the Chief of the Israeli Mossad at the time, Meir Amit, to visit Cairo, for a meeting with 'Abd al-Hakim 'Amir, number two in the Egyptian hierarchy. The meeting, for a variety of reasons, did not take place. Nasser had originally agreed to meet Amit because he hoped that Israel would push for economic aid to Egypt. In exchange, Nasser had agreed with Israel that Egypt moderate its position on the Arab boycott, and at a later stage he would enable Israel to use the Suez Canal, under certain conditions.[100] However, genuine, significant changes in Nasser's economic and political policy occurred only after the June 1967 defeat.

In the initial period after the revolution, Egypt tried to build an open (i.e. free-trade, private capital) economy; the need for economic cooperation dictated its policy. But in 1955, the attitudes of its policy-makers changed. Several factors contributed to this: the growing tension in its relations with the US (after the Americans refused to finance the Aswan High Dam), the nationalization of the Suez Canal, the 1956 War, and Egypt's growing cooperation with the socialist countries.[101]

Egypt's crushing military defeat in June 1967 was accompanied by serious damage to its economy: Egypt suffered considerable losses of military hardware and of foreign currency income. Losses of military equipment included 214 aircraft (including ninety-five MIG 21s and forty MIG 19s) and 600 armoured vehicles.[102] In order to rebuild its army, Egypt was forced to increase its military expenses significantly. Egypt also lost two sources of foreign currency income: the Suez Canal and its income from the Sinai oil fields. Furthermore, its income from tourism declined. But by far its greatest loss was that of the revenues from the Suez Canal: in the fiscal year 1966/7 Egypt's revenues from the Suez Canal amounted to $219 million. In the opinion of IMF economists, if the Suez Canal had continued operations until the end of the fiscal year (another twenty-five days in June 1967), revenues would have topped $230 million. The IMF economists also declared, that considering the fact that in the years prior to 1967 the Suez Canal revenues increased by about 10 percent annually, it would be safe to say that this upward trend would have continued.[103] It was not before 1975 that Egypt once again started earning transit fees from the Canal. Besides the loss of these revenues, the Suez Canal Authority suffered damages to costly equipment during the war, such as: bulldozers, tow trucks, towboats, salvage vessels, passenger liners, service boats, and also rolling material like busses, ambulances, heavy trucks and generators.[104]

The tourism sector was not a total loss. Although the number of tourists staying overnight in Egypt during 1968 was less than half compared to 1966, this recession was temporary: in 1967 and 1968 Egypt's income from tourism diminished, but already by 1969 its tourism revenues increased (see table 5.1), and in 1971 tourism showed a strong recovery.[105] The June War also saw Egypt lose the Abu Rodeis oil fields and oil exploration activity in the Suez Gulf ceased almost completely. Egypt also suffered badly from the destruction of the Canal cities – with a population of 1 million people, who were forced to abandon their homes – and from damage to industry and to the infrastructure in the area.

Kaissouni, the Egyptian Minister of Planning, claimed that lost revenues following the war amounted to $420 million. This figure was comprised of $280 million from the Suez Canal; $84 million from reduced tourism; and $56 million from the closed down oil field.[106] Keissouny certainly exaggerated some of his figures, especially in tourism losses (Keissouny claimed revenues had completely stopped). Keissouny released these figures in July 1967,[107] just before the Arab Summit conference in Khartoum, September 1967. The exaggerated nature of his

data is confirmed in the memoirs of Mahmoud Riad: before the summit conference
he spoke to Nasser and told him that Egypt had lost EgP 120 million annually ($276
million), following the closing of the Suez Canal and the loss of the Sinai oil fields.[108]
If we add to this the loss of tourism revenues, this amount could reach $300 million
a year (table 5.1). Speaking to Nasser, Riad proposed asking the AOC to renew their
oil production, and to apply 10 percent of their income in support of the Egyptian
economy. As Riad told it, Nasser was quiet for some time, and afterwards he said,
that it would be difficult for him, as an Egyptian, to ask the AOC for help. And he
added: "Can you imagine the influence this step would have on the Egyptian people
and on me?"[109]

**Table 5.1**    Egypt's revenues from the Suez Canal and tourism, 1965–1967 (in
millions of EgP)[1]

| Year | Suez Canal | Tourism |
| --- | --- | --- |
| 1965 | 86.2 | 46.7 |
| 1966 | 95.3 | 54.4 |
| 1967 | 47.0 | 50.9 |
| 1968 | — | 46.5 |
| 1969 | — | 57.9 |

*Sources*: Central Bank of Egypt, *Economic Review* (no. 3, 1967 and nos. 2, 3, 1972);
National Bank of Egypt, *Economic Bulletin* (nos. 1–4, 1970).

[1] The data in table 5.1 differ slightly from the IMF data, as quoted above, as they referred
to the calendar years, while the IMF data referred to the fiscal years.

It was clear to Nasser, despite what he had earlier proclaimed, that Egypt needed
urgent assistance from the AOC, and that the Egyptians should review their foreign
policy because of the difficult economic situation the country was in. Egypt's entan-
glement in the Yemen War and the loss of revenues after the June War did not leave
Nasser any options. He had devoted great resources to the war in Yemen, which
included the direct cost of maintaining his army in Yemen; military aid, loans and
foodstuffs he provided to the Yemenite republic; bribes to the Yemenite tribal chiefs
to buy their support, and at the same time, neutralizing their military activities
against him; and caused indirect damage to the local Egyptian economy by mobilizing resources for waging war in Yemen.[110] In 1967, approximately 70,000
Egyptian soldiers (about half his army) were serving in Yemen. Egypt paid a very
high price for the five years of war in Yemen (according to Haddad and Adams,
half a million dollars a day).[111] Adams indicated that these were direct expenses only,
not including aid in material and arms for the Yemenite army. Western observers
estimated the cost of the war to the Egyptian economy at double this sum.[112]

The difficult circumstances in which the Egyptian economy found itself, in addition to Nasser's serious political and personal situation,[113] contributed to his revised
economic–political outlook. Nasser "renounced" his honor, and Riad got "the
green light" to open negotiations for aid with the AOC leaders. Nasser was surprised
by the magnitude of aid the oil countries agreed to grant Egypt at the Khartoum

Summit. Nasser, for his part, paid a price for this aid. His defeat and subsequent requests for aid shattered the socialist–nationalist foundations of his previous policy, and contributed an important dimension to Egypt's realpolitik conception. It was clear to Egypt's policy-makers that the Arabs were not powerful enough "to regain Arab sovereignty" over all Israeli territories, and even Soviet aid was limited. Nasser's etatist economic policy had failed miserably, and after admitting his failure even before the war, but without taking any significant steps, he finally effected a revolution in his economic–political policy after the defeat.

Heikal pushed the Arab states to adopt a new approach toward the US; on the inter-Arab level, Nasser moderated his revolutionary ideology, and he promised to withdraw from Yemen; and on the internal economic level, Nasser communicated the change in his aims to Saudi Arabia and the Western countries, and after a long period of strict socialist control of the local business sector, the government's attention to the private sector started to become apparent. An example of this was the meeting of the Ministers of Economy and Industry with representatives of the private sector in December 1967, in order "to hear complaints and solve problems";[114] and in May 1968 Nasser appointed 'Abd al-'Aziz Hijazi – with his Western economic orientation – as Minister of Finance.

Just before the Arab summit conference in Rabat in late 1969, Nasser declared that the proposed aim of the summit was not to request aid for Egypt, but statements he made since the previous Arab summit, and during the Rabat summit, indicated otherwise. At times Egyptian policy-makers demonstratively brought up the subject of Arab aid: in an interview on *Cairo Radio* in March 1969, King Hussein was asked if in his opinion Arab states not bordering on Israel could do more to support the confrontation states.[115] Hussein was asked this question as co-recipient with Egypt of Arab aid, but indirectly this question was addressed to the oil states.

If Nasser "was ashamed" to ask for aid from the AOC before the Khartoum Summit in 1967, at the Rabat Summit this "shame" was transformed into an aggressive and explicit demand for aid. Nasser came to the conference adamant that he was going to mobilize substantial additional aid from the AOC and he openly announced this before the opening of the conference. There were two reasons that convinced Nasser to demand increased aid, and to believe such a venture would succeed: (i) Nasser's ability to unite Arab resources for a joint effort, which received a significant push after the June 1967 defeat and the War of Attrition. (ii) The Libyan revolution, the toppling of its monarchistic regime and Gaddafi's rise to power.[116]

At the summit Gaddafi actually supported Nasser's views and he attacked the leaders of the conservative states. On the third day of discussions, Nasser attacked Faysal and al-Sabah,[117] and he addressed them sharply: "I want to know if you wish to participate in this campaign? . . . I am preparing for two possibilities: that you fulfill your duty to fight in the campaign together with Egypt or your public announcement that you are rejecting this obligation." After his speech, he angrily left the conference hall,[118] but not before warning the conferees, that if they did not demonstrate their responsibility for Egypt's military and economic needs, he would be forced to "take an independent stand."[119] And so, at a meeting in Benghazi between the leaders of Libya, Egypt and Sudan on their return from the Rabat

Summit, Nasser made good his threat and he was involved in the formation of a block of revolutionary Arab states. The three leaders signed an economic, military and political agreement, and they decided to convene every four months.[120]

Nasser's steps and threats at the Rabat Summit and afterwards signified a sort of final roar at power, rather than any revolutionary intent, and certainly not a return to his policy prior to June 1967. The erosion of the Nasserist ideology and of Nasser's charisma, which had seen failures even before the June War – mainly following events like the breaking up of the UAR, his failed intervention in Yemen and the state of the Egyptian economy[121] – contributed to Nasser's realizing the limits of his strength and his restricted ability to take action, and his understanding that the state of his economy would not allow him to retreat from the "Khartoum revolution." Furthermore, it should be remembered that at the Rabat Summit, he was quoted as explaining to the Arabs – besides his aggressive speeches – that they should leave the door open for the possible regaining of the territories and the solution of the Palestinian problem by peaceful means.[122]

The essential changes in Nasser's policy – which came about because of an additional deterioration of the Egyptian economy after the June War – continued after the Rabat conference. The Arabs and the USSR together did not cover the total damages and economic losses sustained by his previous economic policy and by the Yemen and June 1967 wars. Following their defeat, the Egyptian government increased its defense budget substantially, and Nasser had no other choice but to continue his post-June War policy; that is, the plan of moderation at the Khartoum conference in 1967, the economic and political plan he presented on March 30, 1968, and the budding rapprochement with the US, as demonstrated by Mahmud Fawzi's visit to Washington as Nasser's envoy.[123] Nasser continued acting according to the new policy he had adopted in the second half of 1967. The new economic plan presented by Hasan 'Abbas Zaki, Minister of Economic and Foreign Affairs, in a letter he sent to Schweitzer, head of the IMF, on June 21, 1970,[124] and Nasser's agreement to accept the Rogers Plan signified more than anything the continuation of the positive change in his economic–political policy, assisted by the two economic ministers he had appointed in 1968, Hasan 'Abbas Zaki and 'Abd al-'Aziz Hijazi.

Nasser understood, as indicated by Sadat, that only the Americans were capable of "doing something" about the Arab–Israeli conflict, and therefore he agreed to Rogers' initiative in the summer of 1970.[125] The stalemate developing in the War of Attrition, notwithstanding Soviet aid, and the deteriorating economic condition in Egypt,[126] contributed to Egypt's turn to the West for aid. In a May 1, 1970 speech, Nasser appealed to the US to intervene and force Israel to pull out from the occupied territories, and in July 1970, he accepted Rogers' plan. The Americans hinted that a further rapprochement between the two countries could work in Egypt's favor, with certain economic incentives, and after Rogers' visit to Cairo in 1971, the two countries reached an agreement to defer debts to the tune of $145 million.[127] An extract from the Egyptian minister of economy's letter to the manager of the IMF illustrates the magnitude of the turnaround in Nasser's policy: "The Egyptian authorities believe that the policy presented in the letter is sufficient to obtain the goals of the plan, but [they] will take any further steps necessary. [However] if this policy does not obtain the results desired by the Egyptian government or the manager of the IMF, the Egyptian authorities will consult with the IMF about further suitable steps, to achieve the goals of the plan."[128]

**Table 5.2**   Oil revenues for Egypt, Saudi Arabia, Kuwait, UAE, 1970–1982 (in millions of US dollars)

| Year | Egypt | SA | Kuwait | UAE |
|------|-------|-----|--------|-----|
| 1970 | 1,150.0 | 890.1[1] | — | — |
| 1974 | 22,573.5 | 6,542.6 | 5,536.0 | — |
| 1975 | 25,675.8 | 6,393.1 | 5,960.0 | — |
| 1976 | 311.8 | 30,754.9 | 6,869.5 | 7,010.0 |
| 1977 | 545.6 | 36,538.4 | 7,515.7 | 7,713.2 |
| 1978 | 700.0 | 32,223.8 | 7,699.5 | 8,200.0 |
| 1979 | 950.0 | 57,522.0 | 16,863.0 | 12,862.0 |
| 1980 | 2,648.0 | 102,212.0 | 17,900.0 | 19,344.0 |
| 1981 | 2,800.0 | 113,200.0 | 14,900.0 | 18,850.0 |
| 1982 | 2,700.0 | 70,500.0 | 9,477.0 | 9,400.0 |

*Sources*: Table 4.9: *Arab Oil and Gas*, July 1, 1984, p. 5.

[1]  Data refers to the 1970/1 fiscal year, as quoted from IMF documentation.

Nasser attached great importance to Arab aid: after the Khartoum 1967 conference, he said that the decision for aid "was the main achievement of the summit,"[129] and he emphasized the importance of this aid for the strengthening of "Egypt's ability to resist." In the "October Paper" Sadat presented economic cooperation as one of the main pillars of Arab nationalism, but Nasser had already expressed this sentiment, when he had said in a speech before the People's Council, that Arab aid was the most outstanding achievement of the all-Arab effort.[130] Nasser often described Arab nationalism in his speeches in terms of Arab unity, as a movement and a political–social ideology, but he definitely did not forget the mobilization of economic resources from the rich Arab nations, not before the June 1967 War and certainly not afterward. Of course, the completely different circumstances in the economic sphere that reigned in Nasser's time, compared to Sadat's period, should be taken into account. The oil states did not possess enormous amounts of money during Nasser's time, and therefore it is quite likely that this was one of the reasons contributing to the various emphases in the forming of foreign policy and the Arab national definitions in their respective periods.

## Pragmatism at the expense of doctrinairism under Sadat: 1970–1975

### *Rapprochement between Egypt and the conservative oil countries*
On Sadat's rise to power, he inherited an empty treasury from his predecessor, and he found himself in control of a humiliated nation with its economy mortgaged to war.[131] The Egyptian economy and society were on the edge of bankruptcy: the

Yemen, June 1967 and Attrition wars had all brought in their wake considerable material damages and the loss of sources of income; casualties caused demoralization among the people, to which should be added the low standard of living of the masses; industrial output was low – including food; imports were increasing; the external debt was growing and amounted to over one third of the Egyptian GNP; public services were of a low standard; oppression and social coercion were the same as in Nasser's time; Egyptian intellectuals were alienated; Egypt's inter-Arab status was lower than ever; and Egyptian society felt defeated and humiliated and faced an uncertain future.[132] Sadat wrote in his memoirs: "The economic legacy Nasser left me was worse than the political one," echoing the words of the minister of the economy who said "the Treasury is empty and we are practically bankrupt."[133]

Cooper wrote that there was a basic continuance between Nasser's regime – after his defeat – and that of Sadat.[134] The latter, like his predecessor, put great emphasis on his rising to power, on foreign policy and the economic profit this was supposed to bring, but he used different means. Sadat ironically remarked that Nasser, in his last days, came to realize that the countries who helped him after the June defeat were none other than the conservative states.[135] Sadat realized that export of revolutionary ideas would not solve Egypt's economic problems. According to Heikal, Sadat always thought that Nasser was mistaken in not admitting his June 1967 defeat and in the agreement he made with the Soviets, and Sadat wanted a comprehensive rehabilitation plan for the Egyptian economy, which could only be carried out by the US.[136] Sadat continued many of the politics of his predecessor (after the June 1967 defeat), only differently, with different emphases and intensified processes. Even in the 1971 constitution, part of its economic goals and welfare principles comprised the basis for development projects in Egypt since the mid-fifties. In the "October Paper" Sadat wrote (also from political considerations), that he intended to build on Nasser's heritage, to be able to meet the needs of the future, and he added, on the matter of "the new stage in our lives"[137]: "we are not operating in an empty void, but behind us we have rich experience, which we should examine and we should use anything positive therein, to open it and to add to it, and reject anything which is negative."[138]

Sadat wished to strengthen his ties with the AOC, even with the smaller nations among them. In late March 1971 he sent Sabri al-Khuli to the Gulf States, which later came to form the United Arab Emirates (UAE), to promote inter- and intra-Arab unity, and to guard their stability. The collapse of the AOC threatened the long-term supply of economic aid they provided to Egypt from their oil revenues.[139] Besides civilian aid, Egypt was in need of military aid, because of its diversification of arms sources policy. The problem Egypt faced, as a recipient of Western arms, was financial, and as Sadat saw it, the AOC were supposed to finance Egyptian purchases in the West, as well as assist in the development of an Egyptian arms industry.[140] Egypt needed the investment of the Gulf States governments and their people, and in the mid-1970s it also wanted the AOC to absorb its surplus labor force. These reasons were central to Sadat's considerations in building his relations with the AOC. Besides these factors, there were relatively secondary factors, such as the development of export markets for Egyptian products.

Under Nasser's regime, Egypt exported workers – mostly professionals – to the

AOC, but this strictly low-key phenomenon did not contribute in any vast way to the Egyptian economy. Until the mid-1960s, emigration was not really permitted, except on Government assignment, and total aid from these countries was limited in scope until 1963. The deteriorating economy in Egypt, allied with the demo- graphic switch of power to the AOC after Nasser's death forced Sadat to devote most of his attention to the resources of these countries, and to build up his foreign and domestic policy, in an attempt to acquire a large part of petro-dollar wealth.

Sadat exploited the Saudis' fear of extremist factions in the region, and he tried to prove to the conservative states that he intended to cement good relations with the US at the expense of the USSR, emphasizing Egypt's practical, moderating role. In July 1971, he helped Numeiry to eliminate Soviet influence in Sudan, and in November 1971 he assisted him against the Anya-Anya rebels in the south of the country; he declared openly that Egypt would never recognize a communist Arab government; he banned communism in Egypt; in July 1972 he expelled the Soviet advisors; and he aided North Yemen in their civil war, in coordination with Saudi Arabia. For tactical reasons, Sadat actively praised the Saudi role in the various measures he took, even if the Saudis had not played a decisive role in these events.[141]

The Investment Law of 1971 saw Sadat give priority to Arab capital. It is very likely that this was a criterion for the continuation of his economic policy. Sadat preferred at first to bring in Arab capital and to prevent criticism against his regime after his rise to power, because his critics claimed that he had opened Egypt to the associated evils of imperialism. Arab capital was seen in a different light, because it came from "their sisters." Moreover the small oil states could not "threaten" Egypt by means of their capital, the way Western capital had threatened Egypt throughout modern history – mainly in Isma'il's time. Only later did Sadat open the Egyptian economy to Western investment, primarily because: Egypt saw an opportunity to attain advanced technology. Improved relations with the West, the low level of Arab investments and the ensconcing of Sadat's regime after the October War were also contributing factors in Egypt's economic proto-libarlization.

In 1972, frustration and a lack of political clarity had manifested themselves in Egypt. Sinai was still occupied by Israel, and Sadat's promise that 1971 would be "a decisive year" remained unrealized. In January the government declared a war economy: a ban was imposed on the import of luxury goods and on ministers and officials travelling abroad; the investment budget was curtailed; and they announced military training for students and young volunteers.[142] These steps were meant, among other things, as a signal to the AOC of Egypt's serious intentions. Sadat, writing in his memoirs, understood that if he did not clearly demonstrate his warlike intentions, he would not have received any massive aid from the AOC.[143] The attitude of the AOC merely confirmed this. On January 29, the Emir of Kuwait declared that his country would put all its revenues and capital at the disposal of the struggle against Israel, but it would do this "when it was needed" and at "zero hour." Sadat felt that a situation of "no peace and no war" which had existed since 1967, would cause a steady deterioration of the Egyptian economy. Among the Egyptian elite there was a feeling that Israel and the US would be pleased to see Egypt's economic situation decline, forcing it to make concessions to Israel.[144] Sadat said that in 1970 he read an American report analyzing Egypt's economic position as follows: "Nasser can shout as much as he wants. Very soon he will be on his knees economically."[145]

In late February 1972 the Prime Minister, Aziz Sidki, announced, in a broadcast to the nation, the steps Egypt had taken for an eventual war, and in March Sadat announced in a speech at an air force base in the delta: "Our decision to go to war is final and we will not rescind it. We will not discuss this any more."[146] Egyptian missionaries were sent to the AOC armed with this battle cry. Their purpose was to clarify the seriousness of Egypt's intentions, and to gain military and financial aid. Sadat himself visited Saudi Arabia and Kuwait in early March 1972 at the head of a delegation of eighty-one persons. The Egyptian people were kept in the dark about these visits, and Sadat demanded that their talks be kept secret. In these talks, Sadat proclaimed his despair of ever reaching a political solution, and was critical of the reaction of the Arabs, who were demanding a date for the opening of hostilities with Israel in exchange for their aid. Sadat demanded that Saudi Arabia and Kuwait finance the purchase of front line arms for Egypt, from a third party. On March 19, about a week-and-a-half after Sadat's visit, the Egyptian Minister of War, Muhammad Sadiq, visited Kuwait and Saudi Arabia, to receive their replies to Sadat's requests,[147] and one week later the Saudi Foreign Minister arrived in Cairo with a letter from King Faysal.[148]

After the expulsion of the Soviet advisors from Egypt in July 1972, Libyan leader Colonel Muammar Gaddafi called for the unification of the two nations. Sadat accepted his proposal, and on July 26 Gaddafi sent his first concrete proposals to Sadat. Sadat did not reject them outright, as Gaddafi was willing to provide financial aid – approximately $1 billion for a period of five years, according to Sadat – in exchange for unification. But Sadat was faced with several problems regarding any such deal: besides the lack of sympathy the Egyptian elite had for Gaddafi's proposal, he was considered an extremist. Sadat was aware that unification with Libya could disrupt relations with the Arab monarchies, from whom he received aid, and which he hoped would increase following the expulsion of the Soviet experts. Indeed, Gaddafi demanded that Sadat sever his ties with the conservative oil countries. Though he was not keen to unify, Sadat did not want to lose Libyan aid, and Jalud headed a Libyan delegation to the USSR to purchase arms for both Libya and Egypt, and these arms were meant to reach Egypt. Sadat calculated his steps carefully: he wanted to keep open all possibilities at his disposal for the optimal exploitation of resources, and therefore he chose unification with Libya, although not all at once, but in stages. Sadat flew to Benghazi on August 1, 1972, where the two leaders decided to arrange unification by September 1, 1973.[149]

The rapprochement between Sadat and the AOC leaders resulted in extensive economic and military aid for Egypt. Sadat was satisfied with these developments and with the "unified Arab actions," and he declared before the People's Council and the central committee of the ASU on the anniversary of the revolution (July 23, 1973): "Arab potential is enormous, much has been achieved." He added that they should rely on Egyptian ability and Arab economic potential. In his speech Sadat showed great optimism, and he said that in his opinion Arab resources belonged to the whole Arab nation. "We now produce 55 percent of global oil production, and we hold 85 percent of global oil reserves."[150]

## The influence of Arab rapprochement on the October 1973 War

Sadat tried to organize a unified Arab position before the war, mainly in order to alleviate some of the burden of the campaign off Egypt's shoulders. However, when he saw that not all the AOC agreed to this – especially the conservative oil states opposed to Libya – he cleverly maneuvered around the subject of Arab aid. In order to ensure that every one of the AOC nations kept their promise to give aid, Sadat agreed to unification with Libya in stages. Egypt subsequently received extensive aid from Libya, notwithstanding the fact, as stated by Egyptian political figures, that at first it seemed Sadat did not intend to honor the agreement. In August 1973 – after Sadat returned from his trip to the Gulf – the Egyptian leader met with his Libyan counterpart in Cairo, and there, according to Heikal, it became clear that unification would not be carried out.[151] Sadat had used Libya to strengthen Egypt's financial resources – the unification plan was merely a tool to get Gaddafi's money. On October 6, 1973, Sadat, armed with extensive financial and political aid received from all sides of the Arab world, was ready to go to war.[152]

The difficult economic situation in Egypt just before the war, on top of the fact that the AOC would only grant massive aid in case of war, was a major factor behind Sadat's decision to start the campaign. In August 1974, at a meeting of senior public relations personnel, Sadat said that the economic crisis "was . . . one of my reasons for going to war, because if we had waited until 1974, in our present difficult situation Israel would not have had to fire even one shot."[153] Sadat wrote in his memoirs that several members of the National Security Council, which convened on September 30, 1973, were uneasy about going to war, because there was a shortage of food reserves in Egypt that would worsen in the event of a conflict, but Sadat told them:

> We have commitments (to banks etc.) that we should have kept but we will not be able to do so by the end of this year. In another three months, in early 1974, we won't have enough bread in the breadbox! I cannot ask for even one more dollar from the Arabs; they say that they are giving us aid, in return for lost income from the Canal, although we did not fight, or that we did not want to fight.[154]

In an interview broadcast in December 1975, Sadat said:

> Before the beginning of the war, no Arab was willing to give us even one dollar. They gave us EgP 100 million . . . as agreed in Khartoum, and that this was all they were willing to give. Afterwards the following story circulated: "you will not fight and don't do anything" . . . If I started speaking with them about aid, they would say: wallah, we don't know if you will fight or not. In the first week of the war I received $0.5 billion . . . why? Because they realized we were serious. The Emir of Kuwait spoke with me and he had to stop when he started crying . . . we handled matters with half a billion dollars.[155]

The argument that Sadat was coerced into military action doesn't mean that he had not thought about the possibility of war since his rise to power. Feelings of insult, disgrace, humiliation and lost honor had become a commonplace obsession with the Egyptian people. This national psyche also came to influence the decision-makers in Egypt, and threatened to undermine Sadat's regime. Naguib Mahfouz depicted the Egyptian people's sense of relief after the October War:

> We have regained our spirit after much suffering and tasting the bitterness of death for six years, years in which I saw the Egyptian people walking in the markets, wrapped in the veil of humiliation, muttering unintelligibly, scowling without pride, laughing without joy, living in their country like strangers, advancing in time without a future . . . our friends in this world have shown us mercy, not without contempt.[156]

It was clear to Sadat that without a political solution which would reclaim Sinai, that perennial symbol of Egyptian weakness, there was bound to be another war, especially as Sadat had publicly announced several times "the year of decision," while nothing actually happened. "The world has lost its faith in us and we have started losing faith in ourselves," Sadat declared.[157] On another occasion, before the outbreak of hostilities, Sadat claimed he thought that Egypt would gain some advantages from the war, no matter the reasons behind it.[158] Sadat planned a limited war, which would solve the deadlock of the conflict with Israel, placing it high on the international agenda of the Great Powers. This, Egypt hoped, would persuade the US – possibly with the added incentive of an oil embargo – to urge Israel to retreat from the territories it had occupied since the June 1967 War.

The aid Egypt received was the crucial factor in Sadat's decision to go to war. Western intelligence and diplomatic sources indicated that, before the war, Sadat received a commitment from Faysal that Saudi Arabia would not only finance the war, but it would also cover any debts the Egyptian government incurred from the conflict.[159] After Saudi Arabia's guarantee, Sadat informed the National Security Council of the war just four days before it broke out. The hope that colored Sadat's sudden hunger for war – that the vast increases in military aid from the AOC would be supplanted by economic charity – was soon dispelled. The amount of aid was not as great as Sadat had hoped. In February 1974, *MEED* indicated that the war was also an important part of the *infitah* (open door) strategy. According to this analysis, there were limited goals for a limited war. The conflict's priorities were to restore territories on the east bank of the Suez Canal, to reopen the Canal and to renew commercial traffic, demonstrating Egypt's peaceful intentions and encouraging foreign investment.[160]

It would be pretentious to claim that war would not have broken out without the economic and military aid Egypt had received from the AOC, but without the enlisting of Arab oil resources it is extremely doubtful that Egypt would have had the clout, in terms of wealth or army, to start the October War. Sadat's comments before the National Security Council several days before the war were backed up by a statement made post-conflict, concerning the relationship between the mobilization of resources and the formation of foreign policy: "I say to the Egyptian journalists who complain about the lack of soap in Egypt, that we would not have received any Arab aid whatsoever, if we had not written the glorious chronicle of the crossing in blood . . . without this aid [$500 million], we would have been left without bread or soap today."[161]

*Practical concerns in the "October Paper"*

The shift in Egypt's political and economic situation after the October War saw Sadat formulate a policy that would reflect the new needs and crises facing Egypt. Sadat knew he had to accelerate economic development through modernization. He also had to change the economic framework in Egypt by engineering decentralization of industry and public service sectors, in conjunction with Arab and Western aid. Obtaining Arab and Western aid was essential for financing the rehabilitation of the Canal area, as well as domestic development. The new aims for economic and social development were presented in the "October Paper" and ratified by the People's Council in May 1974.[162] Taking into consideration the new economic conditions which had been created, such as the new levels of Arab capital, Sadat called for increased economic cooperation with the Arab states, with Egypt seeking to absorb a high level of petro-dollar investment. The political and economic liberalization introduced by Sadat was a major part of his efforts to extricate the economy from its rock-bottom state. Following the implementation of the economic reform measures, Sadat thought Arab and Western investment would come flowing into Egypt. His determination to carry out his plan was presented in the "October Paper," and soon after its publication, he decentralized the economic decision-making process, continued to encourage the private sector and permitted the forming of political parties. The investments that Sadat channeled to the rehabilitation of the Suez Canal area were meant to demonstrate to the Egyptian people, and the world, Egypt's intention to reach a settlement with the Israelis by diplomatic means, which was important for the people's morale and for the long-term success of economic development.

After the October War, senior American bankers swarmed into Egypt – including David Rockefeller, Chairman of the Chase Manhattan, Robert McNamara, President of the World Bank, William Simon, Secretary of the American Treasury – and the American administration offered increased aid from the US and from Western states and institutions, if it continued with its open-door policy.[163] In February 1974, Rockefeller remarked that Egypt had now realized that socialism and extreme Arab nationalism did not do much good for most of the 37 million people in Egypt. If President Sadat wanted to help them, he should concern himself with private initiative and with aid. The Israeli leaders, Rockefeller added, felt that there was a better chance to end the war between the two nations if Sadat was able to secure the economic future of his country, encouraging stability, growth and increased levels of prosperity.[164]

Abdel Khalek was opposed to those who were inclined to believe that the *infitah*, as formulated in the "October Paper," was new. According to him, the *infitah* was not a deliberate opening of an economy that was "closed," but a reshaping of its economic relations.[165] The word *"infitah"* in Arabic is the opposite of *"inghilaq"* (closure), and Khalek felt that the dichotomy gave the impression that Egypt's economy had been "closed." He emphasized that, even before 1974, the Egyptian economy was not closed, and the turnabout in economic policy started after attempts at socialism in the 1960s failed. For Khalek, the *infitah* had more to do with reform of the internal economic policy than any external economic relations. The reforming of the Egyptian economy was Egypt's turning "north-west" toward

EGYPT AND THE ARAB PETRO-DOLLAR INFLUENCE

the US and Europe, with various international bodies – such as the IMF – and foreign banks all playing a part in this shift.[166]

The "October Paper" though published in 1974, nonetheless contained policies that had been implemented long before, soon after Sadat's rise to power.[167] However, the "October Paper" reflected a new episode in Egyptian economic history. The dreadful conditions that followed after the October War required the Egyptian policy-makers to try and obtain part of the AOC's petro-dollars wealth. Political pressure exerted by Saudi Arabia and Kuwait on Sadat to open the Egyptian economy to foreign investment[168] was another factor helping him to form his policy. Sadat willingly accepted this "pressure," as he was expecting a massive flow of investment into his economy. Senator Charles Percy's report to the Foreign Relations Committee of the US Senate in April 1975 stated that Sadat was aware that Saudi Arabia, Kuwait and other countries would not be willing to make massive investments in a country with tight controls on its economy.[169]

In the "October Paper," Sadat calls the task of economic development after the war "a matter of life or death." He states that successful development will determine Egypt's regional and global standing. He also argues that the burden would fall squarely on the back of the Egyptian people, but:

We urgently need foreign sources and in this connection, I think that first of all it is important to speak about Arab capital. Arab countries exporting oil have enormous cash reserves, which will be multiplied several times over . . . the owners of these funds want to invest part of their money in Egypt . . . and we welcome and encourage this . . . we want Arab economic cooperation to enter an active and strong period.[170]

The atmosphere reigning in Egypt in 1974, as told by the local manager of Mobile Oil, was one of "there is a smell of money around this place."[171] During a discussion in the legislation committee of the People's Council about the ratification of law 43, one of the participating delegates put forward the case for making Egypt a financial power:

Some of the nations are earning interest on their investments up to $1 million per minute and these states face a real problem in their economy – the problem how and where to invest. So far the existing capital markets in Europe and America and in other places were able to attract these funds, because there were no obstacles, no currency controls and absolute freedom of operations . . . We might very well miss the boat, because money does not wait forever. If capital is diverted to other markets, it will be very difficult to withdraw it. Therefore we must start our efforts now . . . We want Egypt to be a financial market, as London used to be, especially with the Arab states holding reserves of billions.[172]

In a broadcast to the nation in April 1975, Sadat proclaimed that Arab wealth could contribute to the renewal of the socio-economic structure in the Arab world, adding: "Is there any logic [in continuing the controversy between revolutionaries and conservatives] just because the revolutionaries are right? . . . Lately our region has become the source of capital and money, should we withdraw from this development?"[173]

The "October Paper" describes several economic goals, including the strengthening of economic cooperation with the Arab states, encouraging the flow of foreign investment and bringing in technological knowhow to Egypt from any source. Further, the paper outlined plans for developing industrial exports to finance the growing import of foodstuffs; creating free-trade areas to exploit Egypt's geographical location for industrial development; encouraging oil exploration and tourism as leading sectors; and forming a new policy which would influence social development.

In addition to these targets, Sadat often mentioned the term "the sovereignty of the law," which reflected his desire to give the Egyptian public personal security and to improve the atmosphere of stability in the country, an essential condition for attracting both local and foreign investment. As for the institutional–managerial framework, Sadat mentioned the need for firm steps toward "the reallotment of authority," granting the provinces greater authority in their dealings with the central government. These alterations, he said, would bring "a change to the philosophy and the responsibility for planning . . . the private sector is the vanguard of progress and rehabilitation."[174]

The concept of *infitah* was about much more than just an open economy; it was also powered by social and political exposure and freedom. The four main pillars of the policy – economic liberalization, the strengthening of democracy; an alliance with the West;[175] and peace with Israel – all shared a common objective; that is the development of the Egyptian economy. But they also represented a new, more democratic and liberal approach to Egyptian society. Sadat implied that all four precepts were within the framework of Nasserism and the goals of the revolution of 1952; to say otherwise risked a critical feedback from the people. Besides, the wars afforded Sadat the luxury of being able to implement whatever measures he chose to lift Egypt from the economic quagmire:

> In order to repel aggression, the Egyptian people lost more than Egp 10,000 million, this besides the lives of the fallen soldiers, which cannot be evaluated in terms of money. The Egyptians did not pay this price just for their own defense, but in defense of the whole Arab nation . . . the burden of military expenses caused a reduced rate of development of 6–7 percent, the rate [originally] existing in the period between 1956 up to 1965, to less than 5 percent annually.[176]

The *infitah* strategy brought impressive results, mainly an increase in foreign currency income from $1.4 billion in 1973 to about $5.5 billion in 1978. Revenues from oil, earnings from Egyptian workers abroad, from tourism and from transit fees from the Suez Canal proved to be the main new sources of foreign currency.[177] The Egyptian government also succeeded in getting commitments for aid in the sum of $3.4 billion annually for 1975–8, compared to an average of $0.6 billion in the period of 1967–72.[178] The increase of income from foreign currency and aid reduced pressure on the balance of payments and allowed Egypt to increase the level of imports, as there was a greater reserve than previously. This paved the way for a rapid increase of investments, greater domestic consumption, and more efficient exploitation of existing production facilities. Import of products and services went up from approx. $2 billion in 1973 to around $6.7 billion in 1978. Import of capital products went up from $1.2 billion to $4 billion in the same period.[179] The increase in both Egypt's foreign currency sources and foreign aid brought with it a consolidation of its external debts and improved its credit status. Its short-term debts, amounting to $1.4 billion in 1976, decreased to $490 million in 1978, the majority of it paid off using loans from the GFDE.[180]

## Arab aid and the peace initiative: 1976–1978

After the peace treaty between Egypt and Israel, much was written about the difficulties in the relations between Egypt and the Arab countries. What is overlooked is the fact that relations were characterized by economic, political and social traumas long before the peace agreement, even in the period of the "blossoming" of relations after the 1973 war, when the Riyadh–Cairo axis was created. Indeed, the many problems that existed between the AOC and Egypt contributed to Sadat's peace treaty with Israel, as Sadat was displeased with the way the oil countries had treated him, which also hurt Egypt's standing and prestige.

On February 25, 1974 a special delegation on behalf of the US Foreign Relations committee presented a report on its visit to Egypt. The conclusion of the authors of the report gave evidence, in retrospect, of excellent analytical and forecasting ability, as their report was based on multiple-factor analysis, not a blunt evaluation: "if this analysis is valid, most of these factors will continue to help Egypt in its drive for a comprehensive settlement with Israel."[181] First of all and most important, they wrote, it was important for Sadat to be seen as the victor after the October War. The IDF's retreat from the banks of the Suez Canal and the Egyptian army's successful crossing of the canal strengthened Sadat's standing in the eyes of his people,[182] and this meant that Sadat's own position was stable (stability, internally was necessary for peace). Second, Arab aid to Egypt was a sensitive topic:

> While the Egyptians can claim that their Arab brothers are compensating them for the cost of the war and for the loss of income from the Canal, there are signs that Egypt would have preferred not to be so dependent on external aid. The Egyptians are very proud of their historical heritage . . . and they don't like to be dependent on others . . . For example, an Egyptian told us that aid from Saudi Arabia, Kuwait and the Gulf States did not come easily and that "we don't like to receive aid from those Bedouins."[183]

The third point touched on relations with the US. The Egyptians expressed their objections to American arms supplied to Israel "which was often supplied on Egyptian territory." The Egyptian government still showed "an earnest desire for friendship with the US." The report mentioned that Egypt wanted to strengthen its ties with the US because they currently felt over-dependent on the Soviets.[184] The fourth point referred to the Egyptian economy's efforts toward rehabilitation: the report mentioned the Egyptian policy-makers' concern with economic and social development, and added: "It is logical that Sadat would be in a position to concentrate on a solution to serious domestic problems." The report concluded with the nearly prophetic claim that Egypt would seek peace with Israel. The report also warned that certain groups would be opposed to any peace treaty, especially the radical Arab states and the Palestinians, "and a country wanting to play a leading role in the Arab world, could not afford to ignore this pressure."[185]

The cocktail of economic, social, strategic and political factors gave way to what became known as the "Sadat initiative." This initiative was certainly motivated, at least in part, by the Arab states, as well as other factors. The main core of influence the Arabs possessed was their aid, which in turn defined the economic situation in Egypt. Therefore, there is a phenomenon here that can be labeled the "Arab aid factor." This was part of a wider "economic factor" that touched a wide range of subjects, including: the desire to reduce the military burden and to increase revenues from Egypt's resources which were in limbo (the Suez Canal, tourism and foreign investment); the desire to obtain permanent and substantial aid from the West and; various other matters. Sadat even confided to Kissinger in November 1973 that the termination of war with Israel was the first step toward the tackling of chronic poverty.[186]

Many observers have argued that the economic factor was the driving force behind the "Sadat initiative." Gilber stated in November 1977 that:

> The main factors causing the sharp shift in Egypt's attitude toward Israel were the positive economic and social changes that occurred in the land of the Nile in the last few years . . . Only an important element like giving a chance for "economic success" to succeed, can explain Sadat's willingness to take upon himself personal risks and to pay a high price in the field of relations between Egypt and some of the Arab states . . . The Egyptian people's enthusiastic reactions . . . also testify to the fact that the economic-social situation takes a prominent place nowadays in the political experience of the Egyptian community.[187]

*Al-Ahram al-Iqtisadi* wrote in January 1978 that "after thirty years of austerity and wars . . . economic considerations are more important than political considerations for the Egyptian people,"[188] while Kanovsky argued that, "Sadat's initiative was connected, without a doubt . . . to Egypt's serious economic problems and the influence they exerted on the internal situation."[189] Kubursi, writing in 1981, concurred, arguing that the foundations of the Camp David agreement were based on the difficult economic situation in Egypt, on its limited economic achievements, on the gloomy long-term economic forecast, on the poverty that had spread to very wide layers of the population, urbanization, unemployment and an increasing external debt and a deficit in its current account. For Kubursi, the decision to seek peace cannot be extricated from the changes to *infitah* policy that sought to ease Egypt's ills.[190]

Most observers, regardless of their arguments, tended to overlook the Arabs' influential role on "Sadat's initiative,"[191] specifically the timing of aid. Why did Egypt seek peace in 1977 and not in late 1976, or on any other date after the October 1973 War? Sadat's announcement before the Egyptian People's Council in early November 1977, on his willingness to go to Jerusalem, was not the first time he had intimated that that was a path he was willing to take.[192]

In truth, Sadat had no other option, because a deteriorating domestic economic, political and military situation had forced his hand. The peace initiative was the best solution to the difficulties Egypt was facing. This is not to imply that money was the only reason for peace. Sadat's visit to Israel also stemmed from a heart felt desire to resolve the conflict with Israel, and represented a genuine despair over the behavior of his Arab colleagues[193] along with the bitter realization that Egypt could not succeed in defeating Israel by force.[194] Sadat also wanted to regain Sinai, was worried about political extremism in Israel (after the rise to power of the Likud party),[195] and concerned about the consequences of a future war with Israel (especially in light of the Egyptian army's severe situation in 1976[196] and the fear that Israel would use nuclear weapons in the next war[197]). The Soviets were refusing to provide arms any longer to Egypt – this was compounded by the refusal of the West, mainly the US, to supply massive amounts of front-line weapons.

Sadat rejected claims that economic difficulties – including the food riots – hastened his trip to Jerusalem. Before his trip, he painted a bright picture of Egypt's economic situation: "Even if we do suffer from economic problems, we manage very well. Our Arab brothers help us with billions a year, we have paid all our debts, and even big countries like the UK are doing worse than we are";[198] and in his speech in the Knesset, he claimed that he had come to Jerusalem out of humanitarian and ethical motives only.[199] Nafi' then tried, in December 1977, to refute the claim that the "Sadat initiative" stemmed from the deteriorating state of the economy, reasoning Sadat had announced his initiative in "the year of economic victory."[200] Others to step forward and defend Sadat included Mustafa Khalil and 'Abd al-'Aziz Hijazi (former prime ministers) and Mansur Hasan (ex-minister of information), all of whom denied that money was the main motive behind Sadat's seeking peace: Khalil said that the Arab countries' aid was minor and it had not compensated Egypt for its expenses in the wars. There was no connection between that Arab aid and the peace initiative; and even if there was such a connection, it was secondary.[201] But beneath the words and proclamations, there was no denying the dire economic situation: Khalil himself illustrated Egypt's problems in a meeting with Ezer Weizman in November 1977, when he compared Egypt to Bangladesh and Cairo to Calcutta.[202]

The Egyptian politicians' ambiguous attitudes are understandable, considering that many of them had to portray the whole peace process in a very delicate and particular manner. The politicians were uneasy with portraying the peace initiative as an exchange for economic gains because:

1   Admitting the centrality of economic motives lessened the momentum of Sadat's initiative, which would mean that Egypt was seeking peace from a position of weakness, and not from a position of strength, as presented by Sadat in his historical speech on the opening of the People's Council convention on November 9, 1977: "I am ready to go to the end of the world from a position of strength, so that none of my sons, the officers and the soldiers, will be hurt";[203]
2   Acknowledging the existence of economic motives also meant admitting that Egypt had neglected the wider Arab interest in favor of its own interests;
3   Revealing the scope of Arab aid and the influence it had in Sadat's decision would mean that Egyptian foreign policy was influenced by an external factor, which was undesirable.

Not all Egyptian observers were as unwilling to admit that the economic motive was key. Anis Mansour said that "from many and intense conversations" with Sadat, the Egyptian leader's pragmatic outlook – that war was too costly – became apparent. Sadat argued that he preferred to live in peace, while at the same time, with the amelioration of the economy, his international standing would improve considerably, which was very important to him.[204] After Sadat's peace initiative Mansour wrote:

> Who is against war? The soldiers themselves. The war had weakened them, as they were flesh and blood. It had embittered their lives and had denied them their home and street and life like all normal people: picking up the phone and finding the line is busy; opening the tap and there is no running water; standing in the street and waiting hours for the bus, and if it arrives, there is no room on the steps; any young man who cannot find work, and if he does find work – he cannot find a house – he cannot pay the rent and so he gives up the idea of marriage and thinks of emigrating – all these people do not want war. None of them need a political doctrine to curse life and people, and to curse those responsible for spending all of Egypt's capital and resources on the purchase of weapons, while preparing for a war with no end in sight, and to curse those we are defending while God increases their riches more and more.[205]

Abd al-Majid, vice-premier for economic affairs, stressed the economic dimension behind Sadat's peace treaty, even going as far as claiming credit for the idea. The representatives of the AOC asked al-Majid to prepare a plan, detailing the way Egypt intended to exploit the aid it was requesting, in preparation for the meeting of the advisory group in Paris in May 1977. Al-Majid met with Sadat, presented him with the plan and said: "We are building on sand." By this he meant that any plan actioned in a state of war would fail:

> I was not willing to use the money of the people in order to build industries, which would probably be destroyed or to improve land that cannot be cultivated because of the war. I felt that we did not need a five-year plan, but inspired action. He [Sadat] told me later that the nucleus of his idea to go to Jerusalem was born that same evening on the banks of the Suez Canal.[206]

Kamal Hasan 'Ali criticized the poor level of Arab aid to Egypt, claiming:

> Sadat understood very well that he would have to wait a long time before the Arabs reached an agreement; and the Arabs and Egypt would be committing a crime if they were to leave the Arab cause as a hostage to this dream, as the economic situation in Egypt could not be kept waiting and it was necessary to help the people that had been burnt by these wars, to ensure a better future.[207]

Certain Egyptian intellectuals believed that economic stresses and fissures in Egypt would heavily influence the "Sadat Initiative." Muhammad Sid Ahmad wrote in 1975 ("When the guns fell silent") that the Egyptian economy would profit from peace – as the lesser evil – and it would serve the interests of the Arab people. Before and after the initiative, the Egyptian intelligentsia had expressed similar opinions, and many articles were published expounding the urgent economic need for a peace treaty, while expressing their rage at the Arabs who had abandoned

Egypt. Some articles warned that without a political solution, the Egyptian economy would collapse and the great strides made by the country would evaporate.[208] Dessuki made an explicit and controversial statement based on this notion, stating that Sadat was not aiming at Israel with his peace trip but that his goal was to obtain massive economic aid from the US.[209] Menahem Begin, the former Israeli prime minister backed this theory, writing that, "In general it is acceptable to suppose that Egypt chose to sign a peace treaty with Israel also for economic resons, but more than having to do with the AOC, these resons were primarily based on the hope of receiving massive aid from the USA."[210]

Muhammad Sha'lan supported the idea that the Arabs played a major part in the peace process, adding that one could sense the negative mood in Egypt against the Arab nouveaux-rich. Sha'lan felt that many Egyptians believed that "the Arabs wanted to see Egypt on its knees." Egyptian workers felt humiliated when serving the Arabs, and then did not receive fair treatment in return. The Egyptian people felt humiliated when they heard the slogan "we Arabs are one people," because of the glaring differences in standards of living between Egypt and the Gulf States. Sadat was reflecting the opinion of the *fellahin* and the Egyptian workers toward the Arabs when he declared: "We don't want your aid – America will save us when we make peace with Israel." The Egyptian people, Sha'lan observed, were segregated from the rest of the Arab world; in essence, the notion of Arab unity was a lie.[211]

## The disillusionment with petro-dollar aid to the Egyptian economy: 1967–1977

Economic difficulties were routine and part of daily life in the three decades predating the "Sadat Initiative," especially in the last few years before the peace deal. The Egyptian balance of payments took a noticeable turn for the worse after the 1973 October War. The worldwide rise in prices of raw products increased Egypt's revenues from export of cotton, but on the other hand, its increased imports, mainly foodstuffs, weighed heavily against its budget, to the point where the balance was running deep into the red, and the deficit in its trade balance more than doubled in 1974. The worldwide slowdown and the decrease in demand for cotton in late 1974 caused a reduced level of income from exports, while imports remained artificially high. The negative trend in prices, allied with the steps to liberalize the imports market, led to a continued deterioration of its balance of payments: from possessing reserves of $148 million in 1973, the balance of payments registered a deficit of $920 million in 1975. The monetary reserves of the Egyptian Central Bank went down from $264 million in 1973, to $206 million at the end of 1975 – an amount sufficient for less than one month's imports.[212]

In the light of these economic difficulties, contact between Egypt and the IMF was initiated in April 1975;[213] Egypt requested aid, with the IMF demanding reforms in the Egyptian economy in return. In April 1976, the AOC ministers of the treasury, meeting in Riyadh, adopted the position of the IMF regarding reforms.[214] Because the AOC supported the IMF's stand, with both parties making it clear that aid would be halted should Egypt reject reform proposals, the Egyptian leaders were left with no choice but to agree to international supervision of its economic policy, so that it could continue to obtain Arab and Western aid. At first Egypt had protested against cutting down on its subsidies, but it was forced to change its position.

Sadat was disappointed with the size of the GFDE's capital, and with the rejection of his request in October 1976 for aid in the amount of $1.25 billion, which had been earmarked to cover the deficit that had accumulated in the Egyptian economy's debts in the second half of 1976. The heads of the GFDE agreed to transfer only $250 million through the Fund – stressing that this money was not meant to cover the deficit, but for development projects – and to guarantee the loan of an identical sum provided by the Chase Manhattan Bank. Nothing came of the high hopes that Sadat had from the petro-dollars. He did not receive, in terms of amount or conditions, anything like the aid he had hoped for. To compound matters, Arab investment in Egypt was low, while the AOC continued to invest hundreds of billions of dollars in the West. Indeed, Arab investment in Egypt totaled just EgP 84 million in late May 1977 (only $215 million as governmental and civil investments, not including inter-Arab projects in Egypt).[215]

On the threshold of 1977, the Egyptian economy faced especially difficult circumstances: the flow of external capital (grants, loans, deposits on the Central Bank), decreased sharply (especially Arab aid), from $3.1 billion in 1975 to $1.9 billion in 1976. The shortage of foreign currency brought with it a decrease in imports, which fell from $4.5 billion in 1975 to $4.2 billion in 1976. In real terms the decline was bigger – approximately 10 percent. Because of the constant demand for foodstuffs from a hungry populace, luxury imported goods suffered. As a result of the foreign currency shortage, Egypt was unable to pay back its short-term debts, and its arrears on these debts, loaned by commercial banks at very high interest, grew steadily. The IMF evaluated the sum of arrears by the end of 1976 at $453 million,[216] and in late April 1977 at more than $1 billion.[217] In the Five-Year Plan of 1978–82 (published in the summer of 1977), the Egyptian leaders had summarized the country's major economic difficulties, dividing them up into seven areas: inflation, a large deficit in its balance of payments, a low level of savings and investment, traditional practices and customs causing unnecessary delays, reduced efficiency in labor, a growing population and a poor administrative leadership unable to carry out development projects.[218]

The IMF, with the enthusiastic support of the AOC and Western countries, continued pressuring Egypt to execute the reforms proposed to it. For two years the Egyptian leaders resisted and rejected the request to cut subsidies and to devaluate their currency. They were opposed to the cut in subsidies, because officials believed it would hit the areas of Egyptian society already weighted down with poverty, allied with their fear that a cut would lead to massive riots. Their opposition to devaluation was derived from their unwillingness to increase Egypt's internal debt, which was partly linked to foreign currency rates. The Minister of the Treasury at the time, Muhammad Zaki Sha'fi'i declared: "We will not bow to any pressure."[219] The act which finally forced the Egyptian government to cut subsidies, much against their will, was the terrible condition the economy was in, lurching from crisis, and the

AOC's unrelenting support of the IMF's demands. This was not passive support, but actively exerted pressure, with the threat of a complete cessation of aid should Egypt fail to comply. The AOC proved that they were in total control of their situation, by agreeing to provide Egypt with increased aid until they initiated reforms. The appointment of Kaissouni as Vice-Premier for Economic Affairs in November 1976, and an additional reshuffling among the economic leadership – with Salah Hamid as Minister of Finance and Hamid al-Sa'ikh as Minister of Economic Affairs – signaled that Egypt was willing, at last, to begin implementing the reforms, and, with the understanding that in the 1977 budget, Egypt would cut down on subsidies, the IMF and GFDE agreed in December to assist Egypt.[220]

According to the agreement, in January 1977 the Egyptian government announced a raise in taxes and a reduction in subsidies, which was supposed to raise the prices of basic products such as rice, sugar, gas and cigarettes. The planned cut in the budget for subsidies was not carried out, because of the food riots on 18–19 January 1977.[221] The cancellation of the planned reforms created an ironic situation, whereby the budget deficit created was eventually larger than the one projected before reforms were ever brought up. The initial budget, with the reforms, included a deficit of EgP 280 million but the riots and the change in the budget – after cancellation of the reforms – generated an expected deficit of EgP 1.5 billion.[222]

Sadat had good reason to fear the political situation in Egypt, which was a result of the economic crisis, and manifested in a dangerous coalition of the unhappy working masses, and the students, who came together in the food riots. In Egypt a direct link was long established between the economic situation and political stability. It was evident in the food riots, regional strikes and 1975 strikes.[223] Senator Percy, in a report presented to the Foreign Relations Committee of the US Senate, stated that, in lieu of the food riots, the Egyptian economy was in serious trouble, with worrying signs of agitation among the people, which could turn into a major problem for Sadat. Although Egyptian officials told Percy that in general in the Middle East, employees do not start revolutions – "the army does that" – Percy remarked that it had become of growing importance to Sadat and to Egypt to terminate the conflict with Israel, so that Egypt would be free to dedicate itself to its own internal development.[224] Not for nothing did they mention in the discussions of the Subcommittee for European and Middle Eastern Affairs that to survive, Sadat had to make some kind of progress with his economic problems, peace initiatives and military stockpiles.[225]

Foreign observers were not the only ones to conclude that a continuing state of war, with no peace treaty in sight, was dangerous for the Egyptian economy and a direct threat to the stability of the regime: Sadat himself said to the Vice-Premier Hasan Tuhami after the 1977 riots that an immediate settlement of the conflict with Israel was absolutely necessary to make the regime less vulnerable,[226] and 'Abd al-'Azim Ramadan warned after the riots that there was talk of a planned military coup.[227] Then in late November 1977, following Sadat's visit to Jerusalem, the *Ruz al-Yusuf* intimated that if peace was not made with Israel, it was reasonable to assume that riots would erupt again.[228] Egyptian commentators had issued the same warning immediately after the riots, claiming that Egypt could save up to 42 percent of its budget if it signed a peace agreement with Israel and that "Egypt must withdraw from the Israeli–Arab conflict."[229] *The Egyptian Gazette*, expressing the official government line, asked whether Egypt should be in the forefront in war as well as in striving for peace, with material and physical costs at the expense of the people's welfare, adding that the most profitable economic option would be to avoid a war with Israel, this being the fastest way to get the Arab petro-dollars flowing to this country.[230]

In light of its economic crisis, the IMF consented, in April 1977, to grant Egypt with credit, and in May 1977 an international group of consultants met to discuss the level and means of aid required to help Egypt. They decided that Egypt would receive $5 billion, which included leaving deposits (mostly Arab deposits amounting to $2 billion) in the Egyptian Central Bank. The GFDE agreed to loan it a sum of $1.47 billion. These sums allowed Egypt to repay its debt arrears,[231] but did not enable it to pull itself out of dire poverty. This created a scenario which saw Egypt pay off one debt with another. The main difference was that Egypt had obtained the GFDE loan at much easier terms than the terms of its commercial loans. The loans given to Egypt under commercial terms had been granted for a period of between six to twelve months, with interest sometimes reaching peaks of 15 percent, compared with the GFDE loans, which had been given for a period of five years, including a grace period of five years, and at a much lower interest.[232] Payment of debt arrears, however, was not a guarantee of social development or the ameliora-tion of conditions for the Egyptian population. Their living conditions were appalling, generally, and their patience with the leadership had worn thin. Civil debts continued to grow, increasing from $5.8 billion in late 1976 to $8 billion by the end of 1977, of which $1.1 billion was owed by Egypt to the commercial banks. There seemed to be no way out of the escalating debt for the Egyptian economy. Budget subsidies rose steadily: in 1974 amounting to EgP 83 million, in 1975 multi-plying more than seven times, to EgP 622 million, and in 1977 to EgP 642 million.[233] IMF economists estimated the subsidy budget to be even higher, by a further EgP 280 million (the difference was a result of the Egyptian government's calculations based on the official exchange rate).[234] Egypt's foreign currency reserves remained at a critical level, and in September 1977 they amounted to $458 million, which would just about cover one month's budget.[235]

Sadat was aware that the Gulf Fund had exhausted its capital in its last guar-antee to Egypt after the food riots. The Fund's managers were not willing to increase loan capital, or to provide a permanent aid package to Egypt. As witnessed when the Fund vehemently rejected Egyptian calls for a "Marshall Plan" style of aid, the Fund's generosity was limited. At a stretch, the leaders of the oil-producing coun-tries were willing to provide military aid for war purposes and donate "trickles" of economic charity. For Sadat, however, the main purpose of the aid was to rehabil-itate the economy, and not to play the role of the Arab "gendarmerie."[236]

There was a further problem: Arab aid to Egypt was more a problem than a solu-tion. This aid was given largely to help Egypt in its continuing struggle with the Israelis, and this meant that Egypt was forced to prioritize war ahead of valuable and much-needed development of its resources (the Suez Canal, Sinai oil), renouncing any chance of improving the economic and social crises, by capitulating to the status quo. Arab aid was never able to fulfill the needs of the Egyptian economy, in the main because it was not channeled to long-term development, only to urgent problems. Arab aid also tended to be unpredictable in its amount and timing, as Egyptian policy-makers found out. Neither did the AOC's military aid cover all Egypt's military expenses, so Sadat had to divert considerable sums to fund the military's expenses. Resources reallocated to the armed forces represented another burden on the economy. Sadat knew that the situation would at best remain static, at worst, and more realistically, continue to deteriorate, due to the handicaps placed on his ability to carry out reforms.

The extent of Arab aid, the manner in which it was given and interference in its internal affairs all represented blows to Egyptian prestige, and were demonstrative of a desire among the Arab nations to make Egypt a dependent entity, while it slogged away in meaningless and crippling conflict. The financial debt constituted a potential threat to Egypt's standing in the Arab world and to its political manoeuverability. Shamir said: "From Egypt's point of view, even if Arab aid would cover all its direct and indirect losses, Egypt would still be the loser, because this settlement brings with it a large debt to other Arab countries in exchange for aid, which in the end does not help it very much other than making time."[237] Sadat was unhappy with both the timing and the conditions the oil-producing countries attached to their aid, as Egypt was in the midst of a serious crisis and it had no other choice but to accept their dictates.

World Bank reports anticipated a further decline in the level of aid to Egypt: in a research done by the Bank's economists, predictions for the Egyptian economy in the years 1978–81 concluded that the economic aid, in all its forms (cash, goods and aid for projects), would decline from year to year.[238] In their opinion, Egypt would suffer a sharp decline of cash grants, and by 1978, these would be no higher than $150 million.[239] The bank's economists also expected an increase of the commercial deficit and in Egypt's debt payments.[240] The level of Arab investment was a concern to all, especially Sadat, and an atmosphere of fear and helplessness was prevalent, Senator Percy was told: "Everybody talks about [the aid crisis], but nobody is doing anything."[241] Ironically, it seems that by withholding a share of the oil wealth from Egypt, the AOC made plain to Sadat that every Arab nation upheld its own independent interests. By signing two interim agreements with Israel and therefore launching his own peace initiative, Sadat proved that an isolationist policy could be advantegous.

Sadat had, however, failed to gain any ground in the matter of Arab aid after the October War. If, after the euphoria following the "glorious crossing," Egyptian leaders had not managed to get the levels of civil aid so desperately needed, what would they get at a later date? Egypt could have applied considerable pressure after the war and it could have made specific demands. The Mar'i delegation, as we saw, received instructions to obtain resources, but without mentioning an amount, and that is the way they operated. The Egyptian leadership, having failed to obtain commitments for Arab aid, had to settle for aid on an ad hoc basis. The mission to secure aid had not been an easy one, but some of Sadat's associates felt that the Egyptian leader had made an avoidable mistake by refraining from leaning heavily and applying massive pressure on the AOC leaders. As a *fellah*, Sadat's rural traditions and background meant that he would not mention specific figures to the

AOC; they ought to give of their own free will. Also, "the protocol presents" he received did not facilitate the mobilizing of aid. Sadat was aware of this dismal failure, and of the many occasions he had shown gratitude and forgiveness for Arab aid up to mid-1976, such as: "we are satisfied with our brothers' aid."[242] Sadat's decision to make peace with Israel was intended to secure permanent aid from beyond the Arab sphere; sadly, this was, according to Ayubi, "a process which never started properly."[243]

## The blow to Egyptian prestige

Sadat detested the Gulf States' leaders even before the peace process. His main gripe was the way the Arabs treated him, causing him and his people shame and frustration. Sadat's relationship with the AOC leaders prevented him from openly expressing his bitterness and anger. Although he was a sentimental figure with a rural background, Sadat was also a realist. His realistic attitude separated him from Nasser's political idealism. Nasser had also been aware of Egypt's serious economic situation, and though he effected changes in his political and economic policy after the defeat of June 1967, the steps he did take were insignificant. In comparison, Sadat had the moral courage not only to admit the bitter truth – which Nasser also did – but, primarily, he had the courage to work honestly and decisively toward a peace treaty with Israel. Such a policy revealed the depths to which Egyptian pride had sunk, and this was felt by every Egyptian citizen.

There were many ways in which, intentionally or otherwise, the AOC wounded Egyptian pride, including:

1   The manner in which aid was granted immediately after the war (starting with the Mar'i delegation).
2   AOC unwillingness to allocate sufficient resources to a "Marshall Plan" for Egypt.
3   The oil countries' demand that Egypt adopt the reforms of the IMF.
4   The dictate to put Egypt under external supervision.
5   The affair of the Gulf Fund for the Development of Egypt (GFDE).
6   The extent of Arab investment in Egypt compared to their investments in the West.
7   The food riots and the feeling among Egyptian people that "the Arabs have abandoned us."
8   The AOC's readiness to provide economic aid only in times of hardship and military aid for war purposes.
9   The treatment of Egyptian workers in the AOC.

Honor and shame are universal values, but in Middle Eastern society they stand at the summit of the social values pyramid.[244] J. G. Peristiany developed a basic theory of Arab humility and pride, according to which you never ask for what you need except in times of great stress. Your needs are determined by the other party, and this motivates the phenomenon known as "the national honor." Honor is composed, in the main, of the image of weakness subdued by humility.[245] Sadat was in deep trouble, and the Arabs were in no hurry to solve his economic problems. Translated in terms of "pride relations," Sadat was helpless to complain, even though the aid conditions were terrible, and Egypt was being forced to beg again and again from the "Bedouin." The AOC did not live up to Sadat's expectations, but he was not in a position to make specific demands. Although Sadat did not express this openly until 1977,[246] it was not uncommon for him to confide in those close to him in private conversations.

The AOC demanded that Egypt spell out in detail how and for what purposes their aid was used. Anis Mansur stated that "the Arabs asked Egypt for receipts on its expenditures, in other words they were saying they did not completely trust Egypt. This fact humiliated Egypt, the more so considering that before the oil era Egypt had assisted these states on all levels, and their princes and their kings received their salaries from the Egyptian treasury."[247] Tahsin Bashir also said that the AOC leaders requested that foreign institutions manage the loans they were supposed to allocate to Egypt. Sadat was expecting to be rewarded by the Arabs for such financial transparency, "but the Arab world does not operate in this way."[248] Very often the AOC dictated the publications in the Egyptian media a propos their aid. In late 1974, the Saudis demanded that Hijazi advertize in the Egyptian media the fact that the aid they had decided to grant him on a visit to South America "was a grant to the Egyptian people." Hijazi refused, and it was only after Sadat intervened that this item was published in the Egyptian media.[249]

Sadat was angry. In his opinion, he had been forced to renounce both his personal and national pride because of the AOC's decisions and strict aid policies, while the "Bedouin dwarfs," as Sadat called the AOC, became stronger at Egypt's expense. While Egypt was not particularly happy with the demands for economic reform made by the Western nations and major international financial institutions, it had no choice but to agree to some of their proposals; after all, these were not "Arab brothers" – it was not a matter of pride. Accepting dictates from the Arab countries, however, was a different matter.[250] The KD 10 million loan given for the textile project in the village of Al-Dawar, which Egypt borrowed from the Kuwaiti Development Fund is a pertinent example: in a discussion of the People's Council regarding the ratification of the loan, Kuwait was sharply criticized. Mumtaz Nasir declared that the interest the Fund had offered (4%) "was higher than the reduced interest customary between brothers (ashiqqa')," and he added that many clauses of the agreement, "primarily the fourth clause," included "harsh conditions of submission hurting our economic sovereignty." This clause dealt with the necessity of appointing a (Kuwaiti) manager and contractor for the project, who required the total agreement of the lenders.[251] Khalid Muhyi al-Din supported Nasser's position, arguing that "the Fund's conditions were hurting our sovereignty." 'Abd al-Fattah Hasan proposed rejecting the entire agreement "because it conveys custodianship." "Yes, we do need the money," Hasan said, "but this agreement is likely to be an opening to additional agreements with custodianship qualities." Al-Khariri stated that "this agreement perpetuates our dependence (irtibat) on the lender, and this is not cooperation nor partnership . . . the loan conditions are not conditions of an Arab sister state, but imperialistic conditions." 'Abd al-Mun'im Husayn remarked that the loan conditions showed "this is an expression of no-confidence."[252] The AOC leaders also insisted that GFDE capital be invested in specific projects under Fund supervision, and they refused to consent to Egypt's request for a reduction of interest rates. Sadat suggested to al-Sabah (the ruler of Kuwait since 1977) before the Fund was established, that it be managed by David Rockefeller,[253] apparently in order to obtain some flexibility in using the Fund's money, but al-Sabah replied: "We have our own talented Davids for this job, but their names are . . . Ali and Ahmad."[254]

Muhammad Sha'lan wrote in his book *Al-Tibb al-Nafsi wal-Siyasa* about the importance of the psychological aspect of the decision-making process of the Egyptian leaders.[255] Egypt had been the hand giving aid to the Arab states, and now it was experiencing being on the receiving end of aid. Egypt opened schools in the Gulf, sent food and subsidized free meals for the poor, it sent medical staff and teachers to the AOC, the covering of the Ka'aba was made in Egypt (*kiswah*). After the 1960s, however, Egypt found itself forced to repeatedly beg the AOC for aid. Egyptian pride was wounded again after the food riots, when even poor Sudan sent it food and $5 million as support.[256] Sadat also found himself in a position of unmitigated gratitude, filling his speeches with words of praise for his Arab brothers. This was in complete contrast to Nasser's powerful stance in the Arab world, where Arab leaders came to visit him. Sadat travelled several times to the Gulf States and he sent his envoys to knock on the Emirs' doors.[257]

Herman Eilts, the American Ambassador to Egypt and Saudi Arabia, witnessed first-hand Egypt's policy-makers and their attitude toward foreign aid. Eilts said that Egyptian officials treated aid as a sworn commitment of the aid-providing countries to assist them, rather like the images of Pharaonic friezes, showing subjects bringing gifts to the Egyptian rulers.[258] Eilts was speaking in general of foreign aid, but it would be fair to say that there was an especially strong feeling toward the Arab states that they were duty-bound to assist Egypt. It was not just the Egyptian leadership which felt betrayed; many ordinary citizens felt exactly the same. For the average Egyptian, barely able to afford enough to survive, watching the Arabs grow in wealth was humiliating. Amos Ayalon published a book, which included several essays by Egyptian students writing about peace with Israel. These essays illustrated the way poor Egypt's relations with the rich Arabs had penetrated the psyche of the Egyptian people, how the Arabs were perceived by the Egyptian people and how the wars had hurt Egypt's economy and its citizens:

> Those who are opposed to the [peace] treaty are not, as a matter of fact, capable of existing without war, because they are the only ones to derive any benefit from it. But countries at war with each other – both the winning and the losing side – they both lose . . . in casualties and property . . . peace means an end to war, an end to poverty, to backwardness, to sickness and to ignorance. It is impossible to solve these problems while dedicating all our strength to endless wars.

Another pupil in the eighth grade wrote:

> Now, if we could get rid of the Arab states, we would have called for help from anybody willing to do so – after our futile cooperation with people who have no desire for peace.

The hardline states, which oppose the peace treaty, did not participate in any war, they did not experience the taste of war nor did they feel the ravages and the damages caused by war. Those opposed to peace enjoy an easy life.

And a ninth-grader remarked that:

[When] oil prices went sky-high – did Egypt enjoy the fruits of this situation? No. Have those Arabs done anything in the war? We were the only ones to suffer losses in wars for the sake of the Arabs.[259]

Egyptians saw the Arabs from the Gulf States who came to Egypt as tourists, shamelessly flaunting their wealth in front of impoverished Egyptians.[260] This concept of Arab wealth is supported by the Egyptians who worked in the AOC. Many of them were badly treated, and bore witness to the fact that in nearly all sectors the Arabs made it clear to them that "who pays the piper calls the tune." The Egyptians were discriminated against in Arab workplaces, in spite of (or perhaps because of) their contribution to the wealth and the social and economic development of these countries. When Egyptian emigrants came back home, they returned with the impression that the AOC were greedy and demonstrated a lack of respect for Egyptians.[261] 'Ala al-Dib described the mental stress experienced by an Egyptian in the Arab diaspora: "The gulf . . . air . . . struck me in the face . . . the nightmares of mental sickness . . . they are nightmares no more, but a reality that I am experiencing . . . [the employer's] words are courteous and crafty . . . as if he is saying to me . . . I know why and with how much you came." Regarding an Egyptian journalist he met in an Arab country, al-Dib wrote "it hurts to see a person of a high standard who, for money, accepts a lower status than he is worth."[262] Tawfiq al-Hakim said: "The Minister of Education and Culture declared a while ago that in his heart he was sad, knowing that thousands of Egyptian teachers were being humiliated, and how their pride was wounded for a piece of bread in a foreign land, in several Arab countries."[263] Sha'lan stressed the hardships, both mental and physical, of the Egyptians working in the Arab countries, and he related many stories of Egyptian emigrants returning to their homeland and suffering acute mental traumas, unable to cope with the humiliation they encountered in the AOC. Baghdadi, who examined a group of Egyptian workers in Riyadh, commented that more than 60 percent suffered from some kind of mental illness as a result of their work.[264]

## Disillusionment with the Arabs' status as "The Sixth World Power"

Besides Sadat's disillusionment with the contribution of petro-dollar aid to the Egyptian economy, his view of the AOC's role and influence in the Arab–Israel conflict was accurate. Very quickly Sadat became cynical of the Arabs' status as "the sixth world power" – a widespread conception after the 1973 war – and became disillusioned with the possibilities of using Arab aid as a political lever. At first, Sadat had spoken enthusiastically of the Arabs' expanding international status: "It is the first time that the Institute for Strategic Studies in London affirmed, that the Arabs had become the sixth power in the world [after the two Great Powers, Western Europe, Japan and China] . . . We will add another weapon in the future, the weapon of Arab capital."[265] Sadat regularly advanced the idea of a partnership between the Egyptian people and Arab resources, and on the anniversary of the revolution in 1973 he said:

> Arab potential is immense, we have achieved a great deal . . . let us put these facts in figures: we are now producing 55 percent of global oil supplies, and we hold 85 percent of global oil reserves . . . if we use this vast potential wisely, we will be able to mobilize the enormous Arab power for the good of our national problem . . . we will welcome cooperation . . . between Arab powers, whatever their geographical situation or their political regime.[266]

Sadat was well aware that the AOC were not able to have any political clout, acting on Egypt's behalf, on the international stage.[267] The "oil weapon" and Arab capital, as political weapons, were weak and in a poor bartering position *vis-à-vis* the Arab–Israeli conflict. The Arabs did have holdings and vast amounts in Western bank accounts, estimated at their peak [after the peace initiative] at more than $300 billion, but these amounts – large by Middle Eastern criteria – could not compare with the economic, military and political strength of the Great Powers. Mattione examined the possibility of the OPEC countries' harming the Great Powers by gaining control of industries in the US or of the Western financial markets through judicious investing. He concluded that OPEC's assets did not constitute a real threat to American or European interests. Moreover, the OPEC countries were dependent on the West, which was holding their investments. The case of the freezing of Iranian assets in the US, following the affair of the American hostages, was a prime example.[268]

### Economic quid pro quo for political negotiations

Gazit argues that, up to the 1973 war, Sadat did not seek peace in any shape or form, although this is contradicted by the Egyptian–Israeli contacts that had been set up.[269] Whether peace had been actively sought before the war or not, after the war, the chances for peace had improved, and Sadat could plan to apply greater resources to the civilian sector, with the needs of the military reduced, and to establish a long-term plan for the Egyptian economy. Kissinger noted that Fahmi – the Egyptian Minister of Foreign Affairs – told him at their meeting in Washington in October 1973, that Sadat wanted a chance to strengthen relations not only with the US, but also with Israel. In his memoirs he wrote that not only had Egypt accepted the existence of Israel, but Fahmi left no doubt that Egypt would not let the Palestinians interfere in a solution.[270] Heikal also affirmed that in November 1973 Sadat said to him: "This is the last war as long as I am President."[271]

Sadat's two main concerns were, first, the continued development of the Egyptian economy, and, second, the financial quid pro quo that comes with political peace treaties. At first, Sadat wanted to oversee Egyptian growth and investment in stages, but by the end of 1977, he realized that he had no choice other than to adopt a policy of "shock treatment." Sadat's ability to wrest economic benefits from political negotiations is amply illustrated by both his practical economic–political policy and by various documents: in the "October Paper" Sadat spoke about the heavy burden of military expenditures, and he predicted an increase of Egypt's revenues from growing investment, the development of the Suez Canal, oil exports and tourism. This document reflected Sadat's growing belief that only through peaceful settlement with Israel could the economic potential of Egypt be harnessed. It should be remembered that in 1974 – the year the "October Paper" was published – the Suez Canal was closed, oil was not an essential component of the Egyptian economy, the Sinai oil fields were under Israeli control, and it was impossible to develop oil resources in the Suez Gulf without political cooperation. In January 1975, Sadat declared: "The goal of peace should be the goal for all of us . . . and with peace we will be able to build and develop our country";[272] then in August 1975, in a speech to a delegation of the American Congress visiting Egypt, Sadat argued the case of a caterminous relationship between economic development and the need for peace. Sadat said that he saw no way of rehabilitating Egypt while the threat of war existed.[273] In a letter sent by Zaki Shafi'i, the Minister of Economic Affairs to Witteveen, director of the IMF, on January 1, 1976, Shafi'i wrote that Egypt would not be able to continue to bear deficits in its balance of payments on the level of 1975, and he added: "In the near future we expect a significant boost to our income from the opening of the Suez Canal, rapid development of oil exports [inter alia as a result of the return of the oil fields], and a continuing rise in remittances from emigrants and tourism revenues."[274] This letter, as in the "October Paper," highlights the Sadat regime's preoccupation with political settlement and the domestic economy.

In the Egyptian Five-Year Plan for the years 1978–82 – planning started in 1975 and it was published in August 1977 – far-reaching results for Egypt were established, among them the aim to reach a real annual GDP growth rate of 12 percent.[275] There is no way Egyptian policy-makers would have made such an optimistic forecast without the prospect of peace close at hand. In various interviews granted by Sadat to journalists, before his trip to Jerusalem and expecially afterwards, he spoke about the future prosperity Egypt could expect from peace.[276] He spoke about an American Marshall Plan for Egypt, to be called the "Carter Plan," and he declared he would ask for $15 billion (in economic aid) for a period of five years, and he said this aid "will work wonders for this country."[277] The media also pointed out the economic profits Egypt would gain from Sadat's steps, inter alia mentioning American aid, growth of foreign investment and reduced military expenditures. Perhaps some reporters made tendentious observations because of government pressure to support Sadat and his policy. However, there was still some disillusionment about what the future held for the economy, even in peacetime, which predated 1977.

Sadat utilized propaganda through the media channels to try and alter the mindset of the Egyptian masses. In interviews given by Sadat and members of the government they mentioned Egypt's sacrifices in the wars with Israel: tens of thousands of soldiers killed, tens of billions of dollars squandered, and all the while the other Arab countries had offered nothing close to such sacrifices. On the contrary, some of them had even profited from Egypt's suffering.[278] Egypt's economic difficulties, the Sadat regime added, emanated from its wars with Israel. A war with Israel wan an exercise in futility, since the US backed Israel. Sadat often said that he stopped the October War because he was really fighting against the US and not against Israel.[279] The military aid given to Egypt by the USSR was ultimately insignificant, as the weapons given to it by the Soviets were not able to win the war. Sadat had talked fleetingly about peace before the October War, but following the war and the interim agreements in Sinai, he began to preach the need for peace as being the first step in Egypt's economic recovery.[280] The move toward a political settlement with Israel was also reflected in the rearrangement of Egypt's regional and global alliances: on the regional level, the Teheran–Riyadh–Cairo axis replaced the Cairo–Damascus–PLO axis, and on the global stage the US and Western Europe replaced the USSR as its main allies.

Sadat was not acting against the grain of an entire nation when he decided to go to Jerusalem: the intelligentsia also helped to create the foundations necessary for Sadat's initiative to succeed. Previously they had pointed out the unequal share of the burden sustained by Egypt *vis- à -vis* the Arab states regarding the conflict and they pushed to find a remedy for Egypt's troubles, even at the expense of the Arabs. Shamir notes that, after Nasser's death, liberal-minded and leftist elements spoke about the need to reach a political settlement with Israel, with an eye on the disastrous results brought about by the conflict on their society and economy.[281] Tawfiq al-Hakim, for example, wrote in his book *'Awdat al-Wa'y*, that if the resources spent in war had been invested in Egyptian villages, each village would have received EgP 1 million and would have become a "prosperous settlement."[282] The intelligentsia's carefully considered views on the subject of the conflict were also based on other factors beyond the economic crisis. The Egyptian illuminati understood that there was no chance of the Arabs crushing Israel in the foreseeable future because of the IDF's strength, and because of American support for Israel's existence. Other Egyptian reasons for opting for peace included: consciousness of the price in lives of the conflict; the reaction of Egyptian patriotism against pan-Arabism and the feeling that Egypt had become the cannon fodder of the Arab world; the realization that Egypt's resources were not sufficient for simultaneously continuing the conflict and for domestic rehabilitation; the realization that a constant state of war would choke Egypt's political and cultural development; the recognition that the war with Israel could lead to a global military and political crisis; uitilizing Israel's scientific and technological advancements for the good of the whole region.[283]

Up to mid-1977 Sadat strove to settle the Arab–Israeli conflict piece-by-piece, rather than total peace, in order to satisfy the very different demands of the US and Saudi Arabia. Sadat soon realized that this solution would not strengthen the economy and could even threaten his regime. In November 1977, Sadat undertook to settle the conflict quickly and without further delay, as he had done before (the expulsion of the Soviets, the October War). This was known as Sadat's "electric shock policy."[284] This was a desperate–realistic move (with its conflicting meaning) in reaction to the economic–political crisis. A solution for the Egyptian people's suffering was critical. Ever since he had come to power, Sadat had been promising that the people would have to suffer and sacrifice "just a little more," but after the 1977 riots the patience of 40 million Egyptians had worn thin. The Egyptian leadership was faced with a dire situation: the external threat was no longer an effective instrument for diverting attention from the difficult domestic economic situation. During the food riots students held placards proclaiming "a dead Nasser is preferable to a living Sadat."[285] Sadat could not demand any more sacrifices from people who were at breaking point. Nor were the Egyptian commercial bourgeoisie (which had been steadily growing ever since the mid-1970s), sympathetic to the cause. Sadat understood the connection between the military burden, the external debt and growth. The enormous expenditure on security could have been channeled to investments in technology and education, which would have led to economic growth and acted as the catalyst for broad economic–social development.[286]

**Table 5.3**  Egypt's security expenditure before Sadat's visit to Jerusalem and afterwards (in millions of US dollars, 1980)

| Year | SIPRI | IISS | % of GNP | ACDA[1] |
|------|-------|------|----------|---------|
| 1975 | — | 6,901 | 49.6 | 5,512 |
| 1977 | 3,882 | — | — | — |
| 1978 | 2,719 | 2,134 | 11.3 | — |
| 1979 | 2,068 | 2,622 | 11.9 | — |
| 1980 | 1,621 | 1,600 | 7.2 | 3,056 |
| 1981 | 1,647 | 1,930 | 8.6 | — |
| 1982 | 1,820 | 1,996 | 8.6 | — |
| 1983 | 1,882 | 2.097 | 8.6 | 3,011 |

*Sources*: SIPRI *Yearbook 1987*, p. 169; IISS, *The Military Balance 1987–88*, p. 217; US Arms Control, *World Military Expenditure and Arms Transfers*, various issues.

[1] ACDA data came out originally in 1982 prices. They have been adapted by the author to 1980 prices for the sake of uniformity.

All the cards were stacked against Sadat: he knew that an economic débâcle would mean his political collapse. Regaining Sinai could very well restore his prestige, and it could be an economic starting point – by the increase of oil revenues from the Sinai oil fields, the creation of a tranquil atmosphere for investment and Western aid. The considerable efforts Sadat invested in the peace process were aimed at improving the standard of living in Egypt, and he realized that Egypt's future, its stability and prosperity depended, inter alia, on a peaceful conclusion to the war. Although Sadat wanted peace, what attracted him to Jerusalem was not peace itself, but rather the economic, social and political benefits that came with peace;[287] and this in turn was forced by domestic pressures to end Egypt's appalling state of affairs.[288]

Sadat decided to redirect Egyptian resources to long-term social–economic development projects rather than toward the conflict. The wars and military expenses weighed heavily on his economy: besides the pain and bereavement caused, Egypt had for several years allocated almost half of its GNP to security (see table 5.3), in comparison to an expenditure of about 6 percent in the industrialized West. Israel also spent a high percentage of its GNP on security, but there were three basic advantages Israel had that made such a high level of fund allocation feasible: first, the Israeli GNP per capita was more than ten times higher than the Egyptian GNP per capita; Israel received extensive economic and military aid from the US; and Israel did not have to contend with the problem of rapid population growth as Egypt did. Straight after Sadat's visit to Jerusalem, it was already possible for Egypt to mark up a significant reduction in its outlay on security. Table 5.3 presents three estimates for Egypt's security expenses before and after the Sadat initiative: SIPRI in Stockholm, the Center for Strategic Studies in London (IISS), and ACDA. Notwithstanding the differences between the data, they all point to a clear trend – considerably diminished security costs after the trip to Jerusalem, and especially after the signing of the Camp David agreement.

The Egyptian economy was severely affected not only by the direct costs of the wars, but also – no less important – by loss of potential income and postponed development caused by political instability and insecurity, which over the years affected Egypt's GNP. Egyptian leaders argued that the conflict swallowed vast resources, because Egypt had to fund the military sector. Furthermore, the war delayed the return of the Sinai peninsula, with its natural resources as a source of potential profits.[289] As a land embroiled in the great ideological Arab–Israeli conflict, Egypt was similar to Brazil – a land of potential wrecked by brutality, corruption and poverty. Senator Charles Percy stated that the Egyptians believed that their country had enormous potential, with their labor force, varied experience and (potential and realized) market. They spoke about progress, about projects for oil exploration and tourism, and boasted of their mineral reserves, mainly phosphates. But as long as Egypt had to live in the shadow of war, the country's economic potential could not be realized.[290]

In the June 1967 War, Egypt had lost the Sinai peninsula, the Suez Canal's population of one million was uprooted from its homes, and most of the major industries in the Canal area were destroyed, including the refineries. Sinai represented a considerable loss of income for Egypt, following the occupation of the oil fields. The continued state of war in Sinai after the 1967 War ensured a total stagnation of development of the Gulf of Suez, which was within range of military drills, preventing both private and Government investment. The Suez Canal – one of Egypt's few sources of substantial foreign currency at the time – was closed to vessels because of the war. This meant that a large part of Egypt's profit from foreign currency revenues – oil exports, the Suez Canal and tourism – was expunged. In order to realize potential monies, Sadat would have to reach a peace agreement with Israel. This is without taking into consideration the vast economic and military aid from the US (including aid for the Egyptian military industries), and from Western European countries and Western investment that Egypt could reasonably expect after any treaty was signed. As expressed by the Vice-Premier for Economic Affairs in December 1977, a political settlement would enable Sadat to regain Sinai with all its natural wealth,[291] and to develop the oil sector, with its important potential revenue. Sadat probably knew in advance – through Dayan – that his demand for Sinai would be accepted, although this point is still a matter of controversy.[292] Sadat was interested in promoting foreign investment in Egypt, and he saw that, in spite of the investment laws of 1971 and 1974, not many investments were being made. This changed a little for the better after 1975 following the Sinai agreement – the

Egyptian Minister of Economy, Zaki Shafi'i, said that only then were foreign investors provided with a fair opportunity[293] – but the shadow of war remained an anathema to foreign investors.[294]

**Table 5.4**    Current account, 1974–1977 (in millions of US dollars)

|                       | 1974      | 1975      | 1976      | 1977      |
|-----------------------|-----------|-----------|-----------|-----------|
| a. Balance of trade   | –1,841.1  | –2,831.9  | –2,777.6  | –2,723.0  |
| Export FOB            | 1,671.1   | 1,566.0   | 1,609.3   | 1,992.6   |
| Import CIF            | –3,512.2  | –4,397.9  | –4,386.9  | –4,715.6  |
|                       |           |           |           |           |
| b. Net services       | 212.1     | 356.5     | 1,180.4   | 1,463.4   |
| Revenues              | 709.4     | 1,079.7   | 1,976.5   | 2,551.8   |
| Payments –            | 497.3     | –723.2    | –796.1    | –1,088.4  |
|                       |           |           |           |           |
| c. Balance a+b        | –1,629.0  | –2,475.4  | –1,597.2  | –1,259.6  |
|                       |           |           |           |           |
| d. Private transfers  | 41.7      | 90.2      | 87.1      | 60.6      |
|                       |           |           |           |           |
| e. Current balance    | –1,587.3  | –2,385.2  | –1,510.1  | –1,199.0  |

*Source*: IMF, *ARE – Recent Economic Development* (SM/79/53: February 20, 1979), p. 45.

Several positive factors did exist in the Egyptian economy, and these elements also stood to benefit from any peace treaty. Sadat wanted to continue to develop sectors that had contributed to the country's economy in times of peace. Since 1976, current and capital accounts in the balance of payments had improved; the current account deficit had fallen from $2.4 billion in 1975 to $1.2 billion in 1977, and the general deficit was reduced from $2.4 billion in 1975 to $0.7 billion in 1977 (see table 5.4). This improvement stemmed primarily from the reopening of the Suez Canal in June 1975, increased oil exports and revenues from tourism, and increased money transfers from Egyptians residing abroad.

The Suez Canal was reopened in June 1975 after the second interim agreement, and yielded a return of $430 million in 1977. Indeed, the opening of the Canal was a symbol gesture of a new era of stability in Egypt. The Canal attracted investors and made possible the development of the Gulf of Suez (oil reserves located there held great promise for the Egyptian economy). Already in 1976, the oil sector had taken its place as Egypt's prime export product replacing cotton: in 1975, Egypt exported an average of 70,000 barrels of oil per day; by 1979, it was 200,000 barrels a day.[295] Tourism also showed an impressive increase after 1975: in that year revenues increased by 25 percent, in 1976 by another 40 percent, and in 1977 by even higher percentages.[296] The number of tourists from the OECD countries grew steadily: in 1973 there were 149,000 tourists, and their number increased to 362,000 in 1976, and in 1977 to 434,000 tourists[297]. In the first nine months of 1978 the number of tourists from these countries was even higher than the number of Arab tourists – 357,000 compared to 352,000.[298]

Although the road to peace had been difficult to follow, the results had justified the means; notwithstanding an increase in the price of imports in 1979, the current deficit in the balance of payments remained approximately on the same level as in 1978, because Egypt had exported more than double the amount of oil in1979, and there was also the continued income from its emigrants in the Gulf States and from the Suez Canal. The oil factor made a double contribution: it saved Egypt from having to import oil, and contributed to the increase of its foreign currency earnings. In 1980 its income from oil exports reached $2.7 billion,[299] and its combined income in that year from oil exports, the Suez Canal and tourism amounted to about $4 billion. The newfound, independent sources of income had proved to be far more important and beneficial than foreign aid; not only was Egypt not dependent on the wealth and politics of Arabs, Soviets or Americans, but the total revenues of independent sources – tourism, oil and the Suez Canal – had, by 1980, produced earnings higher than total foreign aid. Sadat's trip to Jerusalem was the first step on the long road to rehabilitating the Egyptian economy.

## Aid from Washington: The alternative to Arab and Soviet aid

Sadat was not disappointed only with Arab aid. He soon discovered that the Egyptian economy did not profit very much from its dependence on the USSR. Besides recognizing that the US was more able to contribute to the economy than the USSR, Sadat also feared the Soviets' political intentions. In September 1975, he said: "Since I came to power . . . the Russians have not been satisfied with me. They want another President . . . [from the arms supply viewpoint] I am ten steps behind Israel and three steps behind Syria."[300] The USSR could not supply Egypt with economic and technological aid as advanced as the US. To Egypt's anger, the Soviets opposed a debt repayment postponement offer on a number of occasions.[301] Seceding from the tight Soviet grasp, and the tightening of relations between Egypt and the US, seemed more promising from the standpoint of Egypt's economy.

**Table 5.5** Aid from Soviet bloc countries to Egypt (in millions of US dollars)

| Accumulated aid from 1954 to year | Amount | Yearly increase |
|---|---|---|
| 1961 | 681 | — |
| 1962 | 711 | 30 |
| 1963 | 765 | 54 |
| 1964 | 1,282 | 517 |
| 1965 | 1,408 | 126 |
| 1966 | 1,415 | 7 |
| 1967 | 1,535[1] | 120 |
| 1968 | 1,703 | 168 |
| 1969 | 1,741 | 38 |
| 1970s | 1,844 | 103 |
| 1971 | 2,157 | 313 |
| 1972 | 2,327 | 170 |

*Source*: UN information as quoted by Robert Mabro's "Egypt's economic relations with the socialist countries," *World Development*, (vol. 3, no. 5, May 1975), p. 310, table 4.

[1] As per CIA data, civil aid received by Egypt from the communist bloc in the years 1955–67

amounted to a total of $1,639 million, out of which the Soviet Union guaranteed $1,011 million, and the other countries $628 million. See: CIA, "Memorandum for WHSR, from Paul H. Corsradden (Operation Center) to Smith and Richard," (SDO/CIA: June 8, 1967, declassified 032931). Additional data issued by the CIA mentioned that in the years 1954–85 Egypt received economic aid from the USSR for a total of $1,439 million. See: CIA, *Handbook of Economic Statistics*, 1986. Confirmation of this data can be found in Fahmi's statement to the Foreign Relations Committee of the People's Council in 1976, that the civil debt to the USSR amounted to $1.5 billion. See: *ARR*, March 1, 1976, p. 144. This data matches CIA data, as from 1976 on Egypt did not receive any substantial aid from the USSR.

Soviet military aid to Sadat made up about 75 percent of total Egyptian aid. Total commitments for civil aid that Egypt received from the Soviet bloc in the years 1954–72 amounted to $2.3 billion (table 5.5), but the real sum given to Egypt was less. Up to 1975, actual Soviet aid equaled commitments given by it up to 1972.[302] According to the CIA data, actual economic aid in the years 1954–85 amounted to $1.4 billion.[303] As for military aid received by Egypt from communist bloc countries, the CIA recorded an amount of $1,439 million in the period 1955–67, out of which the USSR gave $1,160 million and the rest of the communist bloc gave $279 million.[304] *Al-Ahram* ran an article stating that Soviet military aid amounted to $5 billion, which is a vast exaggeration.[305] Fahmi declared before the Foreign Affairs Committee of the Peoples Council (fall 1976), that the military debt up to that time amounted to $4 billion, which matched CIA data .[306]

Sadat was unhappy with Soviet military aid. Just six months after the 1973 War, he declared that Egypt was preparing to terminate its dependence on Soviet arms and begin to search for other arms sources.[307] Egypt then began buying large quantities of arms from Western European countries. In March 1976, Sadat proposed to cancel the friendship pact between the two countries, remarking that the USSR had delayed shipments of spare parts and that "they were playing a cat-and-mouse game with me."[308] Sadat's concern for the Egyptian armed forces was tangible: Senator Stevenson, who headed the Senate delegation to the Middle East in February 1976, was privy to the problems faced by the Egyptian army, and detailed a report on the army's status. Stevenson wrote that some of the fighter planes were capable of flying only six hours a month, and that, since May 1975, the Soviets had refused to supply, or to provide maintenance for MIG engines.[309] Fahmi also claimed that the USSR refused to allow India to supply MIG engines to Egypt.[310]

In June 1977 Sadat was still trying to obtain Russian aid. Fahmi, who had discussed the possibility of alleviating Egypt's debts and of receiving arms, received a list of counter-demands as conditions for aid, including: a new friendship pact, cash payment for spare parts and a change in its anti-Russian policy, inter alia by supporting the USSR in suppressing the Eritrean revolt.[311] Sadat was to further distance himself from the Russians, while establishing closer relationships with the US.[312] On October 13, 1977, Ashraf Ghorbal gave Carter a letter from Sadat, in which he promised to make a "bold move."[313]

The Soviet option did not offer Egypt any genuine economic or military opportunities. Mubarak was asked why Egypt had not changed its stance on the peace treaty after emissaries at the 1978 Baghdad conference offered them large amounts of money. He replied: "What are we supposed to do with this money? Will this allow us to purchase arms to fight Israel, and who will sell us arms, the USSR? When they hear that we received $9 billion from the Arabs, [they] will increase the price of their arms three or four times, as they did with Syria, when Algeria paid for it. The Soviet Union will not give us front-line weapons for reclaiming territory."[314]

**Table 5.6** American economic aid[1] to Egypt, 1946–1984 (commitments in millions of US dollars)

| Period[2] | Grants | Loans | Total |
|---|---|---|---|
| 1946–8 | 0.3 | 10.7 | 11.0 |
| 1949–52 | 1.3 | — | 1.3 |
| 1953–61 | 171.1 | 131.2 | 302.3 |
| 1962–78 | 690.3 | 3,151.5 | 3,841.8[3] |
| 1979 | 607.4 | 480.7 | 1,088.1 |
| 1980 | 601.1 | 565.3 | 1,166.4 |
| 1981 | 787.9 | 342.5 | 1,130.4 |
| 1982 | 802.9 | 262.0 | 1,064.9 |
| 1983 | 766.8 | 238.3 | 1,005.1 |
| 1984 | 866.6 | 237.5 | 1,104.1 |
| Total | 5,295.7 | 5,419.7 | 10,715.4[4] |

*Sources*: USAID, *Congressional Presentation, Fiscal Year 1987* (Annex II, Asia and Near East), p. 89; United States General Accounting Office, *Egypt's Capacity to Absorb and Use Economic Assistance Effectively* (report of the Comptroller General of the United States, Id-77–33: September 15, 1977), pp. 1, 3, 11; USAID, *US Overseas Loans and Grants and Assistance from International Organizations* (annual), various issues.

[1] Aid includes assistance by AID and other agencies, "food for peace" aid as per clauses 1 and 2 and additional economic aid.
[2] Fiscal years (USA): July 1 – September 30.
[3] Out of this sum, $3.2 billion was promised for fiscal years 1975–8. In 1967 Egypt received $0.8 million. In the years 1968–74 it did not receive any aid from the US. In 1975 the commitment for aid amounted to $370.1 million, while in 1976 this went up to $991.3 million, and since then it has remained on a level of about $1 billion annually.
[4] During this period, refunds and interest paid by Egypt to the US amounted to $996.2 million, so that after these payments the total came to $9,719.2 million. According to the first source, total economic aid after refunds and interest amounted to $9,522.3 million. In addition to these amounts, Egypt received over this entire period (1946–84) additional aid from the American Bank for Export and Import, and other loans totaling $292.8 million before refunds and interest and $218 million afterwards.

Washington's open door policy suited Sadat. After he had changed Egypt's political–economic orientation toward the West – viewing Western aid as the most promising possibility for a country struggling with urgent economic and political problems[315] – Sadat looked, more than ever, toward Washington for help with Egypt's internal crises. America's promise of economic aid, without military ties, constituted an important component in the peace talks: Harold Saunders, Secretary of State, explained in the American Committee for Foreign Affairs, that Sadat tried to avoid illustrating any relationship between his new pro-West attitude and American aid, but he did acknowledge the economic value of continuing coopera- tion with the US.[316] Indeed, Sadat received aid from Washington even before the peace initiative (see tables 5.6, 5.7), and he perhaps understood that even greater monies from Washington's pockets were waiting for him at the gates of Jerusalem. Sadat would have to be quick. By 1977, Egypt was in economic and political turmoil. The US seemed to offer a quick fix to the many problems dogging the nation, by assisting the Egyptian economy through government aid, as well as encouraging private investment. Most importantly, the US seemed to offer the best chance of reclaiming Sinai, which was the key to restoring his prestige, his regime and his economy. Sadat chose the American option after the 1973 War and, through much criticism and opposition, persevered in this policy. In August 1977, a senior Egyptian official remarked: "If there is no progress toward peace, we will lose all our logical basis to govern. The liberalization, the open-door policy and our new attitude toward Israel were based first and foremost on the American option. If Americans cause us to fail, we will lose our jobs.[317]

Sadat had a sound basis for choosing to realign himself with the Americans: before they had established diplomatic relations, Egypt received American aid in the amount of just $8.5 million between June 1967–74,[318] but during talks leading to the signing of the first interim agreement in Sinai, Kissinger promised Sadat economic and military aid. Kissinger also told Heikal that, while the USSR might be able to supply Egypt with arms, only the United States could provide a fair solu- tion that would allow Egypt to regain its territories.[319] After the renewal of diplomatic relations in 1974, President Nixon promised to provide Egypt with advanced technology, even agreeing to discuss the possibility of selling Egypt a nuclear reactor.[320] During Sadat's visit in the US in November 1975, American officials guaranteed to provide Egypt with nuclear reactors and the uranium for their operation.[321] In 1976, the extent of Western aid to Egypt surpassed that of AOC aid; and American economic aid was increasing all the time. The American administration was attempting, through a financial catalyst, to encourage Sadat to continue on the democratic road and to start working on long-term domestic conomic development.[322]

American policy-makers kept close relations with Sadat after the 1973 War. By the time of his death, more than two thirds of the members of Congress had visited him.[323] Carter recalled that his personal relations with Sadat were "as close as they could possibly be."[324] The Americans proved to Sadat that the road to peace and democracy was profitable for the Egyptian economy, in both the short and long term, and that American aid was more reliable and rewarding than Arab or Soviet aid: within one year of the renewal of relations with Washington, American aid to Egypt was tripled, from $250 million in 1975 to $750 million in 1976. After the food riots, the US agreed to divert $190 million that were destined for development projects into emergency aid for foodstuffs;[325] and according to Ambassador Atherton, the US intervened with the IMF on Egypt's behalf, persuading them to lessen their pressure for reforms in the Egyptian economy, taking into account Sadat's "very delicate" situation.[326]

**Table 5.7**    American military aid[1] to Egypt, 1946–1985[2] (commitments in millions of US dollars)

| Period | Grants | Loans | Total |
|--------|--------|-------|-------|
| 1946–8 | — | — | — |
| 1949–52 | — | — | — |
| 1953–61 | — | — | — |
| 1962–78 | — | 0.2 | 0.2 |
| 1979 | 0.4 | 1,500.0 | 1,500.4 |
| 1980 | 0.8 | — | 0.8 |
| 1981 | 0.8 | 550.0 | 550.8 |
| 1982 | 202.4 | 700.0 | 902.4 |
| 1983 | 426.9 | 900.0 | 1,326.9 |
| 1984 | 466.7 | 900.0 | 1,366.7 |
| Total | 1098.0 | 4,550.2 | 5,648.2[3] |

*Sources*: Same as table 5.6, not incl. source no. 2.

[1] The Military Assistance Program (MAP) includes grants, credits for arms purchases and military instruction.
[2] The data in table refer to the period up to 1984. In 1985 Egypt received military assistance totaling $1,777 million. There is no data available at this time about the division of aid into grants and loans.
[3] After Egypt paid refunds and interest, military aid amounted to $4,642.6 million in 1984.

Apart from the obvious benefits of American economic aid, Sadat realized that peace and political reconciliation with Israel would reap other benefits, such as Western military–technological aid and front-line arms. The conflict was limiting the amount of economic and military aid from the West and also deterring investment from Western businesses, who were not interested in investing their capital in such an unstable region. In 1976, Egypt received six military cargo planes (with Saudi financing) from the US, but aside from this, military supplies were sporadic and there were no front-line arms. Total American aid to Egypt before the peace treaty did not surpass $250 million – most of which represented actual purchases and the confirmation of supply of twenty cargo planes and jeeps.[327] By late April 1977, the US promised to supply several military items to Egypt. Brzezinski, Carter's National Security Advisor, said that this gesture was intended to demonstrate to Sadat that moderation paid off, and that the US was prepared to match its military relations with Israel through closer cooperation with anti-Soviet and politically moderate Arab regimes.[328] Only after his trip to Jerusalem was Sadat able to order F-5E planes. Carter agreed to this deal, then went and exceeded expectations by deciding to supply Egypt with fifty fighter planes, despite the suggestion of some of his advisors that it would be wise to supply Sadat with a smaller number of planes.[329]

Sadat was well aware that the rate of aid to Egypt would parallel the rate of his moves in the peace process. The Foreign Relations Committee of the American House of Representatives insisted that peace and aid be inextricably linked, when it was asked to confirm expanded aid to Egypt. In a discussion in early 1978,

Hamilton, chairman of the Subcommittee for European and Middle-Eastern Affairs, stated:

> Gentlemen, we usually hear that the rationale for the Egyptian aid program is a polit-
> ical rationale . . . Why are we giving so much aid to Egypt?" Veliotes replied: "We
> believe our response to the obvious needs of the Egyptian Government, in its efforts
> to create a better life for its people, will firm up support for the Sadat government as
> it moves to make peace with Israel.[330]

Even after reaching a tentative peace agreement, there was a general consensus amongst Western officials that, without actually signing a treaty, Egypt would not receive any further military aid, over and above the F-5 planes promised it. The following is a discussion regarding the granting of military aid in the Foreign Affairs Committee on March 2, 1979:

> *Chairman F. Church*: "I know, and I was fearful last year that [agreeing to sell
> F-5s] would be the beginning of another policy as mistaken as the Iranian
> policy. I assume that no substantial arms sales are contemplated to Egypt in
> the absence of a peace treaty with Israel. Is that correct?"
> *Draper*: "Again, the F-5."
> *Church*: "Other than the F-5, I mean."
> *Draper*: "That is true, we tend to couch our dialog in terms of what may occur
> after the Egyptian–Israeli treaty is signed."
> *Church*: "I think you should do that because the reports that reach us are that
> Egypt has presented the US with a massive arms shopping list, including 300
> F-16s, hundreds of tanks, short-range technical missiles and armoured
> personnel carriers."[331]

After the final signing of the peace treaty, Brown, the American Secretary of Defense, wrote in a formal document to Kamal Hasan 'Ali on March 23, 1979, that following the peace treaty, the US was willing to strengthen its security ties with Egypt, especially for the sales of arms, and to finance a part of these sales, subject to confirmation by Congress. Brown advised Hasan 'Ali, that the president was going to ask Congress to agree to the shipping of military hardware and accompanying services for a period of three years, for a total of $1.5 billion, out of which credit for up to $500 million would be granted for one year, on very generous terms. He also stated, that the US would be willing to supply the equip-ment "as discussed" and send a military mission to Egypt "soon."[332] In April 1979, Carter sent a document to the Foreign Affairs committee, in which he stated that the American national interest would be served by the confirmation of additional aid to Egypt ($300 million as "a peace dividend") essential to its economic stability, its develpment, and most important, to the continuation of the peace process .[333]

Although Sadat had high hopes for American aid after the peace settlement, he had not completely given up carting Arab aid. Sadat saw American aid as supple-mentary to official Arab assistance (at whatever level), civil investment, as well as the remittances from Egyptian workers in the oil states. Sadat had no real reason to suspect that the AOC would suspend their aid following the peace talks. Saudi Arabia, having declared in public that aid would be suspended, continued to secretly fund Sadat. Before the Camp David agreement, Sadat expressed his belief to Ibrahim Kamal, the Foreign Minister at the time, that Jordan and Saudi Arabia would join the peace process,[334] and so after the first Baghdad Summit Sadat was not worried by the possibility of suspension of aid. In late November 1978, Sadat did not seem to be worried by the Saudis' reaction at the conference, claiming that the relations between Egypt and the Arabs would improve, given time.[335] A report made in early May 1979 by the intelligence division of the American State Department strengthened the supposition that Sadat did not fear a suspension of Arab aid: according to the report, Egypt signed an arms deal with Italy for a total of $225 million just before the peace agreement. The original deal was signed in early 1978, when Saudi Arabia was supposed to finance nearly the entire transaction, but Egypt cancelled the deal, renewing it only just before the peace treaty. The timing of the deal suggests that there was great confidence among the Egyptian policy-makers in the first quarter of 1979, that Saudi Arabia would indeed finance the deal.[336]

The belief that the peace would not have any detrimental effect on Arab aid was advanced by the Americans, not just Sadat. They believed, after Sadat's Jerusalem trip, that the AOC would want to maintain their ties with Egypt and would continue to render their assistance. In a Foreign Relations Committee discussion on September 28, 1978, Hamilton asked Saunders about Saudi Arabia's reaction to the peace process. Saunders replied that Saudi Arabia's policy concentrated on the maintaining of good relations with the US and with Egypt. This belief in a complacent Arab reaction to the peace treaty continued to dominate American and Egyptian political thought up to February and March 1978:

> *Hamilton*: "Arab aid to Egypt in 1978 will amount to $2 billion, is that correct?"
> *Wheeler*: "It may again reach $2 billion this year."
> *Hamilton*: "Will it be on the same level in 1979?"
> *Wheeler*: "We expect it to fall to $1.5 billion in 1979." (Afterwards Veliotes remarked: "We are not sure that the Arabs will cut back on aid." Wheeler was of the opinion that the Arabs "would cut back" on aid to Egypt, but he reckoned that the reason for this would not be the peace talks, but increased Arab aid Egypt had received in 1977).[337]

Besides the US, Egypt received assistance from other Western states. Their aid went up from $540 million in 1976 to $1.1 billion in 1979. The big lenders were the World Bank, West Germany and Japan, who were ready to help Egypt in exchange for a political settlement.[338] In the early 1980s, total commitments from the West (economic aid), including that of the US, amounted to an annual average of $2.1 billion. Furthermore, in 1979 Western businessmen invested about $500 million in Egypt.[339]

## The influence of the Arab economic boycott on the Egyptian economy: 1979–1984

### The attitudes of Egyptian policy-makers and media to the boycott

The economic boycott took place in three stages, and each was accompanied by a different response from the Egyptian policy-makers and official media (herein referred to as the "personalities"). The first period commenced after Sadat's visit to Jerusalem: at this stage they did not yet know where his move would lead, and therefore they hardly occupied themselves with the subject. The second period followed the first Baghdad conference which threatened sanctions if a peace agreement was signed. In this period the media published threats against the stopping of aid and speculated widely on the results of the boycott. In the third period – after the confirmation of the boycott decisions at the second Baghdad conference – some of the Egyptian policy-makers were apprehensive of the boycott, but in order to allay the fears of the Egyptian people, the politicians and the official media declared that the economic boycott would not have a negative influence.

During the first period, before the expression economic boycott was even mentioned, Lutfi 'Abd al-'Azim and Rif'at 'Isam examined the possible outcome of a stoppage of Arab aid to Egypt following Sadat's initiative. 'Abd al-Azim said that there would be no negative influence on the economy if a boycott was imposed. 'Abd al-'Azim compared a future boycott to one previously imposed by Nasser on West Germany after it renewed its diplomatic ties with Israel, calling it "a boycott based on a mistaken estimate of the size of exports and imports between the Arab countries and Germany." Summarizing, he wrote that the boycott would harm economic ties between the Arab states, "ties which Egypt always wanted to develop, but it would not have any real affect on the Egyptian economy."[340]

Rif'at 'Isam concentrated on Arab aid to Egypt. According to him, the Arabs provided aid to compensate Egypt for the loss of income from tourism and from the occupied oil fields of Abu-Rodis. "If Israel withdraws . . . [and the oil fields are returned] what can we expect from Arab aid?" Rif'at stated that Libya had discontinued aid after "the crossing" and it seemed that some of the Arabs would also stop their aid, claiming that the reasons for which it was given did not exist any more. "[In any case], [Arab] aid must not be one of the actual sources on which Egypt bases its economic policy . . . therefore, it is now urgent more than ever . . . to look for . . . an alternative to Arab aid." 'Isam concluded in an optimistic vein, mentioning the expected increase of revenues from oil and tourism, and he emphasized that Egypt must develop a peace economy and not a war economy, in the light of its difficult economic situation.[341]

After the first Baghdad conference (November 1978), many articles were published on the subject of the expected boycott, some of which were pessimistic about the future of the Egyptian economy.[342] But the media remained optimistic and declared that the effects of the imminent boycott would be marginal. One of the arguments for this was that Egypt's foreign trade with the Arab countries was minimal and totaled $621 million a year, e.g. 6 percent of total Egyptian exports. Imports from the Arab states, they wrote, amounted to $436 million, or 4 percent of total imports. The media also stressed that the Americans would cover the loss of Arab aid.[343] After the boycott was officially imposed at the second Baghdad conference (March 1979), the Egyptian media warned the Arab countries not to stop their aid. The Egyptian Minister for Affairs of Economic Cooperation also "mentioned" in early April 1979, that at the end of that year the term of Arab deposits in his country would expire.[344] Egypt actually refused to release AOC deposits totaling $2 billion. Fahd expressed concern over the possibility that Egypt might nationalize the capital of the AOC deposits in its banks, in the event of Arab aid being suspended following the first Baghdad conference.[345] Egyptian media and policy-makers claimed that the Arab countries gave Egypt just $4 billion, while the wars cost its $40 billion.[346]

The message was clear: if Egypt was to be denied Arab aid, then it would not spend enormous amounts on wars. The official Egyptian media stressed that Egypt wanted to establish good economic ties with the Arab states, but that it would not let any boycott hurt the economy. Usama Ghayth examined several decisions taken at the Baghdad conference, quoting "a senior economic personality," who claimed that the decision not to supply oil to Egypt would not affect its economy, as Egypt produced enough oil for domestic use and would even be able to export. After an Israeli withdrawal as part of the peace treaty, Egypt would increase production of the Sinai oil fields. Nor would foreign trade suffer from the boycott, he said, as the extent of trade with the Arabs was minor and Egypt could find alternative export and import markets for those goods in which it traded with the Arabs. The Arab countries, it was argued, and not Egypt, would suffer from the boycott, as the AOC only exported oil to Egypt, while the latter exported a variety of goods to their countries.[347]

The Egyptian policy-makers and the media stressed that in any case Egypt did not receive any significant Arab aid. Jamal al-Natar, Minister of State for Economic Cooperation, said that the boycott would not have any great influence, as Arab aid to Egypt did not exceed 25 percent of total aid received in 1978 from all countries – $750 million of a total $2 billion.[348] Also Mustafa Khalil, the Prime Minister, made an assuring budget speech for 1980, calming concerns about the boycott, stating that the West was "pouring money into Egypt," adding that "in the budget for next year loans and grants from any Arab factor have not been taken into account."[349] Egyptian leaders sometimes intimated that, even if the AOC wanted to, they could not dissociate themselves economically from Egypt, especially because of the Egyptian workers in their countries.[350]

In an article titled "Questions on the subject of the Economic Boycott of Egypt," al-Hasan wrote that not only had Egypt received minimal aid, but that Arab funds made loans to Egypt which were set at harsh terms. Al-Hasan also said that the Arabs interfered in the management of the projects. Even a possible suspension of private Arab investments, however unlikely that was, would not harm Egypt's economy. Private investors obtained favorable terms from the Egyptian government, profiting from the investment conditions without ever helping to genuinely stabilize the Egyptian economy. Furthermore, the investors put most of their money in real estate and in speculative deals, and not in productive projects, exerting a negative influence on the level of inflation. Al-Hasan also stated that boycotting Egypt would strengthen Israel, by showing the Arab world to be divided. "So we are only left with that sad question," he summarized, "is the blood of our beloved ones in a time of Arab solidarity not more precious than all that money?"[351]

**Table 5.8**  Forecast of foreign aid by the Egyptian Ministry for Planning in 1979 (in millions of US dollars)

|  | 1979 | 1980 | 1981 | 1982 | 1983 | 1984 |
|---|---|---|---|---|---|---|
| Aid commitments | 4,300 | 5,155 | 5,750 | 5,990 | 6,580 | 7,380 |
| Actual aid | 1,160 | 1,650 | 2,260 | 2,985 | 3,200 | 3,600 |
| Actual aid after refund of debts | −193 | 250 | 672 | 945 | 690[1] | 950 |

Source: ARE, Ministry of Planning, *Egypt's Development Strategy: Economic Management and Growth Objectives 1980–1984* (November 1979), p. 7, table 2.

[1] In 1983 the Ministry of Planning anticipated a decrease in actual aid, less debt refunding. The reason for this, as mentioned in the report, was that Egypt was supposed to have started repaying its debts to the GFDE, after the termination of the five-year post-ponement period. See: *Ibid.*, p. 6. In actual fact, Egypt did not repay its debts to the GFDE.

The general Egyptian populace was given constant assurances that the Egyptian economy would not be affected by the boycott. An exception to this rule was the report Sadat sent to the Tokyo Conference in June 1979, which brought together the leaders of the European countries with the President of the United States. In this report, Sadat requested aid totaling $17.5 billion over a period of five years, which would help Egypt to contend with the anticipated loss of income through the Arab boycott.[352] This document revealed a deep pessimism and anxiety compared to the brash public statements Egypt made prior and after the report. By cultivating such a pessimistic attitude, Sadat endeavored to mobilize large-scale aid from the West; and it seems that the authors of this report stretched the anticipated negative results of the boycott to the limit, such as listing a concern with the return, en masse, of Egyptian workers from the AOC. A document from the Egyptian Ministry of Planning supported this supposition: an internal report from the Ministry (distrib-uted for debate in November 1979) analyzing future economic strategy, showed signs of optimism. The report stated that in 1979 total refund of debts exceeded total aid from all sources by $193 million, and the forecast for 1984 predicted that aid would exceed refund of debts by $950 million. Forecasts for aid commitments were high. The report anticipated that in 1984 Egypt would receive about $7.4 billion, out of which it would succeed in actually exploiting $3.6 billion. Table 5.8 gives some of the details appearing in this report. The report was distributed for discus-sion before the convening of the Advisory Committee for the Egyptian Economy in Paris on December 19, 1979, in which it was decided that Egypt would receive $2.5 billion in 1980.[353] It is fair to suppose that every declaration served to further a different Egyptian interest: the declarations that the boycott was not affecting Egypt were aimed at proving to the people that peace was essential and would not hurt the economy, and at raising national morale. Expressing concern over the future of the economy was a tactic aimed at gaining increased Western aid.

### An empiric examination of the boycott's influence

The Baghdad boycott did not affect the Egyptian economy, and in some sectors economic ties between Egypt and the oil-producing countries even expanded after its imposition. Furthermore, after the boycott Egypt obtained several new sources of substantial income from the Arab states, such as arms exports to Iraq. The Arabs' decision to maintain economic ties between peoples – the boycott being imposed on a governmental, not civilian level – took the sting out of the boycott; but it should also be taken into account that in several fields Egypt took precautions against any potential damage by freezing AOC assets, as in the case of the Arab deposits amounting to $2 billion in the Egyptian Central Bank.

**Deposits of the Arab oil-producing countries with the Egyptian Central Bank**
From World Bank reports it appears that, already in 1973, the AOC held funds in Egyptian Central Bank (ECB) deposits. According to one of these reports, in late 1973 Egypt's external debt stood at $3.5 billion, with the share of AOC deposits amounting to 9 percent,[354] or $315 million. In April 1975 the *Commerce du Levant* wrote that Libya alone held deposits of $423 million in Egypt,[355] but this data, based on al-Fatah sources in Tripoli, does not match the other reports. In reality, Libya's deposits in Egypt never reached this level.

In the summer of 1975, Arab deposits in Egypt increased sharply, from $300 million in late 1973 to $1.4 billion in mid-1975. According to a memorandum from the Minister of Finance at the time, Ahmed Isma'il, to Sadat, Saudi Arabia agreed to deposit $600 million and Kuwait $500 million. In the agreement with the Saudis (June 19, 1975) it was determined that the ECB would pay its government five percent annual interest, and in the agreement with Kuwait (June 9, 1975) interest of only one percent was fixed.[356] Ayubi stated that in 1979 independent sources estimated Arab deposits in Egyptian banks at about $4 billion. A breakdown of these funds in deposits, however, tells a different story: Kuwait deposited more than $1 billion, Saudi Arabia $900 million, and the UAE $350 million. This is significantly less than Ayubi's estimate, even taking into account Libyan and Iraqi deposits, which amounted to only several tens of millions of dollars, and private Arab deposits.[357] Most reports from both dependent and independent sources (the IMF, the Egyptian, Saudi and Kuwaiti governments, the American Embassy in Cairo), indicated a little over $2 billion as the sum of official Arab deposits made on the ECB, out of which Kuwait deposited $1.1 billion and Saudi Arabia slightly less than $1 billion.[358] In 1975, the last year significant deposits were made in the ECB, total Arab deposits in Egypt came to about $1.4 billion. These deposits became public knowledge after Egypt refused to release them as requested by the AOC, following the Baghdad boycott.

In May 1979 Kuwait advised Egypt that it intended to withdraw its deposits of $1.1 billion.[359] Kuwait's demand threatened to have dire consequences for the Egyptian economy. A report of the IMF indicated that Egypt's liquid foreign currency reserves amounted to less than $400 million in late March 1979. There were also sources claiming that Egypt did not have the ability to return these deposits, even if it wanted to do so, because they were invested partly in Western financial markets.

By the end of 1979 the oil-producing countries, wanting to modernize and affect domestic change, demanded they be allowed to withdraw their deposits. Iraq, with deposits in Egypt amounting to only $30 million, was first to make the request. Egypt refused its request, not because of the amount of money involved, but because it feared setting a precedent that Kuwait and Saudi Arabia would take advantage of. Egypt was acutely embarassed by this matter: the IMF – to whom the subject was referred – made it clear to Egypt that it could reject Iraq's request for reasons of "national interest." Egypt could claim that the request for withdrawal was a polit-ical, not commercial, motive. If Egypt paid Iraq, it would not be able to use the "national interests" card against Kuwait and Saudi Arabia.[360] In the end the Egyptian government froze the deposits by military decree for reasons of "national security." The Minister of Economy, Hamid al-Sa'ikh, declared that the AOC had unilaterally violated agreements with Egypt, adding that in the summer of 1978, Egypt and Saudi Arabia agreed to leave the Saudi deposit in the ECB for an addi-tional period of ten years. As for the Kuwaiti and Iraqi deposits, the minister said that "technically they are available."[361] In December 1979 Sadat denounced the AOC, stating that they had asked the IMF to declare Egypt bankrupt, which would isolate Egypt from the world financial community, and in January 1980 he announced that Egypt had stopped paying interest on the AOC's deposits.[362]

After lengthy discussions, with the mediation of the IMF and in direct talks, the Saudi Minister of Finance Muhammad Aba al-Kha'il announced – after a secret visit to Egypt – that it, along with Saudi Arabia and Kuwait, had reached an agree-ment, according to which the deposits of $2 billion would be released, but they would remain in Egypt. It was decided that it would pay interest on these deposits – a decision which Egypt honored. Prior to the agreement for the release of the deposits (March 1980), Egypt had insisted on an agreement that there would be no sudden withdrawals.[363] The matter of the government deposits was therefore settled, but this was not the case regarding Arab League funds totaling $50 million, which had been deposited before the boycott in Egyptian banks and were subsequently frozen by Sadat's government. Several weeks after the settlement with the AOC, the Arab League took legal steps against Egypt in order to force it to release its deposits,[364] but no decision was taken on the matter.

**The boycott on oil shipments to Egypt and on the use of the Suez–Alexandria oil pipeline** The boycott on oil supplies to Egypt failed to damage its economy. In 1979, annual oil production increased by 25 million tons, out of which Egypt needed only 12 million tons for domestic purposes, leaving the rest for export.[365] Besides, there was no problem obtaining certain kinds of oil that Egypt needed on the international markets. As for the use of the Suez–Alexandria oil pipeline, there were reports that Saudi Arabia and Iraq had stopped using it and that Kuwait was also contemplating a boycott,[366] but only Iraq ever actually kept to its word,[367] and the other Gulf States continued to export oil through this pipeline.[368] The reason for this becomes clear when it is recalled that the Saudis, Kuwait, the UAE and Qatar were partners in this project, and that Saudi Arabia had laid another pipeline along the Red Sea coast in Yanbu', taking into account the use of the Suez–Alexandria pipeline in their planning.

**Expulsion from financial institutions**   In addition to being ousted from the Arab League, Egypt was banned or suspended from membership in the OPEC, the Arab Monetary Fund, the Arab Mining Company, the Arab Development Bank, the Arab African Bank, the Arab Investment Company, all Arab aid funds, the Arab Shipping Agency and from many other bodies.[369] This suspension, however, was more symbolic than damaging to the Egyptian treasury.

**Migration of workers**   After the boycott, there was an increase in both the number of Egyptian workers in the AOC and in the level of foreign currency remittances they transferred to Egypt: in 1978 official remittances amounted to $1.8 billion and in 1980 $2.8 billion. There was a slight decrease in 1981, mainly as a result of the assassination of Sadat, and in 1983 the extent of remittances through official channels exceeded $3 billion; and in 1984 they amounted to approximately $4 billion.

After the boycott, the basis for economic ties between Egypt and the AOC changed. Prior to the boycott, aid was the most important element in their relations; after that period, the remittances of the Egyptian labor force in the AOC fulfilled a central role in the economic relationship between the countries involved. In the years 1979–83 – during the boycott – remittances from Egyptian workers totaling $13 billion in hard currency flowed into the Egyptian coffers, compared to less than $5 billion in the period of 1967–78, or to the approximately $15 billion that Egypt received in aid from the AOC in the period of 1967–78.

**The AMIO**   In May 1979 the Saudi Minister of Defense announced his country's decision to disband the Authority for Arab Military Industrialization (AMIO)[370] as of July 1, 1979. The members of AMIO tried to withdraw the balance of unused funds, but again Egypt froze part of the authority's assets. Kamal Hasan 'Ali, the Egyptian Minister of Defense, announced that the partners in the authority would have to bear the costs of their withdrawal themselves, and that, as compensation, Egypt would protect the rights of foreign members and of the countries that had signed contracts with the organization.[371] Following the dissolution of the AMIO, Sadat established an Egyptian authority for military industrialization, with the intention of filling the gap left by the closure of the AMIO. The US came to Egypt's help and assisted it in renovating factories, in the production of airplane engines and in the reconditioning of Soviet military equipment. Egypt's military industries improved greatly after they terminated their partnership with the AOC.

**Governmental and private investments**   The oil-producing countries continued to invest in Egypt, openly as well as covertly, and the amount of private investment exceeded the pre-boycott level. There was not even a need for the Arab investors to disguise their activities, as Saudi Arabia and Kuwait announced their decision not to interfere in their citizens' private investments in Egypt.[372] An illustrative example for this was the establishment of the Islamic Faysal Bank in Egypt, a few months after the boycott was imposed. The primary backers of this project were the Egyptian government (12.5% of capital) and Prince Muhammad al-Faysal al-Sa'ud, King Faysal's nephew (20.25% of capital). The balance of shares were held by Egyptian nationals and citizens of the Gulf States. The bank succeeded impressively by any standard: its authorized capital went up from $8 million in 1977 to $500 million in 1984; and its total assets increased from $37.4 million in 1979 to $1,861.9 million in 1984. Muhammad al-Faysal, who headed the bank, visited Cairo and always dealt openly, unaware or uninterested in any Arab boycott.[373]

**Aid**   Official aid was one of the only areas in which Egypt saw a level of reduced income, but it did not stop completely. Although Saudi Arabia did not pay for Egypt's F-5E planes, Egypt was able to find an alternative source of funding in the shape of the US, who took care to compensate it and granted it military credit, enabling it to purchase F-4E planes (the F-4E was a superior model to the F-5E). Nor did Egypt repay its debts, the lion's share of which became grants. It did not start paying off its debt of $2 billion to the GFDE until early 1989, instead of in 1982, as originally stipulated.

In April 1982, for the first time since the imposition of the Arab economic boycott, banks with Arab partners started to openly provide loans to Egypt. The first loan for $200 million was given jointly by four banks: Union de Banques Arabes et Francaises; the European Arab Bank; the Arab International Bank; and the United Gulf Bank. Some of the most radical Arab states were among the share-holders of these banks.[374] In May 1982, the *Akhbar Al-Yawm* quoted "a senior Arab official" as stating that various banks in the Gulf intended to grant Egypt several major loans,[375] and at the end of that year the Egyptian Central Bank received an additional loan of $150 million from the International Arab Bank.[376] Many media reports mentioned Arab aid to Egypt, but these sources were not officially confirmed. *Newsweek*, for example, wrote in late January 1982, that Saudi Arabia would probably finance for Egypt a transaction for Mirages totaling $1 billion;[377] in early 1983 *al-Kifah al-'Arabi* wrote that a Gulf State had "recently" granted Egypt a secret loan of $2 billion. The source added that 'Abd al-Muhsin al-Sadir, President of the International Fund for Agricultural Development (who was, incidentally, Saudi), played an important role in securing the loan.[378]

Such information, lacking official credibility, cannot be wholly trusted, but Western diplomats in Egypt maintained that "not insignifcant" sums of money occasionally reached Egypt through covert channels, from anonymous bank accounts in New York. These sums, as per above sources, were not part of any official American aid program, and it is probable that some of these funds came from accounts belonging to Egyptian governmental bodies, such as the Suez Canal Authority or the Egyptian Defense Ministry abroad. However, according to American sources, some of the funds consisted of Arab aid. In 1986 Egypt received $600 million from Saudi Arabia and Kuwait ($400 million from Saudi Arabia and $200 million from Kuwait). This aid was donated covertly, except for the occasional symbolic aid, such as that provided by Saudi Arabia in July 1986, when it openly sent shipments of flour, earning praise in the Egyptian media.[379] After the Islamic conference in Kuwait in 1987, Egypt was promised substantial aid, with talk of the

AOC paying some of Egypt's military debts to the West.[380] The AOC did not halt indirect aid that Egypt received from them through international bodies. This refers primarily to the IMF and various UN institutions, such as: the UNFPA; UN/FAO; UNDP; and many other bodies.[381]

In addition to continued Arab aid, the Western countries also increased their assistance to Egypt. Immediately after the second Baghdad conference, West Germany and Japan showed growing interest in strengthening their economic ties with Egypt. American State Department reports indicate that the Arab confrontation states started applying pressure on Bonn and Tokyo, lest they reacted favorably to Egypt's requests for aid. This pressure became a source of concern to the Germans, and especially, the Japanese.[382] The Japanese found themselves in a difficult dilemma, because they did not want to harm their relations with the Arab states supplying them with oil; but conversely, they did not want to give the impression that additional aid to Egypt stemmed from American pressure. These factors played a role in their request to postpone Sadat's planned visit to Japan in July 1979.[383] After initial doubts, however, West Germany and Japan did not stop their aid to Egypt. On the contrary – they increased it.

**Arab aid funds**   In general, Arab aid funds halted their aid to Egypt after Camp David, but not all the funds followed the same policy. After the imposition of the boycott, Egypt's membership in the funds was cancelled and most stopped their financial support for various projects. Some of the others, however, including the Arab Development Fund, continued financing projects that were already under way. An ADF representative declared that as long as Egypt was not in arrears in interest payments on its previous loans, and as long as it did not violate its commitments, all projects in an advanced state of execution would continue to receive aid. However, it was also made clear that Egypt could not expect to receive new loans.[384] In any case, the loss was not significant. Total loans in the seventies did not exceed $900 million, and from the early 1980s several funds, primarily the Kuwaiti Development Fund, renewed their aid to Egypt.

**Other fields**   Any discussion on the influence of the Arab boycott would not be complete without mentioning the trends in the flow of tourism and commerce between Egypt and the oil-producing countries. Tourism to Egypt was not affected by the boycott, and in the early 1980s Arab tourism to Egypt actually reached record levels. This is remarkable considering that Arab tourism to Egypt did not show any major increase until the 1960s. In 1966 there were 266,000 Arab tourists, which came to 44 percent of the total number of tourists. In the 1970s, Arab tourism to Egypt received additional momentum, marking a record in 1976 – 535,000 Arab tourists, 54 percent of the total number of tourists in that year. In the years 1977–9 there was a decline in the number of Arab tourists. One year after the imposing of the boycott in March 1979, Arab tourism recovered and exceeded the number registered before the boycott: 479,000 tourists in 1980, 579,000 in 1981 and 618,000 in 1982 (see table 5.9). The number of Saudi tourists in Egypt reached a new record in the 1982/3 fiscal year – more than 170,000 Saudis.[385] In 1984 the Saudis made up the second largest group of tourists after the Americans. In that year, 188,000 Americans and 149,000 Saudis visited Egypt. Third place was taken by Sudanese tourists – 140,000.[386]

**Table 5.9**   Arab and other tourists in Egypt, 1952–1984 (in thousands and percentages)

| Year | Arabs | | Others | | Grand total | |
|---|---|---|---|---|---|---|
| | total | % | total | % | total | % |
| 1952 | 21 | 28 | 55 | 62 | 76 | 100[1] |
| 1966 | 256 | 44 | 323 | 56 | 579 | 100 |
| 1967 | 167 | 48 | 178 | 52 | 345 | 100 |
| 1968 | 184 | 58 | 134 | 42 | 318 | 100 |
| 1969 | 194 | 56 | 151 | 44 | 345 | 100 |
| 1970 | 231 | 65 | 127 | 35 | 358 | 100 |
| 1971 | 260 | 61 | 168 | 39 | 428 | 100 |
| 1972 | 314 | 58 | 227 | 42 | 541 | 100 |
| 1973 | 333 | 62 | 202 | 38 | 535 | 100 |
| 1974 | 412 | 61 | 264 | 39 | 676 | 100 |
| 1975 | 437 | 55 | 355 | 45 | 792 | 100 |
| 1976 | 535 | 54 | 449 | 46 | 984 | 100 |
| 1977 | 475 | 47 | 529 | 53 | 1004 | 100 |
| 1978 | 455 | 43 | 597 | 57 | 1052 | 100 |
| 1979 | 397 | 37 | 667 | 63 | 1064 | 100 |
| 1980 | 479 | 38 | 774 | 62 | 1253 | 100 |
| 1981 | 579 | 38 | 797 | 62 | 1376 | 100 |
| 1982 | 618 | 43 | 805 | 57 | 1423 | 100 |
| 1983 | 599 | 40 | 899 | 60 | 1498 | 100 |
| 1984 | 596 | 38 | 964 | 62 | 1560 | 100 |

*Sources*: CAPMAS, *Statistical Handbook, ARE 1952–1971*, p. 218, 1977, p. 196, 1983, p. 240, 1984, p. 244; Ministry of Tourism, *Statistical Bulletin*, various issues; IMF, *UAR Part 1: Staff Report and Proposed Decision – 1968 article XIV Consultation* (April 14, 1969) p. 51; Egyptian General Authority for the promotion of tourism, *Annual Report 1984*, p. 22.

[a] Sometimes there is a discrepancy of less than one percent between data from the bureau of statistics and that of the Ministry of Tourism. Data presented in rounded figures by the author.

The reality is that the extent of commerce between Egypt and its Arab neighbors has historically been marginal. Notwithstanding that no real damage was inflicted on the Egyptian economy following the boycott, the potential for damage was low in any case. Inter-Arab commerce was and remained marginal ever since World War II,[387] and even the enormous boost of oil revenues in the 1970s did not contribute to any significant increase. In the years 1975–80 Arab exports to Arab countries amounted to only five percent, while the lion's share of commerce was with the West.[388]

**Table 5.10**   Tourism revenues, 1974–1978 (in millions of US dollars)[1]

| Year | Revenues |
|------|----------|
| 1974 | 265 |
| 1975 | 332 |
| 1976 | 464 |
| 1977 | 730 |
| 1978 | 702 |

*Source*: World Bank, *ARE, Recent Economic Development and External Capital: Capital Requirements* (report no. 2738–EGT: November 12, 1979), p. 33.

[1] These revenues represent foreign currency exchanged by tourists through official channels only.

In 1960, Egyptian exports to all Near East countries totaled $25 million and imports from the above amounted to $21 million, with the AOC filling a tiny part of these already low figures: Egypt exported goods totaling $1.8 million to Kuwait and $8 million to Saudi Arabia. Total Egyptian exports in that year to all countries totaled $550 million. That is, Egypt exported less than five percent of its goods to all Arab countries combined.[389] Toward the late 1960s Egyptian exports to Arab states increased, but compared to its exports to the rest of the world, it was still at a relatively minor level: out of total exports to all countries of $567 million in the 1967/8 fiscal year, Egypt exported goods for $48 million to the Arab countries – about eight percent – with the combined imports from Egypt to Saudi Arabia and Kuwait amounting to only $12 million.[390] Table 5.11 illustrates the meager extent of commerce between Egypt and the Arabs: total Egyptian exports to all Arab countries in the years 1969–76 amounted to $731 million, or seven percent of total exports for that period, while imports from the AOC came to $658 million in the same period, or four percent of all its imports.[391]

**Table 5.11**   Foreign commerce between Egypt and the Arab countries, 1977–1979  (in thousands of EgP)

| Arab League countries | 1977 | 1978 | 1979 |
|---|---|---|---|
| Exports | 74,140 | 84,644 | 109,100 |
| Imports | 58,948 | 77,529 | 67,900 |
| Rest of the world | | | |
| Exports | 668,478 | 679,754 | 1,287,800 |
| Imports | 1,884,278 | 2,632,180 | 2,686,200 |
| Share of Arab commerce in % | | | |
| Exports | 11.1 | 12.5 | 8.5 |
| Imports | 3.1 | 2.9 | 2.5 |

*Sources*: Central Bank of Egypt, *Economic Review* (vol. 19, nos. 3–4, 1979), p. 253; CAPMAS, *Monthly Bulletin of Foreign Trade* (April 1980); 'Isam Rif'at, "Hijrat Al-'Arab . . . ma' Misr," *al-Ahram al-Iqtisadi* (April 15, 1979), p. 9.

A study of the distribution of Egyptian exports to the Arab countries shows that only Saudi Arabia, Iraq and Syria imported relatively large amounts of goods from Egypt, with Saudi Arabia importing for EgP 15.6 million in 1978; in that same year Kuwait imported only EgP 4.3 million; the UAE under EgP 2 million; and Qatar one million EgP.[392] Saudi Arabia increased its imports from Egypt after the boycott. A similar relationship existed with regards to the goods that Egypt imported from the AOC. The goods were classified as luxury or non-essential items, certainly not valuable commodities that Egypt would encounter difficulty in obtaining elsewhere. In 1978 Egypt imported from Saudi Arabia by transit-commerce mainly TV sets, cars and trucks; from Abu Dhabi and Libya, passenger cars; and from Kuwait, ventilators, TVs and cars.[393] Car imports were prominent because Egyptians working in the Gulf returned to Egypt with cars they had purchased in those countries.[394]

**Table 5.12**   Exports to Saudi Arabia and Kuwait 1978–1982 (millions of dollars)

| Year | Saudi Arabia | Kuwait |
|------|------|------|
| 1978 | 40 | 11 |
| 1979 | 47 | 8 |
| 1980 | 56 | 4 |
| 1981 | 80 | 8 |
| 1982 | 86 | 12 |

*Source*: IMF, *Direction of Trade Statistics Yearbook 1984*, p. 150.

Not only did commerce between Egypt and the AOC not stop completely after the boycott, but Egypt managed to increase its exports to several countries and it even succeeded in augmenting its balance of trade with them. In 1978, before the boycott, Egypt had a trade deficit with Saudi Arabia of EgP 2 million; and in 1981 Egyptian exports to Saudi Arabia reached a total of EgP 56 million as against imports of EgP 38 million. In 1982, Egypt improved its commercial relations with Saudi Arabia even further: it exported goods for a total of EgP 60 million and imported for EgP 37 million.[395] So its pre-boycott trade deficit with Saudi Arabia of $2 million turned into a post-boycott surplus of $30 million, complete with an expanding commerce market. Egypt's exports to Saudi Arabia in the years 1978–81 actually doubled in scope after the boycott (see table 5.12). This trend repeated itself with the UAE;[396] and the Egyptian government improved its commercial ties with Jordan and Iraq following their rapprochement in the early 1980s.[397]

## Reasons for the ineffectuality of the boycott on Egypt
Conclusive evidence has been offered to substantiate the claim that the boycott did not harm the Egyptian economy (see table 5.13). The boycott was difficult to enforce and the AOC was not keen to implement it. Salim al-Hus declared that the general Arab feeling was that by isolating Egypt, with its dominant political, economic and demographic position in the Arab world, the Arabs were suffering a great loss. Al-Hus added that there was legitimate concern that the boycott of the Egyptian regime should not penalize the Egyptian people.[398] In early October 1983, at a meeting that took place in Amman, Dessouki argued that the boycott was a

political and social lever, not an economic weapon.[399] At the same meeting, Sa'ad al-Din Ibrahim remarked that, in retrospect, Sadat's judgment – that the boycott would not really affect the Egyptian economy – had been proved correct.[400]

**Table 5.13** The impact of the boycott by sectors

| Sector | Effect | No effect |
|--------|--------|-----------|
| Deposits | | + |
| Workers | | + |
| Oil supply | | + |
| Tourism | | + |
| Aid | | +[1] |
| SUMED | | + |
| Suez Canal | | + |
| Trade | | + |
| Total[2] | | + |

[1] Including funds and military and civilian aid. This demonstrates that aid was not stopped completely.
[2] Sometimes one negative item can be more dominant than all positive items put together. However, this was not the case in Egypt at the time.

There are four main reasons as to why the Arab economic boycott did not hurt Egypt:

1   The conservative oil states did not want to harm Egypt, and therefore they took a decision not to weaken economic ties on the popular level.[401]
2   Egypt's position toward the Iran–Iraq War forced the AOC to strengthen their ties with Egypt, whilst broadening economic ties between Egypt and Iraq, a stance which boosted trade to unprecedented levels.
3   Egypt did its part to prevent the AOC from damaging its economy. The freezing of funds in deposits, and of some of AMIO's assets, and the non-payment of its debts to the AOC (about $5 billion), all ensured that the Egyptian economy was not damaged by the AOC's boycott.
4   Increased Western aid to Egypt after the Arab boycott.

The AOC needed Egypt as much as Egypt needed them: the Arab countries needed Egyptian workers who were indispensable for the development of their economies; many tens of thousands of Arab students were studying in Egypt and the AOC feared they would be deported; they were concerned that Egypt might exert a ban on the passage of their ships through the Suez Canal, or prevent ships carrying goods to and from the AOC from using the Canal. In 1978 60 Saudi tankers passed through the Canal and in 1979, the year the boycott was imposed, 116 tankers flying the Saudi flag passed through the Canal. One year later the number of tankers went down to 111, but goods they carried showed an increase of 200 tons. The same goes for Kuwait: in 1978, 23 tankers flying the Kuwaiti flag passed through the canal; in 1979, 57 tankers; in 1980, 44 tankers and in 1982, 93 tankers.[402]

Moreover, the Canal services were vital to the AOC for importing goods. For example, in 1984 Saudi Arabia ranked as the prime importer of foodstuff through the Canal, importing 847 tons of food or 24 percent of the total amount of food imported and passing through the Canal. In that year all the conservative Gulf States (including Saudi Arabia) imported about 32 percent of the total amount of foodstuff imported and transported through the Canal.[403]

Egypt's position *vis-à-vis* the Iran–Iraq War brought it substantial financial profits – both through its workers in Iraq and by its arms exports – specifically from a source that previously had not assisted the Egyptian economy in any significant manner. Egypt supplied arms to Iraq in the framework of official contracts,[404] and up to 1984 it exported arms for a value of more than $2 billion. Before the boycott, Egypt's arms exports amounted to less than $100 million annually.[405] These shipments were of great importance to the Iraqi military, and to the oil-producing countries. Besides Egypt, Libya and Syria also possessed Soviet arms, but they supported Iran during the conflict, and up to the beginning of 1983 the USSR refused to ship large quantities of arms to Iraq.[406]

In 1984 Egypt and Iraq signed a (secret) political–military agreement. This was not the first agreement between the two countries. A previous agreement had been signed just after Mubarak came to power, and had concentrated mainly on arms supply.[407] This new agreement dealt with a wide range of subjects, such as cooperation between the two countries in the political, economic, military and security fields. On the subject of the economy, problems arose when the Iraqi government limited the amount of remittances transferable by over one million Egyptian who worked in Iraq. It was then agreed that Egypt would continue to encourage emigration to Iraq, and in exchange the Iraqi government would allow the transfer of hard currency deposits, at the official rate, to Egypt. The two governments would encourage the activities of joint companies and facilitate customs control on their goods. Regarding military matters, about 17,000 Egyptians actually served in the Iraqi armed forces, and Egypt did supply arms and acted as intermediary. Egypt guaranteed to supply "enough" military experts to train Iraqi forces in the use of the Western arms it had purchased in the West; to mediate and to transfer arms and equipment to Iraq; and to allow its citizens to volunteer to serve in the Iraqi armed forces, while guaranteeing their conduct according to Egyptian law.[408]

The war presented Egypt with two opportunities: on the economic level it brought a steep rise in foreign currency income from arms exports and from its workers' remittances from Iraq; and on the political level, the opportunity to bridge some of its differences with the Arab countries. Egypt was very concerned, during the war, with the possible expansion and increase of fundamentalist Islam, together with the underlying fear of growing Soviet influence in the event of an Iranian victory.[409] During the Iran–Iraq War, Egypt emerged as a defender of the Arab cause, in contrast to its portrayal following the peace agreement as forsaking common Arab interests. The war also improved Egypt's strategic value to its Arab neighbors and the Great Powers.

Another factor which facilitated economic and political ties between Egypt and the AOC was the rise to power of Mubarak in October 1981. Mubarak continued Sadat's policy of stabilizing the country, both internally and in terms of external, inter-state relations, remaining faithful to the idiom that peace was the basis for development.[410] The changes Mubarak carried out up to 1983 were not significant. He maintained his good ties with the West, which included receiving economic and military aid, and he honored the peace treaty with Israel. Mubarak's main efforts were directed toward finding a solution for the Egyptian economy and establishing and securing Egypt's regional and global prestige.[411] Mubarak improved Egypt's relations with the Arab countries, mainly by moving to reduce tension with the Arabs, and especially eroding personal animosities between the leaders, who frequently launched verbal attacks on each other. Mubarak responded differently from Sadat to Arab demands. Sadat had once confessed that he was a man who "was not in the mood for conciliation [with the conservative Arab states]," as the AOC maintained an arrogant stance of demanding that Egypt, as a presumed violator of their trust, make the first conciliatory move.[412]

Compared to Sadat, Mubarak initiated symbolic moves to end Egypt's isolation from the Arab world. He met with King Fahd at the funeral of King Khaled, conversed with Arafat after he was banished from Lebanon, supplied arms to Iraq and declared his support for the Iraqi people. Mubarak promised to defend the security of the Gulf, reaffirming his belief that Egypt was part of the Arab nation: "We are not separating ourselves from the Arab world and we are not forsaking the Arab cause, because Egyptian Arabism is not an ornament that we put on when we want to and whoever wishes to do so can take it off."[413] In early 1982, for the first time since the Camp David agreement, Egypt was officially represented at an international conference on Arab soil – the preparatory conference of the non-aligned states which was held in Kuwait[414] – and on January 30, 1984, Egypt received a formal invitation to rejoin the organization of the Islamic Congress. "Of course we accept the invitation," said Mubarak.[415]

Egypt did not focus on normalizing its ties with the AOC, as Boutros Ghali stated,[416] because it realized that in its relations with the AOC, the economic and diplomatic dimentions were not necessarily interrelated. In other words, economic ties endured, despite the economic boycott. The "understanding" Egypt showed toward the oil countries who subsequently chose not to renew their diplomatic relations with it ("they find themselves between the hammer and the anvil. On the one hand they are struggling with the Iranian threat, and on the other hand they are being blackmailed by the revolutionary Arab regimes," in Nafi"s words).[417] This meant that Egypt cooled its offer of the olive branch. Mubarak stated that a reconciliation with the Arab countries would not be obtained "at any price," and the process must take into consideration Egypt's national honor and the peace treaty with Israel. Egypt also stressed that it had no intention of sacrificing human and material resources for a reconciliation with the Arab states.[418] In March 1983, Kamal Hasan 'Ali defined Egypt's official position toward the Arabs as:

> We do not have any plans for renewing our ties with the Arab countries. This depends on the desire of those states to renew their relations with Egypt. We are taking steps accordingly: we talk and consult with them and we receive envoys from the AOC. However, diplomatic relations on an ambassadorial level have still not been resumed, and this matter is their business.[419]

## Summary

Egyptian policy-makers attributed great importance to attracting the resources of the rich Arab countries, and they were active to this end on both the ideological and practical level. Notwithstanding that Nasser as well as Sadat desired to "participate" in the AOC's wealth, the two leaders' policies were very different. Nasser found it difficult to accept that he was forced to request aid from conservative governments, and only after his total defeat in June 1967, did he accept that fate. However, even before June 1967, Nasser moved to attract foreign resources, also from the AOC.

Nasser's rout in the war and the loss of his resources shook the very foundations of his economic and political policies, and contributed to a more realistic outlook. The results of the defeat made it clear to Nasser that he would have to request aid from the AOC, while at the same time he would have to change his policy toward the Arab oil countries, and adopt a new attitude toward the US. The economic policy-makers began to exhibit the first signs of serious consideration for the private sector, following a long period of socialist–nationalist control. The dramatic change in Nasser's policy was made after the 1969 Rabat conference, in spite of his threat to the AOC that he would take "an independent stand," and in spite of the signing of an economic–military agreement between Egypt, Libya and Sudan.

The different circumstances existing under Nasser's and Sadat's regimes should be taken into account. In Nasser's time, the AOC's revenues did not reach the level of the early 1970s, and the aid granted by the Arab nations in this period had already reached the very limits of their capacity. It is quite likely that if they had enjoyed revenues such as those after the Teheran Agreement and the October War, the emphases in Nasser's policy would have been different. Sadat inherited a grave economic situation from Nasser, and the Egyptian economy was on the brink of bankruptcy. The change of political and economic circumstances in the AOC and within Egypt's political and economic spheres compelled Sadat to dedicate most of his efforts to obtaining a share of the AOC's resources. On taking over the reins of power, Sadat spoke about the expected flow of "oil capital" to Egypt, and in the Investment Law of 1971 he gave priority to Arab investment. Sadat was well aware of the AOC's fears of radicalization of the region, and in order to gain their confidence and their assistance, he took steps to moderate revolutionary forces in the area, announcing Egypt's disaffection with communism. Sadat knew that the AOC would not grant him massive aid if he did not seriously intend to go to war, and in early 1972 he started urgent negotiations with their governments, so that they would purchase front-line arms for Egypt. Sadat wanted economic and military aid, from the conservative as well as from the revolutionary Arab states (mainly Libya), and therefore he agreed to unification with Libya in stages. Even before the October War, Sadat showed great optimism about "united Arab action," claiming that Arab resources belonged to the entire Arab nation. Without the massive military and economic assistance that Sadat received before the October War, it is doubtful he could have initiated the campaign.

The October 1973 War and the rise in oil prices caused euphoria among the intellectuals and policy-makers in Egypt, and they made ambitious plans for the development of their economy with the help of the riches of the AOC, whose prestige Egypt had helped to restore. In the "October Paper" Sadat presented plans for economic development. He took into account the new economic conditions that had been created, and according to this strategy, Arab resources were supposed to extricate Egypt from its chronic economic troubles. The enthusiasm and the expectations of Egyptian policy-makers over massive Arab aid and investment was short-lived, however. Egypt attacked the AOC for their delaying tactics in providing it with aid. Sadat showed open forbearance with the extent of the AOC's aid, and he hoped that by January 1976 their donations would extricate Egypt from its economic difficulties with the help of the billions' fund. In private conversations, though, Sadat expressed his bitter disappointment over Arab aid after the 1973 War. The establishment of the GFDE with a total capital of $2 billion, the pressure that the oil countries applied on Egypt to adopt the reforms of the IMF and the food riots in January 1977 were all turning-points for Sadat's political and economic positions. Controversy erupted in the Egyptian media over Egypt's future. Tawfiq al-Hakim called for Egyptian "neutrality," because the Arab states had forced Egypt to go to war, but they had not shared their wealth with it.

Sadat's peace initiative was highly significant because it represented the first move toward detaching Egypt from the Arabs. Sadat had singularly failed to achieve any momentum in the matter of Arab aid after the October 1973 War, and he was well aware of this burning failure. The extent of Arab aid, its conditions, the injury to Egyptian prestige and Sadat's disillusionment with the Arabs' role as "the sixth world power" – contributed to the maneuver away from the AOC. Sadat knew that the Arabs could not reach a consensus on the conflict, and in Egypt's dire economic straits he had no other choice but to try and negotiate a peace agreement with Israel. This way, at least, he could try to obtain direct American aid and private investment from the West, which would help develop Egypt's internal resources. The fear of Sadat's regime collapsing if he did not take this path outweighed any concerns about abandoning the Arab cause.

At first, Sadat was not concerned that Arab economic aid to Egypt would be halted as a result of the peace talks. American policy-makers promised plenty of economic aid, and guarantees for military and technological assistance encouraged him to continue with his peace initiative, especially as he realized that the amount of aid provided would be in direct proportion to the rate of political progress. In spite of this, Sadat was prudent enough to ensure in advance that Egypt would not be affected economically by the peace process, and that Western aid would compensate him, at least at the level of Arab aid. Anticipated aid from the West following the peace initiative seemed to the Egyptian leaders the most promising scenario for dealing with Egypt's severe economic problems, and the one most capable of lifting them from the economic mire. Furthermore, Sadat wished to establish bilateral military ties with the US, to some extent copying the existing Israeli–American model.

From an economic standpoint Sadat's moves were successful, and his decision to continue his efforts toward a peaceful settlement proved correct, notwithstanding threats to stop aid and the imposition of the boycott. The economic boycott the Arabs imposed on Egypt at the 1979 Baghdad conference was more a symbolic gesture than a practical measure. Not only did millions of Egyptians continue to work in the AOC, but their number increased considerably after the peace treaty. The extent of commerce between Egypt and the AOC was not affected, and in several cases it even expanded. AOC citizens continued investing in Egypt, and the AOC did not harm any of their joint projects in Egypt. Tourists from the AOC continued to visit Egypt, and Arab aid was never completely halted. Sadat had ensured against possible harm to the Egyptian economy by freezing the oil countries' funds deposited in Egypt and by non-repayment of former loans.

Political events in the area in the early eighties – primarily the Iran–Iraq War and reduced oil prices – limited the AOC's capacity to provide Egypt with substantial aid, as the majority of Arab aid went to Iraq. On the other hand, the Western countries and Japan increased their aid to Egypt significantly. Egypt profited handsomely, financially and politically, from the Gulf War and succeeded in minimizing the practical influences of the boycott. Egypt's official position on the war and Mubarak's rise to power led to a tightening of economic and political relations – albeit not formally – between Egypt and the AOC. Egyptian leaders even went as far as to declare that Egypt was not focusing on establishing formal relations with the AOC, demonstrating the new strength of Egypt's negotiating position. Moreover, Egypt proclaimed that any formal rapprochement with the AOC would not come at the expense of the peace treaty, and stressed that it was the Arabs who would have to initiate the renewal of formal relations with Egypt. Given that informal relations were relatively healthy and normal between Egypt and the AOC, Mubarak could afford to adopt such a position.

# 6

# Egypt and the Gulf States, 1985–2000

## Political background

### The period 1985–1990

The period 1985–1990 was characterized by two main episodes. The first was the continuation of Egypt's suspension from the Arab League, and the *formal* economic embargo placed upon Egypt, introduced by the Arab states after it had signed the peace treaty with Israel. This formal embargo continued until the end of 1987, when most of the Arab states renewed their diplomatic relations with Egypt, following the Amman Arab Summit Conference in November, which saw the adoption of a resolution that allowed each Arab state to individually decide whether to restore such relations.[1]

While the formal boycott continued, the GCC states maintained *informal* relations with Egypt that included various levels of political, economic, military and cultural contacts.[2] Egypt's suspension from the Arab League lasted until May 1989. However, by the mid-1980s Egypt was reintegrated into regional and multilateral affairs within regional institutions such as the Islamic Conference Organization (ICO).[3] Egypt was readmitted into the Arab League following the Casablanca Summit Conference of May 1989, and on October 31, 1990, the Arab League headquarters moved back to Cairo.

The second episode was the ongoing Iran–Iraq War, and growing fears among the Gulf States of an impeding Iranian military attack on them. This resulted in a desire to secure an Egyptian military commitment of one sort or another. During this period Egypt staunchly supported Iraq – a policy greatly appreciated by the Gulf States, and it reinforced this position in 1987, when it sent military experts to Kuwait at a time of heightened fears of an Iranian attack.[4]

Following the re-establishment of formal relations between Egypt and the Gulf States at the end of 1987, President Husni Mubarak visited his new Arab allies in turn in January 1988, and solemnly pledged to assist in their defense.[5]

The Iran–Iraq War, which broke out on September 22, 1980 with an Iraqi invasion of Iran, came to a final, undetermined end on July 24, 1988. Two years later, in August 1990, Iraq invaded Kuwait. Soon after this invasion, Egypt offered refuge to many Kuwaitis who had fled their country, absorbed their children in its educational system, and became a base for some of the Kuwaiti media, including the *Voice of Kuwait.* Almost overnight, Egypt found itself leader of a group of states, including the GCC states, that was united by a deep unease over Saddam Hussein's aggression and armament, and willingness to become closely aligned with the West.[6]

Immediately after the invasion, Egypt convened an emergency summit meeting of Arab leaders, at which the participants supported a resolution demanding the withdrawal of Iraqi forces from Kuwait. In response to a Saudi request for international assistance to deter potential aggression upon it by Iraq, the meeting voted to send an Arab force to the Gulf region. The Egyptian contingent within the multinational force that was eventually set up numbered 35,000 troops.

## The period 1991 to the present

The second period of recent Egypt–AOC relations began with the Gulf War of January–February 1991,[7] followed by the Madrid Conference of October–November 1991. By now Egypt was fully reintegrated into the Arab world, and had managed to consolidate its position as a central pillar of the inter-Arab system; it was a credible mediator in intra-regional disputes, a staunch fighter against Muslim extremism and a proud exponent of Arab sentiments to the world. In the course of 1991 Egyptian Foreign Minister Ismat 'Abd al-Majid was elected Secretary-General of the Arab League, and Minister of State for Foreign Affairs Boutros Boutros-Ghali was elected Secretary-General of the UN.[8] Egypt also continued to play a major role in the peace process with Israel.[9]

Though the Gulf States followed the footsteps of the United States and the European Community in distributing foreign aid following the outbreak of the Gulf crisis in 1990, Egypt soon began to distance itself from the AOC. Egypt's first disappointment came after a meeting with the GCC states and Syria in Damascus in March 1991, which saw the issuing of the ambitious Damascus Declaration, speaking of a new regional order, but which failed to materialize.[10] This was partially due to different geo-political concerns *vis-à-vis* Iran, which led to a growing measure of mistrust and reluctance on the part of the Gulf States to have Egyptian and Syrian troops permanently stationed on their soil.[11]

However, Egypt's move away from the Gulf States also had economic motives: the relative economic weakening of the Gulf States, on the one hand, and the willingness of the Western industrialized states, headed by the United States, as well as the World Bank and IMF, prompted by the US, to provide Egypt with generous aid in the aftermath of the Gulf War, on the other.[12] The Western states were also Egypt's most important trading partners and source of investment. Only in the sphere of workers' remittances did the Gulf States maintain their predominant position.

In the years that followed the Gulf War, Egypt's relations with the Gulf States were relatively stable, and were influenced by its desire to fortify its own position within the Arab system, advance the peace process with Israel with the goal of stabilizing the Middle East,[13] and generally maintaining a balance between the various forces in the region. It never lost sight of its own economic interests in the region, which were tied up with those of Saudi Arabia and Kuwait.[14] Egypt's decision to boycott the Middle East and North Africa (MENA) Economic Conference in the capital of Qatar, Doha, in November 1997, was the only interruption to relative regional stability during this time. A lack of progress in the Middle East peace process, and the desire to deny Israel any economic standing in the region as long as this stagnation continued, were the reasons for Egypt's abstention.[15]

After 1995, Saudi crown prince Abdallah Ibn Abdel Aziz started trying to usurp Egypt as the regional hegemony, by placing Saudi Arabia in between the radical Muslim countries and the moderate ones. Following September 11, 2001, Abdallah also made proposals for renewing the Middle East peace process. Egypt, in response, insinuated that the Saudis were in part responsible for the emergence of figures like Osama bin Laden, and should not have raised "wild weeds" (i.e. Bin Laden). Egypt also pointed out that Saudi funds supported the activities of radical groups in Egypt, such as Islamic Jihad.

Nevertheless, there is no doubt that, today, it is the US rather than the Gulf States, that plays a central strategic role in Egypt's policy. US–Egypt relations are marked by a significant level of military cooperation, including joint military exercises, a common desire to see progress in the Middle East peace process and a large-scale provision of American economic and development aid.[16]

## Aid

Following Egypt's signing of the peace treaty with Israel in 1979, Western aid to Egypt in the 1980s and 1990s reached significant levels, and replaced Arab aid.[17] This was due, at first, to the official Arab boycott of Egypt, though as time went by the oil-producing states significantly reduced their aid budgets, so that, regardless of the nature of its relationship with Israel, a fall in Arab aid was inevitable for Egypt. By the late 1980s, Arab economic aid to Egypt, which in the 1970s had still been extremely important, became so insignificant that in 1989 UNCTAD stopped publishing data for it. In fact, in the years 1981–5 Arab aid was negative (see table 6.1.)

Rumors began to spread in May 1987, against the background of the continuing Iran–Iraq War, and amid fears among some of the GCC states of an impeding Iranian attack on them, that three Gulf States had agreed to provide Egypt with a loan of $750–$1,000 million to help pay its debts to Western countries. Further speculation suggested that in October and December of the same year, Kuwait and Saudi Arabia gave financial assistance to Egypt. There were also rumors of a negotiated deal on troops-for-aid.[18] However, very little, if any, of this appears to actually have taken place, and there is certainly no reflection of it in the official statistics.

Through 1989/90, official transfers varied between $0.7 billion and $1 billion. The bulk of this civilian foreign assistance was provided by the United States. Largely on account of the expected adverse impact of the Middle East crisis, official transfers surged in 1990/1 to $4.8 billion of which $3.4 billion were provided under the auspices of the Gulf Crisis Financial Coordination Group (GCFCG). This amount included grants totaling $3 billion from Saudi Arabia, Kuwait, the United Arab Emirates and the Gulf Organization for the Development for Egypt (GODE), most of which was untied balance of payments assistance.[19]

**Table 6.1**  Arab aid to Egypt, 1979–1989 (in millions of US dollars)

| Year | Net bilateral aid by Arab donor states | Net multilateral aid by Arab organizations | Total Arab aid |
|------|------|------|------|
| 1979 | 168.9 | 42.1 | 211.0 |
| 1980 | 3.2 | −1.3 | 1.8 |
| 1981 | −14.1 | −8.6 | −22.7 |
| 1982 | −12.6 | −7.8 | −20.4 |
| 1983 | −60.8 | −7.5 | −68.3 |
| 1984 | −19.2 | −8.2 | −27.4 |
| 1985 | −19.3 | −7.7 | −27.0 |
| 1986 | 59.4 | −5.4 | 54.0 |
| 1987 | 73.9 | −8.8 | 65.1 |
| 1988 | −16.8 | 24.9 | 8.1 |
| 1989 | −14.5 | 97.8 | 83.3 |

Based on Pierre van den Boogaerde, *Financial Assistance from Arab Countries and Arab Regional Institutions* (Washington, D.C.: IMF, September 1991), pp. 62–87.

**Table 6.2**  Egypt's external debt to GODE and total, 1986/87–1990/91 (in millions of US dollars)[1]

| Year | GODE | Total |
|------|------|------|
| 1986/7 | 2,449 | 37,565 |
| 1987/8 | 2,529 | 39,980 |
| 1988/9 | 2,598 | 43,054 |
| 1989/90 | 2,592 | 46,105 |
| 1990/1 | — | 35,473 |

*Sources*: IBRD; Debt Reporting System; Central Bank of Egypt; creditor countries; and Fund staff estimates.

[1] Disbursed debt outstanding at end-period, including outstanding principal capital and interest in arrears as well as late interest.

As can be seen in table 6.2, Egypt's foreign debt at the time was enormous. As the GCFCG helped mobilize assistance for Egypt, the US and Arab donors together cancelled nearly $13 billion of Egypt's external debt. This significant aid in the form of debt cancellation resulted in annual savings in debt service of approximately $1 billion in each of the next five years. While nearly all of this debt was in arrears and thus did not have a schedule of debt service obligations, interest savings were about $300 million per annum. The debt cancellation by the US in late 1990 amounted to $6.6 billion. Debt cancellation by regional creditors amounted to around $6.3 billion as follows: GODE $2,592 million, Kuwait $1,896 million, Saudi Arabia $1,139 million, the United Arab Emirates $305 million, the Arab African Bank $279 million and Qatar $93 million.[20]

However, as table 6.3 shows, as the 1990s progressed, Arab aid, both in absolute terms and as a percentage of total aid received by Egypt from all sources, once again dropped to insignificant levels. In some years Egypt received no new commitments

**Table 6.3**  ODA figures for Egypt (in millions of US dollars)

| | 1993 | 1994 | 1995 | 1996 | 1997 | 1998 | 1999 | 2000 |
|---|---|---|---|---|---|---|---|---|
| Total | 2,400.8 | 2,694.9 | 2,022.0 | 2,199.3 | 1,985.2 | 1954.7 | 1,582.1 | 1,328.4 |
| Of which Arab countries | 379.5 | 94.3 | 116.6 | 53.6 | 49.5 | na | na | na |
| Of which Arab agencies | 73.3 | 66.2 | — | — | — | — | — | — |
| Net ODA from Arab sources as % of total | 18.9 | 6.0 | 5.8 | 2.4 | 2.5 | — | — | — |

*Source:* Author's calculations, based on OECD *Geographical Distribution of Financial Flows to Aid Recipients 1993–1997 & 1996–2000.*

or net flows of aid from Saudi Arabia, Kuwait or the UAE,[21] and in 2000/1 it received only $200,000 from Saudi Arabia as a grant,[22] though Saudi Arabia was reported to have contributed about $100 million as a loan for several development projects in Egypt, by means of the Saudi Fund for Economic Development (SFED).[23] Table 6.4 shows that, by the turn of the millennium not a single Gulf State could be found in the list of the ten largest donors of ODA to Egypt.

**Table 6.4** Top ten donors of gross ODA to Egypt (1999–2000 average) in millions of US dollars

| | | |
|---|---|---|
| 1 | United States | 799 |
| 2 | France | 265 |
| 3 | EC | 144 |
| 4 | Japan | 129 |
| 5 | Germany | 102 |
| 6 | Denmark | 41 |
| 7 | IDA | 41 |
| 8 | Austria | 24 |
| 9 | Italy | 20 |
| 10 | Netherlands | 19 |

*Source*: OECD, World Bank.

**Table 6.5** Saudi Arabia foreign direct aid: 1990–1999 (in billions of Saudi riyals)

| Year | |
|---|---|
| 1990–1[1] | 16.2 |
| 1992 | 2.1 |
| 1993 | 1.6 |
| 1994 | 0.5 |
| 1995 | 0.3 |
| 1996 | 0.3 |
| 1997 | 0.3 |
| 1998 | 0.2 |
| 1999 | 0.3 |

*Source*: IMF, *Saudi Arabia – Recent Economic Developments* (SM/00/215, September 25, 2000), pp. 80–1.

[1] As a result of the special circumstances arising from the Gulf War, the Saudi authorities have combined the data for 1990–1.

The drop in GCC aid was not due to malice or ill intentions on the states' part, but more due to a slowdown in economic growth, fiscal deficits, domestic and foreign debts (see table 6.7); falling oil earnings experienced by these states in this period were also to blame for the drop. The value of OAPEC oil exports (expressed in real 1995 prices) in 1980 was $289.2 billion; in 1985 it went down to $129.7 billion; it decreased further to $102.4 million in 1990; it fell again to $93.7 million in 1995; and went up to $188.9 million in 2000.[24] Real 1995 prices of crude oil were $48.40 per barrel in 1980; $42.80 in 1985; $23.40 in 1990; $16.90 in 1995; and $29.90 in 2000.[25]

**Table 6.6** Total gross lending and grants from the Saudi Fund for Economic Development, 1997–1999 (in millions of US dollars)

|  | 1997 | 1998 | 1999 |
|---|---|---|---|
| Total foreign assistance | 460.4 | 461.7 | 399.5 |
| Total grants | 64.6 | 126.6 | 70.5 |
| Arab countries | 41.7 | 108.0 | 51.9 |
| African countries | 2.4 | 4.4 | 7.5 |
| Asian countries | 2.3 | 10.1 | 7.0 |
| Other countries | 18.2 | 4.0 | 4.1 |
| Grants to organizations and programs | 71.4 | 70.8 | 98.6 |
| Multilateral assistance | 130.2 | 128.5 | 115.8 |
| Gross concessional loans | 194.3 | 135.9 | 114.7 |

*Sources*: Saudi Ministry of Finance and National Economy; IMF, *Saudi Arabia – Recent Economic Developments* (SM/00/215, September 25, 2000), pp. 80–1.

**Table 6.7** Saudi Arabia: Central government's domestic and external debt, 1996–2000

| Year | Domestic debt (in billions of SDR) | External debt (in millions of US $) |
|---|---|---|
| 1996 | 446.9 | 15,764 |
| 1997 | 476.7 | 21,315 |
| 1998 | 558.8 | 28,949 |
| 1999 | 624.7 | 30,388 |
| 2000 | 616.2 | 30,388 |

*Source*: IMF, *Saudi Arabia – Statistical Appendix* (SM/01/283, September 18, 2001), pp. 29, 48.

While the six GCC nations earned more than $180 billion in 1980, in 1998 this sum was down to less than $60 billion. Arab Monetary Fund figures show that the official cumulative financial aid provided by the GCC between 1970 and 2001 totaled around $101.8 billion, nearly 94 percent of the overall Arab cash assistance. While in the years 1975–9 the GCC states extended a total of $29.1 billion in aid, and in the years 1980–4 some $30.4 billion, their financial aid fell sharply to $8 billion in the years 1995–2001.[26] This decline means more than one-third of the 1980s level in current prices or less than a fifth considering inflation rates and the real value of the US dollar.

Saudi Arabia extended around 64 percent of the Arab aid, while 16.5 percent was provided by Kuwait and 10.5 percent by the UAE. Official aid transfers by Saudi Arabia, which had been one of the world leaders in the granting of development assistance until the 1980s, decreased from $6.5 billion in 1991 (5.2% of its GDP) to only $600 million in 1994 (0.5% of GDP). In the years 1995–2000 it offered an annual average of around $100 million (table 6.5).[27] In actual terms Saudi aid transfers were actually negative – minus $0.1 billion in 1992, minus $0.8 billion in 1993, minus $0.6 billion in 1994, and around minus $0.1 billion annually in the years

1995–2000.[28] In the fiscal year 1999/2000 Egypt received no new commitments or net flows of grants from Saudi Arabia or the UAE. The Abu Dhabi Development Fund made commitments of $180 million but transferred nil. In the fiscal year 2000/1 Egypt received from Saudi Arabia only $200,000 as grant.[29] Kuwait had been a major aid donor through KFAED. Following Iraq's invasion, KFAED has received no injection of government funds since the late 1980s. The cost of financing the war and subsequent reconstruction led Kuwait to announce plans to borrow up to $33 billion from the international markets in 1991. Kuwait's external debt amounted to $9.3 billion at the end of 2000.[30]

## American and EU aid

The fall in aid from the Gulf States to Egypt was compensated by increased American and European aid. Since 1979, the US has provided Egypt with tens of billions of dollars of aid. As can be seen in table 6.8, total US aid to Egypt has amounted to around $2 billion annually – $1.3 billion in military aid, and around $700 million in economic aid.

**Table 6.8**  US aid to Egypt (in millions of US dollars)

| Year | Commodity export credit guarantee | Economic grant aid | Military grant aid | Total |
|------|-----------------------------------|--------------------|--------------------|-------|
| 1991 | 125 | 781 | 1,300 | 2,371 |
| 1992 | 40  | 892 | 1,300 | 2,382 |
| 1993 | 115 | 747 | 1,300 | 2,162 |
| 1994 | 160 | 592 | 1,300 | 2,052 |
| 1995 | 165 | 815 | 1,300 | 2,280 |
| 1996 | 200 | 815 | 1,300 | 2,315 |
| 1997 | —   | 815 | 1,300 | 2,115 |
| 1998 | —   | 815 | 1,300 | 2,115 |
| 1999 | —   | 775 | 1,300 | 2,075 |
| 2000 | —   | 735 | 1,300 | 2,035 |
| 2001 | —   | 655 | 1,300 | 1,995 |

*Source*: US Embassy, Cairo.

Members of the European Community (now the European Union) became Egypt's second largest providers of aid. European aid has largely taken the form of project aid, including technical assistance. In the years 1977–96 Egypt received a total of EgP 5.6 billion from the EU. In addition, during the years 1986–95, Egypt was granted a EgP 1.68 billion worth of food aid. The EU has also supported other projects through the Social Fund for Development with EgP 700 million.[31]

**Table 6.9**  Egypt: Disbursements of bilateral and multilateral ODA (in thousands of US dollars)

| Year | Bilateral | Multilateral | Total |
|------|-----------|--------------|-------|
| 1989 | 1409.2 | 196.1 | 1605.3 |
| 1990 | 3171.8 | 59.4  | 3231.2 |

**Table 6.9** *(continued)*

| | | | |
|---|---|---|---|
| 1991 | 4157.0 | 283.9 | 4440.9 |
| 1992 | 3000.9 | 355.1 | 3356.0 |
| 1993 | 1823.8 | 346 | 2169.8 |
| 1994 | 2310.7 | 335.2 | 2645.9 |
| 1995 | 1689.4 | 78.2 | 1767.6 |
| 1996 | 1933.3 | 211.9 | 2145 |
| 1997 | 1496.3 | 388.1 | 1884.3 |
| 1998 | 1470.8 | 267.3 | 1738.1 |

*Source*: OECD, *Geographical Distribution of Financial Flows to Aid Recipients*, various issues.

## Investment by the Gulf States in Egypt

In the course of the 1990s, Egypt adopted various measures to encourage foreign investment. Among the measures taken was the enactment of Public Business Law 203 (1991), which established the framework for the privatization of Egypt's massive public sector. This was followed by the legislation of BOT (Build, Operate, Transfer) devices to attract foreign companies to participate in the development of certain infrastructures and public services. Law 95 (1995) enabled foreigners to lease real estate, and thus helps them to circumvent the laws that limited their right to own land.

Investment Law (1997) was designed to simplify the complex legal and regulative framework for investment that had evolved in the previous two decades. In addition, the law offered guarantees against nationalization, confiscation, seizure, requisition, blocking and placing under custody sequestration of all investment, including in real estate and project property. The law also offered tax exemptions, the right to 100 percent ownership, and free repatriation of profits and capital. In addition, Egypt offered foreign investors a five-year corporate tax holiday that could be extended by an additional five years, while projects located in new industrial zones and urban communities, and in remote areas, automatically receive a ten-year tax holiday, that may be extended by another five years.[32]

Despite all the efforts and reforms there is still in Egypt an unfortunate residue of some institutional features left over from the former centralized economy, like its heavy bureaucratic traditions.[33] As recently as May 2002, in the course of a debate on amendments to the Law for Encouraging Investment, Egyptian Members of Parliament accused the Government of frightening off foreign investors as a result of its cumbersome bureaucracy.[34]

In 1986, an increase in Saudi investment in Egypt was marked, despite the fact that diplomatic relations had not yet been renewed between the two countries. While Egypt was in need of foreign investment capital to help it implement its five-year economic plan, Saudi investors found in Egypt the potential for healthy industry and manufacturing. In particular, building contractors were able to use their construction equipment, which stood idle in Saudi Arabia due to the economic recession there.

**Table 6.10**   Total foreign direct investment in Egypt (in millions of US dollars)

| Year | FDI |
|------|------|
| 1977 | 105.0 |
| 1978 | 318.0 |
| 1979 | 1,216.0 |
| 1980 | 548.0 |
| 1981 | 753.0 |
| 1982 | 294.0 |
| 1983 | 490.0 |
| 1984 | 729.0 |
| 1985 | 1,178.0 |
| 1986 | 1,217.0 |
| 1987 | 948.0 |
| 1988 | 1,190.0 |
| 1989 | 1,250.0 |
| 1990 | 734.0 |
| 1991 | 253.0 |
| 1992 | 459.0 |
| 1993 | 493.0 |
| 1994 | 1,256.0 |
| 1995 | 598.0 |
| 1996 | 636.0 |
| 1997 | 891.0 |
| 1998 | 1,076.0 |
| 1999 | 1,065.0 |
| 2000 | 1,235.0 |
| 2000/1 | 541.6 |

*Sources*: IMF, *BOP Statistical Yearbook*, Part 1, pp. 266–70. Data for 2000/1 from Central Bank of Egypt, *Economic Review* (vol. XLI, no. 4, 2000/2001), p. 76.

Against this background the Egyptian–Saudi Investment Conference took place in Cairo in October 1986. Among its many resolutions, the Conference recommended that the Egyptian government prepare a list of the projects required, with feasibility studies to be produced for the guidance of potential investors, and called for the formation of a permanent Saudi–Egyptian committee to tackle any difficulties facing Saudi investments in Egypt. In November, a delegation of top Saudi contractors arrived in Cairo to undertake a number of priority investment projects in the fields of housing, land reclamation and the manufacture of building materials.

One of the steps taken by Egypt to attract both Saudi and Gulf investors in this period was to lift the total ban on the purchase of real estate in Egypt by foreigners, allowing them to own apartments or land of up to 1,000 square meters.[35]

In the years 1987–90 the share of Arab investment in Egypt in total inter-Arab investment, and the share of Arab investment in terms of total foreign direct investment (FDI) in Egypt, started to rise, as a result of Egypt's return to the Arab fold (table 6.11). Arab investors were soon searching for ways to increase their activity

in the Egyptian market.[36] In 1991 – in the aftermath of the Gulf War – Arab investment in Egypt shot up. Out of $922.6 million worth of inter-Arab investments,
$651.3 million (71%) were in Egypt.[37]

According to IMF figures, the total FDI in Egypt was $253 million in that year
(table 6.10). The discrepancy comes from the fact that the Arab institutions also
count investment in real estate, while the IMF does not account for investment in
real estate.

**Table 6.11**   Total foreign direct investment and direct Arab investment in Egypt in
the years 1987–1989 (in millions of US dollars)

|  | 1987 | 1988 | 1989 | 1990 |
|---|---|---|---|---|
| Total FDI in Egypt | 948.0 | 1,190.0 | 1,250.0 | 734.0 |
| Total inter-Arab investment | 227.6 | 222.4 | 258.4 | 400.8 |
| Arab investment in Egypt | 21.7 | 51.9 | 77.8 | 92.0 |
| % of total inter-Arab investment in Egypt | 9.5 | 23.3 | 30.1 | 23.0 |
| % of Arab investment in total FDI in Egypt | 2.2 | 4.4 | 6.2 | 12.5 |

*Sources*: IMF, *BOP Statistical Yearbook*, Part 1, pp. 266–70; IFS (vol. no. 4, 2000/2001),
p. 76. Calculatuion based on reports for 1987–90. See: *al-Muassasa al-Arabiyya Li-Daman
al-Istithmar, Munakh al-Istithmarfi al-Duwal al-Arabiyya* and *al-Safa*, 1987–90; Dr. Ali
Saliman, "Tajribat Al-Istithmar Al-Arabi Al-Mushtarac", *al-Ahram al-Iqtisadi*, December 24,
1990, p. 29; Interview with Dr. Mamoon Hasan, director of the Arab Institute for Investment
Guarantees to *al-Ahram al-Iqtisadi*, August 19, 1991, p. 20.

From table 6.12 we learn that in 1995, 51 percent of all Arab investment in Egypt
was from the Gulf States. This was also the case in 1997.[38]

**Table 6.12**   Distribution of inter-Arab investment in Egypt by investing state in
1995

| Investing state | Share in inter-Arab investment in Egypt |
|---|---|
| Saudi Arabia | 22.0 |
| Kuwait | 19.0 |
| Libya | 9.0 |
| UAE | 7.0 |
| Bahrain | 3.0 |
| Lebanon | 3.0 |
| Syria | 2.0 |
| Palestine[1] | 1.5 |
| Yemen | 1.5 |
| Iraq | 1.0 |
| Other | 21.0 |
| Total | 100. |

*Source*: *Al-Ahram al-Iqtisadi*, August 5, 1996.

[1] Palestinian Authority.

**Table 6.13**  Arab investment in Egypt 2001 by country (in millions of US dollars)

| Country | 2001 |
| --- | --- |
| Bahrain | 2.4 |
| Iraq | 3.8 |
| Jordan | 3.3 |
| Kuwait | 17.6 |
| Lebanon | 3.5 |
| Libya | 4.1 |
| Oman | 2.7 |
| Palestine | 16.3 |
| Qatar | 1.1 |
| Saudi Arabia | 21.7 |
| Sudan | 0.3 |
| Syria | 8.1 |
| UAE | 2.2 |
| Yemen | 1.1 |
| Total | 88.2 |

*Source*: Al-Muassasa al-Arabiyya Li-Daman al-Istithmar, *Munakh al-Istithmarfi al-Duwal al-Arabiyya*, 2001; *Al-Safa*, 2002.

By 2001, there had been a significant slowdown in direct Arab investment in Egypt (table 6.13). At the end of 1999, total Arab investments in the country stood at $3.92 billion. Arab countries had set up 1,799 companies and joint ventures, with a total registered capital of $16.28 billion. According to the Chairman of Egypt's General Authority for Free Zones and Investment, Mohammed al-Ghamrawi, Saudi Arabia was the largest investor among the Arab states with $1.22 billion (38% of the total), followed by Kuwait with $1.02 billion and the UAE with about $380 million.[39] The number of Saudi companies that had invested in Egypt was 521 (29%), and these investments were distributed in industry, agriculture, investment companies, banks, transportation service companies and free zone companies[40]. An internal GAFI study claimed that in 2000/1 Arab investment accounted for 46 percent of new foreign investment in Egypt, and 6 percent of all investment (foreign and domestic).[41]

Arab investors have been taking large stakes in the Toshka project,[42] as well as in the privatization drive in Egypt.[43] In addition to those mentioned above in connection with the Toshka project, the following are some of the main projects: a Saudi touristic project, the "Golden Pyramids Plaza," with an investment of EgP 420 million ($119 million);[44] 44 projects, with a total investment of $300 million, from the Saudi Dala al-Barka group;[45] various projects by the al-Futaim group from the UAE;[46] investments worth EgP 2.5 billion ($725 million) by the Kuwaiti Kharafi Investment Group;[47] and plans by the SGI-Global Saudi group, in which the Emir Fahd Bin Salman Bin Abd el-Aziz holds 20 percent of the capital, to invest $250 million in the spheres of energy, construction and project financing.[48]

It should be noted that while the largest sums of Arab investment in Egypt were private, Arab development funds which in the past had been a main source of such investment, continued to channel funds for specific projects in Egypt. Thus, the

Arab Fund for Economic Development granted Egypt, in the period from the beginning of 1990 until the end of May 1997, KD 291.7 million ($88.6 million), to finance projects in various sectors.[49] The Kuwaiti Fund for Economic Development granted Egypt loans worth KD 166.7 million ($50.8 million) to finance a project to improve 400,000 feddans in Northern Sinai, the Sidi Karir power station, a printing and newspaper paper project in Kuz, a drainage system in Greater Cairo, and several projects of the Social Fund for Development.[50]

From 1990 to 1997, the Abu Dhabi Fund for Arab Economic Development granted Egypt $1.5 million in addition to ED 220.3 million ($60 million) to finance a project to improve 155,000 feddans of land in the Western al-Nubariah area, and the Northern coast, and projects of the Social Fund for Development. The Fund also administered funds granted by the UAE government, which amount to $285 million, in addition to ED 11.5 million ($3.13 million) to finance a project extending the Hamam canal, improving 40,000 feddans east of the Suez Canal, and several construction and housing projects.[51] In June 1988 a protocol was signed, under which the Fund was to grant $200 million to improve 65,000 feddans in the al-Nubaria area, as the first part of a new land improvement plan, in cooperation with the UAE, for an area of 215,000 feddans.[52] Finally, the Saudi Fund for Development granted Egypt in this period loans worth around SDR 265 million ($70.75 million) to finance a beet project in Balakaas, the construction of the Cairo–Asuite road, and an irrigation project in the Sinai desert.[53]

### The New Millennium

Figures for total FDI in Egypt for the financial year 2000/1 showed a sharp fall compared to previous years. The previous year had been a one-time $340 million investment by Mexico. The beginning of a world economic crisis led to a 74% cut in EU investments in Egypt, a 40% cut in US investments, and an 86% cut in Arab investment, to be limited to $14.1 million, due especially to cuts by Bahrain and the UAE (table 6.14). By 2001 the share of Arab investment in total FDI in Egypt was similar to the 1987 figure, namely 2.3%, while Egypt's share in total inter-Arab investments had fallen drastically. In that year total inter-Arab investments reached $2,447.0 million, and Egypt, which was sixth amongst the Arab recipients, receiving only $88.2 million – 3.6% of the total.[54]

**Table 6.14**  Net foreign direct investment in Egypt by country (in millions of US dollars)

| Countries | 1999/2000 | 2000/1 | 2001/2[1] |
|---|---|---|---|
| USA | 459.7 | 277.3 | 159.0 |
| Portugal | 486.0 | 0.0 | 38.8 |
| UK | 178.7 | 169.4 | 12.3 |
| Mexico | 340.0[2] | 0.1 | 0.0 |
| France | 62.4 | 0.1 | 208.1 |
| Spain | 3.6 | 0.0 | 83.8 |
| Germany | 25.6 | 25.2 | 17.5 |
| Bahrain | 64.5 | 0.4 | 0.0 |
| UAE | 29.8 | 5.6 | 0.1 |
| Switzerland | 22.8 | 5.8 | 2.0 |

**Table 6.14** *(continued)*

| | | | |
|---|---|---|---|
| Japan | 3.1 | 11.0 | 0.0 |
| Kuwait | 1.6 | 3.9 | 2.5 |
| Saudi Arabia | 4.7 | 2.2 | 0.9 |
| Italy | 1.4 | 1.5 | 2.7 |
| Tunisia | 0.0 | 0.0 | 0.0 |
| Other | 7.3 | 7.6 | 4.3 |
| Total | 1,691.2 | 510.1 | 532.0 |
| Net Foreign Direct Investment | 1,656.1 | 509.4 | 428.2 |

*Source*: Central Bank of Egypt, *Memo*, October 31, 2002.

[1] Provisional.  [2] Includes the proceeds of selling Assiut Cement Co.

## Egyptian investment in the Arab countries

While Egypt was a major recipient of Arab investment, one cannot ignore the phenomenon of Egyptian investment in other Arab states, and especially the GCC countries. By the end of 2000, joint Egyptian–Saudi investments in Saudi Arabia, in around 30 projects, totaled $84.1 million, constituting 1.7 percent of all foreign investments in Saudi Arabia.[55] By the end of 2001, total Egyptian investmens in Saudi Arabia reached $52.9 million – 7.34 percent of total inter-Arab investments in that year (table 6.15). The remainder of Egyptian investments were directed to non-Gulf Arab states.[56]

**Table 6.15**  Egyptian investments in Arab countries in 2001 and in the years 1985–2000 (in millions of US dollars)

| Country | Egyptian investment in 2001 | % of total Arab investment | Egyptian investment in 1985–2000 |
|---|---|---|---|
| Algeria | 87.5 | 25.00 | 5.911 |
| Bahrain | — | — | 57.590 |
| Iraq | — | — | 31.864 |
| Jordan | 2.0 | 7.20 | 136.821 |
| Kuwait | — | — | 1,119.660 |
| Lebanon | — | — | 87.369 |
| Libya | 1.7 | 2.00 | 176.212 |
| Morocco | — | — | 45.919 |
| Oman | — | — | 68.239 |
| Palestine | — | — | 118.741 |
| Qatar | — | — | 217.401 |
| Saudi Arabia | 52.9 | 7.34 | 1,567.566 |
| Sudan | 31.2 | 5.62 | 50.116 |
| Syria | 1 | 2.30 | 98.763 |
| Tunisia | — | — | 14.086 |
| UAE | — | — | 214.043 |
| Yemen | 1 | 15.90 | 28.562 |
| Total | 177.3 | — | 4,038.863 |

*Source*: Al-Muassasa al-Arabiyya Li-Daman al-Istithmar, *Munakh al-Istithmar fi al-Duwal al-Arabiyya* 2001; *Al-Safa*, 2002, pp. 56–7, 59–60.

## Remittances from Egyptian workers in the Gulf

Economic growth in Egypt was to be slow in order to enable it to absorb the new entrants to the labor market. The combination of the high growth rate of the labor force and low productivity exacerbated unemployment and eroded real wages.[57] Migration continued to offer Egyptians an important source of job opportunities and a large donor of foreign exchange to Egypt's government in the 1990s. Nevertheless, workers' remittances have not grown over time (table 6.16) due to the downturn in oil prices and demand in the GCC, because of lower labor costs in the Asian market.

In 1986 oil prices plummeted, generating a region-wide recession. Although the economic downturn did not bring down the levels of Arab labor migration, immigration patterns have witnessed change, particularly in terms of destination countries. Workers already employed in the oil-rich Gulf States retained their jobs in sectors vital to those countries' economies and their remittances did not only sustain their pre-recession levels, but also increased in the case of some labor-exporting countries. The most significant transformation of the decade was the emergence of Iraq as a major labor importer. The trend was a result of the mobilization of much of Iraq's male workforce to serve in the war against Iran. In the late 1980s Iraq absorbed as many as 1.25 million Egyptian workers. The timing could not have been better for Egypt, as the increase in demand for working hands in Iraq coincided with a slowdown in demand for foreign labor in other Gulf States. Many Egyptian construction workers found themselves out of work in the GCC states as a growing number of Asian workers were taken on for lower wages. Asians were also hired in growing numbers as maintenance workers and domestic helpers.[58] Nearly a third of Egypt's migrant workers were employed in Iraq. In addition, a construction boom in Jordan – itself fueled by growing remittances from Jordanian professionals migrating to the Gulf – drew skilled Egyptian workers to the kingdom.[59]

The Iraqi invasion of Kuwait in August 1990 led to the departure of most of the non-Iraqi Arab workers from Iraq. It was estimated that over 700,000 Egyptians returned to Egypt from Iraq, Jordan and Kuwait.[60] The disappearance of work opportunities in Iraq, and the drop in work opportunities in Jordan resulting from the economic hardships that accompanied domestic political development there, were especially harmful to the Egyptian expatriates, whose total number decreased by about 1 million.[61]

In addition to the loss in income, the large number of repatriates exacerbated the existing unemployment problem in Egypt, and slowed down economic growth further. The combination of the high growth rate of the labor force, accelerated by the return of workers from abroad and low productivity, also eroded real wages to the point that average wages in 1995/6 were only two-thirds their level in 1985/6.[62]

Fortunately for Egypt, following the Gulf War of January–February 1991, Saudi Arabia offered it various economic compensations for its cooperation with the anti-Iraqi coalition, and by the end of April 1991, the number of Egyptian workers in Saudi Arabia had reached 1.25 million – double their pre-war number. Data published by the Saudi Ministry of Interior revealed that of a foreign population of

6.26 million, 2.38 million (38%) were Arabs migrants, and of these around 1.2 million (50.2%) were Egyptians.[63]

In the latter half of the 1990s, according to CAPMAS, the number of Egyptians working abroad in the Arab world dropped by 9 percent between 1996 and 1999. As of January 1, 1999, there were 1.9 million Egyptians working on fixed term contracts in the Arab states compared to 2.1 million in 1996.[64] Saudi Arabia was the largest employer with 924,000 Egyptian workers, followed by Libya with 333,000 and Jordan with 227,000.

It should be noted that as the 1990s progressed, the unemployment troubles of the GCC states and balance of payments deficits encouraged the GCC countries to pursue a policy of trying to substitute their foreign labor forces with local workers. Their success, however, was limited.[65] This was due to the higher pay demanded by local workers and their lack of basic skills,[66] implying that hiring expatriates helped GCC governments realize substantial savings of the wage bills of both the private and public sectors,[67] and that the employment of expatriates has increased in some cases at a faster rate than the employment of nationals.[68] Non-Saudi workers constituted 55.8 percent (4 million) of the total labor force. In the government sector it was only 21.8 percent (0.2 million), and in the private sector 61.3 percent (3.837 million).[69]

**Table 6.16**   Net remittances by Egyptian workers (in million of US dollars)

| Year | Remittances |
| --- | --- |
| 1987 | 3,604 |
| 1988 | 3,770 |
| 1989 | 3,293 |
| 1990 | 4,284 |
| 1991 | 4,054 |
| 1992 | 6,104 |
| 1993 | 5,664 |
| 1994 | 3,672 |
| 1995 | 3,226 |
| 1996 | 3,107 |
| 1997 | 3,697 |
| 1998 | 3,370 |
| 1999 | 3,235 |

*Source*: IMF, *BOP Statistical Yearbook*, Part 1, pp. 266–70.

Outflows of Saudi private transfers increased from $13.7 billion in 1991 to $18.7 billion in 1994, reflecting the rise in workers' remittance as the private sector expanded. Government efforts to reduce the expatriate workforce contributed to a moderate decline in outflows of current transfers to $14 billion in 1999, and to $15.5 billion in 2000.[70]

From table 6.16 we learn that the remittances by Egyptian workers rose sharply from an average of $3.5 billion in the years 1987–9 to $4.3 billion in 1990 and to $6.1 billion in 1992. In the second part of the 1990s the remittances dropped to between $3.1 billion and $3.7 billion. Nevertheless, despite the fall, workers' remit-

**Table 6.17** Egypt's inter-Arab trade (in millions of US dollars)

| | 1990/1 | 1991/2 | 1992/3 | 1993/4 | 1994/5 | 1995/6 | 1996/7 | 1997/8 | 1998/9 | 1999/00 | 2000/1 | 2001/2[1] |
|---|---|---|---|---|---|---|---|---|---|---|---|---|
| Imports | 550.5 | 351.2 | 201.2 | 189.9 | 305.4 | 422.1 | 588.6 | 732.3 | 623.5 | 840.5 | 754.3 | 847.5 |
| % of total | 4.8 | 3.5 | 1.9 | 1.8 | 2.4 | 3.0 | 3.8 | 4.3 | 3.7 | 4.7 | 4.6 | 5.8 |
| Exports | 300.8 | 509.6 | 508.1 | 424.9 | 484.4 | 504.3 | 635.0 | 711.8 | 511.4 | 444.3 | 816.7 | 902.5 |
| % of total | 7.1 | 13.1 | 13.6 | 12.7 | 9.8 | 10.9 | 11.9 | 13.9 | 11.5 | 7.0 | 11.5 | 13.6 |
| Balance | −249.7 | 158.4 | 306.9 | 235.0 | 179.0 | 82.2 | 46.4 | −20.5 | −112.1 | −396.2 | 62.4 | 55.0 |

*Source:* Central Bank of Egypt, *Memo*, December 2002.

[1] Provisional.

tances are by far the most significant source of income to Egypt from the Arab countries than either trade, investment or aid.

The remittance income which Egypt was receiving in this period was much larger than any aid that Egypt might have received from the Arab oil-producing states, had Egypt refrained from signing its peace treaty with Israel, and had no boycott been imposed on it by the Arab states. This is a fair conclusion from the fact that due to the collapse in oil prices, the aid budgets of all the GCC states drastically fell.[71]

## Trade and tourism

### Egyptian trade with the Gulf States

Inter-Arab trade accounts for only 8 percent of the Arab world's total trade. This figure is extremely low compared to other regions and trade blocs. Thus, for example, in 2000 trade amongst members of the EU accounted for 61 percent of all EU trade, trade amongst the members of the North America Free Trade Agreement (NAFTA) acounted for 55 percent of the trade of these states, and the figure for the Association of South-East Asian Nations (ASEAN) was 23 percent.[72] The reason for the paucity in inter-Arab trade is the fact that most of the exports of this group of states are oil exports, and most of its imports are industrial goods from the industrialized states. The potential for trade among the Arab states is thus limited, even though for much of the 1990s regional economic integration continued to be a key strategic goal of most Arab states, and numerous bilateral trade agreements were signed to reduce trade barriers.[73] Egypt, Lebanon and Jordan are the only Arab states who export more than than 10% of their total exports to other Arab states.[74]

The 1990s saw the volume of Egyptian trade with other Arab countries grow in absolute terms (table 6.17). In terms of imports there was a drop in the percentage of imports from the Arab world the year before and the year after the Gulf War, but then they gradually rose again as the 1990s proceeded. In terms of exports the percentage kept vascilating between 7 percent and 13.6 percent. The EU states, the US and various Asian states were, and still are Egypt's predominant trading partners.

**Table 6.18**   Exports by region (in millions of US dollars)

|  | 1999/2000 | 2000/1 | 2001/2[1] |
|---|---|---|---|
| USA | 2,893.8 | 2,889.2 | 2,592.8 |
| European Union | 1,699.7 | 2,007.2 | 1,811.6 |
| Asian States | 917.9 | 765.9 | 834.6 |
| Arab States | 444.3 | 816.7 | 902.5 |
| Other European | 343.4 | 322.8 | 272.5 |
| African States | 37.3 | 41.1 | 51.5 |
| Russian Federation & CIS | 12.2 | 16.5 | 44.4 |

**Table 6.18** (continued)

| | | | |
|---|---|---|---|
| Australia | 5.3 | 3.3 | 3.3 |
| Others | 33.8 | 215.5 | 130.2 |
| Total Exports[2] | 6,387.7 | 7,078.2 | 6,643.4 |

*Source*: Central Bank of Egypt, *Memo*, December 2002.

[1] Provisional.
[2] Includes exports of free zones.

Nonetheless, Egypt does have important trading partners in the Arab world, such as Saudi Arabia and Kuwait. Interestingly, since 1988 Israel has been a larger market for Egyptian exports than both combined, due to its oil purchases from Egypt. Regarding suppliers of goods to Egypt, Saudi Arabia has certainly been Egypt's main trading partner, ahead of the other two states, and most years Egypt has imported more from Israel than from Kuwait.

In 2001, a trade agreement was established between Egypt and Saudi Arabia. The agreement stipulates that the two countries will enjoy customs duties reductions at a rate of 40% in the first year of the agreement's implementation, 20% in the second year, 20% in the third year, 10% in the fourth year, and 10% in the fifth year, when the customs duties will be removed altogether, with the exception of a few items mentioned in the agreement.[75] It will be interesting to observe the effect of this agreement on the volume of trade between the two countries.

**Table 6.19** Egyptian imports by region (in millions of US dollars)

| | 1999/2000 | 2000/1 | 2001/2[1] |
|---|---|---|---|
| European Union | 7,286.4 | 6,145.1 | 5,296.6 |
| USA | 3,821.0 | 4,414.9 | 3,684.0 |
| Asian States | 2,956.1 | 2,553.8 | 2,096.9 |
| Other European | 1,550.0 | 1,266.9 | 1,322.7 |
| Arab States | 840.5 | 754.3 | 847.5 |
| Australia | 269.7 | 246.7 | 225.4 |
| Russian Federation & CIS | 259.3 | 251.4 | 254.6 |
| African States | 118.8 | 124.5 | 132.0 |
| Others | 758.2 | 683.7 | 784.5 |
| Total imports | 17,860.0 | 16,441.3 | 14,644.2 |

*Source*: Central Bank of Egypt, *Memo*, December 2002.

[1] Provisional.

**Table 6.20** Egypt's trade relations with Saudi Arabia, Kuwait and Israel 1988–2001 (in millions of US dollars)

| Year | Export | | | Import | | |
|---|---|---|---|---|---|---|
| | Saudi Arabia | Israel | Kuwait | Saudi Arabia | Israel | Kuwait |
| 1988 | 69 | 146 | 14 | 68 | 28 | 36 |
| 1989 | 76 | 163 | 17 | 46 | 22 | 5 |
| 1990 | 77 | 168 | 11 | 76 | 41 | 6 |

(Table 6.20 continues on p. 251)

**Table 6.21** Number of tourists visiting Egypt (in thousands)

| Area | 1989/ 90 | 1990/ 1 | 1991/ 2 | 1992/ 3 | 1993/ 4 | 1994/ 5 | 1995/ 6 | 1996/ 7 | 1997/ 8 | 1998/ 9 | 1999/ 2000 | 2000/ 1 | 2001/ 2 |
|---|---|---|---|---|---|---|---|---|---|---|---|---|---|
| Europe | 1,154 | 607 | 1,354 | 1,350 | 979 | 1,200 | 1,853 | 2,168 | 1,580 | 2,282 | 3,241 | 3,501 | 2,769 |
| Middle East | 973 | 914 | 1,090 | 971 | 890 | 1,084 | 1,054 | 1,170 | 1,274 | 1,388 | 1,303 | 1,070 | 1,025 |
| Africa | 288 | 246 | 211 | 201 | 152 | 145 | 117 | 121 | 119 | 150 | 148 | 145 | 144 |
| Americas | 210 | 112 | 189 | 216 | 174 | 203 | 261 | 250 | 229 | 244 | 315 | 325 | 184 |
| Asia & Pacific | 157 | 91 | 154 | 179 | 162 | 197 | 263 | 282 | 192 | 200 | 301 | 304 | 217 |
| Others | 1 | 0 | 1 | 2 | 2 | 3 | 1 | 96 | 2 | 2 | 3 | 2 | 2 |
| Total | 2,783 | 1,970 | 2,999 | 2,919 | 2,359 | 2,832 | 3,549 | 4,087 | 3,396 | 4,266 | 5,311 | 5,347 | 4,341 |

*Source*: Central Bank of Egypt, *Memo*, December 2002.

**Table 6.22** Number of tourists from the Middle East visiting Egypt (in thousands)

| Country | 1989/ 90 | 1990/ 1 | 1991/ 2 | 1992/ 3 | 1993/ 4 | 1994/ 5 | 1995/ 6 | 1996/ 7 | 1997/ 8 | 1998/ 9 | 1999/ 2000 | 2000/ 1 | 2001/ 2 |
|---|---|---|---|---|---|---|---|---|---|---|---|---|---|
| Jordan | 62 | 46 | 55 | 44 | 47 | 54 | 49 | 61 | 72 | 82 | 75 | 76 | 81 |
| Kuwait | 72 | 107 | 91 | 8 | 59 | 77 | 71 | 73 | 67 | 71 | 71 | 61 | 64 |
| Palestine[1] | 101 | 68 | 58 | 67 | 111 | 129 | 108 | 162 | 195 | 195 | 155 | 133 | 131 |
| Saudi Arabia | 187 | 170 | 227 | 219 | 198 | 231 | 173 | 221 | 220 | 240 | 258 | 229 | 229 |
| Syria | 0 | 53 | 98 | 95 | 68 | 71 | 70 | 68 | 72 | 70 | 60 | 75 | 71 |
| Other[2] | 551 | 470 | 561 | 461 | 407 | 522 | 583 | 585 | 648 | 730 | 684 | 496 | 449 |
| Total | 973 | 914 | 1,090 | 971 | 890 | 1,084 | 1,054 | 1,170 | 1,274 | 1,388 | 1,303 | 1,070 | 1,025 |

*Source*: Central Bank of Egypt, *Memo*, December 2002.

[1] Palestinian Authority.
[2] Including Israel.

**Table 6.20** (continued)

| 1991 | 114 | 369 | 15 | 135 | 4 | 45 |
|------|-----|-----|----|-----|----|----|
| 1992 | 202 | 290 | 36 | 104 | 12 | 8 |
| 1993 | 197 | 230 | 36 | 133 | 19 | 5 |
| 1994 | 155 | 188 | 26 | 194 | 13 | 7 |
| 1995 | 113 | 174 | 17 | 249 | 23 | 9 |
| 1996 | 123 | 344 | 19 | 291 | 37 | 6 |
| 1997 | 139 | 314 | 19 | 440 | 42 | 7 |
| 1998 | 197 | 134 | 22 | 613 | 20 | 11 |
| 1999 | 121 | 187 | 15 | 698 | 22 | 16 |
| 2000 | 184 | 19 | 18 | 866 | 65 | 20 |
| 2001 | 147 | 190 | 17 | 679 | 19 | 50 |

Sources: IMF, Direction of Trade Statistics, various issues; KSA, SAMA, Annual Report, various issues; Egyptian Trade Point, "Dalil al-Musaddir al-Misri lil-Saudiyya," Al-ahram al-Iqtidadi, October 8, 2001.

## Tourism from the Gulf States

In terms of the number of foreign tourists, and the number of nights spent by foreign tourists in Egypt, the nation receives a greater influx of tourists from Europe than the rest of the Middle East.

**Table 6.23**   Number of nights spent by tourists in Egypt (in thousands)

|  | 1999/2000 | 2000/1 | 2001/2 |
|---|-----------|--------|--------|
| West Europe | 21,560 | 20,910 | 16,560 |
| Middle East States | 6,760 | 5,709 | 6, 080 |
| Americas | 1,926 | 1,979 | 1,294 |
| East Europe | 1,496 | 1,717 | 2,461 |
| Asia and Pacific | 1,320 | 1,441 | 1,130 |
| African States | 966 | 934 | 1,003 |
| Other States | 17 | 12 | 14 |
| Total | 34,045 | 32,702 | 28,542 |

Source: Central Bank of Egypt, Economic Review, vol. 42, 2001/02/.

## Summary

Faced with mounting economic woes, Sadat was the first to realize that salvation would not come from the Arab countries, but rather from the West, and that his *infitah* policy could only be implemented if he were to cooperate with the Americans. This strategic choice was also well understood by his sucessor Mubarak, who two decades later stood shoulder to shoulder with the Americans in the Gulf War. Vindicating this policy, tens of billions of US aid dollars have poured into Egypt since Sadat concluded a peace treaty with Israel in 1979, and this has replaced Arab aid. These funds helped Egypt re-equip its armed forces with modern Western weaponry and develop more sophisticated industries. Egypt has long been under considerable pressure to sever its diplomatic relations with Israel. In response, Mubarak maintains that these ties enable Egypt to hold Israel up to its international obligations. While that may be so, it is also clear that if Egypt were to call off relations with Israel, Cairo's economic partnership with the US would have been put at risk. Considering that the US is Egypt's chief aid donor, biggest export market and main investor, Cairo is hardly inclined to jeopardize this relationship.

In addition to the generous American aid, Arab states have also occasionally bankrolled Egypt's support, as in the case of the anti-Iraq coalition formed in 1990/1. In the aftermath of the Kuwait crisis, the Arab countries joined the generous international debt forgiveness deals granted to Egypt. The large decline in world oil prices in the 1980s created budget deficits that led to increasing poverty within the Gulf States. Facing economic hardship, they were unable to provide Egypt with sufficient aid. The economic situation in Saudi Arabia, for example, did not allow the Kingdom to donate the same amount of foreign aid as in the past. In all but four years from 1983 to 2000, Saudi trade surplus failed to offset its services and transfers deficits, resulting in recurring current account deficits. Expenditure related to the Gulf conflict caused the current account deficit to rise to $27.6 billion. In 1996, 1997, 1999 and 2000 the current account reverted to surpluses, mainly owing to higher oil prices. Kuwait's limited aid resources were further diminished after the Gulf War. Bearing in mind the economic assistance delivered to Iraq in the 1980s, Kuwait has become disillusioned with having financial allies, as the aid donations it made did nothing to prevent Iraq from invading it in 1990. Consequently, the oil-rich emirate redirected its financial resources to fortify its internal security with the help of Western experts.

The Saudis under Crown Prince Abdallah are seeking to extend their influence over other parts of the world. The 1990s have seen the Saudis reassess their obligations in the inter-Arab arena. Shortly after the Gulf War, the Saudis asserted that Egypt's weight in the Arab world was on the wane. They aggressively turned to exert their influence in the Indian subcontinent, Afghanistan and Pakistan. Saudi Arabia and the other GCC countries increasingly turn to provide assistance to Muslim communities outside the Arab world, such as those in Chechnya.[76] Muslim separatist groups in the Southern Philippines and Turkey. Amidst this expansionist program, Egypt receives significant aid from the West and maintains strong trade, investment and technology ties, securing its position as a key supplier of labor to the GCC states. Remittances from Egyptian workers exceed all other sources of foreign income.

Egypt's long-term orientation toward the West was based on the premise that Western aid and trade ties were more reliable than those offered by the Arab world. Faced with tough internal predicaments, Egyptian policy-makers realized that substantial economic support could only come from the West rather than from the Arab world. In its search for substantial partners to support the country's economic development, Egypt reached the obvious conclusion in turning westward rather than eastward. And so, while Arab League discussions still pay tribute to the rhetoric of inter-Arab cooperation, foremost on Egypt's mind are its particular economic interests. While Egypt realized that the best source for considerable economic support is in the West – the US and Europe – it has managed to supplement that income with the remittances repatriated by Egyptian laborers in the GCC countries.

# 7

# AOC Aid: The Shifting Equation

In the past forty years, tens of billions of dollars were transferred from the AOC to the Egyptian economy, mainly in the form of direct civil and military aid, private and state investment, and worker remittances. This bounty was unprecedented in the course of international relations, and represented a unique opportunity for the Egyptian economy.

The flow of aid from the Arab oil-producing states to developing countries in the 1970s was vast. Foreign aid up to that time was restricted to relations between the Great Powers and dependent countries. This relationship was transformed to new geo-political terrains. The first was the manner of inter-relationship between states within the Third World, with aid flows highlighting the new pseudo-class differentiation that had developed between the countries of the region. The second was the sub-global level of relations in the regional entity – that of the Middle East.

An empirical examination of the economic ties between Egypt and the AOC showed an impressive quantitative picture of about $41 billion in the years 1967-84, including aid – $14.2 billion; investments and deposits of $4.5 billion; and worker remittances through official channels – $22 billion. During the late 1980s and the '90s, Arab aid to Egypt was marginal, apart from the 1990-1 Gulf War period. During this time, Arab investment in Egypt was also superseded by European and US investors. Only the remittances remained a significant factor, and continued to encompass the flow of tens of billions of dollars from AOC countries into Egypt.

Although the AOC economic aid to Egypt was ostensibly derived from cross-national motivations and objectives, the national partitions separating Egypt from the AOC were not torn down. Not only was the stated aim of Arab unity stagnant during this time, but isolationist trends were actually strengthened. It is true that oil wealth had a moderating influence on the ideological conflict, but conversly it added a new divisive element in the light of Egypt's demand for a more even-handed sharing of the bounty. The AOC rejected this demand absolutely and tried to delete the subject of oil revenues from the Arab agenda. Important processes of nation-building were simultaneously taking place in the AOC. The prosperity and wealth that came with oil brought with it social modernization and an independent political awareness – the bureaucracy, the technocracy, army officers, the public sector, businessmen and others. Their power was based on the existence of a national oil economy and on national mechanisms and institutions. Therefore these groups were interested in safeguarding and strengthening national independence and its crystal-lization.[1]

Each country was first and foremost protecting its own interests, and pan-Arab concerns were pushed into a corner. The AOC countries helped Egypt not in order to save the economy there, but with the aim of promoting their own interests, while Egypt did not request aid to develop the Arab world, but for its own separate devel-opment. Sadat's peace initiative, taken without consultation or cooperation with the Arab sister states, illustrated conspicuously the dominance of narrow national considerations in the whole complex of pan-Arab relations and especially in the relationship between Egypt and the AOC.

AOC aid to Egypt bagan in the 1960s, and its growth matched the rise in the Gulf States' wealth. Prior to the early 1960s, aid to Egypt was meager. It was actually Egypt who assisted the oil-producing countries in the 1940s and 1950s, primarily in the field of education. Many research scholars seize upon June 1967 as the pivotal point in Arab aid to Egypt and tend to ignore or underestimate aid flows prior to this date. However, official documents present a different picture, showing that Kuwaiti aid started several years before the given date. This first aid flow highlights the motivations behind the AOC money transfers.

In the years 1962-67 Kuwait, which had only become independent in 1961, started the flow of aid to Egypt. The Kuwaiti rulers and the country's national exis-tence were not yet well-established, and they strived to maintain good relations with the Egyptian regime, in order to "buy" the validation of its independence by the Arab world's leader, and to be viewed positively in Cairo – the revolutionary, threat-ening center. Egyptian influence in Kuwaiti government and society reinforced the need for Kuwaiti aid.

The concept of aid as a permanent, extensive phenomenon appeared only after the June 1967 War, following the Khartoum summit (August 1967). At that same conference, Saudi Arabia, Kuwait and Libya guaranteed to provide Egypt about $260 million annually, in quarterly payments, "until the results of Israeli aggression have been eliminated." In addition, up to 1970 Egypt received one-time (minor) aid at the 1969 Rabat summit, and additional small loans and grants.

Up to the end of 1967 Saudi Arabia had not offered aid to Egypt, because of the tense relations between the regimes and the contrasts in their ideological and polit-ical character. After the June 1967 defeat and Nasser's revised moderate stance, Saudi Arabia and other neighboring countries joined the aid circle. At the Khartoum summit the AOC decided to offer Egypt an annual grant in quarterly payments. This method was determined to ensure that Egypt would fulfil its commitment to withdraw from Yemen, as well as to facilitate matters for the trea-suries of the aiding countries. The Khartoum aid compensated Egypt for the loss of revenues by the closing of the Suez Canal, the loss of the oil fields in Sinai and the decline in tourism, but did not help Egypt with regards to damages, security expen-ditures and the heavy economic burden incurred from the June war and the war of attrition.

Aside from the heavy psychological and political pressure created by the trauma of defeat, strategic, political and economic considerations also played a part in the AOC's Khartoum decision. After the rout of war, the AOC felt threatened by Israel and acknowledged the fact that even a defeated Egyptian army could come to their succour in times of need. Secondly, they feared that Nasser, if he did not receive aid, would be a threat to the oil fields and/or increase his dependence on the Soviets; moreover the AOC were concerned that Egypt would attempt to dictate oil policy to them, contrary to their national interests. The AOC anticipated this and neutralized this danger. At the Khartoum conference, Nasser supported the position of the conservative oil states on the subject of oil.

Sadat's coming to power brought with it a strengthening of ties between Egypt and the AOC, especially after the expulsion of the Soviet advisors in July 1972. From this time on the AOC increased their civil and military aid to Egypt, thereby helping it to prepare for the October 1973 war. Contrary to Egyptian expectations, however, there was no significant increase in economic aid after the war. The AOC adopted a calculated policy of "trickles of aid." Only events threatening Egypt's stability moved them to temporarily relax their aid policy. On the other hand, in the sector of military aid the AOC governments manifested greater generosity, and they readily purchased arms for Egypt, mainly on the European market.

In 1976, aid took a turn for the worse in both scope and its pattern. The extent of aid was reduced by half in 1975, and conditioned on Egypt adopting various economic reforms proposed by the IMF. This was seen by Egyptians as an unprecedented manifestation of patronage and interference by the AOC. Furthermore, the funds of the GFDE, founded by the AOC, were set at just $2 billion, instead of the $12 billion that Sadat had expected. Only military aid was not reduced. In 1976 Saudi Arabia guaranteed to finance all military needs for a period of five years.

The decline in aid from the AOC was conspicuous against the rapidly deteriorating economic situation in Egypt. In 1977 the amount of Arab aid was increased again, although it did not reach 1975 levels. The reason for this increase was not a change in approach by the AOC, but the "food riots" in Egypt in January 1977, and the AOC leaders' concern that these riots could have potentially disastrous implications for them. After Sadat's peace initiative, Arab aid did not cease completely, but it did diminish sharply.

The type and extent of AOC economic aid to Egypt was governed by the political considerations of the AOC leaders, who consistently chose to present their aid as stemming from mostly moral and transnational considerations: moral duty, the commandments of Islam, the principle of brotherhood with the Third World and the Muslim world, their feeling of responsibility towards their Arab brothers and reinforcing their stand against Israel. However, the divisions of aid, its channels, extent, timing and exploitation point to a more narrow national interest as the central consideration regarding aid to Egypt.

In the AOC, political stability and national security were the overriding concerns for the local leadership because of their enticing wealth on the one hand, and their narrow authoritarian, demographic and military foundations on the other hand. Foreign aid was the main political means for applying foreign policy, and was seen as central to achieving AOC objectives. The AOC's aid was dynamic and meted out according to contemporary events. Egypt received most Arab aid, with emphases and reasons for this aid differing though key reasons included: a desire to moderate Nasser's regime; warfare against Israel; reinforcing the Egyptian army; to help rid the region, including Egypt, of Soviet influence; and gain economic benefits with the help of Egypt's human resources.

Following the 1967 war, the AOC kept up their yearly payments to Egypt, but they objected to increasing the amount, as demanded by Nasser at the Rabat summit in 1969. Their reasoning was that the aid they were giving Egypt amounted to 10 percent of their oil revenues, and that as Egypt was not actively trying to regain the conquered territories, it was not in need of additional military aid. The AOC also demanded to supervise how their aid was utilized; they preferred to direct funds destined for military aid straight to the European arms suppliers. In light of the relative improvement in the Egyptian economy, in no small way thanks to the AOC, the oil chiefs were concerned that Nasser still supported subversive activities against them, as well as due to the close relations forged between Nasser and the revolutionary Gaddafi, who had risen to power in September 1969. Furthermore, they were worried by increased Soviet activity in Egypt.

After Sadat's rise to power. Saudi Arabia and the US tried to convince him to expel the Soviets from Egypt. Faysal also used his personal relations with Sadat, making promises of economic and military aid, part of which was already given before the expulsion. It seems that Faysal's dogmatic, anti-Soviet stand and his promise to compensate Egypt lent weight to the decision to expel the Soviet advisors from Egypt. And indeed, from the date of the expulsion until the outbreak of the October 1973 War, Arab economic and military aid to Egypt increased sharply. This assistance, mainly military, enabled Egypt to fight in the 1973 war. The AOC even agreed that part of their aid be used for purchasing arms from the USSR, to circumvent the limitations some of the Western countries had imposed on arms exports to the confrontation states.

Crecelius stated that after the war the Saudi treasury was open to Egypt for any sum it needed. In reality things turned out differently: the AOC continued their aid to Egypt, but they carefully calculated the extent of this aid. Even while the guns were thundering during the October War, the AOC made it clear that their funds to Egypt were not limitless. After the war the extent of their aid and investment was reevaluated and fixed at a fairly low level. This in sharp contrast to their burgeoning wealth generated by the post-war oil embargo, and out of all proportion to their investments in the West.

Another flow of petro-dollars to Egypt was the transfer of funds from the AOC to Egypt through "irregular" channels. There exist several testimonies on extensive Saudi "aid" to senior Egyptian officials, to Egyptian newspapers and their editors, and to Islamic associations and institutions (in cash or in goods), all with the aim of winning greater political and social influence for Saudi Arabia with the help of a "correct" article in the paper, by publishing Islamic books and books condemning communism.[2]

Instead of an "Arab Marshall Plan" thought up by Egypt, the AOC governments provided economic aid in trickles. They showed greater generosity when it came to military aid. Many times they paid directly to the arms suppliers, inter alia, to prevent Egypt from appropriating these funds for civilian purposes. The AOC cultivated military aid so that Egypt was maintaining a military balance with Israel. This meant Egypt could come to the AOC's assistance in times of need, to give Sadat greater maneuverability on the international level, and also to block Soviet re-entry into Egypt through arms supply. An important aim of aid was to reinforce Egypt's rapprochement with the West. It was not a coincidence that, in 1976, Saudi Arabia guaranteed to finance all requirements for the Egyptian army for a period of five years, after the abrogation of the friendship treaty between Egypt and the USSR.

In 1976 the supporting governments introduced new and harsher standards for the allocation, transfer and conditions of aid. From that year on most aid was channeled through the GFDE, conditional on the adoption of reforms proposed to Egypt by the IMF. Also, the AOC demanded that the aid funds to be provided be managed by external bodies. Sadat, his nation in economic turmoil, was forced to agree to some of these dictates. Saudi Arabia supported the position taken by the IMF, in the belief that the reforms would guarantee long-term stability in Egypt.

The change in approach of 1976 stemmed, inter alia, from Sadat's "independent" stand toward Israel, which caused a dangerous split in the Arab world from the oil chiefs' point of view. The leaders of the oil-producing countries had no desire to overly strengthen the Egyptian economy, because of their concern that a strong Egypt would threaten their regimes' political stability. They preferred that Egypt be economically dependant on them. Conversely, a collapse of the Egyptian economy could cause domestic instability threatening to spread to their own countries. A middle path for them was a calculated trickle of aid. In addition, the oil chiefs were inclined to view Egypt as a bottomless pit. It seems they assumed that Egypt would never be satisfied with increased aid, because of its complicated problems. They feared that Egypt would become accustomed to receiving aid from them any time it asked for it, leading to pressures threatening the independence of their resources.

Another primary reason for reduced aid was the oil chiefs' evaluation that the conflict with Israel did not constitute a tangible threat to their existence. As evidence for this they stated that in twenty years of aid, Egypt had not received even one third of the aid received by Iraq in the first six years of the war with Iran. This war represented a tangible threat to their well-being, and aid was provided accordingly. However, aid to Egypt received priority, when the AOC felt that Egypt's stability was in danger of being undermined. In these cases, they moved in a limited way from a policy of trickles of aid to increased aid, as was done following the food riots in 1977.

The common interests of Egypt and the AOC were also responsible, ironically, for relatively minor aid. The communist threat and the desire for regional stability were common interests for both. The Saudis believed that Egypt would act, with or without Arab aid, to throw off communist influence, and would strive for regional stability. Egypt would act in a way compatible to the interests of the AOC, without the latter having to make any substantial investment. This theory was proved correct when even after boycott was imposed on Egypt, eliminating the aid factor, Egypt and the AOC continued ccoperating in the suppression of revolutionary elements.

Some of Sadat's close advisors were of the opinion that he was also personally to blame for the low level of aid. They believed that, in most cases, he did not request specific amounts of aid, and he was not aggressive in his demands for aid, as for example Syria and the PLO were. They also claimed that Sadat missed the window of opportunity after the October war to push for and to receive aid "fitting" to the occasion. Some advisors even claimed that he occasionally received "protocol presents" from the Saudis, weakening his bargaining power when discussing aid matters with them.

After the peace initiative, Saudi Arabia declared openly that it would continue aiding Egypt. Even after the Baghdad conference in 1978, when Sadat and the oil chiefs exchanged sharp accusations, aid was not discontinued. After Sadat accepted the peace agreement in mid-March 1979, the Saudis promised Bzhezhinski not to take sanctions against Egypt, in spite of their official opposition to the agreement. In the end, Saudi Arabia changed its stand, joining the boycott resolutions against Egypt at the second Baghdad conference in 1979, and recalling its ambassador from Cairo. Pressure and threats by the confrontation states, Saudi Arabia's feeling that it could not exert real influence on Sadat's position, all forced Saudi Arabia's hand. Other factors included: the feeling that Egypt had become America's preferential partner in the Arab world, their unwillingness to be seen as abandoning the interests of the Palestinians and the holy sites of Islam; and an internal reason, the victory of the "Arab approach" faction in the Saudi royal family.

The AOC joined the boycott resolution to try and satisfy the Arab confrontation states, but they had no desire to damage either the Egyptian or their own economies. Therefore, notwithstanding the formal breaking-off of relations, nearly all kinds of economic (and strategic) relations between the AOC and Egypt continued. Egyptian workers worked in the Gulf, Gulf citizens invested in Egypt, and the flow of commerce and tourism did not cease. Even official aid did not stop completely, and in addition the Gulf States "temporarily" dropped (sometimes for lack of choice) their demand for the repayment of Egypt's debts, constituting in itself aid to the Egyptian economy. Although Saudi Arabia refused to fulfil its commitment to purchase F-5 fighter jets for Egypt, it later had to reconsider its stance because of the publicity given to this deal, and because the US was ready to grant credit to Egypt for the purchase of F-4 Phantom aircraft, more advanced than the F-5. Saudi Arabia also continued financing arms deals for Egypt. Other oil states found ways and means to continue aiding Egypt, including by loans from joint European Arab banks.

One of the factors that lessened the impact of the economic boycott was the decision at the 1979 Baghdad conference not to break off unofficial economic ties with the Egyptian people. The AOC (and Egypt) exploited this clause to the limit. Heads of state therefore resumed their ties with Egypt. The peace treaty did not bring about any change in the oil chiefs' economic, security and political policy toward Egypt. The supply of Egyptian weaponry to Iraq after the break-out of the Iran-Iraq War justified their attitude, primarily when viewed against the background of Syria's support of Iran. Further vindication was given in the 1990-1 Gulf crisis, in which Egyptian troops were sent to protect Saudi Arabia and then fought to retake Kuwait.

Saudi-Egyptian relations were far from being proprietor-client relations, as some observers saw them.[3] Time and again Egypt took steps independent of the AOC attitudes. Egypt lost some of its prestige, mainly in its relations with Saudi Arabia, but it did not take any kind of stand merely because Saudi Arabia demanded it do so, and it definitely did not renounce its independence in taking decisions. In this context, Tuma referred to the difference between "power" and "influence": power points to the capacity of one country to force another country to do as it demands, willingly or unwillingly; in comparison, "influence" describes the capacity of a country to convince other countries to do as it wants. According to Tuma, oil wealth would be a source of influence but not a source of power, and the AOC did not succeed in changing the balance of power existing in the region before the "oil boom."[4]

The limited influence of the AOC on Egypt emanated mainly from the lack of balance in the structure of their economies, besides their demographic, social and military weakness, and their (long-term) dependence on Egypt's demographic and military power. Also after the defeat of June 1967, Egypt retained some elements of its hegemony (e.g. its military and cultural capacity), and the importance of other components grew stronger, such as the significance of the Egyptian workforce for the development of the whole Arab world. The AOC were not capable of taking over Egypt's role as regional leader after the peace treaty with Israel as they did not have the components of a significant power. Except for their financial muscle, the AOC lacked nearly all other distinctions of power, such as a large population, strong military, an advanced administrative structure and professional military manpower. They were dependent on other countries for nearly everything, from bread to weapons. Basic infrastructure works, still under construction, were carried out by foreign labor; and some of these turned native citizens into a minority in their own country.[5]

The desire for a share of the wealth of the oil countries played a central role in the forming of Egypt's national and foreign policies. Egypt demanded a new, regional division of oil revenues, and it took steps to that end on both the ideological and practical levels. Already after the June 1967 war, the Nasser regime implied that it was the AOC's duty to assist the Egyptian economy, and towards the end of his rule, made a specific demand pertaininig to that issue. Sadat, brought up the subject of the AOC's wealth many times, but only hinted at their duty to aid Egypt. The Egyptian media and the intellectuals, however, referred to this subject freely. They implicitly demanded Egypt's fair share, arguing that its material and physical sacrifices for the Arab cause and the enrichment of the AOC with the help of Egypt demanded such a reward.

The disappointment with aid and the bitterness caused by Egypt having to bear the heavy burden of the struggle with Israel grew steadily during the 1970s, particularly in 1976 after the founding of the Gulf Fund, and after the food riots in January 1977. After Sadat's initiative, ideological controversy was aggravated when Tawfiq al-Hakim called for Egyptian "neutrality" in matters pertaining to the Near East, as Egypt had paid its dues, without receiving its rights. After the 1978 Baghdad conference Sadat personally joined in the biting attacks on the AOC. A transition from ideological approach to attacks on a personal level had taken place. Only in Mubarak's time did this approach change; he refused to make personal attacks on the AOC leaders, and in public he hardly touched on the ideological discussion regarding Arab aid to Egypt. The AOC leaders tried to avoid openly discussing ideological matters; when they did do so, they stressed that their capacity for aid was limited, because of the need to develop their own economies. And they also gave voice to the claim that corruption, Egyptian bureaucracy, low absorption capacity, and the risk of future nationalization prevented them from increasing aid.

On a practical level, the Egyptian leadership acted to obtain maximum aid and Arab investments. The idea of Arab nationalism spread by Nasser was meant partly to attract oil resources; and after the 1967 defeat the difficult circumstances made it clear to him that he should reconsider his policy in order to attract Arab aid. Therefore, Nasser adopted a new international policy toward the US; on the inter-Arab level he moderated his subversive activities and his revolutionary ideology; and nationlly he showed greater attention to the private sector.

Sadat, as with Nasser, attached great importance to mobilizing foreign resources, as he viewed economic development in Egypt "as a matter of life and death." But Sadat's emphases, his methods and means to that end, differed from Nasser's. Part of this difference was due to the fact that economic circumstances in the AOC at the time were completely different from those during Nasser's rule. However, Sadat wanted to strengthen his ties with the AOC: he had proved to the conservative states that he had improved his relations with the US at the expense of his relations with the USSR, that he was actively involved in getting rid of communist influence in Egypt and other Arab countries, and that he gave priority to AOC investment over those by other nations.

Besides civil aid, investment and the absorption of Egyptian manpower, Egypt needed military aid because of its policy of "diversification of weapons sources." In January 1972 Sadat sponsored austerity measures to put the Egyptian economy on a war footing. The budget cuts were aimed, inter alia, to illustrate to the AOC Egypt's serious intentions of going to war, without which, Sadat realized, he would not get any substantial aid. Parallel to his declaration of war, Sadat sent his deputies to the AOC in order to coordinate economic and military aid for the war.

In his preparations for the 1973 war, Sadat sought to utilize the resources of the conservative oil-producing states as well as the revolutionary countries (mainly Libya), and therefore he did not reject Gaddafi's proposal of 1972 for a unification between the two countries in exchange for significant financial aid. By so doing, however, Sadat feared the reactions of the conservative oil states' leaders. Therefore he cleverly maneuvered between the possibilities at his disposal, so as to exploit to the maximum all available resources. He agreed to unification with Libya in stages, but from the very beginning he never intended to fulfil their agreement. Sadat therefore received significant aid from Libya and the conservative oil states, paving the way for him to go to war in October 1973.

The political and economic changes after the October war, in an atmosphere of restored Arab pride, inspired Sadat to try and mobilize petro-dollars for the rehabilitation of the Egyptian economy. According to his plan, the petro-dollars would be utilized as the central financial pillar for Egyptian development projects. The Egyptian government willingly agreed to the AOC's demand that it open its economy to foreign investment and anticipated that this would encourage Arab investment. However, the Egyptians were quickly disappointed. The extent of aid continued to be smaller than was necessary for structural economic changes. The AOC emphasis was still on security rather than on the economy, and it continued to be allotted under humiliating conditions.

Many research scholars have stated that the economic factor was central to the "Sadat initiative," but they did not focus on the influence of Arab aid on his initiative and on the method by which it was meted out. Sadat and his associates were soon left disillusioned with Arab aid. Economic difficulties, and the feeling that the Arabs had turned their backs on them, contributed significantly to Sadat seeking a peace settlement. Arab aid to Egypt in 1974, as indicated by Kanovsky, was less than sufficient, even in terms of help, to maintain the Egyptian standard of living, not to speak of any substantial improvement.[6] Through his actions, Sadat expressed his dissatisfaction with the scope of Arab capital flow and the way in which it was provided, notwithstanding Egypt's sacrifices. Furthermore, Sadat correctly saw the AOC's role and influence on the Arab-Israeli conflict, and he lost any illusions he may have had about the Arabs' role as "a sixth world-power," and about their capacity to utilize their resources for the good of Egyptian political purposes.

On top of this disappointment and embitterment there was a feeling of national humiliation in Egypt, because of the need to come begging to these "Bedouin," primarily because of the conditions attached to aid, which Egypt felt was interference in its internal affairs. The Egyptian citizens felt humiliated, witnessing Arab tourists squandering money freely while they lived in poverty. The Egyptians living in the AOC were insulted by the arrogance of the local population. Against this background, the readiness to take a new and independent road developed among the Egyptian population as well as with Sadat and his associates, the road to peace in favor of economic welfare.

Compared with all these factors, Sadat saw that political negotiations had brought positive economic results for the Egyptian economy after the interim agreements. All along Sadat spoke about the heavy military burden, and before his peace initiative in 1977 he spoke many times about the Egyptian economy and its capacity for rehabilitation.Sadat had a talent for political realism and he administered a rational foreign policy aimed at reducing dangers to a minimum and maximizing national benefits.[7] His initiative was a desperate realistic move in light of the economic-political slump, and as Sadat related to Tohami after the riots, an immediate settlement of the conflict with Israel was essential to lessen the regime's vulnerability. The peace treaty guaranteed the return of Sinai, the restoring of Sadat's personal prestige, as well as economic bonuses, with more oil fields, the reduction of the military burden, the creation of a good climate for investment, tourism and suitable recompensation from the US.

Sadat's initiative and his timing were also successful in the context of Arab aid. In the 1980s, after the fall of oil prices, the AOC were not able to significantly increase their aid to Egypt. From reserves of $100 billion in current accounts in 1980, they marked a deficit of more than $10 billion in 1982–3, and in addition they were forced to assist Iraq with tens of billions of dollars.

Following the peace treaty with Israel, the Arab countries imposed an economic boycott on Egypt. The weapon of economic sanctions, however, generally points to a lack of success, from a viewpoint of the realization of the boycott and its economic effectiveness, as well as its political influence.[8] Generally speaking, the Egyptian economy was not affected, and after the boycott Egypt even gained some large, new sources of income from the Arab countries, such as the export of arms to Iraq. The main influences of the boycott were political and the influence on the economical level was limited, primarily thanks to American aid and an increase of remittances by Egyptians working abroad.

Egypt also fought back against the AOC measures by freezing their deposits in the Egyptian Central Bank, and suspending repayments on its debts to them. When the AOC members calculated their anticipated costs from the sanctions, they concluded that they stood to loose the most from the boycott of Egypt: the Egyptian stand regarding the Iran-Iraq war forced them to a rapprochement with Egypt, and also broadened economic ties between Egypt and Iraq; the AOC realized that the Egyptian labor force was vital to the development of their economies; tens of thousands of students received their education in Egypt; and AOC ships passed through the Egyptian-owned Suez Canal. The fact that the Egyptian leadership stressed their commitment to defend the Gulf States, even after the peace agreement with Israel, was essential to the peace of mind of AOC members.

There were groups, particularly in the Egyptian opposition press, who challenged the "peace dividend": for example, in late December 1983 'Adil Mustafa wrote in *al-Sha'b* that the six years since the "peace" initiative had proven that peace had not been attained, and further that plans for economic prosperity following peace had not been successful, military expenditure had not fallen and economic problems had not been solved.[9] In this context, it is important to bear in mind the anticipations created by Sadat's public declarations about "a harvest of peace," such as: "we will make the desert blossom," and numerous similar statements. The danger is that exaggerated anticipations may not materialize. Even if the economic situation on the macro level had improved, the population at large examines, as a matter of course, the micro level, e.g. housing conditions, regular supply of food, the level of public services and so on.[10] Lutfi al-Khuli referred to this during the wave of arrests in Egypt in the summer/fall of 1981: another cause for opposition to the regime, al-Khuli claimed, emanated from Sadat's promises that peace with Israel would bring prosperity; matters were not being resolved this way at all: "the road to peace had not brought prosperity. On the contrary, there are growing economic problems and long-term development has come to a standstill."[11] Kamal Hassan Ali was asked in March 1983: "You said that Egypt had received large amounts of [Western aid]... Why is it that the influence of this money is not clearly felt in the internal situation in Egypt?" Ali's reply illustrated the less glamorous reality:

"That is the question we must ask ourselves. What would our situation have been without this aid, without loans, without easy credit terms and other things? That is the question .... Last year the budget of the Ministry of Housing came to nearly 650 million. Would this sum have been sufficient for the iron and cement we needed without foreign aid? What kind of a housing crisis would we have without this aid? . . . Let me tell you frankly, that we could not have built even one house or repaired the water system [without this aid]."[12]

The question of how Arab aid influenced the economic development of Egypt is complicated and highly contentious. However, if economic development is measured by the reduced dependence of the country receiving foreign aid, Egypt did not prosper. Instead, its dependence on foreign aid steadily grew.

On first impressions it seems that the policymakers in Egypt, observing the wealth of the oil-producing countries over the years, did less than necessary to mobilize Egypt's internal resources. No amount of aid could have extricated Egypt out of its desperate poverty without ground-level reform in fields such as family-planning or streamlining the bureaucracy. However, one also gets the impression from contemporary accounts that, at least in the years of plenty, the AOC could have provided greater aid to Egypt, alleviating the stress on the Egyptian economy, without unduly affecting national treasuries. Aid did indeed prevent a further deterioration of Egypt's unstable economy, but it was far from sufficient in terms of imporoving the economy.

Could the AOC have encouraged institutional change in Egypt, which would have led to a more efficient exploitation of their aid? The AOC had few tools for stimulating institutionalized change in Egypt, just as they had not succeeded in activating a political lever through their aid. Probably because of this they unreservedly supported the reforms proposed to Egypt by the IMF in 1976. American aid to Egypt encountered many difficulties with regards to pressing for domestic change, in spite of the extensive experience accumulated by the Americans in planning and applying economic aid.[13] The AOC and American experience in dealing with Egypt gives at least partial legitimacy to the claim that foreign aid, by its weakening influence, is damaging, because it enables the local leadership to evade painful, economic root treatment. The local bureaucracy was a stumbling block for the efficient and profound utilization of aid (as in many cases in the Third World). In Egypt, the bureaucracy controlled many sectors of society since the days of the Pharaohs, and not always efficiently.[14]

The disappointment of Egypt's leaders with Arab aid was compounded by the level of Arab investments in their country. Their sole investment guidelines were economic, and their investments in Egypt were marginal. In an attempt to gain renewed economic momentum, Sadat declared a policy of *infitah*. The Egyptian government initiated improvements and legislation to attract foreign, primarily Arab, investment. However, this effort was in vain. Egypt received a very small share of petro-dollar investment. The AOC governments viewed investments as a guarantee of the continuation of the flow of revenues to their countries in the post-oil age, and private investors were naturally interested mainly in maximizing their profits. In the years 1973–84 the AOC invested, bilaterally, only $400 million in Egypt. Kuwait held the largest investment portfolio, and after it came Saudi Arabia, the UAE and Qatar.

In addition to the investments of each country separately, in 1975 Saudi Arabia, the UAE and Qatar established jointly with Egypt the AMIO, with a capital of $1.04 billion, for the development of a military industrial base. This project was an utter failure and technical, financial and political problems arose, preventing it from "taking off." After the peace agreement between Egypt and Israel, the oil-producing states washed their hands of this affair and withdrew their financing of the authority. In the final instance, the losses of the AOC from the disbanding of the partnership were greater than Egypt's. The latter, with its developed infrastructure, had no problem in maintaining a developing military industry, even after the above event, and it had the support of the US, whereas the AOC had difficulties setting up a military center without Egyptian experience and know-how. Another large joint project of the AOC and Egypt was the laying of a pipeline between Suez and Alexandria. Moreover, bi-lateral and multilateral Arab aid funds allocated $850 million to development and investment projects in Egypt, particularly to the development of the Suez Canal and to the construction of a fertilizer plant in Talkha.

At the same time that the oil chiefs were economizing on aid and investment in Egypt, they invested hundreds of billions of dollars in the West. Moreover, the AOC established banks jointly with European financial firms, who loaned their money to Arab states as Western monies, and then profit from higher interest rates and better guarantees for the return of their money.

Private investments by AOC citizens exceeded those of their governments. Up to the end of June 1985 private Arab investors made commitments to invest EgP 1.9 billion under Law 43 (most of it intended for the services sector), though actual investments came to about half this amount. Up to 1989 the Egyptian Investment Authority approved the setting up of 1,649 projects (with a combined capital of EgP 7.2 billion), out of which 1,034 projects were operational (with paid up capital of EgP 3.9 billion). The Egyptian contribution to investments amounted to 61 percent of the total capital. Citizens' from Arab countries share was about 25 percent, and American, European and other citizens invested the balance, about 14 percent.

Investments in Egypt by expatriate Egyptians played a major part in total investment under Law 43. Many Egyptians working in the AOC transferred capital for investment in Egypt during the period they worked in the Gulf States as well as on their return to Egypt. In time, the Egyptian government recognized the inherent economic potential in the savings of Egyptians residing abroad, and in 1977 affected changes in Law 43, which enabled, inter alia, Egyptian investors to benefit from all the advantages that foreign investors enjoyed. Long-term, Egyptian private investments comprised the lion's share of "foreign" investment, which Law 43 was designed to promote.

Private Arab investors were attracted to Egypt because of its cultural and geographic proximity, marital ties between investors and Egyptian women and the fact that many of them had received their education in Egypt or from Egyptian teachers working in the Gulf States. Even after the imposition of the boycott the flow of private investments from the AOC in Egypt continued or in some cases increased. The AOC governments quietly backed these investments, turning a blind eye to this matter. The Lebanon war, the Iran–Iraq war and the fall of the *Suk al-Manah* in Kuwait increased the economic attractiveness of Egypt as the attraction of these other states declined.

The economic climate in Egypt, as elsewhere, played an important part in determining the scope of investment. There was no lack of deterring factors for Arab businessmen from the Gulf States: the memory of radicalism and nationalism of the Nasser period, the low level of development and the limited purchasing power of most of the population, mainly in the periphery, a cumbersome bureaucracy and so forth. Under these circumstances it is not surprising that most Arab investment flowed to more attractive sites in the West.

The biggest source of money transfers to the Egyptian economy from the GCC was that of remittances by the millions of Egyptians who went to work in the prosperous oil states. The Egyptian workers in the AOC contributed a vital flow of capital to the Egyptian economy. Particularly great importance can be attributed to the remittances in hard currency they transferred to Egypt, which played an important part in covering the Egyptian balance of payments deficit. The size of these remittances increased steadily, up to $4 billion in 1984, as compared to $310 million in 1974 and $10 million in 1965.

During this entire period, the number of Egyptian workers in the Arab states grew steadily larger, until it reached three million in the early 1980s, compared to 100,000 in the mid-1960s. Up to 1973 Egyptians moved mainly to Libya and Sudan. In the period between the October 1973 War and the Iran–Iraq war, they primarily migrated to Saudi Arabia, Kuwait, the UAE, Libya and Jordan. After the outbreak of war, Iraq, which needed workers to replace their own men fighting at the front, became a chief attraction for Egyptians.

The Gulf States' extensive need for foreign labor was caused by the gap between large development projects envisioned by their leaders, especially after the turn-around in oil prices, and the chronic shortage of local manpower. This shortage in the AOC was caused not only by their small population: about half of its citizens were below employment age, less than 10 percent of the women worked outside their home and about 10 percent of the population were nomads. In addition, only a small percentage of local manpower had any education, technical skills or the modernistic orientation needed for planning, constructing and operating government projects. Egypt, on the other hand, suffered from severe structural problems: high population growth, poverty and unemployment. Especially frustrated were the graduates of the relatively developed higher education system. The rapidly developing labor market of the Gulf States offered them diverse possibilities and high salaries and many accepted the offer. The Egyptian government encouraged this migration out of socio-economic and political considerations: the desire to alleviate the problem of population density, employment and unemployment; the possibility of obtaining foreign currency; a "safety valve," by giving millions of Egyptians a possibility to improve their standard of living and the possibility for university graduates to find suitable employment for their talents; and the desire to strengthen cooperation between Egypt and the AOC. Criticism, that emigration was encouraging "a brain drain," accelerating inflation and affecting work norms, was rejected, especially when the workers' contribution to foreign currency reserves became apparent.

The AOC preferred Egyptian workers to other foreigners (Arabs or Asians). In the eighties, when circumstances in the oil economies dictated a reduction in the number of foreign workers, Egyptian workers were the last to be fired. In the market for foreign workers in the Arab countries the Egyptians had priority because of traditional factors: they were a large workforce, of diverse ability, and were considered to be politically neutral, in contrast to the Palestinians. Also, the AOC considered the migration of Egyptian workers to their territory as an important contribution to the improvement of their ties with the Egyptian regime and the strengthening of the Egyptian economy, especially after the severing of formal diplomatic and economic relations as a result of the peace treaty with Israel.

Nevertheless, in contrast to the locals, the Egyptians were treated as badly as the other foreigners. As far as working conditions and government services was concerned, discrimination was rife (housing, education, etc.), and they were often humiliated. Many of the Egyptians were academics and were employed in skilled professions. The latter were especially sensitive to the humiliating way their Arab brothers related to them. They returned home disappointed by their Arab hosts and the idea of inter-Arab brotherhood and became vocal opponents to the concept of Egyptian "Arab-ness."

## Egypt comes in from the cold: late 1980s and 1990s

Egypt's decade of official censure by its Arab brothers ended in the late 1980s. Egypt was formally readmitted into the Arab League following the Casablanca Summit Conference of May 1989, and on October 31, 1990, the Arab League headquarters moved back to Cairo. Following the Gulf War and the Madrid Conference of 1991, Egypt was again fully integrated into the Arab world, and had managed to consolidate its position as a central pillar of the inter-Arab system. Sela claims that the "speed that marked most Arab government's decision to resume their diplomatic relations with Cairo indicated that Egypt's re-admittance to the Arab League was imminent. Regional crisis gave Egypt an opportunity to promote its drive for regional leadership."[15]

In its 1999 strategic report, the al-Ahram Institute[16] highlighted "the declining stature of Saudi Arabia compared to the rising status of Egypt in the Arab order, as a result of the economic consequences of the Gulf War and of falling oil prices." According to the report, the heavy expenditures incurred by the GCC as a result of the Gulf War, along with the drop in oil prices, let to a deteriorating economic situation among the GCC states in the early 1990s. In stark contrast to the start of the 1980s, when these countries loaned over $200 million to other states, the start of the 1990s saw the GCC nations in debt to others. In addition to their external debts the Gulf States also suffered from high national debts. This economic failure re-focused the internal policies of Gulf States toward reduction in social expenditures and a weakening of the welfare state. This in turn would create internal pressures that could force a redefinition of the social contract between rulers and subjects, giving the subjects the ability to participate in politics, strengthening national democratic systems. The report stressed that the failure of this democratic objective had impacted foreign policy, especially the role that some of these states played in the Arab order; it was thus difficult to talk of a new Saudi period in the Arab hierarchy.[17]

According to the al-Ahram Institute, a marked improvement took place in the economic performance of the Arab countries which were not oil producers, and especially Egypt, a fact that entailed a redefinition of the balance of power within the Arab order, shifting influence to Egypt. The report concluded: "This change in the balance of powers within the Arab system must be utilized to increase the cooperation between member states, to enlarge mutual dependence, and to bring about a situation in which cooperation outweighs conflict."[18]

The question of economic power and performance also came to play a major part in the matter of AOC economic aid. The Arab oil states themselves were therefore facing economic hardships, which limited their ability to provide Egypt with meaningful aid funds. Faced with a significant drop in world oil prices in the 1980s, and with rapid demographic growth at home, local AOC economies were pushed to breaking point.

In addition to a growing scarcity of resources, AOC countries were also disillusioned by the results of economic aid, and turned their focus elsewhere. Kuwait, for example, faced not only diminished economic resources after the Gulf War, but also came to terms with the failure of the massive economic assistance delivered to Iraq in the 1980s in preventing their neighbor from attacking them. Consequently, the oil-rich emirate redirected its financial resources to fortify its internal security with the help of Western experts.

Saudi Arabia also had limited economic resources, and under Crown Prince Abdallah, used these to further new political ambitions. In the 1990s the Saudis reassessed their priorities in the inter-Arab arena. Shortly after the Gulf War, the Saudis asserted that Egypt's weight in the Arab world was on the decline. They then aggressively turned to exert their influence in the Indian subcontinent, Afghanistan and Pakistan. Saudi Arabia and the other GCC countries increasingly turned to provide assistance to Muslim communities outside the Arab world, such as those in Chechnya[19], Muslim separatist groups in the Southern Philippines[20] and Turkey.

Egypt's foreign policies in the 1990s, mainly in playing an active and supportive role in the peace process, and its pivotal role in the formation of the international coalition that reversed Iraq's 1990 invasion of Kuwait, assured both its relationship with the US and its leadership role in inter-Arab affairs. Egypt fully understood that only the US had the capacity to support both its socio-economic development and maintenance of its national security. Mubarak continued Sadat's policy of maintaining the strategic enhancement of Egypt's relations with Washington. Egypt's relationship with the US comes with a dowry in the form of generous military and economic aid. US administrations have also been keen to strengthen their political relationship with Egypt. Consultations on regional issues are frequent and in-depth. The two countries institutionalized a "Strategic Dialogue" at the ministerial level. During the 1990s strong pro-Egyptian bipartisan support in Congress supported a long-term commitment to rebuild and modernize the Egyptian military and to create a modern force capable of acting interoperably with US forces in matters of regional security, peacekeeping and humanitarian operations. The US has invested tens of billions of dollars in this effort, which is transforming the Egyptian military from a Soviet-style mass attack force into a leaner, Western-style defensive-oriented force. Equally strong support has allowed the provision of tens of billions of dollars in economic assistance. The US is Egypt's largest bilateral civil and military aid donor, and largest bilateral trading partner, and also one of the largest investors in the Egyptian economy.

In addition, the US government has been instrumental in putting into place foundations for economic growth such as infrastructure (water, waste water, power and telecommunications) and a favorable economic policy environment for private sector development and economic reform program, including job creation, economic growth and productivity, infrastructure, education, democracy and governance, population, health and nutrition, environment and natural resource management. The US also supported IMF assistance to Egypt and debt forgiveness from foreign donors, which cut the Egyptian budget deficit and inflation from 15–20 percent per year at the start of the 1990s to less than ten percent by the end of the decade.

US assistance to Egypt more than offset the loss of Arab aid. By the late 1980s Arab aid to Egypt became insignificant, and in some of these years the balance of payments was even negative. Moreover, the GCC could not offer Egypt economic reform, the legal foundation vital for facilitating private sector activity as well as for encouraging foreign investment and business in Egypt, or privatization programs. And yet, a major component of GCC transfers to Egypt remained in the form of worker remittances that continued to be channeled home by Egyptian workers in the Gulf. These constituted a major source of foreign exchange to the Egyptian economy.

The reign of Sadat's heir, Hosni Mubarak, has been marked by an overriding quest for political and social stability. The economic field is of key importance to these goals, but government performance has not been stellar. Intensive economic reform measures in the first half of the 1990s gave way to a sluggish economy in the following years. Today Egypt is a country of 70 million people which apparently lacks the institutional ability to foster rapid economic growth. Under Egypt's highly centralized regime, the shortcomings of the all-powerful bureaucracy hinder development and growth. These shortcomings include: personal and ideological conflicts between the government ministries and their heads, a lack of practical responsiveness to changing economic situations, and an overwhelming degree of regulation and procedure.

The successive Egyptian governments never excelled in economic imagination and planning. Even though they gave much thought to the economic subject, the Nasser, Sadat and Mubarak governments never succeeded in initiating and executing a comprehensive economic plan. To a large degree this is understandable. As in a situation in which the masses are clamoring for bread, it is difficult and politically dangerous to carry out painful reform measures or to direct money to long-term projects, instead of focusing on the immediate reduction of economic distress.

# *Notes*

---

Abbreviations are listed on pages xix–xx.

## Preface

1 See, for example, Ragaei El-Mallakh, *Saudi Arabia: Rush to Development* (London: Croom Helm, 1982), p. 367. Various economic dictionaries give the definition for foreign aid, as a transfer of resources from developed countries to developing countries, for promoting economic growth. Naturally, this is not the case in the subject of our research. See, for example, Graham Bannock *et al.*, *Dictionary of Economics* (Harmondsworth: Penguin Books, 3rd edn., 1984), p. 178.

2 One of the central questions brought up by Keohane was when and to what extent cooperation between countries would continue, after the status of the dominant country had diminished. He cast doubts on the necessity of hegemony to maintain cooperation between countries. Furthermore, Keohane did not support the contention that cooperative relations are inevitably impaired by a diminishing of the relative power of the dominating country, stressing that cooperation does not necessarily go hand-in-hand with harmony, but prepares the ground for adapting a mutual policy by the countries concerned. See: Robert O. Keohane, *After Hegemony: Cooperation and Discord in the World Political Economy* (Princeton: Princeton University Press, 1984), pp. 16, 31.

3 See, for example, Marshall R. Singer, *Weak States in a World of Powers* (New York: The Free Press, 1972), pp. 61–2.

4 For the term "interdependence," see: Robert O. Keohane and J. S. Nye, *Power and Interdependence: World Politics in Transition* (Boston: Little Brown, 1977), p. 8.

5 Even before that time Egypt received aid, mainly from Kuwait, but it was not institutionalized. See: chapter 1.

6 Certain research scholars added aid and foreign investments to their calculations, while other researchers separated these components in their economic analysis; some studies concentrated on a specific geographical region, such as the South American countries, and other studies analyzed the influence of foreign capital on the economic development of Third World countries as a single unit. A number of researchers indicated that foreign aid exerted a positive influence on the recipient country's economy and fulfilled a positive role in the growth of the GNP in many developing countries. On the other hand, other researchers found that there was not necessarily a circumstantial connection between aid and growth rates, which were not boosted by aid, on the contrary, aid actually caused a slowdown by aggravating the balance of payments deficit through increased debt payments. They further claimed that aid exerted a negative influence on

NOTES TO P. IX

domestic savings and could damage future economic growth, as the recipient countries allocated capital to sectors that were not always productive. As regards the first group, see, for example, Hollis B. Chenery and Alan M. Strout, "Foreign Assistance and Economic Development," *American Economic Review* (vol. 56, no. 4, September 1966), pp. 679–733; H. B. Chenery and N. G. Garter, "Foreign Aid Assistance and Development Performance," *American Economic Review* (vol. 63, no. 2, 1973), pp. 459–68; Irma Adelman and Hollis B. Chenery, "Foreign Aid and Economic Development: The Case of Greece," *Review of Economics and Statistics* (vol. 18, no. 1, 1966), pp. 1–15; Robert Cassen and Associates, *Does Aid Work? Report to Intergovernmental Task Force* (Oxford: Clarendon Press, 1986). Regarding the second group, see for examples: K. B. Griffin and J. L. Enos, "Foreign Assistance: Objectives and Consequences," *Economic Development and Cultural Change* (vol. 18, no. 3, April 1970), p. 317; Gustav F. Papanek, "The effect of aid and other resource transfers of savings and growth in less developed countries," *Economic Journal* (vol. 82, no. 327, September 1972), p. 941–50; M. B. Dolan and B. W. Tomlin, "First World–Third World linkages: External Relations and Economic Development," *International Organizations* (vol. 34, 1980), pp. 41–63; Paul Stevenson, "External Economic Variables influencing the Economic Growth Rate of seven major Latin American Nations," *Canadian Review of Sociology and Anthropology* (vol. 9, no. 4, 1972), pp. 347–56; Melville J. Ulmer, "Multinational Corporations and Third World Capitalism," *Journal of Economic Issues* (vol. 14, no. 2, 1980), pp. 453–71.

Bauer opposed granting aid and he declared that many countries enjoyed considerable economic development without foreign aid. In his opinion, aid does not alleviate poverty in the Third World, as it does not always reach those who need it most, but ends up in the coffers of the government, whose policy is sometimes the direct cause of the inferior living conditions of the poor. He believes that the rulers channel resources according to their own interests, and the poor have lowest priority. He says that aid only helps to maintain the rulers' policy. See: P. T. Bauer, *Reality and Rhetoric, Studies in the Economics of Development* (London: Weidenfeld and Nicolson, 1984), pp. 38, 49–50. For many other reasons against the granting of aid, see pp. 38–72.

7    Mohammad Fouad Abou Settit, "Foreign Capital and Economic Performance: The Case of Egypt" (Ph.D. dissertation, the University of Texas at Dallas, 1986), pp. v–vi.

8    *Ibid.*, p. 92.

9    *Ibid.*, p. 93.

10   An additional study of the influence of foreign capital on the Egyptian economy is El-Boraiy's research, but he only examined the influence of foreign investments (excluding aid) on a number of indicators in the Egyptian economy in the years 1967–1979, with the help of regressive analysis. See: Esam Badrawe El-Boraiy, "The Egyptian Open Door Policy towards Foreign Investment: An Economic View" (Ph.D. dissertation, University of South Carolina, 1982).

11   In this context, see: Manusi I. Midlarsky, "The Revolutionary Transformation of Agrarianism and its International Behaviour Impact," in Charles W. Kegley Jr. and Pat McGowan (eds.), *The Political Economy of Foreign Policy Behaviour* (California: Sage, 1981), pp. 39–62; C. E. Lindblom, *Politics and Markets: The World's Economic Systems* (New York: Basic Books, 1977).

12   See bibliography by Jamil Matar and 'Ali al-Din Hilal, *Al-Nizam al-Iqlimi al-'Arabi. Dirasa fil-'Alaqat al-Siyasiyya al-'Arabiyya* (Beirut: Markaz Dirasat al-Wahda al-'Arabiyya, al-Tab'a al-Thalitha, 1983), see also various issues of the *Middle East Contemporary Survey* (*MECS*) of the Dayan Center, Tel Aviv University.

13   Researchers like Gilbar, Dessouki, Waterbury and Kanovski (see list of sources) and

others attributed decisive importance to economic factors, particularly in the Egyptian economy, but they did not examine comprehensively the sum total of Egypt's economic ties with the Arab countries in the period dealt with in this study. This picture differs in a study of the inter-relationship of Western countries or of their relations with Third World countries. Since the 1970s many researchers have combined political and economic factors in their studies of international relations. See, for example, Charles P. Kindleberger, *Power and Money* (New York: Basic Books, 1970); Paul A. Bran and Paul M. Sweezy, *Monopoly Capital: An Essay on the American Economic and Social Order* (New York: Modern Reader, 1966); Klaus Knorr, *Power and Wealth: The Political Economy of International Power* (New York: Basic Books, 1973); Robert O. Keohane and Joseph S. Nye, Jr., *Power and Interdependence: World Politics in Transition* (Boston: Little, Brown, 1977); R. O. Keohane, *Beyond Hegemony: Cooperation and Discord in the World Political Economy* (Princeton: Princeton University Press, 1984); J. E. Spero, *The Politics of International Economic Relations* (New York: George, Allen & Unwin, 3rd edn., 1985).

14  Ali E. Hillal Dessouki, "The New Arab Political Order: Implications for the 1980s," in Malcolm H. Kerr and El Sayed Yassin (eds.), *Rich and Poor States in the Middle East: Egypt and the New Arab Order* (Cairo: The American University in Cairo Press, 1982), p. 345, note no. 24.

15  Jack Wien, *Saudi–Egyptian relations: The Political and Military Dimensions of Saudi Financial Flows to Egypt* (Santa Monica: Rand, p. 6327, 1980), p. 82.

16  Adeed I. Dawisha, *Egypt in the Arab World. The Elements of Foreign Policy* (London: Macmillan, 1976).

17  Marguerita D. Ragsdale, "Egypt and the Persian Gulf: A Study of Small States in Coalition" (Ph.D dissertation, University of Virginia, 1978).

18  Fakhry A. Elfiki, "Foreign Economic Assistance and the Egyptian Economy" (Ph.D dissertation, Worcester, Massachusetts: Clark University, 1984), pp. 48–51.

19  Nazih M. M. Ayubi, "OPEC Surplus Funds and Third World Development: The Egyptian Case," *Journal of South Asian and Middle Eastern Studies* (vol. 5, no. 4, Summer 1982); Haim Barkai, "Egypt's Economic Constraints," *The Jerusalem Quarterly* (no. 14, Winter 1980), pp. 123–43.

20  Ibrahim Shihata, *The Other Face of OPEC* (London, 1982); Shireen Hunter, *OPEC and the Third World: The Politics of Aid* (Bloomington: Indiana University Press, 1984); Robert and Pamela Mertz, *Arab Aid to sub-Saharan Africa* (Boulder, CO: Westview Press, 1983); Andre Simmons, *Arab Foreign Aid* (NJ: Fairleign Dickinson University Press, 1981); Robert Stephens, *The Arab's New Frontier* (London: Temple Smith, 1976); Alkazaz, 'Aziz, "The Arab Fund for Economic and Social Development," *Orient*, vol. 17, no. 4 (December 1976); Gitelson, Susan A., "Arab Aid to Africa: How Much and At What Price," the *Jerusalem Quarterly*, no. 19 (Spring 1981); Williams, Maurice J., "The Aid Programs of the OPEC Countries," *Foreign Affairs*, vol. 54 (October 1975); Mohammed Imady, "The Role of Arab Development Funds," *Arab Gulf Journal* (vol. 2, 1982); Anthony M. Underwood, *Inter Arab Financial Flows* (Durham, 1974).

21  The Organization for Economic Cooperation and Development (OECD), for example, did not present any data on aid to Egypt for the years 1969–1973 and up to 1976 OECD data only indicated the total amount of aid received by Egypt from all OPEC countries, without a breakdown of separate countries. See: OECD, *Geographical Distribution of Financial Flows to Developing Countries* (Paris: OECD, 1977), pp. 68–9.

22  The Autobiography was first published in 1977 and was translated into Hebrew by Aharon Amir. See: Anwar al-Sadat, *The Story of My Life* (Hebrew), (Jerusalem: Edanim, 2nd edn., 1978).

## 1  Aid to Egypt, 1967–1978

1  Kamal Hasan 'Ali, *Muharibun wa-Mufawidun* (Cairo: Markaz al-Ahram lil-Tarjama wal-Nashr, 1986), p. 74. (Mr. Ali served as Foreign Minister 1980–4 and Prime Minister 1984–5); speech by the Minister of the Economy to the Egyptian Parliament, December 27, 1977.

2  *Aramco World Magazine*, vol. 30, 1979, p. 3; *United Press International* (*UPI*), (Jedda, May 22, 1979).

3  Ibrahim Nafi', *Nahnu wal-'Alam wa-Nahnu wa-Anfusuna* (Cairo: Markaz al-Ahram lil-Tarjama wal-Nashr, 1986), p. 124.

4  Mohamed H. Heikal, *Autumn of Fury: The Assassination of Sadat* (New York: Random House, 1983), pp. 79–80.

5  International Bank for Reconstruction and Development (IBRD), "Second Bank of Alexandria Project" (report no. P-1670-egt, July 22, 1975), p. 4.

6  Edward R. Sheehan, *The Arabs, Israelis, and Kissinger: A Secret History of American Diplomacy in the Middle East* (New York: Reader's Digest Press, 1976), p. 195.

7  Nazem Abdalla, "The Role of Foreign Capital in Egypt's Economic Development, 1960–1972," *International Journal of Middle Eastern Studies* (IJMES), (vol. 14, 1982), pp. 87–97.

8  Eliyahu Kanovski, "The Economy in Arab Countries and the Arab–Israeli Conflict," Eitan Gilbo'a and Mordechai Naor (eds.), *The Arab–Israeli Conflict* (Hebrew), (Tel Aviv: Ministry of Defence, 1981), p. 70.

9  *Ibid.*, March 15, 1964; April 4 and 15, 1964: the fund granted a number of loans for an amount of KD 35 million, inter alia for plans to widen the Canal; but after examining fund documents, it appears that loans amounted to only KD 9.8 million. Apparently the rest of the money came from Kuwaiti government sources. For additional details regarding aid from the Kuwaiti Fund, see chapter 2.

10  Commutations (exchange trade) were calculated on the basis of the International Monetary Fund (IMF) data, in its publication: IMF, *IFS*.

11  *New York Times News Service* (*NYTNS*), June 23, 1965.

12  Loan was made by the Kuwaiti National Bank. See: *MEED*, January 28, 1966, p. 38; February 4, 1966, p. 55; *Syrie et Monde Arabe* (Damascus), January/February 1966.

13  *MEED*, February 4, 1966, p. 55.

14  *The New York Times News Service* wrote that Kuwait loaned Egypt a total of $224 million in the 1964–5 period. See: *NYTNS* (Cairo), n.d. Taken from "Misr-Kuwait" file, *al-Ahram* Archives, Cairo.

15  *MEED*, December 2, 1966, p. 607.

16  *Petroleum Press Service* (monthly, London), April 1966.

17  *MEED*, July 9, 1965, p. 318.

18  IMF, *IFS Yearbook 1983*, p. 203.

19  IMF, "UAR – 1967 Article XIV Consultation" (December 22, 1967), p. 5.

20  *Ibid.*, p. 25.

21  *Ibid.*

22  *Al-Ahram*, June 12, 1967. Kuwaiti Foreign Minister declared: "Kuwait is ready to exploit its resources whenever required." See: *Ibid.*, June 19, 1967.

23  *Al-Jumhuriyya*, June 19, 1967.

24  The *Algerian News Agency*, June 22, 1967. See: *Arab Report and Record* (*ARR*), June 16, 1967, p. 208.

25  *Al-Ahram*, July 23, 1967.

26  *Ibid.*: June 28 and December 11, 1967; *al-Jumhuriyya*, August 15, 1967.

27  *MEED*, July 20, 1967.

28  IMF, "United Arab Republic. Background material for 1969 article XIV Consultation" (part II, January 20, 1970), p. 28.

29  *The Times* (London), July 4, 1967, p. 4.

30  For complete version of resolutions at the summit conference see: Yehuda Lukacs (ed.), *Documents on the Israeli–Palestinian Conflict, 1967–1983* (London: Cambridge University Press, 1984), pp. 213–14: Fuad Jaber (ed.), *International Document on Palestine, 1967* (Beirut: Institute for Palestine Studies, 1979), pp. 655–7. For a full account of discussions at the summit, see chs. 4 and 5.

31  Lukacs (ed.), *Documents on the Israeli–Palestinian Conflict*, p. 214; Jaber (ed.), *International Document on Palestine*, pp. 656–7.

32  Mahmoud Riad, *The Struggle for Peace in the Middle East* (New York: Quartet Books, 1981), p. 53

33  Mohammed H. Heikal, *The Road to Ramadan* (London: Collins, 1975), pp. 267–8; Anwar el-Sadat, *Those I Have Known* (New York: Continuum, 1984), pp. 64–5; Riad, *The Struggle for Peace in the Middle East,* p. 53.

34  *Al-Difa'* (Jordan), October 11, 1967.

35  *Al-Ahram*, October 20, 1967: *al-Dustur* (Jordan), October 4, 1967; *al-Difa'*, October 11, 1967; Kuwait transferred its payments on a monthly basis, and not every quarter. See: *al-Yawm* (Lebanon), January 21, 1969. For further details, see: *Keesing's Contemporary Archives* (*KCA*), September 23, 1967, p. 2267; *MEED*, October 11 and 26, 1967: *ARR*, September 16, 1967, p. 306: October 16, 1967, p. 340.

36  *MEED*, December 7, 1967, p. 829: *ARR*, December 1, 1967, p. 378. Starting with its first payment in 1968, Saudia Arabia transferred £10.2 million instead of £8.3 sterling, and it continued doing so over the years. See: *al-Ahram*, April 28, 1968; *al-Yawm* (Lebanon), January 21, 1969; *MEED*, February 5, 1968, p. 97. As to Libya, see: *MEED*, January 21, 1970, p. 5.

37  *Al-Risala*, Kuwait, December 17, 1967.

38  *MEED*, June 21, 1968, p. 591.

39  IMF, January 20, 1970, *op. cit.*, p. 28.

40  *Ibid.*, in the 1967/8 fiscal year, the amount did not exceed $251 million, as aid commenced only in October 1967. The fiscal year normally ends on June 30. Khartoum aid is also reflected in the Saudi budget. See: IMF, *Saudi Arabia – An Economic and Financial Survey* (December 3, 1973), p. 38.

41  *Al-Ahram*, October 14, 1967; *al-Hayat* (Lebanon), October 15, 1967.

42  For more on the economic boycott see below. Unlike Egypt, Jordan sometimes suffered from discontinued aid, as in 1970/71, when Kuwait stopped its payments to Jordan, following a dispute about Jordanian attitude to Palestinians.

43  In the first half of 1968 it was rumoured that aid would be stopped, but all parties involved denied this. See: an interview by the Egyptian Foreign Minister to *al-Jumhuriyya*, May 26, 1968; *al-Difa'*, August 7, 1968; *ARR*, April 16, 1968, p. 111; *MEED*, May 31, 1968, pp. 496, 505.

44  According to the report, Dubai gave a grant of £60,000 sterling to the Egyptian and Jordanian war effort. We estimate that Egypt received at least half of that sum. See: *ARR*, April 1, 1968, p. 99.

45  *Middle East and African Economist*, September 1968, p. 123.

46  IMF, January 1970, *op. cit.*, part II, p. 28.

47  See Sadat's speech to the Central Committee of Arab Socialist Union (ASU), July 16, 1977, as reported by *MENA* on the same day. Later Sadat declared that Gaddafi had not honoured Sanusi's promise.

48  Riyad, p. 51.

49  *Al-Hayat*, November 21, 1969. See also a review of the conference by Avraham Sela, *Unity within Separation. Arab Summit Conferences* (Jerusalem: Magnes, 1983), and see also following chapters.
50  *KCA*, December 31, 1970, p. 23808.
51  Sela, *Unity within Separation,* pp. 88, 90.
52  *MEED*, January 2, 1970, p. 26.
53  Nazli Choucri, *International Politics of Energy Interdependence: The Case of Petroleum* (Lexington, MA: Lexington Books, 1976), p. 92.
54  Hamied Ansari, "Egypt in Search of New Role in the Middle East," *American Arab Affairs* (no. 12, spring 1985), p. 44.
55  *Al-Nahar*, December 28, 1969.
56  *Al-Jarida*, December 29, 1969; *Daily News* (Kuwait), December 28, 1969.
57  *MEED*, January 2, 1970, p. 14.
58  *Al-Ahram*, December 25, 1969.
59  *Al-Siyasa*, December 29, 1969.
60  *MENA*, July 16, 1977.
61  *Al-Ahram*, February 26, 1970; *ARR*, February 15, 1970, p. 118.
62  Kuwait's final pledge came to 10 million KD to Egypt, and 5 million to the PLO. In the 1969/70 fiscal year, Kuwait granted 8.6 million KD, and in the 1970/71 fiscal year another 2.5 million. The budget specifically indicated that the sum comprised a transfer according to the Rabat agreement, but it did not indicate the breakdown between Egypt and the PLO. Thus an amount of 3.9 million KD had not yet been transferred. See reports from the Kuwaiti finance and energy ministries and the Kuwaiti Central Bank, as presented to the IMF. IMF, *Kuwait*, 1972, pp. 30–1.
63  *Ibid.*
64  *ARR*, December 16, 1969.
65  *Al-Jadid* (Lebanon), January 9, 1970. *Commerce du Levant* (Lebanon), March 28, 1970.
66  Reports on continued Khartoum payments, see: *al-Ahram*, April 19, 1970; August 10, 1970.
67  *MENA*, March 26, 1970.
68  *ARR*, June 1, 1979, p. 324. An IMF report, titled "UAR-1967 Article XIV Consultation" (December 22, 1967), asserted that in late June 1967 Egypt owed Kuwait $252 million, but two years later Egypt repaid a large part of its debt. It should be remembered that Egypt did not increase its debt to Kuwait, because from 1967 on it received aid in the form of grants.
69  *NYT*, January 24, 1970, p. 1.
70  *Ibid.*
71  *NYT*, January 24, 1970, p. 1, and December 19, 1969.
72  Heikal, *The Road to Ramadan*, p. 159.
73  *Ibid.*, p. 179. See also report by Senator Charles Percy, who stated that Egypt had received large grants from Libya since 1969. *The Middle East* (a report by Senator Charles H. Percy to the Committee on Foreign Relations, United States Senate, April 21, 1975. Washington, D.C.: GPO, 1975), p. 75.
74  *Ha'aretz*, December 17, 1972, p. 1.
75  Saad El-Din el-Shadhli, *The Crossing of the Suez* (San Francisco: American Mideast Research, 1980), pp. 177–8.
76  Heikal, *The Road to Ramadan*, p. 179; *al-Ahram*, April 25, 1972, reported on Iraq's pledge to render aid totaling $5 million, but in the end the Iraqis deposited $7 million for Egypt in a London bank, to cover an urgent purchase of military equipment from the West. See Shadhli, *The Crossing of the Suez*, pp. 146–7.

77 *New Society* (Bahrain), June 19, 1972.

78 *Al-Akhbar*, May 23, 1972.

79 *Al-Anwar* (Lebanon), August 24, 1972.

80 *Ibid.*

81 *Daily News* (Kuwait), August 25, 1972.

82 On 'Aziz Sidqi's visit, see *al-Ahram*, December 1 and 7, 1972. On Ashraf Marwan's visit, see: *ibid.*, November 25, 1972.

83 *MEED*, October 13, 1972, p. 170.

84 *Al-Majlis al-Musawwar* (Kuwait), December 18, 1972; *Ha'aretz*, December 17, 1972; the London *Times* reported that Kuwait, Qatar and Abu Dhabi had guaranteed only £90 million sterling in addition to the £15 million for development projects, a total of £105 million sterling, and not £120 million sterling, as mentioned by other sources. See: Economist Intelligence Unit (EIU), *Quarterly Economic Review* (*QER*): Egypt, Sudan, no. 1 (1973), p. 8; *FT*, December 12, 1972.

85 *Al-Siyasa* (Kuwait), December 9, 1972; *al-Usbu' al-'Arabi*, December 18, 1972, reported that Kuwait had transferred only $28 million for this purpose, loaned for a period of 12 years at 8 percent interest.

86 On promises of military aid, see: Shadhli, *The Crossing of the Suez*, pp. 277–8. On financial aid, see: *al-Hawadith*, March 29, 1973; Alvin Z. Rubinstein, *Red Star on the Nile: The Soviet Egyptian Influence Relationship since the June War* (Princeton: Princeton University Press, 1977), p. 242.

87 Shadhli, *The Crossing of the Suez*, pp. 277–8.

88 Robert Lacey, *The Kingdom: Arabia and the House of Saud* (New York: Harcourt Brace Jovanovich, 1981), pp. 393, 398; Adeed Dawisha, *Saudi Arabia's Search for Security* (*Adelphi Papers*, no. 158. London: IISS, 1979), p. 5; *QER*, Egypt, Sudan, no. 1 (1973), p. 8; no. 3 (1973), p. 5. The Center for Strategic Studies in London reported that on an undefined date between July 1972 and June 1973, Egypt signed an agreement with the USSR for the purchase of 100 MIG 21-MF planes, and in February 1973 it signed another agreement for the purchase of "Scud" missiles, which it was to receive in October 1973. See: IISS, *The Military Balance 1973–1974*, p. 82; *1974–1975*, p. 89.

89 *BBC/ME/4256* (March 28, 1973), p. A5.

90 Roger F. Pajak, "Soviet Arms Aid in the Middle East since the October War," in *The Political Economy of the Middle East: 1973–78* (a compendium of papers submitted to the Joint Economic Committee Congress of the United States, April 21, 1980. Washington, D.C.: GPO, 1980), p. 449.

91 *Al-Ahram*, February 7, 1973; *al-Jumhuriyya* (Iraq), March 8, 1973.

92 *Al-Hawadith*, March 29, 1973.

93 See report in the French pro-government newspaper: *Le Figaro*, April 28, 1973. This report was filed after repeated denials by circles close to the French government. Libya ordered 100 Mirage planes, out of which they received 60. The contract between Libya and France stipulated that they were not to be transferred to any third country that had been involved in the June 1967 war.

94 *Aviation Week and Space Technology* (*AWST*), September 20, 1973, details the purchase of British helicopters, but makes no mention of the fact that it was financed by Saudi Arabia. See also: IISS, *The Military Balance 1974–1975*, p. 89 and SIPRI (Stockholm International Peace Research Institute) Yearbooks. Already in July 1973 Marwan told Shadhli about the Saudis' intention to make these purchases for Egypt. See: Shadhli, *The Crossing of the Suez*, p. 149.

95 Henry A. Kissinger, *Years of Upheaval* (Boston: Little Brown, 1982), p. 225.

96  *MENA*, June 25, 1973. *MEED*, June 29, 1973, p. 746; July 6, 1973, p. 770; *ARR*, June 16, 1973, pp. 270, 273.

97  *QER*, Egypt, Sudan, no. 3 (1973), p. 5; *al-Usbu' al-'Arabi*, September 3, 1973: about Sadat's visit to Riyadh, see also: Steven Emerson, *The American House of Saud. The Secret Petrodollar Connection* (New York: Franklin Satts, 1985), p. 35.

98  *QER*, Egypt, Sudan, no. 4 (1973), p. 5: *BBC/ME/4457* (November 11, 1973), p. A4; Yusuf J. Ahmad, *Oil Revenues in the Gulf: A Preliminary Estimate of Absorptive Capacity* (Paris: OECD, June 1974), p. 108. 'Adil Husayn noted that Kuwait alone forked out $700 million for Soviet arms in October 1973. See: 'Adil Husayn, *Al-Iqtisad al-Misri min al-Istiqlal ila al-Tab'iyya* (Cairo: Dar al-Mustaqbal al-'Arabi, 1982, 2 vols.), vol. 1, p. 79–80.

99  Sadat, *The Story of My Life* (Jerusalem: Edanim, 1978), p. 185; *The Military Balance 1974–75*, p. 90.

100  In late October 1973, *Agence France Presse* reported that up to that date the oil countries had made grants of $3 billion to "Egypt's war efforts." The agency did not elaborate on this figure. See: *Agence France Presse*, October 31, 1973. EIU quoted "Israeli sources," alleging that between 1967 and the October war Egypt had received grants and civil credits totaling $1.8 billion. See: *QER*, Egypt, no. 2 (1975), p. 7.

101  Sayyid Mar'i, *Awraq Siyasiyya* (Cairo: Dar al-Ahram, 1979, 3 vols.), vol. 3, pp. 737, 739–40. Sayyid Mar'i was a technocrat from Nasser's time and chairman of the ruling party during Sadat's reign. For a study on Sayyid Mar'i, see: Robert Springborg, *Family, Power and Politics in Egypt: Sayed Bey Marei – His Clan, Client and Cohorts* (Philadelphia: University of Pennsylvania Press, 1982). Before the October war Mustafa Khalil studied the use of the oil weapon, under the patronage of *al-Ahram*'s Centre for Strategic Studies. He was Egypt's Prime Minister October 1978–May 1980.

102  Mar'i, vol. 3, p. 737, 739–41. Mar'i did not indicate how much was "a little."

103  *Ibid.*, pp. 743–6.

104  *Ibid.*, p. 747.

105  *Ibid.*, pp. 748–50. Also relying on Mar'i, Waterbury wrote that Qatar pledged aid amounting to only $50 million. But, as mentioned, Mar'i added that the figure was doubled. See: John Waterbury, *The Egypt of Nasser and Sadat. The Political Economy of Two Regimes* (Princeton: Princeton University Press, 1983), p. 416.

106  *Newsweek*, March 10, 1975.

107  Riyad, p. 252.

108  See; *MENA*, August 3, 1976, as reported in Jumhuriyyat Misr al-'Arabiyya, al-Hay'a al-'Amma lil-Isti'lamat, *Khutub wa-Ahadith al-Rais Muhammad Anwar al-Sadat, al-Qadaya al-Dakhiliyya wal-Kharijiyya*, vol. 6, 1976 (hereinafter: *Sadat's Speeches*).

109  On October 16, the Kuwaiti National Council approved an allotment of $344 million to the Arab cause. See: *MEED*, October 19, 1973, pp. 1209, 1219; Robert Stephens, *The Arabs' New Frontier* (London: Temple Smith, 1976), p .145.

110  *ARR*, October 1, 1973, p. 448; November 1, 1973, p. 508.

111  Riyad, pp. 264–5, 267.

112  *Daily Telegraph*, January 21, 1974; *The Times* (London), January 22, 8, 1974: *FT*, January 20, 1974.

113  The cheque was presented by the Saudi ambassador in Cairo on April 17. See: *MEED*, April 19, 1974, p. 444; Economist Intelligence Unit (EIU), *Quarterly Economic Review (QER)*, Egypt (no .2 , 1974), p. 7.

114  Ahmad J. Yusuf, *Absorptive Capacity of the Egyptian Economy* (Paris: OECD, 1976), p. 112.

115  *Ibid.* In February, Gaddafi participated in a ceremony in honor of war heroes in Cairo,

but subsequently relations deteriorated rapidly. See: Gideon Gera, *Libya Under Qadhafi* (Hebrew) (published by Hakibbutz Hame'uhad, 1983), p. 195.

116 *Akhbar al-Yawm* (Egypt), March 30, 1974.
117 See interview in *al-Nahar*, April 14, 1974.
118 Excerpts from the letter were published in *al-Ahram*, May 24, 1974.
119 *ARR*, June 1, 1974, p. 220.
120 *Akhbar al-Yawm*, August 3, 1974; IBRD, "The Egyptian Economy in 1974" (Report no. 491a-EGT, September 25, 1974), p. iv; *The Economist*, August 10, 1974, p .69; *MEED*, August 9, 1974, p. 906; August 16, 1974, p. 932.
121 IBRD, *Suez Canal Rehabilitation Project* (report no. P-1488a-EGT, November 19, 1974), p. 3; *ibid.*, Report and Recommendation for a Telecommunications Project (report no. P. 1587a-EGT, April 28, 1975), p. 3.
122 *Al-Jumhuriyya* (Egypt), June 25, 1975. *MEED*, December 13, 1974, p. 1521.
123 *Ibid.* For further details on the plans see chapter 2. On aid by the Abu Dhabi Fund and the Qatar government, see: IBRD, report no. 491a-EGT, *op. cit.*, p. iv; *ibid.*, report no. 1587a-EGT, *op. cit.*, p. 3.
124 *MEED*, November 29, 1974, p. 1440; November 22, 1974, p. 1414.
125 For further details on the project, see: Sayyid Mar'i, *Likay Narbah al-Mustaqbal: al-Mashru' al-'Arabi lil-Tanmiya* (Cairo: Dar al-Ma'arif, n.d.), esp. pp. 138–54. See also his interview with Ibrahim Nafi', *al-Ahram*, May 22, 1975. p. 3.
126 Sadat's words: *Ruz al-Yusuf*, February 3, 1975; Hijazi's interview with Musa Sabri, *Akhbar al-Yawm*, August 17, 1974.
127 *Middle East Economic Survey* (*MEES*), November 1, 1974; January 24, 1975, p. 3.
128 Riyad, p. 283; *Sela*, p. 127; *al-Safir* (Lebanon), November 30, 1977.
129 Riyad, p. 383; *Washington Post* (*WP*), January 14, 1975, p. A1.
130 Heikal, *The Assassination of Sadat*, p. 79. The author wrote that Riyad had warned Sadat that aid was in danger, but Sadat did not heed his proposal that he (Riyad) would participate in the sub-committee's meetings.
131 *MEES*, November 1, 1974; February 21, 1975; April 11, 1975, p. 9.
132 Egypt also received crude oil from Iraq worth $82 million. See: *Reuters*, April 9, 1975; *Ruz al-Yusuf*, April 19, 1976; *MEED*, January 24, 1975, p. 9; *AP*, January 16, 1975. News agency reports were taken from *al-Ahram* Archives in Cairo.
133 Interview with Egypt's Minister of Finance, see: *Akhir Sa'a*, February 11, 1976. pp. 3–5. Sadat also acknowledged that the Arab countries had carried out Rabat aid commitments in full. See: *al-Hawadith* (Lebanon), August 21, 1975.
134 OECD, OPEC (1983), *op. cit.*, p. 55.
135 Ibrahim Nafi', *Nahnu wal-'Alam wa-Nahnu wa-Anfusuna* (Cairo: Markaz al-Ahram lil-Tarjama wal-Nashr, 1986), p. 123.
136 *Ibid.*, p. 122.
137 *Ibid.*, p. 123.
138 In a personal interview with Hijazi (Cairo, July 1987), he stated that he had resigned. He said one of the reasons for his decision was the riots against him organized by Mamduh Salem, who succeeded him in his position. On the riots see: *MEED*, January 3, 1975.
139 *Al-Ahram*, January 21, 1975; *MEED*, January 24, 1975; *MEES*, January 24, 1975, p. 3 and February 21, 1975, p. 8. The entire amount was presented to Hijazi in February by the Saudi ambassador in Egypt. See personal interview and *al-Ahram*, February 15, 1975.
140 *Al-Ahram*, April 28, 1975; *MEED*, May 2, 1975, p. 10.
141 *MEED*, May 16, 1975, p. 10.

142 Remarks by the Egyptian Minister of Finance. See: *al-Ahram*, August 15, 1975.

143 *MEED*, July 25, 1975, p. 14.

144 *Al-Ahram*, July 21, 1975; *MEES*, July 25, 1975, pp. 2–3.

145 *Al-Ahram*, September 21, 1975. After this loan, *MEED* reported (July 25, 1975, p. 13) that total financial aid provided by Saudi Arabia to Egypt since the October war exceeded $5 billion, as follows: military aid totaling $2.5 b.; $600 m. promised by Khaled; commitments for $1.5 b. given before Khaled's visit; and $400 m. in investments and economic development. This estimate is misleading, not in the final figures, but in the method used. First, the report, published in July 1975, stated – quoting Saudi sources – that Egypt had been guaranteed $1.5 billion in direct aid, but this was only a commitment and it cannot be seen as actual aid. Secondly, the $400 million was pledged in the form of investments and this was also a case of a commitment. However, the figures presented by *MEED* would be realistic, if aid from the other oil countries was added.

146 See the declaration by Egypt's finance minister, as quoted by: *al-Ahram*, August 15, 1975. See also: *FT*, August 22, 1975.

147 *MEED*, September 5, 1975, pp. 11–12: September 26, 1975, p. 9; *FT*, June 19, 1975; *Inter Press Service* (Beirut), September 25, 1975.

148 *MEED*, November 7, 1975.

149 *Al-Qabas*, October 7, 1975.

150 IBRD, "Egypt. Textile Project Development" (report no. P-1835-EGT, 1976), p. 7.

151 *ARR*, August 16, 1974, p. 343.

152 *SIPRI* (1975), pp. 193, 222–3; IISS, *The Military Balance 1974–1975*, p. 89; *United Press International* (Beirut), September 15, 1974; *MEED*, November 15, 1974, p. 1389: November 22, 1974, p. 1414: December 20, 1974, p. 1565; *ARR*, August 16, 1974; *NYT*, November 20, 1974. See also Sadat's speech before the National Assembly of ASU, Cairo Radio, July 23, 1975 (*al-Ahram* Archives). In 1979 a report of the Intelligence Department of the American State Department asserted that in 1974 the Gulf States gave a commitment to purchase for Egypt military equipment at a cost of over $1 billion. The authors of this report opined that this commitment had not yet been fulfilled. The report gave no further details, so it is not clear if this commitment was given in the framework of the $1 billion indicated above, or in addition to this sum – which indeed seems to have been the case, as Egypt received considerable quantities of Western arms in the mid-1970s, according to data quoted above. For the intelligence report, see: United States, Department of State, Bureau of Intelligence and Research, "Egypt: Sadat's Millitary Requirements and Funding Problems" (Secret, RDS-2/2/99 Multiple Sources, report no. 1209, July 2, 1979), pp. 1–2.

153 *NYT*, December 19, 1975; *WP*, January 30, 1975.

154 *ARR*, 1975, p. 332.

155 Interview on Kuwaiti TV, as quoted by *MENA*, May 15, 1975, and as published in Sadat's Speeches, vol. 5, 1975.

156 *WP*, October 17, 1974: *International Herald Tribune* (*IHT*), October 18 and 21, 1974; *ARR* (1975), p. 279; *MEED*, December 20, 1975, p. 1565; *SIPRI* (1975), pp. 222–3; *L'Orient le Jour*, December 13, 1975.

157 *WP*, November 9, 1975.

158 Herbert Coleman, *Aviation Week and Space Technology* (*AWST*), November 17, 1975, p. 22. For other agreements between the UK and Egypt, see: IISS, *The Military Balance 1975–76*, p. 94.

159 *Al-Ahram*, August 13 and 14, 1976; *Daily News* (Kuwait), February 2, 1976.

160 *Al-Ahram*, June 25, August 13 and September 14, 1976: *MEED*, October 29, 1976, p. 17.

161 *NYT*, February 26, 1976. Israeli wrote that during his visit Sadat had succeeded in obtaining financing for this fund totaling $10 billion. But in fact there was only a decision in general terms to establish the fund, and no specific amount was promised to Sadat. See: Raphael Israeli, *Man of Defiance: A Political Biography of Anwar Sadat* (1985), p. 203.

162 *Al-Ahram*, June 15, 1976; *MEED*, March 5, 1976. According to World Bank data, Sadat obtained $700 million on his February visit, and not $720 million. See: IBRD, "Egypt. Textile Project Report" (report no. P-1835-EGT, 1976), p. 7.

163 *MENA*, March 25, 1976, as reported in *Sadat's Speeches*).

164 *Akhbar al-Yawm*, April 3, 1976, p. 5; compare with July 2, 1976.

165 The protocol of the fund was ratified on August 21, 1976. For the activities of the fund, see: National Bank of Egypt, *Economic Review* (Cairo), (vol. 17, nos. 1–2, 1977), pp. 80–1; 'Adil Husayn, *Al-Iqtisad al-Misri min al-Istiqlal ila al-Taba'iyya* (Cairo: Dar al-Mustaqbal al-'Arabi, 1982, 2 vols.), vol. 1, pp. 162–85; Sabah Nabil, "Tasawwurat hawla Hay'at al-Khalij lil-Tanmiya," *al-Ahram al-Iqtisadi*, September 1, 1976, pp. 10–13; Samira Behar, "Misr . . . wa-Hay'at al-Tamwil al-'Arabi," *al-Siyasa al-Duwaliyya*, October 1978, pp. 108–13.

166 For reports on these debts, see: World Bank, *Arab Republic of Egypt, Economic Management in a Period of Transition* (vol. IV – Financial Resources, May 8, 1978, report no. 1815-EGT), pp. 39, 93.

167 IBRD, *ARE*, "Recent Economic Development and External Capital Requirement" (report no. 2738-EGT, November 12, 1979), p. 13; *ibid.*, report no. 1815-EGT, *op. cit.*, p. 94.

168 *MEED*, August 20, 1976, p. 12 and January 21, 1977; *Reuters*, October 3, 1976.

169 *Al-Akhbar*, November 15, 1976; *Akhir Sa'a*, October 27, 1976; *al-Musawwar*, December 31, 1976, p. 26; *MEED*, October 15 and December 31, p. 17, 1976: *MEES*, October 18 and December 20, p. 10, 1976.

170 *Al-Musawwar*, December 31, 1976, p. 26; *An-Nahar Arab Report and Memo*, February 20, 1978, p. 4; *MEED*, January 7, 1977. The last source indicated that the loan was given for a period of 7.5 years. Compare: World Bank, *ARE: Economic Management in a Period of Transition* (in six volumes. Report no. 1815-EGT, May 8, 1978), vol. IV, p. 37, table 16.5, note B.

171 *MEED*, June 6, 1978, p. 6.

172 *MEED*, January 21, 1977, p. 19; *Kuwait Times*, January 10, 1977.

173 *Al-Siyasa* (Kuwait), February 8, 1977.

174 *MEED*, February 25, 1977, p. 18; *The Times* (London), February 28, 1977.

175 *MEED*, April 1, 1977, p. 17; *An-Nahar Arab Report and Memo*, February 20, 1978, p. 4; International Monetary Fund (IMF), *ARE – Recent Economic Development* (report no. Sm/79/53, February 20, 1979), p. 8.

176 *Al-Sayyad* (Lebanon), April 21, 1977. *MEED* (April 15, 1977, p. 17) report on postponement of debts of more than $2 billion. Probably part of this sum or all of it represented Saudi and Kuwaiti deposits on the Egyptian Central Bank. See chapter 5 about these deposits.

177 *Al-Anwar*, February 23, 1976; *Middle East Money*, March 3, 1976. In April 1976 the US agreed to sell six C-130 cargo planes to Egypt, see: IISS, *The Military Balance 1975–76*, p. 94.

178 The speech was given on May 4, 1977, and was broadcast by *MENA*, See: *Sadat's Speeches*, vol. 7, 1977.

179 *MEED*, August 20, 1976, p. 12 and January 21, 1977; *Reuters*, October 3, 1976; *Daily Telegraph*, September 7, 1977: *SIPRI* (1977). The latter source mentioned 39 planes.

180 Sadat's speech to ASU, July 16, 1977, see: *Sadat's Speeches*, vol. 7, 1977. Quoted also by: *NYT*, July 17, 1977, p. 13; *MEED*, July 22, 1977, p. 15; *Observer* (London), July 17, 1977.

181 *MEED*, December 31, 1977, pp. 27–30.

182 US Department of State, Bureau of Intelligence and Research, "Egypt: Sadat's Military Requirements and Funding Problems" (Secret, RDS-2, 7/2/99 multiple sources, report no. 1209, July 2, 1979), p. 2.

183 *Ibid.*, on arms agreements between Egypt and France and England, see also: IISS, *The Military Balance 1975–76*, p. 94; *1977–78*, p. 97.

184 ACDA, Expenditure and Arms Transfer 1968–1978, 1985.

185 *Al-Sayyad*, April 21, 1977.

186 For further details see: *al-Ahram*, May 12 and 13, 1978; *NYT*, May 10, 1978, p. A4; *MEES*, July 3, 1978; "Egypt Waiting for Godot," *The Economist*, June 3, 1978, p. 95.

187 *Egyptian Gazette*, July 31, 1978, p. 3; *MEES*, August 21, 1978, p. 9.

188 *Al-Ahram*, August 11, 1978; *FT*, August 15, 1978; *An-Nahar Arab Report and Memo*, August 7, 1978, p. 2; *MEES*, August 21, 1978, p. 9.

189 Wheeler, a senior official in the Middle East department of USAID: Economic and Military Aid Programs in Europe and the Middle East: Egypt (Hearings and Markup before the Sub-committee on Europe and the Middle East of the Committee on Foreign Affairs, House of Representatives. 96th Congress, first session. February 14, 1979. Washington, D.C.: GPO, 1979), pp. 130–1. See also the report from American Embassy in Cairo, made up in February 1979, which pointed out that the multilateral level of aid from Saudi Arabia and Kuwait stood at $300 million in 1978. American Embassy in Cairo, *Economic Trends Report*, February 5, 1979, p. 9.

190 *Ibid.*, the two sources: first source, p. 139, second source p. 9: data in first source (testimonies) referred to period of January–September 1978 only. The ECB report indicated that in the last six months of 1978, Arab aid to Egypt amounted to $432 million. See: *al-Ahram*, October 6, 1979, see also: *Egyptian Gazette*, October 8, 1979. Egypt's Minister for Economic Cooperation, 'Ali Jamal Al-Natar, gave slightly different figures. He said that Arab aid in 1978 amounted to $750 million, out of which $150 million in direct aid, and another $600 million constituted the last payment by the Gulf Fund. See an article by 'Abid Nafisa, *al-Ahram al-Iqtisadi*, April 15, 1979, pp. 14–17. See also: *October*, September 2, 1979, pp. 26–7; *MEES*, April 16, 1975, p. 10.

191 Arab Monetary Fund, *First Annual Report* (Abu Dhabi, 1978). See also: *FT*, August 16, 1978; FBIS, *DR*, August 14, 1978; *BBC*, August 22, 1978.

192 Report by the Bureau of Intelligence of the American Department of State, as quoted above, p. 2.

193 *Strategic Middle East Affairs*, February 15, 1978.

194 Economic and Military Aid Programs in Europe and the Middle East, *op. cit.*, pp. 361–2.

195 See report attached to *ibid.*

196 *Al-Akhbar* (December 5, 1978) reported that Saudi Arabia would keep its commitments to finance the purchase. See also: *MEED*, December 8, 1978; *FT*, January 17, 1979.

197 Middle East Peace Package (hearings before the Committee of Foreign Affairs, April 11 and 25, 1979. CIS document no. S 381–15, 1979), p. 43.

198 Among other things, Saudi Arabia was reported to have objected to the high price of the planes fixed by the US. The value of the transaction skyrocketed as a result of inflation and other costs to $590 million. The report also said that Saudi Arabia refused to go through with the transaction because of limitations imposed by Congress on arms sales to the Middle East. See: *FT*, July 7, 1979; *Le Monde*, July 8–9, 1979.

199 For a comprehensive study of Egypt's foreign debts and their influence on its economy,

see: Ramzi Zaki, *Buhuth fi-Duyun Misr al-Kharijiyya* (Cairo: Maktabat Madbuli, 1985).

200 Al-Bank al-Duwali, *Taqrir 'an al-Tanmiya fil-'Am 1983* (Cairo: Al-Tab'a al-'Arabiyya, 1983), p. 41.

201 *Ibid*. The report included the private sector's debts and noted that a considerable share of the above, $455 million, originated from Arab sources, and was applied mainly to tourism and construction, see: *Ibid.*, p. 34.

202 World Bank, *Arab Republic of Egypt. Recent Economic Developments and External Capital Requirements* (report no. 2738-EGT, November 12, 1979), p. 38. (hereinafter, WB, 2738-EGT); IMF, *ARE – Recent Economic Developments* (SM/79/53, February 20, 1979), appendix III, table 64, p. 126.

203 OECD, *External Debt of Developing Countries in 1984* (DCD/85.43, W.1304D/arch. 0307D, 32.823. Paris: OECD, December 1985), p. 79.

204 See, for example, UNCTAD, Financial Solidarity for Development. Development Assistance from OPEC Members and Institutions to Other Developing Countries, 1973–1981 (report by the secretariat of UNCTAD. New York: United Nations, 1984), annex, table 4, p. 10.

205 "The Gulf Fund" actually granted only $1,725 million, see: *World Bank report*, no. 2738-EGT, as quoted above, p. 38. However, later on the Fund enabled Egypt to exploit interest payments that it was to have reimbursed to the Fund, and it also guaranteed several loans Egypt had taken on the international money markets. In the end, the Fund's entire capital of $2 billion was exploited. On aid by funds and bilateral and multi-lateral institutions, see chapter 2. From conversations held with Western diplomats in Cairo, it appears that Egypt's debts of more than $5 billion to Arab countries and institutions were, at this stage, "a write off."

206 Khalid Ikram (coordinating author), *Egypt. Economic Management in a Period of Transition* (Baltimore and London: Johns Hopkins University Press), p. 351. This book was composed from a study by the World Bank, published in six volumes in the same format in 1978, and quoted above. A comparison of the two sources shows up insignif-icant disparities in the figures. For example: the 1980 book, p. 351, reports that grants in 1973 stood at $700 million, whereas the 1978 research – vol. 4, p. 48 – indicated $725 million. Studies by the IMF also reported slightly different amounts, but mostly insignif-icant, and it seems they emanated from different rates of exchange and dates. So, for instance, it is quite probable that the World Bank calculated its rates of exchange as of January, while the IMF did the same based on October values.

207 Many researchers referred to GFDE aid as regular direct aid, and not as aid applied to specific projects. There are several reasons for this: first, this aid was granted like any other direct aid, despite the fact that it was destined from the beginning to be channeled to development projects. Second, the monies were provided as support for the balance of payments. Third, the scope of aid from this fund was much bigger than that chan-neled by various aid funds to Egypt or to any other country. Fourth, in the years 1977–8, this was really the only assistance Egypt received from the oil countries. Fifth, the highest echelons of power in the oil countries determined the scope of aid and its timing, in contrast to the way aid was channeled from the development funds.

208 *The Middle East*, December 1979, p. 73.

209 OECD, Development Co-operation, Annual Report, various issues: *ibid.*, Flows of Resources from OPEC Members to Developing Countries. Statistical tables, 1978–1980 (secretariat working document, DCD/ 81.34. Drafted: October 12, 1981).

210 On Iranian aid, see: OECD, *Aid from OPEC Countries* (Paris: OECD, 1983), pp. 78–80; S. Hunter, *OPEC and the Third World, The Politics of Aid* (Bloomington: Indiana University Press, 1984), pp. 106–22.

211 G. Abdel-Khalek, "Foreign Economic Aid and Income Distribution in Egypt, 1952–1977," in G. Abdel-Khalek and R. Tignor (eds.), *The Political Economy of Income Distribution in Egypt* (New York: Holmes and Meier Publishers Inc., 1982), p. 440.

212 UNCTAD, Financial Solidarity for Development, *op. cit.*, 1984, p. 4 and *ibid.*, 1977–1983 (1985), p. 19. The first report (1984) also deals with this period, but the second report's (1985) figures for the 1977–8 period are more up to date.

213 Economic and Military Aid Programs in Europe and the Middle East, Hearings, *op. cit.*, p. 517.

214 John Waterbury, *The Egypt of Nasser and Sadat. The Political Economy of Two Regimes* (Princeton: Princeton University Press, 1983), p. 418.

215 The calculations were made according to tables presented by Abdel-Khalek, "Foreign Economic Aid and Income Distribution in Egypt, 1952–1977," table 13.2, p. 439 (see also comment 'a' on table) and table 13.3, p. 440. Abdel-Khalek also included Iranian aid in this data, but this was not included.

216 *Ibid.*, p. 440, table no. 13.3.

217 Yusif A. Sayigh, *The Economies of the Arab World: Development since 1945* (London: Croom Helm, 1978), p. 697.

218 R. D. Mclaurin, J. M. Price, "OPEC Current Account Surpluses: Assistance to Arab Front-line States," *Oriente Moderno* (vol. 58, 1978), p. 542.

219 *Ibid.*, p. 543.

220 Ibrahim Nafi', *Nahnu wal-'Alam wa-Nahnu wa-Anfusuna* (Cairo: Markaz al-Ahram lil-Tarjama wal-Nashr, 1986), pp. 121–2.

221 *Ibid.*, pp. 122–4.

222 Paul Jabber, "Oil, Arms, and Regional Diplomacy: Strategic Dimensions of the Saudi–Egyptian Relationships," in Malcolm H. Kerr and El-Sayed (eds.), *Rich and Poor States in the Middle East: Egypt and the New Arab Order* (Boulder, CO: Westview Press, 1982), pp. 424, 446 note 21, and pp. 428–9.

223 Economist Intelligence Unit, *QER Egypt* (no. 2, 1979), p. 5.

224 *Al-Fajr* (Saudi Arabia), May 7, 1979.

225 *Al-Watan al-'Arabi*, April 13, 1979. My study showed that the sums Egypt received for the summit conferences slightly exceeded $3.5 billion.

226 Elias T. Ghantus, *Arab Industrial Integration. A Strategy for Development* (London: Croom Helm, 1982), p. 69.

227 Marguerita D. Ragsdale, "Egypt and the Persian Gulf: A Study of Small States in Coalition" (Ph.D. dissertation), p. 292.

228 Hanspeter Mattes, "Libya's Economic Relations as an Instrument of Foreign Policy," in Bichara Khader and Bashir el-Wifati (eds.), *The Economic Development of Libya* (London: Croom Helm), p. 97.

229 'Adil Husayn, *Al-Iqtisad al-Misri min al-Istiqlal ila al-Tab'iyya 1974–1979* (Cairo: Dar al-Mustaqbal al-'Arabi, 1982, 2 vols.), vol. 2, pp. 79–80.

230 Heikal, *The Assassination of Sadat*, pp. 78–9.

231 *Al-Riyad*, May 22, 1979, p. 1. See also: *UPI* (Jedda), May 22, 1979; *al-Ba'th* (Syria), May 23, 1979, quoting Saudi sources.

232 *Al-Qabas* (Kuwait), April 14, 1979, p. 3.

233 See, for example, *al-Nahar al-'Arabi wal-Dawli* (Paris), November 10, 1978, p. 18.

234 For Ali's remarks, see: *al-Hawadith*, December 15, 1978, pp. 38, 43: Gamasi's speech to the Council for National Security and Foreign Relations of the Egyptian People's Assembly, see: *al-Akhbar*, March 16, 1977. The Egyptian leadership spoke about military aid even after the Camp David agreement and the breaking off of relations with the Arab states. See, for example, Sadat's words regarding the financing of 39 Mirage

planes, which Saudi Arabia purchased for Egypt, and this in one of his most militant speeches to the oil countries in general, and to Saudi Arabia in particular. See also in earlier chapter, when in July 1977 Sadat revealed that Saudi Arabia had pledged to finance all Egyptian military expenditures for a period of five years.

235 See: *al-Riyad*, May 22, 1979, p. 1.
236 *The Economist*, October 6, 1979, p. 70.
237 *Al-Qabas*, March 18, 1975.
238 Nazih N. M. Ayubi, "OPEC Surplus Funds and Third World Development: The Egyptian Case," *Journal of South Asian and Middle Eastern Studies* (vol. 5, no. 4, summer 1982), p. 46.
239 Haim Barkai, "Egypt's Economic Constraints," *The Jerusalem Quarterly* (no. 4, winter, 1980), p. 136.
240 *Ibid.*
241 Abdel-Khalek, "Foreign Economic Aid and Income Distribution in Egypt, 1952–1977," p. 438.
242 Kamal Hasan 'Ali, *Muharibun wa-Mufawidun* (Cairo: Markaz al-Ahram lil-Tarjama wal-Nashr, 1986), p. 74.
243 A personal interview by the author, Cairo, July 1987.
244 *World Bank*, Suez Canal Expansion Project (report no. P-2030-EGT, July 27, 1977), p. 3.
245 *Ibid.*, p. 4.
246 World Bank, *Egypt*, report no. 1815, *op. cit.*, vol. IV, pp. 36–9, 48.
247 American Embassy in Cairo, *Economic Report* (July 1979), p. 3.

## 2  Arab Investment in Egypt

1 Patrick O'Brien, *The Revolution in Egypt's Economic System: from Private Enterprise to Socialism, 1952–1966* (London: Oxford University Press, 1966), p. 68.
2 Robert E. Driscoll *et al.*, *Foreign Investment in Egypt: An Analysis of Critical Factors with Emphasis on the Foreign Investment Code* (New York: Fund for Multinational Management Education, 1978), pp. 6–7; Robert L. Tignor, "Foreign Capital, Foreign Communities, and the Egyptian Revolution of 1952," paper presented at the conference "Egypt from Monarchy to Republic: Structural Continuity and Dynamics of Change," Tel Aviv University: The Dayan Center for Middle Eastern and African Studies and the Kaplan Chair in the History of Egypt and Israel, June 8–10, 1987.
3 The dividing into stages with details, see O'Brien's book, pp. 227–30, and in many other sources. On Nasser and Arab socialism see, for example: Shimon Shamir, "Arab Socialism and Egyptian-Islamic Tradition," in S. N. Eisenstadt and Y. Atzmon (eds.), *Socialism and Tradition* (Atlantic Highlands: Humanities Press, 1975), pp. 193–218. On domestic savings, see: George K. Kardouche, *The U.A.R. in Development: A Study in Expansionary Finance* (New York: Praeger, 1966).
4 Waterbury, *The Egypt of Nasser and Sadat: the Political Economy of Two Regimes*, p. 67. Besides the agrarian reform of 1961, this data also refers to the reform of 1952. See also: Gabriel Baer "New Data and Conclusions from the Results of Agrarian Reform in Egypt," *The New East* (1966), pp. 238–43.
5 *Ibid.*, pp. 73–4; O'Brien, in many places; Hussein H. El Said and M. S. El-Hennawi, "Foreign Investment in LDCs: Egypt," *California Management Review*, vol. 24, no. 4 (summer 1982), p. 86; Charles Issawi, *Egypt in Revolution: An Economic Analysis* (London: Oxford University Press, 1954), p. 60; R. Tignor, *State, Private Enterprise, and Economic Change in Egypt, 1918–1952* (Princeton: Princeton University Press, 1984), p. 243.

6  Waterbury, *ibid.*; G. Abdel-Khalek, "Looking Outside or Turning Northwest? On the Meaning and External Dimensions of Egypt's *Infitah*," *Social Problems* (vol. 28, no. 4, April 1981), pp. 394–409.
7  Waterbury, *ibid.*, p. 69.
8  John Waterbury, "The 'Soft State' and the Open Door: Egypt's Experience with Economic Liberalization, 1974–1984," *Comparative Politics* (vol. 18, no. 1, October 1985), p. 66. See also articles by Ajami and Dessouki, in Abdel-Khalek and R. Tignor (eds.), *The Political Economy of Income Distribution in Egypt* (New York: Holmes and Meier Publishers Inc., 1982).
9  Raymond William Baker, *Egypt's Uncertain Revolution under Nasser and Sadat* (Cambridge, MA: Harvard University Press, 1978), p. 151.
10  Quote appeared in *MEED*, November 4, 1966, pp. 558–9. See also: *ibid.*, October 7, 1966.
11  *ARE*, "Policy on the Economics of Egyptian Expatriate Savings," *op. cit.*, p. 11.
12  Marvin G. Weinbaum, "Egypt's *Infitah* and the Politics of U.S. Economic Assistance," *MES* (vol. 21, no. 2, April 1985), p. 206.
13  See the constitution of the Arab Republic of Egypt (translated by Varda Ben-Zvi), *The New East* (vol. 22, 1972), pp. 307–24.
14  Ali E. Hillal-Dessouki, "Policy Making in Egypt: A Case Study of the Open Door Economic Policy," *Social Problems* (vol. 28, no. 4, 1981), p. 411.
15  For text of the law, see: *al-Jarida al-Rasmiyya* (no. 39, September 30, 1971).
16  *MENA*, March 23, 1975 (*Sadat's Speeches*, 1975).
17  Personal interview, Cairo, February 1987.
18  It is well known that Sadat's economic policy was met with hostility, mainly from left-wing circles, who exploited the platform of the ideological monthly *al-Tali'a* for this purpose. See, for example, Adel Hassin, *al-Tali'a* (vol. 2, 1975), pp. 10–23. See also an article in the opposition paper *al-Sha'b* June 17, 1980, pp. 8–9; Rashad Kamil Tadras, "Al-Jihaz al-Markazi lil-Muhasabat . . . wa-Mawqi'uh min al-Infitah," *al-Ahram al-Iqtisadi*, April 15, 1978, pp. 10–17, 25. Left-wing circles were ideologically opposed to this policy. But there was also pertinent criticism of the *infitah* policy, primarily in the weekly – formerly bi-weekly – *al-Ahram al-Iqtisadi* and in the periodical *Misr al-Mu'asira*, which wrote in essence: the foreign companies have not lived up to expectations and they should be put under supervision; the government plans to implement a certain policy but fails to take any practical steps towards this end; there is no comprehensive strategic planning for economic development, therefore the *infitah* is a failure; most investments are channeled to services, instead of being applied to the productive sector; *infitah* plans do not provide employment as originally expected; the level of investments is low; the rich are becoming richer while other strata of society suffer a drop in their standard of living; the *infitah* boosted inflation and a flowering black market; the *infitah* brought with it greater dependence on the West and a loss of values (mainly Galal Amin), and so on. For a treatise on the opponents of the *infitah*, see also an article by Waterbury, as quoted above. See also: Hamdallah Ahmad al-Saman, *al-Ahram al-Iqtisadi* (no. 871, September 23, 1985), pp. 34–5; Mustafa Imam and others, *al-Ahram al-Iqtisadi* (no. 669, November 9, 1981), pp. 14–15; Muhammad 'Ali Rif'at, *al-Ahram al-Iqtisadi* (no. 677, January 4, 1982), pp. 18–19; 'Ali al-Sayyid 'Abd al-Mali, *Misr al-Mu'asira* (no. 400, April 1985), pp. 105–20; Mahmud 'Abd al-Fadil, *Misr Al-Mu'asira* (no. 400, April 1985), pp. 5–40; Ulfat Sa'd, *Ruz al-Yusuf* (vol. 57, no. 2823, July 19, 1982), pp. 28–30; Mahmud al-Muraj, *Ruz al-Yusuf* (no. 2790, November 30, 1981) pp. 8–9, 62–3; 'Abdallah Diab, *al-Yasar al-'Arabi* (no. 38, December 1981), pp. 13–14; Galal A. Amin, "Some Economic and Cultural Aspects of

Economic Liberalization in Egypt," *Social Problems* (vol. 28, April 1981), pp. 430–41.

19 *MENA*, October 8, 1974 (*Sadat's Speeches*, 1974).

20 *Al-Hawadith*, May 2, 1975.

21 An interview to the weekly *Ruz al-Yusuf*, September 23, 1974.

22 See especially Waterbury, *The Egypt of Nasser and Sadat: the Political Economy of Two Regimes*, pp. 57–204. See also: Ibrahim 'Amar, "Al-Raqaba al-Idariyyah lil-Infitah al-Iqtisadi," *al-Ahram al-Iqtisadi*, April 15, 1978, pp. 8–9, 25; *ibid.*, February 15, 1974, pp. 20–1; Fuad Sultan, "Ashwak 'ala Tariq al-Infitah," *al-Ahram al-Iqtisadi*, December 1, 1974, pp. 14–16; Lutfi 'Abd al-'Azim, "Kashf al-Istithmarat al-'Arabiyya wal-Ajnabiyya," *al-Ahram al-Iqtisadi*, May 1st, 1975, pp. 29–35; Driscoll *et al.*, *Foreign Investment in Egypt*; Kate Gillespie, *The Tripartite Relationship* (New York: Praeger, 1984); David W. Carr, *Foreign Investment and Development in Egypt* (New York: Praeger, 1979); Jeswald W. Salacuse and Theodore Parnall, "Foreign Investment and Economic Openness in Egypt: Legal Problems and Legislative Adjustment of the First Three Years," *International Lawyer* (vol. 12, no. 4, 1978), pp. 759–78; G. E. Bushnell, "The Development of Foreign Investment Law in Egypt and its Effect on Private Foreign Investment," *Georgia Journal of International and Comparative Law* (vol. 10, 1980), pp. 301–32; Abdel-Meguid Adly, "Egypt's Policy towards Foreign Investment," *Vanderbilt Journal of Transnational Law* (vol. 10, no. 1, 1977), pp. 97–107.

23 In 1945 the Arab League established the "Permanent Boycott Committee," and prohibited imports of Israeli goods. In 1952 the boycott was extended to companies trading with Israel. The boycott committee can only make recommendations, whereas companies can decide as they see fit. On the boycott committee and the list of boycotted firms, see: Edward Hotaling, *The Arab Blacklist Unveiled* (New York: Landia, 1977).

24 On talks with these companies see: *MEED*, October 24, 1975; January 28, May 13, August 19, September 16, November 11, 1977.

25 John Waterbury, *Egypt: Burden to the Past, Option for the Future* (Bloomington: Indiana University Press, 1978), pp. 217–19. As for item C, the average weekly salary in the non-agrarian sector was only EgP 5.6. See: International Labour Organization (ILO), *Yearbook of Labour Statistics* (Geneva: ILO, 1982), p. 497.

26 *ARE*, General Authority for Investment and Free Zone (GAFIZ), *Investment Review* (vol. 6, no. 2, July 1985), pp. 1, 3.

27 John Law, *Arab Investors: Who They Are, What They Buy and Where* (New York: Chase World Information Corporation, 1981, 2 vols.), vol. 2, p. 8.

28 He was quoted by Munir Nasif, *al-Akhbar*, May 23, 1982.

29 Quoted by *Law*, vol. 2, p. 8. In the same sense, see also: *MEED* Special Report, August 1977, p. 22.

30 Further on this subject, see: UN/ECWA, *Economic Integration in Western Asia* (London: Frances Pinter, 1985), pp. 132–4.

31 For a description of this body, see: 'Abd al-'Aziz al-Mazhari, "Al-Jihaz al-'Arabi li-Himayat al-Istithmarat wa-Imkaniyyat al-Ta'awun ma' al-Duwal al-Sina'iyya," *al-Naft wal-Ta'awun al-'Arabi* (al-Sana 4, al-'Adad 3, 1978), pp. 71–82: UN/ECWA, 1985, pp. 134, 260; Elias T. Ghantus, *Arab Industrial Integration* (London: Croom Helm, 1982), pp. 72–3; Traute Wohlers-Scharf, *Arab and Islamic Banks* (Paris: OECD, 1983), pp. 54–5.

32 UN/ECWA, 1985, p. 136. See list of these bodies in appendix. See also: Samih Mas'ud, "Al-Mashru'at al-'Arabiyya al-Mushtaraka: Waqi'uha, Ahmiyyatuha, Mu'awwaqatuha wa-Mustaqbaluha," *al-Mustaqbal al-'Arabi* (al-'Adad 103, September 1987), pp. 26–44; K. A. Mingst, "Regional Sectorial Economic Integration: The Case of OPEC," *Journal of Common Market Studies* (vol. 16, no. 2, December 1977), pp.

95–113; I. F. Shihata, *Joint Ventures among Arab Countries* (UNCTAD, TD/B/AC-19/R. 5, October 21, 1975).

33   *Law*, vol. 2, p. 176.

34   The law was published in a special appendix to *al-Ahram al-Iqtisadi*, February 1, 1978. See also: *al-Jerida al-Rasmiyya* (no. 23) June 9, 1977.

35   *Law*, vol. 1, p. 1. On the acumen of Arab investors, see also report by American Senate, as quoted by: Fouad Ajami, "The Open-Door Economy: Its Roots and Welfare Consequences," in Abdel-Khalek and Tignor (eds.), *The Political Economy of Income Distribution in Egypt* (New York: Holmes and Meier Publishers Inc., 1982), pp. 508–9.

36   *Law*, vol. 2, p. 46.

37   "Kuwait Adopts Measures to Adjust to the Impact of Reduced Oil Revenues," *IMF Survey* (August 8, 1983), pp. 236–8; *The Middle East*, July 1986, p. 22; "Investment abroad makes up for Oil Revenue Shortfalls," *The Arab World Weekly* (Beirut), (no. 694, November 26, 1983), pp. 9–12. For the scope of Kuwait's and Saudi Arabia's oil revenues in the 1980s, see: *Middle East and North Africa 1987* (Europa Publication, 1987), p. 125.

38   Anthony H. Cordesman, *The Gulf and the Search for Strategic Stability* (Boulder, CO: Westview Press, 1984), p. 7.

39   Studies on OPEC investments were made by the Bank of England and Mattione: "Deployment of Oil Exporters Surpluses," *Bank of England Quarterly Bulletin* (vol. 25, no. 1, March 1985), pp. 69–74; Richard P. Mattione, *OPEC's Investments and the International Financial System* (Washington, D.C.: The Brookings Institution, 1985). For further studies see, for example: Ibrahim 'Uways, "Fawaid al-Batrudularat – Wujhat Nazar Iqtisadiyya," *al-Naft wal-Ta'awun al-'Arabi* (al-Sana 12, al-'Adad 3–4, 1986), pp. 136–77; "The Surpluses of the Oil Exporters," *Bank of England Quarterly Bulletin* (June 1980), pp. 154–9; Ibrahim Oweiss, "Petrodollar Surpluses: Trends and Economic Impact," *L'Egypte Contemporaine* (nos. 393–4, October 1983), pp. 5–35; I. M. Oweiss, "Impediments to Arab Investment in the United States," in Michael R. Czinkota and Scot Marciel (eds.), *U.S.-Arab Economic Relations. A Time of Transition* (New York: Praeger, 1985), pp. 138–58; John E. Logan *et al.*, "Arab Investment in the United States: A Case Study," in Salah el Sayed (ed.), *International Business and the Middle East* (Cairo: The American University in Cairo, 1979), pp. 13–35; Alan Stoga, "The Foreign Investments of OPEC and the Arab Oil Producers," *American Arab Affairs* (vol. 3, 1982/83), pp. 60–7; John Law, *Arab Investors, Who They Are, What They Buy and Where* (New York: Chase World Information Corporation, 2 vols., vol. 1, 1980, vol. 2, 1981); Barry W. Blank and Lila Sein, "U.S. Banking Adjustment to Changes in Gulf Liquidity," in Michael R. Czinkota and Marciel Scot (eds.), *U.S.-Arab Economic relations. A Time of Transition* (New York: Praeger, 1985), pp. 101–28; Harry P. Guenther, "Arab Investment in the United States and U.S Public Policy," in Czinkota and Marciel, pp. 159–82.

40   *Mattione*.

41   *Law*, vol. 2.

42   *Ibid.*, p. 2. This sum probably includes Kuwait's deposits in Egypt.

43   For details on this subject, see: Steven Emerson, *The American House of Saud. The Secret Petrodollar Connection* (New York: Franklin Watts, 1985), chapter 16, pp. 312–33; "Saudi American Affairs," *International Currency Review* (vol. 12, no. 4), pp. 37–43. See also, *The Middle East*, April 1981, p. 66 and I. M. Oweiss, in Czinkota and Marciel, *U.S.-Arab Economic Relations*, pp. 140–1.

44   IMF, *Kuwait – Recent Economic Development* (SM/80/146, June 20, 1980), table 24, p. 55.

45 *Wall Street Journal* (*WSJ*), October 26, 1982; Stoga, "The Foreign Investments of OPEC," p. 65.

46 IMF, *IFS* (vol. 37, no. 11, November 1984), pp. 292, 393.

47 According to him, by the end of 1982 reserves totaled $71.6 billion. See: *MEES*, June 6, 1983, p. B5.

48 *The Middle East*, July 1986, p. 22. Compare: "Investments Abroad make up for Oil Revenue Shortfalls," *The Arab World Weekly* (Beirut), (no. 694, November 26, 1983), pp. 9–12, which reported that total Kuwaiti investments by the end of 1982 amounted to between 80 and 90 million dollars.

49 See quote of research data: *WSJ*, September 16, 1987; *MEES*, September 21, 1987.

50 *Law*, vol. 1, pp. 29–30. See also: "Investment Abroad," *op. cit.*; *The Middle East*, April 1981, p. 65. The above source reported that at the time, the fund's assets had been evaluated at about $20 billion. For a treatise on investments by the Kuwaiti government, see: *Neue Zuericher Zeitung*, September 17, 1980; *The Middle East*, April 1981, pp. 65–6: *MEED* Special Report, August 1977, pp. 21–2.

51 These institutions were in addition to the body established by Kuwait in London in the late 1950s, as consultants for the channeling of Kuwait's oil revenues. For more details on these bodies, see: M. W. Khouja and P. G. Gadler, *The Economy of Kuwait: Development and Role in International Finance* (London: Macmillan, 1979), pp. 195–6. Arab capital from other countries was invested in these companies. The Kuwaiti Corporation for Real Estate was also involved in banking, and it owned 10 percent of the capital of the "Egyptian Gulf Bank," established in 1982, with a capital of $20 billion. About this bank, see: EGB, *La Documentation Africaine* (Paris), Fevrier 1986.

52 *MEES*, February 1, 1974, p. 9; March 22, 1974, p. 18; *MEED*, February 8, 1974.

53 *QER*, Egypt (no. 4, 1978), p. 8; *MEED*, September 6, 1974, p. 1019.

54 Details on nature of plans, see: *MEED*, December 13, 1974, p. 1521; *MEES*, December 6, 1974, pp. 9–11.

55 *Akhbar al-Yawm*, April 12, 1975, p. 7; *MEED*, April 4, 1975, p. 12; UN/ECWA, 1985, annex IV, pp. 308–9.

56 *MEED*, January 31, 1975, p. 26; "KEIC," *La Documentation Africaine*, Janvier 1984; *MEES*, May 17 and August 2, p. 7, 1974: February 5, 1976: August 4, 1980, p. 4; *ARR*, February 1, 1974, p. 45; *Law*, vol. 2, pp. 22–3.

57 IBRD, International Finance Corporation, *Project Appraisal report. Arab Ceramic Company, SA–Egypt* (report no. 289, 19 78); *Law*, vol. 2, pp. 31–2.

58 *Al-Ra'y al-'Amm* (Kuwait), March 2, 1976; *UN/ECWA*, 1985, pp. 300–1; *ARR*, 1975, p. 548; *MEED*, February 21, 1975, p. 11. The above reported that the company's capital stood at $7 million only.

59 *Ibid.*, *ibid*; *Law*, vol. 2, p. 39; *MEES*, December 6, 1974; March 7, 1975, p. 12.

60 *Law*, vol. 2, p. 39.

61 *MEED*, December 19, 1982, p. 22; *Law*, vol. 2, p. 40; *MEES*, December 20, 1976, p. 10.

62 About these projects, see: *Law*, vol. 2, pp. 32, 40; *MEED*, November 19, 1982, p. 22.

63 *Al-Anba* (Kuwait), February 14, 1976.

64 'Uthman Ahmad 'Uthman, *Safahat min Tajribati* (Cairo: al-Maktab al-Misri al-Hadith, 1981), pp. 495–8.

65 *Ibid.*, pp. 499–506. After 1976, Arab citizens did not encounter this kind of difficulty. As for the dispute between 'Uthman Ahmad 'Uthman and 'Abd al-'Aziz Hijazi, these two gentlemen often presented contradictory views, and they continued with their dispute even after the termination of their respective functions in the Egyptian government. See, for example, Hijazi's sharp criticism of 'Uthman's book, which appeared in *al-Ahram*, April 21, 1981.

66  *MEED*, November 19, 1982, p. 22.

67  *MEED*, September 23, 1983, p. 19 and May 31, 1986.

68  It was agreed that Kuwaiti subjects would also participate in the financing. See: Jian Dab'i, "Hal Saham al-'Arab wal-'Uruba fi Inqadh al-Iqtisad al-Misri al-Mut'ab?," *al-Mustaqbal* (vol. 6, no. 269, April 24, 1982), p. 37; *An-Nahar Arab Report and Memo*, March 8, 1982, pp. 11–12; *MEED*, March 19, 1982, p. 13; *MEES*, March 1, p. 10.

69  *An-Nahar Arab Report and Memo*, July 26, 1982, p. 11; *Arab Oil and Gas* (vol. 11, no. 26, August 1, 1982), p. 7. This was not a one-time investment in this sector. In 1986 the Kuwaiti government alone allocated $200 million to oil-drilling in Egypt. It was determined that the Kuwaiti "Santa Fe" company would carry out the works, concentrating on the "Al-'Amal al-Jadid" oil fields in the Gulf of Suez. For this see: *al-Ahram*, May 10, 1986; *MEED*, May 17, 1986.

70  *MEED*, November 12, 1982, p. 30; November 19, 1982, p. 22. In a publication in *ibid*., November 12, 1982, it was mistakenly reported that the total sum amounted to $200 million. On bureaucratic difficulties regarding this project, see *ibid*., November 19, p. 22.

71  *Ibid.*, March 16, 1984.

72  IMF, *IFS* (vol. 37, no. 11, November 1984), p. 399. A record level of foreign investments by the Saudi Monetary Agency was reached in the last part of 1982, totaling $145.1 billion. See: *ibid.* This agency manages a major part of Saudi government overseas investments.

73  Cordesman, *The Gulf and the Search for Strategic Stability*, p. 7.

74  *WSJ*, September 16, 1987; *MEES*, September 21, 1987. In August 1987, the International Clearing Bank (BIS) in Basel reported that, up to late March 1987, its deposits (excluding assets) in Western banks amounted to $46 billion. See: *MEES*, August 10, 1987.

75  See the declaration by 'Abd al-'Aziz al-Qurayshi, governor of the Saudi Monetary Agency, as quoted in: "Lifting the Veil in Saudi Arabia," *Euromoney*, April 1979, p. 60.

76  *Law*, vol. 1, p. 65.

77  D. Wells, *Saudi Arabia Development Strategy* (Washington: American Enterprise Institute for Policy Research, 1976), p. 60.

78  *Egyptian Gazette*, January 1, 1975: *MEED*, January 24, 1975, pp. 9–10.

79  *UN/ECWA*, 1985, pp. 304–5. In the second company, private investors owned 25 percent of the shares; the Egyptian government – 40 percent; and the Saudi government – 35 percent. See: *ibid.*, pp. 308–9.

80  David Shireff, "The Flight into Egypt," *Euromoney*, May 1984, p. 177.

81  *MEES*, September 21, 1987.

82  The company was established in 1971 with a capital of $50 million, which was increased to $100 million in 1976. See: *MEES*, May 17, 1976.

83  *UN/ECWA*, 1985, pp. 296–7; *MEED*, June 22, 1979; July 6, 1979, p. 21; *Law*, vol. 2, pp. 69–70.

84  *MEES*, September 21, 1987.

85  *UN/ECWA*, 1985, pp. 296–7.

86  For additional details on this bank, see: Financial Times Business Publishing, The Banker Research Unit, *Banking Structures and Sources of Finance in the Middle East* (London, 2nd edition, 1980), p. 181: *MEES*, January 30, 1978, p. 13.

87  On the Bahrain subsidiary and the financial system in that country, see: "Albaab," *La Documentation Africaine*, January, 1984; *MEED*, Bahrain Special Report, September 1980.

88  *MEES*, April 17, 1978, p. 12: June 5, 1978, p. 10.

89 Further details on this bank, see: *ibid.*, October 1, 1971; August 11, 1972, p. 9: *MEN Economic Weekly* (Cairo), August 3, 1974; *Wohlers-Scharf*, 1983, pp. 30–1.

90 The AMIO was liquidated after the peace agreement. See below.

91 Oil pipelines in the Middle East received a boost in the early 1930s with the laying of the pipeline across Iraq and Syria. For a description of the development of the oil pipeline network in the area, see: 'Abdallah al-Tikriti, "Ahammiyyat Shabakat Khutut al-Anabib fil-Sina'a al-Naftiyya al-'Arabiyya," *al-Naft wal-Ta'awun al-'Arabi* (al-Sana 12, al-'Adad 1, 1986), pp. 94–111.

92 Sadat, *Those I Have Known*, p. 111.

93 *Al-Ahram*, March 20, 1971; *MEES*, March 19, 1971, p. 1; March 26, 1971, p. 7.

94 *Al-Ahram*, April 9, 1971; *MEES*, April 16, 1971, pp. 5–6.

95 *Al-Usbu' al-'Arabi* (Lebanon), September 24, 1973; *FT*, July 29, 1973.

96 Kuwait demanded that 49 percent of shares be held by foreign investors. *MEES*, August 3, 1973, p. 3. "Bechtel's" bid was only $15.5 million lower, but on top of that the American Export-Import Bank pledged to grant a loan to the project. On this subject, see remarks by the Egyptian Minister of Energy, Ahmad 'Izz al-Din: *ARR*, October 1, 1973, p. 448; January 1, 1974, p. 4. The Chase Manhattan Bank also promised a loan to the project, after Rockefeller, the president of the bank, met with Sadat. See: *al-Ahram*, February 5, 1974. See also: *MEES*, October 5, 1973; December 21, 1973, p. 6.

97 *ARR*, April 1, 1974, p. 126.

98 On the company and on further contacts between the countries, see: *MEES*, December 14, 1973; *MEED*, April 21, May 5, June 16 and 30, July 14, August 11, October 20, 1972 and January 4 and 18, February 1 and 8, 1974. Salacuse stated that the oil countries provided aid to the Suez Alexandria project on commercial terms, but the oil countries, as noted, were partners in the project, and they did not provide aid on commercial terms. See: Jeswald W. Salacuse, "Arab Capital and Trilateral Ventures in the Middle East: Is Three a Crowd," in Malcolm H. Kerr and El-Sayed Yassin (eds.), *Rich and Poor States in the Middle East. Egypt and the New Arab Order* (Cairo: The American University in Cairo Press, 1982), p. 140.

99 *MEES*, January 4, 1974, pp. 6–7: January 18, 1974, pp. 4–6.

100 *Le Monde*, December 22, 1976; *Middle East Reporter*, June 6, 1977.

101 *Al-Ahram*, May 6, 1978: *Law*, vol. 2, p. 21; on the profits, see also: Sadat, *Those I Have Known*, p. 112; William B. Quandt, *Saudi Arabia in the 1980s: Foreign Policy, Security, and Oil* (Washington, D.C: The Brookings Institution, 1981), p. 16: Giacomo Luciani (ed.), *The Mediterranean Region. Economic Interdependence and the Future of Society* (London: Croom Helm, 1984), pp. 20, 22. Up to the beginning of 1988 the Egyptian government's revenues from the oil pipeline amounted to $633 million. See: *MEES*, May 16, 1988.

102 Dueij headed delegations of investors from the Gulf many times. On September 12, 1983, he was killed in a traffic accident in Egypt. About the company, see: *MEED*, October 15, 1982, p. 8; *MEED*, Egypt Special Report, July 1983, p. 14; David Shireff, "The Flight into Egypt," *Euromoney*, May 1984, p. 174.

103 For a list of these bodies and companies, see: Jami'at al-Duwal al-'Arabiyya, al-Amana Al-'Amma, *Dalil al-Mashru'at al-'Arabiyya al-Mushtaraka wal-Ittihadat al-Naw'iyya al-'Arabiyya wal-Mashru'at al-'Arabiyya wal-Ajnabiyya al-Mushtaraka* (Cairo: Jami'at al-Duwal al-'Arabiyya, 1979); on joint companies initiated by OPEC, which specialized mainly in ship-building and repairs, maritime transport, oil investments and services, see: 'Ali Ahmad 'Atiqa, "Al-Ta'awun al-Iqlimi fi Majal al-Istithmarat fil-Sina'at al-Naftiyya al-Aqtar lil-Intaj mithl . . . Munazzamat al-Aqtar al-'Arabiyya al-Musadira lil-Batrul," *al-Naft wal-Ta'awun al-'Arabi* (al-Sana 4, al-'Adad 2, 1978), pp. 16–32;

Samih Mas'ud, "Al-Mashru'at al-'Arabiyya al-Mushtaraka bayn al-Waqi' wal-Mustaqbal . . . ," *al-Naft wal-Ta'awun al-'Arabi* (al-Sana 7, al-'Adad 2, 1981), pp. 111–34.

104 'Abd al-'Izz al-Dardari, "The Arab Military Industries between Ambitions and Reality" (translation of title from Arabic), *Shu'un 'Arabiyya* (no. 30, August 1983), pp. 221–4.

105 Shadhli, *The Crossing of the Suez*, p. 196.

106 *Ibid.*

107 Muhammad Anis, "Al-Hay'a al-'Arabiyya lil-Tasni' wa-Tahyi'at al-Amn al-Qawmi," *al-Siyasa al-Duwaliyya* (no. 56, April 1979), pp. 130–4.

108 *Al-Musawwar*, December 16, 1983; *Defence and Armament (DAA)*, (December 1981). Dessouki, in contrast to other sources, stated that the authority's capital exceeded $1.4 billion. See: Ali E. Hillal Dessouki, "The Primacy of Economics: The Foreign Policy of Egypt," in Bahgat. Korany and Ali Dessouki (eds.), *The Foreign Policies of Arab States* (Boulder, CO: Westview Press, 1984), p. 127. Waterbury, *The Egypt of Nasser and Sadat: the Political Economy of Two Regimes*, p. 420, wrote that Kuwait was a member of the AMIO. However, at no stage did Kuwait join the authority, even after Egyptian policy makers had made great efforts in this direction. About two weeks after the founding of the authority, Sadat, on his trip to the Gulf, discussed the subject with Kuwaiti leaders, but with no result. Furthermore, in early September 1975 and early January 1977, Marwan tried, unsuccessfully, to persuade Kuwait to join. On Kuwait's refusal to join the authority, see: *KCA* (1975), p. 27235; *Reuters*, January 11, 1977; *ARR*, September 1, 1977, pp. 719, 724; *MEED*, November 11, 1977; *Defence and Armament (DAA)*, (December 1981). Already in the 1960s Kuwait opposed the ratification and the financing of several pan-Arabic plans. See: Miguel S. Wionczek (ed.), *Economic Cooperation in Latin America, Africa, and Asia* (Cambridge, MA: MIT Press, 1969), p. 286.

109 See speech by the Saudi Minister of Defence, Prince Sultan, at the conference of the High Committee of the AMIO, which convened in Cairo in September 1975: *Aviation Week and Space Technology (AWST)*, September 15, 1975, p. 18.

110 *Al-Ahram*, May 18, 1979.

111 "Egypt. A Special Economic Report," *IHT*, June 14, 1984; *DAA* (December 1981).

112 Especially General Fernbacher, Messerschmidt, Eckhardt and Gerka.

113 On the military industries in Egypt in the 1950s and 1960s, see: 'Abdu Mubashir, *Ruz al-Yusuf* (vol. 60, no. 2945, November 19, 1984), pp. 7–10; *al-Nahar al-'Arabi wal-Dawli*, December 4, 1978, p. 13; *al-Musawwar*, May 19, 1978, pp. 13–16, 48: see also Isser Harel's interview with Yeshayahu Ben-Porat, *Conversations* (Hebrew), (Tel Aviv: Edanim, 1981), pp. 269–72; Robert R. Ropelewski, "Improvisation Key to Egyptian Growth," *AWST*, November 13, 1978, pp. 38–47; Raimo Vaerynen, "The AOI: A Case Study in the Multinational Production of Arms," *Current Research on Peace and Violence* (vol. 2, no. 2, 1979), pp. 66–78; Richard F. Nyrop, *Egypt. A Country Study* (U.S. Government: fourth edn., 1983), pp. 225–8; Joe Stork, "Arms Industries of the Middle East," *MERIP* (no. 144, January–February 1987), p. 13.

114 Israel contributed to the departure of the German scientists, by taking various actions against them. Moreover, the West German government did its bit, by deciding to annul citizenship rights of any German scientist opting to stay and work in the Egyptian military industries. On this, see also Isser Harel's interview with Yeshayahu Ben-Porat, as quoted above, p. 272; *SIPRI* (1971), p. 736. On other factors, see Stork (1987), p. 13.

115 *AWST*, August 15, 1978, p. 15. The decision to transfer the Egyptian military industries to the AMIO was opposed by the Egyptian workers, who feared losing their jobs. See: Muhammad Anis, "Al-Hay'a al-'Arabiyya lil-Tasni' . . . " *al-Siyasa al-Duwaliyya* (no. 56, April 1979).

116 Muhammad Anis, *ibid*.

117 *ARR*, October 10, 1978, p. 722.

118 Marwan returned to Riyadh with him. On this affair, see: *Tishrin* (Syria), January 4, 1979; *Foreign Report*, November 1, 1978, pp. 2–3. Jack Wein, *Saudi-Egyptian Relations: the Political and Military Dimensions of Saudi Financial Flows to Egypt* (Santa Monica: The Rand Corporation P-6327, 1980), p. 63, noted that the Saudis were probably concerned with the high operating costs and with the Egyptian bureaucracy, and they urged Sadat to change the management of the joint authority. But on p. 62 he contradicts himself, stating that Marwan's dismissal exacerbated the tense relations existing between them.

119 *Strategic Middle East Affairs*, November 22, 1978; *Tishrin*, January 4, 1979, reported that the reason for this was American pressure on Egyptian policy-makers, because of its concern about arms manufacture in the area without its supervision.

120 Sadat was also not happy with Marwan's close relationship with Khashoggi. *Foreign Report, ibid.*, pp. 2–3.

121 *ARR*, October 1, 1978, p. 722.

122 Wein, p. 13.

123 *Ibid*.

124 *AWST*, March 6, 1978, p. 17: May 15, 1978, p. 15: *Defence et Diplomatie*, March 9, 1978: Maurizio Cremasco, "The Middle East Arms Industry: Attempts at Regional Cooperation," *Lo Spettatore Internazionale* (vol. 16, October 1981), p. 301. The latter source stated that the final goal was the assembly of 250 helicopters. In mid-September 1974, even before the official establishment of the AMIO, Egypt and England discussed the possibility of assembling Lynx helicopters in Egypt. See: *FT*, September 14, 1974; *DT*, September 15, 1974. One week later, Anderson, a senior British official, paid a visit to Egypt, where he met with President Sadat, Marwan and Faysal's advisor. At this meeting it was agreed that Britain would start supplying Lynx helicopters to Egypt, and at a later stage Egypt would be licensed to manufacture them. See: *ARR*, September 16, 1974, p. 397.

125 *AWST*, May 15, 1978, p. 15.

126 Talks with the "Rolls-Royce" Co. commenced during Sadat's visit to Britain in November 1975. See: *al-Safir* (Lebanon), October 10, 1975, which quoted British sources. See also: *Cremasco*, as quoted above, p. 302.

127 *FT*, December 8, 1977.

128 *MENA*, September 17, 1978.

129 *Cremasco*, p. 303.

130 *MEED*, June 1, 1979, p. 8; *FT*, November 20, 1978; *AWST*, November 27, 1978, p. 17; *Le Monde*, March 16 and August 3, 1978.

131 "Multi-million Shut-down," *The Middle East* (June 1979), p. 91: R. Popelewski, "Arab Seek Arms Suffiency," *AWST*, May 15, 1978, p. 14.

132 *FT*, July 25, 1978; *AWST*, July 3, 1978, p. 24; *Defence et Diplomatie* (*DED*), July 13 and September 21, 1978.

133 *MEED*, October 6, 1978, p. 40.

134 Howard Schissel, "French Arms Lead Trade Drive," *Eight Days*, March 7, 1981, pp. 34–5. On France's arms dealings with the Arab world, see also: "Paris Arms Drive will Continue," *ibid.*, July 25, 1981.

135 *IHT*, January 16, 1978, p. 1.

136 Quoted by *Tishrin*, January 4, 1979.

137 *WP*, August 9, 1979, pp. A-1, A-7; *Africa Contemporary Record* (1979–1980), p. B-41; "Egypt will Build its Arms Industry with Western aid," *An-Nahar Arab Report and*

Memo, June 25, 1979, p. 11; *Defence et Diplomatie*, august 30, 1979; Dessouki, in Korani and Dessouki, as quoted above, p. 140; *NYT*, October 22, 1979; *MEED*, February 8, 1980, p. 23; *AWST*, January 11, 1982, pp. 42–9; *DED*, November 5, 1979; *Egyptian Newsletter*, October 29–November 11, 1979, pp. 5, 8.

138  R. Popelewski, "Arabs Push Arms Industry Despite Peace," *AWST*, November 6, 1978, pp. 16–18.

139  *IHT* (Special Supplement, June 1979), p. S-16; *An-Nahar Arab Report and Memo* (vol. 3, no. 21, May 21, 1979), pp. 3–4.

140  *The Middle East* (June 1979), p. 91.

141  *An-Nahar Arab Report and Memo*, May 21, 1979, p. 3.

142  In October 1980, the problem of compensation to the British Westland co. had still not been settled. See: *MEED*, October 24, 1980, p. 26; *An-Nahar Arab Report and Memo*, May 21, 1979, p. 3.

143  About this, see also Kamal Hasan 'Ali's remarks in this connection: *al-Ahram*, June 21, 1979; *MEED*, June 15, 1979, p. 21; *FT*, May 11 and 16, 1979; *BBC/SW*, April 19, 1979; *DED*, June 28, 1979, p. 2; *An-Nahar Arab Report and Memo* (vol. 3, no. 28, July 9, 1979), p. 3.

144  *ARR*, July 18, 1979, p. 29.

145  *MEED*, August 17, 1979, p. 19. In 1981 Egypt was still utilizing authority funds. McLaurin noted that, despite the fact that the international monetary community took a dim view of these steps, Egypt received a guarantee from the creditors that they would ignore the freeze, and would view it as an essential political step. See: A. Mclaurin *et al.*, *Middle East Foreign Policy* (New York: Praeger, 1982), p. 61.

146  *Strategic Mid-East and Africa*, September 5, 1979, p. 1. On the Egyptian Industrial Authority, after it was liquidated, see: *Akhir Sa'a*, October 24, 1980, pp. 70–7; articles by Lutfi Hamdi, *Akhir Sa'a*, October 10, 1980, pp. 44–6: October 24, 1980, pp. 86–7; Huda Husayn, *al-Hawadith* (vol. 26, November 19, 1982), pp. 33–5; *al-Watan al-'Arabi* (no. 299, November 5, 1982), pp. 29–32, and October 14, 1983; *al-Watan al-'Arabi* (no. 348, October 14, 1983), pp. 46–7; 'Ali Muhammad Qasim, *al-Dustur* (Lebanon–London) (vol. 13), March 21, 1983 and August 15, 1983, pp. 28–30, and *al-Majalla*, August 11, 1984, pp. 28–31; interviews by Abu Ghazala, Egyptian Minister of Defence and Military Industry, with Samir 'Izzat, *Ruz al-Yusuf* (no. 2887, October 10, 1983), pp. 18–19, and to *al-Siyasi* (Egypt), October 16, 1983; *al-Musawwar*, October 24, 1980, and December 16, 1983; *al-Nasser* (Egypt), November 1980; *Mayo*, August 1, 1983, and December 5, 1983: Tawfiq Hasan Ibrahim, *al-Ahram al-Iqtisadi* (no. 829, December 3, 1984), pp. 20–1: Munir Nawwaf, *al-'Arabi* (no. 314), January 1985), pp. 36–50; *Foreign Report*, March 18, 1982, pp. 5–6; *MERIP Reports* (vol. 13, February 1983), pp. 26–8; *Mideast Markets* (vol. 11, January 23, 1984), pp. 9–10; *An-Nahar Arab Report and Memo*, November 26, 1984; *MEN Economic Weekly* (vol. 24, no. 41, October 11, 1985), pp. 2–3; Michael Dunn, "Arming for Peacetime: Egypt's Defense Industry Today," *Defence and Foreign Affairs*, October–November 1987, pp. 20–4.

147  Ropelewski, *AWST*, November 6, 1978, pp. 16–18.

148  Muhammad Anis, *al-Siyasa al-Duwaliyya*, as quoted above, pp. 130–4.

149  *DED*, October 22, 1979, p. 6.

150  *Al-Dustur* (Lebanon/London), August 15, 1983; *al-Qabas*, January 19, 1984.

151  Muhammad Anis, *al-Siyasa al-Duwaliyya*, as quoted above; *Business Week*, November 20, 1978. Vaeyrynen, as quoted above, p. 73, stated that the AMIO did not appear to have any financial difficulties, and that in 1976–7 it showed profits of $41 million. But this fact alone is not an indication of whether or not there were financial difficulties;

there is always the likelihood of a situation in which there are profits on the one hand and a non-honoring of commitments by the oil countries on the other hand.

152  About the dependence of the Arab oil countries on external arms sources, in regard to the AMIO, see: 'Abd al-'Izz al-Dardari, *Shu'un 'Arabiyya* (no. 30, August 1983), pp. 221–4.

153  *FT*, May 15, 1979; "Egypt. A Special Economic Report," *IHT*, June 14, 1984.

154  On the manufacture of these items, see: *Al-Taqrir al-Istratiji al-'Arabi 1985* (Cairo: Al-Dirasat al-Siyasiyya wal-Istratijiyya bil-Ahram, 1986), pp. 398–9, and see also details in cross-reference 147.

155  *MEED*, February 1, 1980, p. 15; *FT*, January 29, 1980; *DED*, February 4, 1980.

156  Mohammad 'Abd al-Wahab said that in 1979 Kuwait, Iraq, Saudi Arabia, UAE and Qatar had established a joint arms industry with a capital of $8 billion. See: *al-'Arabi* (no. 314, January 1985), pp. 55–60. But this industry was never set up. In the early 1980s the GCC countries discussed jointly setting up a military factory, but up to early 1988 nothing came of this venture.

157  On the Saudi military industry see, for example: Gharib Wahib, *al-Balad*, December 16 and 23, 1980; Yusuf al-Shihab, *al-'Arabi* (no. 317, April 1985), pp. 36–45; *Newsweek* (international edition), (vol. 106, no. 17, October 21, 1985), p. 54; J. Fitchett, *IHT*, December 17, 1983; *Middle East International* (no. 226, June 1, 1984), p. 84.

158  *Al-Yaqza*, February 5, 1982, pp. 14–15; 'Ali Hashim, *al-Nahar al-'Arabi wal-Dawli*, October 18, 1982. pp. 22–4.

159  See, for example, James Pringle, "Abdulla Bishara: `We May Create an Arms Industry," *Newsweek* (vol. 101, no. 15, April 11, 1983), p. 56; "GCC Military Coordination," *BBC*, *SW*, June 1, 1983; Robert C. Allen, "Regional Security in the Persian Gulf," *Military Review* (Kensas), (vol. 63, no. 12, December 1983), pp. 2–11.

160  Ahmad Abu al-Hasan Khali, *al-Siyasa Al-Duwaliyya* (vol. 21, no. 80, April 1985, pp. 182–5; FBIS, *DR*, February 1, 1984; *The Middle East* (no. 119, September 1984), pp. 15–18.

161  "GCC States to Form Joint Defence Force," *Monday Morning* (vol. 12, no. 645, December 3, 1984), pp. 26–7.

162  "GCC Secretary-General on Military Industries," FBIS, *DR*, December 27, 1985.

163  "Multi-Million Shut-down," *The Middle East* (June 1979), p. 91.

164  *Al-Ahram*, May 21, 1982, p. 1.

165  *Al-Taqrir al-Istratiji al-'Arabi 1985*, quoted above, p. 417; *SIPRI* (1986), p. 340.

166  Personal interview, Paris, August 1986.

167  On the Kuwaiti Fund see, for example: 'Abd al-Latif al-Hamid, "Khamsat 'Ashar 'Aman min al-'Amal al-Inma'i al-Duwali, al-Sunduq al-Kuwayti lil-Tanmiya al-Iqtisadiyya al-'Arabiyya," *al-Naft wal-Ta'awun al-'Arabi* (al-Sana 3, al-'Adad 1, 1977), pp. 14–32.

168  KFAED, *Twenty Third Annual Report*, 1984/1985, table d.

169  KFAED, *Annual Report 1977–1978*, p. 27.

170  The Permanent Mission of the State of Kuwait to the U.N, press release no. 2/77 (October 11, 1977), as cited by Soliman Demir, *Arab Development Funds in the Middle East* (New York: Pergamon Press published for UNITAR, 1979).

171  IBRD, Suez Canal Rehabilitiion Project (report no. P-1488a-EGT. November 19, 1974), p. 12; *ARR*, March 1, 1974, p. 81.

172  *MEED* (vol. 2, no. 41, 1978), p. 13.

173  Demir, *Arab Development Funds*.

174  In late 1984 the Kuwaiti Fund agreed to provide the Egyptian Electric Authority with a loan of $8.5 dollars, to purchase spare parts for the Abu Kir power station. See: *al-*

*Ahram*, December 10, 1984; *MEED*, December 14, 1984. In late December 1985, Egyptian government representatives and the Kuwaiti Development Fund reached an agreement on a loan to Egypt of $35 million, as aid for the Egyptian national plan to increase sugar-cane production. Total cost of the project was $94 million. The main regions to be developed were Kana, Aswan and al-Minya. Talks on the financing of this plan commenced in November 1984. See: *al-Ahram*, December 18 and 25, 1985; *MEED*, November 9, 1984.

    In October 1986 the Kuwaiti Fund agreed to grant a loan of $37 million, as financing for a pharmacological industry. The agreement was for the loan to be channeled to seven companies in the public sector and to two marketing companies. The loan was to be repaid over a period of 20 years – including 5 years postponement – at 3 percent annual interest. See: *al-Ahram*, October 9, 1986.

175   At the same time, veteran funds such as the Kuwaiti Fund, cooperated with international financial institutions. See, for example, Ibrahim Shahata, "Ma'unat Duwal al-Ubik wal-Ta'awun ma'a Masadir al-Tamwil al-Tijari," *al-Naft wal-Ta'awun al-'Arabi* (al-Sana 5, al-'Adad 1, 1979), pp. 7–22. In the period 1973–83 OPEC aid agencies, the World Bank and the OECD jointly financed 275 projects, totaling $4 billion. See: M. Abalkhail, "OPEC Aid: A Question of Solidarity," *OAPEC Bulletin* (vol. 12, nos. 8–9, 1986), p. 14.

176   *MEED*, November 22, 1974, p. 1414; *MEES*, November 22, 1974 and February 21, 1975, p. 8.

177   World Bank, *ARE Telecommunication Organization (ARETO)*, (report no. 631a-EGT, April 11, 1975), pp. 15, 18–19.

178   IBRD, *Report and Recommendation for Second Railway Project* (report no. P. 1552a-EGT, March 10, 1975), p. 13.

179   World Bank, *report no. P-2780-EGT*, April 18, 1980, annex II, p. 28.

180   IBRD, *Egypt Textile Project* (report no. P-1835-EGT, 1976), p. 5; World Bank, *Appraisal of Kafr el Dawar and El Beida Textile Project, Egypt* (report no. 1131-RGT, June 7, 1976).

181   On this affair, see details: "Al-Qurud wal-Tanmiya," *al-Ahram al-Iqtisadi* (no. 523, June 1, 1977), pp. 8–14. For further sentiments in this spirit, see chapter 5.

182   USAID, *ARE Canal Cities Water and Sewerage* (Project Paper Factsheet, n.d.), p. vii. Egypt received these convenient terms even before Sadat's trip to Jerusalem. For the loan for gas turbines in Talkha and Helwan ($50 million) given in May 1976 on the same conditions, see: USAID, *Helwan and Talkha Gas Turbine Plants*, n.d., p. 1.

183   IBRD, *Tourah Cement Expansion Project* (report no. P-1540a-EGT, January 15, 1975), pp. 11–12: see also: *ibid., Egypt Appraisal of Tourah Cement Expansion Project* (report no. 608-egt, December 30, 1974, 2 vols.).

184   In 1984 Egypt imported 5.5 million tons of cement, for about $350 million. See: *MEED*, February 1, 1985.

185   World Bank, report no. P-2780-EGT, *op. cit.*, annex II, p. 30.

186   Additional details, see chapter 1, and: UNCTAD, Financial Solidarity, *op. cit.* 1984, pp. 30, 32–6 and 1985, pp. 55–6.

187   Ibrahim Shihata (ed.), *The OPEC Fund for International Development: The Formative Years* (London: Croom Helm, 1983), annex 1, p. 176, annex 2, pp. 267, 269.

188   See tables 8 and 10. On the Islamic Development Bank, see also: *Daily Star* (Beirut), December 24, 1974; *MEES*, April 17, 1978; *Middle East Money*, April 12, 1975.

189   See, for example, the loan for $100 million in 1974, given to the ECB for various industrial projects. *ARR*, August 16, 1974, p. 345.

190   The other rich oil countries also exported oil through the Canal, see: *ARE, Suez Canal*

*Authority, annual report, various issues.* For detailed figures, see chapter 5, in the part dealing with the Arab boycott's influence on the Egyptian economy.

191  See the extensive interview with 'Izzat 'Adil, Chairman of the Board of Directors of the Suez Canal Authority, *al-Musawwar* (no. 3113, June 8, 1984), pp. 55–8. Note that works on the widening of the Canal started under Nasser's regime, in February 1967, and were supposed to be finished by 1972. But work stopped when the June 1967 war broke out.

192  IBRD, Industrial Project Department, *Appraisal of Talkha 2 Fertilizer Project* (report no. 456-UAR, May 28, 1974), pp. 17–21.

193  World Bank, report no. P-2780-EGT, *op. cit.*, annex 2, p. 28.

194  For a comprehensive study of Egyptian bureaucracy see: Nazih N.M. Ayubi, *Bureaucracy and Politics in Contemporary Egypt* (London: Ithaca Press, 1980).

195  Report of the Comptroller General of the United States, *Egypt's Capacity to Absorb and Use Economic Assistance Effectivly* (id-77-33, September 15, 1977), pp. 18–19.

196  *Akhbar al-Yawm*, October 27, 1979, p. 10.

197  N. Ayubi, "Implementation Capability and Political Feasibility the Open Door Policy in Egypt," in Malcolm H. Kerr and El-Sayed (eds.), *Rich and Poor States in the Middle East: Egypt and the New Arab Order* (Boulder, CO: Westview Press, 1982), pp. 370–1.

198  Jeswald W. Salacuse, "Arab Capital and Trilateral Ventures in the Middle East: Is Three a Crowd?," in Kerr and Yassin (eds.), *Rich and Poor States in the Middle East: Egypt and the New Arab Order* (Boulder, CO: Westview Press, 1982), p.139

199  See, for example, Chase Bank, Guide to Doing Business in Egypt (Cairo, 1980); International Trade Consulting Co. (Egypt), *The Green Business Guide* (Cairo, 1986); United States and Foreign Commercial Service, *Business Directory for Egypt* (Cairo: United States Embassy-Cairo and American Consulate-General-Alexandria, February 1986); Fiani and partners, *Egypt Investment Directory 1980/81* (Cairo, 1980), and *ibid.*, Egypt Investment and Business Directory 1983/84 (Cairo 1983).

200  Gillespie based herself on the Fiani directory of 1980. See: Kate Gillespie, *The Tripartite Relationship* (New York: Praeger, 1984).

201  More material on the authority and its bodies, see: US Department of Commerce, *Investing in Egypt* (International Marketing Information Series, Overseas Business Reports 81–108, May 1981), pp. 3–5.

202  Jumhuriyyat Misr al-'Arabiyya (JM'), al-Hay'a al-'Amma lil-Istithmar wal-Manatiq al-Hurra, Qita' al-Manatiq al-Hurra, "Haqa'iq wa-Arqam 1984" (no date). For additional details, see research work as ordered by the Egyptian Investment Authority: Farouk Shakeer and Mona Ghalib Mourad, *Cost/Benefit Assessment of Free Zones. A Case Study on Egypt* (Cairo, May 1981), pp. 3–22.

203  Alternatively, some view the free-trade zones as private and public. See: Reynolds, Smith and Hills, *Scoped Environmental Assessment of Arab Republic of Egypt* (prepared for Gafiz, Ministry of Cooperation, Cairo and Jacksonville, Florida, USAID, report no. 263-0042, 1980).

204  *ARE*, GAFIZ, Statistics and Information Department, *Report on the Arab and Foreign Investment until 31/12/1977* (Cairo, 1978), p. 7.

205  JM', Al-Hay'a al-'Amma lil-Istithmar wal-Manatiq al-Hurra, Qita' al-Buhuth wal-Ma'lumat, *al-Taqrir al-Sanawi 1980*, p. 77.

206  The authority set up branches in the US, Canada, Sweden, the UK, France, West Germany and Japan.

207  The figure includes domestic plans and plans for the free-trade zones. Capital for domestic plans only totaled EgP 180.8 million. See: GAFIZ, *Investment Review* (vol. 6, no. 2, July 1985), p. 1; GAFIZ, *Facts and Figures* (no. 1, September 1977).

208 See report by Egyptian Ministry of Investment, Ahmad 'Abd al-Fattah, *Akhbar al-Batrul wal-Sina'a* (Abu Dhabi), February 1978, pp. 19–21.
209 On Egyptian investments, see: Al-Hay'a al-'Amma lil-Istithmarat wal-Manatiq al-Hurra, *al-Taqrir al-Sanawi 1979*, pp. 56–60.
210 Calculations based on diagrams which appeared *ibid.*, p. 38.
211 Total according to authority figures is only about 97 percent. See: *ibid.*, pp. 88–90.
212 Al-Hay'a al-'Amma lil-Istithmar wal-Manatiq al-Hurra, *al-Taqrir al-Sanawi 1980*, p. 52.
213 *Ibid.*, pp. 79, 83.
214 *Ibid.*, p. 76.
215 On the free-trade zones, see: ARE, CAPMAS, *Status of the Open Door Economy up to 31.12.1981* (Cairo, February 1982), pp. 56–65.
216 *MEN Economic Weekly* (Cairo), (vol. 20, no. 19, May 8, 1981), p. 22.
217 Wizarat al-Istithmar wal-Ta'awun al-Dawli, al-Hay'a al-'Amma lil-Istithmar wal-Manatiq al-Hurra, *al-Taqrir al-Sanawi 1982/1983* (April 1984), p. 36.
218 *MEED*, June 1, 1984.
219 *Ibid.*, p. 21.
220 Al-Hay'a al-'Amma lil-Istithmar wal-Manatiq al-Hurra, Qita' al-Buhuth wal-Ma'lumat, *al-Taqrir al-Sanawi 'Am 1983/1984* (Cairo, September 1984), p. 30.
221 *Ibid.*, p. 67.
222 *Ibid.*, p. 86.
223 Processed as per data from al-Hay'a al-'Amma lil-Istithmar wal-Manatiq al-Hurra, Qita' al-Buhuth wal-Ma'lumat, *al-Taqrir al-Sanawi, 1984/85* (Cairo, September 1985), pp. 18, 35.
224 The Egyptian Investment Authority quarterly periodical, as quoted above (vol. 7, no. 1, April 1986), p. 8.
225 See also: *International Policy Analysis, An Assessment of Investment Promotion Activities* (Final Report. Washington: SRI International, January 1984), p. 196; American Embassy in Cairo, Economic Section, "Egypt. Economic Trends Report" (January 1981) p. 10; Olfat Tohamy, "Improved Arab Ties Spur Foreign Investment," *International Herald Tribune*, Egypt Special Survey, June 14, 1984; Sa'ad el-Din Ibrahim, *The New Arab Social Order. A Study of the Social Impact of Oil Wealth* (Boulder, CO: Westview Press, 1982), p. 73. Hansen and Radwan declared that the building "boom" in Egypt in recent years can be credited both directly and indirectly to the emigrants, many of whom returned and invested the money they saved in real estate. See: Bent Hansen and Samir Radwan, *Employment Opportunities and Equity in a Changing Economy: Egypt in the 1980s* (Geneva: ILO, 1982), p. 241.
226 *The EIA Quarterly* (vol. 4, no. 3, October 1983), p. 5; (vol. 6, no. 3), pp. 6–7; *MEED*, September 30, 1983, p. 22.
227 *MEED*, March 4, 1977, p. 18; *FT Survey*, July 24, 1978, p. 21; J. Birks and C. Sinclair, "Migration and Development. The Changing Perspection of the Poor Arab Countries," *Journal of International Affairs* (vol. 33, 1979), p. 301.
228 Processed according to EIA data, as published in *al-Taqrir al-Sanawi 1983/1984*, pp. 32, 56.
229 *Ibid.*, p. 58.
230 Even today priority is given for the same reasons, although not always openly declared, for the development of the municipal sector. See, for example, World Bank, *ARE, Current Economic Situation and Medium-term Prospects*, March 18, 1985, p. 10.
231 On bureaucracy and investments in Egypt, see: Chase National Bank (Egypt), "Investment Constraints Report," March 16, 1983.

232 Quoted by author: Nabil Megalli, "Western Bankers Irked by Difficulties in Egypt," *Burroughs Clearing House* (Detroit), (vol. 59, September 1975), pp. 42, 44.

233 N. Ayubi in Kerr and Yassin (eds.), *Rich and Poor States in the Middle East*, p. 374.

234 *Al-Ahram al-Iqtisadi*, September 1, 1974, p. 5.

235 *Ibid.*, July 23, 1984.

236 Ayubi in Kerr and Yassin (eds.), *Rich and Poor States in the Middle East*, pp. 376–7. See also: David Ignatius, "Course of Cairo," *WSJ*, March 24, 1983. A comprehensive study by Ayoubi on Egyptian bureaucracy, see: N. M. Nazih, *Bureaucracy and Politics in Contemporary Egypt* (London: Ithaca Press, 1980).

237 A. D. Little International, "Investment Information Center-Updated Project Plan," July 1981.

238 *MEED*, April 29, 1983; June 1, 1984.

239 The latter ministry was cancelled with the forming of the new government in July 1984, headed by Kamal Hasan 'Ali. See Kamal Hasan 'Ali's statement to *al-Ra'y al-'Amm*, January 5, 1985, p. 15. See also: US, Department of State, *Investment Climate Statement: Egypt* (Department of State Airgram, state no. 248830, October 16, 1984), pp. 7, 13; GAFIZ, *Investment Review* (vol. 6, no. 2, July 1985), p. 2; *MEED*, July 20 and October 12, 1984.

240 See: JM`, *Jadwal Muqaran lil-Mazaya al-Muqarrara bi-Qanun al-Istithmar wa-ma Yuqabiluha min Ahkam fi Qanun al-Sharikat al-Jadid* (Cairo: Raqm al-Ida' bi-Dar al-Kitab al-Qawmiyya 3596, 1984).

241 About the conference, see also: *al-Ahram al-Iqtisadi*, October 20, 1986, p. 22; Suhayr Abu al-`Ala, *al-Jumhuriyya*, October 12, 1986.

242 *MEED*, February 8, 1974, p. 151; February 22, 1974, p. 201.

243 *MEED*, August 16, 1974, pp. 938, 941; *MEES*, August 2, p. 6–7 and 9, p. Z3, 1974; *An-Nahar Arab Report and Memo*, January 18, 1974; *al-Ahram*, June 19, 1975; *al-Ta'akhi* (Iraq), May 17, 1975. Ahmad declared that total joint Egyptian–Iraqi investment plans came to $1 billion. See: Yusuf J. Ahmad, *Absorptive Capacity of the Egyptian Economy* (Paris: OECD, 1976), p. 122.

244 *MEED*, November 19, 1982, p. 22.

245 The World Bank classified Kuwait, Libya, Qatar, Saudi Arabia and the UAE as countries with a low absorptive capacity. See: World Bank, *World Development Report 1985*, p. 89. For a treatise on the domestic absorptive capacity of the oil-producing countries, see: Ragaei el Mallakh *et al.*, *Capital Investment in the Middle East, The Use of Surplus Funds for Regional Development* (New York: Praeger Publishers, 1977), pp. 14–48.

246 *Law*, vol. 2, p. 15.

247 *MEED*, November 11, 1977, p. 20; August 19, 1977, p. 21; September 16, 1977, p. 22. For the "Coca Cola" co.'s bid see: Sam Ayub, *The Coca Cola Co., A Proposal to the ARE for the Development of Arid Lands for Agriculture Purposes* (Atlanta, Sept. 1976).

248 *MEED*, May 18, 1979, p. 24. The American administration assisted Sadat, by granting incentives to American investors and companies operating in Egypt. For example, the Xerox company received an American government guarantee against political risks to its property in Egypt. See: *ibid.*, November 1979, p. 28.

249 *ARE*, Ministry of Planning, *The Detailed Frame of the Five Year Plan for Economic and Social Development 1982/83–1986/87* (Cairo, December 1982), part 1, p. 14.

250 Farouk Shakweer, Mona Ghaleb Mourad, *Cost/Benefit Assessment of Free Zones. A Case Study on Egypt* (Cairo, May 1981), p. 100–2.

251 *Ruz al-Yusuf*, May 15, 1978, pp. 12–13.

252 *Ibid.*, September 18, 1978, pp. 22–5.

253 About the delegations see: *Akhbar al-Yawm*, May 22, 1982: June 19, 1982: April 21,

1984; *al-Ahram*, June 15, 1982; *al-Mustaqbal*, June 26, 1982; *al-Jumhuriyya*, June 12, 1982; *al-Akhbar*, May 24, 1984; *al-Hawadith*, March 23, 1984; *al-Ahram al-Iqtisadi*, March 22, 1984; *MENA*, February 17, 1982; *MEED*, March 19, 1982, p. 13; *Emirate News*, February 18, 1983.

254  *Al-Ahram al-Iqtisadi*, October 12, 1986, p. 22.
255  *UPI* (Kuwait), May 26, 1979.
256  *MEED*, May 18, 1979, p. 26.
257  Personal interview, Cairo, September 22, 1986.
258  *Egyptian Newsletter*, November 26–December 9, 1979, p. 9.
259  David Shireff, "The Flight into Egypt," *Euromoney* (May 1984), pp. 174, 181.

## 3  Labor Migration to the Arab Oil Countries

1  See, for example, Gabriel Baer, *Arabs of the Middle East – Population and Society* (Tel Aviv: Hakibbutz Hame'uhad, 1973), pp. 40–1; Ya'akov Shimoni, *The Arab States. Chapters of Political History* (Hebrew), (Tel Aviv: Am Oved, 1977), pp. 445–6; W. Cleland, *The Population Problem in Egypt: A Study of Population Trends and Conditions in Modern Egypt* (Lancaster, 1936), pp. 52, 88; Nazih Ayubi, "The Egyptian Brain Drain: A Multi-dimensional Problem," *IJMES* (vol. 15, no. 4, November 1983), p. 431.

2  M. A. El-Badri, "Trends in the Components of Population Growth in the Arab Countries of the Middle East: A Survey of Present Information," *Demography* (vol. 2, 1965), p. 158.

3  Mahmud 'Abd al-Fadil, *Al-Naft wal-Wahda al-'Arabiyya: Ta'thir al-Naft al-'Arabi 'ala Mustaqbal al-Wahda al-'Arabiyya wal-'Alaqat al-Iqtisadiyya al-'Arabiyya* (Beirut: Markaz Dirasat al-Wahda al-'Arabiyya, 1979), p. 21; Nazli Choucri with the collaboration of Peter Brecke, "Migration in the Middle East: Transformation and Change," *Middle East Review* (vol. 16, no. 2, winter 1983/4), p. 17; Bent Hansen and Samir Radwan, *Employment Opportunities and Equity in a Changing Economy: Egypt in the 1980s* (Geneva: ILO, 1982), p. 81. Choucri pointed out that data referred to 1962. Hansen and Radwan and Abdel Fadil claimed that data referred to 1965.

4  According to a population census conducted in May 1966. See economic and social anthology, *The New Orient* (vol. 17, 1967), p. 321.

5  J. S. Birks, C. A. Sinclair and J. A. Socknat, "The Demand for Egyptian Labour Abroad," in A. Richards and P. Martin (eds.), *Migration, Mechanization and Agricultural Labour Market in Egypt* (Cairo: AUC and Westview Press, 1983), p. 118.

6  Hansen and Radwan mentioned 149,000 temporary emigrants, with an additional 70,000 Egyptians, who they think went abroad to look for employment, on the pretext of going on a Hajj or as tourists. See Hansen and Radwan, *Employment Opportunities and Equity in a Changing Economy: Egypt in the 1980s* (Geneva: ILO, 1982), table no. 30, p. 85.

7  Ralph R. Sell, *Gone for Good?* (Cairo: Cairo Papers in Social Science, vol. 10, Monograph 2, summer 1987), pp. 1, 58, 68, 77, 83–4. For a further study on this subject, see: Georges Sabagh, "Immigrants in the Arab Gulf Countries: 'Sojourners' or 'Settlers'?," in Giacomo Luciani and Ghassan Salame (eds.), *The Politics of Arab Integration* (London: Croom Helm, 1988), pp. 159–82

8  For data on contracts drawn up as per agreements between the governments of Egypt and the oil countries, see: *MEN Economic Weekly* (Cairo), (vol. 22, no. 47), p. 13.

9  See the Egyptian Minister of Labor's remarks, when he spoke about Egyptians looking for gainful employment, on the pretext of going on a Hajj. Quoted by: *al-Ahram*, September 18, 1978, p. 5.

10 Data was processed according to table 3.1.

11 On December 15, 1981, the Jordanian Minister of the Interior abolished restrictions on Egyptians employed in Jordan. See: *MEED*, January 24, 1982. See also a working paper presented by Ahmad Qasim al-Ahmad at a conference that took place in Jordan in October 1983, on the subject of ties between Egypt and the Arab world. Quoted by *al-Sharq al-Awsat* (London), October 23, 1983, p. 3.

12 *MEED*, April 18, 1975, p. 39.

13 John A. Shaw and D. E. Long, *Saudi Arabian Modernization, The Impact of Change on Stability* (Washington Papers, vol. 10, no. 89, 1982), p. 36; J. S. Birks and C. A. Sinclair, *The Kingdom of Saudi-Arabia and the Libyan Arab Hamhiriya: The Key Countries of Employment* (Geneva: ILO, WEP 2-26/*WP*, 1979), pp. 5–13.

14 Gil Feiler, "The Migration from Egypt to the Arab Oil Economies, 1974–1983: Demographic and Economic Characteristics" (MA thesis, Department for the History of the Middle East, Haifa University, June 1985), pp. 27–8. See also: *ibid.*, The Number of Egyptian Workers in the Arab Oil Countries, 1974–1983: A Critical Discussion (Tel Aviv: The Dayan Center for Middle Eastern and African Studies, occasional paper, October 1986), pp. 10–11. A 1976 census gave a figure of 1.425 million Egyptians residing abroad at the time, but the census did not provide a breakdown of the number of tourists, workers, pilgrims on a Hajj, and so on. See: ARE, Central Agency for Public Mobilisation and Statistics (CAPMAS), *Statistical Yearbook 1952–1984* (Cairo, June 1985), p. 6.

15 See the following three estimates: 'Abd al-Fattah al-Jibali, "Al-Athar al-Iqtisadiyya li-Hijrat al-'Amala al-Misriyya," *al-Siyasa al-Duwaliyya* (no. 73, July 1983), pp. 87–8.

16 For an evaluation by the Ministry of Labor, see: *al-Ahram*, August 5, 1982, p. 9.

17 See various data and the way they were examined by G. Feiler 1985 and 1986.

18 Muhsin Khalil Ibrahim, "Hawla Tajribat al-'Iraq fil-'Amala al-Wafida," *al-Mustaqbal al-'Arabi* (no. 51, May 1983), pp. 93–104.

19 Ali Hillal Dessouki, "The Shift in Egypt's Migration Policy, 1952–1978," *MES* (vol. 18, no. 1, 1982), p. 53; Suzanne A. Messiha, *Export of Egyptian School Teachers* (Cairo papers in Social Science, vol. III, monograph IV, April 1980), p. 3; FBIS, *JPRS*, November 7, 1978, p. 16, cited *al-Ahram*, September 18, 1978.

20 See: *al-Ahram*, August 13, 1983, p. 3; October 12, 1984, p. 11; *al-Siyasa* (Kuwait), May 15, 1984; *MEED*, February 24, 1984; Victor Lavy, "The Economic Embargo of Egypt by Arab states: Myth and Reality," *MEJ* (vol. 38, no. 3, summer 1984), p. 431.

21 *Arab Oil and Gas* (vol. 13, no. 307, July 1, 1984), pp. 4–5.

22 Philip L. Martin and A. Richards, "The Laissez-faire Approach to International Labor Migration: The Case of the Arab Middle East," *Economic Development and Cultural Change* (vol. 31, no. 3, 1983), p. 461.

23 In this context, see: Sa'ad el-Din Ibrahim, "Superpower in the Arab World," *The Washington Quarterly* (summer 1981), esp. p. 84.

24 United Nations, Department of International Economic and Social Affairs, Statistical Office, *Demographic Yearbook 1982* (New York, 1984), pp. 134, 137.

25 IMF, *UAE – Recent Economic Development* (sm/83/108, May 31, 1983), p. 16.

26 IMF, *Kuwait – Recent Economic Development* (sm/83/151, July 7, 1983), pp. 17–18.

27 International Labour Organisation (ILO), *Yearbook of Labour Statistics 1978* (Geneva: ILO), pp. 37–8. Data on the industrialized nations, see *ibid* and also: World Bank, *World Tables* (from the data files of World Bank, Baltimore and London, 1980), p. 436.

28 ILO, *Yearbook of Labour Statistics 1978*, pp. 19, 21, 37–8.

29 Further data, see: Paul R. Shaw, *Mobilisation Human Resources in the Arab World* (London, 1983), pp. 141–2.

30 ILO, *Yearbook 1981*, p. 13.
31 Data on Bahrein, Egypt and other Arab countries, see: UNESCO, *Statistical Digest* (Paris, 1983), pp. 22–3, 46–7, 178–9, 200–3, 207–8, 212–13, 232–47, 309; ibid., *Statistics of Science and Technology – latest available data* (December 1983), pp. 31–2.
32 See: Ibrahim M. Oweiss, "The Migration of Egyptians," in A. B. Zahlan (ed.), *The Arab Brain Drain* (London: Ithaca Press, 1981), pp. 164–5; William Quandt, *Saudi Arabia in the 1980's*, p. 6.
33 See: *Financial Times Survey: Saudi Arabia*, April 28, 1980, pp. xv–xvi; Al-Eassa, "Toward Manpower Planning in Kuwait" (Ph.D. dissertation, Fletcher School of Law and Diplomacy, 1978), p. 3; *MEED*, June 18, 1976.
34 See following and other data: State of Kuwait, Ministry of Planning, *Annual Statistical Abstract 1978*, pp. 109–25.
35 A comprehensive review of the Egyptian labor market, see: Hansen and Radwan, *Employment Opportunities and Equity in a Changing Economy,* as quoted above.
36 Processed on the basis of ILO data, 1978 yearly, *passim*.
37 L. H. Hadley, "The Migration of Egyptian Human Capital to the Arab Oil-Producing States: A Cost Benefit Analysis," *International Migration Review* (vol. 11, 1977), p. 293.
38 ARE, Ministry of Planning follow-up report 1977, as cited by Sa'ad el-Din Ibrahim, *The New Arab Social Order. A Study of the Social Impact of Oil Wealth* (Boulder, CO: Westview Press, 1982), p. 75.
39 Sa'ad el-Din Ibrahim, *The New Order*, p. 69.
40 Ali Hillal Dessouki, "The Shift in Egypt's Migration Policy, 1952–1978," *MES* (vol. 18, no. 1, 1982), pp. 54–5, 58.
41 For example, the Egyptian government decided to establish a special department, under the supervision of the Minister for Social Affairs, to promote migration, and the Egyptian People's Assembly recommended increasing the number of Egyptian experts loaned to the Arab states. See: Azriel Karni, "Developments Relating to the Control of the Birth Rate in the Middle East," *The New Orient* (vol. 17, pamphlet 3–4, 1967), p. 231; economic and social anthology, *The New Orient* (vol. 5, pamphlet 3, 1954), p. 289; (vol. 9, pamphlet 3, 1958/59), p. 189.
42 "Policy of the Economics of Egyptian Expatriate Savings," Presidency of the Arab Republic of Egypt, *The Specialised National Councils' Magazine* (no. 13), p. 11. From 1965 on, Egyptian policy-makers devised many plans in order to attract expatriates' funds to Egypt, and the media called for encouraging the Egyptians working abroad to invest in Egypt. See, for example, *ibid.*, pp. 10–24; Nabil Saba'i, "Suk al-Mal," *al-Ahram al-Iqtisadi*, February 1st, 1974, pp. 56–9.
43 *Ibid.* (vol. 18, pamphlet 3–4, 1968), p. 259; (vol. 19, pamphlet 3, 1969), p. 253.
44 See resolution no. 364 in 1968 presented by the Minister of Economy and Foreign Trade, as translated and as a supplement to the *Middle East Observer*.
45 *Ibid.* (vol. 19, pamphlets 1–2, 1969), p. 125.
46 On the resolution, see: *ibid.* (pamphlet 4, 1970), p. 83. See also: *al-Jumhuriyya*, June 24, 1969; Paul Rivlin, *The Dynamics of Economic Policy Making in Egypt* (New York: Praeger), p. 157.
47 Dessouki, "Migration Policy," pp. 60–2; Hansen and Radwan, *Employment Opportunities and Equity in a Changing Economy*, 241–2.
48 Notwithstanding the above, even before that the Egyptian government encouraged emigration. Hansen and Radwan noted, for instance, that already after 1967 permanent emigration was being promoted by the government. See Hansen and Radwan, *Employment Opportunities and Equity in a Changing Economy*, p. 84.
49 See item no. 52, in the chapter "General Fundamentals," as it appears in: The

Constitution of the Arab Republic of Egypt, translated and published in *The New Orient* (vol. 22, pamphlet 3, 1972), p. 311.

50  Dessouki, "Migration Policy," pp. 53–4; *al-Ahram*, November 17, 1981 (taken from file – "Egypt: Population and Manpower" in the Shiloah Institute).

51  Dessouki, "Migration Policy," pp. 63–5.

52  *Al-Ahram*, February 24, 1982, p. 1.

53  *Al-Ahram*, May 24, 1982 ("Egypt: Population and Manpower" file, Shiloah Institute).

54  For excerpts from Mubarak's speech, see: *al-Akhbar*, August 15, 1983 (*Hasav*, August 16, 1983). See also: *Akhir Sa'a*, August 17, 1983, p. 6 ("Egypt Abroad" file, Shiloah Institute). Similar words used by Mubarak in his speech to a meeting of expatriates held in August 1984. See: Sulayman Hasan, Salwa Ma'tu, "Al-Misriyyun fil-Kharij bayna al-Akhdh wal-'Ata," *October* (no. 408, August 19, 1984), p. 16. Further details on the conference, see: *al-Ahram al-Iqtisadi*, August 20, 1984, pp. 30–5.

55  In the press and in research literature, many arguments against migration can be found. See, for example, Sa'ad el-Din Ibrahim, as quoted above, Mahmud Abdel Feisal, as quoted above; Ayubi, "The Brain Drain," as quoted above; Nazli Choucri, *Migration in the Middle East: Transformation, Policies and Processes* (Cairo: Cairo University and MIT Technology Adaptation Program, July 1983, 2 vols.) One can also find contradictory opinions, claiming that in the end emigration was a blessing for the Egyptian economy. See: Khalid Ikram, *Egypt, Economic Management in a Period of Transition* (Baltimore: Johns Hopkins University Press, 1980), p. 139. See also: G. Feiler, "Migration from Egypt to the Arab oil Economies, 1974–1983," pp. 184–207.

56  Mustafa Imam, Jamal Za'ida, "al-Misriyyun al-'Amilun fil-Duwal al-'Arabiyya – al-Mustaqbal fi Sallat al-Qalaq!!," *al-Ahram al-Iqtisadi* (no. 747, May 9, 1983), p. 9.

57  Kamal Jibala, *al-Ahram al-Iqtisadi* (no. 745, 1983), p. 12.

58  An interview by Mubarak to *al-Siyasa* (Kuwait), February 20, 1983, pp. 14–15.

59  For a summation of reasons see: Dessouki, "Migration Policy," p. 60; Hansen and Radwan, *Employment Opportunities and Equity in a Changing Economy*, p. 84: Ibrahim Sa'ad El-Din, "Asbab wa-Nata'ij Tasdir al-Yad al-'Amila fi Misr," *al-Mustaqbal al-'Arabi* (no. 35, January 1982); 'Abd al-Fattah al-Jibali, "Al-Athar al-Iqtisadiyya li-Hijrat al-'Amala al-Misriyya," *al-Siyasa al-Duwaliyya* (no. 73, July 1983), pp. 87–91; *al-Sha'b*, February 21, 1984, p. 6 (the "Egyptians Abroad" file, the Shiloah Institute); Philip Geyelin, "Population and Policy in Egypt," *IHT*, January 27, 1982; Ibrahim M. Oweiss, "The Migration of Egyptians," in A. B. Zahlan (ed.), *The Arab Brain Drain* (London: Ithaca Press, 1981), p. 165; Deena T. Khatkhate, "The Brain Drain as a Social Safety Valve," *Finance and Development* (vol. 7, no. 1, march 1970), pp. 38–9.

60  *MEED*, July 28, 1978, p. 13.

61  On the migration policy of the oil countries see, for example: Nazli Choucri, "Demographic Changes in the Middle East," in *The Political Economy of the Middle East: 1973–78* (a compendium of papers submitted to the joint economic committee, Congress of the United States, April 21, 1980), pp. 34–9; "Sedentarisation as a Means of Detribalisation: Some Policies of the Saudi Arabian Government towards the Nomads," in Tim Niblock (ed.), *State, Society and Economy in Saudi Arabia* (London, 1982), p. 208; *The Times* (London), August 30, 1980; "Expatriate Recruitment Procedures Amended," *QER of Saudi Arabia* (no. 3, 1982), p. 14.

62  "Immigration Rules Get Tighter Still," *Saudi-Arabia Newsletter*, September 15–28, 1980, pp. 4–5; A. Dhaher, "Expatriate Labor in the Arab Gulf States: The Citizens and Political Status," *the Arab Gulf* (vol. 16, 1984), pp. 185–92; R. Franklin, "Migrant Labor and the Politics of Development in Bahrain," *MERIP Reports* (vol. 15, 1985), pp. 7–13, 32.

63 *Al-Sharq al-Awsat*, March 11, 1980, p. 30 (*Hasav*, June 14, 1980); July 27, 1984; UN Department of International Economic and Social Affairs, *National Experience in the Formulation and Implementation of Population Policy: 1958–1979, Saudi Arabia* (New York, 1981), pp. 40–2; "Control on Immigration Labour," *ARR* (no. 14, July 16–31, 1978), p. 525; *Birks and Sinclair*, p. 84; "Saudi curbs on Families of Foreign Workers," *The Times* (London), August 30, 1980.

64 Kingdom of Saudi Arabia, Ministry of Planning, *Third Development Plan 1980–1985.* Saudi Arabia failed to obtain this goal. Furthermore, the number of foreign workers in the kingdom increased by another 1.6 million during this Five-Year Plan.

65 Sa'ad Eddin Ibrahim, "Oil, Migration and the New Arab Social Order," in Kerr and Yassin (eds.), *Rich and Poor States in the Middle East: Egypt and the New Arab Order* (Boulder, CO: Westview Press, 1982), pp. 56–7.

66 *Al-Jumhuriyya*, August 14, 1983.

67 *The Arab World Weekly* (Beirut), October 18, 1980, p. 17.

68 N. Choucri, "The New Migration in the Middle East: A Problem for Whom?," *International Migration Review* (vol.2, no. 4, 1977), p. 423.

69 "Gulf Limits on Palestinians," *Foreign Report* (no. 1783, July 21, 1983), p. 5.

70 Tah Yassin Ramadan's interview to *al-Musawwar*, June 10, 1983. p. 44.

71 *Ibid.*

72 See tables 3.6, 3.7, 3.9, 3.10.

73 Many research works have been published which dealt with the profit and loss balance of migrants' remittances. Besides the considerable help to the balance of payments of the country exporting workers, many economists claim that remittances bring with them a substantial increase in consumption and accelerate inflation. Many researchers emphasized the negative influence of remittances made by non-conventional means. For a general and specific survey of the Arab world and a survey of Egypt on these points see: Sharon Stanton Russell, "Remittances from International Migration: A Review in Perspective," *World Development* (vol. 14, no. 6, June 1986), pp. 677–96; Nazli Choucri, "The Hidden Economy: A New View of Remittances in the Arab World," *World Development, op. cit.*, pp. 697–712; Gil Feiler, "The Scope and Some Effects of Remittances of Egyptians working in the Arab Oil Producing Countries, 1973–1984," *Asian and African Studies (AAS)*, (vol. 21, no 3, 1987), pp. 305–25; Gala A. Amin and Elizabeth Awny, *International Migration of Egyptian Labour. A Review of the State of the Art* (Ottawa: International Development Research Centre, May 1985), chapter III.

74 See data on remittances and commercial exports: IMF, *IFS 1983 Yearbook*, pp. 204–5.

75 *Ibid.*

76 *NYT*, January 28, 1983; Alan McDermatt, "Egypt," *Middle East Review 1983*, p. 156.

77 National Bank of Egypt, *The Egyptian Economy in Brief*, Cairo, 1981.

78 Hansen and Radwan, *Employment Opportunities and Equity in a Changing Economy*, p. 241.

79 Paul R. Shaw, *Mobilization Human Resources in the Arab World* (London, 1983), p. 30.

80 National Bank of Egypt, *Economic Bulletin* (vol. 32, nos. 3–4, 1979), p. 271; see also: Nazih Ayubi, "The Egyptian 'Brain Drain': A Multi-dimensional Problem," *IJMES* (vol. 15, November 1983), p. 147. See also: *al-Siyasi* (Cairo), June 26, 1983, p. 6; *al-'Amal* (monthly, Cairo), March 1983, as quoted by: FBIS, *JPRS*, April 11, 1983.

81 Sa'ad el-Din Ibrahim, *New Order*, p. 87; A. Richards and Philip Martin, "The Laissez-Faire Approach to International Labor Migration: The Case of the Arab Middle East," *Economic Development and Cultural Change* (vol. 31, no. 3, 1983), p. 467.

82 'Abd al-Fattah al-Jibali, "al-Athar al-Iqtisadiyya li-Hijrat al-'Amala al-Misriyya," *al-Siyasa al-Duwaliyya* (no. 73, July 1983), p. 90.

83  On these steps see: Michael H. Davies, "Implications of Egypt's New Exchange Rate System," *Middle East Executive Reports* (vol. 11, no. 1, January 1988), pp. 9–11.

84  Sa'ad el-Din Ibrahim, *New Order*, p. 73.

85  *Ibid*. From research data on remittances published in *al-Ahram*, it appears that 44 percent of remittances in 1981 were channeled to the black market. See: 'Abd al-Rahman 'Aql, "Mudhakhirat al-Misriyyin fil-Kharij, ayna Tadhhab . . . ila man?," *al-Ahram*, November 21, 1982, p. 3.

86  Alice Brinton, "Up to 3.5 million Workers Abroad," *IHT*, June 7, 1983.

87  "War against Black Market Continues," *Mideast Markets*, April 30, 1984. *Al-Qabas*, July 10, 1984 (*Hasav*, August 3, 1984), also mentioned in July 1984 that capital remitted to the free market amounted to 3 billion dollars annually. See also: *FT Survey, Egypt*, June 25, 1984, p. iv.

88  See: *al-Ahram*, August 13, 1983, p. 3, which reported that total wages for 3.4 million expatriates amounted to $7 billion, of which $2.5 b. was transferred to Egypt. There is no evidence that all remittances were made to the free market, because migrants need some of their wages for living expenses in the Gulf States. See also: *al-Ahram*, December 28, 1983, which noted that out of $5 billion earnings, Egyptian migrants remitted only $2.85 billion through official channels. See also: McDermatt, "Egypt," p. 156.

89  'Abd al-Rahman 'Aql, *al-Ahram*, as quoted above.

## 4  Aid Policy of the Arab Oil Countries toward Egypt: Containment and the Construction of Arab Unity

1   Ali Rustum, "The Use of Oil as a Weapon of Diplomacy: A Case Study of Saudi Arabia" (Ph.D. dissertation: The American University, 1975), p. 122; Norman C. Walpole *et al.*, *Area Handbook for Saudi Arabia* (Washington, D.C.: American University, 1971), p. 164.

2   *MEED*, July 9, 1965, p. 318.

3   M. Field, *A Hundred Million Dollars a Day* (London: Sidgwick and Jackson, 1975), p. 150.

4   Egyptian teachers comprised about 85 percent of all teachers in Libya. On Egyptian aid to Libya, see: IBRD, *The Economic Development of Libya* (report of a mission organized by the IBRD at the request of the government of Libya. Baltimore: Johns Hopkins Press, 1960), pp. 48–9, 263. On aid to Abu Dhabi, see: Abdullah Omran Taryam, *The Establishment of the United Arab Emirates 1950–85* (London: Croom Helm, 1987), pp. 18–19. For further details, see chapter 3.

5   Nadav Safran, *Saudi Arabia: The Ceaseless Quest for Security* (Cambridge, MA: Harvard University Press, 1985), pp. 103–4, 105.

6   *Ibid.*, p. 96.

7   Saudi Arabia complained to the UN about these attacks. See correspondence between Saudi delegates and the UN Secretary-General in following documentation: UN, Security Council, S/7749, February 2, 1967; S/7793, February 27, 1967; S/7816, March 11, 1967; S/7842, April 6, 1967; S/7889, May 17, 1967; see also UN, Economic and Social Council, E/CN. 4/941, April 7, 1967.

8   Safran, *Saudi Arabia*, p. 121; *UPI* (Jedda), February 5, 1967.

9   See: A. I. Dawisha, "The Role of Propaganda in Egypt's Arab Policy 1955–1967," *International Relations* (vol. 5, November 1975), p. 898.

10  A. M. Said and M. W. Wenner, "Modern Islamic Reformed Movements. The Muslim Brotherhood in Contemporary Egypt," *MES* (vol. 36, 1982), p. 347; Hamied Ansari, *Egypt. The Stalled Society* (New York: SUNY, 1986), p. 93.

11  F. Shehab, "Kuwait: A Super Affluent Society," *Foreign Affairs* (April 1964), p. 474.

12  David Holden, *Sand-Glass. Stormy South Arabia* (Hebrew), (IDF: Ma'arachot, 1967), pp. 204–5. On relations between Kuwait and Iraq during the former country's first years of independence see: Martha Ducas: *Azmat al-Kuwayt: al-'Alaqat al-Kuwaytiyya al-'Iraqiyya 1961–1963* (Beirut: Dar al-Nahar, 1973); Harold and Richard Dickson, *Kuwait and her Neighbours* (London: Allen and Unwin, 1968).

13  IBRD, Kuwait, *op. cit.*, p. 147. On Egyptian dominance in Kuwait and its implications on the forming of that country's public opinion, see also: Tawfiq Farah *et.al.*, "Alienation and Expatriate Labor in Kuwait," *Journal of South Asian and Middle Eastern Studies* (vol. 4, no. 1, fall 1980), p. 25.

14  IBRD, *The Economic Development of Kuwait* (Baltimore: Johns Hopkins Press, 1965), p. 25; Ragaei El-Mallakh, *Economic Development and Regional Cooperation.* Kuwait (Chicago: The University of Chicago Press, 1970), p. 173.

15  Holden, *Sand-Glass*, pp. 207–8.

16  This occurred at the first Arab oil congress, which convened in Cairo in April 1959. See: Field, *A Hundred Million Dollars,* pp. 4, 149–50. Kuwaiti citizenship laws determined that one could attain Kuwaiti citizenship in one of the following cases: a foreign resident living in Kuwait for 40 years, his children and grandchildren; the wives of Kuwaiti citizens; and in certain cases, Arabs living in Kuwait for ten years as of 1959 or foreigners living there for 15 years. Furthermore, in exceptional cases, the individual must have a profession vital to the Kuwaiti economy, should be fluent in Arabic (reading and writing), economically independent and with a clean record. In 1970, only 50 Arabs received Kuwaiti citizenship. On the strict laws for foreigners, see: *MER 1968,* p. 617. On citizenship laws, see: *al-Ra'y al-'Amm*, February 5, 1969; March 3, 1970.

17  *Al-Ahram*, January 19, 1964; Leila S. Kadi, *Arab Summit Conferences and the Palestine Problem, 1936–1950, 1946–1966* (Beirut, 1966), p. 101.

18  Kadi, *Arab Summit Conferences*, p. 138. On Kuwaiti aid in general in the 1960s, see: Y. S. F. Al-Sabah, *The Oil Economy of Kuwait* (London: Kegan Paul International, 1980), pp. 75–9.

19  On this affair, see: *al-Ahram*, March 15, 1965.

20  See, for example, attacks by Heikal – Nasser's mouthpiece – on the regimes of Syria, Saudi Arabia, Jordan and Lebanon: *al-Ahram*, August 21 and 28, 1964: April 18, 1965. See also: *Ruz al-Yusuf*, December 16, 1963, which attacked the Syrian, Saudi and Jordanian regimes.

21  *NYT News Service* (Cairo), 1965 (n.d.), as gleaned from the "Misr-Kuwayt" file, *al-Ahram* Archives in Cairo.

22  *Al-Ra'y al-'Amm* (Kuwait), February 2, 1966; *al-Ahram*, February 3, 1966; *al-Muharrir* (Egypt), April 26, 1966. *MEED*, February 2, 1967, p. 100. By Western standards, the Kuwaiti National Assembly did not represent parliamentary democracy. Nevertheless, the Kuwaiti Assembly did have influence on the various steps taken by its ruler, such as: a reduction of 20 percent in his defence budget in 1962, and refusing to compromise with foreign oil companies, in January 1965. See: Holden, *Sand-Glass*, p. 204.

23  *MEED*, February 11, 1966, p. 62.

24  Egypt was in arrears with the reimbursement of its short-term debts, amounting to $200 million. See: *ibid.*, September 16, 1966, p. 440.

25  *Ibid.*, February 16, 1966, p. 142; *BBC*, February 11, 1967; *Keesing's Contemporary Archive* (*KCA*), May 6, 1967, pp. 22019, 21004.

26  The Egyptian government announced that it would not export any goods to Saudi Arabia before receiving payment in advance. On Egypt's steps, see: *al-Ahram*, February

11, 1967; *KCA*, May 6, 1967, p. 22019; *MEED*, February 16, 1967, p. 142; *BBC*, February 14, 1967.

27   *ARR* (1967), p. 83.

28   *Al-Ahram*, June 6, 1967. On the thaw in relations, see: Harold Jackson, "King Feisal gives Nasser Brotherly Backing," *Guardian*, May 24, 1967.

29   Riyad, p. 53.

30   *Al-Ahram*, August 31, 1967. On the annulment of sanctions, see: *al-Dustur* (Jordan), September 28, 1967.

31   David Holden and Richard Johns, *The House of Saud* (London: Sidgwick and Jackson, 1981), pp. 252–4. Holden and Johns noted that the meeting between Nasser and Feisal took place on August 31, 1969, and not the day before, as stated by *al-Ahram*. A few months before the June war, Sudan and Kuwait tried, unsuccessfully, to reach a similar agreement. See: *ARR* (1967), p. 103.

32   Mohammed Heikal, *The Road to Ramadan* (London: Collins, 1975), pp. 267–8. See following chapter for details of damages.

33   IBRD, *Current Economic Position and Prospects of the Arab Republic of Egypt* (December 30, 1972), p. iii.

34   IMF, document from the secretary of IMF to the members of the executive board, July 14, 1970.

35   Riyad, p. 51. Compare statement by Qaysuni, Minister of Planning, in early July 1967, when he indicated that the losses Egypt incurred by the stoppage of revenues from the Suez canal, tourism and oil amounted to $35 million per month, or $420 million annually (*The Times*, July 4, 1967, p. 4. But Riyad's statement was based on calculations made on the eve of the Summit conference, compared to Qaysuni's statement, made in early July and which turned out to be unfounded, according to other available sources.

36   Sela, *Unity within Separation. Arab Summit Conferences* (Jerusalem: Magnes, 1983), pp. 8–9.

37   Adeed I. Dawisha, "Saudi Arabia's Search for Security," in Charles Tripp (ed.), *Regional Security in the Middle East* (New York: St. Martin's Press, 1984), p. 4.

38   John Waterbury, *The Egypt of Nasser and Sadat. The Political Economy of Two Regimes* (Princeton: Princeton University Press, 1983), p. 415.

39   Fouad Ajami, "The Arab Triangle," *Foreign Policy* (no. 29, winter 1977–8), p. 100.

40   Nazli Choucri, *International Politics of Energy Interdependence: The Case of Petroleum* (Lexington, MA: Lexington books, 1976), p. 93.

41   Nadav Safran, "The War and the Future of the Arab–Israeli Conflict," *Foreign Affairs* (vol. 52, no. 2, January 1974), p. 220.

42   P. J. Vatikiotis, *Arab and Regional Politics in the Middle East* (New York: St. Martin's Press, 1984), p. 88.

43   Malcolm Kerr, *The Arab Cold War* (London: Oxford University Press, 1971), p. 139.

44   Safran, *Saudi Arabia*, pp. 122, 124; see also Kerr, *The Arab Cold War*, p. 139.

45   Michael C. Hudson, *Arab Politics: The Search for Legitimacy* (New York: Yale University Press, 1977), p. 2. For an in-depth discussion on this subject, see *Hudson*, *passim*, esp. pp. 1–30.

46   *Al-Ahram*, March 15, 1965.

47   In July 1967, Yamani, the Saudi Minister of Energy, declared that exploiting the oil weapon after the June 1967 war was negative. See: *MEES*, July 21, 1967. The boycott collapsed after a fortnight, when the oil countries decided on a selective boycott, which also folded after 90 days. Moreover the boycott imposed following the Suez affair of 1956 had no effect. In this connection, see also the statement of the Kuwaiti deputy Foreign Minister: *MEES*, August 11, 1972.

48  Sela, *Unity within Separation*, pp. 69, 71.
49  On the summit resolutions, see: *ibid.*, pp. 73–9.
50  *Al-Ahram*, October 14, 1967; *al-Haya*, October 15, 1967. The Egyptian banks only resumed operations in the second half of 1969. See: *MEED*, August 1, 1969, p. 977; November 11, 1969, p. 1481.
51  For example: Husayn al-Shafi'i, Nasser's envoy, who met four times with King Faysal in less than a month. *Al-Ahram*, October 31, 1967; November 1 and 3, 1967, as well as the meetings of Hasan 'Abbas Zaki, the Egyptian Minister of Economy, with Faysal. To this meeting he was accompanied also by the governor of the Egyptian Central Bank: *al-Ahram*, November 30, 1967.
52  *Al-Jumhuriyya*, December 2, 1967; *al-Ahram*, December 3, 1967.
53  *Jewish Chronicle*, January 26, 1968.
54  See: *al-Ahram*, November 15, 1969; December 4, 1969.
55  *MEED*, December 19, 1969. In 1968 Saudi Arabia's revenues from oil exports through the Tapline came to $100 million. See: *MEED*, June 6, 1969; *ARR*, June 16, 1969, p. 214. In September 1968, Faysal, in referring to aid, remarked: "It is our solemn duty to provide aid, we are prepared to sacrifice our blood, and the more so our wealth." See: *Radio Jedda*, September 17, 1968, as quoted by: *BBC*, September 19 and 25, 1968.
56  Statements by the Kuwaiti Minister of Finance, see interview with *al-Anwar*, June 9, 1968. On the discussion in the Kuwaiti National Council in January 1969, see: *al-Usbu' al-'Arabi*, January 6, 1969. On proposals to provide aid to the Palestinians with Egyptian and Jordanian financing see: *Al-Usbu' al-'Arabi*, *ibid.*: *al-Ra'y al-'Amm*, February 2, 1969; November 25, 1969; February 11, 1970; March 1, 1970. On putting the blame for aid that turned out to be detrimental to the Kuwaiti economy, see: *ibid.*, July 16, 1969; September 12, 1969; *Daily News* (Kuwait), November 14, 1969.
57  *Al-Usbu' al-'Arabi*, January 6, 1969.
58  This idea came up for discussion several times in the Kuwaiti press. See, for example, *Al-Usbu' al-'Arabi*, *ibid.*, *al-Ra'y al-'Amm*, February 2, 1969; November 25, 1969; February 11, 1970; March 1st, 1970; Kuwait also stopped all aid to Jordan, following the civil war in 1970 and renewed it only after the fighting had stopped.
59  *Al-Ra'y al-'Amm*, July 16, 1969; September 12, 1969; *Daily News*, November 14, 1969.
60  Interviews to *al-Anwar*, May 12, 1968; June 9, 1968; *al-Haqiqa*, June 12, 1968; *BBC*, June 14, 1968.
61  On the visit, see: *al-Ahram*, December 16–21, 1969.
62  Heikal, *Ramadan*, pp. 77–9. The National Front took responsibility for the sabotage. See: *MEED*, June 13, 1969.
63  IMF, document from the secretary to the members of the executive board, *Saudi Arabia – An Economic and Financial Survey* (December 3, 1973), p. 17; *ibid.*, *SM/75/157* (June 24, 1975), p. 10.
64  Saudi Arabia Monetary Agency (SAMA), *Annual Report 1390/91 and 1391/92 (1970/71 and 1971/72)*; IMF Report, *Saudi Arabia, no. SM/76/57* (March 26, 1976), p. 37. SAMA and IMF reports showed that up to the end of the 1974/5 fiscal year Saudi Arabia provided aid only to Arab countries.
65  *IMF document*, December 3, 1973, p. 52 and table no. 30, p. 53. In 1970 the balance of payments showed a surplus of slightly more than $100 million, and in subsequent years this surplus increased considerably. See: IMF Report, *Saudi Arabia, no. SM/75/175*, p. 34.
66  IMF, *Kuwait Recent Economic Development* (May 19, 1975), pp. 19, 25, 33.
67  IMF report, *Kuwait*, 1972, p. 29.
68  *Al-Haqiqa*, May 18, 1968.

69    Sela, *Unity within Separation*, p. 82.
70    "Khilaf al-Urdun wal-Kuwayt," *al-Hawadith* (no. 618, September 13, 1968), p. 9.
71    Sela, *Unity within Separation*, p. 89.
72    IMF, *Secretary Document*, July 14, 1979.
73    A letter from the Egyptian Minister of Economy to the administrative director of the International Monetary Fund, written on June 21, 1970. This letter was added as an appendix to IMF document, no. EBS/70/197.
74    *Al-Ahram*, September 5 and 9, 1969.
75    *Al-Muharrir*, October 6, 1969.
76    *NYT*, August 5 and 12, 1969.
77    Alvin Z. Rubinstein, *Red Star on the Nile* (Princeton: Princeton University Press, 1977), pp. 100–2.
78    On the Cairo–Riyadh axis, which he often mentioned in the 1970s, see: Ali E. Hillal Dessouki, "The New Arab Political Order: Implications for the 1980s," in Kerr and Yassin (eds.), *Rich and Poor States in the Middle East: Egypt and the New Arab Order* (Boulder, CO: Westview Press, 1982), pp. 319–48; Paul Jabber, "Oil, Arms, and Regional Diplomacy: Strategic Dimensions of the Saudi–Egyptian Relationship," in Kerr and Yassin (eds.), pp. 430–5.
79    William B. Quandt, *Saudi Arabia in the 1980s: Foreign Policy, Security, and Oil* (Washington, D.C.: The Brookings Institution, 1981), p. 15.
80    Heikal, *Ramadan*, pp. 119–20.
81    *Ibid.*, p. 120. On this affair, see also: Holden and Jones, *The House of Saud*, p. 392; Robert Lacey, *The Kingdom* (New York: Avon Books, 1982), p. 393.
82    A. H. Cordesman, *The Gulf and the Search for Strategic Stability* (Boulder, CO: Westview Press, 1984), p. 34.
83    *Washington Post*, February 22, 1977. In a personal interview with Tahsin Bashir in Cairo, he expounded on the extensive and close ties that existed between Kamal Adham, Ashraf Marwan, Sadat and liaison personnel of the CIA. As we will see in due course, according to him Sadat received "protocol presents" from Adham and other Saudi personalities. John Pass, who according to him was the head of the CIA in Egypt in the 1970s, afterwards worked for Kamal Adham, a member of the Saudi royal family.
84    Sela, *Unity within Separation*, p. 102.
85    Jamal Ali Zaharan, *Al-Siyasah al-Khariyya li-Misr, 1970–1981* (Cairo: Madbuli, 1987), p. 283; Safran, *Saudi*, p. 146; Rubinstein, p. 154 claimed that the visit took place in June and not in May.
86    Rubinstein, *Red Star on the Nile*, p. 154.
87    Sadat, *Those I Have known*, pp. 66–7. In the end, the planes never arrived. The reason for this, according to Sadat, was their bad state of repairs and high operation costs. Saudi Arabia bought this type of plane from the UK in 1966. See: *MEED*, January 7, 1966, p. 9.
88    Heikal, *Ramadan*, pp. 157–8.
89    *Ibid.*, p. 158.
90    Edward R. F. Sheehan, *The Arabs, Israelis and Kissinger* (New York, 1976), p. 65.
91    On the visit, the contract and the reaction of the Iraqi media, see: *al-Jumhuriyya* (Iraq), February 18, 1972; *al-Thawra* (Iraq), April 16, 1972: September 13, 1972; FBIS, *DR*, April 18, 1972.
92    See chronology of these visits, as given in: *MEJ* (1972), p. 434. On Prince Sultan's stopover in Cairo, on his return from Washington, see interview he granted to the Lebanese *al-Hawadith* in May 1980, as quoted by Zahran, *ibid.*, p. 284. On talks between Sadat and Sultan, see also Quandt, *Decade of Decisions*, p. 162.

93 Heikal, *Ramadan*, p. 194.

94 *Izvestia*, August 28, 1972. Russia accused the conservative states of driving a wedge between her and Egypt, even before the Russians were expelled. See: *Pravda*, August 18, 1971. These two sources were quoted by Hamied Ansari, *Egypt* (1986), comment 26, p. 283.

95 Saad El-Din el-Shadhli, *The Crossing of the Suez* (San Francisco: American Mideast Research, 1980), pp. 147–9.

96 Heikal, *Ramadan*, p. 184. Sadat wrote in his memoirs: "Of course, the Americans were astonished to hear of my decision on July 16, 1972, to expel the Soviet experts." See: Anwar Sadat, *The Story of My Life* (Jerusalem: Edanim, 1978), p. 216.

97 On relations between Egypt and the Soviet Union, see Sadat's books, *My Life*; Heikal, *Ramadan*; Heikal, *The Sphinx and the Commissar. The Rise and Fall of Soviet Influence in the Arab World* (Tel Aviv: Am Oved, 1981); Rubinstein, *Red Star on the Nile*; on descriptions of relations before the expulsion, see also: *al-Ahram*, December 3, 1976, p. 6; *Akhbar al-Yawm*, August 19, 1972; Fuad Matar, *Rusiya al-Nasiriyya wa-Misr al-Misriyya* (Beirut, 1972); Shimon Shamir, "The Reorientation of Egypt towards the United States – Dynamics of Decision Making on the Inter-Bloc Issue," from Itamar Rabinovitz and Haim Shaked (eds.), *The Middle East and the United States* (published by Am Oved and the Shiloah Institute, 1980), pp. 278–80; M. M. El Hussini, *Soviet–Egyptian Relations, 1945–1985* (London: Macmillan, 1987); *NYT Magazine*, August 6, 1972, p. 11.

98 Sadat in a speech on May 1, 1979, in Safaja.

99 Rubinstein, *Red Star on the Nile*, p. 241.

100 No details on this view, see: Sheehan, *The Arabs, Israelis and Kissinger*, p. 65; Cordesman, *The Gulf and the Search*, pp. 333–4; Dale R. Tahtinen, *National Security Challenge to Saudi-Arabia* (Washington, D.C.: American Enterprise Institute for Public Policy Research, 1978), p. 8.

101 Personal interview conducted by author with Tahsin Bashir, Cairo, July 1987.

102 Rustum, "The Use of Oil as a Weapon of Diplomacy," p. 126.

103 Bahgat Korany, "Dependence Financiere et Comportement International," *Revue Française de Science Politique* (vol. 28, no. 6, December 1978), pp. 1078–9.

104 At this conference – February 15, 1971 – with the participation of the oil countries and oil companies, the oil producers decided to raise prices by 35 cents a barrel, and they agreed on a creeping price rise for oil, at the rate of 3 percent annually, to compensate for inflation. On the agreement see : Shukri Ghanem, *OPEC: The Rise and Fall of an Exclusive Club* (London: KPI, 1986), pp. 126–8.

105 Shadhli, *The Crossing of the Suez*, pp. 167–9.

106 Riyad, pp. 234–5; Shadhli, *The Crossing of the Suez*, pp. 106–9.

107 For details on this plan, see: Shadhli, pp. 106–9.

108 *Ibid.*, p. 109.

109 On this see: *ibid.*, pp. 122–5.

110 Adeed Dawisha, *Saudi Arabia's Search for Security* (*Adelphi Papers*, no. 158. London: IISS, 1979), p. 5.

111 *MEED*, May 4, 1973, p. 515.

112 On the various visits and Sadat's visit to Saudi Arabia, see: *Al-Usbu' al-'Arabi*, September 3, 1973, p. 21; *MEED*, May 18, 1973, p. 575; *ARR*, May 1, 1973, p. 200; June 16, 1973, p. 269; July 1, 1973, p. 293; July 16, 1973, p. 326, 340; August 16, 1973, p. 363, 372; September 16, 1973, p. 410.

113 Bahgat Korany, "The Glory That Was? The Pan-Arab, Pan-Islamic Alliance Decisions, October 1973," *International Political Science Review* (vol. 5, no. 1, 1984), p. 60.

114 Heikal, *Ramadan*, p. 268. On the agreement to exploit the oil weapon, see also Sheehan, *The Arabs, Israelis and Kissinger*, p. 82; *al-Hawadith*, September 30, 1973; *ARR*, September 1, 1973, p. 387. For Sadat's version of this visit, see: Anwar el-Sadat, *Those I Have Known* (New York: Continuum, 1984), pp. 69–70.

115 *Al-Hawadith*, August 30, 1973.

116 *US News and World Report*, September 10, 1973, p. 57.

117 *Ibid.*, September 30, 1973.

118 R. D. Mclaurin *et al.*, *Foreign Policy Making in the Middle East: Domestic Influence on Policy in Egypt, Iraq, Israel and Syria* (New York: Praeger, 1977), p. 9.

119 Heikal, *Ramadan*, p. 268.

120 A summary of the history of decisions for and against using the oil as a diplomatic weapon, see: Pierre Terzian, *OPEC: The Inside Story* (London: Red Books, 1985).

121 *ARR*, September 1, 1973, p. 387.

122 On the contacts of the delegation, see: Sayyid Mar'i, *Awraq Siyasiyya* (Cairo: Dar al-Ahram, 1979), vol. 3, pp. 741–9. On the Saudi stand *vis-à-vis* the oil boycott, see also Korany, "The Glory That Was," pp. 47–74.

123 Daniel Crecilius, "Saudi Arabian-Egyptian Relations," *International Studies* (vol. 14, 1975), p. 580.

124 Mar'i, *Awraq Siyasiyya* , vol. 3, pp. 743–6.

125 For detailed figures of aid, see chapter 1.

126 *Al-Anwar*, November 28, 1975, p. 1.

127 For an in-depth review of the Arab Marshall Plan, see: Sayyid Mar'i, *Likay Narbah al-Mustaqbal: al-Mashru' al-'Arabi lil-Tanmiya* (Cairo: Dar al-Ma'arif, n.d.), esp. pp. 138–50. See also interview he gave to Ibrahim Nafi', *al-Ahram*, May 22, 1975, p. 3.

128 See declaration by Egypt's Minister of Finance, *al-Ahram*, August 15, 1975; see also: *FT*, August 22, 1975.

129 A preliminary agreement was signed on September 1, 1975. For the agreement, see: Israel, Ministry of Foreign Affairs, *Documents*, vol. 3, pp. 281–6.

130 On the Saudi dilemma, see: Quandt, *Saudi Arabia in the 1980s*, p. 112.

131 Holden and Jones, *The House of Saud*, p. 422.

132 Sela, *Unity with Separation*, p. 142.

133 *Al-Qabas*, October 7, 1975.

134 For the text of the Egyptian announcement, see: "Israel, Ministry of Foreign Affairs," *Israel Foreign Relations. Selected Documents, 1947–1974*, ed. Meron Medzini (Jerusalem, 1976), vol. 2, pp. 1054–5.

135 *ARR*, October 16, 1973, p. 478. On resolution no. 242 of November 22, 1967, see: "Israel, Ministry of Foreign Affairs," *Documents*, vol. 2, pp. 824–30.

136 *Daily News* (Kuwait), September 20, 1975.

137 *Reuters*, November 13, 1975.

138 Personal interview with Tahsin Bashir in Cairo, 1987.

139 *MENA*, March 25, 1976, as printed in: Jumhuriyyat Misr al-'Arabiyya, al-Hay'a al-'Amma lil-Isti'lamat, *Khutub wa-Ahadith al-Ra'is Muhammad Anwar al-Sadat* (Cairo, 1976), vol. 6. Hereinafter: *Sadat's Speeches*, by years.

140 *NYT*, February 26, 1976.

141 *Akhbar al-Yawm*, July 2, 1976.

142 Nabil Sabbagh, "Tasawwurat hawla Hay'at al-Khalij lil-Tanmiya," *al-Ahram al-Iqtisadi* (September 1, 1976), pp. 10–13; *Al-Akhbar*, November 15, 1976; *Akhir Sa'a*, October 27, 1976; *MEED*, October 15, 1976; December 31, 1976, p. 17.

143 *Al-Musawwar*, December 31, 1976, p. 26.

144 Personal interview with 'Abduh Mubashir, Cairo, January 27, 1988.

145 Sela, *Unity with Separation*, p. 160.

146 *Kuwait Times*, January 10, 1977; *MEED*, January 21, 1977, p. 19.

147 *Ibid.*, two sources.

148 *The Banker*, March 1975, p. 299.

149 *An-Nahar Arab Report and Memo*, January 26, 1978, pp. 5–6.

150 Jaber in Kerr, *The Arab Cold War*, p. 429.

151 Fiscal year 1980 International Security Assistance Authorization. 1980 Foreign Assistance Request (United States Senate, Committee on Foreign Relations, FY 1980. 96th Congress, 1st session, Friday, March 2, 1979. Washington, D.C.: GPO, 1979), p. 158.

152 Personal interview, Cairo, 1986.

153 Personal interview, Cairo, 1987.

154 *Washington Post*, August 15, 1976.

155 John Waterbury, *Hydropolitics of the Nile Valley* (Syracuse: Syracuse University Press, 1979), pp. 172–3.

156 *ARR*, August 1, 1974, p. 337.

157 These issues were discussed in a personal interview with Mansur Hasan, Sadat's Minister of Information and a businessman who enjoyed close ties with the oil-producing countries, Cairo, 1987. In this context, see also: Kerr, in Kerr and Yassin (eds.), *Rich and Poor States in the Middle East*, pp. 9–10; Gad G. Gilbar, "Wealth, Want, and Arab Unity: Saudi–Egyptian Relations, 1962–1985," *The Jerusalem Journal of International Relations* (vol. 9, no. 3, 1987), p. 76.

158 US Department of Commerce, *Foreign Economic Trends and their Implication for the US, Iraq* (Washington D.C., June 1986, FET 86–50. Prepared by the American Embassy, Baghdad), p. 6.

159 Kamal Hasan 'Ali, *Muharibun wa-Mufawidun* (Cairo: Markaz al-Ahram lil-Tarjama wal-Nashr, 1986), p. 75. There are many evaluations on the extent of aid granted to Iraq by the oil countries. In several cases, the latter made their own announcements on aid they had given to Iraq, like in the case of the *Kuwaiti News Agency* on April 21, 1981, when it reported that Kuwait had loaned Iraq $2 billion, free of interest, "for the rehabilitation of positions damaged in the war." See: FBIS, *DR*, April 23, 1981; *FT*, April 22, 1981. Hasan 'Ali, p. 99, stated that in September 1980 Kuwait granted Iraq an interest-free loan of $4 billion. But in most cases the oil countries did not refer to details of their aid to Iraq, and there are many estimates, given for various periods. Following are a few estimates: Eilts noted that, since the beginning of the war until late 1983, Saudi Arabia alone granted Iraq around $12 billion. See: Hermann Frederick Eilts, "Saudi Arabian Foreign Policy toward the Gulf States and Southwest Asia," in Hafeez Malik (ed.), *International Security in Southwest Asia* (New York: Praeger, 1984), p. 82. Gur, quoting from IDF Intelligence Branch data, said that Iraq received $16 billion just in 1981. See: Avraham Gur, "The Oil Weapon – Reality or Myth?" (in his MA thesis, Tel Aviv University, July 1982), p. 30. In July 1983, *MEED* reported (in a special review) that the oil countries, primarily Saudi Arabia, granted Iraq $20 billion. The yearbook on the 1984 military balance in the Middle East indicates that during the first two years Iraq received $20–25 billion from the oil countries. See: Mark Heller (ed.), *The Military Balance in the Middle East 1984* (Tel Aviv: The Jaffe Center for Strategic Studies, Tel Aviv University, 1985), p. 39. Hasan 'Ali specified a sum of $ 22 billion up to the end of 1983, and Anthony named a figure of $35 billion granted by the GCC states to Iraq up to the fall of 1984, of which Saudi Arabia donated about two thirds. See: Hasan 'Ali, p. 65; John Duke Anthony, "The Gulf Cooperation Council," *Orbis*, vol. 28 (Fall 1984), p. 447. King indicated that aid given as "loans," amounted to at least $35 billion up to

early 1987. See: Ralph King, *Adelphi Papers,* p. 33. Besides aid in cash, the conservative oil countries assisted Iraq by providing port facilities – as some of the ports were closed – by transferring goods, and by selling oil on its account from the neutral region. Since 1983, the oil countries sold on its account about 0.3 million barrels of oil per diem. See: *al-Majalla,* no. 208 (February 4–10, 1984), pp. 45–7.

160 In a personal interview with Mustafa Khalil, the former Egyptian Prime Minister (Cairo, September 22, 1986), this matter came up.

161 As came up in personal interviews with them in Cairo.

162 The word was stressed, to emphasize that these personalities, like Tahsin Bashir, were not hostile to Sadat or condemning his work. They discussed the facts from a sober-minded view on the subject, and not out of opposition to Sadat.

163 See the words of the Egyptian Minister of Defense, 'Abd al-Ghani al-Jamasi, as published in the *New York Times*, June 11, 1978, p. 5; interviews with the Minister of Defense, Abu Ghazala in the following places: *al-Musawwar,* June 4, 1982, pp. 18–21 and October 29, 1982, pp. 16–19; *October*, December 27, 1981; *Armed Force Journal International*, September 1981, pp. 46–51.

164 Further details on this affair, and on general relations between Sadat and Sabri, see: Mohamed H. Heikal, *The Sphinx and the Commissar: The Rise and Fall of Soviet Influence in the Middle East* (NY: Harper & Row, 1978), p. 220; Anwar Al-Sadat, *In Search of Identity: An Autobiography* (NY: Harper & Row, 1978), p. 216; Rubinstein, *Red Star on the Nile*, p. 149: P. J. Vatikiotis, "Egypt's Politics of Conspiracy," *Survey* (vol. 18, no. 2, 1972), p. 89. Further attempts to remove him, see: *NYT*, July 29, 1984; *US News and World Report*, June 6, 1976; *Middle East Intelligence Survey*, May 1, 1973 and April 15, 1974.

165 See, for example, Tohami: Ibrahim A. Karawan, "Egypt's Defence Policy," in Stephanie G. Neuman (ed.), *Defence Planning in Less-Industrialized States. The Middle East and South Asia* (Lexington: Lexington Books, 1984), p. 124, note no. 38, and see p. 160. On Sadat's fears of communism and the Soviets, see also: *NYT*, January 22, 1977, p. 3; *al-Jadid* (Lebanon), May 7, 1971. *Department of State Bulletin* (vol. 81, no. 2054, September 1981), p. 57. *WP*, August 1, 1977; *The Middle East*, September 1977, pp. 36–40; Efraim Karsh, *The Cautious Bear. Soviet military engagement in Middle East Wars in the post-1967 Era* (JCSS study no. 3, Tel Aviv: the *Jerusalem Post* and Westview Press, 1985), p. 82. Jamasi expressed his concern about Soviet and Cuban activities in Ethiopia, which, he said, were aimed against Sudan and could become "an indirect threat to Egypt." Jamasi added that the USSR had sent sophisticated arms to Libya, suggesting that the Russians were stepping up activity in that region, as the Libyans were not capable of operating those arms by themselves. See: Drew Middleton, "Egyptian Aide Worried over Soviet's Moves in Africa," *NYT*, June 11, 1978, p. L5. Abu Ghazala, in an interview to *al-Musawwar*, October 8, 1982, declared that it was the the USSR's goal to encircle Egypt with a belt of pro-Soviet countries, and to use Libya, Ethiopia and South Yemen to isolate Egypt from Africa. Abu Ghazala expressed his deep concern with the enormous amounts of arms in the possession of these countries, "far above their absorption capacity," as well as with the Soviet and Cuban forces based in these countries. He said: "Egypt is in the very critical position of being surrounded by a threat from the west and the south." See his interviews to *October*, December 27, 1982; *Armed Force Journal International*, September 1981, p. 49. On the riots, see the official press in the week following the food riots. For an external description of the riots, see *The Times* (London), January 20, 1977, and also below.

166 *MENA*, May 15, 1978, as cited by: FBIS, *DR*, May 15, 1978.

167 A Senate delegation headed by Claiborne Pell visited Cairo on November 24–25, 1978,

and met with Sadat, Mustafa Khalil and Sufi Abu Talib – the spokesman of the National Assembly. Claiborne Pell, *Visit to Eastern Europe and the Middle East by the Senate Delegation to the Twenty-fourth Meeting of the North Atlantic Assembly* (a report to the Committee on Foreign Relations, United States Senate, 96th congress, 1st session. Washington, D.C.: GPO, May 1979), p. 25.

168 About the common concept of the communist threat, see: R. K. Ramazani, "Security in the Persian Gulf," *Foreign Affairs* (Spring 1979), p. 822.

169 Charles H. Percy, *The Middle East* (a report to the Committee on Foreign Relations, United States Senate. 94th congress, 1st session. Washington, D.C.: GPO, April 21, 1975), p. 60. Hoagland stated that Saudi Arabia had transferred $100 million to Democratic Yemen via Egypt. See: Jim Hoagland, "Shah's Force Jolted in Oman," *Washington Post*, December 16, 1974. The island of Prim is located in the entrance to the Indian Ocean, and Saudi Arabia and the US feared that if the USSR had bases in Aden, Prim, and Mogadishu-Somalia, they could easily control all shipping movements passing through the Red Sea and the oil lines to East Africa. The fact that Egypt occupied Prim made this more difficult. Egypt's location on this island was an additional advantage for the Arabs *vis-à-vis* Israel. The situation gave Egypt control of Israel's eastern sea lines, enabling it to impose a naval embargo, and damaging Israel's position in Sharm al-Sheikh. See: Charles Percy, *The Middle East* (a report by Senator Charles H. Percy to the Committee on Foreign Relations, United States Senate, April 21, 1975. Washington, D.C.: GPO, 1975), p. 60.

170 Sadat declared more than once that any aggression against Sudan would be considered as aggression against Egypt. Moreover, Abu Ghazala said in an interview in June 1982 that Egypt would intervene with its military if Sudan was endangered. See: *al-Musawwar*, June 4, 1982.

171 On the food riots, see Egyptian press one week later, and in chapter 5. For a description of the riots by Western researchers, see: Harold Alderman *et al.*, *Egypt's Food Subsidy and Rationing System: A Description* (research report no. 34. Washington, D.C.: International Food Policy Research Institute, October 1982).

172 *Al-Siyasa* (Kuwait), February 8, 1977. Waterbury indicated that the visit took place immediately after the riots. See: Waterbury, *Egypt under the Nasser and Sadat Regimes*, p. 419.

173 See, for example, Tawfiq al-Hakim, *al-Ahram*, January 20, 1977. See also in this volume, chapter 5.

174 *Al-Ra'y al-'Amm*, January 20, 1977.

175 *Al-Wahda* (Abu Dhabi), January 20, 1977.

176 Waterbury, *Egypt under the Nasser and Sadat Regimes*, p. 419.

177 *Al-Ra'y* (Kuwait), January 25, 1977.

178 *MEED*, February 25, 1977, p. 18; *The Times* (London), Feb. 28, 1977. Qatar's Minister of Finance came to Cairo earlier to discuss increase of aid. See: *IHT*, January 26, 1977.

179 *MEED*, April 1, 1977, p. 17; *An-Nahar Arab Report and Memo*, February 20, 1978, p. 4.

180 IMF, *ARE-Recent Economic Development* (SM/79/53, February 20, 1979), p. 8; *MEED*, November 11, 1977, p. 18.

181 *Al-Sayyad* (Lebanon), April 21, 1977; *MEED*, April 15, 1977, p. 17. On the deposits in connection with the Arab economic boycott of Egypt, see chapter 5.

182 *MEED*, April 15, 1977, p. 17.

183 See Sadat's speech to the Arab Socialist Union – Egyptian ruling party (ASU) on July 16, 1977, as published by Egypt's Ministry of Information, *Sadat's Speeches* (vol. 7, 1977). See also: *NYT*, July 17, 1977, p. 13; *MEED*, July 22, 1977, p. 15.

184 Adlai E. Stevenson (senator), *The Middle East: 1976.* A Report to the Committee on Banking Housing and Urban Affairs, United States Senate on His Study Mission to the Middle East Conducted Between February 10 and February 25, 1976. Washington, D.C.: GPO, April 1976, p. 4.

185 *MEED*, December 31, 1977, pp. 27–30.

186 See his speech to ASU, on July 16, 1977, as quoted by: *MEED*, July 22, 1977, p. 15. See also: *ARR*, March 1, 1976, p. 144.

187 *Department of State Bulletin* (vol. 76, June 27, 1977), p. 673.

188 See interview to *al-Safir*, January 9, 1980.

189 *NYT*, June 22, 1979; *al-Nahar*, July 15, 1980. Dayan wrote in his memoirs that Sadat told him that he decided to visit Jerusalem only after he had left Saudi Arabia. See: Moshe Dayan, *Ha-Lanetzah Tokhal Herev: Sihot ha-Shalom, Reshamim Ishiyim* (Hebrew), (Jerusalem: Edanim, 1981), p. 107. Saudi officials indicated that if Sadat had consulted with them they would have been in an awkward position: opposing his initiative would have created tension between Sadat and the Saudis, and if they had supported him, the leaders of the confrontation states would have considered them as cooperating with Sadat. See: Salim al-Luzi, *al-Hawadith*, December 9, 1977, p. 4. In this connection see: Jacob Goldberg, "Saudi Arabia and the Egyptian-Israeli Peace Process," *Middle East Review* (vol. 18, no. 4, 1986), p. 26. Tahsin Bashir stated that Kamal Adham, Faysal's brother-in-law and chief of Saudi Intelligence, had advance knowledge of Sadat's initiative, but he did not report it to the Saudi leaders. Adham, according to Bashir, apparently did not believe that Sadat would actually do this and so he did not report it, for which he paid by being dismissed. At the same time, Adham did not lose his influence in Saudi policy, as his brother-in-law replaced him. Also Haber *et al.* wrote in their book that Adham knew about the move from Sadat, but in their opinion he did not report it to the Saudis, as he was afraid to hurt relations between the two countries. See: Eitan Haber, Ehud Ya'ari and Ze'ev Schiff, *The Year of the Dove. The Story behind Peace* (Hebrew), (Tel Aviv: Zemora, Bitan, Modan, 1980), pp. 52–5.

190 *Wall Street Journal*, January 27, 1978, p. 1.

191 Cyrus Vance, *Hard Choices. Critical Years in America's Foreign Policy* (New York: Simon and Schuster, 1983), p. 195.

192 Fahd in an interview to *al-Ra'y al-'Amm*, March 9, 1978. Further discussion on this subject, see article by Goldberg, "Saudi Arabia and the Egyptian–Israeli Peace Process," *Middle East Review* (vol. 18, no. 4, 1986), and also: *MECS* 1976/77, pp. 88, 580–2; 1977/78, pp. 165–7; *NYT*, March 10, 1978, p. 16 (S2). On Fahd's attempts to arbitrate a compromise between Egypt and Syria, see: *al-Nahar*, August 29, 1978. On the Arab countries' approach in general to the peace process, see: Jiryis Sabri, "The Arab World at Crossroad: An Analysis of the Arab Opposition to the Sadat Initiative," *Journal of Palestine Studies* (vol. 7, no. 2, winter 1978).

193 Jonathan C. Randal, *Washington Post*, January 13, 1978, p. 20: David E. Long, "Saudi Foreign Policy and the Arab–Israeli Peace Process: The Fahd (Arab) Peace Plan," in Willard A. Beling (ed.), *Middle East Peace Plans* (New York: St. Martin's Press, 1986), p. 60: *NYT*, June 29, 1978, p. 25. In this connection, see also: *al-'Ukaz* (Jedda), April 9, 1979; Sela, *Unity within Separation*, pp. 159–61.

194 *Al-'Ukaz*, December 8, 1977, p. 1; *al-Safir*, December 7, 1977: *Radio Riyad*, December 7, 1977, as quoted by: FBIS, *DR*, December 7, 1977.

195 Interview to *al-Riyad*, December 21, 1977, as cited by Goldberg, "Saudi Arabia and the Egyptian–Israeli Peace Process," p. 26.

196 Muslim Students Following the Law of the Imam, *Documents from the U.S. Espionage Den* (vol. 54, n.p., n.d.), p. 94. (hereafter: *Seized Documents* from the American Embassy

in Teheran). In the end, Egypt cancelled the deal, but the State Depratment's report specified that the cancellation reflected Sadat's certainty in the first quarter of 1979 that Saudi Arabia would finance the deal.

197 On the planes affair, see below. On aid from the Gulf Fund and from the Khartoum and Rabat summits, see in chapter 1.

198 As to the difficulties, see the memoirs by Weizman, Dayan, Carter and Brzezhinski

199 *NYT*, August 3, 1978, p. 6.

200 On preparations for the summit, see: Sela, *Unity within Separation*, pp. 169–71.

201 Vance, *Hard Choices*, p. 229.

202 Quoted by: FBIS, *DR*, October 3, 1978, p. C3.

203 *BBC*, October 15, 1978.

204 *Al-Riyad*, October 26, 1978.

205 *Al-Qabas*, October 27, 1978. Same subject, see: FBIS, *DR*, October 31, 1978.

206 *Washington Post*, October 29, 1978; FBIS, *DR*, October 25, 1978.

207 Jimmy Carter, *Keeping Faith: Memoirs of a President* (New York: Bantam Books, 1982), p. 408.

208 On discussions at the summit, see: Sela, *Unity within Separation*, pp. 159–80.

209 *Al-Safir*, November 6, 1978. Sela specified that the fund's assets came to $3.6 billion. Sela, *Unity within Separation*, p. 172. From data provided to OECD by the oil countries it appears that out of this sum Saudi Arabia pledged $1 billion a year, with the following breakdown: Syria – $589 million, Jordan – $357 million and the PLO – $114 million. UAE pledged $400 million, of which: $212 million to Syria, $143 million to Jordan, $46 million to the PLO. Kuwait pledged $487 million, but no breakdown was given. See: OECD, *Aid from OPEC countries* (Paris: OECD, 1983), pp. 44, 55, 63. Sela gave slightly different figures, according to which Saudi Arabia committed $1 billion, Kuwait – $550 m., UAE – $450 m., Iraq – $500 m., Algeria – $250 m., Qatar – $250 m., Libya – $550 m. See: Sela, *Unity within Separation*, pp. 172–3.

210 *Al-Dustur*, November 19, 1978; *ARR*, November 1, 1978, p. 802.

211 Carter did not explain the term "directly ." See: Carter, *Keeping Faith*, pp. 410–11.

212 C. Pell, *Report to the Committee on Foreign Relations of the American Senate, Visit To Eastern Europe and the Middle East by The Senate Delegation To The 24th Meeting of the North Atlantic Assembly* (United States Senate, Washington, D.C.: GPO, May 1979), p. 25.

213 *Radio Cairo*, December 30, 1978, as quoted by: FBIS, *DR*, January 2, 1979, p. C2.

214 Above-mentioned testimonies, February 1979.

215 Zbigniew Brzezhinski, *Power and Principle: Memoirs of the National Security Adviser, 1977–1981* (New York: Farrar, Straus and Giroux, 1983), p. 286.

216 *Newsweek*, March 26, 1979; *NYT*, March 31, 1979.

217 Sela, *Unity within Separation*, p. 184.

218 Y. Lucas (ed.), *Documents on the Israeli–Palestinian Conflict 1967–1983* (London: Cambridge University Press, 1984), pp. 232–6.

219 *Ibid.*

220 *FT*, April 20, 1979.

221 The Syrian threat, see: *Syrian News Agency*, March 28, 1979, as quoted by Sela, *Unity within Separation*, p. 184; the Iraqi threat, see: *al-Thawra* (Iraq), March 23, 1979: *NYT*, April 1, 1979.

222 Quandt, *Saudi Arabia in the 1980s*, pp. 17–18.

223 Foreign Affairs and National Defence Division, Saudi Arabia and the United States, p. 55. This testimony was also reported in the *Washington Post*, April 12, 1979.

224 *NYT*, May 8, 1979.

225 *Al-'Ukaz*, January 20, 1979.

226 The Israeli cabinet ratified the peace treaty and its appendices on March 19, 1979. The next day Begin presented the text to the Knesset and asked for its approval. See Begin's speech: Israel, Foreign Ministry, *Documents*, vol. 5, pp. 665–85. The Knesset discussed the peace agreement for two days, with the particpation of 108 members out of 120. On March 22, 1979, 95 voted for the peace agreement, 2 abstained and 3 were absent. On March 26, 1979, the peace agreement between Egypt and Israel was signed. The text of the agreement *ibid.*, pp. 696–711.

227 Comments by Saudi personalities on this subject, see: J. K. Cooly, "Iran, the Palestinian and the Gulf," *Foreign Affairs* (vol. 57, no. 4, 1979), p. 1027. Similar concern was expressed by Saudi officials in the early 1970s. See: *al-Hawadith*, April 27, 1973. In July 1979, Arafat said: "We own a part of this oil," see: *al-Safir*, July 23, 1979. For frther comments by Arafat, see: *Shu'un Filastiniyya*, January 1980.

228 Heikal, *al-Anwar*, May 23, 1977.

229 *Ibid.*, on the Jerusalem problem, see also: *MECS* 1976/77, p. 581.

230 Anis Mansur, *October*, October 21, 1979, p. 8.

231 *Al-Hawadith*, April 13, 1979, p. 14.

232 On the controversy, see Jim Hoagland's article, *Washington Post*, April 15, 1979. Hoagland indicated that Fahd's position on this subject had weakened.

233 The Saudis denied there was a dispute. On this affair, see: Safran, *Saudi Arabia*, pp. 280, 306, 312.

234 Safran, *Saudi Arabia*, p. 264; Sela, 187; John Law, *Arab Investors: Who They Are, What They Buy and Where*, New York: Chase World Information Corporation, vol. 2, 1981, p. 10.

235 A memorandum from the Secretary of State which was sent to American Embassies in the Middle East and in several Western capitals, May 4, 1979, as appears in documents seized from the American Embassy in Teheran, p. 50.

236 Relations between Israel and African countries continued secretly after 1973 (mainly in the defense sector), in spite of broken-off diplomatic relations. See: David Blumberg, "Bilateral Relations in the Absence of Diplomatic Ties: Africa and Israel in the post-1973 Era" (Senior Thesis, Harvard University, 1981); *CSM*, December 27, 1982.

237 About forgiving debts, the parties corresponded via the IMF. See personal interview with Alfred Atherton – the American ambassador in Egypt from 1979 to 1983. Tel Aviv, October 30, 1986.

238 Data received from the economic attaché at the American Embassy in Cairo, and from Egyptian politicians, who wished to remain anonymous. Personal interviews in Cairo, 1986–7. This figure is also mentioned in data on Egypt's debts to the oil countries in ECB and IMF reports. For details see chapter 1.

239 On this date, *Radio Riyadh* announced the Saudi leadership's decision to break off diplomatic relations with Egypt. See: FBIS, *DR*, April 24, 1979. On the renewal of contracts with Egyptian employees, see: *al-Ahram*, June 2, 1979; *al-Jazira*, June 2, 1979; *al-Riyad*, June 20, 1979; see also chapter 3.

240 *Al-Ahram* and *al-Jazira*, June 2, 1979; *al-Riyad*, June 20, 1979.

241 Sadat, *Those I Have Known*, p. 110.

242 Quandt, *Saudi Arabia in the 1980s*, p. 15.

243 Patrick E. Taylor, *WP*, October 8, 1981, p. A21.

244 A memorandum from the Secretary of State of May 3, 1979, as quoted above, p. 50.

245 *Afro Asian Affairs*, May 1979, as appears in the dossier on Saudi Arabia/The Arab World, Shiloah Institute.

246 See testimony by Marbod, who served as head of the American Aid Agency for military

equipment, to the allotment committee of Congress: Foreign Assistance and Related Program (part 4), (96th congress, 2nd session, April 1980), p. 168. Tuma indicated that Saudi Arabia paid the US $100 million a year for Egyptian arms purchases, after the Camp David agreement. See: Elias H. Tuma, *Economic and Political Change in the Middle East* (California: Pacific Books, 1987), p. 206.

247  *Al-Jumhuriyya* (Egypt), June 21, 1979; *Davar, Ha'aretz, Al-Hamishmar*, June 20, 1979; *Jerusalem Post*, June 21, 1979.

248  "Al-Qussa al-Kamila li-Liqa al-Sadat – Fahd," *al-Kifah al-'Arabi*, June 16, 1980, pp. 8–12. The item stated that an internal report of *Newsweeek* and the *NBC* TV network had reported a two-day meeting between Fahd and Sadat on May 3, 1980, but that it had taken place in Khartoum. See: *ibid.*, pp. 11–12. In a personal interview with Hasan Mansur, he denied the reports connected with him.

249  *Afro Asian Affairs*, July 1979, as appears in the dossier on Saudi Arabia/The Arab World, the Shiloah Institute.

250  US, Department of State, Bureau of Intelligence and Research, "Egypt: Sadat's Millitary Requirements and Funding Problems" (report no. 1209, RDS-2, July 2, 1979).

251  Eilts, "Saudi Arabian Foreign Policy" in Malek (ed.), *International Security in Southwest Asia,* p. 77.

252  Kissinger, *The Years of Upheaval* (Boston: Little Brown and Company, 1982),.p. 659.

253  FBIS, *DR*, April 25, 1979, as quoted by Safran, *Saudi Arabia*, p. 308.

254  *MENA*, May 23, 1979.

255  *MEED*, January 4, 1980, p. 24.

256  A memorandum of the American Secretary of State sent to American Embassies in the Middle East, and in London, Madrid, Caracas, Buenos Aires, Brasilia, Athens, Ankara and Paris, May 3, 1979. As published in dossier taken away by the Iranians from the American Embassy in Teheran, p. 40.

257  An IMF document in my possession.

258  Ibrahim Sa'ada, *Akhbar al-Yawm*, May 31, 1980, p. 3.

259  On the transfer of the American "Hercules" plane, see: *SIPRI*, 1982, p. 212; Y. Yarom (ed.), *Arms Transactions with Eastern and North African countries in 1981* (CSS Digest no. 1, Tel Aviv: CSS, December 1982), p. 3. On the loan to the Egyptian military industries for armoured cars, some of which were destined for Iraq, see: *SIPRI*, 1986, p. 414.

260  Forty percent of bank capital is Egyptian and sixty percent Saudi. See: *al-Mustaqbal*, February 24, 1982; May 22, 1982; *al-Jumhuriyya*, May 6, 1982.

261  See: *al-Wafd* (Egypt), August 13, 1987, which specified that Egypt still owed the Fund $1.9 billion.

262  See: *Radio Riyad*, October 29, 1981, as quoted by: FBIS, *DR*, October 29, 1981.

263  This opinion, see also: "Egypt's Surprising Cash Flow," *Business Week*, September 24, 1979, p. 86.

264  OECD, Development Co-operation, *1985 Review* (Paris: OECD, 1985), p. 114.

265  See: *Arab Times* (Kuwait), February 12, 1984.

266  *IHT*, October 9, 1979, pp. 1–2.

267  *Ibid.* See also articles in *Business Week*, on following dates: May 28, 1979; September 17, 1979.

268  On the two memoranda, see: *al-Usbu' al-'Arabi* (Lebanon), April 21, 1980.

269  A personal interview with the author, Cairo, 1986.

270  *Ruz al-Yusuf*, January 28, 1980, pp. 3–6. See also: *ibid.*, January 13, 1980, pp. 3–5.

271  *Al-Watan al-'Arabi*, October 14, 1983: Hermann Frederick Eilts, "Defence Planning in Egypt," in Neuman (ed.), *Defence Planning in Less-Industrialized States*, p. 176: Dale R. Tahtinen, *National Security Challenges to Saudi-Arabia* (Washington, D.C.:

American Enterprise Institute for Public Policy Research, 1978), p. 4: Drew Middleton, "Egyptian Aide Worried over Soviet's Moves in Africa," *The New York Times*, June 11, 1978, p. L5; *IHT*, May 25, 1977; *SIPRI* (1980), p. 86; (1983), p. 332; Ned Temke, *CSM*, December 6, 1978; *MEED*, Egypt Special Report (May 1978), p. 54.

272 US Department of State, *Department of State Bulletin* (May 1984), p. 65; Eilts in Neuman, p. 176; *NYT*, April 29, 1986.

273 Anis Mansur, *October*, April 26, 1982; *al-Watan al-'Arabi*, October 14, 1983; *SIPRI* (1981), p. 78; (1982), pp. 181, 188; David Ignatius, *WSJ*, December 9, 1981, p. 1; Ned Temke, *CSM*, December 6, 1978; James Dorsey, *CSM*, July 8, 1983, p. 7; Joe Stork and Jim Paul, *MERIP Reports*, no. 112, p. 9; William Claiborne, *WP*, January 9, 1980, p. 16; *IHT*, May 25, 1977; *FT*, September 3, 1979.

274 *MECS,* 1979/1980, p. 190.

275 See: *Radio Cairo*, June 6, 1981, as quoted by: *SWB*, June 8, 1981. See also: FBIS, *DR*, May 19 and June 12, 1981.

276 See: FBIS, *DR*, October 2, 1980; *Radio Cairo*, July 9, 1981, as quoted by: FBIS, *DR*, July 10, 1981, p. D2; *SWB*, July 11, 1981. See also statement by a senior Egyptian official in early 1981: "We pledge that our forces will assist in case of any subversive actions threatening Saudi Arabia," as quoted by: David Ignatius, *WSJ*, February 9, 1981, p. 12. On the position of the Egyptian press, official and opposition, *vis-à-vis* the Iranian revolution, see: Mohga Machhour and Alain Roussillon, *La Revolution Iranienne dans la Presse Egyptienne* (Cairo: Cedej dossier no. 4, Mars 1982).

277 *MENA*, November 7, 1980.

278 *Al-Kifah al-'Arabi* (Lebanon), November 17, 1980; *al-Hurriyya* (Lebanon), November 10, 1980.

279 *Al-Siyasa*, February 16, 1981, p. 1. See complete interview, pp. 12–14.

280 *Al-Safir*, November 8, 1980; *al-Kifah al-'Arabi*, November 3, 1980. These newspapers are hostile to the Saudi and Egyptian regimes. *Al-Kifah al-'Arabi* is close to the Libyan elite. It is very likely that the reports lacked any substance and were published with the aim of harming the Saudi regime, and maybe even as a warning against deviating from its policy against Egypt.

281 FBIS, *DR*, January 21, 1981, p. D-5.

282 *Ibid.*, April 1, 1981, p. H-1. See also the statement by Abu Ghazala in an interview to *al-Musawwar*, June 4, 1982. For the report by the *Iraqi News Agency*, see as quoted by: FBIS, *DR*, April 2, 1981, p. E3. On arms supply to Iraq under Sadat, see also: *al-Sharq al-Awsat*, March 28, 1981; *Ruz al-Yusuf*, September 7, 1981, pp. 13–14; *The Guardian*, April 1, 1981, quoting Sadat who officially confirmed (March 31, 1981) the military aid to Iraq via a third party; *MENA*, May 23, 1981, as quoted by *SWB*, May 27, 1981.

283 FBIS, *DR*, March 11, 1981, p. I-3; March 26, 1981, p. I-3; November 18, 1981, pp. I-4–I5.

284 *D & Faw*, July 11–17, 1983, p. 1.

285 *MECS* 1981/82, pp. 795–6. Even before that time the Saudis talked about the need to bring Egypt back to the Arab fold, but with Mubarak there was a feeling of "turning over a new leaf," as they put it. On January 18, 1981 – before Mubarak's rise to power – the Saudi Minister of Information said that it was important for Egypt to return to the Arab ranks. See: *MENA*, January 18, 1981, as quoted by: FBIS, *DR*, January 18, 1981, p. D 1.

286 *Al-Madina* (Saudi Arabia), October 28, 1981. Even after the withdrawal from Sinai, *al-'Ukaz* (April 30, 1982) called for the building of bridges between Egypt and the Arab countries, inter alia to weaken the "enemy."

287 *October*, December 27, 1981. Later on Abu Ghazala explained that threats to stability

in the Gulf were crucial to Egypt. Besides stability in the Gulf, Egyptian policy-makers had in mind the consolidation of Egypt's status and image in the Arab world, as well as financial rewards from arms sales to Iraq.

288  *Al-Musawwar*, April 9, 1982; *Al-Ahram*, May 14, 1982; *Washington Post*, May 21, 1982.

289  *Radio Cairo*, April 26, 1982. See also Mubarak's interview with the Kuwaiti *al-Siyasa*, as quoted by *MENA*, October 19, 1983.

290  *Al-Musawwar*, June 4, 1982.

291  *Ibid.*, April 30, 1982, p. 21; *al-Madina*, October 31, 1982, p. 21. Speeches conveying the same message continued throughout the 1980s. See the interview by the Saudi Foreign Affairs Minister, Sa'ud al-Faysal, to *al-Majalla* (London/Saudi Arabia), December 24, 1983. Kuwait also conformed to this view. See *Kuwaiti News Agency*, August 2, 1983, as quoted by: FBIS, *DR*, August 2, 1983, p. C1 and August 5, 1983, p. A6; *Arab Times* (Kuwait), August 2, 1983.

292  *Al-Ahram*, May 21, 1982. On the supply to Iraq under Mubarak's regime, see also: *al-Sharq al-Awsat*, April 29, 1982, p. 1; July 25, 1983, p. 1; *Mayo* (Egypt), August 2, 1983; *al-Watan al-'Arabi*, October 14, 1983; *FT*, June 3, 1982; *Washington Post*, May 12, 1982; *SIPRI*, various volumes; *Akhbar al-Usbu'* (Oman), July 7, 1983, pp. 1, 28; *al-Ra'y al-'Amm*, November 3, 1985; *al-Majalla* (London/Saudi Arabia), May 21–27, 1986, p. 23; *AWST*, January 1, 1982, p. 44. On the supply of Egyptian arms to other Gulf States and military cooperation with them, see: *al-Watan al-'Arabi*, October 14, 1983; *al-Dustur* (Lebanon), October 15, 1983; *MEED*, October 12, 1982.

293  Anis Mansur, *October*, April 5, 1981, pp. 8–11. According to "classified sources in the American Department of Defense," Israel was the source of the Soviet tanks that Egypt bought from Romania. The Egyptian Minister of Defense, Abu Ghazala, was embarrassed, when he announced to the Egyptian press that Egypt had not ordered the tanks for itself, but that this was an arrangement to ship the tanks to Iraq. See: *Mideast Markets* (vol. 10, no. 25, December 12, 1983), p. 13. Milavnews, May 1981, p. 17.

294  On the Omani Foreign Minister's visit, see: *Al-Sharq al-Awsat* (London), April 29, 1982, p. 1. On Kabus's visit, see: *An-Nahar Arab Report and Memo*, May 17, 1982, p. 1. See in this connection Mubarak's statement as quoted by the *New York Times*, May 30, 1982 and Abu Ghazala's statement: *MEES*, May 24, 1982.

295  *Akhir Sa'a*, November 9, 1983. See also Abu Ghazala's remarks, *al-Nahda* (Kuwait), April 9, 1983. Mubarak's words, see: *Al-Anba'* (Kuwait), January 19, 1987, p. 15: Tariq Aziz's statement in this connection, see: *al-Hawadith* (Lebanon), August 10, 1984; *al-Watan al-'Arabi*, March 4, 1983; see also: FBIS, *DR*, November 5, 1986, p. E3; *MEES*, February 8, 1982.

296  *The Economist*, December 19, 1987, p. 54.

297  *Sunday Times* (London), January 14, 1973. In this context it is worth noting St. John's basic thesis, which considered that small Libya had tried to play a global role and failed. See: Ronald Bruce St. John, *Qaddafi's World Design: Libyan Foreign Policy, 1969–1987* (London: Al-Saqi, 1987).

298  These matters came up during an interview with Dr. Ali Hillal Dessouki in Cairo.

299  Elias H. Tuma, "The Rich and the Poor in the Middle East," *MEJ*, vol. 34 (Fall 1980), pp. 413–17.

300  Quandt, *Saudi Arabia in the 1980s*, p. 15.

301  Kerr, in Kerr and Yassin (eds.), *Rich and Poor States in the Middle East*, p. 6.

302  *Ibid.*, p. 11.

303  *Al-Ra'y al-'Amm*, April 20, 1984.

304  Cited by *al-Ahram*, international issue, December 28, 1984, p. 1.

305  *Al-Mustaqbal*, December 1, 1984.

306 *Davar*, July 29, 1986.
307 Mubarak's interview to *Al-Anba*, Kuwait, January 19, 1987, p. 15.
308 *Al-Iqtisad al-'Arabi*, no. 59, May 1981; *al-Mustaqbal*, vol. 6, no. 279 (June 26, 1982), p. 35; *al-Ahram al-Iqtisadi*, August 29, 1983, p. 7: no. 836, January 21, 1985, pp. 36–9; *al-Ahram*, December 21, 1986, p. 1; January 10, 1987, p. 16; *al-Ra'y al-'Amm* (Kuwait), October 12, 1986, p. 1; *al-Watan* (Kuwait), January 7, 1987, p. 11; *al-Ittihad* (UAE), January 5, 1987, p. 5; *al-Majalla*, May 29–June 4, 1982; March 5–11, 1986, pp. 38–9; *Akhir Sa'a* (Egypt), January 21, 1987, p. 59; *al-Masa* (Egypt), August 1, 1986, p. 1; *Ruz al-Yusuf*, March 24, 1986, pp. 28–9; January 19, 1987, p. 15; 'Abd al-Qadir Shahib, *Ruz al-Yusuf*, February 2, 1987; *Davar*, April 27, 1987; *Yedi'ot Aharonot*, October 28, 1987; *MEED*, March 15, 1985; May 24, 1985; 28 September, 1985; June 7, 1986; July 12, 1986; Olfat Tohamy, "Debt Burden Grows to an All-time High as Resources Decline," *IHT*, Special News Report, Egypt's Critical Path, June 11, 1986; *An-Nahar Arab Report and Memo*, January 12, 1981; *MEN Economic Weekly*, vol. 24, December 27, 1985, p. 27; vol. 25, January 3, 1986, p. 22.
309 See *al-Ahram*, as quoted by the *BBC*, August 26, 1987, and *Radio Cairo*, which quoted *Radio Riyad*, August 20, 1987, as reported by *Hasav*.
310 Hallwood Paul and Stuart Sinclair, *Oil, Debt and Development: OPEC in the Third World*, (London: George Allen and Unwin, 1981), p. 105.
311 *The Middle East*, May 1978, p. 24.
312 S. Hunter, *OPEC and the Third World, The Politics of Aid* (Bloomington: Indiana University Press, 1984), p. 141.
313 A. Z. Rubinstein, *Red Star on the Nile*, p. 331.
314 It should be noted that the oil countries were sometimes quite successful. Through their aid to developing countries, all Arab states profited greatly, mainly by mobilizing public opinion on the subject of the Arab–Israeli conflict. It seems that among the outstanding successes was the Saudis' successful campaign to oust Soviet advisers from Somalia in exchange for aid, and furthermore, the influence of Arab aid on African countries to break off relations with Israel. In Emerson's view, the oil-producing countries, through their investments in the US, succeeded in influencing the political process in that country. Emerson gave great importance to this influence and he was concerned with the emerging "pro-Saudi petro-dollar lobby." See: Steven Emerson, *The American House of Saud* (New York: Franklin Watts, 1985). Quote was taken from p. 5. Contrary to Emerson, Mattione, as quoted above, rejected the claim that petro-dollars had any great influence in the US.

## 5 Egypt and the Arab Petro-Dollar Influence

1 On the importance of economic considerations in Egypt's policy, see: Waterbury in the Yudovich dossier; Ali E. Dessouki, "The Primacy of Economics: The Foreign Policy of Egypt," in Bahgat Korany and Ali Dessouki (eds.), *The Foreign Policies of Arab States* (Boulder, CO: Westview Press, 1984); A. Rubinstein, "The Egypt of Anwar Sadat," *Current History* (January 1977), p. 19.
2 In this context, see also Philip Ghalib, who noted that "there can be no Arab unity without economic linkage," *al-Tali'a*, July 1974.
3 A speech on the occasion of the anniversary of the revolution, July 26, 1976, from *Sadat's Speeches*.
4 Quoted by Faysal Salman, in an article in *al-Safir*, December 7, 1977, p. 11.
5 Kamal Hasan 'Ali to *al-Musawwar*, March 25, 1983. See also Hijazi's statement on the importance of money, "the fourth branch of the armed forces," in an interview to Egyptian TV, as published by: *MENA*, October 9, 1974.

6 Emile Bustani, *Marche Arabesque* (London: Robert Hale, 1961), p. 159; Robert W. Macdonald, *The League of Arab States. A Study in the Dynamics of Regional Organization* (Princeton: Princeton University Press, 1965), p. 204. Saudi Arabia opposed this idea and in the end it was rejected by the Economic Assembly of the Arab League which convened in March 1960. See: Macdonald, *The League of Arab States*, p. 204.

7 Transit agreements, including the oil pipeline which crossed Jordan, Lebanon and Syria, put \$35 million annually in their coffers, and since 1960 Egypt earned more than \$100 million a year from passage of tankers through the Suez Canal. See Macdonald, *The League of Arab States*, pp. 194–5; on demands for a share in oil revenues, see: Bustani, *Marche Arabesque,* p. 141. This claim was also made in the 1970s. See the statement of a senior Syrian official to *al-Hadaf*, Beirut, August 12, 1975, as reported by: David Hirst, *Oil and Public Opinion in the Middle East* (London: Faber and Faber, 1966), p. 106.

8 Gamal Abd al-Nasser, *The Philosophy of the Revolution* (Hebrew), (IDF: Ma'arachot, 1961), pp. 37, 47–9.

9 In the first oil congress, the participants were the Arab oil countries, the countries through which the oil flowed in transit and Libya, before it was considered an oil country. Further details, see: Shukri Ghanem, *OPEC: The Rise and Fall of an Exclusive Club* (London: KPI, 1986), pp. 21–2; Michael Field, *A Hundred Million Dollars a Day* (London: Sidgwick and Jackson, 1975), pp. 4, 149–50.

10 See data in: Tawfiq Y. Hasou, *The Struggle for the Arab World. Egypt's Nasser and the Arab League* (London and Boston: Routledge and Kegan Paul, 1985), pp. 25–6. Up to 1946, even Saudi Arabia received cash from Egypt totaling \$1.1 million. See: Raymond F. Mikesell, "Monetary Problems of Saudi Arabia," *MEJ* (vol. 1, no. 2, April 1977), p. 176.

11 Nazih N. M. Ayubi, "OPEC Surplus Funds and Third World Development: The Egyptian Case," *Journal of South Asia and Middle Eastern Studies* (vol. 15, no. 8, Summer 1982), pp. 43–4.

12 *Al-Ahram*, January 12, 1968.

13 *BBC*, May 30, 1970.

14 *MENA*, June 22, 1971.

15 A broadcast to the nation, *Radio Cairo*, September 9, 1971 (*Sadat's Speeches*, vol. 1, the Egyptian Ministry of Information).

16 See article by Talal Salmani, *al-Sayyad* (Lebanon), March 25, 1971.

17 *Al-Akhbar*, July 31, 1972.

18 Saad El-Din el-Shadhli, *The Crossing of the Suez* (San Francisco: American Mideast Research, 1980), pp. 195–6.

19 *Al-Ahram*, October 9, 1973.

20 *Ibid.*, November 16, 1973.

21 *Ibid.*, November 1, 1974.

22 Fuad Marsi, "Al-Tanmiya al-Iqtisadiyya wal-Istithmarat al-Ajnabiyya," *al-Tali'a* (vol. 11, no. 3, March 1975), pp. 16–17.

23 On the changes in the global ecomony after the October war, see: al-Dayrut 'Abd al-'Aziz, "al-Iqtisad al-Misri wal-Mutaghayyarat al-Duwaliyya," *al-Ahram al-Iqtisadi*, January 15, 1974, pp. 6–7.

24 *Al-Ahram*, November 16, 1974.

25 Fouad Ajami, *The Arab Predicament* (Cambridge, 1981), pp. 7–8.

26 Translation taken from the Shimon Shamir and Matti Peled (eds.), *Egyptian Writers and Intellectuals on New Aspects of the National Goals* (Jerusalem: Truman Institute, the Arab and Israel series, 1978), pp. 87–91.

27   *Al-Akhbar*, December 11, 1974.
28   Jake Wien, *Saudi–Egyptian Relations: The Political and Military Dimensions of Saudi Financial Flows to Egypt* (Rand Corporation, p-6327, Santa Monica, 1980), p. 17.
29   *Radio Cairo*, October 23, 1974 (*Sadat's Speeches*, vol. 4).
30   *Le Figaro* (France), January 1, 1975. See also Sadat's interview with the editor of *al-Anwar*, Basam Fariha, January 7, 1975.
31   The Marshall Plan was front-page news many times in Egypt. See Sadat's interview to the Kuwaiti *al-Siyasa*, as quoted by *MENA*, April 11, 1975, and see *al-Anwar* (Lebanon), January 7, 1975. However, Sadat often stressed that he would not name specific sums. "I will behave like an Egyptian fellah, I will not ask for any help, I will only present my situation." The fellah motif comes up repeatedly in Sadat's speeches and interviews. He said many times that fellahin are proud people, who prefer to suffer and not ask for help: "The pride of our people knows no bounds" – "We refrain from asking" – are only a small sample of Sadat's utterances on this subject.
32   *Al-Ahram*, December 19, 1975.
33   *Al-Akhbar*, December 22, 1975. See also: *The Middle East*, no. 59 (June 1979), p. 26. According to the second source, the Egyptian officials stated that they had spent $40 billion in the period from 1967–1976, and the Arabs gave $4 billion.
34   'Abd al-Fattah al-Qindil, "Iltizam Ra's al-Mal al-'Arabi Nahw al-Mintaqa al-'Arabiyya," *Misr al-Mu'asira*, April 1975, p. 87.
35   John Waterbury, *Egypt Burden of the Past, Option for the Future* (American Universities Field Staff, 1978), p. 230.
36   *Al-Ahram*, January 29, 1975.
37   In the end, Iranian credit amounted to half of its commitment.
38   See at length Shamir's article on the October Paper, in Shimon Shamir, *Egypt under Sadat*, (Hebrew) *Mizraim be-Hanhagat Sadat. Ha-Biqush ahar Oryentazya Hadasha. Asufat Maamarim* (Tel Aviv: Dvir, 1978), pp. 117–39, especially pp. 128–31.
39   *The Middle East*, June 1979, p. 26.
40   *Radio Cairo*, March 14, 1976 (*Sadat's Speeches*). In reality, as can be seen in the previous chapter, this visit was not successful, from Sadat's point of view.
41   A speech to the forces of the Third Army Corps in Suez, see: *MENA*, March 24, 1976.
42   *The Times*, June 4, 1976; *MENA*, June 7, 1976. The same message, see also Sadat's May 1 speech, *Radio Cairo*, May 1, 1976.
43   *MENA*, July 26, 1976. A similar message, see: *Radio Cairo*, August 3, 1976, which broadcast Sadat's speech to delegations of Egyptian researchers and students studying in the US, at the Ras al-Tin palace in Alexandria. In this speech, Sadat was very moderate and several times he thanked "our Arab brothers for their help." At the same time he indicated that the amount of the fund was not sufficient, stating: "They should reconsider the amount in this fund." He repeatedly mentioned that he wanted a comprehensive plan, similar to the "Marshall Plan." See his interview to the Lebanese weekly *al-Sayyad*, published by *MENA*, December 30, 1976.
44   *MENA*, October 13, 1976.
45   *Ruz al-Yusuf*, August 9, 1976, as quoted by FBIS, *JPRS*, and published by Jack Wein, *Saudi-Egyptian Relations: the Political and Military Dimensions of Saudi Financial Flows to Egypt* (Santa Monica: The Rand Corporation P-6327, 1980), p. 18. On the claim that funds were applied to Western money markets, see also: *Ruz al-Yusuf*, October 9, 1978.
46   *Al-Ahram al-Iqtisadi*, September 1, 1976, pp. 10–13.
47   *Al-Ahram*, July 24, 1976.
48   *Ibid.*, January 20, 1977.
49   See *al-Akhbar*, January 24, 1977, p. 6.

50 *Al-Ahram*, January 24, 1977.

51 *Ruz al-Yusuf*, January 31, 1977, p. 16.

52 *Al-Ahram al-Iqtisadi*, February 1, 1977. Criticism was also leveled at the ostentatious life style of the oil country leaders. See: Ibrahim Nafi', *Nahnu wal-'Alam wa-Nahnu wa-Anfusuna* (Cairo: Markaz al-Ahram lil-Tarjama wal-Nashr, 1986), p. 126.

53 See: *al-Ahram al-Iqtisadi*, January 14, 1978; Rushdi Salah, *Akhir Sa'a*, January 26, 1977, p. 4.

54 *Nafi'*, pp. 121–2.

55 This motif appears in many articles by Tawfiq al-Hakim, see for instance: *al-Ahram*, March 2 and 18, 1978.

56 See Hakim's ideas also in *al-Ahram*, March 13, 1978; April 21, 1978; *al-Akhbar*, March 23, 1978. For further details and statements by other intellectuals see: Sa'ad al-Din Ibrahim, *Ittijahat al-Ra'y al-'Amm Nahw al-Wahda al-'Arabiyya* (Cairo: Markaz al-Dirasat al-Siyasiyya wal-Istratijiyya bil-Ahram, 1978). On oil wealth in the context of Arab unity, see: Muhammad 'Abd al-Fadil, *al-Naft wal-Wahda al-'Arabiyya* (Beirut: Markaz Dirasat al-Wahda al-'Arabiyya, 1979).

57 *Al-Ahram*, April 7, 1978.

58 See opposition by Wahid Rifa't in *al-Akhbar*, March 11 and 25, 1978.

59 Nadav Safran, *Saudi Arabia: The Ceaseless Quest For Security* (Cambridge, MA: Harvard University Press, 1985), p. 311.

60 As cited by J. Wien, *Saudi Egyptian Relations: The Political and Military Dimensions of Saudi Financial Flows to Egypt* (Rand Corporation, p-6327, Santa Monica, 1980), quoted above, in Safran, p. 17.

61 *Al-Ahram*, November 9, 1978. See also, *al-Siyasa* (Kuwait), November 8, 1978.

62 *Ruz al-Yusuf*, November 14, 1978; *October*, November 12, 1978; *Radio Cairo*, November 14, 1978, as quoted by *DR*, November 15, 1978, pp. D3–D4.

63 This speech was made in Sapagia on the Red Sea, see: *MENA*, May 1, 1979, as published by the Egyptian Ministry of Information (*al-Ahram* archives).

64 *Al-Balad* (Jedda), May 2, 1979.

65 *NYT*, May 21, 1979. The American ambassador in Egypt met with Fahd in Western Europe, and he informed him of Sadat's agreeing to discontinue his public altercations with the Saudi leadership. In addition, Egypt's newspaper editors were requested to cease publishing hostile articles against the Saudi elite. See: *Facts on File*, 39/2010 – May 18, 1979, p. 378.

66 *MENA*, January 1, 1980, as quoted by *DR*, January 2, 1980. See Sadat's interviews to *October*, and his speech to the Egyptian National Assembly, as quoted by *DR*, December 31, 1979 and January 29, 1980, as well as his interviews to *Ruz al-Yusuf*, February 22, 1980, *Washington Post*, April 3, 1980. Besides the verbal attacks, the Egyptian cabinet made a statement, referring to the attack on the Great Mosque in Mecca, to the effect that it hoped that "our Saudi brothers would punish the perpetrators." See: *Reuters*, Cairo, November 22, 1979.

67 *Al-Ahram*, January 28, 1980.

68 See the statement by the chairman of the Suez Canal Authority, Mashhur Ahmad Mashhur: "Confusion in Arab Economic Relations," *The Arab Economist* (vol. 12, no. 128, June 1980), p. 80.

69 *Daily Telegraph*, May 2, 1980; *DR*, October 8, 1980 and November 26, 1980.

70 *Al-Riyad*, May 19, 1981.

71 Kamal Hasan 'Ali, *Muharibun wa-Mufawidun* (Cairo: Markaz al-Ahram lil-Tarjama wal-Nashr, 1986), p. 74.

72 See the article by Jamil George, *al-Akhbar*, April 13, 1979.

73 Kamal Hasan 'Ali, *Muharibun wa-Mufawidun*, p. 74.

74 *Saudi Gazette*, July 23, 1985.

75 See interview Prince Fahd – the Saudi Crown Prince – gave to *al-Nahar* (Lebanon), July 19, 1976.

76 *Al-Dustur* (Lebanon), August 25, 1975.

77 *Ruz al-Yusuf*, April 19, 1967.

78 Mohammed Imady, "The Role of Arab Development Funds," *Arab Gulf Journal* (vol. 2, 1982), p. 30.

79 John Waterbury and Ragai El-Mallakh, *The Middle East in the Coming Decade. From Wellhead to Well Being?* (New York: McGraw-Hill, 1978), pp. 75–6. Waterbury declared that he could not accept the picture painted by Yamani in view of the extent of petro-dollar revenues: "Any problem in Saudi Arabia can be solved . . . with money. They can desalinate sea-water, cement is imported while they are constructing [cement] factories, and they mobilize great numbers of employees and technically skilled personnel from neighbouring countries and from the whole world . . . SA will try to invest – year in, year out – twice as much as the present Egyptian GNP." See Waterbury and El-Mallakh, *The Middle East in the Coming Decade*, p. 76.

80 *MECS*, 1976/77, p. 572.

81 Sa'ad El-Din Ibrahim, *The New Arab Social Order* (Boulder, CO, 1982), p. 126.

82 N. N. M. Ayubi, "OPEC Surplus Funds and Third World Development" (1982), pp. 52–3. See also: Sa'ad El-Din Ibrahim, *The New Order*, p. 126.

83 Ibrahim Nafi', *Nahnu wal-'Alam*, pp. 124–5.

84 *Ibid*.

85 Sa'ad El-Din Ibrahim, *The New Order*, p. 126.

86 Ibrahim, *The New Order*, p. 127.

87 World Bank, *ARE Economic Report* (report no. 1624-EGT, March 22, 1977), p. 1.

88 See: *Egyptian Gazette*, December 22, 1965.

89 *NYT*, May 5, 1966.

90 IMF, *UAR. Exchange System and Use of Fund's Resources* (EBS/70/179, July 14, 1970), p. 2. On Egypt's economic situation in this period, see: Bent Hansen and Karim Nashashibi, *Foreign Trade Regimes and Economic Development: Egypt* (New York: Columbia University Press, 1975), ch. 5; Hansen and G. Marzouk, *Development and Economic Policy in UAR* (Amsterdam: North-Holland Publishing Co., 1975); Robert Mabro and Samir Radwan, *The Industrialization of Egypt, 1939–1973: Policy and Performance* (Oxford: Clarendon Press), chs. 3–4; Patrick O'Brien, *The Revolution in Egypt's Economic System: from Private Enterprise to Socialism, 1952–1966* (London: Oxford University Press, 1966); John Waterbury, *The Egypt of Nasser and Sadat*, part 2, chs. 4–5. On Egypt's development strategy since the 1952 revolution, see also: Iliya Hariq, "Azmat al-Tahawwul al-Ishtiraki wal-Ighma fi Misr," *Majallat al-'Ulum al-Ijtima'iyya* (Jami'at al-Kuwayt, al-Mujallad 15, al-'Adad 1, Rabi' 1987), pp. 15–142.

91 Nasser, *al-Ahram*, November 20, 1964.

92 See a detailed description by Miles Copeland, *Game of the Nations* (Jerusalem: Shocken, 1970), chs. 8–9, pp. 103–72. Quote taken from pp. 131–2.

93 Paul Rivlin, *The Dynamics of Economic Policy Making in Egypt* (New York: Praeger), p. 40.

94 Hamied Ansari, *Egypt: The Stalled Society* (New York: SUNY, 1986), p. 91.

95 *Al-Ahram*, January 14, 1966, as quoted by: Raymond William Baker, *Egypt's Uncertain Revolution under Nasser and Sadat* (Cambridge, MA: Harvard University Press, 1978), p. 45.

96 See quote by Baker, *Egypt's Uncertain Revolution under Nasser and Sadat*, p. 253,

comment no. 5 and other sources quoted by him in this connection, and see *ibid.*, p. 46.

97 Gad Zilberman, "Changes in the Forming of National Identity in the Nasserist Ideology, 1952–1970," *The New Orient* (vol. 28, 1971), pp. 113–39.

98 M. Kerr, "Egyptian Foreign Policy and the Revolution," in P. J. Vatikiotis (ed.), *Egypt since the Revolution* (New York: Praeger, 1968), pp. 126–7.

99 Report by the *AP* agency from Damascus, June 4, 1964 (taken from *al-Ahram* Archives).

100 On this affair, see memoirs by Yisrael Lior, Levy Eshkol and Golda Meir's military secretary, as published by Eitan Haber, *War will Break Out Today* (Hebrew), (Tel Aviv: Edanim, 1987), pp. 64–5.

101 On the deterioration of economic relations with the US, see analysis by Burns: William J. Burns, *Economic Aid and American Policy toward Egypt 1955–1981* (Albany: State University of New York Press, 1985), pp. 36–107. See also the foreword to this book, written by ambassador Herman Eilts, esp. pp. xiii–xiv.

102 SIPRI, Arms Trade Registers. *The Arms Trade with the Third World*, pp. 43–6.

103 IMF, UAR. *Background Material for 1969 article XIV Consultation* (part II, January 20, 1970), p. 27.

104 A complete list of damaged equipment at the Suez Canal as a result of the war, see: IBRD, *Appraisal of the Rehabilitation of the Suez Canal. ARE* (reports no. 578-EGT and p-1488a, November 19, 1974), annex II, pp. 1–2.

105 For data on this sector see: Khalid Ikram, *Egypt Economic Management in a Period of Transition* (World Bank, 1980), pp. 284–314. For a discussion on tourism to Egypt, see further on in this chapter.

106 *Middle East and African Economist* (October 1967), p. 134. See also Kanovski's analysis of Egypt's losses in the wake of the June 1967 war: Eliyahu Kanovski, *The Economic Impact of the Six-Day War. Israel, The Occupied Territories, Egypt Jordan* (New York: Praeger, 1970), pp. 279–91.

107 *The Times* (London), July 4, 1967, p. 4.

108 Mahmoud Riad, *The Struggle for Peace in the Middle East* (New York: Quartet Books, 1981), p. 51.

109 *Ibid.*

110 Dana Adams, *Yemen: The Unknown War* (London: Dabby Heel, 1968), p. 234; Yael Vered, *Revolution and War in Yemen* (Hebrew), (Tel Aviv: Am Oved, 1967), pp. 50, 70. On Nasser's involvement in the Yemen war, see: Muhammad 'Ali al-Shahri, *'Abd al-Nasir wa-Thawrat al-Yaman* (Cairo: Madbuli, 1976); Ahmad Yusuf Ahmad, *Al-Dawr al-Misri fil-Yaman (1962–1967)* (Cairo: al-Hay'a al-Misriyya al-'Amma lil-Kitab), 1981.

111 George M. Haddad, *Revolution and Military Rule in the Middle East: The Arab States. Part II: Egypt, The Sudan, Yemen and Libya* (New York: Robert Spetler and Sons, 1973), p. 257; D. Adams, *Yemen*, p. 234.

112 Y. Vered, *Revolution and War in Yemen*, p. 70.

113 On Nasser's personal condition, see Sadat's description, *The Story of My Life* (Jerusalem: Edanim, 1978), pp. 153–5.

114 *MEED*, December 14, 1967, p. 851. An in-depth study of the steps taken, see chapter on investments, and quoted sources. See also J. Waterbury's book, *The Egypt of Nasser and Sadat: The Political Economy of Two Regimes* (Princeton: Princeton University Press, 1983) and Cooper's article: Mark Cooper, "Egyptian State Capitalism in Crisis: Economic Policies and Political Interests, 1967–1971," *IJMES* (vol. 10, 1979) pp. 481–516.

115 *Radio Cairo*, March 18, 1969, quoted by the *BBC*, March 20, 1969.

116 On ties between the leaders, see: Fathi al-Dib, '*Abd al-Nasir wa-Thawrat Libiya* (Cairo: Dar al-Mustaqbal al-'Arabi, 1986).

117 Nazli Choucri, *International Politics of Energy Interdependence: The Case of Petroleum* (Lexington, MA, 1976), p. 92.

118 *NYT*, December 24, 1969.

119 Hamied Ansari, "Egypt in Search of New Role in the Middle East," *American Arab Affairs* (no. 12, Spring 1985), p. 44.

120 *ARR*, December 12, 1969.

121 On Nasserism and its decline, see: Shimon Shamir, "The Decline of Nasserist Messianism," in Shimon Shamir (ed.), *The Decline of Nasserism, 1965–1970* (Tel Aviv: Shiloah Institute, 1978), pp. 1–60; Nissim Rejwan, *Nasserist Ideology* (New York: John Wiley, 1974); John P. Entelis "Nasser's Egypt: The Failure of Charismatic Leadership," *Orbis* (vol. 28, no. 2, summer 1974), pp. 451–64.

122 *NYT*, December 24, 1969.

123 On this visit, see: Richard Nixon, *The Memoirs of Richard Nixon* (New York: Warner Books, 1979, 2 vols.), vol. 1, p. 592.

124 For text of the letter and development plan, see a letter from Muhsan Abas Zaki to Schweitzer, June 21, 1970. A photostat is enclosed with the IMF document ( letter from the secretary to the fund's board of directors), no. EBS/70/197 of July 14, 1970. See also Zaki's letter to Schweitzer of Feb. 15, 1968 (IMF document, without further details).

125 *MENA*, December 14, 1976 (Al-Ahram Archives). On the change in Nasser's policy towards the Americans, see: Shimon Shamir, "Egypt's Re-orientation towards the United States – Dynamics of Decision-making on the Inter-Bloc Issue," in Itamar Rabinovitch and Haim Shaked (eds.), *The Middle East and the United States* (Tel Aviv: Am Oved and the Shiloah Institute, 1980), pp. 266–7.

126 In April 1970, Egypt's debts to commercial banks totaled $280 million. Egypt's Minister of the Economy wrote to the head of the IMF: "Because of the grave situation of our foreign currency reserves, the government was forced to obtain large sums from foreign commercial banks on a short-term basis . . . the government is aware of the difficulties likely to emanate from an increasing dependence on short-term loans . . . " See Zaki's letter to Schweitzer, as quoted above.

127 U.S. Department of State, US Foreign Policy 1971 (a report of the Secretary of State, general foreign policy series 260, Department of State publication released March 1972), p. 100. On Fawzi's visit to Washington, see: Richard Nixon, *The Memoirs of Richard Nixon* (New York: Warner Books, 1979, 2 vols.), vol. 1, p. 592.

128 Zaki's letter to Schweitzer.

129 *Al-Ahram*, March 14, 1968: April 11, 1968.

130 Broadcast by *Radio Cairo*, January 20, 1969. Quoted by the *BBC*, January 22, 1969.

131 Pierre Mirel, *L'Egypte des Ruptures: L'Ere Sadate, de Nasser a Moubarak* (Paris: Editions Sindbad, 1982), p. 263. Mirel also noted that Sadat "left behind [after his death] a confused people, on the verge of a social upheaval."

132 See Shimon Shamir, *The Decline of Nasserist Messianism*, esp. pp. 16–38: J. Waterbury, *Egypt: Burdens of the Past, Options for the Future* (Bloomigton: Indiana University Press, 1978), pp. 202–5.

133 Sadat, *My Life*, pp. 162–3.

134 Cooper, "Egyptian State Capitalism in Crisis: Economic Policies and Political Interests, 1967–1971," *IJMES*, 1979.

135 Sadat, *My Life*, p. 161.

136 Mohamed H. Heikal, *Autumn of Fury: The Assassination of Sadat* (New York: Random House, 1983), pp. 42–3.

137 Sadat, *October Paper* (*Hasav*), May 1974, p. 17.
138 *Ibid.*, p. 23.
139 *Middle East Monitor*, May 1, 1971, p. 2.
140 In this context see: Yitzhak Oren, "Sales of Western Arms to the Arab States," *Ma'arachot* (no. 267, January 1979), p. 45. Oren noted that Egypt also took into consideration the potential benefits of Libyan and Saudi arms for its military needs. See *ibid.*
141 Personal interview with Tahsin Bashir, Cairo. In this connection see also chapter 4.
142 *ARR*, January 16, 1972, p. 27.
143 Sadat, *My Life*, p. 185.
144 Waterbury, *Egypt: Burdens of the Past*, pp. 205–6.
145 Sadat, *My Life*, p. 163.
146 *ARR*, March 1, 1972, p. 106: March 16, 1972, p. 135.
147 *Al-Nahar*, April 12, 1972: *ARR*, March 16, 1972, p. 136.
148 *ARR*, March 16, 1972, pp. 136–7.
149 On the preparations for the unification with Libya, see: Mohammed H. Heikal, *The Road to Ramadan* (London: Collins, 1975), pp. 190–8. See also: 'Abd al-'Aziz Rifa'i, *Al-Wa'y al-'Arabi wa-Wahdat Misr-Libiya* (Cairo: Maktabat al-Wa'y al-'Arabiyya, 1973).
150 *Radio Cairo*, July 23, 1973, from *Sadat's Speeches* published by Egypt's Ministry of Information.
151 Heikal, *The Road to Ramadan*, p. 196.
152 See figures on war aid in chapter 1. See same opinion by: Guy F. Erb and Helen C. Low, "Resource Transfers to the Developing World," in J. C. Hurewitz (ed.), *Oil, the Arab–Israel Dispute, and the Industrial World: Horizons of Crisis* (Boulder, CO: Westview Press, 1976), pp. 231–2: Don Peretz in Russel A. Stone (ed.), *OPEC and the Middle East: The Impact of Oil on Societal Development* (New York: Praeger, 1977), p. 24. In this connection see also: Eliyahu Kanovski, "The Economy of the Arab States and the Arab–Israeli Conflict," in Gilboa and Naor (eds.), *The Arab–Israeli Conflict* (Tel Aviv: Misrad ha-Bitahon ha-Hozaa la-Or, 1981), pp. 69, 74.
153 Quoted in Efraim Ahiram's "Trends in the Egyptian Economy," *Economic Quarterly* (vol. 25, 1978), p. 99.
154 Sadat, *My Life*, p. 185.
155 *Radio Cairo* and *MENA*, December 22, 1975 (*Al-Ahram* Archives). Sadat (see his memoirs) made similar statements several days before the October war, speaking before the Egyptian Defense Council. See Sadat, *My Life*, p. 185.
156 *Al-Ahram*, October 10, 1973, as quoted by Emmanuel Sivan in *Arab Conclusions from the October War* (Jerusalem: Am Oved, the Arab Israel series, no. 22, 1974). For extensive material on the defeat and the frame of mind, see Yehoshafat Harkavi dossier, Lessons learned by the Arabs from their Defeat (Tel Aviv, 1969).
157 *MENA*, October 9, 1974 (Ministry of Information, Sadat's Speeches, 1974).
158 *Al-Ahram*, October 3, 1975. These explanations were given after the war, and it is entirely possible that they were "adapted" after the event.
159 *Al-Usbu' al-'Arabi*, September 3, 1973, p. 21: David Binder, *NYT*, October 21, 1973.
160 *MEED*, February 22, 1974, p. 199.
161 An interview with the editor of *Al-Nahar*, September 7, 1974. For a similar view, see: *MENA*, October 8, 1974 (Ministry of Information, Sadat's Speeches, vol. 1974).
162 An analysis of the October Paper, see: in Shimon Shamir, *Egypt under Sadat*, (Hebrew) *Mizraim be-Hanhagat Sadat. Ha-Biqush ahar Oryentazya Hadasha. Asufat Maamarim* (Tel Aviv: Dvir, 1978), pp. 117–39.

163 On the American role in developing the *infitah*, see: J. Waterbury, *The Egypt of Nasser and Sadat*, pp. 156, 402–4.

164 "La Nouvelle Loi sur les Investissements," *Economie des Pays Arabes* (vol. XVII, June 1974), p. 197, as quoted by MERIP staff, "Open Door in the Middle East," *MERIP Reports* (no. 31, 1974), p. 25.

165 Gouda Abdel Khalek, "The Open Door Economic Policy in Egypt: A Search for Meaning, Interpretation and Implication," in, H. M. Thompson (ed.), *Studies in Egyptian Political Economy* (Cairo: Cairo Papers in Social Science vol. 2, monograph 3, 2nd. edn., July 1983), pp. 73–100: Khalek, "Looking Outside or Turning Northwest? On the Meaning and External Dimensions of Egypt's Infitah," *Social Problems* (vol. 28, no. 4, April 1981), pp. 394–409. On the failure of socialism and the *infitah*, see also Waterbury, *The Egypt of Nasser and Sadat*.

166 Abdel Khalek, article from April 1981, pp. 394–409.

167 On economic policy and the focus on development in Egypt before and after the 1973 war, see chapter 2. See also: Ya'ir Menzali, *The Changes in Planning and in Economic Policy in Egypt after the Yom Kippur War* (Tel Aviv: Horovitz Institute, Tel Aviv University, 1977).

168 Osama Hamed, "Egypt's Open Door Economic Policy: An Attempt at Economic Integration in the Middle East," *IJMES* (vol. 13, 1981), p. 3.

169 Chares H. Percy (Senator), *The Middle East* (A Report to the Committee of Foreign Relations, United States Senate, Washington D.C.: GPO, April 21, 1975), p. 11. On this subject in depth, see chapter 2.

170 Sadat, *October Paper*, translation by *Hasav*, May 1974, pp. 32, 37.

171 Quoted by Hamed, "Egypt's Open Door Economic Policy," *IJMES* (vol. 13, 1981), p. 1.

172 Discussions of the Egyptian People's Council Committee, as quoted by: Marc N. Cooper, *The Transformation of Egypt* (London: Croom Helm, 1982), pp. 94–5, 96.

173 Broadcast to the nation, *Radio Cairo*, April 14, 1975 (Ministry of Information), *Sadat's Speeches*, vol. 1975).

174 *October Paper* (*Hasav*). On security of the citizen, see pp. 10–11, 24–5; economic development, see pp. 32–9.

175 On Egypt's Western orientation, the stages of change towards the US with an analysis, see: Shimon Shamir in Rabinovitch and Shaked, *The Middle East and the United States*.

176 Sadat, *October Paper* (*Hasav*), p. 33.

177 World Bank, *Report and Recommendation of the WB to the Executive Directors on a Proposed Loan to the Egyptian General Petroleum Corporation* (report no. P-2580-EGT, June 7, 1979), p. 2.

178 *Ibid.*

179 *Ibid.*, p. 3.

180 *Ibid.* Intermediate and long-term debts increased sharply in the same period from $9.2 billion in late 1973 to $23.1 billion in late 1978. But the reimbursement of debts relative to GNP decreased from 33 percent to 24 percent, respectively. This was thanks to the more favorable repayment terms as well as an increase in foreign currency sources. See: *ibid.* On loans from the GFDE and the easing of short-term debts, see: Claiborne Pell (Senator), Visit to Eastern Europe and the Middle East by the Senate Delegation to the 24th Meeting of the North Atlantic Assembly (A Report to the Committee of Foreign Relations, United States Senate, Washington, D.C: GPO, May 1979). On these achievements, see also letter from Mamduh Salem, the Egyptian Prime Minister, to the head of the IMF, June 10, 1978, and see correction to this letter of June 15, 1978 (IMF document, no number. A copy of the letter is in my possession).

181 Report of Special Study Mission to the Middle East (pursuant to H. Res. 267, authorizing the Committee on Foreign Affairs to conduct thorough studies and investigations of all matters coming within the jurisdiction of the committee, February 25, 1974. Washington:x GPO, 1974), p. 3.

182 The authors of the report noted that Israel should be credited for its desire for peace and for the fact that it had not given prominence to its military achievements "which were extraordinary." "The Israeli government understands the importance of letting Sadat proclaim a victory." See: *ibid.*

183 *Ibid.*

184 The Egyptian policy-makers complained to the delegation that the Soviets had not provided Egypt with arms in the October war, in the same quantity as the Americans had supplied Israel. See *ibid.*

185 *Ibid.* David Rockefeller (he visited the region at least once a year, meeting with policy-makers in Egypt, Saudi Arabia and Israel) also anticipated that after the war the economic situation in Egypt would hasten the peace process, and he tried to convince Israeli policy-makers of this view. The above was gleaned by the author from an interview with Arnon Gafni – the former Governor of the Bank of Israel, Tel Aviv, 1987.

186 Harold H. Saunders, *The Other Walls. The Politics of the Arab–Israeli Peace Process* (Washington, D.C.: American Enterprise Institute for Public Policy Research, 1985), p. 96.

187 Gad Gilbar, "Economic Background to the Change in Egyptian Policy," *Monthly Review*, November 1977, pp. 28, 36.

188 *Al-Ahram al-Iqtisadi*, January 1, 1978, p. 15.

189 Eliyahu Kanovski, "The Economic Aspects of Peace between Israel and the Arab Countries," in Aluf Har'even (ed.), *If Peace Breaks Out* (Hebrew), (Jerusalem: Van Leer, 1978), p. 96.

190 Atif Kubursi, *The Economic Consequences of the Camp David Agreements* (Beirut: Institute for Palestine Studies, 1981), pp. 93–6. Besides the researchers mentioned, other researchers also pointed out the dominance of the economic factor in the peace process. See: Ya'ir Menzali, "The Influence of the Economic Factor on Egypt's Striving for a Peace Agreement," *International Problems* (vol. 17, 33, 1978), pp. 18–29; Fuad Marsi, "Al-Athar al-Iqtisadiyya lil-Mu'ahada al-Isra'iliyya al-'Arabiyya," *al-Mustaqbal al-'Arabi* (August 1980), p. 28; Haim Barkai, "Egypt's Economic Constraints," *The Jerusalem Quarterly*, no. 14 (Winter 1980), pp. 123–43.

191 Korany related to this point but only in a superficial way. He noted that from 1976 on there was mutual disillusion: "the Arabs" or the "the Sheikhs" saw Egypt as a bottom-less pit. Therefore if the "gladiators of the Arab world" had failed to carry out their mission, why shouldn't Egypt be able to choose another road with other neighbors, even Israel? That was the reason, according to the author, for the "psycho-historical shock" of Sadat's trip to Jerusalem in 1977. See: Korany, "Political Petrolism and Contemporary Arab Politics, 1967–1983," *JAAS*, p. 75. Ayubi noted that the fact that Egypt never benefitted from "an Arab Marshall Plan" to the extent requested by Sadat, "gives credibility" to this being one of the reasons for the continuing peace process. See: N. N. M. Ayubi, "OPEC Surplus Funds and Third World Development," 1982, p. 56. Gilbar also referred indirectly to this matter. See: Gad G. Gilbar, "Wealth, Want, and Arab Unity: Saudi–Egyptian Relations, 1962–1985," *The Jerusalem Journal of International Relations* (vol. 9, no. 3, 1987), p. 77.

192 In July 1977 Sadat declared in a speech to ASU that he was ready to accept Israel "as a Middle East state," and around the same time he said to an American delegation: "Five years after the end of the war everything is open, including the path to the signing of a

peace treaty and stability." See: *MEED*, July 22, 1977, p. 15. See following for similar utterances in the mid-seventies.

193 The Americans, who participated in the Camp David talks and discussed Sadat's visit to Jerusalem with Dayan, told him that the primary factor for his decision was his despair with his Arab colleagues, and the refusal of Syria and Jordan to participate in the Geneva talks. They said that Sadat believed that Washington could force Israel, S. Arabia and Jordan to make concessions in order to reach an agreement. See: Moshe Dayan, *Ha-Lanetzah Tokhal Herev: Sihot ha-Shalom, Reshamim Ishiyim* (Jerusalem: Edanim, 1981), p. 89. Eilts, the American ambassador to Egypt, sent a cable to the State Department, stating "that Sadat was bitter about the Syrians not wanting to cooperate with him or showing even the slightest moderation in anything to do with the Geneva conference." See: Haber *et al.*, *The Year of the Dove* (Hebrew) (Tel Aviv: Zemora, Bitan, Modan, 1980), p. 53; William B. Quandt, *Camp David. Peace and the Political Game* (Jerusalem: Keter, 1988), p. 132. Ibrahim Kamel also wrote in his memoirs that Sadat told him that he despaired of the Arabs reaching a unified stand on the matter of the Geneva conference: See: Mohammed Ibrahim Kamel, *The Camp David Accord. A Testimony* (London: KPI, 1986), p. 42. And as quoted by Quandt, Sadat said in this connection "We will explode." See Quandt, *Camp David*, p. 84. Egypt was apprehensive of the Geneva conference for two main reasons: a dictate of a policy close to that of the Syrians and the PLO and a return of the USSR to a pivotal role in Middle East politics, while Sadat wanted to restrict the Soviets' role (Quandt: *Camp David*, p. 57). In the summer of 1974, the Brookings Institute in Washington invited a group of American researchers, diplomats and public figures, to discuss how the US could be of assistance in reaching a settlement in the Middle East. The report exerted great influence on American foreign policy in the Middle East during President Carter's administration. One of the team – Zbigniew Bzhezhinsky – was appointed as Carter's National Security Adviser. For contents of the document see: Israel, Foreign Office, *Dossier of Documents* (edited by M. Medzini, vol. 3), 403–16. The Brookings document destined a place to the USSR, and on October 1, 1977, a joint American-Soviet statement was published on the convening of the Geneva conference no later than December 1977. Sadat feared that if the conference failed, it would lead to another war, as he realized (see Quandt, *Camp David*) that he would not regain territory this way. See: Cyrus Vance, *Hard Choices. Critical Years in America's Foreign Policy* (New York: Simon and Schuster, 1983), p. 162.

194 Safran wrote that Sadat realized that if the Arabs had not succeeded in gaining a decisive victory under the ideal conditions of the October war, they certainly would not succeed in the foreseeable future. According to Safran, Sadat also assumed that even if the Arabs succeeded in closing their ranks against the common enemy and building up a powerful military force, Israel, under Begin, would probably make a preemptive strike. See: Safran, *Saudi Arabia*, p. 256.

195 Vance, *Hard Choices*, p. 178, noted the tension caused by the Likud taking over the helm in Israel in May 1977, which expressed itself, inter alia, in the meeting of Fahd, Sadat and Asad in Riyadh.

196 On Egypt's fears that Israel would attack in the light of Egypt's weakness see: *US News and World Report*, August 15, 1977, p. 24.

197 Khalil and Jamasi warned against this trend. Mustafa Khalil told Yigael Yadin and Ezer Weizman (during Sadat's visit to Jerusalem in 1977) "we know that we cannot win in war and we also know that you have an atomic bomb" and he added: "Why are you so afraid of us? Obviously we cannot beat you! Egypt does not have a military solution, so we must look for another solution. You must believe Sadat." On their talks, see: Haber

*et al.*, *The Year of the Dove*, pp. 139–40; Ezer Weizman, *The Battle for Peace. A Personal Observation* (Jerusalem: Edanim, third edn., 1982), pp. 42, 84. Heikal several times expressed his concern, in Beirut's *al-Anwar*, of Israel's exploiting this weapon in the future. See: *al-Anwar*, June 12, 15, 19, 22, 1977. See also: Melvin A. Friedlander, *Sadat and Begin. The Domestic Politics of Peacemaking* (Boulder, CO: Westview Press, 1983), p. 306.

198 See his interview to *al-Akhbar*, November 17, 1977.

199 Sadat's speech in the Knesset, November 20, 1977. See: *Israel Foreign Relations. Selected Documents, 1947–1974*, ed. Meron Medzini (Jerusalem: Israel, Ministry of Foreign Affairs, 1976) (Hebrew), vol. 4, pp. 182–90. In connection with these points, see also his interview to *al-Ahram*, January 22, 1978.

200 *Al-Ahram*, December 23, 1977. See also Nafi's article, *ibid.*, November 25, 1977.

201 Personal interviews with Khalil, Hijazi and Hasan held in Cairo.

202 Ezer Weizman, *The Battle for Peace*, p. 41.

203 See his speech: Israel, Min. of Foreign Affairs, *Documents Dossier*, vol. 4, pp. 162–3. See also: *al-Ahram al-Iqtisadi*, January 1, 1978, p. 15.

204 A personal interview, Cairo, 1987.

205 Anis Mansur wrote this in *October*, November 27, 1977. Quote from Shamir and Peled (eds.), pp. 158–9.

206 See his statements in a closed session: "Near East Development Forum" (Sheraton-Carlton Hotel, Washington, D.C., May 8, 1981, morning session), pp. 49–50. See also pp. 53–4.

207 Kamal Hasan 'Ali, *Muharibun wa-Mufawidun*, p. 75.

208 See above. See also: *al-Ahram al-Iqtisadi*, December 1, 1977, p. 7; *Ruz al-Yusuf*, November 28, 1977, p. 10.

209 Personal interview, Cairo, October 15, 1986.

210 A letter from Menahem Begin to Gil Feiler, Jerusalem, October 12, 1987.

211 Personal interview, Cairo, August 1987.

212 An IMF document from the secretariat to members of the board of directors: IMF, document no. EBS/76/257, June 2, 1976, p. 3.

213 On relations between the IMF and Egypt, see: Paul Rivlin, *The Dynamics of Economic Policy Making in Egypt* (New York: Praeger), pp. 177–83.

214 At this meeting, it was decided to establish the Gulf Fund for the Development of Egypt. See chapter 4 and: Ali E. Hillal-Dessouki, "Policy Making in Egypt: A Case Study of the Open Door Economic Policy," *Social Problems* (vol. 28, no. 4, 1981), pp. 413–14.

215 Tah 'Abd al-'Alim, *al-Ahram al-Iqtisadi*, December 1, 1977, pp. 14–16. See further details provided in chapter 2.

216 World Bank, *ARE. Recent Economic Development and External Capital Requirements* (report no. 2071-EGT, May 19, 1978), pp. 1, 22.

217 IMF, *ARE. Recent Economic Development* (SM/79/53, February 20, 1979), p. 49; US, Aid, *Arab Republic of Egypt* (263-0047, December 9, 1978), p. 76.

218 *Draft Five Year Plan (1978–1982)*, vol. 1, pp. 1-2.

219 Dessouki, "Policy Making in Egypt" (1981), p. 415.

220 Joe Stork, "Bailing out Sadat," *MERIP Reports* (no. 56, April 1977), p. 11.

221 On the riots, see in previous chapters. See also: Shimon Shamir and Ran Segev, *MECS*, 1976/1977, pp. 289–92; Mark Cooper, *The Transformation of Egypt*, chapter 13, pp. 235–45; J. Waterbury, *The Egypt of Nasser and Sadat*, pp. 229–31; Roger Owen, *Middle East International* (no. 69, March 1977), pp. 4–6.

222 IMF, *ARE. Recent Economic Development* (SM/78/21, January 23, 1978), p. 19. Compare, *The Times* (London), February 2, 1977; *MEED*, February 25, 1977, p. 18.

223 In early October 1984 the Egyptian government announced it was retracting food price increases after the riots in Kafr al-Dawar. See: *NYT*, October 2, 1984.

224 *The Middle East* (C. H. Percy's report, 1975), p. 11.

225 See dialogue between Hamilton and Valiotis, hearing before the sub-committee on Europe and Middle East of the committee on Foreign Affairs, House of Representatives, 96th Congress, first Session, February–March 1979, Washington, D.C.: GPO, 1979, p. 363.

226 Quoted by: Martin Indyk, *To the Ends of the Earth. Sadat's Jerusalem Initiative* (Cambridge, MA: Harvard Middle East Papers, 1984), p. 54, note 14.

227 A personal interview with an Egyptian historian, Cairo, 1987.

228 *Ruz al-Yusuf*, November 28, 1977, p. 10.

229 Among the commentators was Mustafa Amin, a well-known Egyptian journalist. Amin *et al.* were quoted by: *'Al Hamishmar*, January 23, 1977, p. 1; *CSM*, January 25, 1977.

230 *Egyptian Gazette*, January 21, 1977.

231 World Bank, report of May 19, 1978 (as quoted above), p. 22.

232 Sa'id Sinbal, *akhbar al-Yawm*, July 2, 1977.

233 IMF, report of January 23, 1978 (as quoted above), table 4.

234 *Ibid.*, p. 25. In this connection, it should be noted that in the early 1970s Egypt was a net exporter of agricultural products. In the eighties Egypt imported over half of its agricultural goods. See: U.S. Department of Agriculture, Foreign Agricultural Service, *Annual Situation Report: Egypt* (March 6, 1986), p. 1.

235 IMF, report of January 23, 1978, p. 40.

236 Sadat expressed this in a speech before Egyptian students from the US. See: FBIS, *DR*, August 12, 1981, pp. D3–D4.

237 Shimon Shamir, "Departure from Nasserism," in Shamir, *Egypt under Sadat*, p. 211. On the conflict and the Arab states' economic contribution to Egypt see also *ibid.*, pp. 210–11.

238 World Bank, report of May 19, 1978, p. 26.

239 *Ibid.*, p. 27.

240 *Ibid.*, p. 28.

241 *The Middle East* (C. H. Percy's report, 1975).

242 See: *MENA*, September 8, 1975, which quotes an interview Sadat gave to *al-Siyasa* (*al-Ahram* archives).

243 N. N. M. Ayubi, "OPEC Surplus Funds and Third World Development," p. 56.

244 For a discussion on honor and shame in Middle Eastern society, see: J. G. Peristiany (ed.), *Honour and Shame. The Values of Mediterranean Society* (London: Weidenfeld and Nicolson, 1965).

245 I wish to thank Prof. Dan Sagra for bringing several problems in connection with this subject to my attention.

246 Sadat, as we saw, did not name any specific sums for aid. Yisraeli wrote in this context: "Sadat also derived his sense of shame, honor and his values of productive labor from the village . . . He admits that even he needs help sometimes, but he does not 'beg'. He talked about his acrimonious situation with his Arab brothers. But far from asking them for financial contributions, he let them 'draw their own conclusions' because 'we Egyptian farmers are too proud to ask for help'." Refael Yisraeli, "Sadat: Image of a Leader," in Eitan Gilboa and Mordechai Naor (eds.), *The Arab–Israeli Conflict* (Tel Aviv: Misrad ha-Bitahon ha-Hozaa la-Or, 1981), p. 15.

247 Anis Mansur, a personal interview with the author, Cairo, 1987.

248 Tahsin Bashir, a personal interview with the author, Cairo, 1987.

249 Personal interview with the author, Cairo, 1987.

250 For example, the dispute between Musa Sabri, among Sadat's close associates, and 'Abd al-Rahman al-'Atiqi, Kuwait's Finance Minister, as quoted by Ayubi, "OPEC Surplus Funds and Third World Development," p. 54.

251 *Al-Ahram al-Iqtisadi* (no. 325, June 1, 1977), pp. 8–13.

252 *Ibid.* In the end the loan was approved.

253 Heikal, *The Assassination of Sadat*, p. 85.

254 *Ibid.* The end result was that Chase Manhattan acted as Egypt's representative with the Fund.

255 Muhammad Sha'lan, *Al-Tibb al-Nafsi wal-Siyasa* (Cairo: al-'Arabi, 1979). On the psychological dimension, see the Brecher model: Michael Brecher, *Decisions in Israel's Foreign Policy* (London: Oxford University Press, 1974), pp. 3–8, and passim.

256 Lipman, *Washington Post*, January 30, 1977.

257 On visits in the Arab world, see: William Thompson, "Center-Periphery Subsystems: The Case of Arab Visit 1946–1975," *International Organization* (vol. 35, no. 2, spring 1981) and *ibid.*, "Delineating Regional Subsystems: Visit Networks and the Middle East Case," *IJMES* (vol. 13, no. 2, May 1981).

258 See Eilts' foreword to William J. Burns, *Economic Aid and American Policy toward Egypt, 1955–1981* (New York: SUNY Press, 1985), p. xv.

259 Amos Ayalon, *The Finding of Egypt* (Hebrew) *Meziat Mizraim: Masa* (Jerusalem: Schoken, 1980), pp. 127–8.

260 The Egyptians' hatred of the Gulf Arabs' extravagant spending was obvious. About this, see: Paul Jabber, "Oil, Arms, and Regional Diplomacy: Strategic Dimensions of the Saudi–Egyptian Relationships," in Kerr and Yassin (eds.), *Rich and Poor States in the Middle East: Egypt and the New Arab Order* (Boulder, CO: Westview Press, 1982), p. 432.

261 On discrimination against foreigners and Egyptians in the oil countries, see: al-Farah *et al.*, "Alienation and Expatriate Labor in Kuwait," *Journal of South Asian and Middle Eastern Studies* (vol. 4, no. 1, fall 1980), esp. pp. 29–33, and also: Jacquelin S. Ismael, "The Condition of Egyptian Labor in the Gulf," *Arab Studies Quarterly*, vol. 8, no. 4 (1986), pp. 390–403.

262 See translation of article from *Sabah al-Khayr*, January 28, 1982, by Yona Shilo, as published by Rivka Yadlin, *Portrait of an Egyptian* (Jerusalem: Magnes, 1986), pp. 102–5.

263 *Al-Akhbar*, March 18, 1978, as quoted in the Peled and Shamir dossier, p. 164.

264 Author's interview with Sha'lan. As regards Baghdadi's research, Baghdadi did not describe their mental condition before their emigration. See a summary of the thesis in English: Maher Abdalla Baghdadi, "Study on Psychological Problems of Egyptian Workers Abroad using Sample from Riyadh, Saudi Arabia" (MA Thesis, al-Azhar University, Cairo, 1987).

265 *Akhbar al-Yawm*, September 14, 1974. See further speeches in this spirit, interview to *Ruz al-Yusuf*, September 23, 1974; *ibid.*, September 2, 1975; a speech to Egyptian students abroad during their stay in Alexandria, as broadcast by *Radio Cairo*, August 3, 1976 (Ministry of Information, *Sadat's Speeches*, vol. 1976); see also: *Ibrahim Kamel*, p. 11.

266 Speech broadcast by *Radio Cairo*, July 23, 1973 (*al-Ahram* Archives).

267 On the influence of the oil weapon, see: Douglas Feith, "The Oil Weapon De-mystified," *Policy Review* (no. 15, 1981), pp. 19–39.

268 On this subject in depth, see: Richard P. Mattione, *OPEC's Investments and the International Financial System* (Washington, D.C: The Brookings Institution, 1985), pp. 38–58. On the freezing of Iranian deposits, see: Gary Sick, *All Fall Down. America's*

*Tragic Encounter with Iran* (New York: Random House, 1985), pp. 227–9, 241, 289.

269  Mordechai Gazit, *The Peace Process, 1969–1973* (Hebrew), (published by Hakibbutz Hame'uhad, 1984).

270  H. Kissinger, *Years of Upheaval* (Boston: Little Brown and Co. 1982), p. 618.

271  M. H. Heikal, "Egyptian Foreign Policy," *Foreign Affairs* (vol. 56, no. 4, July 1978), p. 726.

272  Sadat statement on January 14, 1975, as quoted by Jamal Ali Zaharan, *Al-Siyasah al-Khariyya li-Misr, 1970–1981* (Cairo: Madbuli, 1987), p. 125.

273  Raphael Israeli, *Man of Defiance. A Political Biography of Anwar Sadat* (London: Weidenfeld and Nicolson, 1985), p. 209.

274  Shafi'i's letter to Witteveen, February 1, 1976 (appendix to IMF document no. EBS/76/52, February 10, 1976).

275  IMF, a report of February 20, 1979 (quoted above), p. 22.

276  See interviews with Anis Mansur, *October*, December 18 and 25, 1977.

277  *Al-Ahram*, November 5, 8, 9 and 16, 1978. The *Washington Post* reported on November 8, 1978, that Sadat had already asked Carter for this sum.

278  See below. After the peace treaty, Kamal Hasan 'Ali stated: "Our four wars with Israel cost us a hundred billion dollars. I hope that every Egyptian is aware of this figure. This in addition to the casualties we suffered." Kamal Hasan 'Ali – Foreign Minister – in an interview to an *al-Musawwar* panel (no. 3050), March 25, 1983, p. 24.

279  See Sadat, *My Life*, pp. 196–7.

280  See quotes from *Sadat Speeches* on subject of peace, as published by Jamal 'Ali Zaharan, *al-Siyasa al-Kharijiyya li-Misr 1970–1981* (Cairo: Madbuli, 1987), pp. 124–5. See also below.

281  See in depth: Shimon Shamir, "Some Arab Attitudes toward the Conflict with Israel, between 1967 and 1973," in Gabriel Sheffer (ed.), *Dynamics of a Conflict* (Atlantic Highlands, NJ, 1975), pp. 185–95.

282  Shamir, *Egypt under Sadat*, pp. 184–5. For a further analysis on this subject, see also: *ibid.*, chs. 14 and 16: S. Shamir and Matti Peled (eds.), *Egyptian Writers and Intellectuals on New Aspects of the National Goals* (Jerusalem: Truman Institute, the Arab and Israel series, 1978).

283  Shamir, "Introduction," in Shamir and Peled (eds.), *Egyptian Writers and Intellectuals,* p. 14.

284  See the article by Patrick Seale, "Sadat's Shock Therapy," *New Statism* (vol. 94, no. 2436, December 21, 1977), pp. 760–1. One can see similarities in Sadat's decision to go to war in October 1973 and his initiative of 1977. The years 1973 and 1977 were years of disappointment for him; in these two years Egypt suffered a combination of political and economic stagnation, and a sharp turnabout was needed to generate a positive evolution in Egypt. The main difference was that in 1973 Sadat exercised the military option as against the political option in 1977.

285  Hearst, *Guardian*, January 20, 1977.

286  On the theoretical aspect of this subject, see: S. Chan ,"The Impact of Defense Spending on Economic Performance: A Survey of Evidence and Problems," *Orbis* (vol. 27, no. 3, 1985), pp. 403–34: Ron Huisken, "Armaments and Development," in Helena Tuoni and Raimo Vayrynen (eds.), *Militarization and Arms Production* (New York: St. Martin's Press, 1983). For other opinions aiming to prove that military expenditures do not necessarily harm a country's situation, and conditions for this, see: Robert E. Looney and Peter C. Fredriksen, "Defence expenditures, External Public Debt, and Growth in Developing Countries," *Journal of Peace Research* (vol. 23, no. 4, December 1986), pp. 329–38. On the growth of the bourgeoisie in Sadat's time, see: Cooper, *The*

*Transformation of Egypt*, p. 202; Raymond Hinnebusch, *Egyptian Policy under Sadat* (Cambridge: Cambridge University Press, 1985), p. 89.

287 Economic and Military Aid Programs in Europe and the Middle East (Hearings and Markup before the Sub-committee on Europe and the Middle East of the Committee of Representatives, 96th Congress, first session February 1, 13, 14, 22, 26, 28 and March 1, 5, and 6, 1979. Part 3, Washington, D.C.: GPO, 1979), p. 59.

288 Cooper, *The Transformation of Egypt*, p. 255.

289 On peace, investments and the reduction of the military burden, see comments by the Egyptian Minister of Finance and Economy, *al-Musawwar*, December 2, 1977, p. 11. On the exploitation of resources in Sinai, see comments by the Vice-Premier on economic matters, *al-Jumhuriyya*, December 19, 1977, p. 9.

290 A report by Senator Charles Percy to the Senate Committee on Foreign Affairs, April 21, 1975, p. 11.

291 *Al-Jumhuriyya*, December 19, 1977, p. 9.

292 Uzi Benziman, *Ha'aretz*, March 1, 1978. Elyakim Rubinstein who accompanied Dayan on his trip to Morocco on December 2, 1977, stated that it was only then that Dayan showed Tohami a peace plan which recognized Egyptian sovereignty over Sinai. See *Ma'ariv*, special supplement for the tenth anniversary of the peace initiative, November 13, 1987. In this connection, Begin commented: "He [Dayan] did not speak about returning [Sinai]. But you might say that this was the drift of his words." See: *Yedi'ot Aharonot* (Shabbat supplement, November 13, 1987), p. 3.

293 *Al-Jumhuriyya*, April 25, 1976.

294 In his Ph.D. thesis, Seif el-Din interviewed American businessmen operating in Egypt, and they emphasized the crucial importance of political and social factors on their investments. See: Ashraf Emam Seif el-Din, "Investment Climate in Egypt as Perceived by Egyptian and American Investors" (Ph.D. thesis, Ohio State University, 1986).

295 IMF, report of February 8, 1980 (as quoted above), p. 2.

296 *Ibid.*, report of January 23, 1978, p. 34.

297 *Ibid.*

298 *Ibid.*, p. 80, table no. 18 and report of February 20, 1979. More on tourism to Egypt see below.

299 World Bank, *ARE. Recent Economic Development and External Capital Requirements* (report no. 3252-EGT, December 19, 1980), pp. 12–13. It should be remembered that Egypt also increased its oil revenues by raising prices: in January 1979 a barrel of oil cost $12.50, in June 1979 – $18.50 and at the end of that year – $29.20.

300 Sadat as quoted by the *Washington Post*, September 10, 1975.

301 See Sadat's speech to the People's Council on March 14, 1976, with his proposal to annul the friendship treaty between the two countries. *ARR*, March 1, 1976, p. 144.

302 Robert Mabro, "Egypt's Economic Relations with the Socialist Countries," *World Development* (vol. 3, no. 5, May 1975), p. 310.

303 CIA, *Handbook of Economic Statistics, 1986*. On Soviet aid, see also: 'Adil Husayn, *Al-Iqtisad al-Misri min al-Istiqlal ila al-Tab'iyya, 1974–1979* (Cairo: Dar al-Mustaqbal al-'Arabi 1982, 2 vols.), vol. 1, pp. 44–58. On military aid, see also: Roger F. Pajak, "Soviet Arms Aid in the Middle East since the October War," In *The Political Economy of the Middle East: 1973–1978* (A compendium of papers submitted to the Joint Economic Committee, Congress of the United States. Washington: GPO, April 21, 1980), pp. 446–62.

304 CIA, "Memorandum for WHSR, from Paul H. Corsradden (Operation Center) to Smith and Richard" (SDO/CIA, June 8, 1967. Declassified 032931).

305 *Al-Ahram*, March 30, 1972.

306 Fahmi's speech, see: *ARR*, March 1, 1976, p. 144. The CIA data referred to the years 1955–1977. See: CIA, *Communist Aid to Less Developed Countries of the Free World, 1977* (Washington, November 1978), p. 28. Since mid-1975, Egypt did not receive any significant amounts of arms from the USSR. See: CIA, *Communist Aid to Less Developed Countries, 1976* (August 1977), p. 28.

307 *NYT*, April 19, 1974.

308 *ARR*, March 1, 1976, p. 144.

309 Adlai E. Stevenson, *The Middle East: 1976* (a report to the committee on banking, housing and urban affairs, United States Senate, on his mission to the Middle East conducted between February 10 and and February 25, 1976, April 1976. Washington: GPO, 1976), p. 4.

310 *ARR*, March 1, 1976, p. 144. See also interview granted by Ashraf Ghorbal, Egypt's ambassador to the US: US News and World Report, April 19, 1976, p. 57.

311 *Washington Post*, July 17, 1977; *NYT*, June 25, 1977.

312 In October Sadat announced that starting in early 1978, Egypt would discontinue payments on its debt of $4.4 billion to Moscow for a period of 10 years, and stop shipments of cotton to the USSR and Czechoslovakia. See: *MEED*, October 29, 1977, p. 17. Sadat wanted to reach an agreement with the Soviets on a moratorium already in early 1975, but they refused, so in the end Sadat took unilateral steps. See: *The Economist*, June 28, 1975, p. 67; the CIA, *Communist Aid to Developing Countries, 1976* (August 1977), p. 29. On March 20, 1987, Egypt and the USSR signed a long-term agreement for the repayment of Egypt's debts, which were to be spread out over 25 years. The Russians, who owed Egypt $500 million for commercial transactions between them, suggested deducting this amount from the debt, but Egypt refused, claiming that it was a military debt and the two sectors should be kept separate. See: Abdel Rahman Akl, *Middle East Times* (March 29–April 4, 1987).

313 W. B. Quandt, *Camp David*, p. 130.

314 *Al-Siyasa* (Kuwait), February 16, 1981. There are several versions of the amounts Sadat was offered to cancel the peace talks. The figure of $5 billion was the largest (see chapter 4); and see also Elias H. Tuma, *Economic and Political change in the Middle East* (California: Pacific Books, 1987), p. 201. Sa'ad El-Din Ibrahim even quoted a report on $15 billion offered to Sadat, for a period of 5 years. See: Sa'ad El-Din Ibrahim, *The New Order*, p. 157.

315 Marvin G. Weinbaum, *Egypt and the US – Economic Aid*.

316 Evidence from January–March 1980, p. 90.

317 *US News and World Report*, August 15, 1977, p. 24.

318 U.S. Department of State, US Foreign Policy 1971 (a report of the Secretary of State, general foreign policy series 260, Department of State publication released March 1972), p. 100.

319 Quoted by Shamir in Rabinovich and Shaked, *The Middle East and the United States*, p. 284. See also: Eilts in Stephanie G. Neuman (ed.), *Defence Planning in Less-Industrialized States. The Middle East and South Asia* (Lexington: Lexington Books, 1984), p. 175, and Crowan in *ibid.*, p. 159.

320 R. Nixon, *Memoirs*, vol. 2, p. 591. See also: Henry Kissinger, *Years of Upheaval*, p. 1129.

321 Henry M. Schuler, "Will Egypt be Denied its Peace Dividend," *American Arab Affairs* (no. 7, winter 1983/84), pp. 36. On the transfer of technology from the US to Egypt, see following reports: Congress of the United States, Office of Technology Assessment, *Technology Transfer to the Middle East* (OTA-ISC-173, Washington, D.C: GPO, September 1984); congressional research division, science policy research division, *Technology Transfer to the Middle East O.P.E.C Nations and Egypt 1970–1975* (back-

ground study prepared for the subcommittee on domestic and international scientific planning and analysis, Washington, D.C.: GPO, 1976).

322 Comptroller General, *Meeting U.S. Political Objectives through Economic Aid in the Middle East and Southern Africa* (report to the Congress of the United States, id-79–23, May 31, 1979), p. 2. Israel utilized nearly the entire amount of aid as it was provided in cash, whereas Egypt only utilized a small part of it. See also report by American Comptroller General, September 15, 1977, as quoted above, p. 1. Aid to Egypt at that time was provided from security supporting funds, and not from development assistance funds. See: *ibid.*, p. 2. See also: *report by State Comptroller*, July 31, 1985, p. 1, and testimony by Murphy, the Assistant Secretary of State for Middle Eastern and South Asian Affairs, to the Sub-Committee for Foreign Operations of the Allocations Committee, on March 15, 1984: *Department of State Bulletin*, May 1984, pp. 66–7.

323 Saunders, *The Other Walls*, p. 98.

324 J. Carter, *Public Papers of the President of the US*, February 4, 1978, p. 368.

325 *Washington Post*, February 3, 1977.

326 *The Economist*, December 9, 1978.

327 They decided also to set up a joint production line for jeeps, see: State Department report no. 1209, as quoted above, in the *Seized Documents*, taken from the American embassy in Teheran.

328 Zbigniew Brzezhinski, *Power and Principle: Memoirs of the National Security Adviser, 1977–1981* (New York: Farrar, Straus and Giroux, 1983), p. 94.

329 *Ibid.*, pp. 247–8. This was in late February 1978. The Saudis were to have financed the planes transaction.

330 Hearings before the Sub-Committee on Europe and the Middle East, February–March 1979, as quoted above, p. 363.

331 Fiscal year 1980 International Security Assistance Authorization (1980 foreign assistance request. US Senate Committee on Foreign Relations, Friday, March 2, 1979), p. 152–3.

332 *In Search of Peace in the Middle East: Document and Statement, 1967–1979* (Washington, D.C.: GPO, 1979), p. 59. The military delegation went to Cairo in the summer of 1979 and presented a report on its return (June) on the type of arms demanded by Egypt. See: State Department report no. 1209, as quoted above in the *Seized Documents*. See also: Henry F. Jackson, *From the Congo to Sweto: US Foreign Policy toward Africa since 1960* (New York: Morrow, 1982), p. 104.

333 "Communication from the President of the USA" (referred to the Committee of Foreign Affairs, April 9, 1979. Washington, D.C. GPO, 1979), pp. 7–8. See also: U.S. General Accounting Office, *The U.S. Economic Assistance Program for Egypt poses a Management Challenge for Aid* (report to the administrator agency for international development, GAO/NSIAD-85–109, July 31, 1985), p. 3.

334 Ibrahim Kamel, *The Camp David Accord*, p. 368.

335 The delegation noted that, during its visit, the oil countries were still providing assistance to Egypt. See: *Visit to Eastern Europe and the Middle East by the Senate Delegation* (a report to the Committee on Foreign Relations, United States Senate by Senator Claiborne Pell, May 1979. Washington: GPO, 1979), pp. 25, 28–9.

336 U.S., Department of State, Bureau of Intelligence and Research, "Egypt: Sadat's Military Requirements and Funding Problems" (secret, report no. 1209, RDS-2 7/2/99 multiple sources, July 2, 1979). This report, together with others, was seized by the Iranians from the American embassy in Teheran, and published in one batch (hereafter: *Seized Documents*). This particular report can be found in the *Seized Documents* on pp. 90–7. When the Saudis did not honor their commitments to finance arms for Egypt,

Sadat was of little help to the American administration in its efforts to persuade the Saudis to keep their part of the bargain. On the contrary, according to Quandt and Tahsin Bashir as quoted by Crowan, Sadat attempted to disrupt these efforts, with the aim of attaining direct military relations with the US similar to those between the US and Israel. See: Crowan in Neuman, *Defence Planning in Less-Industrialized States*, p. 159 and p. 164, note no. 35.

337 Testimonies before the Sub-Committee for Europe and the Middle East, the Committee for Foreign Relations of the House of Representatives, February–March 1979, pp. 375, 365–7. Valiotis' comments, see p. 375.

338 For example, in September 1977 the West German Chancellor supported increasing European aid (technical and financial) to Egypt, after a peace settlement had been reached. See: *al-Ahram*, December 23, 1977, p. 3. Egypt was the second largest recipient of aid from West Germany after India. On German aid to Egypt, see: *al-Ahram al-Iqtisadi*, April 6, 1987, p. 10; *An-Nahar Arab Report and Memo* (April 1, 1985). On World Bank aid to Egypt, see: *al-Ahram al-Iqtisadi*, April 6, 1987, p. 10; *al-Ahram*, March 23, 1978, p. 1; May 13, 1987, p. 1; comprehensive data on Western and Japanese aid, see O.E.C.D. data.

339 At least half of this sum came from foreign oil companies, according to AID data. See: *Weinbaum*, p. 38; *FT*, June 5, 1985.

340 Lutfi 'Abd al-'Azim, "Duwal al-Rafd . . . wa-Muqata'at Misr Iqtisadiyyan!," *al-Ahram al-Iqtisadi*, December 15, 1977, pp. 4, 8.

341 'Isam Rif'at, *Al-Ahram al-Iqtisadi*, January 1, 1978, pp. 15–17, 61.

342 Jean Debji, *Al-Nahar Al-'Arabi wal-Duwali*, November 20, 1978, p. 18.

343 *Ibid*. For similar points, see 'Abd al-Rahman 'Aql's review. The opinions of Egyptian economists on the Egyptian economy in peacetime, *al-Ahram*, May 4, 1979, p. 5.

344 *Al-Akhbar*, April 3, 1979.

345 J. Debji, *Al-Nahar Al-'Arabi wal-Duwali*, p. 18.

346 The figure of $40 billion that the wars with Israel cost Egypt figured in the headlines many times. As indicated by publications, this amount included both direct and indirect damages, as well as defense budgets. See: *Al-Ahram*, May 10, 1975; *Al-Akhbar*, December 22, 1975, and see above.

347 Usama Ghayth, *al-Ahram*, April 3, 1979, p. 9. See also: *Egyptian Gazette*, April 10, 1979. Egypt imported small amounts of cooking gas from Italy and Greece. On trade relations between Egypt and the Arab countries, in connection with the boycott, see also: 'Isam Rif'at, *al-Ahram al-Iqtisadi*, April 15, 1979, pp. 8–13, and below.

348 'Abid Nafisa, *October*, September 2, 1979, pp. 26–7.

349 *Al-Ahram*, December 16, 1979.

350 See *Radio Cairo*, April 16, 1980, as quoted by *DR*, April 7, 1980. See also chapter 3.

351 Abu al-Hasan 'Abd al-Rahman Abu al-Hasan, "Tasa'ulat hawla al-Muqata'a al-'Arabiyya li-Misr," *al-Ahram al-Iqtisadi*, April 15, 1979, pp. 14–17.

352 *FT*, July 9, 1979.

353 The US was to have granted $1.1 billion of this sum. See: *MEED*, January 4, 1980, p. 23.

354 IBRD, *The Egyptian Economy in 1974, Its Position and Prospects* (report no. 491a-EGT, September 25, 1974), p. 8.

355 *Commerce du Levant*, April 30, 1975.

356 'Adil Husayn, vol. 1, p. 158. On deposits, see also *ibid*., pp. 159–62.

357 Nazih N. M. Ayubi, "Implementation Capability and Political Feasibility the Open Door Policy in Egypt," in Kerr and Yassin (eds.), *Rich and Poor States in the Middle East: Egypt and the New Arab Order* (Boulder, CO: Westview Press, 1982), pp. 370–1.

358 See: American Embassy in Cairo, *Economic Trends Report, Egypt* (February 5, 1979), p. 9.
359 *NYT*, May 11, 1979, pp. A1, A9.
360 In any case, the IMF was not ready to accept automatically the argument of "national interest" against Kuwait and Saudi Arabia. On this matter, see: *Akhbar al-Yawm*, February 2, 1980; *al-Ahram*, February 6, 1980; *MEED*, October 10, 1979, p. 25; *An-Nahar Arab Report and Memo*, October 15, 1979, p. 3.
361 *Ruz al-Yusuf*, December 30, 1979. In June 1978, *MEED* reported that there was Egyptian-Saudi agreement on a further extended period of only one year for the Saudi deposit ($980 million). See: *MEED*, June 2, 1978, p. 25. In April 1977, *al-Ahram* wrote that Kuwait agreed to postpone the withdrawal of its deposits (the paper did not specify the period of time), so that $2 billion pertaining to Kuwait and Saudi Arabia would remain in Egypt. In this connection, see: *Jaridat al-Misr*, July 25, 1977, p. 6; *al-Sayyad*, April 21, 1977.
362 *Financial Times, Daily Telegraph, International Herald Tribune*, December 31, 1979; *DR*, January 29, 1980.
363 *FT*, Feb. 5, 1980; *MEED*, Jan. 4, 1980, p. 23; Feb. 1, 1980, p. 22; Feb. 8, 1980, p. 23; March 28, 1980, p. 28; *An-Nahar Arab Report and Memo*, Feb. 2, 1980; *MEES*, April 4, 1980, p. 7; *Egyptian Newsletter*, April 14, 1980, p. 11; "Al-Qussa al-Kamila li-Liqa' al-Sadat – Fahd," *al-Kifah al-'Arabi*, June 16, 1980, p. 11. The last report indicated that deposits stood at $2.3 billion. On correspondence between Saudi Arabia and the IMF on the freezing of deposits by the Egyptian government, see chapter 4.
364 *Egyptian Newsletter, op. cit.* April 14, 1980.
365 *Egyptian Gazette*, April 10, 1979; *October*, September 2, 1979, pp. 26–7.
366 See report from the American embassy in Jedda to State Department, and same from American bankers to their embassy in Cairo, according to the report received from their colleagues in Jedda. These facts came to light from a message sent by the Secretary of State (May 4, 1979) to American embassies in the Middle East and in several European countries, as published in the *Seized Documents*, p. 50. See also: *al-Yaqza* (Kuwait), April 19, 1979.
367 *Middle East Newsletter*, May 20, 1979, p. 7.
368 Ray Vicker, "Beating the Boycott," *WSJ*, February 14, 1980.
369 See, for example, message from the Secretary of State (May 3, 1979), to American embassies in the Middle East and in several European countries, as published in *Seized Documents*, pp. 40–2; *al-Watan* (Kuwait), April 17 and 20, 1979; *Egyptian Newsletter*, October 29, 1979.
370 See in depth (also on boycott) in the part on the AMIO in the chapter on investments. See also State Department report no. 1209, as quoted above.
371 *FT*, May 18, 1979; *Middle East Newsletter*, May 20, 1979, p. 7. There are various versions on the sum of money already spent on the project. The sources quoted above mentioned $400 million. Sheikh Faysal al-Qasimi proclaimed that only $200 million of company capital had been exploited and the balance had been invested in various banks, *ibid*. A report by the Intelligence and Research Bureau of the Department of State estimated that at least $780 million had been spent or were under direct Egyptian control. See report no 1209 as quoted above, p. 1, as appeared in the *Seized Documents*, p. 92.
372 See chapter 2 and: *IHT*, October 9, 1979: *UPI* (Kuwait), May 26, 1979.
373 On the Islamic Feisal Bank in Cairo and its impressive achievements over the years, see: Ahmed Abdel-Fattah El-Ashker, *The Islamic Business Enterprise* (London: Croom Helm, 1987), pp. 115–40, 163–8, 174–85, 227–8. See also *MEED*, August 17, 1979, p. 19; *Ruz al-Yusuf*, February 23, 1981.

374 Three of these banks torpedoed the loan of $250 million to Egypt in the spring of 1979. Further details, see document the American Secretary of State sent to about 30 American embassies on May 3, 1979, mostly in the Middle East, as appears in message sent by the Secretary of State to the above, as quoted above, in the *Seized Documents*, p. 41; *al-Sha'b* (Egypt), May 4, 1982; *An-Nahar Arab Report and Memo*, May 10, 1982; *Facts on File* (52/2166, May 21, 1982), p. 368; *Egyptian Newsletter*, May 26, 1980, p. 11. Except for the first- and last-named sources, the others specified that the loan that had been rescinded was for $300 million.

375 *Akhbar al-Yawm*, May 22, 1982.

376 *Al-Ahram*, December 24, 1982.

377 *MENA* denied this, and noted that the financing of the Mirage planes was French, and not Saudi. On this affair, see: *DR*, January 26, 1982, pp. D1–D2. On the other hand, in October 1982 officials of the American administration stated that they had urged Saudi Arabia to loan Egypt $2 billion, so they could start joint production of American fighters, which were to be supplied to Middle East countries. See: *Washington Post*, October 5, 1982.

378 *Al-Kifah al-'Arabi*, January 3, 1983.

379 *Al-Ahram* and *al-Akhbar*, July 14, 1986.

380 *Davar*, April 27, 1987, p. 3.

381 On the activities of UN funds in Egypt, see: US, AID, *Summary of the Activities of the United Nations Development Programme and Associated Programmes in Egypt, 1972–1985* (October 1983); UN, *United Nations Development Co-operation, 1950–1985. Focus on Egypt* (n.d).

382 A communication from the Secretary of State (May 3, 1979), to about 30 American embassies, mostly in the Middle East, as in the *Seized Documents*, p. 40.

383 A communication from the Secretary of State (May 4, 1979) to American embassies in the Middle East and in several European countries, as quoted: *ibid.*, pp. 50–1.

384 *Al-Siyasi* (Egypt), July 8, 1979.

385 Central Bank of Egypt, *Annual Report 1983/84* (Cairo), p. 82.

386 Egyptian General Authority for the Promotion of Tourism, *Annual Report 1984* (Cairo), pp. 14, 24.

387 See: Joseph D. Coppock, *Foreign Trade of the Middle East, 1946–1962* (Beirut: American University of Beirut, 1966).

388 IMF, *Direction of Trade Statistics*, Various Issues and Yearbooks; *An-Nahar Arab Report and Memo*, June 7, 1982, p. 4.

389 IMF and IBRD, *Direction of Trade, Annual 1958–1962*, pp. 264–5. Until the early 1970s, the IMF and the World Bank jointly published trade data, after which the IMF has been responsible for publication.

390 IMF, *UAR part 1. Staff Report and Proposed Decision – 1968* (article XIV consultation, April 14, 1969), pp. 49–50.

391 KFAED, *Geographical Distribution of Arab Foreign Trade, 1969–1976* (Kuwait, 1977), p. 7. Other data see, League of Arab States/ECWA, *Statistical Indicators of the Arab World for the period 1970–1979* (Beirut 1981), pp. 103, 121.

392 'Isam Rif'at, *al-Ahram al-Iqtisadi*, April 15, 1979, pp. 8–13.

393 For detailed figures see in monthly publication: al-Jihaz Al-Markazi lil-Ta'bi'a al-'Amma wal-Ihsa, *al-Nashra al-Shahriyya lil-Tijara al-Kharijiyya* (Cairo).

394 National Bank of Egypt, *Economic Bulletin* (vol. 36, no. 4, 1983), p. 364.

395 *Ibid.*

396 *Ibid.* (vol. 36, no. 1, 1983), p. 15.

397 For further data see: Federation of Egyptian Industries, *Yearbook 1981*, pp. 100, 105–6.

Data on Jordan and Iraq, including trade details, see: *al-Ahram*, December 4, 1983, p. 15; December 28, 1983, p. 3.

398 Salim al-Hoss, "The Political Element in U.S.-Arab Economic Relations," in Michael R. Czinkota and Marciel Scot (eds.), *U.S.–Arab Economic relations. A Time of Transition* (New York: Praeger, 1985), p. 299.

399 The conference was covered by *al-Sharq al-Awsat*, October 23, 1983, p. 3.

400 *Ibid.* Lavy also noted that the boycott had not harmed Egypt in the intermediate period, except for a drastic drop in aid. See: Victor Lavy, "The Economic Embargo of Egypt by Arab States: Myth and Reality," *MEJ* (vol. 38, no. 3, September 1984), pp. 419–32.

401 The conservative oil states paid lip-service to the confrontation states with declarations such as: "We remain committed to the political and economic embargo imposed on Egypt," as announced in 1984 by Jabir al-Sabah, the Kuwaiti Foreign Minister. See: *MEED*, February 17, 1984.

402 ARE, Suez Canal Authority, *Suez Canal Report, Yearly Report 1979*, p. 161; 1980, n.p, 1982, p. 159.

403 *Ibid.*, 1984.

404 *Al-Ahram*, May 21, 1982, p. 1; *al-'Arabi*, October 14, 1983.

405 See the section on the Arab Industrialization Authority, in chapter 2.

406 Anthony H. Cordesman, *The Gulf and the Search for Strategic Stability* (Boulder, CO: Westview Press, 1984), p. 716; *FT*, May 15, 1984.

407 *Al-Sharq al-Awsat*, April 29, 1982, p. 1.

408 The secret agreement was published by the Iraqi *Al-Rafidin* in London, October 6, 1984.

409 Philip H. Stoddard, "Egypt and the Iran–Iraq War," in Thomas Naff (ed.), *Gulf Security and the Iran–Iraq War* (Washington,D.C.: National Defence University Press, 1985), p. 41.

410 See editorial, *al-Jumhuriyya*, July 10, 1987.

411 On the development and the distinctive features of Egyptian foreign policy in the eighties, see symposium held at the Centre for Political Studies of Cairo University, as published by *al-Siyasa al-Duwaliyya*, April 1987 issue, p. 264.

412 Message from the American Secretary of State in May 1979, as quoted above, in the *Seized Documents*, p. 40.

413 A speech to the People's Council, November 6, 1983, as quoted by: FBIS, *DR*, November 8, 1983, pp. D1–D9.

414 *Emirate News* (Dubai), April 8, 1982.

415 *MEED*, January 27, 1984, p. 12; February 3, 1984.

416 *Al-Usbu' al-'Arabi* (Lebanon), July 11, 1983.

417 See Ibrahim Nafi', *al-Ahram* (international edition), December 28, 1984, pp. 1, 3.

418 See Mubarak interview to the *Washington Post*, February 15, 1984.

419 *Al-Musawwar* (no. 3050), March 25, 1983, pp. 73–4.

## 6 Egypt and the Gulf States, 1985–2000

1 Jordan had renewed relations with Egypt already in September 1984. The UAE renewed relations with Egypt on November 11, 1987, Iraq on November 13, Kuwait and Morocco on November 14, the Yemeni Arab Republic and Bahrain on November 16, Saudi Arabia and Mauritania on November 17 and Qatar on November 18. The two Arab states that did not follow suit at the stage were Syria and Libya. Itamar Rabinovich and Haim Shaked (eds.), *Middle East Contemporary Survey*, vol. XI, 1987 (Boulder, CO and Oxford: Westview Press, for the Moshe Dayan Center, the Shiloah Institute, 1989 [*MECS*, 1987]), p. 341.

2  See also Paul Sullivan, "Contrary Views of Economic Diplomacy in the Arab World: Egypt," *ASQ* (*Arab Studies Quarterly*), vol. 21, no. 4, Fall 1999, p. 65; Itamar Rabinovich and Haim Shaked (eds.), *Middle East Contemporary Survey*, vol. X, 1986 (Boulder, CO and Oxford: Westview Press, for the Moshe Dayan Center, the Shiloah Institute, 1988 (*MECS*, 1986), p. 559; Itamar Rabinovich and Haim Shaked (eds.), *Middle East Contemporary Survey*, vol. IX, 1984–5 (Westview Press, for the Moshe Dayan Center, the Shiloah Institute, 1987 [*MECS*, 1984/85]), p. 604.

3  *MECS*, 1986, p. 109.

4  *MECS*, 1987, p. 135.

5  Ami Ayalon and Haim Shaked (eds.), *Middle East Contemporary Survey*, vol. XII, 1988 (Boulder, CO and Oxford: Westview Press, for the Moshe Dayan Center, the Shiloah Institute, 1990 (*MECS*, 1988), p. 403.

6  *MECS*, 1990, p. 335. It should be noted that Egyptian–Iraqi relations soured even before the invasion of Kuwait, when early in November 1989, reported Iraqi maltreatment of Egyptian workers in Iraq prompted a massive flight of Egyptians back home (*MECS*, 1989, p. 313).

7  Avraham Sela (ed.), *The Decline of the Arab–Israeli Conflict: Middle East Politics and the Quest for Regional Order* (NY: SUNY, 1998). pp. 273–4.

8  Ami Ayalon (ed.), *Middle East Contemporary Survey*, vol. XV, 1991 (Boulder, CO and Oxford: Westview Press, for the Moshe Dayan Center, the Shiloah Institute, 1993 [*MECS*, 1991]), p. 339.

9  Weitzman Bruce Maddy (ed.), *Middle East Contemporary Survey*, vol. XX, 1996 (Boulder, CO and Oxford: Westview Press, for the Moshe Dayan Center, the Shiloah Institute, 1998 [*MECS*, 1996]) p. 279, and EIU, country profile, October 9, 2001.

10  *MECS*, 1991, p. 141.

11  Ami Ayalon (ed.), *Middle East Contemporary Survey*, vol. XVI, 1992 (Boulder, CO and Oxford: Westview Press, for the Moshe Dayan Center, the Shiloah Institute, 1994 [*MECS*, 1992]), p. 163.

12  *MECS*, 1991, pp. 344–7.

13  Weitzman Bruce Maddy (ed.), *Middle East Contemporary Survey*, vol. XXIII, 1999 (Tel Aviv: The Moshe Dayan Center, the Shiloah Institute, 2001 [*MECS*, 1999], p. 219.

14  Weitzman, Bruce Maddy (ed.), *Middle East Contemporary Survey*, vol. XXI, 1997 (Boulder, CO and Oxford: Westview Press, for the Moshe Dayan Center, the Shiloah Institute, 1999 [*MECS, 1997*]), p. 330.

15  *Ibid.*, p. 247.

16  "*U.S. Policy Toward Egypt,*" Hearing before the Committee on International Relations of the House of Representatives, Washington D.C, held on April 10, 1997.

17  It should be noted that as of the beginning of the year 2002 the receipt of aid by Egypt is the responsibility of the International Cooperation Sector within the Ministry for Foreign Affairs, headed by a newly appointed Minister of State – Ms. Dayza Abulnaga. Prior to December 2001, aid coordination in the Egyptian government was the responsibility of the Ministry of International Cooperation, with the Ministry of Foreign Affairs responsible for UN agencies. The organization was changed largely because donors expressed general dissatisfaction with the quality of government aid coordination, and the Government's desire to make aid coordination more efficient. See: Nicola Pratt, "Egypt, A Country Case Study Prepared for the OCD DAC Task Force on Donor Practices," September 2002. At the Consultative Group meeting in Feburary 2002 donors pledged $10 billion over three years in order to support the Egyptian economy in the context of the post-9/11 period, pp. 8–9.

18  Itamar Rabinovich and Haim Shaked (eds.), *Middle East Contemporary Survey*, vol.

XI, 1987 (Boulder, CO and Oxford: Westview Press, for the Moshe Dayan Center, the Shiloah Institute, 1989), p. 345.

19  IMF, *Arab Republic of Egypt – Recent Economic Developments*, SM/92/155, August 11, 1992, pp. 41–4.

20  *Ibid.*

21  In some other years Egypt received small credit lines. See, for example, credit line of $20 million that the National Bank of Egypt has signed with the Arab Trade Finance Programme, *Middle East Economic Digest*, February 27, 1998.

22  Central Bank of Egypt, *Economic Review 2000/2001* (vol. XLI, no. 4), p. 81.

23  "*100 Milyun Dular min al-Sunduq al-Saudi li-Mashruaat al-Tanmiya fi Misr*," *Al-Ahram Al-Iqtisadi*, November 20, 2000.

24  *OAPEC Monthly Bulletin* (August/September 2002), p. 30.

25  *Ibid*, p. 28.

26  Nadim Kawach, "GCC aid down sharply between 1995–2001," *Gulf News*, February 7, 2002.

27  EIU, *Saudi Arabia – Country Profile*, December 20, 1996, December 30, 1997, June 1, 2001, April 15, 2002.

28  IMF, *Saudi Arabia, Statistical Appendix*, SM/01/283, September 18, 2001. pp. 27 and 43.

29  Central Bank of Egypt, *Economic Review 2000/2001* (vol. XLI, no. 4), p. 81.

30  EIU, *Kuwait Country Profile* (August 8, 2002).

31  For detailed analysis of EU aid to Egypt, see: Nicola Pratt, "Egypt, A Country Case Study Prepared for the OCD DAC Task Force on Donor Practices," September 2002. At the Consultative Group meeting in Feburary 2002 donors pledged $10 billion over three years in order to support the Egyptian economy in the context of the post-9/11 period.

32  Antoine Basile, "Regulatory and Institutional Framework for Investment in the Arab World (Revisited)," *The Arab Bank Review*, vol. 4, no. 1, April 2002, pp. 18–29.

33  *Ibid,.* p. 31.

34  "Ittiham al-Hukuma bil-Tasabub fi Hurub al-Istithmarat," *Masrawy News* (internet version), May 12, 2002.

35  *MECS*, 1986, pp. 559–60.

36  See, for example, the Saudi–Egyptian committee, Ahmad al-Razaz, "Al-Taawun al-Misri Al-Saudi . . . Namudhaj Arabi," *Al-Ahram Al-Iqtisadi*, December 7, 1992, p. 50.

37  Shahira Al-Rafiii, "Misr Aula Fi Al-Istithmarat," *Al-Ahram Al-Iqtisadi*, August 24, 1992, p. 25, and *Middle East Economic Digest*, November 11, 1994.

38  "Al-Istithmarat Al-Arabiyya fi Misr," *Al-Ahram Al-iqtisadi*, February 23, 1998, p. 20.

39  *Al-Yaum*, April 12, 1998, *Al-Hayat*, December 7, 1998, *SPA* news agency, Riyadh (in Arabic), June 6, 1999, and *Xinhua News Agency Bulletin*, June 12, 2000.

40  "Al-Alaqat Al-Misriyya Al-Saudiyya Wa-Hulm Al-Takattul Al-Arabi," *Al-Ahram Al-Iqtisadi*, November 20, 2000, p. 40.

41  *Business Today* (Egypt), October 2002.

42  Regarding the Toshka project, on August 18, 1997, *Al-Ahram Al-Iqtisadi*, reported the establishment of a Saudi company headed by the Emir Walid bin Tallal in Egypt, with an approved capital of one billion Egyptian pounds (US$ 295.85 million) to invest in the improvement of land in the Toshka area, the raising of live-stock, poultry and fish, and other industrial and agricultural activities. The Toshka project attracted many other investors. On October 6, 1997 the same publication reported that a Kuwaiti company – The Gulf Company for Agricultural Investment and Development – was also established to improve and cultivate land in Toshka. This company had an

approved capital of one billion Egyptian pounds (US$ 295.8 million), and an issued capital of 100 million Egyptian pounds (US$ 29.58 million).

43  Paul Sullivan, "Contrary Views of Economic Diplomacy in the Arab World: Egypt," *ASQ*, volume 21, no. 4, Fall 1999, pp. 65–7. The author dealt with the years 1974–96.

44  *Al-Ahram Al-Iqtisadi*, March 11, 1996.

45  *Ibid.*, December 22, 1997, p. 12.

46  *Ibid.*, April 6, 1998, p. 15.

47  *XINHUA News Agency Bulletin*, Decebmber 6, 1999.

48  *Al-Ahram Al-Iqtisadi*, November 20, 2000, p. 7.

49  "Al-Istithmarat Al-Arabiyya fi Misr," *Al-Ahram Al-Iqtisadi*, February 23, 1998, p. 21. The main projects to which this fund contributed were the al-Karimat power station project, sanitary drainage services in 46 towns, a high quality steel project, and several projects of the Egyptian Social Fund for Development.

50  "Al-Istithmarat Al-Arabiyya fi Misr," *Al-Ahram Al-Iqtisadi*, February 23, 1998, p. 21.

51  *Ibid.*.

52  Ahmad al-Razaz, "Al-Jusur Al-Mumtadda Bayna Misr Wa-Duwal Al-Khalij Al-Arabiyya," *Al-Ahram Al-Iqtisadi*, January 22, 1990, p. 35.

53  "Al-Istithmarat Al-Arabiyya Fi Misr," *Al-Ahram Al-Iqtisadi*, February 23, 1998, p. 21.

54  Al-Muassasa Al-Arabiyya Li-Daman Al-Istithmar, *Munakh Al-Istithmar fi Al-Duwal Al-Arabiyya, 2001, Al-Safa*, 2002, p. 36.

55  "Al-Alaqat al-Misriyya al-Saudiyya wa-Hulm al-Takattul al-Arabi," *Al-Ahram Al-Iqtisadi*, November 20, 2000, p. 40.

56  Al-Muassasa Al-Arabiyya Li-Daman Al-Istithmar, *Munakh Al-Istithmar fi Al-Duwal Al-Arabiyya 2001, Al-Safa*, 2002, p. 59.

57  *Employment and Unemployment jin Egypt* (Policy Viewpoint, no. 11, Cairo: ECES, June 2002).

58  In Kuwait, for example, in 1989, out of a total of 783,094 foreign workers 45 percent were Arab and 54 percent Asian. By the year 2000, out of 1,004,721 foreign workers the Arabs constituted 31.8 percent and the Asians 67.1 percent. See Kuwait, Public Authority for Civil Information, *Population and Labor Force*, December 1989 and January 2000.

59  Gil Feiler, "Migration and Recession: Arab Labor Mobility in the Middle East, 1982–89." *Population and Development Review*, vol. 17, no. 1, March 1991.

60  At the same time over 800,000 Yemenis were expelled from Saudi Arabia and other GCC countries, and about 350,000 Palestinians from Jordan left Kuwait and the other Gulf countries. See: Gil Feiler, *Labour Migration in the Middle East Following the Iraqi Invasion of Kuwait* (Jerusalem: IPCRI, 1993); Nader Fergany, *Aspects of Labor Migration and Unemployment in the Arab Region* (Cairo: Almishkat Center for Research, 2001), pp. 3–4.

61  Nader Fergany, *Aspects of Labor Migration and Unemployment in the Arab Region* (Cairo: Almishkat Center for Research, 2001), pp. 3–4.

62  *Employment and Unemployment in Egypt* (Policy Viewpoint, no. 11, Cairo: ECES, June 2002).

63  KSA, *SAMA annual report 1997*; *MECS*, 1991, p. 634.

64  According to the 1996 census 2.18 million Egyptians lived abroad as temporary migrants. See EIU, *Egypt Country Forecast*, January 25, 2000.

65  On efforts in Saudi Arabia to replace foreign workers (the "Saudization process"), see: IMF: *Saudi Arabia, Selected Issues and Statistical Appendix*, SM/02/255, August 13, 2002, pp. 34–5.

66  In Oman, for example, in the period 1998–2000 around 71 percent of the male Omanis seeking jobs for the first time only had an elementary education or less. (See: *Oman*,

paper presented by the Minister of Social Development in the conference Employing National manpower, October 2001).

67 According to official Saudi report, the government had realized savings of about SR 12 billion as a result of employing non Saudis instead of Saudis during 1999. See: Maurice Girgis, "The GCC Factor in Future Arab Labor Migration," *Memo*, 2002.

68 In Kuwait, total population decreased by 1.7 percent from 2.255 million at the end of 1999 to 2.217 million at the end of 2000. This decrease resulted from the decline in non-Kuwaiti population by 4.7 percent from 1.443 at the end of 1999 to 1.375 million at the end of 2000. The rate of Kuwaitis to total population rose from 36 percent at end of 1999 to 38 percent at end of 2000. See: Kuwait, Central Bank of Kuwait, *Economic Report*, 2000, pp. 55–7.

68 KSA, SAMA, *37 Annual Report 1422* (2001 G), 2001 Riyadh, pp. 265, 271, 274.

69 147 EIU, *KSA, Country Profile*, 15/4/2002, 1/6/2001, 30/12/1997, 20/12/1996.

70 Paul Sullivan, "Contrary Views of Economic Diplomacy in the Arab World: Egypt," *ASQ*, vol. 21, no. 4, Fall 1999, p. 67.

71 UNCTAD, *Handbook of Statistics 2001*.

72 Kemal Dervish, Peter Bocock and Julia Devlin, *Intraregional Trade among Arab countries: Building Competitive Economic Neighborhood*, Paper presented at the Middle East Institute 52nd Annual Conference, Washington, DC, October 17, 1998. For in-depth discussion see Roger Owen, "Inter-Arab Economic Relations during the Twentieth Century: World Market versus Regional Market? In *Middle East Dilemma: The Politics and Economics of Arab Integration,* ed. Michael Hudson (New York: Columbia University Press, 1999).

73 IMF, *Direction of Trade Statistics.*

74 Dalil al-Musaddir al-Misri lil-Saudiyya," *Al-ahram Al-Iqtidadi*, October 8, 2001.

75 Victor Lebedev, *ITAR-TASS*, November 29, 1999 .

76 *AFP*, January 8, 1999.

## 7  AOC Aid: the Shifting Equation

1 Gad Gilbar, "One Arab State, Many Arab States: The Impact of Population Growth and Oil Revenues," in E. Kedourie and S. G. Haim (eds.), *Essays on the Economic History of the Middle East* (London: Frank Cass, 1988), pp. 201–2, 204, 206.

2 See, for example: *Shadhli*, p. 191; Heikal, *The Assassination of Sadat*, pp. 80, 115–16; Osama Hamed, "Egypt's Open Door Economic Policy: An Attempt at Economic Integration in the Middle East," *IJMES* (vol. 13, 1981), p. 6; Henry F. Jackson, "Sadat's Perils," *Foreign Policy* (no. 42, spring 1981), pp. 64–5. Extensive funds are transferred by the Gulf States also to Islamic banking institutions, and outstanding among them are Al-Riyan, Al-Sharif, Al-Sa'ad. The Egyptian government is aggravated by this investment channel – through which billions of dollars have been transferred in recent years – which reaches, inter alia, extremist Islamic groups. The Egyptian government finds itself in a kind of Catch 22 situation. With the objective of not harming real investments, it allows the funneling of Islamic capital to Egypt to continue, while at the same time it is aware that part of these "investments" are sometimes contrary to the state's interests. See: A personal interview by the author with the Supreme Court Judge Sa'id 'Ashmawi in Cairo. The following details show the increase of activities by these banks. In 1971 one Islamic bank was doing business in Egypt, in 1975 three banks, in 1980 – 25 banks and in 1987 – 95 banks and Islamic companies. On the Islamic banks and companies in Egypt and the government's attempts to handle them, see: *al-Ittihad*, UAE, August 19, 1987, p. 3; *al-Jumhuriyya*, Egypt, September 2, 1987, p. 23; *MEED*, January 9, 1988, p. 9; *The Middle East*, January 1988, pp. 22–4.

3   Kerr, in Kerr and Yassin (eds.), *Rich and Poor States in the Middle East: Egypt and the New Arab Order* (Boulder, CO: Westview Press, 1982), pp. 10–11.

4   Elias Tuma, *Economic and Political Change in the Middle East* (California: Pacific Books, 1987), pp. 198–202.

5   Sharaby in *the A. Ibrahim dossier*, pp. 301–4; Kerr, in Kerr and Yassin, *Rich and Poor States in the Middle East*, pp. 11–12; Dessouki, in *Kerr and Yassin*, p. 343; Ya'akov Goldberg, "Saudi Foreign Policy in the Inter-Arab arena: Continuity and Change", in Ya'akov Goldberg and Yosef Kostiner (eds.), *Decade of Reduction - The Middle East in the shadow of a Declining Oil Economy* (Tel Aviv: Dayan Centrer, January 1987), pp. 58–63; 'Abdallah Fahd al-Nafisi, *Al-Kuwayt, al-Ra'y al-Akhar* (London: Ta Ha, 1978), pp. 13, 27–35; Bahgat Korany, "Political Petrolism and Contemporary Arab Politics, 1967–1983," *Journal of Asian and African Studies* (vol. 21, nos. 1–2, 1986), pp. 66–80; Muhammad Rumaihi, *Beyond Oil: Unity and Development in the Gulf* (trans. James Deckins. London: Al-Saqi Books, 1986), passim.

6   Eliyahu Kanovsky, "'Arab Haves' and 'Have-nots'," *Jerusalem Quarterly* (Fall 1976), p. 104.

7   On the realism school of thought, see: H. Morgenthau, *Politics between Nations* (Tel Aviv: Yahdav publications, Fourth Edition, 1968); S. Hofman, "Notes on the Limits of Realism," *Social Research* (vol. 48, no. 4, 1982), pp. 653–9.

8   Hufbaur and Schott critically examined 103 boycott cases, from 1914 (the US against Germany) up to 1985 (the USA et al. against Grenada), and they arrived at the conclusion that the sanctions were successful in only 36 percent of the cases. Other studies gave even much lower success rates. See: Gary C. Hufbaur, Jeffrey J. Schott, Economic Sanctions Reconsidered: History and Current Policy (Washington, D.C.: Institute for International Economics, 1985): Robert Gilpin, "Structural Constraints on Economic Leverage: Market-type System," in Gordon H. Mccormick and Richard E. Bissell (eds.), *Strategic Dimensions of Economic Behavior* (New York: Praeger, 1984), pp. 115–126.

9   *Al-Sha'b*, December 27, 1983, p. 12.

10  On this, see for example Shimon Shamir's words at following meeting: "Two years after the signing of the peace treaty between Israel and Egypt" (Tel Aviv University Peace Papers, May 20, 1981), p. 8.

11  Quoted in: Helena Cabban, *CSM*, September 2, 1981.

12  Kamal Hasan 'Ali, *al-Musawwar*, March 25, 1983, pp. 25–7.

13  See an in-depth description in the Ph.D. thesis of: Dennis Joseph Sullivan, "American Economic Aid to Egypt, 1975-86: Political and Bureaucratic Struggles over Aid Disbursement and Development Choices," Ph.D. dissertation, the University of Michigan, 1987), ch. 4–5.

14  Ayubi, *Bureaucracy in Egypt*, 1980, p. 80. On this subject, see also: Morroe Berger, *Bureaucracy and Society in Modern Egypt* (Princeton: Princeton University Press, 1957).

15  Avraham Sela, *The Decline of the Arab–Israeli conflict: Middle East Politics and the Quest for Regional Order* (New York: SUNY, 1998), pp. 315–20.

16  Few sources provide as precise an insight into the thinking of the Egyptian leadership as the Al Ahram Institute. A state think tank under the wings of the government's official newspaper, the Al Ahram Institute has a long history of accurately reflecting the current line of thinking among Egyptian decision makers on issues ranging from foreign relations to domestic economics

17  "Al-Nizam al-Arabi Bayna Furas al-Waqi wa-Quyud al-Madi," in Dr. Wahid Abd al-Majid (ed.), *Al-Taqrir al-Istratiji al-Arabi, 1999* (Cairo: Markaz al-Dirasat al-Siyasiyya wal-Istratijiyya, January 2000), p. 144

18  "Al-Nizam al-Arabi Bayna Furas al-Waqi wa-Quyud al-Madi," in Dr. Wahid Abd al-Majid (ed.), *Al-Taqrir al-Istratiji al-Arabi, 1999* (Cairo: Markaz al-Dirasat al-Siyasiyya wal-Istratijiyya, January 2000), p. 144
19  Victor Lebedev, ITAR-TASS, November 29, 1999
20  AFP, January 8, 1999

# Bibliography

---

The Bibliography is organized into the following sections (abbreviations are listed on pages xix–xx):

Official Egyptian Sources
    In Arabic
    In English
Researches by Egyptian Ministries or American Aid Agencies
al-Ahram Archive (Cairo) media files, 1960–1985
Reports from Gulf and Other Arab States
    In Arabic
    In English
Reports by Inter-Arab Institutions
    Aid Funds
    Yearbooks and Quarterlies
    Research Institutions
        In Arabic
        In English
The World Bank
The International Monetary Fund (IMF)
    Correspondence
    Documents and Publications
Other Financial Bodies
OECD Documents and Reports
United Nations
    Papers, Publications and Reports
    Correspondence
    International Labor Organization (ILO)
Official American Institutions and Agencies
    Congress Delegations, Hearings before Senate Committees and Reports Submitted to the American Congress
Guides and Directories (Including Official Guides)
Personal Interviews
    Correspondence
Memoirs
Conferences
Books in Arabic

Articles in Arabic
Books in Hebrew
Articles in Hebrew
Books in Other Languages
Articles in Other Languages

## Official Egyptian Sources

### In Arabic

Jumhuriyyat Misr al-'Arabiyya, *Jadwal Muqaran lil-Mazaya al-Muqarrara bi-Qanun al-Istithmar wa-ma Yuqabiluha min Ahkam fi Qanun al-Sharikat al-Jadid*, Raqm al-Ida' bi-Dar al-Kutub al-Qawmiyya, 3596, Cairo: 1984.

Jumhuriyyat Misr al-'Arabiyya, *Yumkin al-Mustathmir al-Ajnabi an Ya'mal fi Misr bi-Ahad al-Ashkal al-Qanuniyya al-Atiya*, Cairo: n.d.

Jumhuriyyat Misr al-'Arabiyya, al-Jihaz al-Markazi lil-Ta'bi'a al-'Amma wal-Ihsa', *al-Atlas al-Ihsa'i li-Jumhuriyyat Misr al-'Arabiyya,* Marja' Raqm 16000/79, Cairo: October 1979.

————, *al-Nashra al-Rub' Sanawiyya lil-Ihsa'at al-Siyahiyya*, Cairo: August 1971.

————, *al-Ta'dad al-'Amm lil-Sukkan wal-Iskan 1976,* Marja' Raqm 1978–15111–93, Cairo: September 1978.

————, *al-Nashra al-Shahriyya lil-Tijara al-Kharijiyya*, Cairo: 1976–1984, various volumes.

Jumhuriyyat Misr al-'Arabiyya, al-Hay'a al-'Amma lil-Istithmar wal-Manatiq al-Hurra, Qita' al-Manatiq al-Hurra, *Haqa'iq wa-Arqam 1984*, Cairo: n.d.

————, Qita' al-Buhuth wal-Ma'lumat, *al-Taqrir al-Sanawi*, Cairo: 1979–1984/1985.

————, *Khutub wa-Akhadith al-Rais Muhammad Anwar al-Sadat, al-Qadaya al-Dakhiliyya wal-Kharijiyya,* Cairo: n.d., 7 volumes.

————, *Khutub wa-Akhadith al-Rais Muhammad Husni Mubarak fi al-Fatra min Uktubar 1981–Disambar 1984*. Cairo: n.d., 7 volumes.

Jumhuriyyat Misr al-'Arabiyya, Wizarat al-Iqtisad wal-Tijara al-Kharijiyya, "Qarar Raqm 501 li-Sanat 1985 bi-Shan Ta'dil al-La'iha al-Tanfidhiyya li- Qanun Nizam Istithmar al-Mal al-'Arabi wal-Ajnabi wal-Manatiq al-Hurra," *al-Waqai' al-Misriyya al-'Adad 280 fi 10 Disambar,* Cairo: 1985.

Jumhuriyyat Misr al-'Arabiyya, Ma'had al-Takhtit al-Qawmi, *Taqwim Mawqif al-Istithmarat al-'Arabiyya wal-Ajnabiyya fi al-Sab'inat*, Mudhakkara Kharjiyya Raqm 1326, Cairo: June 1982.

### In English

Arab Republic of Egypt (ARE), Central Agency for Public Mobilization and Statistics (CAPMAS), *Egypt Statistical Indicators (1952–1979)*, Cairo: July 1980.

————, *Statistical Yearbook*, Cairo: 1967–1985, various issues.

————, "A Statement on the Population of the ARE," *Memo*, Cairo: July 1, 1986.

————, *Status of the Open Door Economy up to 31.12.1981,* Cairo: February 1982.

ARE, Central Bank of Egypt, *Annual Report*, Cairo: various issues.

————, *Economic Review,* Cairo: various issues.

ARE, General Authority for Investment and Free Zones (GAFIZ), *Facts and Figures,* Cairo: September 1977-June 1985, various issues.

————, *Investment Review, A Quarterly on Investment Condition in Egypt,* Cairo: various issues until volume 7, 1986.

————, *Decree of the Minister of Economy and Economic Cooperation no. 375 1977, for Issuing the Executive Regulation for the Law of Arab and Foreign Investment and Free Zones*, Cairo: 1977.

————, *Law no. 43 of 1974 Concerning the Investment of Arab and Foreign Funds and the Free Zones As Amended by Law no. 32 of 1977*, Cairo: n.d.

————, Statistics and Information Department, *Report on the Arab and Foreign Investment Until 31.1 .1977,* Cairo: 1978.

ARE, General Authority for the Promotion of Tourism, *Annual Report 1984,* Cairo: n.d.

————, Information Department, *Total Number of Tourists,* Cairo: various issues.

ARE, Institute of National Planning, *Industrialization in Egypt and the New International Economic Order,* Memo no. 1248, Cairo: August 1979.

Arman, Ismail M. I., *Manpower and Employment of Egypt, 1980–2000,* Memo no. 1320, Cairo: March 1982.

ARE, Ministry of Economy, *Aswan Aid Donors' Meeting,* Cairo: 1981.

ARE, Ministry of Economy and Economic Cooperation, *A Report on the New Investment Policies According To Law no. 43 of 1974,* Cairo: December 1979.

ARE, Ministry of Economy, Foreign Trade and Economic Cooperation, Economic Studies Unit, *Insufficiency of Saving or Shortage of Foreign Exchange,* Cairo: August 1980.

ARE, Ministry of Industry and Mineral Wealth, General Organization for Industrialization, *Industrial Investment Opportunity in Egypt,* Cairo: June 1982.

ARE, Ministry of Information, State Information Service (SIS), *Egypt: Facts and Figures, 1985,* Cairo: n.d.

————, *The October Paper*, Cairo: 1974.

ARE, Ministry of Planning, *The Detailed Frame of the Five Year Plan for Economic and Social Development 1982/83–1986/87,* Cairo: December 1982.

————, *The Five Year Plan*, Cairo: August 1977, 13 volumes.

————, *Egypt's Development Strategy. Economic Management and Growth Objectives 1980–1984*, Cairo: November 1979.

————, *List of Projects of the Second Five Year Plan With Foreign Investment Component,* Cairo: October 1987.

ARE, Ministry of Tourism, Central Directory for Information, Research and Training Information Center, *Statistical Bulletin*, Cairo: various issues.

ARE, Presidency of the Republic, The Specialized National Council, *Policy on the Economics of Egyptian Expatriate Savings,* Report Submitted To the Council on 19.12.1982, Cairo: December 1982.

ARE, Suez Canal Authority, *Suez Canal Yearly Report*, Cairo: 1979–1984, various issues.

ARE, Federation of Egyptian Industries, *Yearbook*, Cairo: 1976–1983/4, various issues.

ARE, National Bank of Egypt (NBE), *Economic Bulletin*, Cairo: various issues.

ARE, UNDP, *Suez Canal Region Plan 1976*, Cairo: n.d.


## Researches by Egyptian Ministries or American Aid Agencies

Bolin, Richard. *The Assessment of Free Zones in Egypt,* A report presented to GAFIZ, Cairo: February 1980.

Coopers and Lybrand. *Egyptian Industrial Free Zones, Interim Report.* Contract no. Aid/otr-C-1773, Work Order no. 4, Washington, D.C.: September 15, 1980.

Shakeer, Farouk and Mona Ghaleb Mourad. *Cost/benefit Assessment of Free Zones, A Case Study on Egypt*, Cairo: May 1981.

Reynolds, Smith and Hills. *Scoped Environmental Assessment of the Public Free Zones At El Ameria, Port Said, and Nasr City, ARE,* A report presented to GAFIZ, Ministry of

Economic Cooperation, Cairo, USAID Grant no. 263 263-0042, Jacksonville (Florida): n.d.

Ullman, A. *The Assessment of Free Zones in Egypt,* A report presentend to GAFIZ, Cairo: 1980.

## al-Ahram Archive (Cairo) media files, 1960–1985

Milaffat Misr/Saʻudiya

Milaffat Misr/Kuwait

Milaffat Misr/Khalij

Milaffat Misr/ʻIraq

Milaffat Qurud/Kharijiyya

Milaffat Misr/ʻUmmal

Milaffat Misr/Infitah

Milaffat Misr/Iqtisad Dawli

Milaffat Misr/al-Wilayat al-Muttahida

## Reports from Gulf and Other Arab States

### In Arabic

al-Mamlaka al-Arabiyya al-Saudiyya, al-Muʻassasa al-ʻAmma lil-Batrul wal-Maʻadin, *Al-Taqrir al-Sanawi 1983/1984*, al-Riyadh: Batrumin, 1985.

al-Mamlaka al-Arabiyya al-Saudiyya, Majlis al-Ghuraf al-Tijariyya wal-Sinaʻiyya al-Suʻudiyya, *Wafd Rijal al-Aʻmal al-Suʻudiyyin ila Jumhuriyyat Misr al-ʻArabiyya, 8–11 Safar 1407 (11–14 October 1986),* al-Riyadh: n.d.

Munazzamat al-Khalij lil-Istithmarat al-Sinaʻiyya, Bank al-Maʻlumat al-Sinaʻiyya, *Dalil al-Bayanat al-Ijtimaʻiyya wal-Iqtisadiyya fi Duwal al-Khalij al- ʻArabiyya*, 1984.

Munazzamat al-ʻArabiyya lil-Tarbiya wal-Thaqafa wal-ʻUlum, Maʻhad al-Buhuth wal-Dirasat al-ʻArabiyya, *Istikhdamat ʻAwaʻid al-Naft al-ʻArabiyya hata Nihayat al-Sabʻinat*, Cairo: 1985.

al-Qiyada al-Qawmiyya li-Hizb al-Baʻth al-ʻArabi al-Ishtiraki, *al-Jamiʻa al-ʻArabiyya wa-Muʻtamarat al-Qimma*, Damascus: 1985.


### In English

Kingdom of Saudi Arabia (KSA), Ministry of Finance and National Economy, *Statistical Yearbook*, Riyadh: various issues.

KSA, Ministry of Information, *Higher Education: On the Road to the Future*, Riyadh: n.d.

KSA, Ministry of Planning, *The Third Development Plan, 1400–1405 (1980–1985),* Riyadh: n.d.

KSA, Saudi Arabia Monetary Agency (SAMA), *Annual Report*, Riyadh: various issues.

————, *Statistical Summary*, Riyadh: various issues.

Kuwait, The Planning Board, Central Statistical Office, *Annual Statistical Abstract*, Kuwait: 1978.

————, *Quarterly Statistical Bulletin*, Kuwait: 1978–1979, various issues.

————, Central Bank of Kuwait, *Economic Report*, Kuwait: various issues.

Kuwait, Kuwait Oil Company (KOC), *Annual Report*, Kuwait: 1977, 1978.

Kuwait, Public Authority for Civil Information, *Population and Labor Force*, Kuwait: December 1989, January 2000.

United Arab Emirates (UAE), Central Bank, *Annual Report*, Abu Dhabi: December 31, 1980.

————, *Fourth Anniversary*, Abu Dhabi: 1975.

UAE, Ministry of Petroleum and Mineral Resources, *UAE Oil Statistical Review*, Abu Dhabi: 1981.

## Reports by Inter-Arab Institutions

### Aid Funds

Abu Dhabi Fund for Arab Development, *Annual Report*, Abu Dhabi: various issues.

Arab African International Bank, *Annual Report*, Cairo: various issues.

Arab Bank for Economic Development in Africa, *Annual Report*, Khartoum: various issues.

Arab Fund for Economic and Social Development, *Annual Report*, Kuwait: various issues.

Arab International Bank, *Annual Report*, Cairo: various issues.

Arab Monetary Fund, *Annual Report*, Abu Dhabi: various issues.

Faisal Islamic Bank of Egypt, *Annual Report*, Cairo: various issues.

Kuwait Fund for Arab Economic Development (KFAED), *Annual Report*, Kuwait: various issues.

————, *Geographical Distribution of Arab Foreign Trade 1969–1976,* Kuwait: 1977.

Organization of the Petroleum Exporting Countries (OPEC), Fund for International Development, *Annual Report*, Vienna: various issues.

Organization of Arab Petroleum Exporting Countries (OAPEC), ENI, *The Interdependence Project Report 14: The Labor Market in Arab Countries,* Kuwait: December 1985.

### Yearbooks and Quarterlies

League of Arab States/Economic Commission for Western Asia (ECWA), *Statistical Indicators of the Arab World for the Period 1970–1979*, Beirut: 1981.

OPEC, *Annual Report*, Vienna: various issues.

————, *Annual Statistical Bulletin*, Vienna: various issues.

————, *Official Resolution and Press Releases, 1960–1983*, Oxford: Pergamon Press, 1983.

————, *Statistical Time Series*, Vienna: various issues.

————, *OPEC Bulletin* (including supplemental *Member Country Profiles*), Vienna: various monthly issues.

————, *OPEC Review*, Vienna: various quarterly issues.

OAPEC, *OAPEC Bulletin*, Kuwait: various issues.

### Research Institutions

### In Arabic

al-Muassasa al-Arabiyya Li-Daman al-Istithmar, *Munakh al-Istithmar fi al-Duwal al-Arabiyya*, Safat (Kuwait): various issues.

### In English

Bureau of Lebanese and Arab Documentation, *Argus of the Arab Economy, Economic Review of the Arab World*, Beirut: 1970–1981, various quarterly issues.

Council of Arab Economic Unity (CAEU), General Secretariat, *Direct Investment and Joint Venture in View of Arab Experience,* Amman: 1980.

————, Arab Central Statistical Bureau, *Statistical Yearbook for Arab Countries 1978*, volume III, Cairo: December 1978.

## The World Bank

International Bank for Reconstruction and Development (IBRD), *Appraisal of the Rehabilitation of the Suez Canal, ARE,* Reports no. 578-Egt and P-1488a, Cairo: November 19, 1974.

————, Industrial Projects Department, *Appraisal of Talkha II Fertilizer Project, Egypt*, Report no. 456-UAR, May 28, 1974.

————, *ARE: Current Economic Situation and Growth Prospects*, October 1983.

————, *The Economic Development of Libya*, Report of a Mission Organized by the IBRD at the Request of the Government of Libya, John Hopkins Press for IBRD, 1960.

————, International Finance Corporation (IFC), *Project Appraisal Report, Arab Ceramic Company S.A-Egypt*, Report no. Ifc/t-169, April 8, 1976.

————, *ARE, Recent Economic Development and External Capital Requirement*, Reports no. 2071-Egt, May 19, 1978; 2738-Egt, November 12, 1979.

————, *Egypt Appraisal of Tourah Cement Expansion Project*, Report no.608-Egt, 2 volumes, December 30, 1974.

————, *Egypt Textile Project*, Report no. P-1835-EGT, 1976.

————, *The Egyptian Economy in 1974: Its Position and Prospects*, Report no. 491a-Egt, September 25, 1974.

————, *Report and Recommendation for a Second Railway Project*, Report no. P-1552a-Egt, March 10, 1975.

————, *Report and Recommendation for a Telecommunications Project*, Report no. P-1587a-Egt, April 28, 1975.

————, *Second Bank of Alexandria Project*, Report no. P-1670-Egt, July 2, 1975.

————, *Suez Canal Expansion Project*, Report no. P-2030-Egt, July 27, 1977.

————, *Tourah Cement Expansion Project*, Report no. P-1540a-Egt, January 15, 1975.

————, *UAR*, R71-188, July 19, 1971.

————, *UAR, Document of International Development Association*, Report no. P-1410a, June 6, 1974.

World Bank (WB), *Annual Report*, Washington D.C.: various issues.

————, *Appraisal of the Bank of Alexandria, Egypt*, Report no. 797-EGT, June 27, 1975.

————, *ARE Economic Management in a Period of Transition*, 6 volumes, Report no. 1815-Egt, May 8, 1978.

————, *ARE Economic Report*, Report no. 870a-EGT, January 5, 1976; Report no. 1624-Egt, March 22, 1977.

————, *ARE Recent Economic Development and External Capital Requirement*, Report no. 2071-Egt, May 19, 1978: 2738-EGT, November 12, 1979; 3252-EGT, December 19, 1980.

————, *ARE. Current Economic Situation and Economic Reform Program*, Report no. 6195-Egt, October 22, 1986.

————, *ARE. Current Economic Situation and Medium-Term Prospects*, Egypt Division (draft), March 18, 1985.

————, *ARE Telecommunication Organization (ARETO)*, Report no. 631a-Egt, April 11, 1975.

————, *Industrial Imports Project*, Report no. P-2017-Egt, May 24, 1977.

————, *Petroleum and Gas in Non-OPEC Developing Countries: 1976–1985*, WB Staff Working Paper no. 289, Washington D.C.: 1978.

————, *Report and Recommendation of the WB to the Executive Directors on a Proposed Loan to the Egyptian General Petroleum; Corporation*, Report no. P-2580-Egt, June 7, 1979.

————, *World Debt Tables. External Debt of Developing Countries 1985–86 Edition*, Washington D.C.: 1986.

————, *World Economic Outlook*, Washington D.C.: various issues.

————, *World Development Report*, Washington D.C.: various issues.

# The International Monetary Fund (IMF)

## Correspondence

Letters of the Saudi Finance Minister, Muhammad Aba al-Kha'il, to the director of the IMF, Jacques de Larosiere:

————, Appendix to the IMF document no. EBD/79/237, December 19, 1979.

————, December 1, 1980 (no number).

Letter from the Egyptian Minister of Economy, Hasan 'Abbas Zaki, to the director of the IMF, Pierre-Paul Schweitzer, dated June 21, 1970, Appendix to the IMF document no. EBS/70/197, July 14, 1970.

Letter from Shafi'i, Egyptian Minister of Economy, to the director of the IMF, Johannes Witteveen, January 1, 1976, Appendix to the IMF document no. EBS/76/52, February 10, 1976.

Letter from the Egyptian Vice Premier for Economic Affairs, 'Abd al-Mun'im Qaysuni, to the director of the IMF, Witteveen, March 4, 1977, Appendix to the IMF document no. TR/77/9, April 1, 1977.

Letter from the Egyptian Prime Minister, Mamduh Salim, to the director of the IMF, Witteveen, June 10, 1978, plus correction from June 15, 1978.

## Documents and Publications

IMF, ARE, *Recent Economic Development,* SM/71/105, May 3, 1971; Sm/72/135, June 19, 1972; May 7, 1973; July 22, 1974; SM/75/193, July 23, 1975;sm/78/21, January 23, 1978; SM/79/53, February 20, 1979; SM/80/49, February 25, 1980; SM/92/155, August 11, 1992.

————, Document EBS/76/257, June 2, 1976.

————, Document EBS/77/90, January 4, 1977.

————, Document SM/78/9, January 6, 1978.

————, *ARE, Staff Report for the 1979 Article IV Consultation,* Sm/80/41, February 8, 1980.

————, *Balance of Payments Statistics*, various issues and yearbooks.

————, *Direction of Trade Statistics*, various issues and yearbooks.

————, *Government Finance Statistics Yearbook*, various issues.

————, *IMF Survey*, various issues.

————, *International Financial Statistics*, various issues and yearbooks.

————, *Kuwait, Recent Economic Developments*, February 15, 1979; Sm/80/146, June 20, 1982.

————, *Saudi Arabia, an Economic and Financial Survey*, SM/73/269, December 3, 1973; SM/75/157, June 24, 1975; Sm/76/57, March 26, 1976.

————, *Saudi Arabia, Recent Economic Developments*, SM/00/215, September 25, 2000.

————, *Saudi Arabia, Selected Issues and Statistical Appendix*, SM/02/255, 13 August 2002.

————, *Saudi Arabia, Statistical Appendix*, SM/01/283, September 18, 2001.

————, *United Arab Emirates, Recent Economic Developments,* SM/ 80/128, June 6, 1980; SM/81/110, May 28, 1981; SM/82/108, June 10, 1982.

————, *UAR, Exchange System and Use of Fund's Resources,* EBS/70/197, July 14, 1970.

————, *UAR, 1967 Article XIV Consultation,* December 22, 1967.

————, *UAR, Background Material for 1969 Article XIV Consultation,* January 20, 1970.

————,*UAR Part I. Staff Report and Proposed Decision-1968,* Article XIV Consultation, April 14, 1969 and Correction 1, SM/69/47, April 23, 1969; 1969 Article XIV, Sm/70/23, January 22, 1970; 1970 Article XIV, Sm/71/97, April 19, 1971; 1972 Article XIV, April 30, 1973; 1974 Article XIV, Sm/74/172, July 11, 1974.

## Other Financial Bodies

Bank of England, *Quarterly Bulletin*, "The Surpluses of the Oil Exporters," London: June 1980, pp. 154–9.

————, "Oil Exporter's Surpluses and their Deployment," London: March 1985, pp. 69–74.

Deutsche Bank, *OPEC: Facts, Figures and Analyses*, Frankfurt: May 1975 and revised, October 1975.

La Documentation Africaine, *Fichier Des Banques Arabes,* Paris: various issues.

Morgan Guaranty Trust, *World Financial Markets*, New York: various issues.

## OECD Documents and Reports

Organization for Economic Cooperation and Development (OECD), *Aid from OPEC Countries*, Paris: 1983.

————, *Apports De Ressources Des Pays Membres De L'opep Aux Pays En Voie De Developpement. Tableaux Statistiques,* Paris: 1977.

————, *Apports De Ressources Des Pays Membres De L'opep Aux Pays En Voie De Developpement. Tableaux Statistiques 1976–1978,* Dcd/79.31, Paris: 1979.

————, *The Co-Financing of Development Projects by DAC and OPEC Members and International Financial Institutions*, Paris: 1980.

————, *Development Co-Operation Review*, Paris: 1975–1985, various issues.

————, *External Debt of Developing Countries in 1984*, Paris: 1985.

————, *The Flow of Investments, Loans, Development Assistance, Technical Co-Operation and Balance of Payments Support from Middle Eastern Surplus Oil Countries to Arab and non-Arab Developing Countries, CD/eds-74*, Paris: 1974.

————, *Geographical Distribution of Financial Flows to Developing Countries*, Paris: 1984, 1986.

————, *OPEC Countries As Aid Donors, Dd-479*, Paris: February 5, 1976.

————, Secretariat Working Document, *Flows of Resources from OPEC Members to Developing Countries. Statistical Tables 1978– 1980, DCD/81.34*, Paris: October 12, 1981.

## United Nations

### Papers, Publications and Reports

United Nations Development Program, *Summary of the Activities of the United Nations Development Program and Associated Programs in Egypt 1972–1983,* (draft), Geneva: October 1983.

————, *UN Development Coopration 1950–1985. Focus on Egypt*, Geneva: n.d.

————, *Suez Canal Regional Plan 1976,* Geneva: n.d.

United Nations Economic Commission for Western Asia (ECWA), *Development Planning Division, Survey of Economic and Social Development in the ECWA Region, 1976–1977,* Beirut: May 1978.

————, *External Trade Bulletin of the ECWA Region*, 2nd issue, Baghdad: 1984.

————, *1970–1979 Statistical Abstract of the Region of the Economic Commission for Western Asia*, 4th Issue, Beirut: 1981, and 1973–1982; 7th Issue, Baghdad: 1984.

————, Development and Planning Division, *Survey of Economic And Social Development in the ECWA Region, 1976–1977*, Beirut: May 1978.

————, *Survey of Economic and Social Developments in the ESCWA Region, 1998–1999,* New York: 1999.

UN Economic and Social Council, *Multilateral Institutions Providing Financial and Technical Assistance to Developing Countries,* E/ac.54/l.75, Geneva: March 28, 1975.

————, *Memorandum Submitted by the Permanent Representative of Saudi Arabia at the UN,* E/cn.4/941, April 7, 1967.

United Nations Educational, Scientific and Cultural Organization (UNESCO), *Science and Technology in the Development of the Arab States,* Science Policy Studies and Documents no. 41, Paris: 1977.

United Nation Conference on Trade and Development (UNCTAD), *Debt Problems of Developing Countries, Report by the UNCTAD Secretariat,* Td/b/c.3/195, December 14, 1984.

————, *Flow of Financial Resources to, from and among Developing Countries, Including Official Development Assistance: General Monitoring and Review of Measures Contained in Conference Resolution 164 (vi),* Report by UNCTAD Secretariat, Td/b/c.3/198, December 5, 1984;

————, *Private Capital Flows,* Td/b/c.3/196, December 14, 1984.

————, *Tripartite Industrial Cooperation and Cooperation in Third World Countries,* Td/243/supp. 5, April 20, 1979.

### Correspondence

United Nations Security Council, *Letter from the Deputy Permanent Representative of Saudi Arabia [DRSA] addressed to the Secretary General, February 14, 1967,* S/7749, February 15, 1967 and May 16, 1967, S/7889, May 17, 1967.

————, *Exchange of Cables With the DRSA,* S/7793, February 27, 1967.

————, *Letter from DRSA to the President of the UN Security Council,* March 10, 1967, S/7816, March 11, 1967.

————, *Exchange of communication with the DRSA,* S/7842, April 6, 1967.

### International Labor Organization (ILO)

Eldin, Amr Mohie, *External Migration of Egyptian Labor, A Paper Submitted to ILO Strategic Employment Mission to Egypt,* Geneva: September 1980.

International Labour Office (ILO), *World Labor Report,* Geneva: 1984.

## Official American Institutions and Agencies

International Policy Analysis, *An Assessment of Investment Promotion Activities,* Report submitted to Bureau of Private Enterprise, Agency for International Development, January 1984.

Muslim Students Following the Line of the Imam, *Documents from the US Espionage Den,* n.p., n.d., vol. 54.

*Public Papers of the President of the US,* Weekly Compilation of Presidential Documents, J. Carter, Washington, D.C.: GPO, 1977, 1978, various issues.

*The Search for Peace in the Middle East, Document and Statement,* 1967–1979, Washington, D.C.: GPO, 1979.

US Agency for International Development (USAID), Department of State, *Annual Budget Submission FY 1981, Egypt,* June 1979.

————, *Congressional Presentation, FY 1984, Egypt, Annex IV: Near East,* April 1982.

————, *Arab Republic of Egypt,* 263–0047, December 9, 1978.

————, *Egypt: Country Development Strategy Statement, FY 1983,* January 1981.

————, *Memorandum from NE/E, Edward J. Krowitz, Egypt Economic Situation and Debt Repayment Prospects, March 25,* 1982.

————, *United States Economic Assistance to Egypt. Status Report,* April 1987.

————, *Egypt: Industrial Free Zones,* Project Number 263-0093, Cairo: February, 18, 1981.

————, *Canal Cities Water and Sewerage*, Project Paper Factsheet no. 263-0048, September 12, 1978.

————, *Helwan and Talka Gas Plants*, Project Paper Factsheet, May 27, 1976.

————, *Port of Suez*, Project Paper Factsheet no. 263-0047, September 12, 1978.

US Arms Control and Disarmament Agency, *World Military Expenditures and Arms Transfers*, Washington D.C.: various issues.

US Central Intelligence Agency (CIA), *Arms Flows to LDCs: US Soviet Comparison, 1974–1977*, Washington, D.C.: GPO, 1980.

————, *Communist Aid Activities in Non-Communist Less Developed Countries, 1976, 1977 and 1979*, Washington, D.C.: GPO, 1977, 1978 And 1980.

————, *Handbook of Economic Statistics*, 1986.

————, *International Energy Statistical Review,* November 25, 1986.

————, *Memorandum for WHSR from Paul Corsradden (operation Center) to Smith and Richard,* SDO/CIA, June 8, 1967 (declassified 032931).

————, *World Factbook 1983,* Washington, D.C.: May 1983.

US Department of Commerce (USDOC), *Investing in Egypt*, International Marketing Information Series, Overseas Business Reports 81-08, May 1981.

US Department of Agriculture (USDA), Foreign Agricultural Service, *Annual Situation Report: Egypt,* March 6, 1986.

US Department of State, *Atlas of US Foreign Relations*, Washington, D.C.: GPO, 1982.

————, *Department of State Bulletin*, various issues.

————, *Investment Climate Statement: Egypt*, Department of State Airgram, State 248830, October 16, 1984.

————, Bureau of Intelligence and Research, *Egypt: Sadat's Military Requirement and Funding Problems, Report no. 1209*, Rds-2, July 2, 1979.

————, *US Foreign Policy 1971*, A Report of the Secretary of State, General Foreign Policy Series 260, Department of State Publication Released March 1972.

US Department of the Treasury, *Middle Eastern Multinational Financial Institutions*, Washington, D.C.: July 1976.

US Embassy, Cairo, *Economic Trends Report: Egypt,* Cairo: 1978–1987, various issues.

US General Accounting Office, *Egypt's Capacity to Absorb and Use Economic Assistance Effectively*, September 15, 1977.

————, *The US Economic Assistance Program for Egypt Poses a Management Challenge for Aid*, Report to the Administrator Agency for international Development, GSA/nsiad-85–109, July 31, 1985.

### Congress Delegations, Hearings before Senate Committees and Reports Submitted to the American Congress

Comptroller General, *Meeting US Political Objectives Through Economic Aid in the Middle East and Southern Africa*, Report to the Congress of the United States, Id-79-23, May 31, 1979.

————, *US Assistance to Egyptian Agriculture: Slow Progress After Five Years,* Report to the Congress, Id-81–19, March 16, 1981.

Congress of the United States, Office of Technology Assessment, *Technology Transfer to the Middle East*, Ota-Isc-173, Washington, D.C.: GPO, September 1984.

Congressional Research Division, Science Policy Research Division, *Technology Transfer to the Middle East OPEC Nations and Egypt 1970–1975*, Background Study Prepared for the Subcommittee on Domestic and International Scientific Planning and Analysis, Washington, D.C.: GPO, 1976.

United States House of Representatives, Committee on Foreign Affairs, *Economic Support Fund Program in the Middle East,* April 1979.

————, *Fiscal Year 1980 International Security Assistance Authorization*, Hearing Before the Committee of Foreign Relations 96th Congress, February-April 1979.

————, *Fiscal Year 1980 International Security Assistance Authorization 1980 Foreign Assistance Request*, Hearings Before the Committee on Foreign Relations, United States Senate, 96th Congress, 1st Session, March 2, 1979.

————, *Fiscal Years 1980–81 (Part 3), Economic and Military Aid Programs In Europe and the Middle East*, Hearings and Markup Before the Subcommittee on Europe and the Middle East of the Committee of Foreign Affairs, House of Representatives, 96th Congress, First Session, February 1, 13, 14, 22, 26, 28, March 1, 5 and 6, 1979, Washington, D.C.: GPO, 1979.

————, *Fiscal Year 1981 Foreign Assistance Legislation*, Hearings Before the Committee on Foreign Affairs, 96th Congress, 2nd Session, Washington: GPO, 1980.

————, *Fiscal Year 1983 Securing Assistance*, Hearings Before the Committee on Foreign Affairs, 97th Congress, 2nd Session, Washington: GPO, 1982.

————, Foreign Affairs Committee Print, *Chronologies of Major Development in Selected Areas of Foreign Affairs*, Cumulative Edition 1979, n.d.

————, Foreign Affairs and National Defense Division, Congressional Research Service, *Saudi Arabia and the United States, The New Context in an Evolving Special Relationship,* Report Prepared for the Sub committee on Europe and the Middle East of the Committee of Foreign Affairs, Washington, D.C.: GPO, August 1981.

————, *Foreign Assistance Legislation for Fiscal Year 1979 (Part 5), Economic and Military Aid Programs in Europe and the Middle East*, Hearings Before the Subcommittee on Europe and the Middle East of the Committee on International Relations, House of Representatives, 95th Congress, Second Session, February 6, 8, 15, 28; March 1, 6, 13 and 16, 1978. Washington, D.C.: GPO, 1978.

————, *Foreign Assistance and Related Programs: Appropriations for 1981 (Part 4),* Hearings Before the Committee on Appropriations, 96th Congress, 2nd Session, April 1980. Washington, D.C.: GPO, 1980.

————, *Foreign Assistance and Related Programs: Appropriations for 1988 (Part 1 and 2),* Hearings Before a Subcommittee of the Committee on Appropriations, House of Representatives, 100th Congress, 1st Session, Washington, D.C.: GPO, 1987.

————, *International Security and Development Cooperation Act of 1984*, report of the Committee on Foreign Relations, United States S. 2582, Washington, D.C.: GPO, 1984.

————, *The Middle East, 1974: New Hopes, New Challenges*, Hearings Before the Subcommittee on the Near East and South Asia of the Committee on Foreign Affairs, House of Representatives, 93rd Congress, Second Session, April 9, May 7, 14, 23, and June 27, 1974. Washington, D.C.: GPO 1974.

United States Senate, *Middle East Aid Package for Israel and Egypt*, Hearing and Markup 8, 9, before the Committee on Foreign Affairs, April 26 and May 1, 2, 1979. CIS Document no. H 381–32, 1979.

————, *Middle East Peace Package*, Hearings Before the Committee of Foreign Affairs, April 11 and 25, 1979. CIS Document no. S 381-15, 1979.

————, Pell Claiborne (Senator), *Visit to Eastern Europe and the Middle East by the Senate Delegation to the 24th Meeting of the North Atlantic Assembly*, A Report to the Committee of Foreign Relations, United States Senate, Washington, D.C.: GPO, May 1979.

————, Percy, Charles H. (Senator), *The Middle East*, A Report to the Committee of Foreign Relations, United States Senate, Washington, D.C.: GPO, April 21, 1975.

————, *The Political Economy of the Middle East: 1973–1978,* A Compendium of Papers

Submitted to the Joint Economic Committee Congress of the US, Washington: GPO, April 21, 1980.

————, *Report of Special Study Mission to the Middle East,* Pursuant to H. Res. 267, Washington, D.C.: GPO, February 25, 1974.

————, *State Sponsored Terrorism,* Report Prepared for the Subcommittee on Security and Terrorism, US Senate, 99th Congress 1st. session, Washington: GPO, 1985.

————, Stevenson, Adlai E. (Senator), *The Middle East: 1976,* A Report to the Committee on Banking, Housing and Urban Affairs, United States Senate on Study Mission to the Middle East Conducted Between February 10 and February 25, 1976. Washington, D.C.: GPO, April 1976.

————, *United States Arms Policies in the Persian Gulf and Red Sea Areas: Past, Present, and Future,* Report of a Staff Survey Mission to Ethiopia, Iran and the Arabian Peninsula Pursuant to H. Res. 313. Washington, D.C.: GPO, December 1977.

————, *US Foreign Aid in Ten Middle Eastern and African Countries,* Committee of Government Operations, 88th Congress, 1st Session, Washington, D.C.: GPO, 1971.

————, *World Hunger, Health, and Refugee Problems,* Summary of Special Study Mission to Asia and the Middle East, Report Prepared for the Subcommittee on Health and the Subcommittee on Refugees and Escpees, United States Senate, Washington, D.C.: GPO, January 1976.

## Guides and Directories (Including Official Guides)

Jami'at al-Duwal al-'Arabiyya, al-Amana al-'amma, *Dalil al-Mashru'at al-'Arabiyya al-Mushtaraka Wal-Ittihadat al-Naw'iyya al-'Arabiyya Wal-Mashru'at al-'Arabiyya Wal-Ajnabiyya al-Mushtaraka*, Cairo: 1979.

*The Arab Business Yearbook 1984*, London: Graham & Trotman Ltd, 1984.

Arab Modern House for Foreign Trade, *Directory of Government and Public Sector 1984*, Cairo: 1986.

Arab Petroleum Research Center, *Arab Oil and Gas Directory,* Paris: 1981, 1985.

ARE, GAFIZ, *Legal Guide to Investment in Egypt*, Cairo: 1977.

Committee for Middle East Trade (COMET), *Directory of Inter Arab Organizations*, Special Report, London: 1985, 2nd edition.

Chase Bank, *Guide to Doing Business in Egypt*, Cairo: 1980.

Fiani and Partners, *Egypt Investment and Business Directory,* Cairo: 1980 and 1983/1984.

Financial Times Business Publishing, The Banker Research Unit, *Banking Structures and Sources of Finance in the Middle East*, London: 1980, 2nd Edition.

International Trade Consulting Company, *The Green Business Guide*, Cairo: 1986.

*Middle East Annual Review*, London: Saffron Walden, various issues.

*The Middle East and North Africa*, London: Europa Publication, various issues.

*Middle East Economic Digest (MEED) Financial Directory of the Middle East,* London: 1975/76–1981, various issues.

Office Arabe de Presse et de Documentation, *Rapport Economique Arabe, 1975–1979*, Syria: 1980.

Union de Banques Arabes et Francaises (UBAF), *Arab Banking Directory,* Paris: 1977.

United States and Foreign Commercial Service, *Business Directory for Egypt,* United States Embassy, Cairo, American Consulate-General, Alexandria: February 1986.

## Personal Interviews

The following individuals have consented to the publication of their names. Other inter-viewers requested to be sourced as anonymous.

'Ashmawi, Sa'id, Egyptian Supreme Court Judge. Cairo, July 1987.

Atherton, Alfred, US Ambassador to Egypt, 1979–1983. Tel Aviv, October 30, 1986.

Bartsch, Juergen, OECD official commissioned to collect the information on Arab aid. Paris, August 1986.

Bashir, Tahsin, Sadat's spokesman, Egyptian Ambassador to Canada and to the Arab League. Cairo, July 1987.

Ben Elisar, Eliyahu, Israel's first Ambassador to Egypt. Jerusalem, September 1987.

Desuqi, 'Ali Hilal, Professor at the University of Cairo. Cairo, October 1986.

Gafny, Arnon, Governor of the Bank of Israel during the signing of the Peace Treaty. Tel Aviv, April 1987.

Hasan, Mansur, Minister of Information in the late 1970s. Cairo, July 1987.

Hijazi, 'Abd al-'Aziz, Egyptian Finance Minister during the late 1960s and the early 1970s, Egyptian Vice Premier and Prime Minister of Egypt until April 1975. Cairo, July 1987.

Jacobini, A., American Economic Attache in the US Embassy in Cairo. Cairo, July 1987.

Khalil, Mustafa, Egyptian Prime Minister during the signing of the Peace Treaty. Cairo, September 1987.

Mubashir, 'Abduh, former *al-Ahram* military correspondent, senior journalist at the *al-Ahram* editorial board. Cairo, January 27 and February 2, 1988.

Mansur, Anis, editor of *October* until 1985, close to Sadat. Cairo, July 1987.

Ramadan, 'Abd al-'Azim, historian. Cairo, July 1987.

Sha'lan, Muhammad, Psychiatrist, head of the Faculty of Psychiatry, al-Azhar University. Cairo, July 1987.

Tawila, 'Abd al-Sattar, Assistant editor of *Ruz al-Yusuf*. Cairo, July 1987.

### Correspondence

Letters from Menachem Begin, Prime Minister of Israel during the years 1977–1984, to the author. Jerusalem, October 12, 1987.

## Memoirs

'Ali, Kamal Hasan, *Muharibun wa-Mufawidun*, Cairo: Markaz al-Ahram lil-Tarjama wal-Nashr, 1986.

Brezinski, Zbigniew, *Power and Principle: Memoirs of the National Security Adviser, 1977–1981,* New York: Farrar, Straus and Giroux, 1983.

Carter, Jimmy, *Keeping Faith: Memoirs of a President*, New York: Bantam Books, 1982.

Dayan, Moshe, *Halanezah Tokhal Herev: Sihot ha-Shalom, Reshamim Ishiyim*, Jerusalem: 'Idanim, 1981.

Din, Ahmad Baha' al-, *Muhawarati ma' al-Sadat,* Cairo: Dar al-Hillal, 1986.

Fahmy, Ismail, *Negotiating for Peace in the Middle East,* Cairo: American University in Cairo Press, 1983.

Heikal, Mohamed H., *Autumn of Fury: The Assassination of Sadat*, New York: Random House, 1983.

————, *The Road to Ramadan*, London: Collins, 1975.

Kamel, Mohamed Ibrahim, *The Camp David Accord, A Testimony*, London: Kegan Paul International, 1986.

Khomeini, Ayatollah Sayyed Ruhollah Mousavi, *A Clarification of Questions: An Unabridged Translation of Resaleh Towzih al-Masael,* J. Borujerdi, trans., Boulder, CO: Westview Press, 1984.

Kissinger, Henry, *The Years of Upheaval*, Boston: Little, Brown And Company, 1982.

Mar'i, Sayyid, *Awraq Siyasiyya*, Cairo: Dar al-Ahram, 1979, 3 vol.

Nixon, Richard, *The Memoirs of Richard Nixon*, New York: Warner Books, 1979. 2 vols.

Quandt, William B., *Camp David, ha-Shalom veha-Mimshak ha-Politi* (Hebrew), Jerusalem: Keter, 1988.

Riad, Mahmoud, *The Struggle for Peace in the Middle East,* New York: Quartet Books, 1981.

Riyad, Mahmud, *Mudhakkirat Mahmud Riyad (1948–1978)*, 2 vol. vol. 1, Cairo: Dar al-Mustaqbal al-'Arabi, 1985; vol. 2, ibid., 1986.

Sadat, Anwar al-, *Sipur Hayay*, Jerusalem: 'Idanim, June 1978, 2nd edition.

Sadat, Anwar El-, *Those I Have Known*, New York: Continuum, 1984.

Saunders, Harold H., *The Other Walls, The Politics of the Arab-Israeli Peace Process*, Washington, D.C.: Americna Enterprise Institute for Public Policy Research, 1985.

Shazly, Saad El, *The Crossing of the Suez*, San Francisco: American Mideast Research, 1980.

Vance, Cyrus, *Hard Choices. Critical Years in America's Foreign Policy*, New York: Simon and Schuster, 1983.

Weizman, 'Ezer, *ha-Qrav 'al ha-Shalom. Tazpit Ishit*, Jerusalem: 'Idanim, 1982, 3rd edition.

'Uthman, Ahmad 'Uthman, *Safahat min Tajribati*, Cairo: al-Maktab al-Misri al-Hadith, al-Tab'a al-Khamisa, May 1981.

## Conferences

The Arab Planning Institute and Kuwait Economic Society, "Seminar on Investment Policies of Arab Oil Producing Countries," Kuwait: February 18–20, 1974.

The Center for Strategic and International Studies, Georgetown University, "Near East Development Forum," Washington, D.C.: Sheraton-Carlton Hotel, May 8, 1981.

DAC Task Force on Donor Practices, "*Egypt – A Country Case Study*," Workshop on Donor Practices, Paris: OECD, September 11–13, 2002.

Dervish, Kemal, Peter Bocock and Julia Devlin, "*Intra-regional Trade among Arab countries: Building Competitive Economic Neighborhood*," Paper presented at the Middle East Institute 52nd Annual Conference, Washington, D.C.: October 17, 1998.

The Economic Research Forum (ERF) for the Arab Countries Iran and Turkey, "*Trade with Europe*," Second Annual Conference, Istanbul: September 16–18, 1995. In ERF Forum, 2:4 (December 1995), pp. 7–8.

The Economic Research Forum (ERF) for the Arab Countries, Iran and Turkey, "*Economic Trends in the MENA Region*," Cairo: 1998.

Farid, Samia, "The Inter-Arab Investment Guarantee Corporation," Paper presented at the Inter-governmental Expert Group Meeting on the Industrialization of the Least Developed Countries, Vienna: UNIDO, November 22–24, 1976.

Gazit, Shlomo, "Arab Forces Two Years after the Yom Kippur War," in *Military Aspects of the Israeli-Arab Conflict*, Proceedings of An International Symposium, October 12–17, 1975. Tel Aviv: University Publishing Projects, 1975, pp. 188–95.

Handoussa, Heba Ahmad, "The Impact of Foreign Aid on Egypt's Economic Development: 1952–1986," Paper presented to the Conference on Aid, Capital Flows and Development, Jointly Sponsored by the World Bank and International Center for Economic Growth, Tallories, France: September 13–17, 1987.

———, "The Public Sector in Egyptian Industry, 1952–1977," Paper presented to the Annual Conference of Egyptian Economists, Cairo: March 23–25, 1978.

Munro, John (ed.), "*Trade and Peace in the Middle East*," Professors World Peace Academy, Pomezia: August 2–4, 1984, New York, 1984.

Oman, paper presented by the Minister of Social Development at the conference "Employing National Manpower," October 2001.

OPEC, Proceedings of the "OPEC Workshop for Journalists," Mexico City: February 27–29, 1984, Vienna: OPEC, 1985.

Rodenbeck, Max, "An Emerging Agenda for Development in the Middle East and North Africa," Paper presented as part of the workshop on Challenges and Opportunities for Development in the MENA Region, IDRC, Middle East Regional Office, Cairo: January 26, 1999.

Shamir, Shimon and Eliahu Ben-Elissar, "Two Years After the Signing of the Peace Treaty Between Israel and Egypt," Lectures Delivered at the Annual Meeting of the Board of Governors, Tel Aviv University: May 20, 1981.

Tel Aviv University Peace Papers, "Text of Two Symposiums Held With Dr. Mustapha Khlil, Dr. Boutros Ghali and Egyptian and Israeli Professors and Businessmen," At Tel Aviv University: December 19, 1980, June 1, 1982.

Tignor, Robert L., "Foreign Capital, Foreign Communities, and the Egyptian Revolution of 1952," Prepared for Delivery At the Egypt from Monarchy to Republic: Structural Continuity and Dynamics of Change Conference, Tel Aviv University: The Dayan Center for Middle Eastern and African Studies and the Kaplan Chair in the History of Egypt and Israel, June 8–10, 1987.

Weinbaum, Marvin G., "Egypt's Adjustment to a Global Market Economy: The Role of US Economic Assistance," Prepared for Delivery at the 1983 Annual Meeting of the American Political Science Association, The Palmer House, September 1–4, 1983.

## Books in Arabic

Ibrahim, Sa'ad al-Din, *Ittijahat al-Ra'y al-'Amm al-'Arabi nahwa Mas'alat al-Wahda: Dirasa Maydaniyya*, Beirut: Markaz Dirasat al-Wahda al-'Arabiyya, 1981.

Ibrahim, Sa'ad al-Din (Ishraf), *'Urubat Misr Hiwar al-Sab'inat*, Cairo: Markaz al-Dirasat al-Siyasiyya wal-Istratijiyya bil-Ahram, 1978.

Ahmad, Ahmad Yusuf, *al-Dawr al-Misri fil-Yaman (1962–1967)*, Cairo: al-Hay'a al-Misriyya al-'Amma lil-Kitab, 1981.

Ahmad, Kamal, *al-Nasiriyya wal-'Alam al-Thalith*, Beirut: Dar al-Raqy, 1986.

Imam, Silmiya Sa'id, *Man Yamluk Misr',* Cairo: Dar al-Mustaqbal al-'Arabi, 1986.

Butrus, Ghali Butrus, *Dirasat fil-Diblumasiyya al-'Arabiyya*, Cairo: Maktabat al-Anjlu al-Misriyya, 1973.

Dukas, Martha, *Azmat al-Kuwayt: al-'Alaqat al-Kuwaytiyya al-'Iraqiyya 1961–1963,* Beirut: Dar al-Nahar, 1973.

Dib, Fath al-, *'Abd al-Nasir wa-Thawrat Libya*, Cairo: Dar al-Mustaqbal al-'Arabi, 1986.

Din, Ahmad Baha al-, *Muhawarati ma'a al-Sadat*, Cairo: Dar al-Hilal, 1987.

Haykal, Hasanin Muhammad, *Li-Misr . . . La li-'Abd al-Nasir (al-Tab'a al-Rabi'a)*, Beirut: Shrikat al-Matbu'at lil-Tawzi' wal-Nashr, 1984.

Hilal, 'Ali al-Din (ed.), *al-Tatawwur al-Dimuqrati fi Misr,* Cairo: Maktabat Nahdat al-Sharq, 1986.

Zahran, Jamal 'Ali, *al-Siyasa al-Kharijiyya li-Misr, 1970–1981,* Cairo: Madbuli, 1987.

Zaki, Ramzi, *Azmat Misr al-Iqtisadiyya*, Cairo: Madbuli, 1983.

————, *Buhuth fi Duyun Misr al-Kharijiyya*, Cairo: Madbuli, 1985.

Khuli, Lutfi al- (ed.), *Safhat al-Hiwar al-Qawmi. Muntahi al-Fikr al-'Arabi. al-Maziq al-'Arabi,* Cairo: Markaz al-Ahram lil-Tarjama wal-Nashr, 1986.

Husayn, 'Adil, *al-Iqtisad al-Misri min al-Istiqlal ila al-Tab'iyya, 1974–1979 (al-Tab'a al-Thaniya),* Cairo: Dar al-Mustaqbal al-'Arabi, 1982, 2 vol.

Yasin, al-Sayyid (Mushrif), *al-Taqrir al-Istratiji al-'Arabi, 1985,* Cairo: Markaz al-Dirasat al-Siyasiyya wal-Istratijiyya bil-Ahram, 1986.

Labib, Shuqayr, *al-Wahda al-Iqtisadiyya al-'Arabiyya: Tajaribuha wa-Tawaqqu'atuha,* Beirut: Markaz Dirasat al-Wahda al-'Arabiyya, 1986.

Lutskiqtish, F. A, *'Abd al-Nasir wa-Ma'rakat al-Istiqlal al-Iqtisadi* (translated from Russian, Salwa Abu-Sa'da w-Wasil Bakhr), Cairo: Dar al-Kalima lil-Nashr, 1980.

Matar, Jamil wa-'Ali al-Din Hilal, *al-Nizam al-Iqlimi al-'Arabi. Dirasa fil-'Alaqat al-Siyasiyya al-'Arabiyya (al-Tab'a al- Thalitha),* Beirut: Markaz Dirasat al-Wahda al-'Arabiyya, 1983.

Matar, Fuad, *Rusiya al-Nasiriyya wa-Misr al-Misriyya,* Beirut: 1972.

Markaz Dirasat al-Wahda al-'Arabiyya, al-Qawmiyya al-'Arabiyya fi al-Fikr wal-Mumarasa, Buhuth wa-Munaqashat al-Nadwa al-Fikriyya allati Nazzamaha Markaz Dirasat al-Wahda al-'Arabiyya.

Marsi, Fuad, *Hadha al-Infitah al-Iqtisadi (al-Tab'a al-Thaniya),* Cairo: Dar al-Thaqafa al-Jadida, 1984.

Mar'i, Sayyid, *Awraq Siyasiyya,* Cairo: Dar al-Ahram, 1979, 3 vol.

Mar'i, Sayyid, *Likay Narbah al-Mustaqbal,* Cairo: Dar al-Ma'arif, n.d.

Nafi', Ibrahim, *Nahnu wal-'Alam wa-Nahnu wa-Anfusuna,* Cairo: Markaz al-Ahram lil-Tarjama wal-Nashr, 1986.

Salama, Ghassan, *al-Siyasa al-Kharijiyya al-Su'udiyya mundhu 'Am 1945: Dirasa fil-'Alaqat al-Dawliyya,* Beirut: Ma'had al-Inma' al-'Arabi, 1980.

'Ali, Kamal Hasan, *Muharibun wa-Mufawidun,* Cairo: Markaz al-Ahram lil-Tarjama wal-Nashr, 1986.

'Uthman, Ahmad 'Uthman, *Safahat min Tajribati (al-Tab'a al-Khamisa),* Cairo: al-Maktab al-Misri al-Hadith, May 30, 1981.

Fadil, Mahmud 'Abd al-, *al-Naft wal-Mushkilat al-Mu'asira lil-Tanmiya al-'Arabiyya,* Kuwayt: al-Majlis al-Watani lil-Thaqafa wal-Funun wal-Adab, 1979.

————, *al-Naft wal-Wahda al-'Arabiyya 'ala Mustaqbal al-Wahda al-'Arabiyya wal-'Alaqat al-Iqtisadiyya al-'Arabiyya,* Beirut: Markaz Dirasat al-Wahda al-'Arabiyya, 1979.

Sabri, Musa, al-Sadat. *al-Haqiqa wal-Ustura,* Cairo: al-Maktab al-Misri al-Hadith, 1985.

Rifa'i, 'Abd al-'Aziz, *al-Wa'y al-'Arabi wa-Wahdat Misr-Libya,* Cairo: Maktabat al-Wa'y al-'Arabiyya, 1973.

Ratib, 'A'isha, *al-'Alaqat al-Dawliyya al-'Arabiyya,* Cairo: Dar al-Nahda al-'Arabiyya, 1968.

Ramadan, 'Abd al-'Azim, *Misr fi 'Asr al-Sadat,* Cairo: Madbuli, 1986.

Shakir, Ihab (Tasmim al-Ghulaf wal-Ishraf al-Fanni), *Shuhud al-'Asr,* Cairo: Markaz al-Ahram lil-Tarjama wal-Nashr, 1986.

Shihari, Muhammad 'Ali al-, *'Abd al-Nasir wa-Thawrat al-Yaman,* Cairo: Madbuli, 1976.

Sha'lan, Muhammad, *al-Tibb al-Nafsi wal-Siyasa,* Cairo: al-'Arabi, 1979.

Shuqayri, Ahmad al-, *'ala Tariq al-Hazima ma'a al-Muluk wal-Ru'asa',* Beirut: 1972.

## Articles in Arabic

Abd al-Majid, Wahid. "al-Nizam al-Arabi Bayna Furas al-Waqi wa-Quyud al-Madi", in Wahid Abd al-Majid (ed.), *al-Taqrir al-Istratiji al-Arabi,* Cairo: Markaz al-Dirasatal-Siyasiyya wal-Istratijiyya, 2000.

"al-Alaqat al-Misriyya al-Saudiyya Wa-Hulm al-Takattul al-Arabi," *al-Ahram al-Iqtisadi,* (November 20, 2000).

Amer, Hasan, "Suq Iqarat Arabiyya wa-Duwaliyya," *al-Ahram al-Iqtisadi* (October 27, 1997).

Anis, Muhammad, "al-Hay'a al-'Arabiyya lil-Tasni' wa-Tahyi'at al-Amn al-'Arabi," *al-Siyasa al-Dawliyya,* no. 56 (April 1979), pp. 130–4.

'Atiqi, 'Ali Ahmad, "al-Ta'awun al-Iqlimi fi mjal al-Istithmarat fi al-Sina'at al-Naftiyya al-Lataqar lil-Intaj Mithl... Munazzamat al-Aqtar al-'Arabiyya al-Musaddira lil-Batul," *al-Naft wal-Ta'awun al-'Arabi,* al-Sana 4, al-'Adad 2, (1978), pp. 16–32.

'Awis, Ibrahim, "Fawa'id al-Batrudularat Wujhat Nazar Iqtisadiyya," *al-Naft wal-Ta'awun al-'Arabi*, al-Sana 12, al-'Adad 3–4, (1986), pp. 136–77.

'Azim, Lutfi 'Abd al-, "Duwal al-Rafd... wa-Muqata'at Misr Iqtisadiyyan!," *al-Ahram al-Iqtisadi* (December 15, 1977), pp. 4, 8.

———, "Kashf al-Istithmarat al-'Arabiyya wal-Ajnabiyya," *al-Ahram al-Iqtisadi* (May 1, 1975), pp. 29–35.

'Aziz, Hamdi 'Abd al-, "1500 Misri fi 'Barlaman Maftuh," *Ruz al-Yusuf*, al-'Adad 2986 (September 2, 1985), pp. 60–1.

'Aziz, al-Sirwat 'Abd al-, "al-Iqtisad al-Misri wal-Mutaghayyirat al-Dawliyya," *al-Ahram al-Iqtisadi* (January 15, 1974), pp. 6–7.

Bahr, Samira, "Misr... wa-Hay'at al-Tamwil al-'Arabiyya," *al-Siyasa al-Dawliyya* (October 1978), pp. 108–13.

Dabghi, Jan, "Hal Yusahim al-'Arab wa-Uruba fi Inqadh al-Iqtisad al-Misri al-Mut'ab'," *al-Mustaqbal*, al-Sana 6, al-'Adad 269 (April 17, 1982), p. 37.

"Dalil al-Musaddir al-Misri lil-Saudiyya," *al-ahram al-Iqtidadi* (October 8, 2001).

Din, Ahmad Sharif al-, "Istithmar al-Mal al-'Arabi," *Misr al-Mu'asira*, al-'Adad 393–394 (1983), pp. 53–100.

Hakim, Tawfiq al-, "al-Wahda al-'Arabiyya bayn al-Wahda wal-Hiy'ad," *al-Ahram* (April 21, 1978), pp. 12–13.

Hamd, 'Abd al-Latif al-, "Khamsat 'Ashr 'Aman min al-'Amal al-Inma'i al-Dawli, al-Sunduq al-Kuwayti lil-Tanmiya al-Iqtisadiyya al-'Arabiyya," *al-Naft wal-Ta'awun al-'Arabi*, al-Sana 3, al-'Adad 1 (1977), pp. 14–32.

Hammad, Khalil, "al-Musa'adat al-Amrikiyya li-Isra'il wal-Aqtar al-'Arabiyya: Dirasa Muqarana," *al-Mustaqbal al-'Arabi*, al-Sana 9, al-'Adad 89 (July 1986), pp. 45–60.

Hamza, Isam, "al-Imaratiyun Yastathmirun 463 Milyun Dular fi Misr," *al-Quds al-Arabi* (January 13, 2003).

Hasan Abu al-Rahman 'Abd-Hasan al-, "Tasa'ulat hawl al-Muqata'a al-'Arabiyya li-Misr," *al-Ahram al-Iqtisadi* (April 15, 1979), pp. 14–17.

Hariq, Ilya, "Azmat al-Tahawwul al-Ishtiraki wal-Aghma fi Misr," *Majallāt al-'Ulum wal-Ijtima'iyya*, Kuwayt, al-Mujallad 15, al-'Adad 1 (Rabi' 1987), pp. 15–42.

Hitti, Nasif, "Mafahim al-Takamul fi Itar al-Nizam al-Iqlimi al-'Arabi," *Shu'un 'Arabiyya*, al-'Adad 13 (March 1982).

Husayn, 'Adil, "al-Mal al-Nafti 'A'iq lil-Tawhid wal-Takamul," *al-Mustaqbal al-'Arabi* (January 1979), pp. 16–31.

Ibrahim, Sa'ad al-Din, "al-Athar al-Salbiyya al-Furuq al-Dakhiliyya bayn al-Aqtar al-'Arabiyya 'ala al-Tanmiya fil-Aqtar al-Aqall Dakhlan... Halat Misr," *al-Naft wal-Ta'awun al-'Arabi*, al-Sana 3, al-'Adad 4 (1977), pp. 17–33.

Istithmarat al-Amir al-Walid fi Misr Kimatuha AL-Ijmaliyya 500 Milyun Dular," *al-Jazira* (Decmeber 24, 2002).

"al-Istithmarat al-'Arabiyya fi Misr Tatada'af khilal al-Sanawat al-Thalath al-Muqbila," *al-Majalla* (May 29, 1982).

"al-Istithmarat al-Arabiyya fi Misr," *al-Ahram al-Iqtisadi* (February 23, 1998), pp. 20–1.

Jabir, Bul, "al-Batrul wal-Asliha al-Diblumasiyya al-Iqlimiyya: al-Ab'ad al-Istratijiyya fil-'Alaqat al-Misriyya al-Su'udiyya," *al-Siyasa al-Dawliyya* (October 1980), pp. 106–110.

Jadawi, Ahmad Kismat al-, "al-Shrikat al-'Arabiyya al-Munbathiqa 'an Munazzamat al-Aqtar al-'Arabiyya al-Musadira lil-Batrul," *al-Naft wal-Ta'awun al-'Arabi*, al-Sana 2, al-'Adad 2 (1976), pp. 83–115.

Khuli, Lutfi al-, "al-Batru Dular wal-Batru Dam," *al-Ahram*, (January 29, 1975).

Marsi, Fu'ad, "al-Athar al-Iqtisadiyya lil-Mu'ahada al-Israiliyya al-Misriyya," *al-Mustaqbal al-'Arabi* (August 1980), pp. 27–53.

Marsi, Fu'ad, "al-Tanmiya al-Iqtisadiyya wal-Istithmarat al-Ajnabiyya," *al-Tali'a* (1975), pp. 12–27.

Mas'ud, Samih, "al-Mashru'at al-'Arabiyya al-Mushtaraka: Waqi'uha, Ahammiyyatuha, Mu'awwiqatuha wa-Mustaqbaluha," *al-Mustaqbal al-'Arabi,* al-Sana 10, al-'Adad 103 (September 1987), pp. 26–44.

Mathari, 'Abd al-'Aziz al-, "al-Jihaz al-'Arabi li-Himayat al-Istithmarat wa-Imkaniyyat al-Ta'awun ma' al-Duwal al-Sina'iyya," *al-Naft wal-Ta'awun al-'Arabi,* al-sna 4, al-'Adad 3 (1978), pp. 17–82.

"Misr Ta'ud ila al-'Arab fi Tuffaha Lubnaniyya," *al-Mustaqbal,* al-Sana 7, al-'Adad 352 (November 19, 1983), pp. 61–3.

"Mu'awwiqat al-Istithmar al-'Arabi wal-Ajnabi," *al-Ahram al-Iqtisadi* (October 15, 1978), pp. 4.

Nashashibi, Hikmat al-, "Tawtin al-Arsida al-'Arabiyya... Daruratuhu wa-Wasa'iluhu," *al-Naft wal-Ta'awun al-'Arabi,* al-Sana 2, al-'Adad 1 (1976), pp. 11–29.

Nawwar, Ibrahim, "al-Musa'adat al-Amirikiyya ila Misr: al-Wahm wal-Haqiqa," *al-Iqtisad al-'Arabi,* no. 63 (September 1981), pp. 15–18.

Qara'i, Muhammad Yusuf al-, "Munazzamat al-'Amal al-'Arabi wa-Qadayaha al-'Ajila," *al-Siyasa al-Dawliyya,* al-Sana 5, al-'Adad 27 (January 1972).

"al-Qussa al-Kamila li-Liqa' al-Sadat- Fahd," *al-Kifah al-'Arabi* (16 June 1980), pp. 8–12.

al-Rafii, Shahira , "Misr Aula Fi al-Istithmarat," *al-Ahram al-Iqtisadi* (August 24, 1992).

Rahman, Abu al-Hasan al-, "Tasa'ulat hawl al-Muqata'a al-'Arabiyya li-Misr," *al-Ahram al-Iqtisadi* (April 15, 1979), pp. 14–17.

Ramadan, Suliman Muhammad, "al-Mashru'at al-Mushtaraka bayn Misr wal-Sudan ka-Sigha Mula'ima lil-Takamul," *Misr al-Mu'asira,* al-'Adad 389–90 (1982), pp. 139–60.

al-Razaz, Ahmad, "al-Jusur al-Mumtadda Bayna Misr Wa-Duwal al-Khalij al-Arabiyya," *al-Ahram al-Iqtisadi* (January 22, 1990).

————, "al-Taawun al-Misri al-Saudi... Namudhaj Arabi," *al-Ahram al-Iqtisadi* (December 7, 1992).

Rif'at, 'Isam, "Tijarat al-'Arab... ma' Misr," *al-Ahram al-Iqtisadi* (April 15, 1979), pp. 8–13.

Sabbagh, Nabil, "Suq al-Mal," *al-Ahram al-Iqtisadi* (February 1, 1974), pp. 56–9.

————, "Tasawwurat hawl: Hay'at al-Khalij lil-Tanmiya," *al-Ahram al-Iqtisadi,* (September 1, 1976), pp. 10–13.

Sa'dun, Jasim Khalid al-, "Mustaqbal al-Naft wal-Maliyya al-'Amma fi Aqtar Majlis al-Ta'awun al-Khaliji," *al-Mustaqbal al-'Arabi,* al-Sana 10, al-'Adad 99 (May 1987), pp. 4–27.

Sakit, Basam Khalil al-, "Tahwilat al-'Amala al-Muhajira wa-Istikhdamatuha: Halat al-Urdunn," *al-Mustaqbal al-'Arabi,* al-Sana 4, al-'Adad 35 (January 1982).

Saliman, Ali "Tajribat al-Istithmar al-Arabi al-Mushtarac," *al-Ahram al-Iqtisadi* (December 24, 1990).

Samih, Mas'ud, "al-Mashru'at al-'Arabiyya al-Mushtaraka bayn al-Waqi' wal-Mustaqbal," *al-Naft wal-Ta'awun al-'Arabi,* al-Sana 7, al-'Adad 2 (1981), pp. 111–34.

Shaawi, Khalid al-, "al-Mashru' al-'Arabi al-Mushtarak fil-Sina'a al-Naftiyya," *al-Naft wal-Ta'awun al-'Arabi,* al-Sana 11, al-'Adad 4 (1985), pp. 13–31.

Shahata, Ibrahim, "Mu'unat Duwal al-Ubik wal-Ta'awun ma' Masadir al-Tamwil al-Tijari," *al-Naft wal-Ta'awun al-'Arabi,* al-Sana 5, al-'Adad 1 (1979), pp. 7–22.

————, and Robert Mabru, "Mu'unat Duwal al-Ubik Dirasa Tahliliyya," *al-Naft wal-Ta'awun al-'Arabi,* al-Sana 1, al-'Adad 1 (1978), pp. 100–26.

Sharabini, Na'im al-, "Tadaffuqat al-'Ummal wa-Ras al-Mal fil-Watan al-'Arabi," *al-Naft wal-Ta'awun al-'Arabi,* al-Sana 3, al-'Adad 4 (1977), pp. 35–59.

Sultan, Fu'ad, "Ashwak 'ala Tariq al-Infitah," *al-Ahram al-Iqtisadi* (December 1, 1974), pp. 14-16.

"Suq al-Iqarat Yantaziru al-Arab," *al-Ahram al-Iqtisadi* (July 15, 2002).

Tadrus, Rashad Kamil, "al-Jihaz al-Markazi lil-Muhasabat... wa-Mawqi'uhu min al-Infitah," *al-Ahram al-Iqtisadi* (April 15, 1978), pp. 10–17, 25.

Tah, 'Abd al-'Alim Tah, "Amwal al-'Arab fil-Iqtisad al-Misri," *al-Ahram al-Iqtisadi* (December 1, 1977), pp. 14–16.

Taysir, 'Abd al-Jabir, "Intiqal al-Quwwa al-'Amila bayn al-Aqtar al-'Arabiyya. Nazra Mustaqbaliyya," *al-Naft wal-Ta'awun al-'Arabi,* al-Sana 12, al-'Adad 2 (1986), pp. 13–47.

Tikriti, 'Abdalla al-, "Ahammiyya Shabakat Khutut al-Anabib fi al-Sina'a al-Naftiyya al-'Arabiyya," *al-Naft wal-Ta'awun al-'Arabi*, al-Sana 12, al-'Adad 1 (1986), pp. 94–111.

'Umar, Ibrahim, "al-Riqaba al-Idariyya lil-Infitah al-Iqtisadi," *al-Ahram al-Iqtisadi* (April, 15, 1978), pp. 8–9, 25.

Zalzala, 'Abd al-Hasan, "al-Takamul al-Iqtisadi al-'Arabi amam al-Tahaddiyat," *al-Mustaqbal al-'Arabi*, al-'Adad 11 (1980), pp. 6–21.

———, "al-Dawr al-Iqtisadi li-Jami'at al-Duwal al-'Arabiyya," *al-Mustaqbal al-'Arabi*, al-'Adad 8–10 (1982), pp. 147–65.

## Books in Hebrew

Eylon, 'Amos, *Meziat Mizraim: Masa'*, Jerusalem: Schoken, 1980.

Ben-Porat, Yeshayahu, *Sihot*, Tel Aviv: 'Idanim, 1981.

Charney, Leon H., *Yo'ez Meyuhad*, Israel: Revivim, 1985.

Goldberg, Asher (editor), *ha-Sozializm ha-Arvi Kovez*, Jerusalem: Beit Berl, 1970.

Gur, Avraham, "Nesheq ha-Neft Meziut o Mitos," MA Thesis, Tel Aviv University: Social Science Faculty, Political Science Department, July 1982.

Gazit, M., *Tahalikh ha-Shalom 1969–1973,* Tel Aviv: Ha-Kibbuz ha-Meuhad, 1984.

Gal, Yizhak, *Kalkalat Mizraim le-Nokhah ha-Sankziyot ha-'Arviyot,* Tel Aviv: Skirot Mekhon Shiloah, December 1980.

Gilboa, Eytan and Mordekhay Naor (editors), *ha-Sikhsukh ha-'Arvi-Yisreeli,* Tel Aviv: Misrad ha-Bitahon ha-Hozaa la-Or, 1981.

Gera, Gideon, *Derekh Qadafi be-Luv*, Tel Aviv: ha-Kibbuz ha-Meuhad, 1983.

Haber, Eytan, Ehud Yaari and Zeev Shif, *Shnat ha-Yona, Ha-Sipur she-meahorey ha-Shalom,* Tel Aviv: Zemora, Bitan, Modan, 1980.

Holden, David, *Sheon ha-Hol: Drom 'Arav ha-So'eret,* IDF: Ma'arakhot, 1967.

Haykal, Muhammad Hasanin, *ha-Sfinks veha-Komisar. 'Aliyata u-Shqiata shel ha-Hashpa'a ha-Sovyetit ba-'Olam ha-'Arvi*, Tel Aviv: 'Am 'Oved, 1981.

Halperin, Ariel, *Hitpathut Melaey ha-Hon ha-Zevaiyim shel Israel u-Medinot ha-'Imut,* Maamar le-Diyun 86.01, Jerusalem: ha-Makhon le-Mehkar Kalkali 'al Shem Moris Falk, January 1986.

Heler, Mark (editor), *ha-Maazan ha-Zevai ba-Mizrah ha-Tikhon 1984*, Tel Aviv: ha-Merkaz le-Limudim Astrategiyim 'al Shem Yafe, Tel Aviv University, 1985.

Hareven, Aluf and Yehi'am Padan (editors), *beyn Milhama le-Hesderim,* Tel Aviv, Mekhon Shiloah, Zmora, Bitan, Modan, 1977.

Harkavi, Yehoshafat, *Leqah ha-'Arvim mi-Tevusatam*, Tel Aviv: 1969.

Vered, Yael, *Hafikha u-Milhama be-Teyman*, Tel Aviv: 'Am 'Oved, 1967.

Yadlin, Rivka, *Dyoqan Mizri*, Jerusalem: Magnes, 1986.

Morgentau, H., *Politika beyn Umot (4th edition),* Tel Aviv: Hozaat Yahdav, 1968.

Manzeli, Yair, *ha-Shinuyim ba-Tikhnun uva-Mediniyut ha-Kalkalit be-Mizraim leakhar Milhemet Yom ha-Kipurim,* Tel Aviv: Mekhon Horoviz, Tel Aviv University, 1977.

Misrad ha-Ozar, *ha-Rashut le-Tikhnun Kalkali, ha-Mesheq ha-Mizri Skira Kalkalit,* Jerusalem: Misrad ha-Ozar, January 1978.

Naqdimon, Shlomo, *Tamuz be-Lehavot: Hafzazat ha-Kur ha-'Iraqi Sipur ha-Mivza,* Jerusalem: 'Idanim, 1987.

Sivan, 'Imanuel (editor), *Leqahim 'Arviyim mi-Milhemet Oktober,* 'Arav ve-Israel series, number 2, Hebrew University: 'Am 'Oved, 1974.

Sela, Avraham, *Ahdut betokh Perud. Ve'idot ha-Pisga ha-'Arviyot,* Jerusalem: Magnes, 1983.

————, *The Decline of the Arab–Israeli Conflict: Middle East Politics and the Quest for Regional Order*, New York: SUNY, 1998.

Kopland, Mayls, *Mishak ha-Umot,* Jerusalem: Schoken, 1970.

Shamir, Shim'on, *Mizraim be-Hanhagat Sadat. Ha-Biqush ahar Oryentazya Hadasha, Asupat Maamarim,* Tel Aviv: Dvir, 1978.

Zeva *'Iraq be-Milhemet Yom ha-Kipurim* (Translated from Iraqi book), IDF: Ma'arakhot, 1986.

## Articles in Hebrew

Oren, Yizhak, "Mekhirat Nesheq Ma'aravi li-Medinot 'Arav," *Ma'arakhot,* number 267 (January 1979), pp. 41–7.

Ahiram, Efraim, "Megamot be-Kalkalat Mizraim," *Reva'on le-Kalkala,* volume 25 (1978).

Ber, Gavriel, "Netunim u-Masqanot Hadashim bi-Devar Tozeot ha-Reforma ha-Agrarit be-Mizraim," *ha-Mizrah he-Hadash,* 16 (1966), pp. 238–243.

Goldberg, Ya'akov, "Mediniyut ha-Huz ha-Sa'udit ba-Zira ha-Beyn-'Arvit: Hemshekhiyut u-Temura," in Ya'akov Goldberg and Yosef Kostiner (editors), *'Asor shel Zimzum ha-Mizrah ha-Tikhon be-Zel Nesigat Mesheq ha-Neft,* Tel Aviv: Sqirot Merkaz Dayan (January 1987), pp. 58–63.

Gilbar, Gad, "ha-Kalkala shel Telut Gomlin Arzot ha-Berit veha-'Olam ha-'Arvi," in Itamar Rabinovich and Haim Shaked (editors), *ha-Mizrah ha-Tikhon ve-Arzot ha-Berit* 'Am 'Oved u-Mekhon Shiloah (1980), pp. 191–226.

————, "ha-Reqa' ha-Kalkali la-Mifne bi-Mediniyut Mizraim," *Sqira Hodshit* (November 1977), pp. 27–36.

————, "'Asor ha-Neft ba-Mizrah ha-Tikhon, 1973–1982," in Goldberg and Kostiner, pp. 3–14.

Dimelbi, Yonatan, "Bediduto ha-Mazhira shel Sadat," [translated from *New Statesman*], Migvan, volume 13, number 8 (October 1977).

Zilberman, Gad, "Temurot be-'Izuv ha-Zehut ha-Leumit ba-Ideologya ha-Nazerit, 1952–1970," *ha-Mizrah he-Hadash,* volume 28 (1971), pp. 113–139.

Waterbury, John, "Hashlakhot Mediniyut ha-Infitah 'al Yahasey Arzot ha-Berit-Mizraim," in Itamar Rabinovich and Haim Shaked (editors), pp. 350–71.

Israeli, Refael, "Sadat: Demuto shel Manhig," in Eytan Gilboa and Mordekhai Naor (editors), pp. 13–32.

Manzeli, Yair, "Hashpa'at ha-Gorem ha-Kalkali 'al Hatirata shel Mizraim le-Heskem Shalom," *Be'ayot beyn-Leumiyot,* 17, 33 (1978), pp. 19–28.

*Mizraim*, Dapey El'azar 9, lectures presented at Tel Aviv University Conference (June 3, 1986). Hozaat Yad David El'azar, 1986.

Kanovski, Eliyahu, "ha-Hebetim ha-Kalkaliyim shel Shalom beyn Israel le-Arzot 'Arav," in Aluf Hareven (editor), *Im Yikon Shalom,* Jerusalem: Van Lir, 1978, pp. 96–118.

————, "Kalkalat Medinot 'Arav veha-Sikhsukh ha-'Arvi-Isreeli," in Gilboa and Naor (editors), pp. 69–82.

Shamir, Shim'on, "ha-Reoryentazya shel Mizraim le'ever Arzot ha-Berit Dinamiqa shel

Qabalat Hahlatot ba-Nose ha-Beyn-Gushi," in Itamar Rabinovich and Haim Shaked (editors), pp. 261–302.

————, "Sheqi'at ha-Meshihiyut ha-Nazeristit," in Shim'on Shamir (editor), *Yeridat ha-Nazerizm, 1965–1970*, Tel Aviv, 1978.

## Books in Other Languages

'Abdel Fadil, Mahmoud, *The Political Economy of Nasserism,* Cambridge: Cambridge University Press, 1980.

'Abdel-Khalek, G. and Robert Tignor (eds.), *The Political Economy of Income Distribution in Egypt,* New York: Holmes and Meier, 1982.

'Abdel Malek, Anour, *Egypt: Military Society,* trans. Charles Lam Markmann, New York: Random House, 1968.

Abir, Mordechai, *Oil, Power, and Politics: Conflict in Arabia, the Red Sea, and the Gulf,* London: Frank Cass, 1974.

'Abo-El-Sabou, Mohammad Aly, "An 'Open Door' Policy and Foreign Direct Ivestment: The Recent Egyptian Experience," Ph.D. Dissertation, Colorado State University, 1984.

Achili, Michele and Mohamed Khaldi (eds.), *The Role of the Arab Development Funds in the World Economy,* London: Croom Helm, 1984.

Adams, Dana, *Yemen: The Unknown War,* London: Dabby Heel, 1968.

Ahmad, Yusuf, *Absorptive Capacity of the Egyptian Economy,* Paris: OECD, 1976.

————, *Oil Revenues in the Gulf,* Paris: OECD, 1974.

Ajami, Fouad, *The Arab Predicament,* New York: Cambridge University Press, 1981.

Alloush, Khaled Mahmoud al-, "Labor Migration and Income Distribution: The Case of the Arab Region," Ph.D. Dissertation, Johns Hopkins University, 1981.

Alderman, Harold et al., *Egypt's Food Subsidy and Rationing System: A Description,* Washington, D. C.: International Food Policy Research Institute, Research Report no. 34, October 1982.

Aliboni, Roberto et al. (eds.), *Egypt's Economic Potential,* London: Croom Helm, 1984.

Allam, Ezzat, "Les Fonds InterArabes De Developpement Du Moyen-Oreint, Leurs Objectifs et Leurs Activites," Ph.D. Dissertation, Universite de Lausanne, 1974.

Almomani, Riad 'Abdullah, "External Borrowing and Economic Development: The Case of Jordan," Ph.D. Dissertation, Utah State University, 1985.

Alnasrawi, Abbas, *OPEC in a Changing World Economy,* Baltimore: The Johns Hopkins University Press, 1985.

Altaf, Gauhar (ed.), *The Challenge of Islam,* London: Islamic Council of Europe, 1978.

Amin, Galal A., *The Modernization of Poverty: A Study in the Political Economy of Growth in Nine Arab Countries, 1945–1970,* Leiden: 1974.

————, and Elizabeth Awny, *International Migration of Egyptian Labour, A Review of the State of the Art,* Ottawa: IDRC-108e, May 1985.

Amin, Samir, *L'economie Arabe Contemporaine,* Paris: Les Editions De Minuit, 1980.

Amin, Sayed Hassan, *Political and Strategic Issues in the Gulf,* Glasgow: Royston, 1984.

Amirsaderghi, Hossein (ed.), *The Security of the Persian Gulf,* London: Croom Helm, 1981.

Ansari, Hamied, *Egypt: The Stalled Society,* New York: SUNY, 1986.

Anthony, John Duke, *The Middle East: Oil, Politics, and Development,* Washington, D.C.: American Enterprise Institute, 1975.

————, *Saudi Arabia's Influence in the Arab World,* New York: Praeger, 1982.

Arkes, Hadley, *Bureaucracy, the Marshall Plan and the National Interests,* Princeton: Princeton University Press, 1973.

Ashker, Ahmed 'Abdel Fattah El, *The Islamic Business Enterprise,* London: Croom Helm, 1987.

Askari, Hossein, *Oil, OECD and the Third World: A Vicious Triangle,* Austin, Texas: 1980.

Ayalon, Ami (ed.), *Middle East Contemporary Survey*, Boulder, Colorado, and Oxford: Westview Press, 1991–1995, various editions.

————, and Haim Shaked (eds.), *Middle East Contemporary Survey*, Boulder, Colorado, and Oxford: Westview Press, 1998.

————, and Bruce Maddy Weitzman (eds.), *Middle East Contemporary Survey*, Boulder, Colorado, and Oxford: Westview Press, 1996.

Ayoob, Mohammed (ed.), *Regional Security in the Third World, Case studies from Southeast Asia and the Middle East,* London: Croom Helm, 1986.

Ayubi, Nazih N. M., *Bureaucracy and Politics in Contemporary Egypt,* London: Ithaca Press, 1980.

Baghdadi, Maher 'Abdalla, "Study on Psychological Problems of Egyptian workers Abroad Using Sample from Riyadh, Saudi Arabia," MA Thesis, al-Azhar University Cairo, 1987.

Baker, Raymond W., *Egypt's Uncertain Revolution Under Nasser And Sadat,* Cambridge, MA.: Harvard University Press, 1978.

Barnett, Michael, *Dialogues in Arab Politics: Negotiations in Regional Order,* New York: Columbia University Press, 1998.

Baur, P. T., *Equality, the Third World and Economic Delusion,* Cambridge, MA.: Harvard University Press, 1981.

————, *Reality and Rhetoric: Studies in the Economics of Development,* London: Weidenfeld and Nicolson, 1984.

Becker, Abraham S. et al., *The Economics and Politics of the Middle East,* New York, 1981.

Beblawi, Hazem and Giacomo Luciani (eds.), *The Rentier State,* London: Croom Helm, 1987.

Belig, Willard (ed.), *King Faisl and the Modernization of Saudi Arabia,* Boulder, CO: Westview Press, 1980.

————, (ed.), *Middle East Peace Plans*, New York: St. Martin's Press, 1986.

Bhattacharya, Anindya K., *The Myth of Petropower,* New York: Lexington Books, 1977.

Bidwell, Robin, *The Two Yemens,* Boulder, CO: Westview Press, 1983.

Binder, Leonard, *In a Moment of Enthusiasm: Political Power and the Second Stratum in Egypt*, Chicago: University of Chicago Press, 1978.

Blumberg, David, "Bilateral Relations in the Absence of Diplomatic Ties: Africa and Israel in the Post-1973 Era," Senior Thesis, Harvard University, 1981.

Bohi, Douglas R. and William B. Quandt, *Energy Security in the 1980s: Economic and Political Perspectives,* Washington, D.C.: Brookings Institution, 1984.

Brahimi, 'Abdelhamid, *Dimensions et Perspectives Du Monde Arabe,* Paris: 1977.

Braillard, Phillippe and Mohammad-Reza Djalili (ed.), *The Third World and International Relations,* London: Frances Pinter, 1984.

Braun, Ursula, *Der Kooperationsrat Arabischer Staaten Am Golf: Eine Newe Kraft',* Baden-Baden: Nomos Uerlagsgesellschaft, 1986.

Brozoska M. and T. Ohlson (eds.), *Arms Production in the Third World,* London: Taylor and Francis, 1986.

Bulloch, John, *The Gulf: A Portrait of Kuwait, Qatar, Bahrain And the UAE,* London: Century Publishing, 1984.

Burns, William J., *Economic Aid and American Policy Toward Egypt 1955–1981,* Albany: State University of New York Press, 1985.

Bustani, Emile, *Marche Arabesque,* London: Robert Hale, 1961.

Carr, David W., *Foreign Investment and Development in Egypt,* New York: Praeger, 1979.

Carter, J. R. L., *Leading Merchant Families of Saudi Arabia,* New York, 1981.

Casodio, Gian P., *The Economic Challenge of the Arabs,* London: Saxon House, 1976.

Cassen, Robert and Associates, *Does Aid Work?* Oxford: Clarendon Press, 1986.

Chatelus, Michel, *Strategies Pour Le Moyen-Orient,* Paris: 1974.

Chibwe, E. C., *Arab Dollars for Africa,* London: 1976.

Chubin, Shahram (ed.), *Security in the Persian Gulf: Domestic Political Factors,* vol. 1, New Jersey: IISS, 1981.

————, *Security in the Persian Gulf: The Role of Outside Powers,* vol. 4, New Jersey: IISS, 1982.

Choucri, Nazli, *International Politics of Energy Interdependence: The Case of Petroleum,* Lexington, MA.: Lexington Books, 1976.

Cleron, J. P., *Saudi Arabia 2000: A Strategy for Growth,* New York: 1978.

Cline, Ray S. and Yonah Alexander, *Terrorism: The Soviet Connection,* New York: Crane RUSAK, 1984.

Copley, G. R (ed.), *Defense Foreign Affairs Handbook,* Washington, D.C.: The Perth Corporation, 1986.

Copper, John Franklin, *China's Foreign Aid: An Instrument of Peking's Foreign Policy,* Lexington: 1976.

Cooper, Mark N., *The Transformation of Egypt,* London: Croom Helm, 1982.

Coppock, Joseph D., *Foreign Trade of the Middle East: Instability and Growth, 1946–1962,* Beirut: American University of Beirut, 1966.

Cordesman, Anthony H., *The Gulf and the Search for Strategic Stability,* Boulder, CO: Westview Press, 1984.

Cottrell, Alvin J. (ed.), *The Persian Gulf States: A General Survey,* Baltimore: The Johns Hopkins University Press, 1980.

————, and Frank Bray, *Military Forces in the Persian Gulf,* Beverly Hills: Sage Publications, 1978.

Craig-Harris, Lillian (ed.), *Egypt: Internal Challenge and Regional Stability,* London: Routledge & Kegan Paul, 1988.

Currie, Lauchlin Bernard, *The Role of Economic Advisers in Developing Countries,* Greenwood Press, 1981.

Czinkota, Michael R. and Marciael Scot (eds.), *US Arab Economic Relations. A Time of Transition,* New York: Praeger, 1985.

Daniels, Clive, *Egypt in the 1980's: The Challenge,* London: EIU Special Report no. 158, 1983.

Daoudi, M. S., and M. S. Dajani, *Economic Diplomacy,* Boulder, CO: Westview Press, 1985.

Darius, Robert G. et al. (eds.), *Gulf Security into the 1980s: Perceptual and Strategic Dimensions,* Stanford, CA.: Hoover Institution Press, 1984.

David, Steven R., *Third World Coups D'etat and International Security,* Baltimore and London: The Johns Hopkins University Press, 1987.

Dawisha, Adeed I., *Egypt in the Arab World: The Elements of Foreign Policy,* London: Macmillan, 1976.

————, (ed.), *Islam in Foreign Policy,* Cambridge: Cambridge University Press, 1983.

Dekmejian, Harir, *Egypt Under Nasir: A Study in Political Dynamics,* Albany: SUNY Press, 1971.

Demir, Soliman, *Arab Development Funds in the Middle East,* New York: Pergamon Press Published for UNITAR, 1979.

————, *The Kuwait Fund and the Political Economy of Arab Regional development,* New York: Praeger, 1976.

Deutsch, Karl W., *The Analysis of International Relations,* New Jersey: Prentice-Hall, 2nd edition, 1978.

Diab, Muhammad A., *Inter-Arab Economic Cooperation 1951–1960,* Beirut: American University of Beirut, 1963.

Dickenson, J. P. et al., *A Geography of the Third World,* London: Methuen, 1983.

Dickson, Harold and Richard, *Kuwait and Her Neighbours,* London: George Allen and Unwin, 1968.

Din, Ashraf Emam Seif al-, "Investment Climate in Egypt As Perceived by Egyptians and American Investors," Ph.D. Dissertation, Ohio State University, 1986.

Driscoll, Robert et al., *Foreign Investment in Egypt: An Analysis of Critical Factors with Emphasis on the Foreign Investment Code,* New York: Fund for Multinational Management Education, 1978.

Dutt, Srikant, *India and the Third World: Altruism or Hegemony,* London: Zed Books, 1984.

Ebraheem, Hassan Ali al-, *Kuwait and the Gulf: Small States and the International System,* London: Croom Helm, 1984.

Economist Intelligence Unit, *KSA Country Profile,* London: EIU, 15/4/2002, 1/6/2001, 30/12/1997, 20/12/1996.

El-Agraa, Ali M., *International Economic Integration,* New York: St. Martin's Press, 1982.

El-Boraiy, Badrawe Esam, "The Egyptian Open Door Policy Towards Foreign Investment: An Economic View," Ph.D. Dissertation, University of South Carolina, 1982.

Economic Research Forum (ERF) for the Arab Countries, Iran and Turkey, *Economic Trends in the MENA Region,* Cairo: ERF, 1998.

Emerson, Steven, *The American House of Saud: The Secret Petrodollar Connection,* New York: Franklin Watts, 1985.

Evron, Yair, *The Middle East,* London: Elek, 1973.

Fallon, Nicholas, *Middle East Oil Money and its Future Expenditure,* London: Graham & Trotman, 1975.

Farah, Tawfic E. (ed.), *Political Behavior in the Arab States,* Boulder, CO: Westview Press, 1983.

Fargues, P., *Reserves De Main-D'oeuvre et Rente Petroliere: Etude Demographique des Migrations de Travail vers les Pays Arabes du Golfe,* Beirut: Cermoc, 1980.

Fergany, Nader, *Aspects of Labor Migration and Unemployment in the Arab Region,* Cairo: Almishkat Center for Research, 2001.

Field, Michael, *A Hundred Million Dollars a Day,* London: Sidgwick and Jackson, 1975.

First, Ruth, *Libya, the Elusive Revolution,* Harmondsworth: Penguin Books, 1974.

Freedman, Robert O. (ed), *The Middle East Since Camp David,* Boulder, CO, 1984.

Friedlander, Melvin A., *Sadat and Begin. The Domestic Politics of Peacemaking,* Boulder, CO: Westview Press, 1983.

Fukuyama, Francis, *The New Marxist-Leninist States in the Third World,* The Rand Paper Series, Santa Monica, California: Rand Corporation, 1984.

Gaelli, Anton, *Die Sozio-Oekonomische entwicklung der OPEC-Staaten, Auswirkungen und Prspektiven des Devisinreichtums,* Munich: 1979.

Garthoff, Raymond L., *Detente and Confrontation: American-Soviet Relations from Nixon to Reagan,* Washington, D.C.: Brookings Institution, 1985.

Gellner, E. and J. Waterbury (eds.), *Patrons and Clients in Mediterranean Societies,* London: Duckworth, 1977.

Ghanem, Shukri, *OPEC: The Rise and Fall of an Exclusive Club,* London: KPI, 1986.

Ghantus, Elias T., *Arab Industrial Integration: A strategy for Development,* London: Croom Helm, 1982.

Ghosh, Pradip K. (ed.), *Foreign Aid and Third World Development,* Westport, CN: Greenwood Press, 1984.

Gilani, Ijaz Shafi, "From Khartoum to Rabat: The Development of Pragmatic Arabism in

Inter-Arab Relations (1967–74)," Ph.D. Thesis, MIT, January 1977.

Gillespie, Kate, *The Tripartite Relationship: Government, Foreign Investors, and Local Investors During Egypt's Economic Opening,* New York: Praeger, 1984.

Gilpin, Robert, *The Political Economy of International Relations,* Princeton: Princeton University Press, 1987.

Gimbel, John, *The Origin of the Marshall Plan,* California: Stanford University Press, 1976.

Girgis, Maurice, *Industrialization and Trade Patterns in Egypt,* Tuebingen: Mohr, 1977.

Glassner, Martin I. (ed.), *Global Resources,* New York: Praeger, 1983.

Golub, David B., *When Oil and Politics Mix: Saudi Oil Policy, 1983–1985,* Harvard Middle East Papers, Modern Series, no. 4, 1985.

Guecioueur, Adda (ed.), *The Problems of Arab Economic Development and Integration,* 1984.

Guy, Arnold, *Aid in Africa,* London: Kogan Page, 1979.

Halliday, Fred, *Arabia Without Sultans: A Survey of Political Instability in the Arab World,* New York: Vintage, 1974.

Hallwood, Paul and Stuart Sinclair, *Oil, Debt and Development: OPEC in the Third World,* London: George Allen and Unwin, 1981.

Hammad, Khalil, "Foreign Aid and Economic Development: The Case of Jordan," Ph.D. Dissertation, Southern Illinois University at Corbondale, Illinois, 1981.

Hammond, P. Y. and S. Alexander, *Political Dynamics in the Middle East,* New York: 1972.

Hansen, Bent, *Economic Development in Egypt,* Rand Corporation, 1969.

————, and K. Nashashibi, *Foreign Trade Regimes and Economic Development: Egypt,* New York: Columbia University Press, 1975.

————, and Samir Radwan, *Employment Opportunities and Equity in a Changing Economy: Egypt in the 1980s,* Geneva: ILO, 1982.

Haseeb, Khair al-Din and Samir Makdisi (eds.), *Arab Monetary Integration,* London: Croom Helm, 1982.

Hasegawa, Sukehiro, *Japanese Foreign Aid: Policy and Practice,* New York: Praeger, 1975.

Hasou, Tawfig Y., *The Struggle for the Arab World,* London: KPI, 1985.

Hawkins, E. K., *The Principles of Development Aid,* Hamondsworth: Penguin Books, 1970.

Heller, Mark and Nadav Safran, *The New Middle Class and Regime: Stability in Saudi Arabia,* Harvard Middle East Paper, Modern Series, no. 3, 1985.

Hewett, Edward A., *Energy, Economics, and Foreign Policy in the Soviet Union,* Washington, D. C.: Brookings Institution, 1984.

Hinnebusch, Raymond A., *Egyptian Politics Under Sadat,* London: 1985.

Hirst, Daviv, *Oil and Public Opinion in the Middle East,* London: Faber and Faber, 1966.

————, and Irene Beeson, *Sadat,* London: Faber and Faber, 1982.

Hobday, Peter, *Saudi Arabia Today, An Introduction to the Richest Oil Power,* London, 1978.

Holbik, Karel, *West German Foreign Aid, 1956–1966,* Boston: Boston University Press, 1970.

Holden, David and Richard Johns, *The House of Saud,* London: Sidgwick and Jackson, 1981.

Holsti, O. R. et al, *Unity and Disintegration in International Alliances,* London: Lanham, 1985.

Hosmer, Stephen and Thomas Wolfe, *Soviet Policy and Practice Toward Third World Conflicts,* Lexington: Lexington Books, 1983.

Hotaling, Edward, *The Arab Blacklist Unveiled,* New York: Landia, 1977.

Hudson, Michael C., *Arab Politics: The Search for Legitimacy,* New Haven: Yale University Press, 1977.

————, (ed.), *Middle East Dilemma: The Politics and Economics of Arab Integration.* New York: Columbia University Press, 1999.

Hufbaur, Gary C. and Jefferey Schott, *Economic Sanctions Reconsidered: History and Current Policy*, Washington, D.C.: Institute for International Economics, 1985.

Hunter, Shireen, *OPEC and the Third World: The Politics of Aid,* Bloomington: Indiana University Press, 1984.

————, (ed.), *Political and Economic Trends in the Middle East. Implication for US Policy,* Boulder, CO: Westview Press, 1985.

Hurewitz, J. C. (ed.), *Oil, the Arab-Israel Dispute and the Industrial World,* Boulder, CO: Westview Press, 1976.

Hyman, Anthony, *Security Constraints in the Gulf States,* Conflict Studies no. 188, London: Institiute for the Study of Conflict, 1986.

Ibrahim, Ibrahim (ed.), *Arab Resources: The Transformation of a Society,* London: Croom Helm, 1983.

Ibrahim, Saad Eddin, *The New Arab Social Order: A study of the Social Impact of Oil Wealth,* Boulder, CO: Westview Press, 1982.

————, *The Vindication of Sadat in the Arab World,* Policy Focus, no. 22, the Washington Institute, 1993.

Ikram, Khalid, *Egypt: Economic Management in a Period of Transition,* Baltimore: Johns Hopkins Press, 1980.

Indyk, Martin, *To the Ends of the Earth: Sadat's Jerusalem Initiative,* Harvard Middle East Papers, Cambridge, MA., 1984.

Islami, Reza and Rostam Kavoussi, *The Political Economy of Saudi Arabia,* Seattle: 1984.

Israeli, Raphael, *Man of Defiance: A Political Biography of Anwar Sadat,* London: Weidenfield and Nicolson, 1985.

Issawi, C. (ed.), *The Economic History of the Middle East, 1800–1914,* Chicago: 1966.

Jackson, Henty F., *From Congo to Soweto: US Foreign Policy toward Africa Since 1960,* New York: Morrow, 1982.

Jureidini, Paul A. and R. D. Mclaurin, *Beyond Camp David,* New York: 1981.

Kadi, Leila S., *Arab Summit Conferences and the Palestine Problem, 1936–1950, 1964–1966,* Beirut: 1966.

Kanovski, E., *The Economic Impact of the Six-Day War,* New York: Praeger, 1970.

————, *Saudi Arabia's Dismal Economic Future: Regional and Global Implications,* Tel Aviv: Dayan Center, Occasional Papers, April 1986.

Kapoor, A., *Foreign Investments and the New Middle East,* Princeton: Darwin Press, 1975.

Kardouche, George K., *The UAR in Development,* New York: Praeger, 1966.

Karsh, Efraim, *The Cautious Bear: Soviet Military Engagement In Middle East Wars in the Post-1967 Era,* JCSS Study no. 3, Tel Aviv: The Jerusalem Post and Westview Press, 1985.

Kawaz, Ahmad al- and Imed Limam, *The Arab Economies in Multi–Country Models: Survey of Some Regional and Global Experiences,* ERF Working Paper Series, 9602, Cairo: Economic Research Institute, 1996.

Kegley, Charles W., Jr. and Pat Mcgowan (eds.), *The Political Economy of Foreign Policy Behavior,* Beverly Hills: Sage, 1981.

Kelly, J. B., *Arabia, the Gulf and the West,* New York: Basic Books, 1980.

Keohane, Robert O., *After Hegemony: Cooperation and Discord in the World Political Economy,* Princeton: Princeton University Press, 1984.

————, and J. S. Nye, *Power and Interdependent,* Boston: Little Brown, 1977.

Kerr, Malcolm, *The Arab Cold War,* 3rd edition, Oxford: Oxford University Press, 1971.

————, et al., *Inter-Arab Conflict Contingencies and the Gap Between the Arab Rich and Poor,* Rand-2371–Na, December 1978.

Kerr, M. and El Sayed Yassin (eds.), *Rich and Poor States in the Middle East: Egypt and the New Arab Order,* Boulder, CO: Westview Press, 1982.

Khader, Bichara (coordinator), *Monde Arabe Et Developpement Economique,* Paris: Editions Le Sycomore, 1981.

————, and Bashir El-Wifati (eds.), *The Economic Development of Libya*, London: Croom Helm, 1987.

Khalidi, R. and C. Mansour (eds.), *Palestine and the Gulf: Proceedings of an International Seminar Held at the Institute for Palestine Studies,* Beirut: Institute for Palestine Studies, 1982.

Khouja, M. W. and P. G. Sadler, *The Economy of Kuwait: Development and Role in International Finance,* London: Macmillan, 1979.

Kindleberger, Charles P., *Power and Money,* New York: Basic Books, 1970.

King, Ralph, *The Iran-Iraq War: The Political Implications,* Adelphi Papers no. 219, London: IISS, Spring 1987.

Knauerhase, R., *The Saudi Arabian Economy,* New York: 1975.

Kodmani, Bassma (ed.), *Quelle Securite Pour Le Golfe,* Paris: Institut Francais Des Relations Internationales, 1984.

Korany, Bahgat and Ali E. Hillal Dessouki (eds.), *The Foreign Policies of Arab States,* Cairo: The American University in Cairo Press, 1984.

Kosman, William Youssef, *Sadat's Realistic Peace Initiative,* New York: 1981.

Koury, Enver M. and Emile A. Nakhleh, *The Arabian Peninsula, Red Sea, and Gulf: Strategic Considerations,* Hyattsville, Maryland: Institute of Middle Eastern and North African Affairs, 1979.

Kubursi, Atif, *The Economies of the Arabian Gulf: A Statistical Source Book,* London: Croom Helm, 1984.

————, *The Economic Consequences of the Camp David Agreements,* Beirut: Institute for Palestine Studies, 1981.

Kuniholm, Bruce R., *Persian Gulf and United States Policy: A Guide to Issues and References,* Claremont, CA.: Regina Books, 1984.

Laanatza, Mariamme et al., *Egypt Under Pressure,* Uppsala: Scandinavian Institute of African Studies, 1986.

Lacey, Robert, *The Kingdom,* New York: Avon Books, 1982.

Law, John, *Arab Aid: Who Gets It, for What, and How,* New York: Chase World Information Corporation, 1978.

Law, John, *Arab Investors: Who They Are, What They Buy and Where,* 2 vols. New York: Chase World Information Corporation, 1980, 1981.

Lawrence, Robert G., *US Policy in Southwest Asia: A Failure In Perspective,* Washington: National Defense University, 1984.

Le Vine, Victor T. and Timothey W. Luke, *The Arab–African Connection: Political and Economic Realities,* Bouler, CO: Westview Press, 1979.

Litwak, Robert, *Security in the Persian Gulf: Sources of Inter-State Conflict,* vol. 2, New Jersey: IISS, 1981.

Looney, Robert E., *Saudi Arabia's Development Potential: Application of an Islamic Growth Model,* Lexington, MA.: D.C. Heath 1982.

Loup, Jacques, *Can the Third World Survive?* Baltimore: Johns Hopkins, 1980.

Luciani, Giacomo and Ghassan Salame (eds.), *The Politics of Arab Integration,* London: Croom Helm, 1988.

Luciani, Giacomo. (ed.), *The Mediterranean Region: Economic Interdependence and the Future of Society,* London: Croom Helm, 1984.

Lukacs, Yehuda (ed.), *Documents on the Israeli-Palestinian Conflict 1967–1983*, London: Cambridge University Press, 1984.

Lyon, Peyton V. and Tareq Y. Ismael, *Canada and the Third World,* Maclean-Hunter Press Book, 1976.

Mabro, Robert, *The Egyptian Economy 1952–1972,* Oxford: Clarendon Press, 1974.

————, and Samir Radwan, *The Industrialization of Egypt, 1939–1974: Policy and Performance,* Oxford: Clarendon Press, 1976.

Macdonald, Robert W., *The League of Arab States: A Study in the Dynamics of Regional Organization,* Princeton: Princeton University Press, 1965.

Machhour, Mohga and Alain Roussillon, *La Revolution Iranienne Dans La Presse Egyptienne,* Cairo: Cedej Dossier no. 4, March 1982.

Madani, Nizar O., "The Islamic Content of the Foreign Policy of Saudi Arabia: King Faisal's Call for Islamic Solidarity (1965–1975)," Ph.D. Thesis, The American University, 1977.

Mallakh, Ragaei el-, *Capital Investment in the Middle East,* New York: Praeger, 1977.

————, *Economic Development and Regional Cooperation, Kuwait.* Chicago: The University of Chicago Press, 1970.

————, *Kuwait: Trade and Investment*, Boulder, CO: Westview Press, 1979.

————, *Saudi Arabia: Rush to Development*, Baltimore: The Johns Hopkins University Press, 1982.

————, and Dorothea El Mallakh (eds.), *Saudi Arabia: Energy Developmental Planning and Industrialization*, Lexington, MA.: D. C. Heath, 1982.

Mallakh, R. el-, Jacob K. Atta, *The Absorptive Capacity of Kuwait: Domestic and International Perspectives,* Lexington, MA.: D. C. Heath, 1981.

Marayati, Abid A. al- (ed.), *International Relations of the Middle East and North Africa,* Cambridge, MA.: 1984.

Martens, Andre, *L'economie Des Pays Arabes,* Paris: Economica, 1983.

Martin, Lenore G., *The Unstable Gulf: Threats from Within,* Lexington, MA.: Lexington Books, 1984.

Mattione, Richard P, *OPEC's Investments and the International Financial System,* Washington, D.C.: The Brookings Institution, 1985.

Mclachlan, Keith, *Economic Development of the Middle East Oil Exporting States,* London: 1978.

————, and 'Abdulrasool al-Moosa, *Immigrant Labour in Kuwait,* London: Croom Helm, 1985.

Mccloud, Donald G., *System and Process in Southeast Asia,* Boulder, CO: Westview Press, 1986.

Mclaurin, R. D. et al., *Middle East Foreign Policy,* New York: Praeger, 1982.

Mclin, Jon, *Social and Economic Effects of Petroleum Development in Non-OPEC Developing Countries.* Synthesis Report, Geneva: ILO, 1986.

Mead, Donald C., *Growth and Structural Change in the Egyptian Economy,* Homewood: R. D. Irwin, 1967.

MERI Report, *Egypt, Middle East Research Institute,* University of Pennsylvania, London: Croom Helm, 1985.

Mertz, Robert and Pamela, *Arab Aid to Sub-Saharan Africa,* Boulder: Westview Press, 1983.

Mikesell, Raymond F., *The Economics of Foreign Aid,* London: Weidenfeld and Nicolson, 1968.

Mirel, Pierre, *L'Egypte Des Ruptures: L'ere Sadate, De Nasser Moubarak,* Paris: Editions Sindbad, 1982.

Montazer-Zouhour, M., *Petrole et Developpement au Moyen-Orient,* Paris: 1978.

Mufti, Muhammed Ahmed, "United States Foreign Policy Toward Egypt Under Sadat: 1970–1981," Ph.D. Thesis, University of California at Riverside, 1983.

Muna, Farid A., *The Arab Executive,* London: Macmilan, 1980.

Musry, Alfred G., *An Arab Common Market: A Study in Inter-Arab Trade Relations, 1920–67,* New York: Praeger, 1969.

Nagger, Sa'id al-, *Foreign Aid and Economic Development of the United Arab Republic,* Cairo: 1964.

Naguib, Mohamed Fathi, *L'integation De L'Egypte Dans Le Marche: A Anglais Et Les Repercussions Sur Le Systeme Monetaire Egyptien,* Paris: 1972.

Neaim, Hamed 'Abdulaziz al-, "An Analysis of Recruitment of Foreign Employees in the Civil Service of Saudi Arabia," Ph.D. Thesis, North Texas State University, 1980.

Niblock, Tim (ed.), *Social and Economic Development in the Arab Gulf,* New York: St. Martin Press, 1980.

———, (ed.), *State Society and Economy in Saudi Arabia,* New York: St. Martin's Press, 1982.

O'brien, Patrick, *The Revolution in Egypt's Economic System,* New York: Oxford University Press, 1966.

Oehme, Joachim, *Deutsche Stiftung Fuer Internationale Entwicklung,* Dok 1276c, Bonn: Arabische Institutionen, 1984.

Oweiss, Ibrahim M. (ed.), *The Dynamics of Arab-United States Economic Relation in the 1970s,* Washington, D.C.: 1980.

Packenham, Robert A., *Liberal America, and the Third World,* Princeton: Princeton University Press, 1973.

Peristiany, J. G. (ed.), *Honour and Shame. The Values Of Mediterranean Society,* London: Weidenfeld and Nicolson, 1965.

Peterson, J. E., *Oman in the Twentieth Century: Political Foundations of an Emerging State,* London: Croom Helm, 1978.

Plascov, Avi, *Security in the Persian Gulf: Modernization, Political Development and Stability,* vol.3, New Jersey: IISS, 1982.

Presley, John R., *A Guide to the Saudi Arabia Economy,* London: Macmillan, 1984.

Price, David Lynn, *Oil and the Middle East Security,* Washington papers, vol.IV, no. 41, Beverly Hills: Sage Publications, 1976.

Pridham, B. R. (ed.), *Oman: Economic Social and Strategic Development,* London: Croom Helm, 1987.

Proctor, Harris (ed.), *Islam and International Relations,* New York: Praeger, 1965.

Quandt, William B., *Saudi Arabia in the 1980s: Foreign Policy, Security, and Oil,* Washington, D.C.: The Brookings Institution, 1981.

———, *Saudi Arabia Oil Policy: A Staff Paper*, Washington, D.C.: The Brookings Institution, 1982.

Ra'anan, Uri et al., *Arms Transfers to the Third World,* Boulder, CO: Westview Press, 1978.

Rabinovich, Itamar and Haim Shaked (eds.), *From June to October: The Middle East Between 1967 and 1973,* New Jersey: Transaction Books, 1978.

———, (eds.), *Middle East Contemporary Survey*, Boulder CO and Oxford: Westview Press, 1987–1989.

Ragsdale, Marguerita Dianne, "Egypt and the Persian Gulf: A Study of Small States in Coalition," Ph.D. Dissertation, University of Virginia, 1978.

Ramazani, R. K., *Beyond the Arab-Israeli Settlement: New Direction for US Policy in the Middle East,* Cambridge: Institute for Foreign Policy Analysis, 1977.

Ranney, Sue, *The Open Door Policy and Industrialization in Egypt: A Preliminary Investigation,* Ann Arbor, Center for Research on Economic Development, Discussion Paper no. 87, August 1980.

Rejwan, Nissim, *Nasserist Ideology,* New York: John Wiley, 1974.

Riddell, Roger C., *Foreign Aid Reconsidered,* Baltimore: The Johns Hopkins University Press, 1987.

De Rivera, Joseph H., *The Psychological Dimension of Foreign Policy,* Columbus, OH.: 1968.

Rivlin, Paul, *The Dynamics of Economic Policy Making in Egypt,* New York: Praeger, 1985.

Roett, Riordon, *The Politics of Foreign Aid in the Brazilian Northeast,* Vanderblitt University Press, 1972.

Ro'i, Yaacov, *The USSR and Egypt in the Wake of Sadat's July Decision,* Tel Aviv University, *Slavic and Soviet Series,* no. 1, 1975.

Rubinstein, Alvin, *Red Star on the Nile: The Soviet Egyptian Influence Relationship Since the June War,* Princeton: Princeton University Press, 1977.

Rugh, William A., *The Arab Press,* Syracuse: Syracuse University Press, 1979.

Rumaihi Muhammad, *Beyond Oil: Unity and Development in the Gulf* (trans. James Deckins), London: al-Saqi Books, 1986.

Russell, S.S. *International Migration in Europe, Central Asia, the Middle East, and North Africa: Issues for the World Bank,* Washington, DC: World Bank, 1992.

Russett, B. and H. Starr, *World Politics: The Menu for Choice,* San Francisco: W. H. Freeman, 1981.

Rustum, Ali, *Saudi Arabia and Oil Diplomacy,* New York: Praeger, 1976.

————, "The Use of Oil as a Weapon of Diplomacy: A Case Study of Saudi Arabia," Ph.D. Dissertation, The American University, 1975.

Sabah, Y. S. I. al-, *The Oil Economy of Kuwait,* London: Kegan Paul International, 1980.

Safran, Nadav, *Saudi Arabia: The Ceaseless Quest for Security,* Cambridge, MA.: Harvard University Press, 1985.

Sardar, Ziauddin, *Science and Technology in the Middle East,* Essex: Longman, 1982.

Sayed, Salah El-, *Egypt Strategies for Investment,* Cairo: American University in Cairo Press, 1977.

Sayegh, K. S., *Oil and Arab Regional Development,* New York: Praeger, 1968.

Sayigh, Yusif A., *The Arab Economy: Past Performance and Future Prospects,* New York: Oxford University Press, 1982.

————, *The Economics of the Arab World: Development since 1945,* London: Croom Helm, 1978.

Sela, Avraham , *The Decline of the Arab-Israeli Conflict: Middle East Politics and the Quest for Regional Order,* Albany: SUNY Press, 1998.

Sell, Ralph R., *Gone for Good,* Cairo: Cairo Papers in Social Science, vol. 10, Monograph 2, Summer 1987.

Settit, Mohammad Fouad Abou, "Foreign Capital and Economic Performance: The Case of Egypt," Ph.D. Dissertation, The University of Texas at Dallas, 1986.

Sheehan, Edward R. F., *The Arabs, Israelis and Kissinger: A Secret History of American Diplomacy in the Middle East,* New York: Reader's Digest Press, 1976.

Shihata, Ibrahim, *The Other Face of OPEC,* London: 1982.

————, et al., *The OPEC Fund for International Development: The Formative Years,* London: Croom Helm, 1983.

Shoukri, Ghali, *Egypt: Portrait of a President. Sadat's Road to Jerusalem,* London, 1981.

Sicherman, Havey, *Broker or Advocate: The US Role in the Arab-Israeli Dispute 1973–1978,* Foreign Policy Research Institute, Monograph no. 25, Philadelphia, 1978.

Sid-Ahmed, Mohammed, *After the Guns Fall Silent,* London: Croom Helm, 1976.

Simmons, Andre, *Arab Foreign Aid,* London: Associated University Press, 1981.

Singer, Marshall R., *Weak States in a World of Powers,* New York: The Free Press, 1972.

Sirageldin, Ismail and Eqbal al-Rahmani (eds.), *Population and Development Transformations in the Arab World*, Research in Human Capital and Development, Greenwich and London: JAI Press Inc., 1996.

Smithies, Arthur, *The Economic Potential of the Arab Countries,* Rand Publication no. R-2250-Na, Santa Monica, November 1978.

Spero, Joan Edelman, *The Politics of International Economic Relations,* 3rd edition, London: George Allen & Unwin, 1985.

Springborg, Robert, *Family, Power, and Politics in Egypt: Sayed Bey Marei-His Clan, Client and Cohorts,* Philadelphia: University of Pennsylvania Press, 1982.

St. John, Ronald Bruce, *Qaddafi's World Design: Libyan Foreign Policy, 1969–1987,* London: al-Saqi, 1987.

Stephens, John W. and P. F. Hayek (eds.), *Investment in Egypt: Law no. 43 and Its Implications for the Transfer of Technology,* New York: Fund for Multinational Management Education, 1974.

Stephens, Robert, *The Arab's New Frontier,* London: Temple Smith, 1976.

Stevens, P. J., *Joint Ventures in Middle East Oil 1957–1975,* Beirut: Middle East Economic Consultants, 1976.

Stoddard, Philip H. (ed.), *The Middle East in the 1980's: Problems and Prospects,* Washington, D.C., 1985.

Stone, Russel A. (ed.), *OPEC and the Middle East: The Impact of Oil on Societal Development,* New York: Praeger, 1977.

Sullivan, Denis Joseph, "American Economic Aid to Egypt, 1975–86: Political and Bureaucratic Struggles over Aid Disbursement and Development Choices," Ph.D. Dissertation, University of Michigan, 1987

Taher, 'Abdullah Mahmoud, "External Borrowing and Economic Growth in Jordan During the Period 1955–1975," Ph.D. Dissertation, University of Illinois at Urbana-Champaign, 1979.

Tahir-Kheli and S. Ayubi (eds.), *The Iran-Iraq War: New Weapons, Old Conflicts,* New York: Praeger, 1983.

Tahtinen, Dale R., *National Security Challenges to Saudi-Arabia,* Washington, D.C.: American Enterprise Institute for Public Policy Research, 1978.

Tansky, Leo, *US and USSR Aid to Developing Countries,* New York: Praeger, 1976.

Taryam, 'Abdullah Omran, *The Establishment of the United Arab Emirates 1950–85,* London: Croom Helm, 1987.

Taylor, Alan R., *The Arab Balance of Power,* New York: Syracuse University Press, 1982.

Thompson, Herbert M. (ed.), *Studies in Egyptian Political Economy,* Cairo: Cairo Papers in Social Science, vol. 2, Monograph 3, 2nd edition, July 1983.

Tuma, Elias H, *Economic and Political Change in the Middle East,* California: Pacific Books, 1987.

Turner, Louis, *Middle East Industrialization: A Study of Saudi And Iranian Downstream Investment,* London: 1979.

Udovitch, Abram L. (ed.), *The Middle East: Oil Conflict and Hope,* Lexington, MA.: Lexington Books, 1976.

Underwood, Anthony M., *Inter Arab Financial Flows,* Durham: 1974.

Van den Boogaerde, Pierre, *Financial Assistance from Arab Countries and Arab Regional Institutions*, Washington, DC: IMF, September 1991.

Vatikiotis, P. J., *Arab and Regional Politics in the Middle East,* New York: St. Martin's Press, 1984.

————, *Conflict in the Middle East*, London: Allen and Unwin, 1974.

Wai, Dunstan M. (ed.), *Interdependence in a World of Unequals: African-Arab-OECD Economic Cooperation for Development,* Boulder, CO: Westview Press, 1982.

Wall, David, *The Charity of Nations: The Political Economy of Foreign Aid,* London: Macmillan, 1973.

Walpole, Norman C. et al., *Area Handbook for Saudi Arabia,* Washington, D.C.: American University, 1971.

Waterbury, John, *Egypt Burdens of the Past, Options for the Future,* American University Field Staff, 1978.

———, *Hydropolitics of the Nile Valley*, Syracuse: Syracuse University Press, 1979.

———, *The Egypt of Nasser and Sadat: The Political Economy of Two Regimes*, Princeton: Princeton University Press, 1983.

———, and Ragei El-Mallakh, The *Middle East in the Coming Decade: From Wellhead to Well-Being*, New York: Mcgraw-Hill, 1978.

Wien, Jack, *Saudi-Egyptian Relations: The Political and Military Dimensions of Saudi Financial Flows to Egypt,* Santa Monica: The Rand Corporation P-6327, 1980.

Weinbaum, Marvin G., *Egypt and the Politics of US Economic Aid,* Boulder, CO: Westview Press, 1986.

———, *Food, Development, and Politics in the Middle East,* Boulder, CO: Westview Press, 1982.

Weissman, Steve et al., *The Trojah Horse: A Radical Look At Foreign Aid,* Ramparts Press, 1974.

Weitzman, Bruce Maddy, (ed.), *Middle East Contemporary Survey*, Boulder, CO and Oxford: Westview Press, 1995–2000.

White, John A., *The Politics of Foreign Aid,* New York: St. Martin's Press, 1974.

Wilson, Rodney, *Trade and Investment in the Middle East,* London: Macmillan, 1977.

Wionczek, Miguel S. (ed.), *Economic Cooperation in Latin America, Africa, and Asia,* Cambridge: MIT Press, 1969.

Wohlers-Scharf, Traute, *Arab and Islamic Banks: New Business Partners for Developing Countries,* Paris: OECD. Development Centre Studies, 1983.

———, *Trilateral Co-Operation,* 2 vol., Paris: OECD, 1978.

Yarom, Y., *Arms Transaction with Middle Eastern and North African countries in 1981,* CSS Digest no. 1, Tel Aviv: CSS, December 1982.

Ziwar-Daftary, May, *Issues in Development: The Arab Gulf States,* London: MD Research and Services, 1980.

## Articles in other languages

Abalkhail, M., "OPEC Aid: A Question of Solidarity," *OAPEC Bulletin,* vol. 12, No. 8–9 (1986), pp. 12–20.

'Abdalla, Nazem, "Egypt's Absorptive Capacity," *IJMES,* vol. 16, no. 2 (May 1984), pp. 177–98.

———, "The Role of Foreign Capital in Egypt's Economic Development: 1960–1972," *IJMES,* vol. 14 (1982), pp. 87–97.

'Abdel-Meguid, Adly, "Egypt's Policy Towards Foreign Investments," *Vanderbilt Journal of Transnational Law,* vol. 10, no. 1 (1977/78), pp. 97–107.

Abed, T., "Arab Financial Resources: An Analysis and Critique of Present Deployment Policies," in I. Ibrahim (ed.), *Arab Resources: The Transformation of a Society,* London: Croom Helm, 1983, pp. 43–70.

Aburdene, Odeh, "Small Shift in Arab Investment Overseas," *The Banker* (December 1979).

———, and Alan Stoga, "Arab Foreign Investment," *OAPEC News Bulletin* (Kuwait), no. 12 (December 1979).

Adams, R. "The Economic Uses and Impact of International Remittances in Rural Egypt." *Economic Development and Cultural Change*, vol. 39, no. 4, (July 1991).

Addo, Herb, "Foreign Policy Strategies for Achieving the New International Economic Order: A Third World Perspective," in Kegley, Charles W., Jr. and Pat Mcgowan (eds.), *The Political Economy of Foreign Policy Behavior,* Beverly Hills, CA: Sage, 1981, pp. 233–54.

Adelman, Irma and Hollis B. Chenery, "Foreign Aid and Economic Development: The Case of Greece," *Review of Economics and Statistics,* vol. 18, no. 1 (1966), pp. 1–15.

Adly, 'Abdel-Meguid, "Egypt's Policy Towards Foreign Investment," *Vanderbilt Journal of Transnational Law,* vol. 10, no. 1 (1977), pp. 97–107.

Ahmad, Ghafoor 'Abdul, "Economic Cooperation Among Islamic States," *The Criterion* (Karachi), vol. 11, no. 4 (1976).

Ajami, Fouad, "The Arab Triangle," *Foreign Policy,* no. 29 (Winter 1977–8), pp. 90–108.

———, "The End of Pan Arabism," *Foreign Affairs,* vol. 57, no. 1 (October 1978), pp. 355–73.

———, "Retreat from Economic Nationalism: The Political Economy of Sadat's Egypt," *Journal of Arab Affairs,* vol. 1, no. 1 (1981), pp. 27–52.

———, "The Struggle for Egypt's Soul," *Foreign Policy,* no. 35 (Summer 1979), pp. 3–36.

Aly, 'Abdel Monem, "Egypt: A Decade after Camp David," in William B. Quandt (ed.), *The Middle East: Ten Years after Camp David,* Washington: The Brookings Institute, 1988.

Alkazaz, 'Aziz, "The Arab Fund for Economic and Social Development," *Orient,* vol. 17, no. 4 (December 1976), pp. 85–108.

Ameen, 'Abdul Whahab al-, "Kuwait's Role in International Development Finance: With a Special Reference to Kuwait Fund for Arab Economic Development," *Journal for Arab and Islamic Studies,* vol. 4, Nos. 1–2 (1983), pp. 61–72.

Alnasrawi, Abbas, "The Arab Economies: Twenty Years of Change and Dependency," *Arab Studies Quarterly,* vol. 9, no. 4 (1987), pp. 357–82.

Alnasrawi, Abbas, "Dependency Status and Economic Development of Arab States," *Journal of Asian and African Studies,* vol. 21, No. 1–2 (1986), pp. 17–31.

———, "The Rise and Fall of Arab Power," *Arab Studies Quarterly,* vol. 6, No. 1–2 (Winter/Spring 1984), pp. 1–12.

Anbari, 'Abdul Amin al-, "OPEC and the Third World," *OPEC Bulletin* (September 1980), pp. 14–20.

Ansari, Hamied, "Egypt in Search of a New Role in the Middle East," *American Arab Affairs,* no. 12 (Spring 1985), pp. 43–9.

Anthony, John Duke, "The Gulf Cooperation Council," *Orbis,* vol. 28 (Fall 1984).

"Arab Aid in 1978," *Arab Oil and Economic Review,* vol. 12, no. 4 (February 1978), p. 33.

"Arab Aid to Arabs," *The Arab Economist,* vol. 10, no. 106, pp. 12–18.

"Arab and Soviet Aid: A Comparison," *Arab Oil and Economic Review,* vol. 2, no. 6 (June 1979), pp. 23–5.

"Arab Common Market Still at Square One," *The Middle East* (July 1979), pp. 90, 92.

Askari, Hussein and John T. Cummings, "The Future of Economic Integration Within the Arab World," *IJMES,* vol. 8 (1977), pp. 285–315.

Ayubi, Nazih N. M., "OPEC Surplus Funds and Third World Development: The Egyptian Case," *Journal of South Asian and Middle Eastern Studies,* vol. 5, no. 4 (Summer 1982).

———, "OPEC and the Third World: The Case of Arab Aid," in Robert W. Stookey (ed.), *The Arabian Peninsula: Zone of Ferment,* Stanford: Hoover Institution Press, 1984, pp. 109–38.

Barkai, Haim, "Egypt's Economic Constraints," *The Jerusalem Quarterly,* no. 14 (Winter 1980), pp. 123–43.

Basile, Antoine, "Regulatory and Institutional Framework for Investment in the Arab World (Revisited)," *The Arab Bank Review,* vol. 4, no.1 (April 2002).

De Beauce, Thierry, "Trois Fonds Arabes De Cooperation," *Politiqe Etrangere,* no. 1 (1976), pp. 47–50.

Beaud, Michael, "Les Pays Mediterraneens Dans Le Systeme National Mondial Hierarchise," *Revue Tiers-Monde,* vol. 24 (1983) pp. 861–878.

Benchenane, Mustapha, "L'integration Economique Arabe," *Revue Tiers-Monde,* vol. 24 (1983), pp. 899–908.

Bill, James A., "Resurgent Islam in the Persian Gulf," *Foreign Affairs* (1984).

Bill, Paul, "Arabs Buying Up US," *Wall Street Journal* (August 18, 1980).

Boudroua, Ahmed, "Outlook for Industrialization of the Arab World," *Journal of Arab and African Studies*, vol. 21, Nos. 1–2 (1986), pp. 32–43.

Bouri, Wahbi El, "La Cooperation Regionale et Interregionale: Experience De L'opaep," *Revue Tiers-Monde,* vol. 24 (1983), pp. 813–18.

Boyd, D., "Saudi Arabia Broadcasting: Radio and Television in a Wealthy Islamic State," *Middle East Review,* vol. 12, no. 4 (Summer 1980), pp. 20–27.

Bruton, Henry, "Egypt's Development in the 1970's," *Economic Development and Cultural Change*, vol. 34, no.4 (July 1983), pp. 679–703.

Bundy, William, "Element of Power," *Foreign Affairs,* vol. 56, no. 1 (October 1977).

Burrell, Robert M. and Abbas R. Kelidar, "Egypt: The Dilemmas of a Nation (1970–1977)," *The Washington Papers,* vol. 5, no. 48 (1977).

Burt, Richard, "US Planning $3 Billion for Egypt," *New York Times* (December 7, 1979).

Bushnell, George E, "The Development of Foreign Investment Law in Egypt and Its Effect on Private Foreign Investment," *Georgia Journal of International and Comparative Law,* vol. 10, no. 2 (1980), pp. 301–24.

Calchi Novati, Giampaolo, "The Gulf Area: Instability and Conflict," *Politica Internazionale* (Florence), vol. 2, no. 1 (Spring 1981).

Campbell, John, "Oil Power in the Middle East" *Foreign Affairs*, vol. 56, no. 1 (October 1977), pp. 89–110.

Campbell, Bruce and Lynn K. Mytelka, "Petrodollar Flows, Foreign Aid and International Stratification," *Journal of World Trade Law* (1976).

Cantori, Louis J., "Egypt Reenter the Arab System," in Robert O. Freedman (ed.), *The Middle East from the Iran-Contra Affairs to the Intifada,* Syracuse: Syracuse University Press, 1991, p. 356.

————, "Unipolarity and Egyptian Hegemony in the Middle East," in Robert O. Freedman (ed.), *The Middle East after Iraq's Invasion of Kuwait,* Gainesville: University of Florida Press, 1993.

Cayre, Genvieve, "Le Fonds Special De L'OPEC," *Magreb Machrek* (March 1978).

Chan, S., "The Impact of Defense Spending on Economic Performance: A Survey of Evidence and Problems," *Orbis,* vol. 29, no. 3 (1985), pp. 403–34.

Chenery, H. B. and E. Carter, "Foreign Assistance and Development Performance, 1960–1970," *American Economic Review*, vol. Lxiii (1973), pp. 459–68.

Choucri, Nazli, "Energy and Arab Development," in I. Ibrahim (ed.), *Arab Resources: The Transformation of a Society,* London: Croom Helm, 1983, pp. 43–70.

Choucri, Nazli and Richard S. Eckaus, "Interactions of Economic and Political Change: The Egyptian Case," *World Development,* vol. 7 (Aug.-Sept. 1979), pp. 783–97.

"Confusion in Arab Economic Relations," *The Arab Economist,* no. 12 (1980), pp. 77–80.

Cooley, J. K., "Iran, the Palestinian and the Gulf," *Foreign Affairs,* vol. 57, no. 4 (1979).

Cooper, Mark, "Egyptian State Capitalism in Crisis: Economic Policies and Political Interests, 1967–1971," *IJMES,* vol. 10, no. 4 (November 1979), pp. 481–516.

————, "State Capitalism, Class Structure, and Social Transformation in the Third World: The Case of Egypt," *IJMES,* vol. 15, no. 4 (November 1983), pp. 451–69.

Crecelous, Daniel, "Saudi Arabian-Egyptian Relations," *International Studies*, vol. 14 (October/December 1975), pp. 563–85.

Cremasco, Maurizio, "The Middle East Arms Industry: Attempts at Regional Cooperation," *Lo Spettatore Internazionale*, vol. 16 (October 1981).

Cummings, John et al., "An Economic Analysis of OPEC Aid," *OPEC Bulletin,* supplement (September 25, 1978).

"Cut Off Without a Piaster," *The Economist* (April 7, 1979), pp. 18–19.

Dhaher, A. et al., "Expatriate Labor in the Arab Gulf States: The Citizens and Political Status," *The Arab Gulf,* vol. 16 (1984), pp. 185–92.

Dawisha, Adeed I., "The Role of Propaganda in Egypt's Arab Policy 1955–1967," *International Relations,* vol. 5 (November 1975).

——, "Saudi Arabia's Search for Security," *Adelphi Papers,* no. 158, London: IISS, (1979). (also Published in Tripp, Charles (ed.), *Regional Security in the Middle East,* New York: St. Martin's Press, 1984.)

Dethier, Jean-Jacques and Kathy Funk, "The Language of Food: Pl 480 in Egypt," *MERIP Reports,* no. 145 (March April 1987), pp. 22–7.

"The Development of Foreign Investment Law in Egypt and Its Effect on Private Foreign Investment," *Georgia Journal of International and Comparative Law,* vol. 10 (1980), pp. 301–24.

Dunn, Michael, "Arming for Peacetime: Egypt's Defense Industry Today," *Defense and Foreign Affairs* (October, November 1987), pp. 20–4.

"Egypt Supporting Gulf Federation," *Middle East Monitor* (May 1, 1971), p. 2.

"Egypt's Surprising Cash Flow," *Business Week* (September 24, 1979), pp. 86, 90.

"Egypt: A Tightrope Economy Caught Between Internal Ineptitude and External Reluctance," *The Arab Economist,* vol. 12, no. 124 (January 1980).

Eilts, Hermann Frederick, "Defense Planning in Egypt," in S. G. Neuman (ed.), *Defense Planning in Less-Industrialized States, the Middle East and South Asia*, Lexington: Lexington Books, 1984, pp. 167–80.

——, "Saudi Arabian Foreign Policy toward the Gulf States and Southwest Asia," In Hafeez Malik (ed.), *International Security In Southwest Asia*, New York: Praeger, 1984, pp. 77–106.

Eliot, Theodore, Jr., "Afghanistan After the 1978 Revolution," *Strategic Review*, vol. 7 (Spring 1979).

Entelis, John P., "Nasser's Egypt: The Failure of Charismatic Leadership," *Orbis,* vol. 28, no. 2 (Summer 1974), pp. 451–64.

Epstein, Edward J., "Secrets from the CIA Archive in Tehran," *Orbis* (Spring 1987), pp. 33–41.

Erb, Guy F. and Helen C. Low, "Resource Transfers to the Developing World," in J. C. Hurewitz (ed.), *Oil, the Arab-Israel Dispute and the Industrial World*, Boulder, CO: Westview Press, 1976, pp. 212–230.

Faksh, Mahmud A., "Saudi Arabia and the Gulf Crisis: Foreign and Security Policy Dilemma," *MER,* vol. 19, no. 4 (1987), pp. 47–53.

Feige, E. L., "Economic Consequences of Peace in the Middle East," *Challenge*, vol. 21 (January 1979), pp. 5–12.

Feith, Douglas, "The Oil Weapon De-Mystified," *Policy Review,* no.15 (1981), pp. 19–39.

Feoktistov, A., "Saudi Arabia and the Arab World," *International Affairs* (Moscow), (July 1977), pp. 101–7.

Ferror, Robert L., "Foreign Investments in the Egyptian Economy," *Middle East Review* (Winter 1975–76), pp. 57–68.

Faini, R. and A. Venturini. "Trade, Aid, and Migrations." *European Economic Review* , vol. 37 (1993).

Feiler, G. "Migration and Recession: Arab Labor Mobility in the Middle East, 1982–89." *Population and Development Review*, vol.17, no. 1 (March 1991).

Field, M., "Where the Arabs Are Putting Their Money," *The Director,* vol. 27 (September 1974).

Finch, M.H.J. "The Latin American Free Trade Association," in Ali M. El–Agraa, (ed.) *International Economic Integration,* London: Macmillan, 1982.

"The Follow Up of Investment Projects in Egypt," *National Bank of Egypt Economic Bulletin,* vol. 31, no. 2 (1978), pp. 137–45.

Franklin, R., "Migrant Labor and the Politics of Development in Bahrain," *MERIP Reports,* vol. 15 (1985), pp. 7–13, 32.

Franko, Lawrence G, "Multinational Enterprises in the Middle East," *Journal of World Trade Law,* vol. 10 (1976).

Gauhar, Altaf, "Arab Petrodollars: Dashed Hope for a New Economic Order," *World Policy Journal,* vol. 4, no. 3 (1987), pp. 443–64.

Gerakis, Andrea S. and S. Thayanithy, "Wave of Middle East Migration Raised Questions of Policy in Many Countries," *IMF Survey* (September 4, 1978), pp. 260–2.

Gerner, Deborah J., "Petro-Dollar Recycling: Imports, Arms, Investment and Aid," *Arab Studies Quarterly,* vol. 7, no. 1 (Winter 1985), pp. 1–25.

Gilbar, Gad G., "Egypt's Economy: The Challenge of Peace," *The Jerusalem Quarterly,* no. 12 (Summer 1979), pp. 6–19.

————, "The Oil Boom and Pan-Arabism," in *The Middle East Oil Decade and Beyond: Essays in Political Economy,* London: Frank Cass, 1997.

————, "One Arab State, Many Arab States: The Impact of Population Growth and Oil Revenues," in Elie Kedourie and Sylvia G. Haim (eds.), *Essays on the Economic History of the Middle East,* London: Frank Cass, 1988, pp. 196–211.

————, "Wealth, Want, and Arab Unity: Saudi-Egyptian Relations, 1962–1985," *The Jerusalem Journal of International Relations,* vol. 9 no. 3 (1987), pp. 65–84.

Gilpin, Robert, "Structural Constraints on Economic Leverage: Market-Type System," in Gordon H. Mccormick and Richard E. Bissell (eds.), *Strategic Dimensions of Economic Behavior,* New York: Praeger, 1984, pp. 105–28.

Girgis, Maurice, "The GCC Factor in Future Arab Labor Migration," *Memo,* 2002.

Gitelson, Susan A., "Arab Aid to Africa: How Much and At What Price," *The Jerusalem Quarterly,* no. 19 (Spring 1981), pp. 120–7.

Goldberg, Jacob, "Saudi Arabia and the Egyptian-Israeli Peace Process," *Middle East Review,* vol. 18, no. 4 (Summer 1986), pp. 25–33.

Gray, Albert L, "Egypt's Ten Year Economic Plan, 1973–82," *Middle East Journal,* vol. 30 (1976), pp. 36–48.

Greig, Ian, "A New Shadow Falls on the Gulf," *Foreign Affairs Research Institute* (London), vol. 20 (1981).

————, "The Security of Gulf Oil," *Foreign Affairs Research Institute* (London), vol. 4 (1980), also published in the *Atlantic Community Quarterly,* vol. 18, no. 2 (1980), pp. 193–200.

Griffin, Keith and J. L. Enos, "Foreign Assistance: Objectives and Consequences," *Economic Development and Cultural Change,* vol. 3, no. 18 (1970), pp. 313–27.

Hamed, Osama, "Egypt's Open Door Economic Policy: An Attempt at Economic Integration in the Middle East," *IJMES,* vol. 13 (1981), pp. 1–9.

Handoussa, Heba and Nemat Shafic, "The Economics of Peace: The Egyptian Case," in Stanley Fischer et al. (eds.), *The Economics of Middle East Peace,* Cambridge, MA.: MIT Press, 1993.

Hart, Jeffrey A., "Interpreting OECD Policies Toward the New International Economic Order," in Kegley, Charles W., Jr. and Pat Mcgowan (eds.), *The Political Economy of Foreign Policy Behavior,* Beverly Hills: Sage, 1981, pp. 215–32.

Hashim, Jawad M., "Economic Imbalances in the Arab World," *Arab Gulf Journal*, vol. 2 (1982), pp. 13–24.

Heikal, M. H., "Egyptian Foreign Policy," *Foreign Affairs,* vol. 56, no. 4 (July 1978), pp. 714–27.

Hein, John, "OPEC Surpluses Recycling and the Dollar," *The Banker Magazine* (January/February 1981), pp. 86–9.

Hillal-Dessouki, Ali E., "Egypt and Gulf Security: The Dilemma of Two Role Perceptions," in Hafeez Malik (ed.), *International Security in Southwest Asia*, New York: Praeger, 1984, pp. 141–52.

————, "Policy Making in Egypt: A Case Study of the Open Door Economic Policy," *Social Problems,* vol. 28, no. 4 (1981).

————, "The New Arab Political Order: Implication for the 1980's," in Kerr, M. and El Sayed Yassin (eds.), *Rich and Poor States in the Middle East: Egypt and the New Arab Order*, Boulder, CO: Westview Press, 1982, pp. 319–48.

————, and Adel al-Labban, "Arms Race, Defence Expenditures and Development: The Egyptian Case," *Journal of South Asian and Middle Eastern Studies,* vol. 4 (1981), pp. 65–77.

Hoffman, S., "Notes on the Limits of Realism," *Social Research,* vol. 48, no. 4 (1982), pp. 653–59.

Horn, G. H., "Egypt's Investment Potential," *WSJ* (October 21, 1985).

Hottinger, Arnold, "Behind the Grand Mosque Incident," *Swiss Review of International Affairs,* vol. 39 (January 1980).

————, "The Great Powers and the Middle East," in William E. Griffith (ed.), *The World and Great-Powers Triangles,* Cambridge, MA: MIT Press, 1975.

————, "Political Institutions in Saudi Arabia, Kuwait and Bahrain," in S. Chubin (ed.), *Security in the Persian Gulf: Domestic Political Factors,* vol. 1, New Jersey: IISS, 1981. pp. 1–18.

Hout, Shfiq El, "Palestine and the Gulf: A Palestinian Perspective," in R. Khalidi and C. Mansour (eds.), *Palestine and the Gulf*, Beirut: Institute for Palestinian Studies, 1981.

Huisken, Ron, "Armaments and Development," in Helena Tuoni and Raimo Vayrynen (eds.), *Militarization and Arms Production*, New York: St. Martin's Press, 1983.

Ibrahim, Saad Eddin, "Superpowers in the Arab World," *Washington Quarterly* (Summer 1981), pp. 81–96.

Imady, Mohammed, "Patterns of Arab Economic Aid to Third World Countries," *Arab Studies Quarterly,* vol. 6, no. 1–2 (Spring/ Winter 1984), pp. 70–123.

————, "The Role of Arab Development Funds," *Arab Gulf Journal,* vol. 2 (1982), pp. 27–40.

Inoguchi, Kunido Y., "Exit and Voice: The Third World Response to Dependency Since OPEC's Initiative," in Kegley, Charles W., Jr. and Pat Mcgowan (eds.), *The Political Economy of Foreign Policy Behavior,* Beverly Hills: Sage, 1981, pp. 255–75.

Ireland, Jenny, "The Top 100 Arab Banks," *The Banker,* vol. 131, no. 670 (December 1981).

Iskandar, Grant, "Arab and Foreign Investments Achievement in 1975," *The Middle East Observer* (Cairo), (May 26, 1976).

Ismael, J. S., "The Condition of Egyptian Labor in the Gulf," *ASQ*, vol. 8, no. 4, pp. 390–403.

Jackson, Henry F., "Sadat's Perils," *Foreign Policy,* no. 42 (Spring 1981).

Janka, Les, "Security Risks and Reactions," *AEI Foreign Policy and Defence Review,* vol. 2, no. 3 (1980), pp. 82–8.

Kharafi, Jassim Mohamed Al-, "South-South Cooperation with Special Reference to the Role of OPEC Countries," *OAPEC Bulletin,* vol. 12, no. 8–9 (1986), pp. 21–9.

Kanovski, Eliyahu, "Arab 'Haves' and 'Have-Nots'," *The Jerusalem Quarterly*, no. 1 (Fall 1976), pp. 93–105.

Karawan, Ibrahim A., "Egypt's Defence Policy," in Stephanie G. Neuman (ed.), *Defense Planning in Less-Industrialized States: The Middle East and South Asia*, Lexington: Lexington Books, 1984, pp. 147–66.

Kassem, Omar, "Arab Aid Funds Represent the Spirit of Islam," *Euromoney* (December 1981).

Katouzian, Homayoun, "The Political Economy of Oil Exporting Countries," *Peuples Mediterraneens* (Paris), (July–September 1979).

Kaufman, R. H. et al., "A Preliminary Test of the Theory of Dependency," *Comparative Politics*, vol. 7 (April 1975), pp. 303–30.

Kawach, Nadim, "GCC aid down sharply between 1995–2001," *Gulf News* (February 7, 2002).

Kennedy, Charles and A. P. Thirwall, "Foreign Capital, Domestic Savings, and Economic Development: A Reply," *Bulletin of the Oxford University Institute of Economics and Statistics*, vol. 33, no. 2 (1970), pp. 120–34.

Kerr, Malcolm, "Egyptian Foreign Policy and the Revolution," in P. J. Vatikiotis (ed.), *Egypt Since the Revolution*, New York: Praeger, 1968.

————, "Rich and Poor in the New Arab Order," *Journal of Arab Studies*, vol. 1, no. 1 (October 1981).

Khadra, Rajai M. Abu, "Une Evaluation Des Investissements Lies Au Developpement Dans Quelques Pays Du Golfe Persique," *Revue De L'energie* (Paris), vol. 31, no. 321 (1980).

Khalek, Gouda 'Abdel, "Foreign Economic Aid and Income Distribution in Egypt, 1952–1977," in 'Abdel-Khalek, G. and Robert Tignor (eds.), *The Political Economy of Income Distribution in Egypt*, New York: Holmes and Meier, 1982, pp. 435–68.

————, "The Open Door Economic Policy in Egypt: A Search for Meaning, Interpretation and Implication," In H. M. Thompson (ed.), *Papers in Social Studies in Egyptian Political Economy*, Cairo: Cairo Science vol. 2, Monograph 3, 2nd Edition (July 1983), pp.73–100.

————, "The Open Door Economic Policy in Egypt: Its Contribution to Investment and Its Equity," in Kerr, M. and El Sayed Yassin (eds.), *Rich and Poor States in the Middle East: Egypt and the New Arab Order*, Boulder, CO: Westview Press, 1982, pp. 259–84.

————, "Looking Outside or Turning Northwest: On the Meaning and External Dimensions of Egypt's Infitah," *Social Problems*, vol. 28, no. 4 (April 1981), pp. 394–409.

Khouja, Mohamad, "Some Observation on the Flow of Financial Resources to Developing Countries," *OAPEC News Bulletin*, vol. 6, no. 3 (March 1980).

Kinley, David L. and Frances Moore, "The Myth of Humanitarian Aid," *The Nation* (July 11–18), 1981.

Kleiman, David T., "Oil Money and the Third World," *The Banker* (September 1974).

Knauerhase, Ramon, "Saudi Arabia's Economy At the Beginning of the 1979s," *Middle East Journal*, vol. 28 (Spring 1974).

Korany, Bahgat, "The Arab World and the New Balance of Power," in Michael Hudson (ed.), *Middle East Dilemma: The Politics and Economics of Arab Integration*, New York: Columbia University Press, 1999.

————, "Dependance Financiere Et Comportement International," *Revue Francaise De Science Politique*, vol. 28, no. 6 (December 1978), pp. 1067–93.

————, "The Glory That Was' the Pan-Arab, Pan-Islamic Alliance Decisions, October 1973," *International Political Science Review*, vol. 5, no. 1 (1984), pp. 47–74.

————, "Political Petrolism and Contemporary Arab Politics, 1967–1983," *Journal of Asian and African Studies*, vol. 21, Nos. 1–2 (1986), pp. 66–80.

Koury, Enver M., "The Gulf Security and the Linkage Process," in E. M. Koury and E. A.

Nakhleh (eds.), *The Arabian Peninsula, Red Sea, and Gulf: Strategic Considerations,* Washington, D.C.: Institute of Middle Eastern and North African Affairs, 1979.

Krazl, Ladislau, "Hospodarska Spoluprace Arabskych Zemi," *Novy Orient,* vol. 38, no. 5 (1983), pp. 132–4.

Kuczynske, P. P., "Recycling Petrodollars to the Third World," *Euromoney* (November 1974).

Kuniholm, B., "What the Saudis Really Want: A Premier for the Reagan Administration," *Orbis,* vol. 25 (Spring 1981).

Lenci, Marco, "Inter-Arab Relations Form 1945–1982," *Politica Internazionale* (English edition.), vol. 3, no. 1 (1983), pp. 125–58.

Lavy, Victor, "The Economic Embargo of Egypt by Arab States: Myth and Reality," *MEJ,* vol. 28, no. 3 (Summer 1984).

———, "The Savings Gap and the Productivity of Foreign Aid to a Developing Economy: Egypt," *The Journal of Developing Areas,* vol. 19 (October 1984), pp. 21–34.

Logan, John E. et al., "Arab Investment in the United States: A Case Study," in Salah El Sayed (ed.), *International Business and the Middle East,* Cairo: The American University in Cairo, 1979, pp. 13–35.

Long, David E., "Saudi Foreign Policy and the Arab–Israeli Peace Process: The Fahd (Arab) Peace Plan," in Willard A. Beling (ed.), *Middle East Peace Plans,* New York: St. Martin's Press, 1986.

Looney, Robert E. and Peter C. Fredriksen, "Defence Expenditures, external Public Debt, and Growth in Developing Countries," *Journal of Peace Research,* vol. 23, no. 4 (December 1986), pp. 329–38.

Lottem, Emanuel, "Arab Aid to Less Developed Countries," *Middle East Review* (Winter 1979–80), pp. 30–9.

Mabro, Robert, "Egypt's Economic Relations with the Socialist Countries," *World Development,* vol. 3, no. 5 (May 1975), pp. 299–313.

———, and E. Monroe, "Arab Wealth from Oil: Problems of its Investment," *International Affairs* (January 1974).

Magnus, Ralph H., "Afghanistan and Gulf Security: A Continuing Interrelationship," in Robert G. Darius et al. (eds.), *Gulf Security into the 1980s,* Stanford: Hoover Institution Press, 1984, pp.7–30.

———, "Societies and Social Change in the Persian Gulf," in Cottrell, Alvin J. (ed.), *The Persian Gulf States: A General Survey,* Baltimore: The Johns Hopkins University Press, 1980, pp. 369–413.

Makdisi, Samir A., "Arab Economic Co-Operation," in Roberto Aliboni (ed.), *Arab Industrialization and Economic Integration,* London: Croom Helm, 1979.

Mallakh, Ragaei El and Mihssen Kadhim, "Arab Institutionalized Development Aid: An Evaluation," *MEJ,* vol. 30, no. 4 (1976), pp. 471–84.

———, "Capital Surpluses and Deficits in the Arab Middle East: A Regional Perspective," *IJMES,* vol. 8, no. 2 (1977), pp. 183–93.

Malone, Joseph J., "The Islamic Republic of Iran and the Gulf Security," in Hafeez Malik (ed.), *International Security in Southwest Asia,* New York: Praeger, 1984, pp. 43–54.

Mchale, T. R., "Changing Financial Institution in the Arab Oil States," in J. C. Hurewitz (ed.), *Oil, the Arab-Israel Dispute and the Industrial World,* Boulder, CO: Westview Press, 1976, pp. 231–45.

Mclaurin, R. D. and James M. Price, "OPEC Current Account Surpluses: Assistance to the Arab Front-Line States," *Oriente Moderno,* vol. 58 (1978), pp. 533–46.

Mcqueen, C., "Egyptian Investment Climate," *Business America,* vol. 4 (March 9, 1981), pp. 12–14.

Megalli, Nabil, "Western Bankers Irked by Difficulties in Egypt," *Burroughs Clearing House* (Detroit), vol. 59 (September 1975).

Midlarsky, Manus I., "The Revolutionary Transformation of Foreign Policy: Agrarianism and Its International Impact," in Kegley, Charles W., Jr. and Pat Mcgowan (eds.), *The Political Economy of Foreign Policy Behavior,* Beverly Hills: Sage, 1981, pp. 39–62.

Mikdashi, Zuhayr, "Surplus Funds and the Strategy of Oil-Exporting Countries," in Naiem A. Sherbiny and Mark A. Tessler (eds.), *Arab Oil: Impact on the Arab Countries and Global Implications,* New York: Praeger, 1976, pp. 202–24.

Mikesell, Raymond F., "Monetary Problems of Saudi Arabia," *MEJ,* vol. 1., no. 2 (April 1947), pp. 169–79.

Mishlawi, Tewfik and Assem 'Abdul Mohsen, "Arab Ventures Without Egypt," *The Middle East,* June 1979, pp. 90–2.

Mohsen, A. A., "Arab Boycott Far from Fatal to Egypt," *The Middle East* (December 1979), pp. 73-73.

Munoz, Heraldo, "Strategic Dependency: Relations Between Core Powers and Mineral-Exporting Periphery Countries," in Kegley, Charles W., Jr. and Pat Mcgowan (eds.), *The Political Economy of Foreign Policy Behavior,* Beverly Hills: Sage, 1981, pp. 191–214.

Nag, Mostafa H., "Development With Unlimited Supplies of Capital: The Case of OPEC," *The Developing Economies,* vol. 20, no. 1 (March 1982), pp. 3–20.

Naguib, Mohamed Fathi, "Les Investissements Etrangers en Egypte," *CEDEJ Bulletin* (Cairo), vol. 16, (November 1984), pp.19–41.

Nashashibi, Hikmat Sharif, "Investing Arab Financial Surpluses in the 1980s," *OAPEC News Bulletin,* vol. 6, no. 4 (April 1980).

Neumayer, Eric, "What factors determine the allocation of aid by Arab Countries and Multilateral Agencies?" (Forthcoming).

Noble, Paul, "The Prospects for Arab Cooperation in a Changing Regional and Global System," in Michael Hudson (ed.), *Middle East Dilemma: The Politics and Economics of Economic Integration,* London: I.B. Tauris, 1999.

Nowais, Nasser al-, "The Experience of the Abu Dhabi Fund in the Aid Process," *Arab Gulf Journal,* vol. 4, no. 1 (April 1984), pp. 22–27.

Oded, Arye, "Arab Aid to Africa," *International Problems, Society and Politics,* vol. 24, no. 1–4 (1985).

Ojo, Olusola, "Afro-Arab Economic Relations," *International Problems, Society and Politics,* vol. 24, Nos. 1–4 (1985).

"OPEC's Lending Record: A Review," *Arab Oil and Economic Review* (February 1978), pp. 34–5.

"Open Door in the Middle East," *MERIP Reports,* no. 31 (October 1974), pp. 3–21.

Oweiss, Ibrahim M., "Petrodollar Surpluses: Trends and Economic Impact," *L'Egypte Contemporaine,* no. 393–4 (October 1983), pp. 5–35.

Owen, Roger, "Egypt After the Riots," *Middle East International,* no. 69 (March 1977), pp. 4-6.

————, "Inter-Arab Economic Relations During the Twentieth Century: World Market versus Regional Market", in Michael Hudson (ed.), *Middle East Dilemma: The Politics and Economics of Arab Integration,* New York: Columbia University Press, 1999.

————, "The Political Environment for Development," in I. Ibrahim (ed.), *Arab Resources: The Transformation of a Society,* London: Croom Helm, 1983, pp. 139–46.

Pajak, Roger F., "Soviet Arms Aid in the Middle East since the October War," in *The Political Economy of the Middle East: 1973–78, A Compendium of Papers Submitted to the Joint Economic Committee Congress of the US,* Washington D.C.: GPO, April 21, 1980.

Papanek, Gustav, "The Effects of Aid and Other Resource Transfers on Savings and Growth in Less Developed Countries," *Economic Journal,* vol. 82 (September 1972), pp. 934–50.

Paul, Jim, "The Egyptian Arms Industry," *MERIP Reports,* no. 112 (February 1983), pp. 26–8.

Peck, Malcolm, "Saudi Arabia's Wealth: A Two-Edged Sword," *New Middle East* (January 1972), pp. 5–7.

Perry, Glan, "Inter-Arab Relations: Cooperation and Conflict," in Abid al-Marayati (ed.), *International Relations of the Middle East and North Africa,* Cambridge, MA.: 1984.

Peterson, J. E., "The Arab Response to the Iranian Challenge in the Gulf," in Philip H. Stoddard (ed.), *The Middle East in the 1980s: Problems and Prospects,* Proceedings of a Conference Held at the National Defence University, Washington, D.C.: June 8–9, 1983.

Piscatori, James P., "Islamic Values and National Interest: The Foreign Policy of Saudi Arabia," in Adeed I. Dawisha (ed.), *Islam in Foreign Policy,* Cambridge: Cambridge University Press, 1983.

Pitt-Rivers, Julian, "Honour and Social," in J. G. Peristiany (ed.), *Honour and Shame: The Values of Mediterranean Society,* London: Weidenfeld and Nicolson, 1965, pp. 19–78.

Podeh, Eli, "The Emergence of the Arab State System Reconsidered," *Diplomacy and Statecraft,* vol. 9, no. 3 (November 1998), pp. 50–82.

—————, and Onn Winckler, "The Boycott that Never Was: Egypt and the Arab System, 1979–1989," *Occasional papers of the Middle East Center,* Durham University, (Forthcoming).

Price, David Lynn, "Arab Arms Production," *Middle East International,* no. 80 (February 1978).

Ramazani, R. K., "Security in the Persian Gulf," *Foreign Affairs,* Spring 1979, pp. 821–35.

—————, "The Arab-Iranian Conflict: The Ideological Dimensions," in Hafeez Malik (ed.), *International Security In Southwest Asia,* New York: Praeger, 1984, pp. 55–75.

—————, "The Relationship Between OPEC Aid and the Increase in the Net Oil Import Bill of Developing Countries Resulting from the Oil Price Adjustment Since 1973," *OAPEC News Bulletin,* vol. 5, no. 10 (October 1979).

Robana, 'Abderrahman, "The Flow of Inter-Arab Financial Assistance," *Maghreb Review,* vol. 5, no. 2–4 (1980), pp. 57–62.

Roberts, John, "How Kuwait Widens Its Portfolio," *MEED,* February 20, 1981.

Rondot, Pierre, "Traits Originaux et Vocatin Arabe de L'Egypte," *Defence Nationale,* vol. 33 (February 1977), pp. 25–38.

Roy, Delwin A, "Private Industry Sector Development in Egypt: An Analysis of Trends, 1973–1977," *Journal of South Asian and Middle Eastern Studies,* vol. 1, no. 3 (Spring 1978), pp. 11–33.

Rubin, B., "Iran's Revolution and Persian Gulf Instability," in S. Tahir-Kheli and S. Ayubi (eds.), *The Iran-Iraq War: New Weapons, Old Conflicts,* New York: Praeger, 1983.

Rubinson, Richard, "The World Economy and the Distribution of Income within States: A Cross-National Study," *American Sociological Review,* vol. 41 (1976), pp. 638–59.

Rubinstein, Alvin Z., "Egypt's Search for Stability," *Current History,* vol. 76, no. 443 (1979), pp. 19–21.

—————, "The Egypt of Anwar Sadat," *Current History* (January 1977), pp. 19–21, 36–8.

Sabagh, George, "Immigrants in the Arab Gulf Countries: Sojourners' or Settlers," in Giacomo Luciani and Ghassan Salame (eds.), *The Politics of Arab Integration,* London: Croom Helm, 1988, pp. 159–82.

Sabri, Jiryis, "The Arab World at the Crossroad: An Analysis of the Arab Opposition to the Sadat Initiative," *Journal of Palestine Studies,* vol. 7, no. 2 (Winter 1978).

Sadat, Anwar, "Where Egypt Stands," *Foreign Affairs,* vol. 51, no. 1 (October 1972).

Sadik, Ali Tawfic, "La Cooperation Financiere Entre Les Pays Du Sud: La Cas Des Donateurs Arabes," *Revue Tiers-Monde,* vol. 24 (1983), pp. 859–60.

Sadik, Ali Tawfik, "Managing the Petrodollar Bonanza: Avenues and implications of Recycling Arab Capital," *Arab Studies Quarterly,* vol. 6, no. 1–2 (Winter/Spring 1984), pp. 13–38.

Safran, Nadav, "Engagement in the Middle East," *Foreign Affairs,* vol. 53, no. 1 (October 1974), pp. 45–63.

———, "The War and the Future of the Arab-Israeli Conflict," *Foreign Affairs,* vol.52, no. 2 (January 1974), pp. 215–36.

Said, Hussein H. El and M. S. El-Hennawi, "Foreign Investment in LDC's: Egypt," *California Management Review,* vol. 24, no. 4 (Summer 1982), pp. 85–91.

Salacuse, Jeswald W., "Arab Capital and Middle Eastern Development Finance," *Journal of World Trade Law,* vol. 15 (1981), pp. 283–309.

———, and Theodore Parnall, "Foreign Investment and Economic Openness in Egypt: Legal Problems and Legislative Adjustments of the First Three Years," *International Lawyer,* vol. 12, no. 4 (1978), pp. 759–78.

Saliba, Najib, "The Decline of Naserism in Sadat's Egypt," *World Affairs* (Summer 1975), pp. 51–9.

Sambar, David H., "Arab Investment Strategies," *Arab Gulf Journal,* pp. 13–21.

Sarkis, Nicolas, "Les Arabes Riches et les Arabes Pauvres," *Le Monde Diplomatique* (August 1978).

Saudi, 'Abdulla A., "Arab Banking's Role in OPEC Countries' Investment Strategies," *OAPEC News Bulletin,* vol. 10, no. 4 (April 1984).

Sayeh, Hamed El, "The Economic Background. Egypt: The Foundations of the Economy," *The Washington Quarterly,* Special Supplement (Spring 1979), pp. 5–9.

Sayigh, Yusif A., "A New Framework for Complementarity Among the Arab Economies," in I. Ibrahim, Ibrahim (ed.), *Arab Resources: The Transformation of a Society,* London: Croom Helm, *1983,* pp. 147–67.

Schuler, Henry M., "Will Egypt Be Denied its 'peace Dividend'," *American Arab Affairs,* no. 7 (Winter 83/84), pp. 31–9.

Schwartz, Eleanor Brantley, "Kuwait: A Capital Surplus Economy," *Atlanta Economic Review,* vol. 26 (May/June 1976), pp. 40–5.

Seale, Patrick, "Sadat's Shock Therapy," *New Statism,* vol. 94, no. 2436 (December 21, 1977), pp. 760–1.

Selim, Hassan, "Surplus Funds and Regional Development," in Ragaei El-Mallakh and Carl Mcgure (eds.), *Energy and Development,* Boulder, CO: International Research Center for Energy and Economic Development, 1974.

Seven, S, "Egypte: La Paix Cache Misere," *L'economiste Tiers Monde* (1979), pp. 8–11.

Severiens, Jacobus T., "Foreign Investment in Egypt: What Are the Dividends of Peace?" *Middle East Review,* vol. 12, no. 2 (1980), pp. 45–55.

Sindi A. M. Al, "King Faisal and Pan-Islamism," in Willard A. Beling (ed.), *King Faisal and Modernization of Saudi Arabia,* London: Croom Helm, 1980.

Shafik, Nemat, "Labor Migration and Economic Integration in the Middle East," in Michael Hudson (ed.), *Middle East Dilemma: The Politics and Economics of Arab Integration,* New York: Columbia University Press, 1999.

Shamir, Shimon, "Arab Socialism and Egyptian-Islamic Tradition," in S.N. Eisenstadt and Y. Atzmon (eds.), *Socialism and Tradition,* Atlantic Highlands: Humanities Press, 1975, pp. 193–218.

Sharabi, Hisham, "The Poor Rich Arabs," in I. Ibrahim (ed.), *Arab Resources: The Transformation of a Society,* London: Croom Helm, 1983, pp. 301–4.

Shaw, Paul, "The Political Economy of Inequality in the Arab World," *Arab Studies Quarterly*, vol. 6, no. 1–2 (Winter/Spring 1984), pp. 124–54.

Sheffer, G., "Independence and Dependence of Regional Power: The Uncomfortable Alliance in the Middle East before and after the October 1973 War," *Orbis*, vol. 19 (Winter 1976), pp. 1519–38.

Shireff, David, "The Flight Into Egypt," *Euromoney* (May 1984), pp. 174–81.

Stevenson, Paul, "External Economic variables Influencing the economic Growth Rate of Seven Major Latin American Nations," *Canadian Review of Sociology and Anthropology*, vol. 9, no. 4 (1972), pp. 347–56.

Stoddard, Philip H., "Egypt and the Iran-Iraq War," in Thomas Naff (ed.), *Gulf Security and the Iran-Iraq War*, Washington, D.C.: National Defence University Press, 1985.

Stoga, Alan, "The Foreign Investments of OPEC and Arab Oil Producers," *American Arab Affairs*, vol. 3 (1982–3), pp. 60–7.

Stoneman, Colin, "Foreign Capital and Economic Growth," *World Development*, vol. 3, no. 1 (1975), pp. 11–26.

Stork, Joe, "Arms Industries of the Middle East," *MERIP Reports*, no. 144 (January-February 1987), pp. 12–16.

Stork, Joe, "Bailing Out Sadat," *MERIP Reports*, no. 56 (April 1977), pp. 8–11.

————, "Sadat's Desperate Mission," *MERIP Reports*, no. 64 (February 1978).

Sullivan, Paul, "Contrary Views of Economic Diplomacy in the Arab World: Egypt," *Arab Studies Quarterly*, vol. 21, no. 4 (Fall 1999), pp. 65–93.

Taylor, Lance, "The Political Economy of Egypt: An Opening to What?" *Middle East Review*, vol. 10, no. 4 (1978), pp. 10–15.

Thompson, William, "Center Periphery Interaction Patterns: The Case of Arab Visits, 1946–1975," *International Organization*, vol. 35, no. 2 (Spring 1981).

————, "Delineating Regional Subsystems: Visit Networks and the Middle East Case," *IJMES*, vol. 31, no. 2 (May 1981).

Tovias, Alfred, "Egypt's Trade Policies," *Journal of World Trade Law*, vol. 15 (1981), pp. 471–89.

Travies, Tom A., "A Comparison of the Global Economic Imperialism of Five Metropoles," in Charles W., Jr and Pat Mcgowan (eds.), *The Political Economy of Foreign Policy Behavior*, Beverly Hills: Sage, 1981, pp. 165–90.

Tripp, Charles, "Egypt and the Region in the 1980s," in Charles Tripp and Roger Owen (eds.), *Egypt under Mubarak*, London: Routledge, 1989.

Troxler, Nancy C., "The Gulf Co-Operation Council: The Emergence of An Institution," *Journal of International Studies*, vol. 16, no. 1 (Spring 1987), pp. 1–19.

Tuker, J., "Economic Decay, Political Ferment in Egypt," *MERIP Reports*, no. 65 (March 1978), pp. 3–9.

Tuma, Elias H., "The Rich and the Poor in the Middle East," *MEJ*, vol. 34 (autumn 1980), pp. 413–37.

————, "The Palestinians in America," *The Link*, vol. 14, no. 3 (July–August 1981), pp. 1–14.

Ulmer, Melville J., "Multinational Corporations and Third World Capitalism," *Journal of Economic Issues*, vol. 14, no. 2 (1980), pp. 453–71.

"US National Security," in Harry F. Young, *Atlas of US Foreign Relations*, United States Department of State, Washington, D.C.: GPO, 1982.

"U.S. Treasury Suppression of Sensitive Arab Official Investment Data," *International Currency Review*, vol. 12, no. 4 (1980), pp. 37–43.

Vatikiotis, P. J., "Egypt's Politics of Conspiracy," *Survey*, vol. 18, no. 2 (1972).

————, "Inter Arab Relations," in A. L. Udovitch (ed.), *The Middle East: Oil, Conflict and Hope,* Lexington, MA: Lexington Books, 1976, pp. 145–79.

Vayrynen, Raimo, "The Arab Organization of Industrialization: A Case Study in the Multinational Production of Arms," *Current Research on Peace and Violence,* vol. 2, no. 2 (1979), pp. 66–78.

Wassef, M., "Vers L'integration De L'Egypte Et Du Soudan," *Maghreb Machrek,* no. 14 (1979).

Waterbury, John, "The 'Soft State' and the Open Door: Egypt's Experience With Economic Liberalization, 1974–1984," *Comparative Politics,* vol. 18, no. 1 (October 1985), pp. 65–84.

Weinbaum, Marvin G., "Dependent Development and US Economic Aid to Egypt," *IJMES,* vol.18, no. 2 (1986), pp. 119–34.

Weinbaum, Marvin G., "Egypt's Infitah and the Politics of US Economic Assistance," *MES,* vol. 21, no. 2 (April 1985), pp. 206–22.

———, "Politics and Development in Foreign Aid: US Economic Assistance to Egypt, 1975–1982," *MEJ,* vol. 37, no. 4 (1983), pp. 636–55.

Vicker, Roy, "Beating the Boycott," *WSJ* (February 14, 1980).

Williams, Maurice J., "The Aid Programs of the OPEC Countries," *Foreign Affairs,* vol. 54 (October 1975), pp. 308–24.

Wilson, Rodney, "Whither the Egyptian Economy?" *British Journal of Middle East Studies,* vol. 20, no. 2, (1993).

Wissa-Wassef, Ceres, "Le Pouvoir et les Etudiants en Egypte, I," *Maghreb-Machrek,* no. 56 (Mars–Avril 1973), pp. 65–71.

Wright, C., "The Implications of the Iran-Iraq War," *Foreign Affairs,* vol. 59, no. 2 (Winter 1980–1).

Young, George B., "Profile of Egypt," *Industrial Marketing,* vol. 62 (July 1977), pp. 79–83.

Zahlan, Antoine B, "Labor Migration and Economic Integration in the Middle East," in Michael Hudson (ed.), *Middle East Dilemma: The Politics and Economics of Arab Integration,* New York: Columbia University Press, 1999.

Zagoria, Donald, "Into the Breach: New Soviet Alliances in the Third World," *Foreign Affairs,* vol. 57. no 4 (1979).

# Index